WORKER-WRITER
IN AMERICA

WORKER-WRITER IN AMERICA

Jack Conroy and the Tradition of
Midwestern Literary Radicalism,
1898–1990

DOUGLAS WIXSON

UNIVERSITY OF ILLINOIS PRESS
Urbana and Chicago

Publication was supported by a grant from the National Endowment for the Humanities, an independent federal agency.

This book is printed on acid-free paper.

Library of Congress Cataloging-in-Publication Data

Wixson, Douglas C.
    Worker-writer in America : Jack Conroy and the tradition of
midwestern literary radicalism, 1898-1990 / Douglas Wixson.
        p.   cm.
    Includes bibliographical references (p.) and index.
    ISBN 0-252-02043-X (alk. paper)
    1. Conroy, Jack, 1899-1990. 2. Working class writings, American—
History and criticism. 3. Radicalism—Middle West—History—20th
century. 4. Authors, American—20th century—Biography.
5. Radicals—Middle West—Biography. 6. Middle West in literature.
7. Radicalism in literature. I. Title.
PS3505.053Z95   1994
813'.52—dc20
    [B]   93-3684
                                                                         CIP

For Suzanne

Vixere fortes ante Agamemnona multi; sed omnes illacrimabiles urgentur ignotique longa nocte, carent quia vate sacro.

—Horace, *Odes* iv.9.25

Contents

Preface

Jack Conroy's work and life ranged broadly in diverse areas of human activity and interest; a knowledge of labor history, folklore, literature, sociology, and literary politics is necessary to explore them adequately. To bring these separate disciplines together in a coherent analysis that does not miss its very human target was a challenge. Primary source materials were uncollected and uncataloged. No archives existed housing the correspondence of the principal figures. Copies of little magazines were scattered in several dozen libraries, often in incomplete runs. Little had been written on the subject of the worker-writer in America. It was necessary to look abroad for relevant theoretical studies; I discovered several of my most important secondary sources in France and Belgium. I have made every effort to seek the best guides in framing appropriate social, historical, literary, and political contexts.

My quest for living testimonials led me to two continents, to a sun-bleached barrio on the Mexican border, a commune on a New Mexico mesa, Jack London's Valley of the Moon, Chicago's Loop, Missouri's boot-heel, Oregon's Puget Sound, nursing homes, and, having arrived too late, gravesites. My traveling companions were a tape recorder and a stenographer's notebook.

When, near the end of his life, Conroy named me his literary executor and released his papers to me, including several thousand letters, I was faced with the task of sorting, filing, and copying them, as well as interpreting obscure references. The work of many good novelists from the 1930s had been forgotten; their writings were hard to locate. It was tempting to rely upon Conroy's prodigious memory and entertaining performances, in which he recounted past associations in lively, colorful detail. I wished, however, to write a critical study, not a hagiography.

To remove the natural bias I felt toward this extraordinary individual, I made extensive use of primary documentation, critical studies, and interviews with a wide range of contemporary writers, critics, friends, and colleagues. I found myself in an odd role: with no intention at first of writing such a study, I gained the trust of my subject and became, I think, his friend. Later, when I felt more and more the task of doing this book thrust upon me, I thought it necessary to achieve critical objectivity about Conroy's work and life—without losing the great affection I felt for the man. The success of my task seemed always to rest on the issue of trust: Conroy and his contemporaries were neglected (and occasionally reviled) in the post-1930s period of revisionism. Many were blacklisted in the degrading time of congressional and FBI investigations during the 1950s. The extent to which I gained the trust of my informants is reflected in the nature of the detail and the accuracy of the telling. In a sense, this is their story, as I heard it. Whenever possible, I weighed the accounts of informants and sought corroboration. I accept the responsibility for having attempted to find the connections and coherence that make my study a critical history of their achievements.

Acknowledgments

Whatever merit this book possesses owes mainly to fortuitous timing and the goodwill of those listed under "Interviews" in the Bibliography. All of these individuals shared their memories generously and greeted me warmly. The informants include the main subject of this study, Jack Conroy, with whom I spent a hundred afternoons during the last fifteen years of his life; his friends, former colleagues, and contemporaries; and his family. To have started my project at another time would have produced a much different result. The perspective that writers often hope to gain on their literary professions seemed difficult to achieve in the case of Conroy and the literary radicals of his generation. Seldom have politics and personal circumstance met on such intimate terms as with these writers, and seldom has a generation of writers produced so much misunderstanding or suffered such enforced neglect. It was my good fortune to meet these people not too soon to miss that perspective, and not too late to miss knowing them.

Simone Weil's factory journals, which I read in St. Étienne, France, in 1971, introduced me to worker-writing. At a film conference in Chambéry, Michel Fabre drew my attention to Conroy's *The Disinherited*. My father-in-law, Judge Richard J. Chamier, guided me around the mines and railroad yards of northern Missouri. Archie Green urged me at a critical moment to declare the direction my study would take. David Anderson published my early excursions on Conroy and encouraged my further efforts. Alan Wald, Cary Nelson, Fred Whitehead, Jim Bogan, Jack Morgan, Alex "Sandy" Primm, and Larry Vonalt offered counsel and criticism. Meridel Le Sueur tutored me in the art of interviewing. My wife, Suzanne Chamier, gave encouragement, drew my attention to critical texts, and shared in getting to know Conroy's friends and colleagues.

The many librarians and archivists who assisted my project include André Blavier (Bibliothèque de Verviers, Belgium); Robert A. Hull (University of Virginia Library); John P. Beck (Institute of Labor and Industrial Relations, Ann Arbor, Michigan); Lowell L. Cantrell (Brotherhood Railway Carmen, Kansas); Carolyn A. Davis (George Arents Research Library, Syracuse University); Neal W. Moore (Ozarks Labor History Society, Springfield, Missouri); Leslie F. Orear (Illinois Labor History Society, Chicago); Edward C. Weber (Labadie Collection, University of Michigan); Stephen C. Jones and David E. Schoonover (Beinecke Library, Yale University); Rosemary L. Cullen (Brown University Library); Archie Motley (Chicago Historical Society); Diana Haskell and Paul Saenger (Newberry Library); Jannette Fiore (Michigan State University Libraries); Ann Allen Schockley (Fisk University Library); Randall C. Jimerson, Ellen E. Embardo, Darlene Berardi, Richard H. Schimmelpfeng, and Richard C. Fyffe (University of Connecticut Library–Storrs); Steve Nielsen and Alissa Wiener (Minnesota Historical Society, St. Paul); Alice R. Cotten (Wilson Library, University of North Carolina–Chapel Hill); Gene M. Gressley (University of Wyoming Library); Alan K. Lathrop (University Libraries, University of Minnesota); Daniel Traister (Van Pelt Library, University of Pennsylvania); Sharon Scott (Vivian G. Harsh Collection, Chicago Public Library); Lynn Wolf Gentzler, Nancy Lankford, Mark Stauter, and John Bradbury (Western Historical Manuscript Collection, University of Missouri); Laurel G. Bowen and Carl Oblinger (Illinois State Historical Library, Springfield); Frank Paluka (University of Iowa Library); Mary Allcorn and James Goodrich (State Historical Society of Missouri, Columbia); David A. Cobb (Library, University of Illinois at Urbana-Champaign); James H. Hutson, Charles Kelly, and Mary L. Vass (Manuscript Division, Library of Congress); Terry L. Shoptaugh, Alan Nourie, and James Zink (Southeast Missouri State University); William H. Runge (Tracey W. McGregor Library, University of Virginia); Thomas A. Staley (Harry Ransom Humanities Research Center, University of Texas–Austin); Gene DeGruson (Pittsburg State University Library); Joan Parks and Kathryn Stallard (Southwestern University Library); Valerie Darst (Moberly Area Community College); and Janet McKean, Andy Stewart, and Georgia Bieniek (University of Missouri Library–Rolla).

I wish to express my gratitude to the following libraries, agencies, and individuals for granting me permission to quote: Patricia Powell of Harold Ober Associates (Arna Bontemps–Conroy letters); Cleo Paturis, executor to Farrell estate, and Edgar Branch of Miami University (Farrell-Branch letter); Special Collections, Van Pelt Library, University of Pennsylvania (Conroy-Farrell letters); Rodney Dennis, Curator of Manuscripts, Houghton Library, Harvard University (Philip Rahv letters); Special Collections, Northwestern University Library (Conroy manuscripts and letters); Special Collections, The Newberry Library (Malcolm Cowley–Conroy letters; Conroy–Dale Kramer letters); Manuscripts Division, University of Minnesota Libraries (Frederick Manfred–Conroy letters); Manuscript Division, Harry Ransom Humanities Research Center (J. Frank Dobie–Conroy letters; John Lehmann–Conroy letter); Barbara A. Filipac, Manuscripts Division, Brown University Library (Conroy–John Brooks Wheelwright letters; Conroy–Willard Maas letter); Special Collections, Washington University (Conroy–George O'Donnell letter; Conroy–Josephine Johnson letter; Conroy–David Wagoner letter); Western Historical Manuscript Collection, University of Missouri–Columbia (W. W. Wharton papers); Labadie Collection, University of Michigan (Conroy–Jo Labadie letters; Agnes Inglis–Conroy letters); Special Collections, Mugar Memorial Library, Boston University (Conroy–Joseph North letter; Conroy–Abraham Burack letters); Special Collections, University Library, Ohio State University (Conroy–Nelson Algren letters; Nelson Algren manuscripts); Manuscript Division, Special Collections Department, Alderman Library, University of Virginia (Conroy–John C. Rogers letters; Rogers manuscripts and photos); Rare Book and Manuscript Library, Butler Library, Columbia University (Conroy–Millen Brand letters); Rare Books and Special Collections, University Library, University of Michigan (Conroy letters); Historical Manuscripts and Archives, University Library, University of Connecticut–Storrs (Snow correspondence and manuscripts; transcripts of "Semester of the Thirties"); Yale Collection of American Literature, Beinecke Rare Book and Manuscript Library, Yale University (Conroy–Richard Wright letters; H. H. Lewis letters; *Partisan Review*–H. H. Lewis letter; Joe Kalar–Norman Macleod letters; Norman Macleod manuscripts and clippings); H. H. Lewis Papers, Kent Library, Southeast Missouri State University (H. H. Lewis correspondence and manuscripts); Enoch Pratt Free Library, Baltimore (H. L. Mencken–Conroy correspondence); National Archives and Records Service, Washington, D.C. (Federal Writers' Project records); Special Collections, University of Nebraska Library (Benjamin A. Botkin Papers); Manuscript Collection, University of Oregon (Conroy–Verne Bright letters; Earl Conrad–Conroy letters; James Rorty papers; Kenneth Porter papers); Jerre Mangione Papers, Manuscript Collection, University of Rochester Library; Dorothy Canfield Fisher Papers, Special Collections, Bailey-Howe Library, University of Vermont (Conroy–Dorothy Canfield Fisher letters); and Paul Corey Papers, Special Collections, University of Iowa Library.

In addition, I thank the following individuals for allowing me to

xiv   Acknowledgments

quote from letters and interviews: Stanley Burnshaw (Burnshaw–Paul
Corey letter; Burnshaw–Orrick Johns letter; Burnshaw-Conroy letters);
Robert and Janet Cruden (letters and interview); Betrenia Watt Bowk-
er (letters and interviews); Elisabeth Humeston (Mike Gold letters); Ray
B. and Lucille M. West (Ray B. West letters and interview); Flora Snow
and Maurice Isserman (Walter Snow correspondence and manuscripts);
Priscilla Ruth MacDougall (Curtis D. MacDougall letters and interview);
Erskine and Virginia Caldwell (Erskine Caldwell letters and interview);
Catharine L. Bock and H. H. Lewis (Lewis letters and interviews); James
F. Light (letters and interviews); Judith A. Getz (Emerson Price letters);
Edith Vanko (Walt Carmon letters); Joseph Vogel (letters and inter-
view); Alexandra Wharton Grannis and Minerva Wharton Durham
(W. W. Wharton papers and interviews); Elvena Kalar (Joseph Kalar pa-
pers); Paul Falkowski (Edward Falkowski letters and interviews); Norman G. Macleod (Norman Macleod letters and interviews); Annette
M. Porter (Kenneth Porter papers); Frank Sandiford (letters and interviews); Dorothy B. Farrell (interview; James T. Farrell interview and
papers); Abe Aaron (letters and interviews); Sanka and Kenneth Bristow (letters and interviews); Christine and Neal Rowland (letters and
interviews); Robin Rogers (John C. Rogers letters and manuscripts);
Jerre Mangione (papers and interviews); Paul Corey (letters and interviews); Raymond J. and Charlotte Koch (letters and interviews); Lillian Friedman (letters and interview); Maxim Lieber (letters and interview); Flora E. Mercil (Ben Hagglund letters); Sanora Babb (letters and
interview); Mildred Kresensky Allen (Raymond Kresensky letters and
interview); Geraldine Wolf (interview; Howard Wolf letters); Meridel
Le Sueur (letters and interviews); Mark Harris (letters and interview);
J. F. Powers (letters and interview); Betty Rahv (Philip Rahv letters);
and Gertrude Botkin (Botkin papers).

In addition to those already named, my deep gratitude goes to the fol-
lowing people who have aided me over the years in various ways: Ches-
ter Aaron, Daniel Aaron, Russell Ames, L. E. Anderson, Sr., Julie At-
kinson, Al Baumgartner, Mrs. Catharine Lewis Bock, Kay Bonetti, Merlin
Bowen, Edgar M. Branch, Roger Bresnahan, Gwendolyn Brooks, George
W. Burgin, Stanley Burnshaw, Lowell Cantrell, Ted and Nuna Cass,
Lawrence Christensen, Shirley Cloyes, Malcolm Cowley, John Crawford,
Olga Davidson, Frank Marshall Davis, Harold Dellinger, Zena Dorinson,
Sabrina Gray Doster, D.V. R. Drenner, Bettina Drew, David Eppelsheimer,
Helen Falkowski, Paul Falkowski, Robert Farnsworth, Robert Fleming,
Barbara Foley, Marcia Folsom, Eric Foner, Mary Diggles Forsmark, Lewis
Fried, Cliff Garland, Ralph Gerhard, Larry Goldberg, Don Gordon, Mary

Guggenheim, Paul Guggenheim, Jim Gunn, Kathy Hickman Hale, Don Harington, Mark Harris, Bettye Hawley, Carolee Hazlet, Mike Hecht, Agnes Hickman, Bill Hickman, Lawrence Hill, Carl Hirsch, Fred Hobson, Barbara Hogan, Maurice Isserman, Stella Jacoby, Curt Johnson, W. K. Jordan, Dick Kalar, Ed Kalar, Henry Kisor, David Kropf, Red Kruck, Tom Kruck, F. Vernon Lamson, Carla Appel Levine, Milton Lomask, Mary McAnally, Robert McCullough, Zahava K. McKeon, James McKinley, Frederick Manfred, Howard Marshall, Lynn Miller, Harry T. Moore, Neal Moore, Dan Morris, Archibald Motley, Jr., Verle Muhrer, Kiyo Murayama, James L. Murphy, Winona Nation, Douglas Nicholls, Hank Oettinger, Leslie Orear, Leland Payton, William and Margaret Sayers Peden, Harry Mark Petrarkis, Joe Popper, Annette Porter, J. F. Powers, David and Judy Ray, Milton Reigelman, Paula Reingold, Karl and Cecy Rice, Walter B. Rideout, Dave Roediger, Robin Rogers, Alexander Saxton, Dolph and Becky Schroeder, Hope and Frank Scrogin, Jack M. Sherby, Ruth Sheridan, Orville Sittler, Flora Snow, Leonard C. Spier, Thomas F. Staley, Al Stein, Robert Stewart, Jack L. Stoll, Chris Suggs, Judith Suther, Studs and Ida Terkel, Edith Vanko, Stephen Wade, Amelie Weinfeld, and Melvin Yoken. Those not mentioned here are not neglected in my heart.

Professors David Thelen, Elizabeth Schulz, and Tom Mayer arranged for me to present lectures at the University of Missouri–Columbia, the University of Kansas, and the University of Colorado, respectively. Professors Richard Miller, Lon Pearson, and Robert Horick shared their considerable computer expertise. Linda Webster ably provided the index to this book.

The generosity of the Conroy family made possible the formation of two important permanent collections of Conroy's papers and the contents of his personal library. I wish to thank Jack Conroy, Jr. (deceased), Thelma Conroy, Jim Swartz, Jerry and Rene Swartz, Jack and Peggy Swartz, Tom Conroy, and Carolyn Conroy. Paul Saenger and Charles Cullen of the Newberry Library, Chicago, and Andrew Komar, president of the Moberly Area Community College, showed wisdom and vision in establishing Conroy collections.

Thanks, too, to the people of Moberly, the administration and staff of Moberly Area Community College, members of the Jack Conroy Memorial Literary Society, and above all, Elizabeth W. Chamier for her wise counsel and generous hospitality.

My gratitude to Jim Wise and Elizabeth Cummins, chairpersons of the English department; Marvin Barker, former dean of arts and sciences; and Chancellor John Park of the University of Missouri at Rolla for helping to arrange research leaves and course releases.

I extend my thanks to Lyman Field and Stephen J. Campbell for permission to reproduce Thomas Hart Benton's lithograph *The Boy* on the jacket of this book.

I wish to acknowledge the financial support I have received in connection with this book from the National Endowment for the Humanities; the University of Missouri; and the Missouri Committee for the Humanities.

It was an honor and a personally rewarding experience to work with the editors and staff of the University of Illinois Press. Carol Bolton Betts employed the highest standards of her craft in editing the manuscript. With sensitivity, expertise, and tact, Richard L. Wentworth, director of the press, steered the manuscript through to publication. In addition I wish to thank Theresa L. Sears, Janice Roney, and Karen Hendricks for their faith, diligence, and care.

WORKER-WRITER
IN AMERICA

Introduction

THIS IS A BOOK THAT I, and many others, had hoped Jack Conroy would write—but then, the subject was intensely personal, and painful, given the losses that he and many others suffered with the eclipse of radical literature in the Cold War years and its treatment in the hands of revisionists. A number of the revisionists, ex-Stalinists in some cases, subsequently turned their critical skills to promoting European modernism, existentialism, and abstract art, politically safe subjects, as things turned out, in the inquisitional postwar period. The "vulgarians" of the 1930s, unknowns from the hinterland who flouted fine writing with locutions of "crude vigor" and controversial subject matter, were banished into obscurity when the academy and the literary cliques closed ranks against rude interlopers—just as the guardians of traditional canons of learning in ancient times denied lingua vulgaris (the dialect of the common people) the status of literary language.[1]

Conroy, in the years that I knew him (beginning in the early 1970s), was a "disappeared" writer, owing partly to Cold War politics, partly to the popular tastemakers in harmony with hegemonic forces in society. In the early 1930s Conroy's literary magazine, The Anvil, had offered a nonhierarchical, noncentrist, egalitarian alternative to these forces. Jack's own life opposed them in thought and deed. By the 1960s, his novel The Disinherited had won admirers in Japan and Europe, where it was first recommended to me.[2] In the United States, however, Conroy was a neglected writer whose work was obscured by past associations with the radical left in the 1930s. These things I knew, but little else when I first met Jack Conroy in his Missouri home. A native of Moberly, it was there that he had returned to live with his wife, Gladys, in retirement after leaving Chicago in 1965. Conroy had hoped to complete his autobiography, but he was never able, as he said, to "get out of Monkey Nest." So much of a fascinating story risked being lost, and yet to tell it entailed great risks too. I made up my mind finally to attempt it—an account of his life and work in the contexts, social, literary, and historical, I felt they deserved—ignorant of the size of the task that lay before me.

Jack Conroy was a large, robust man with bright, twinkling blue eyes that looked kindly and knowingly on a harsh, resisting world. He was a compulsive storyteller who concluded his anecdotes in boisterous laughter that echoed through the two-story stone house on Fisk Avenue where I spent many an afternoon during the last thirteen years of his life (he died in 1990 at age ninety-one). His personality competed on equal terms with his vast acquaintanceship with literature and literary figures. We were friends (how could one *not* become his friend?), but I cannot say truthfully that I (or few others) ever penetrated the closely held inner reserve beneath his affability, good-natured congeniality, and love of companionship. Conroy was a profoundly decent man who in appearing to enjoy the world's shows, submitted them to humorous, sometimes devastating appraisal. He felt obliged to perform for visitors in a style—oratorical, playful, sly—that reminded some people of W. C. Fields. For years I heard his entertaining stories of people he had known, including Nelson Algren, James T. Farrell, Maxwell Bodenheim, H. H. Lewis, and the "Fallonites," who were a group of rowdy East St. Louis mill workers. He had a prodigious memory, quoting long passages from a most astonishing range of poetry, from Shakespeare to English music-hall song to bawdy miners' ballad. It was not until several years before his death that he shared feelings with me, confessed long-held disappointments, and furnished detail that would have otherwise perished with him.

Jack Conroy was the last of the village bards; he kept language alive and interesting in an age of declining literacy. He had his finger on the pulse of the community, his ear pitched to the accents of the common people. He collected sentimental verse and religious tracts, valuing them for their verbal peculiarities; he hated cant and would review an entire book in less than an hour. He was entirely devoted to writing but he disliked the actual task. First thinking the entire story out in his head, he would pull himself over to his battered, sweat-stained Underwood typewriter, and with his two index fingers flying, compose the first and final version, which he would check for misspellings.

I was privileged to know this man, as were many, and through him many others of his generation. Friendship had a special significance for Jack Conroy. His long friendships with colleagues in the writing trade (he never saw writers as competitors) opened doors for me to those who had, in many cases, become involuntary exiles in their own land during the Cold War era, with its inquisitional spirit and irrational anticommunism. It was enough to have Conroy's personal introduction to receive a warm welcome among former contributors to the *Anvil*, radical writers, and labor activists. I saw it my task to help reclaim the midwestern radicals, the long-suppressed voices of "the other 1930s." They are the rightful mentors of young people who grow up in an age without idealisms and with little in the way of inspiring examples, just as many of the midwestern radicals of Conroy's generation looked to earlier generations for mentors and models.

Someone asked me once whether knowing Jack Conroy would distort the objectivity of my writing. I thought about that and wondered how anyone could ever write about Conroy *without* knowing him, since researchers like myself are products of our own, usually middle-class culture and educations. Even if we grow up in working-class families and environments, we are taught to write and think in a manner that denies this background. Conroy was a mentor to me at a time when I longed for literary companionship. Intriguing clues buried in his storytelling steered me in new scholarly directions. His "method" was not by precept but by casual reference, which, when followed up, exposed broken fragments needing reconstruction, as if something whole—a dream, an ideal, a tentative but powerful movement—had somehow been shattered. Conroy was a believable person, unpretentious, unsentimental, honest with himself, without bitterness. Terrible personal blows rained upon his broad back during his long lifetime, but always he picked himself up, ready, as the English barroom song said, "to fight with you again." In his eighties, nursing his semi-invalid wife, Gladys, at home, Conroy received "pilgrims" come to glean his encyclopedic recollection of radical history, and the people who made it, for their dissertations and books.

For reasons that I relate in the present study, Jack decided to remain within the culture that was his birthright, to valorize what in fact was his by virtue of his childhood in a mining camp, his early apprenticeship in a railroad shop, his involvement in labor strikes and years of migratory labor. At a certain point in his life he had consciously and deliberately decided to remain firmly in that "space" of his experiences and choices, and to create from within it. Both of his novels deal with this choice, and what a momentous choice it was, given his intellectual abilities and literary ambition. Pulled in two conflicting directions—between the world of manual labor and the status of professional man of letters—Conroy attempted a conjunction that in American society seems impossible or undesirable to achieve.

To join worker and writer in hyphenated condition entailed contradictions for Conroy that were never quite resolved. Financial need dictated that he spend most of his waking hours on the assembly line or laying bricks on a road or digging pipeline ditches. The desire to accede to the status of writer, on the other hand, offered a possibility of escape from the exhausting routines of menial labor and entry into the domain of literature with its vertical structures of prominence. To make one's way into a literary career, however, meant ascending in solitary isolation a hierarchical scale of reputation within an unfamiliar literary system of production and publication from which his status as worker-writer excluded him.

Conroy's earliest mentor and sponsor was H. L. Mencken, the iconoclastic editor of the prestigious *American Mercury*. Mencken was scarcely a votary of working-radicalism, but he admired the fresh vitality and authenticity of Conroy's writing drawn from personal experience. Conroy, in turn, sponsored and encouraged new writers through his own editorial work. The Rebel Poets (1928–32), an organization that he cofounded and whose magazine he edited, strove to accommodate the interests of literary radicals as diverse as the midwestern worker-writer Joe Kalar and the New York intellectual radical Philip Rahv. When this project foundered on the shoals of factionalism, Conroy focused his attention, as writer and editor, on fostering a new literature that explored the lives of society's marginalized people. The men and women who appear as the characters of Conroy's fiction and in the *Anvil* stories he edited rarely leave written records of their existence to posterity. Workers, migrants, the homeless, drifters, prostitutes, eccentrics, these people have little access to channels of communication and few literary examples to guide them should they wish to tell their stories on paper, assuming that they possess the (teachable) writing skills to do so, which few have. Conroy gave voice to the voiceless, permitted them to be heard.

By the mid-thirties, however, "the human condition" and mythopoeic versions of "the people" regained ascendancy as literary topics in place of realistic, often cheerless portrayals of working-class existence. The proletarian school had produced too many poorly written, dogmatic novels, eliciting broadside attacks by Mencken and others. Second chances were not readily granted talented writers like Conroy and Algren, for whom the term proletarian had become a liability obscuring their larger creative designs. Depressed about the critical reception of *Somebody in Boots* (1935), sections of which had appeared in the *Anvil*, Algren attempted suicide. Before year's end, Conroy would lose the *Anvil* in an unfriendly takeover and drop from public view to face obscurity and impoverishment. Released from the humiliation of asking friends for help, he was invited to join the ill-starred Missouri Writers' Project in the spring of 1936. Neither Conroy nor Algren was officially invited to the second American Writers' Congress in 1937. Jack had become a "wounded guerrilla," Meridel Le Sueur said, for whom "no-one struggled."[3]

Fundamental differences distinguished Conroy's writing from orthodox proletarian literature. The left attempted to create an ideological space for the insertion of a literature that, termed proletarian, was too varied to merit a single name. Lacking a proper title, this new literature could be identified nonetheless by its view of society in class terms and its sympathy with the outcast, the unemployed worker, the marginalized people in society. Conroy's writing differed from the orthodox strains of proletarian writing with its facile convictions and two-valued perspective (for example, worker/bourgeois, social justice/oppressive capitalism, the literature of commitment/pure art). With all their warts and carbuncles, his workers are individuated, not idealized figures composing the vanguard of a revolutionary class. Defined by concrete circumstances, speaking in the vernacular of the workplace, they are awkward, unheroic historical actors enduring the consequences of real social forces propelling them into a newer world where the safety of custom, family, trade union, skill, and status is lost.

Conroy knew this brave new world of the industrial worker intimately—its uprootedness, alienation, deskilling. He spoke like the figures of his stories because, except for his literary aspirations (on that qualification hangs the tale of the worker-writer), he was one of them, experiencing the transition between an older, artisanal world of labor and a newer, factory world. The authorial voice of his texts is only one among many voices existing on the same level. His literary work contains no single subject but a multiplicity of utterances in collective arrangements, characteristic of the workplace.[4] Inscribed in Conroy's writing are the circumstances of its production, the situation of a worker-writer who crossed boundaries within both the domain of his everyday working-class existence and the domain of literature, in which his status was still undefined and his work, sensitive to the marginalized voices of his culture, fundamentally anticanonical.

What were Conroy and the literary radicals of his generation after, and what was their fate? To find responses to these and many other questions meant collecting material that did not exist conveniently in library archives and interviewing hundreds of people scattered widely, many in their eighties, some healthy, others quite ill. Some I reached too late. I knew that Conroy had kept nearly every letter he had received over sixty years, but these were in his basement and unavailable. Many of those I interviewed had destroyed their correspondence to protect themselves and their correspondents during the inquisition years of the Cold War and McCarthyism. Toward the end of Conroy's life, when it appeared finally that he would not complete the autobiography he hoped to write, he decided to appoint me his literary executor, allowing me, with the help of Nancy Lankford and Lynn Wolf Gentzler, of the Western Historical Manuscript Collection at the University of Missouri–Columbia, to retrieve the letters and manuscripts from beneath a dripping basement water pipe that had begun to do its work of destruction. A few weeks later and most of the letters would have been a mass of sodden pulp. These now reside permanently in the Newberry Library, Chicago. In one sense, my study is a guide to these letters as well as a forum for the contributors to Conroy's magazines, his friends and colleagues of the 1920s and 1930s, to tell their stories. Their confidence in and fondness for Conroy gave them heart to tell their stories to me, just as they had felt trust in Conroy's purposes and editorial abilities in submitting their work to his magazines. These writers of Conroy's generation thus became contributors to my own work, enlarging its scope with their knowledge and experience, but most of all with their humanity.

* * *

My critical-biographical study of Conroy and the midwestern radicals focuses on what Robert Weimann calls the "genesis" and "impact" of their work.[5] Conroy's birth and childhood in a midwestern mining camp, his apprenticeship at age thirteen in a railroad shop, his involvement in the Great Railroad Strike of 1922, and his subsequent years as a laborer in mines, mills, and auto factories were components of the "worker" term of the hyphenated "worker-writer" status that defined his exceptionality as a worker and writer. The "writer" term grew out of his early exposure to socialist publications like the *Appeal to Reason*, the Haldeman-Julius magazines (where numerous midwestern writers, including James T. Farrell, saw their early work published), his contacts in Ohio with editors of "little magazines," and the new group of leftist publications appearing in the late 1920s, for instance, *New Masses*. Perhaps the most important shaping influences in the genesis of Conroy as a writer were his mother and father. His father, an Irish immigrant who died in a mining accident when Jack was nine, was an eloquent speaker and strike leader; his mother, a consummate reader of Victorian sentimental women's novels, nourished his literary interests and encouraged him to further his own education through correspondence courses. Self-taught, Conroy carried inexpensive editions of the world's classics—"The Little Blue Books"—in his work jacket to read during stolen moments in the railroad shops.

Conroy, Meridel Le Sueur, Joe Kalar, H. H. Lewis, and others were part of a loose-knit group of young midwestern literary radicals who knew one another through epistolary contact only. In the late 1920s, they began to express their dissatisfaction with the dominant culture and the lopsided affluence that had left millions, like themselves, exiles in their native land. Attracted to the emerging eastern intellectual radicalism of Mike Gold, *New Masses*, and the cultural programs of the Communist Party of America, these midwesterners nonetheless remained independent of close Party ties. Their roots were, after all, in the independent Socialist-Populist-anarchist traditions of Eugene Debs, Julius Wayland's *Appeal to Reason*, and the Non-Partisan League. Several were factory workers, millhands, and farmers: workers by day, writers by night. The midwestern radicals attempted to keep alive a grassroots literary and cultural movement, grouped around editors like Conroy who demonstrated that cheap printing, wide distribution, social content, and popular readership were the ingredients of a democratic culture. Unnurtured by either the establishment press or the Party's cultural apparatus, they were actively undermined by elements within the left's cultural movement, a fact that raises questions about the left's position on working-class culture as the 1930s wore on. Whatever that position might have been at any one time, the effect was that the cultural left began to ignore the importance of creating an authentic working-class literature sensitive to regional difference, such as Conroy attempted in the *Anvil*. That story, so far as I know, has never been told adequately, in part because many of those whom it affected never, for various reasons, had an opportunity to speak, or were unwilling to speak.

Jack, who generally supported Party aims, particularly its interventions on behalf of the unemployed, was an undependable "element" from the Party's point of view. Independent, rebellious, impatient with theorizing, devoted to people rather than to ideologies, he was admired for his working-class background and literary achievements but criticized as an unreliable "bohemian." In its search for a proletarian culture, the left-wing movement had played a crucial role in fostering worker-writers like Jack, Joe Kalar, Harold H. Lewis, John Rogers, Ed Falkowski, and others. Walt Carmon and Mike Gold had opened the pages of *New Masses* to them for a time, but Carmon had eventually gone to Moscow to work for the publications of the International Union of Revolutionary Writers, and Gold was no longer actively involved as editor. The fresh perspectives of the left's cultural movement, evident in its early promotion of the worker-writers, gave way to ambition and political maneuvering that, together with the changing climate of reception, altered profoundly the evolution of literary radicalism. The inattention or indifference of the bourgeois press toward the worker-writers was not in itself fatal to them; shifting priorities and ambivalence within the left-wing cultural movement were deadfalls that caught the worker-writers.

When Conroy traveled by bus to New York City in late April 1935 to deliver one of the principal speeches at the first American Writers' Congress, held at Mecca Temple on West Fifty-fifth Street and at the New School for Social Research on West Twelfth, he was something of a celebrity. New York journalists cast him as a working-class bard, a rural genius from the hinterland. At the congress he was greeted variously with wonder, affection, and condescension. Reading from food-smeared notes and delivering anecdotal remarks to reporters in a booming longshoreman's voice, Conroy effortlessly played the roles into which the press and the left cast him. With sincere conviction, if perhaps naiveté, he spoke of the possibility of the worker as literary producer. Six feet tall, barrel-chested, his hands roughened by work, Conroy was the very figure of the proletarian hero-writer. His working-class credentials, Mike Gold had said a few years earlier, were impeccable. Yet as Conroy stood awkwardly at the podium in New York, defending the role of the worker-writer to an audience of several hundred fellow writers, editors, and critics, most of whom had never so much as stepped inside a mine or factory, the left's literary politicians were charting a future that boded unfair for "the old daddy of rebel writing," as Richard Wright called him.

The traditions of midwestern literary radicalism, Conroy's status as worker, his struggle for recognition, his evolution as worker-writer comprise this book's first sixteen chapters, whose subtitle might be: the voyage from Monkey Nest to Mecca Temple. In three concluding chapters I focus on the contexts of loss and recovery affecting Conroy's reception and the status of worker-writing. A brief afterword summarizes the significance of what has been said.

Attempting to avoid the presentation of a unitary self, I reflect the multiple "knowings" of Conroy in the mirrors of those who knew him and those who wrote about him—both favorably and unfavorably. I suggest that the democratic, rhizomatous mode of literary expression represented by Jack Conroy and certain others of his generation of literary radicals runs like an underground stream throughout American society, disappearing for a time, but always reappearing in new manifestations, in ephemeral publications, grass-roots initiatives, and individual writers, most recently in the work of minority writers. The nature of worker-writing itself, intimately connected with the conditions of employment and the status of workers in society, has altered fundamentally in the present postindustrial, information age. Yet the deeper impulse to find a means of self-expression among those who do not (ordinarily) write remains, assuming different forms.

The methodological focus of the present study is on evolution, process, and reception: how Conroy, the son of an immigrant Irish coal miner, apprenticed at age thirteen, developed a consuming passion in writing, eventually decided to align himself with the interests of the working class, participated in the labor struggles of the 1920s and 1930s, formulated an alternate system of literary production whose intent was to encourage and advance unknown writers and controversial subjects of social content, produced a flawed but powerful classic of working-class existence, and for a brief period achieved literary prominence in the mainstream press.[6] I discuss the concept of the worker-writer, the tradition of worker narrative, and questions regarding the insertion of worker-writers in a system of literary production that made no place for them. In broader terms, I examine the problems having to do with recognition on the part of the dominant literary system of writers and subjects that challenge the arborescent system of authorial reputation itself. Since my topic is Conroy's significance as worker-writer, not the events of his life per se, the hinge-point of my study is the 1935 American Writers' Congress, coinciding with the precipitous shift in the literary reception of worker-writing.

Despite the fact that the base of support and recognition the worker-writer had briefly enjoyed in the early 1930s was effectively destroyed, Conroy's projects, both as writer and editor, provided new directions for American letters in realizing a democratic culture worthy of its name. A half century earlier, Walt Whitman had called for "a programme of democratic culture, drawn out, not for a single class alone, or for the parlors or lecture-rooms, but with an eye to practical life, the west, the working-men, the facts of farms and jack-planes and engineers, and of the broad range of the women also of the middle and working strata, and with reference to the perfect equality of women and of a grand and powerful motherhood."[7] We seem no closer in our own time to achieving such a culture. Publishing conglomerates, perishing literary magazines, and nightly television dim possibilities even further. The directions, nonetheless, are printed should we wish to read them.[8]

1

Monkey Nest Mine:
The Father's World

You are brought now to fit earth's intestines, stoop
like a hunchback underneath. . . .
—Tillie Olsen, *Yonnondio*

JOHN WESLEY "JACK" CONROY, who bore the name of Methodism's
founder, was born in a coal-mining camp in northern Missouri, on 5
December 1898. Monkey Nest was one of many mining communities
scattered throughout Illinois, Iowa, Missouri, and Indian Territory
(Oklahoma) at the turn of the century. These were tightly knit work
communities, subcultures shaped by immigrant populations, the particular nature of mining, class structure, and union activity. Named by the
miners, Monkey Nest (Eagle mine) shaped Jack's early years so profoundly that again and again throughout his long life he drew upon memories of his childhood to sustain him and provide material for his writing. To acknowledge that the impoverished, isolated, dangerous life of
miners and the resourcefulness of their families shaped his character and
provided him a source of emotional and moral strength is to grasp an
essential truth of his life and thought.

The coal camp in which Jack was raised was bound together in a
community of work, shared danger, class struggle, and the special nature of mining itself. Jack's childhood "family" was not only his parents
but the people of the coal camp. His first novel, the working-class equivalent of a *Bildungsroman*, is not about a nuclear family, characteristic
of the middle class, but about this larger family of miners and their families. He assumed adult responsibilities when at age thirteen he began
an apprenticeship in the Wabash Railroad shops. His childhood was

brief, circumscribed by deprivation, strikes, and death. Because of its brevity it was all the more intense, yet happy. The warm, communal life of the miners, the nurturing intelligence of his mother, the woods and hollows surrounding the ugly, denuded mining camp—these "shadows of childhood" would, as the Danish novelist Martin Andersen Nexö said about his own youth, "stretch over the whole of life."

* * *

Monkey Nest coal camp was a small cluster of tiny houses next to the Eagle mine, a mile northwest of Moberly, Missouri. One of Jack's earliest memories was the terror of being suspended by his legs over the black hole of the mine shaft by a prankish miner. The Eagle coal mine, which "raised steam" for the first time in the winter of 1894, was small, dirty, and dangerous.[1] The central feature of the camp was the pithead with its cathedral-like tipple. To arrive at the pithead was itself hazardous. From there, a rope elevator was used to reach the shafts some 125 feet deep. Far beneath the earth, the miner had to walk, sometimes crawl, as much as a half mile. "Potrocks" worked loose from the ceilings and fell on the men. Black damp contaminated the air in the shaft. Several shafts some hundred feet distant provided air to the pit. Up on the surface, discolored soapstone and dirt were piled in a large hillock near the pithead. Close by was a pond to provide water for the steam engine that drove the elevator and ventilators. William Hendren, at age ninety-seven, remembered the mine as it was some seventy years earlier: "I decided to look for a job at Monkey Nest, and went down into the pit. The rooms were about four feet and full of rock. I said I didn't want to work in a rocky room, would have had to shovel the rock out first. No, I said to the superintendent, this ain't nothing for me, and I left it."[2]

Mining in northern Missouri was a cottage industry in the 1890s, late in the hand-loading era. Miners used the room-and-pillar method, blasting loose the coal with black powder. Men walked stooped through narrow passageways, barely three feet high, to reach a "room" where, lying on their sides, they hewed coal with a pick, shoveling it into small cars to be connected to a string of cars pulled by pit mules.[3] It was a highly skilled craft that miners practiced with great pride and autonomy. Missouri ranked twelfth in total coal production by states in 1896.[4] The entire country depended on coal; by 1899, 270,000 miners were employed nationwide, digging 193 million tons of bituminous coal.[5] Hauled into town in horse-drawn wagons, Monkey Nest coal supplied mainly local demand for heating. During the summer, layoffs were common. The eight-hour day, won by the United Mine Workers in 1898, improved things for the miner, but safety and health conditions were execrable by today's standards. Militant and effective, the UMW fought for better safety conditions and pay, leading 260 strikes in 1898, and winning 160.[6] The most experienced miners and militant union leaders were immigrant miners, mainly from Great Britain and Ireland.[7] Among these was Jack Conroy's father.

Tom Conroy, born on 6 April 1855, in one of the midland counties of Ireland, probably Roscommon, immigrated in the early 1880s to Montreal, Canada, where his brother Michael worked as a "trader."[8] As was the practice then, Tom spent a week in the so-called fever sheds, a precautionary quarantine imposed by the government.[9] Afterward he set out to look for an aunt named Margaret, married to James Woodhouse, an administrator at the Montreal docks. He was already twenty-five years of age, well read and Catholic. Family history has it that he had studied for the Jesuit priesthood. If so, the evidence points toward Jesuit schooling in Ireland, not Montreal, given his age when he emigrated. Furthermore, the Jesuit archives for the province of Quebec contain no record of him.[10] Little is known about this period in Tom's life—how he supported himself, and so forth. Tom Conroy is listed in *Lovell's Montreal Directory* for the first time in 1884–85, living on Dalhousie Street with his brother, Michael.

One dramatic event stands out from this period of his life. The American evangelist Dwight L. Moody came to Montreal during his urban revival campaigns of 1875–85. With Ira D. Sankey directing lachrymose choir music, Moody, his voice vibrant with emotion, fired his gospel message's heart-rending stories of conversion at young Catholics like Tom Conroy. Night after night Tom attended the revivals, his clerical collar turned around, so the family story goes. Moody's talks were virulently anti-Catholic; the Roman Catholic church was the "harlot of Rome." The evangelist spoke luridly about nuns who buried their illegitimate babies in the convent yard in unmarked graves, and he urged his listeners to look directly to the Bible for assistance. Tom must have been experiencing dissatisfaction with the church, for Moody's appeal took hold and Tom renounced his priestly vows.[11]

It was scandalous to leave the priesthood. Added to the stigma was the bitter animosity that existed between Protestants and Catholics, such as was promulgated at the time by the American Protestant Association.[12] Tom would not even be able to obtain a position as a school-teacher in Quebec, a position for which his Jesuit training prepared him. Free of church obligation, he decided to seek his fortune in the United States. Tom left Montreal with a trunk that reminded his mother of a casket; she feared she would never see him again.[13] His brother, Michael, left Canada not long after. For a number of years the Conroys and Woodhouses were able to keep track of Michael's wanderings through Montana and California, but then the letters dwindled and finally no more was heard of Mike, the family's "black sheep." Tom, on the other hand, stayed in touch with his Montreal relatives, despite what they regarded as the scandal of his conversion.

The Wabash railroad ran west from Montreal through Detroit to Illinois and beyond to Moberly and Kansas City. This was the route that many immigrants followed from Montreal to the American Middle West, and it was likely Tom's route too.[14] He first joined Irish and British immigrants heading for the coalfields of southern Illinois, where he learned the craft of mining and sealed his conversion to Methodism, initiated by the Moody revival in Montreal.[15] British immigrants virtually controlled mining in southern Illinois at the time. Most of them had been active unionists before coming to the United States. Many of them, as Amy Zahl Gottlieb points out, "were sympathetic to the philosophies of Chartism, the radical movement in England that espoused a variety of social and labor reforms."[16] Several of these British immigrant miners rose to positions of leadership in the mining union. One authored mining law for the state of Illinois. A "spirit of commonality" characterized these miners, who lived in coal communities such as Braidwood and Streator. Methodists were active in the mining areas, teaching miners how to preach, one effect of which was to produce eloquent miner leaders.[17] These were never "famous" men but they nevertheless made great contributions, ensuring safety standards and improving the material conditions of the miners' lives. Terrible conflicts arose when mine owners tried to break the union, founded in Belleville in the 1860s. The owners imported inexperienced black workers from Alabama and hired thugs from Chicago to protect the strike breakers. Perhaps it was because of these conflicts that Tom Conroy moved on to the bituminous fields of northern Missouri in about 1893. Whatever his motivation, mining in southern Illinois had been a school in collective action, radicalism, and leadership, qualities that were evident in his subsequent activism.[18]

Once in Missouri, Tom took a room in a Huntsville boardinghouse. In this small town he met and married the "widow McKiernan," born Eliza Jane McCollough, who had lost her first husband, Joseph McKiernan, in a mine accident. Not long after, the new family moved to Monkey Nest coal camp, where Tom, Jack, and Margaret were born.

Tom Conroy was an educated man. How then did he end up in a dangerous and dirty profession, in one of the poorest mines? Mining was one of the few trades open to unskilled Irish workers when Tom left

Canada. Perhaps he was atoning for having "disgraced" his family.[19] He was a restless man, rebelling against Jesuit discipline and authority. Methodism appealed to the emotions, as Edward Eggleston's *The Circuit Rider* (1874) makes clear, offering a fresh democratic spirit.[20] The denomination's tradition of individual empowerment of workers through literacy and education had played a powerful role in English working-class history during the nineteenth century. Methodism "seems to have been best adapted to the miners' mentality and their emotional and spiritual needs."[21] Tom apparently parted from Moody's teachings. The evangelist was more concerned with winning souls and inculcating Christian virtues of meekness and self-restraint than with empowering working-class leaders, whose reforms he seemed to hold in contempt.[22] Most literate workers, particularly labor activists like Tom Conroy, were able to separate political belief from religious sentiment, giving their own interpretation to Scripture, as Ken Fones-Wolf points out.[23] Perhaps it was simply the experience of an awakening that appealed to Tom, a lonely immigrant in a new land, who was eager to break with long-held beliefs, welcoming the new.[24] American Methodism encouraged personal responsibility for one's own life. It is entirely possible that such a notion would have appealed to a young man seeking his fortune. W. J. Rorabaugh has noted that "the triumph of evangelicalism heralded the waning of traditional society. That society had functioned on the basis of hierarchy, subordination to authority. . . ."[25] Moreover, Methodism's social gospel movement, whose culmination was a "social creed" calling for equal rights, the principle of arbitration, and safe working conditions for workers, had more to offer a young labor activist than did Catholicism as Tom had known it, which "remained suspicious of state intervention and social reform."[26]

Perhaps the confluence of Methodist conversion and exposure to the traditions of British miners in Illinois mining areas explains why Tom Conroy eventually assumed a leadership role in the United Mine Workers' local at Monkey Nest. During the week, he met with his fellow unionists; on Sundays, he took his children regularly to the Northern Methodist Church in Moberly.[27] He must be counted among those respectable workers who, as Fones-Wolf says, "were imbued with a commitment to respectability and self-help ideology," yet were active trade unionists. "The ideals of liberal Protestantism complemented a wide spectrum of political and class positions."[28]

We know the exterior dimensions of his life, but we can only speculate on Tom's motivations. Fluent in French, able to read Latin, an avid reader, Conroy must have been frustrated by the exhausting routines of mining. Perhaps the close-knit community of fellow miners replaced the community of Jesuits. Discipline, ritual, and study found substitutes in danger, hardship, and the solidarity of strikes. When his close friend, a French-Canadian miner, was crushed in a mine accident, Tom administered the last rites; there was no time to send for a priest.[29] The mine tipple was Tom's cathedral spire; the task fell to him, the lapsed Jesuit, to bless the dying man. The promise of social justice on earth requires intermediaries too. Here was a church Tom Conroy could serve.

Tom E Conroy—who added "E" as a middle name since another miner was named Tom Conroy—was just one of the educated immigrant miners who were instrumental in labor organization in midwestern coal camps. Their generation followed earlier labor leaders who had come to America from Great Britain and Ireland and led the struggle for mine safety laws, shorter hours, and collective bargaining.[30] These included Daniel Weaver, Thomas Lloyd, James Braidwood, Daniel McLaughlin, John Mitchell (later head of the UMW), and, later, John Brophy and Phil Murray.[31] The tiny union local in Monkey Nest, then, had direct antecedents in earlier labor radicalism in the British Isles to which Tom Conroy was, by a peculiar series of events, linked. Noted for his speaking ability and even-temperedness, Tom died too young to make his mark in union activity other than in Monkey Nest, where he was esteemed and loved by his fellow miners.

*   *   *

Monkey Nest was a tiny "United Nations," as Jack called it, an immigrant community isolated from the town and rural life. Black miners lived apart but labored in the mines on equal terms with whites.[32] Miners in Illinois and Missouri represent a separate tradition from the Jeffersonian yeoman tradition of the nineteenth-century farmer. For example, miners did not cultivate the individualistic outlook of the farmers, who generally regarded the miners as inferior beings because their work was dirty and because the close living conditions of the camps drew attention to their ethnicity. The farmers, on the other hand, prized self-sufficiency and independence. They would join voluntarily to raise a barn or put out a neighbor's fire; but unions, class attitudes, strikes were foreign to them. The miners were artisans, comrades in the mines and in the tavern. "The mine worker," writes Carey McWilliams, "served as the exemplar of proletarian brotherhood and virtue—yet the miner was himself an atavism. The U.M.W. was not a true industrial union, it was a civic union, reflecting a society that came close to complete community. Miners shared not only battle and the intimate presence of death, they had a pride in skill and lived in communities where home and recreation were part of a whole whose center was the mine."[33]

The farmers were closer to mainstream American values and attitudes than were the miners. The frequent mine strikes, sometimes violent when strikebreakers were imported, the dangerous and dirty life, even the close-knit communities aroused suspicion among farmers and the middle class of nearby towns.

The coal-camp community, the craft system of mining, and the spirit of fraternity were anachronistic in the new industrial order of the wage earner. Yet mining shared a common feature with the factory system in that large numbers of miners worked for a single employer. Thus a kind of protoproletarianism was characteristic of miners, like the early wage-earning stage among factory workers. Class consciousness evolved without ideology. Class divisions were unequivocal. On the one side was the mine owner (and his superintendent); on the other were the miners who, although their work was stratified, felt on equal terms with one another owing to the shared dangers and nature of the work, in which one miner was hardly distinguishable from another in his suit of coal dust (women did not work in American mines in 1890).

Tom Conroy's education set him apart in one respect from the other miners in Monkey Nest. If he wished for a safer, more comfortable existence, however, he displaced these aspirations on his sons. A member of the working-class intelligentsia, with a fondness for Sir Walter Scott and Charles Dickens, he nonetheless chose to remain a miner, do his reading in his spare time, and work through the union local for change. He remained inside working-class experience while possessing the attributes making social mobility possible should he have chosen it. In an era of self-help, individual aggrandizement, and middle-class aspirations, Tom Conroy was an exception. Here was an individual whose achievement, however modest, lay within the bounds of his class, a man who provided leadership to his fellow miners while he continued to work as a miner, indeed accepted extraordinary risks to increase his pay. The world of the exceptional worker-intellectual in a working-class milieu is largely obscured in traditional and popular fiction. Dreiser, Lawrence, and London describe such individuals, but the tale is usually of their efforts to escape their class.[34]

The social and work structure of mining in the hand-loading era, despite differentiation in pay according to the tasks, placed miners on the same level. The mine tunnels themselves extended out horizontally through the earth. At the coal face, the miner was entirely on his own. His contacts with the mine manager were rare; with the owner, perhaps nonexistent. His entire work life played out in a tightly integrated group of workers whose lives depended upon one another.[35] The miner worked essentially without scrutiny, dependent upon his own skill, alertness, judgment, and strength, yet in a collective body of artisans performing similar tasks autonomously. Mining offered Tom Conroy independence in a dirty and dangerous but proud occupation, and community within the fraternity of miners.

The Eagle mine was to last only some eighteen years. In 1894, the state mine inspector, Charles Evans, reported that the business depression had lowered the profit margin, already narrow, of most Missouri coal mines. Miners earned $17.60 per month after paying for blasting powder, lamp oil, the blacksmith, and the doctor. Eagle mine (Monkey Nest) was unsafe. Successive operators cut corners on equipment in order to meet falling coal prices. Evans, a Welsh immigrant and miner, labored to see that safety standards were met, encountering resistance from both the miners and the operators.[36]

The "roofs" of the mine shafts were soapstone and shale. To save time, the miners would neglect to shore up their "rooms" with adequate timbers. To meet rising competition, Monkey Nest miners relied increasingly on blasting powder to loosen the coal. Poor ventilation caused fire-damp gas to accumulate. When "shots" were fired (using blasting powder), there was always the risk of a catastrophic explosion. Operators, hungry for greater profits, changed mines frequently, sometimes twice in a single year. Few improvements were made either in the hoisting equipment or in providing air shafts to improve ventilation. Year after year the inspector complained of the poor conditions at Monkey Nest. Makeshift improvements were undertaken simply to keep the mine running. Northern Missouri had relatively few fatal accidents in comparison to other coalfields, but this was because its miners still worked with picks and shovels, and were experienced. Conditions in the mining industry, however, were changing fast in the 1890s. The small operator was no longer able to compete with syndicates of operators and corporations. Even in miserable operations such as Monkey Nest, miners had some influence on the operators. Miners worked in substandard conditions, but both they and the operators knew how far to push their luck. Increased coal production and falling prices brought about vast changes. Organized miners demanded higher wages. Corporate mine owners imported black workers from southern farms to replace striking miners. These workers, lacking mining experience, had no idea where the line lay between relative safety and disaster. Immigrant workers from Poland and Italy joined the older British and Irish immigrant miners; as long as there were enough of the latter, apprenticeship could continue. But experienced miners were quitting the mines, or moving elsewhere. Conditions at Monkey Nest were appalling; they would have been a great deal worse without Charles Evans. Strikes were the sole recourse on the part of the miners; they were a regular feature of Jack's childhood.

Contemporary "life-histories" of workers lend the impression of half-educated miners struggling to maintain their existence, reluctantly entering strikes. A popular magazine called the *Independent* printed such life-histories of "undistinguished Americans," editing out remarks of a militant nature, shaping the stories as illustrations of democracy in action. Democracy to the editor obviously meant knowing one's place within the status quo, not acting collectively for change. In reading life-histories printed in union journals and in the state mine inspector's report, however, one finds an entirely different picture.[37] Charles Evans, for instance, proudly notes that members of the UMW in neighboring Macon County refused to accept the coal company's invitation to scab. Efforts to hire farmers proved "an expensive experiment" owing to the lack of skilled miners working with them.[38] After the Macon County mine operator left, a successor company recognized the eight-hour day and the union local.

Tom Conroy held several offices in the UMW Local 419 at Moberly. He and Charles Evans were the "earnest minority" that Richard Hoggart discusses in *The Uses of Literacy*—those workers who involved themselves voluntarily in trade union activity, who read not simply the cheap popular fiction of their day but Macaulay's *History* in popular editions, probably those of Henry George and Edward Bellamy, and subscribed to the pro-union *Indianapolis News*, Wayland's *Appeal to Reason* (published in Girard, Kansas, likewise a mining area), and the *United Mine Workers' Journal*. This small number reached out beyond the common fare "for a more nourishing food";[39] they believed in self-improvement and the empowering acts of language. Their speaking ability made them natural leaders in union meetings. Jack's sister Margaret remembered their father practicing his speeches at home.[40] In neighboring Huntsville, where the Conroys first lived, the newspaper cited the number of impressive speeches in the union meetings, underscoring the importance of eloquence and education.[41] Apparently Tom divided his time between union work and the mine, avoiding the "tavern life" that took up the evening hours of most of his fellow miners. And when he was not engaged in either, he worked in his garden.

Coal prices in the period in which Tom Conroy was a miner did not keep pace with demand, since mines were overproducing. Blasting, cheap labor, and the introduction of machines only worsened the miner's situation. The strike seemed to be the miner's only defense; yet strikes, sometimes lasting months, reduced the miner to poverty and left the mines in worse condition than before owing to the lack of maintenance.

Things improved briefly in 1898 when tracks were laid connecting Monkey Nest to the Wabash line so that coal could be sold to the railroad. At one point, however, the mine operators simply decamped without paying the miners. They returned later, paid up, and the mining resumed. Nearby coal-producing states like Illinois had "thicker seams of coal, better roof and other advantages all tending to a cheaper and more economical method of mining."[42] In 1899, Monkey Nest once again changed operators. Evans's inspection the next year revealed the mine to be in "a deplorable condition."[43] He ordered the mine closed, but the miners persuaded him to wait while a new air shaft was made. Monkey Nest continued to tread a fine line between solvency and failure. "I inspected it on the 18th of April," Evans wrote in his 1902 report, "and, as usual, found it full of black damp."[44] He added that "machinery, drum, pulleys and cages are all in a dilapidated condition full of patches, looking like a makeshift from one day to another." Evans, who had started as a trapper boy at age eight in the mines, was pulled between his responsibilities as mine inspector and his sympathy for the miners who were willing to work a dangerous mine in order to preserve their jobs.[45]

Eliza Jane's sons from her first marriage, Everett and Joseph McKiernan, both worked in Monkey Nest mine. In September 1906 the Moberly paper reported that Everett's right hand was crushed by a rock fall.[46] Both brothers would die eventually in the mine. The UMW revised its constitution in 1904, calling for a minimum age of fourteen for workers in the mines. In 1906, Missouri voted the minimum age into law. The two McKiernan boys had started younger; the family needed their income. Jack might have gone into the mine, except that important changes were taking place, both at Monkey Nest and in the coal industry nationwide.

In the years when Jack was growing up, all of these events shaped his earliest impressions of miners as a class of workers struggling to improve their lot in the face of an economic system that desperately needed regulation. Monkey Nest was an affliction to most of the miners working in its depths, but for Jack as a boy it was a school that taught social justice, class loyalty, and resistance. The number and length of the strikes increased. Tom's kitchen meetings grew more frequent. Blacks, most of whom had been imported as strikebreakers, had gradually assimilated into Monkey Nest life and joined the union. Tom invited leaders among them to his home, which violated the customs of farmers and townspeople in "Little Dixie" but seemed quite ordinary to the miners. After all, the UMW constitution expressly forbade discrimination according to "the color line." Most of the British and Irish im-

migrants held little prejudice, apart from their anger when blacks un-
wittingly acted as strikebreakers. In Monkey Nest, the politics of class
superseded those of ethnicity and race, which is not to say that ethnic
and racial differences were ignored.

Years of deteriorating equipment, strikes, changing operators, and
intense competition took their toll at Monkey Nest. The mine depended
greatly upon winter consumption of coal. The winter of 1907/8 was
unseasonably warm; consumers were beginning to use natural gas and
petroleum. From April through part of June the mine lay idle as the
UMW sought a new labor agreement. Evans again complained: "This
mine has given me a great deal of trouble in trying to see to it that it
is kept in a safe condition for the men to work in. I have closed it down
until a new air shaft is sunk at the head of the works."[47] New management raised his hopes: "I found the foreman devoting his entire time
to looking after the mine, and if Mr. Hyde [the foreman] is given proper encouragement and assistance from the management, the mine will
lose its nom de plume, 'Monkey Nest.'"[48] Yet by September, the mine
had again changed its superintendent and foreman. Evans discovered
black damp gas in the entries and noted again the mine's depressed condition.

Underbidding among competing mines was driving out the small
operators and lowering safety standards. Fatalities increased and so did
the amount of wasted coal, Evans remarked in his 1909 annual report.
He called for the regulation of coal prices in order to improve safety.
Of the three to six dollars per ton of coal paid by the consumer, only a
dollar was returned to be divided among the operator, the miner, and
the landowner. Miners were using increasing amounts of explosives to
speed up production, and in their haste more and more shots were "missing," or misfiring.

In May of 1909, a fateful year for the Conroys, ninety men labored
in Monkey Nest mine. The air was bad as usual—the new operator,
Moberly Coal Company, had returned to the older system of ventilat-
ing using a furnace—the "roadways were low and dirty, and in several
places broken timbers were found."[49] Again Evans threatened to close
the mine, and again the miners prevailed upon him to allow time for
repairs. The degraded condition of Monkey Nest represented the decline of small mines in the twenty or thirty years since British miners
had led the way to unionization. Evans came from this earlier generation, had known better times, and for that reason felt sharply the pitiable condition of the Monkey Nest miners attempting to keep a dying
enterprise alive.

The last years of the mine at Monkey Nest, from about 1900 to 1910, saw a steady degradation of the miner's condition. His world of worker autonomy and skilled artisanship was dying, more quickly at Monkey Nest by virtue of obsolescence and neglect. New nonunion mines in Kentucky and Tennessee produced cheaper coal. The ranks of the miners, once largely immigrants, were swelling with American-born workers who could master the new machines in much less time and who offered little resistance to stratification of tasks and status. Relations between management and workers at Monkey Nest had always been informal. The owners were absentee landlords, "the Smith heirs," living in Nebraska. Operators had come and gone, but the mine superintendents were usually on good terms with the miners. Strikes involved belt-tightening but no actual strife. If World War I had come several years sooner, perhaps demand for coal would have picked up for a while; but petroleum was replacing coal as a primary fuel.

Union activity at Monkey Nest had meant solidarity, meetings, speechmaking, leadership in strikes, gains and losses. Now, however, mine operators were hiring nonunion workers in greater numbers to break the picket lines. In the past, the Monkey Nest miners had persuaded the scabs to go home and had depended upon their own capacity to endure on food scavenged in the nearby woods. It had once been too costly for the operators to hire "armed guards and inefficient workers who would themselves eventually organize."[50] But now operators were employing such methods. Jack tells in *The Disinherited* of a strike-breaker's appearing at the door of the Donovans (Conroys), seeking directions. The father explodes in anger, and with a burst of shotgun fire sends the scab running off into the night. He then makes his sons solemnly promise never to become scabs.

During a strike in 1908, the superintendent offered Tom Conroy the job of pit boss if he would break the strike. Tom refused. Debts piled up. The Conroys owed rent money and the butcher. Eliza and Tom had hoped to keep Jack out of the mine. By this time, both Everett and Joseph McKiernan had died as a result of mining accidents. Joseph had been crushed under rock on 29 January 1907. Everett, recording secretary of the union local, followed him on 23 February 1908. Crushed by a pit mule in the pit elevator, he died of Bright's disease soon after. The deaths of the two brothers greatly reduced the family's income. To make up the loss, Tom decided to work after hours as a shot firer, a job usually reserved for single men.

No activity in mining bore more risks. The UMW had insisted on regulations specifying that shot firers work in teams of two, that they take precautions to avoid a "windy shot," which resulted from overcharging. Shot firers entered the mine after the day's work when all the miners had left. The incentive was of course additional pay. A shot firer could earn a day's wage in fifteen minutes of firing.

On 6 July 1909, two days after the miners' traditional July Fourth picnic, Tom and his partner, J. M. Morris, went into the mine to fire shots. The evening before, in the Conroys' kitchen, Jack had watched his father roll newspaper cartridges around a pipe, filling them with powder and crimping the ends. Whenever firing occurred, the miners' children would listen to the dull thudding of the explosions, their ears pressed to the cracks between the planks of a wood shed placed over an air shaft. Shouting the customary "fire in the hole" warning, the two miners would move from roof to room, blasting loose the coal. In a sense, they were in a race with other shot firers in more productive mines since everything now depended upon maximum productivity with the least expenditure of effort. It was desperate work and Tom knew it, but it was the first time that he could pay the butcher's bill on time and buy new clothes for his children. Perhaps, too, Jack could continue in school, become an accountant.

The inspector called the accident that took Tom's life and injured his partner "a result of pure carelessness."[51] Morris, as reported in the Moberly newspaper, said that Tom had decided to place a shot despite the appearance of a thin wall. The miners, he said, would have "marked it with a danger signal" if it presented a hazard. While Tom and his partner were tamping shots in an adjoining room, the explosion occurred, shattering the wall between and igniting the shots that Tom had just placed.[52] Morris crawled out of the mine in the dark, feeling his way toward fresh air. Blowing the signal horn, he called for help. Miners and their wives gathered at the pithead, waiting for rescuers to bring Tom to the surface.

Tom lay unconscious in his bed five days, dying on 11 July, early in the morning. He was fifty-four, "one of the best known and best liked men of this community," the paper reported. Eliza Jane had now lost two husbands and two sons in the mines around Huntsville. Several years later, the mine was closed permanently, the shafts covered over with dirt and loose rock. "So the Monkey Nest's mouth is stopped with dust," Jack wrote in his first novel, "but in its time it had its pound of flesh. Yes, I figure it had its tons of flesh, all told, if laid side by side in Sugar Creek graveyard."

2

Monkey Nest Coal Camp:
The Mother's World

The shadows of childhood stretch over the whole of life.
—Martin Andersen Nexö

JACK ADMIRED THEODORE DREISER and often referred to his memoir, *A Hoosier Holiday* (1916), in which Dreiser returns to the house where he was born, sees a sleeping child, and thinks of himself when he was a baby asleep in the same room. Numerous writers born in working-class settings—Dreiser, Maxim Gorki, D. H. Lawrence, Michael Gold, Edward Dahlberg—have left unforgettable impressions of childhood and especially of their mothers, usually strong figures on whom fell the main responsibility for holding the family together and managing its economy. The fathers rose early and returned home exhausted; many were intemperate and thriftless men who preferred the camaraderie of the saloon to the intimacy of marriage. The miners of Monkey Nest coal camp lived in a particular world: the mine, the garden, the tavern, bed. The daylight world on the surface belonged to the women. Women raised the children, took them along on errands to town, read to them, disciplined and encouraged them, and saw that they got as much schooling as the family could afford, usually not more than eight years.

Jack spent the main part of each day in the company of his mother, to whom he was very attached. Conroy left many vignettes of his mother in his writing. His younger sister Margaret, who was their mother's closest companion for years, remembered her as stubborn, convivial, shrewd, fastidious, plain, hard-working, and intelligent, despite her lack of formal education. She read a great deal and had pretensions of becoming a writer herself. A proud and healthy spirit in a blighted environment, she led a life in Monkey Nest coal camp that was devoid of any luxury except human warmth and companionship.

* * *

Born 3 September 1859, in Greene County, Pennsylvania, daughter of Rachel Ann Throckmorton and John Wesley McCollough, Eliza Jane McCollough was one of nine children, two of whom died in infancy. Eliza remembered her father being mustered out of the army after the Civil War. When she was nineteen, the family moved to Missouri in a covered wagon, traveling by way of Illinois and Iowa, and settling on a farm near Moberly sometime around 1878–79. Eliza worked in the Huntsville County Courthouse recording deeds, a job that her fine "Spencerian" script won her. Left with four children, Everett, Joseph, Isabelle, and Cora, after the death of her husband, Joseph, Eliza faced the task of supporting a family alone. To increase her income she ran a boardinghouse in Huntsville. The "widow McKiernan," as she was known, was not an attractive woman but she was gregarious and intelligent. After she became acquainted with one of her boarders, an Irish miner named Tom Conroy, they decided to marry, in October 1894. In 1896, the Conroys moved to live in a camp house in Monkey Nest where Tom Conroy, Jr., was born in 1897. A year later Jack was born, followed by Margaret in 1903. Jack always wondered why his father married a widow with four children. "Having been trained for the priesthood," Jack concluded, "he probably didn't know much about women and their wiles."[1]

Eliza was a quietly determined woman who had almost complete authority in matters affecting the welfare of the family, including bartering with merchants and choosing and purchasing a horse. When Charley, the family horse, was near death, Eliza administered one of her mail-order medicines while "Father sat glumly nearby. He had stood by helplessly as Mother tried frantically to minister to Charley."[2] Nurturing her family, she nonetheless made no attempt to shield them from the world.[3] Maternal and paternal instincts coincided in Jack in his intellectual life, the editor-hero who aided young, marginalized writers generously, yet was a patient, demanding "father figure" to those whom he chose to mentor.[4]

* * *

Jack was a *jambot*, a miner's son, to borrow the richly suggestive expression of the borinage mines in Belgium. The term embraces a wealth of cultural, social, and linguistic meanings. To be born in a mining camp is to grow up in the shadow of the mine tipple, to experience the separate worlds of the father and mother. The father's world is the warm intimacy of the pit among his fellow miners, which usually carries over into the tavern; the mother's is the busy daylight world of resourcefulness, economy, sociability, and nurturing. To be a miner's son is to know death and hardship at a very early age, to view the year's seasons in terms of fatigue, strikes, and long periods of idleness. A strike mobilizes the entire community. A mine disaster touches all mining families directly or indirectly. Such an education is deeply political; from the beginning, the family's livelihood is determined by the miners' organized efforts to gain a fair wage under safe conditions in the face of cyclical market prices and often exploitive mine operators.

Miners' children are granted a brief space in their early lives; they see their older brothers and sisters enter the mines or take up domestic work. Their childhood is an interstice in the world of work and the struggle for existence around them. It takes place in a setting of bleak houses, a despoiled mine patch, and pastoral surroundings that provide temporary escape and, for children, material for the imagination. Responsibility laid its mantle early on Jack. His father's death when Jack was ten was warning that his childhood would end early. Because childhood was brief in Monkey Nest it was all the more memorable. Like Lawrence and Dreiser, he was never able to release the grip of his childhood; like Tolstoy, Nexö, and Gorki, he never wished to.

Except for an initial period in Tom and Eliza's marriage, the Conroys did not live in the four-room coal-camp houses. The home in which Jack was born belonged to the Smith heirs, the absentee landlords who also owned the property on which Monkey Nest was located. "Our Irish parents," Jack mused in one of his Monkey Nest tales, "still had old country misgivings about absentee landlords."[5] Situated about two hundred yards to the east of Monkey Nest camp, the storey-and-a-half house faced a large field called the "Tramway" by the miners because a railroad spur once crossed it, joining a mine nearby with the main track. From the dormer bedroom Jack could view the footpath cutting across the Tramway toward Moberly along which his mother would go on her errands, her small figure disappearing into the distance. In this upstairs bedroom slept the Conroy children. In the other dormer bedroom were Tom and Eliza. The McKiernan children had their beds downstairs, since Everett (and soon Joseph) was already working in the mine and therefore needed more freedom to come and go.

For a time things seemed to go fairly well for the Conroys. When a superintendent of the Eagle mine, Mr. Elvin, vacated his large white house located on the end of the Monkey Nest camp opposite the Smith heirs' house, the Conroys rented it. The Elvin house had eight rooms, a curving staircase, and an orchard. It seemed "inexpressibly grand" to Jack and the other children.[6] A separate alcove contained a desk where Tom could put his books and write letters to his Montreal relatives. A thick hedge of Osage orange trees surrounded the house, hiding it from the ugliness of the mine dump and tipple, reminders of Monkey Nest's tyranny over the miners' lives. The Conroys' idyll was brief. A strike placed Tom and fellow miners against the mine operators and their superintendent, Elvin, and once again the Conroys were forced to move. Yet, their luck held for a time. A house owned by a man named Vaughan, who had no connection with mining, would be available for several months. The two-storey Vaughan house, with its neat white picket fence, was located in Kimberly, a nearby mining camp. Vaughan was an eccentric, one of the many "weeds" that seemed to flourish so generously in Conroy's Missouri. Predicting what day he would die, Vaughan had built a concrete tomb for himself along a road adjacent to his house.[7]

The Conroy children were unwelcome newcomers to Kimberly. Kimberly mine was down at the heel even more than was the mine at Monkey Nest. Accidents were frequent, the coal veins played out. Most of the miners had left or had begun to work their own drift mines, tunnels dug by hand into the side of a hill. Those who remained were a hard-bitten lot; their children terrorized their peers from Monkey Nest. Jack soon learned not to venture far from the Vaughan property. When a black miner named Charlie Thomas, an officer in the UMW local, came to talk about the strike with Tom, the Kimberly "toughs" marched like young Klansmen in front of the Conroy house to protest. It was a relief when the strike was settled and the Conroys could move back to the Elvin house, despite the damage inflicted by strikebreakers who had lived there in the Conroys' absence.

The community life of Monkey Nest coal camp was centered on the mother, as was family life. All early midwestern coal camps were similar in this respect.[8] Women formed the social network in the coal camp and bonded the family together in good times and bad. The cohesion of the family was fundamental to the well-being of working-class life in preindustrial communities and midwestern mining camps. Family structures served as a means to face contingencies such as unemployment, separation, death, privation, and migration. In Monkey Nest such patterns of cohesion among family members—and in a wider kinship circle—were adaptations of old-world attitudes toward family life and kinship roles.[9] In contrast to the middle-class family of today, which, according to Richard Sennett, tends to shield its members from invasive conflicts by forming an intensely private unit, isolated from the community, Conroy's family was social, community oriented, and deeply dependent upon sharing, goodwill, and mutual aid.[10] There was little inclination among the miners to protect their families in a defensive posture against a confusing or hostile outside world. The antagonists were very real and immediate: the mine and the mine operator. Struggle was cast almost exclusively in existential and class terms.

The mining families of Monkey Nest lived in a workers' world of insecurity "in which family and community concerns were paramount, and where it seemed difficult and impractical to consider matters in a long-term perspective."[11] Members of the United Mine Workers perhaps felt more empowered than other workers, but up to the 1930s, as John Bodnar points out, most workers felt largely powerless and isolated in their communities. The cyclical nature of the demand for coal and the precarious condition of tiny Monkey Nest created an atmosphere of uncertainty about the future. Survival and security therefore hinged upon the help one might receive within one's family, through larger kinship networks, and from the community.[12] The solidarity expressed through these connections was analogous to the miners' solidarity; both were grounded in a perception of shared dangers and a collective destiny. An accident might take the life of any miner and leave the family destitute; every family felt this truth deeply. The larger family within the community, one's relatives and friends, were policy against accidental death, permanent injury, and unemployment in mining camps.

The family functioned as a productive unit, all the members contributing as they could to their material life.[13] Working-class children started work at age twelve or thirteen, boys often apprenticing to their father. Indeed, a boy's sense of identity was grounded in his awareness of his father's work. In such a setting, where childhood is circumscribed by work and the productive life of the family, the loss of one or both parents is a catastrophe. Such loss is inevitably accompanied by the loss of material security and a large part of family productivity. Death was a familiar presence among the Conroys. Eliza suffered terribly the mining deaths of two of her sons.[14] Grief was a luxury not permitted her; she turned again to the family's well-being.

The family was always the stable center for the Conroys; its well-being derived from the resiliency and resourcefulness of the parents. Beyond the scope of the family were larger kinship ties that remained paramount for the Conroys long after the closing of Monkey Nest. These ties provided a sense of psychological security and functioned in very practical ways, helping the Conroys and their extended family locate jobs, for instance. The community of Monkey Nest itself was galvanized by collective action in strikes and by the common hazards of mining

that tended to forge loyalties, a sense of community, and class consciousness. Jane Humphries studies this special characteristic of working-class
families in England. Her conclusion applies as well to immigrant coal
camps in the American Midwest where British miners often occupied
leadership roles. "Rather than promoting individualism," she writes, "the
mutual dependence of the family could well point up class community
and class interest."[15] The kinship attachments were to persist under the
new conditions Jack experienced when he later entered factory work.
"In the new division of labor," Stanley Aronowitz argues, ". . . the family
became the heart of the heartless world."[16]

Another attachment, no less decisive in Jack's life, was to physical
place, the coal camp and its surroundings. The Monkey Nest mine dump
was an ugly hillock of discolored rock and dirt, the camp a drab assem-
blage of monotone shacks, but the woods and fields around the camp
were a child's paradise. The close juxtaposition of ugliness, a savaged
landscape, and the pastoral, almost untouched wilderness explored by
Jack and his childhood companions provided altogether a different experience from that of the child growing up in an urban center without
natural sanctuaries. Moreover, small midwestern coal camps were different from larger coal communities in, say, Pennsylvania.

One of the earliest studies of coal-mining communities grew out of
William Graham Sumner's sociology seminars at Yale at the turn of the
century. Peter Roberts, a student of Sumner's, studied Pennsylvania coal
communities, using Sumner's folkways perspective. He discovered in
them a denuded landscape—poisonous streams, despoiled hillsides, discolored soil—something entirely different from the physical environment of urban or small-town communities. The defacement of the landscape, he reported in 1904, corresponded to moral degeneration among
the immigrant mining families. Despite the depravity, coalfields provided
opportunities for social and economic mobility, he said, according to
"the law of social capillarity."[17] More interested in the "moral life" of
the miners than in describing individuals, Roberts, following Sumner's
methodology, portrayed the customs, living conditions, and work patterns as a function of the folkways conditioned by environment, ethnicity, and habit. The ethnic groups regard one another with suspicion,
he said, clinging to old customs, seldom learning English, sending their
children into the mines early, frequenting saloons, and selling their
votes. "Sclavs [sic]," Roberts concluded, "are ignorant, clannish, unclean,
suspicious of strangers, revengeful and brutal."[18] Similarly, some twenty
years later, George Korson's study of Appalachian coal camps notes the
blighted earth and the rigid social lines separating miners according to
ethnic and racial identity.[19] While Roberts is content to describe su-

perficial features of the miners' existence, ignoring their cultural life, Korson discovers a rich folklife, recording the miners' music, storytelling, and superstitions.

Ed Falkowski, a worker-writer who was to play a crucial role in Jack's Rebel Poets, grew up in the "Sclav" mining community of Shenandoah, Pennsylvania, where he acted in dramas produced by the Polish miners. Falkowski remembered two miners' sons, Tommy and Jimmy Dorsey, playing in the local miners' band.

For those who experienced it, life in the coal camps was far different from the way it appeared to outside observers, even those trained to observe. This was certainly true of Conroy, Falkowski, and other worker-writers who left autobiographical accounts. John Burnett wrote of British miners: "In their autobiographies miners also write with feeling of the beauty of the countryside which could transcend the ugliness of pit-workings and slag-heaps, and of the intimate life of the mining community where work and leisure, birth, marriage and death all occurred with a kind of extended family group with a network of relationships. To this extent the mining community re-created much of the social pattern of the pre-industrial village, and provided satisfactions which were often lacking in the anonymity of the industrial city."[20]

Both Peter Roberts and George Korson neglect the political culture of resistance proceeding from a fundamental class conflict between the producers and the owners. In Appalachia, this conflict was particularly severe, as Harry Caudill, John Gaventa, and other have shown. Mining companies bought land from the original Scots-Irish settlers, people who prized independence and lived in equality. Deceitfully "structuring inequalities," the companies brought violence, class differences, racism, and environmental destruction to the mountains.[21] Coal companies exercised virtual dominion over the mountain people turned miners, forcing them to shop in company stores and buy company houses.[22] "Mining," Seltzer writes, "became an occupational prison from which there was no escape, upward or outward."[23] The miners lived like serfs.

But no such "total institution," as Seltzer termed it, characterized Monkey Nest (or, it appears in Falkowski's view, the immigrant mining community of Shenandoah, Pennsylvania), despite Conroy's reference, in *The Disinherited*, to "the dump [that] dominated Monkey Nest camp like an Old World cathedral towering over peasants' huts."[24] The suggestion of feudality is imagistic; Monkey Nest miners were not serfs in any sense of the word. Many were part-time farmers, independent entrepreneurs. Monkey Nest coal camp was no mountain enclave, locked in by ignorance and impoverishment. Between Monkey Nest and

Moberly there was economic, social, and cultural interaction. Moberly was within easy walking distance, and Tom Conroy could send his children to school there. Tom was often invited to speak at the Northern Methodist Church in Moberly, but he refused; he saved his speeches for the union hall.[25] The economic insecurity endured by Tom Conroy and his pitmates was not unique to miners; it was shared by factory workers during economic depressions, and in some cases by the mine operators. Some merchants, like the butcher, gave credit to the miners on strike. Harmony generally existed between the town and the coal camp. This was the Midwest, after all, where ethnic groups, and to a lesser extent, races, mixed freely, unwilling to grant one's neighbor, rich or poor, any privilege, discounting the idea of social-class difference.

Yet the nature of mining, which created a class of workers bound by collective political consciousness, created friction between the Monkey Nesters and their rural neighbors.[26] Few outsiders actually penetrated the miners' world. Mining was perceived as a necessary occupation about which most people were content to know nothing. The miners as a class were scorned by the farmers, who bore prejudices against "foreigners," dirt, and strange ways. The miners' children seemed to the farmers' children to embody all these undesirable features. Differences grew acute in the one-room schoolhouse at Sugar Creek where Jack suffered through the annual Christmas program in the company of his Monkey Nest peers and the children from nearby farms. The children of the farmers received ice skates and coaster wagons; the miners' children were given "small mesh bags shaped like stockings and filled with hard, cheap candies."[27] Humiliated in school in the presence of their arch-rivals, the Monkey Nest children were richly compensated when they returned home. "Each year," Conroy recalled, "poverty-harried miners' wives performed a miracle as wondrous as that of the loaves and fishes. From out of the comparative nothing left of their husbands' wages after prosaic necessities had been accounted for, they brought forth gaudy rag dolls, a monkey-on-a-string, a jack-in-the-box, picture books with colors more brilliant than the hues of summer. The pungent, exotic smell of oranges filled the air, and there were sometimes bananas and Brazil nuts."[28] The farmers may have had fleeting doubts about their puritanical repugnance toward dirt and foreignness. "Farmers drove their sleighs past the camp, sometimes halting their horses to listen to the singing and dancing. Most of the miner boys could play a musical instrument of some kind—a 'tater bug' striped mandolin, a guitar, an accordion, mouth organ or jewsharp. When we heard, during a lull in the music, the dying tinkle of sleigh bells, we ran to the eight-paned windows to gaze out across the field toward the road. When we returned to school the farmer kids would be sure to say, with a slight tinge of envy, 'Niggers and coal diggers have more fun than white folks.'"[29]

The notion, portrayed in early sociological studies, of an isolated mining camp, entirely self-contained and anomalous, has little validity then for midwestern coal camps, which interacted with a larger literate market community, vital to its existence. The interaction between Monkey Nest camp and Moberly was economic, social and cultural. Coal fed the Wabash steam engines and the town dwellers' furnaces. It was slightly over a mile to reach town and the miners often made the march, groping their way home in after dark along the "Tramway."

*   *   *

Community in Monkey Nest was characterized as much by its cultural and linguistic differences as by geography and sociological distinction. Language in part defined the subculture of Monkey Nest, for as Joyce O. Hertzler argues, "People live in their social class intuitively, habitually, and *verbally*."[30] Language was primarily spoken discourse in preindustrial communities like Monkey Nest. Miners' speech reflects a particular linguistic subculture centered on work. Their speech is a rich field of idiomatic expression, as George Korson and others have shown. Folk naming was an important component of Monkey Nest community life, reflecting cultural difference, local knowledge, communal identity. "Monkey Nest" itself was a locution bestowed by the miners on the Eagle mine, probably based upon the mining term "monkey drift," a ventilation shaft, joined with the pejorative meaning suggesting the nature of the work.

Folk names were attached to the pathways, hollows, and tiny communities around Monkey Nest. The "Nation" was a small group of Irish families—woodcutters—whose sons were considered wild by the Monkey Nesters, "whiskey drinkers and women chasers."[31] "Happy Hollow" contained drift mines where, when the shaft mines were shut down, one could eke out a livelihood. A folk map of Monkey Nest contains "Stinkin' Creek," "Butler Hollow," "Hell's Tater Patch," and the "Jungle," all of which figure in Jack's writing. Trees, plants, and animal life were given special names in Monkey Nest, in some cases coinciding with traditional Missouri folk names. In the woods, hollows, and fields, the camp children harvested berries. "We had our own names for most flowers," Conroy writes in "Fields of Golden Glow," "not having access to precise botanical information." Farmers cursed plants like "golden glow" as weeds, but Jack viewed them with appreciation and sharp scrutiny. Miners' wives searched in the pastures and woods for plants from which they would make their salads. Not all weeds were edible, of course, requiring local knowledge on the part of the forager to discriminate. Mullein, pokeweed, carpenter's square, dock, lamb's quarter, ragweed, sumac, burdock, plantain, smartweed, jimsonweed, and buck brush were all familiar to Monkey Nesters. Blackberries, gooseberries, hazel nuts, hickory nuts, and walnuts were delicacies that cost nothing but an expedition into the woods.

To Eliza Conroy, a weed was simply a plant for which no use had yet been found. To the farmers, weeds were a nuisance to be destroyed. Of these same lowly plants, despised by some, valued by others, Jack said many years later, "We enjoyed the lees of their abundance."[32] Indians had fashioned arrow shafts from the Osage orange tree, a homely creation of nature with sharp thorns and a bizarre, ugly fruit. The wood also made excellent weather-resistant fence posts. Buck brush had served earlier settlers as material for basketmaking. Root diggers furnished herb medicine from nature's abundance, requiring an intimate knowledge of plant life, a lore that exceeded the miners' own knowledge of weeds.

The weed serves in Conroy's writing as an emblem of the common, often scorned world of his observation. His art is an effort to portray the dignity and beauty of "weeds," the uncommon common people, and their experience, giving renewed meaning to Wordsworth's sentiment that "the meanest flower that grows can give rise to thoughts that lie too deep for tears." Hummingbirds, as Conroy points out, sip from the "long evil-smelling" jimsonweed.[33] A presence familiar to rural Missourians, weeds symbolize in Conroy's writing the persistence, tough resiliency, and individual variety of the folk denizens of Monkey Nest and surroundings. You can kill a Spanish nettle by pulling it from the earth, a young boy in "The Weed King" discovers, but its seeds will drift in the wind, "scattering seeds from the bursting pods in all directions."[34] This dense world of weeds that sting, burn, lash, prickle, stick, or choke was an intimate, private realm to the miners' children. "Among the high-rising stalks," Conroy writes, "we trampled out secret rooms, secure from adult intrusion or inspection."[35]

Jack occupied an intensely personal and concrete "life-world" as a child, a world of lived experience, fundamentally social and contextual.[36] He was a sensitive, impressionable youth, as his autobiographical tales gathered in the collection *The Weed King and Other Stories* (1985) abundantly reveal. In these tales the reader is aware of Conroy's keen sense of an external world, his knowledge of an objective world existing beyond himself and shaped by human associations. It is a real and durable world in which, as Christopher Lasch says, people see their accomplishments, not their desires, reflected, a world before mass consumerism.[37] The essence of working-class existence, Richard Hoggart notes, is the "'dense and concrete life,' a life whose main stress is on the intimate, the sensory, the detailed and the personal."[38] When, as a writer, Jack attempted to recreate this life-world and place it in the construction of his young protagonist's growing consciousness, it was the materiality of existence that he described. Daniel Aaron, in his introduction to the 1963 edition of *The Disinherited*, notes Conroy's attraction to concrete depiction. He is "so intent on rendering exactly the texture of his hero's surroundings that he seems to be constantly forgetting the ideological purpose of his narrative."[39] The neglect of ideology in favor of "texture" may have raised concern on the part of orthodox critics on the left in the 1930s, but it makes Conroy's best writing accessible to us today, freeing it from narrowly defined categories of "proletarian fiction" as these were conceived by those critics.[40]

Jack and his companions were lucky in one particular sense: their playground was not the broken glass or the sun-baked concrete of the ghetto where, as urban dwellers, their poverty would have assigned them. The woods were thick with briars and brush behind Happy Hollow in a valley the miners called Skinner Bottoms. Here among trees "festooned," as Conroy writes, with wild grape vines, one could play hide-and-seek or attempt to catch indolent possums gorged with paw-paw fruit.[41] The "dark and mysterious reaches" of the abandoned drift mines of Happy Hollow posed a hazard to children and animals. The Conroys lost a horse named Riley who in straying from the pasture fell into a deep shaft.[42] In contrast to the traditional pastoral, which defines an ideal against which to measure the corrupt realities of a fallen world, the pastoral in Conroy's life-world and writings is simply what it appears to be: a decidedly real place with thorns where an imaginative person might discover both good and evil, inextricably woven together, and contemplate the riddled existence of lonely eccentrics like Kurt Leischer, Monty Cass, and "the Weed King."[43]

Footpaths threaded through the woods and fields, "avoiding any orientation on a culminating point or towards an exterior end."[44] The network of paths brought the coal-camp-dwellers in close contact with the physical world surrounding the camp and on occasion led to unexpected encounters with hoboes, who dropped off passing freight cars, as well as with eccentric characters, like the mad Hade Pollard (who murdered his family), gypsies, and the mean "Kimberly boys." These are people nourished on failure, ignorance, near-poverty, superstition. Like weeds, they are tough and resilient, possessing clearly delineated features; those who appreciate their value see that they even have a certain dignity. The pathways formed what Deleuze and Guattari call *lignes de fuite* (lines of freedom).[45] They followed no imposed plan, connecting merely with the beyond. Connectable, crisscrossing, they represented movements of deterritorialization and destratification.[46]

Contrasting with these rhizomatous connections are the "dark inner landscapes" of the mine.[47] In Monkey Nest's room-and-pillar system, the miner descended from the pithead down a vertical shaft to the coal seam in a rudimentary cage whose winding gear was powered by steam. The elevator stopped at various levels, called galleries, discharging the miners, who stooped and crawled along narrow roadways. The air was foul, damp, close. Miners moved with alacrity and familiarity to their rooms. When the shift was over, they slogged wearily through the muck, stooped and coughing, back to the elevator shaft. The underground roadways formed a network of interconnecting lines, but they were lines of articulation, part of a hierarchical, "arborescent" structure of exploitation and profit. Corresponding to the underground roadways was the organization of the mining enterprise itself, an "overcoded" system with a centralized administration comprising the mine owners, the mine operator, indeed, even the miners' union itself, which by seeking arbitration helped continue the arborescent structure (and justify its own existence), that is, the stratified class system that separated worker and owner. These two conflicting structures, the rhizomatous and the arborescent, were to play fundamental roles in the shaping of Jack's consciousness, in his role as editor, and in the reception of his own literary work.

Beyond the deterritorialized pathways of Monkey Nest Camp and the mining enterprise's hierarchical stratifications lay the real (and mythic) American West "with its Indians free of hierarchy," in the words of Deleuze and Guattari, "and with its fleeting boundaries, its shifting, displaceable borders" (translation mine).[48] The coal-camp children acted out the mythic freedom of the West and other distant frontiers in their games. Among the dirt dumps, in the woods and hollows, they performed the popular fictions that celebrated the anarchic freedom and violent justice of those frontiers. Cheap editions of *Robin Hood and His Merry Men* and Macaulay's *Lays of Ancient Rome* arrived by mail or were discovered fortuitously, feeding Jack's vivid imagination. Only a few paces separated the short-lived freedom of childhood play from the rigorous articulations of the mine. At age thirteen or fourteen, a miner's son was customarily presented with a pair of boots so that he could begin to work. The daughters scarcely fared better; they were occupied with household work, married early, and followed the patterns of their mothers, who, like Eliza, aged prematurely.

In the enclave surrounding Monkey Nest camp, Jack fashioned a rich imaginative world, prompted by his reading and the strange eccentrics who actually lived there. Sentimental and popular fiction, directed to a new reading public of literate workers, sparked his imagination with characters, situations, and plots. Publishers like Beadle and Adams mass-produced cheap editions of novels with titles such as *Desperate Dan, the Dastard; or, The Pirates of the Pecos*, and *Texas Jack, the Prairie Rattler; or, the Queen of the Wild Riders*. Exemplars of "easy" fiction, the stories were simply told, with lurid characterizations, crude dialogue, and suspense involving as many as twenty deaths per novel. Russel Nye describes these immensely popular novels: "All laws of credibility were suspended, for dime-novel readers accepted anything. The cavalry was never late, the hero's gun never missed; Rocky Mountain Sam, at half a mile, once shot the flint and steel an Indian was about to use to light the torture fire right out of his hand."[49] The best of these stories rewarded virtue and punished vice, encouraged "a chivalrous devotion to woman," and in general were not considered objectionable or detrimental to morality, except to Eliza, who placed them on her proscribed list.[50] Reading dime novels *in camera* only added to the sense of adventure for her children. Thus, in acting out the fantasies portrayed so dramatically in dime novels, Jack and his brother Tom would sneak upon Kimberly coal camp, "skulking as cautiously as Diamond Dick. . . . 'Watch out for twigs snapping underfoot,' Tom whispered." Conroy wrote, "In our customary fiction fare a snapping twig often could be a dead giveaway to a lurking redskin. It did not matter to us that the terrain through which we were traveling was almost bare of human presence."[51]

There was always an abundance of popular fiction around the Conroy home, since Eliza avidly consumed it. Thus the Conroys' horse, Charley, became in the children's imaginations Kentucky Belle, the equine hero of Constance Fenimore Woolson's story of the same name. On other occasions Jack and his friends would pretend that the horse-drawn wagons in which drovers hauled coal to Moberly were pioneer wagon trains like the ones they read about. As "bloody savages," the boys "skulked from tree to tree, sometimes shying stones at the drivers, who swore thunderously and shook their blacksnake whips."[52]

"It is impossible," wrote Hamlin Garland, "for any print to be as magical to any boy these days as those weeklies were to me in 1871."[53] The "weeklies" provided ready-made fictional characters for Jack and his playmates, who staged amateur theatricals, organizing themselves as the "Scorpion Mighty Art Players." Taking parts in what he later called his "cornstalk theatricals," Jack, his half sister Cora, his brother Tom, and his nephews, Fred and Harvey Harrison, staged rough improvisations of the adventures of Kit Carson, Diamond Dick, and the Cheyenne Kid.[54] Popular culture inspired the lively oral culture of the camp children's play. Jack was later celebrated among his friends for his ability to recite long poems from memory, but in fact such exercises were common to working-class homes and to schools when he was a child. Hamlin Garland remembers schoolroom recitations:

> With terror as well as delight I rose to read *Lochiel's Warning, The Battle of Waterloo* or *The Roman Captive*. Marco Bozzaris and William Tell were alike glorious to me. I soon knew not only my own reader, the fourth, but all the selections in the fifth and sixth as well. I could follow almost word for word the recitations of the older pupils and at such times I forgot my squat little body and my mop of hair, and became imaginatively a page in the train of Ivanhoe, or a bowman in the army of Richard the Lion Heart battling the Saracen in the Holy Land.[55]

Garland and Conroy were children of the midlands; in the absence of sea or castle or city, they voyaged in their minds.

Isabelle McKiernan, Jack's half sister, was especially adept in quoting long poems, usually sentimental ballads and songs like "The Blind Child," "Put My Little Shoes Away," and "The Drunkard's Child." But the "star elocutionist," according to Conroy's autobiographical story "The Morphadite," was his father.[56] When memory failed them, the Conroys could turn to their small library of books, including "recitations" from which Tom Conroy frequently drew his poems, such as "The Murderer, an Unpublished Poem by Edgar Allen [sic] Poe." His delivery of this apocryphal poem sent terror coursing through the imaginations of the Conroy children on stormy nights. No brush-arbor preacher, Conroy adds, could conjure up such a graphic portrayal of hell and its torments.[57]

Orality, the preeminence of the spoken word, was an essential feature of nineteenth-century small-town culture, with its political oratory, public lectures, and recitation in schools. Oratory, according to Kent and Gretchen Kreuter, "was one of the art forms of democracy. The man who could speak well and animate a crowd had plenty of opportunities to do so."[58] As Alice Donaldson argues, public speaking was woven into the fabric of midwestern town life, in Sunday services, temperance lectures, schools, and political campaigning.[59] "Do all states have the same exalted idea of speech-making Missouri and Missourians entertain?" asked Walter Williams, who founded the school of journalism at the state university in Columbia.[60]

Miners shared in the public life of both town and coal camp, as pointed out earlier, sending their children to Moberly schools in later grades and making their visits to shop, drink, hear speeches, and vote. In Monkey Nest camp, orality lacked the formal character of urban rhetoric, by contrast representing deeper communal attachments and folk customs. A kind of preliterate oral culture existed there, soon to disappear with the closing of the mine. Social bonds had the spontaneity and immediacy of the spoken word, not yet diluted by mass culture and factory proletarianism. Industrialization and urbanization changed the nature of orality, transforming without destroying it, as Conroy showed much later in his industrial folklore collections.

This liminal quality, the threshold between folk community and fragmented factory existence, created no radical discontinuity, producing instead creative transformations in which new forms of orality appeared, as Jack discovered in the Wabash Railroad shops where he apprenticed, beginning at age thirteen. The transformations taking place were apparent in the *United Mine Workers' Journal* and in socialist publications like *The Coming Nation*. Poetry in the *UMWJ*, for instance, reveals a weakening distinction between folk poems of oral tradition and newspaper doggerel. Daniel Kelliher, a young miner-poet from nearby Renick, Missouri, appeared occasionally in the *UMWJ*. His "The Death of Miner," for example, is a traditional topic recast in newspaper doggerel.[61] The *UMWJ* editor describes Kelliher, whom Conroy remembered, as "one of the *Journal's* bright young poets. Though but 13 years old he has written some good labor poems—poems that teem with bright thoughts."[62] A ballad by the miner-poet D. E. Griffith, of Connellsville, Missouri, begins:

> I would not wed that fellow, she said
> Called drunken miner Jack
> Why, says the girl, as she turned awhirl
> And flung tresses back. . . .[63]

For most of his life Conroy collected ballads, mawkish verse, and bawdy songs, which he valued for both their humor and their social commentary. The comic and the tragic stand in close juxtaposition in working-class productions, albeit on a lower register than in great art, yet with no less truth to workers' existence. Working-class poets like Kelliher and Griffith tended to use genteel models for their writing, so that the formal language of the poem unconsciously burlesques the nature of the subject. An important task lay before worker-writers like Jack, raised on popular fiction, genteel poetry, and the classics: to experiment with ways to represent oral expression in writing. The balladry, popular fiction, and doggerel Jack collected and studied constitute intertexts in his writing just as they were elements in the working-class culture he knew in mines and factories. His achievement as a writer lay in reconstituting the spoken word as literary dialogue so that it *sounded* like oral discourse.[64]

The editors of the *UMWJ* evidently thought it necessary to elevate the cultural standards of the miners. They initiated a column entitled "Poems You Ought to Know," which included Leigh Hunt's "Jenny Kissed Me."[65] William Dean Howells's essay on unemployment, "A Sorry Figure of a Sovereign,"[66] was reprinted. Readers, for their part, contributed well-known ballads, such as "Put My Little Shoes Away,"[67] and sentimental poems, including one on a mine disaster that pictured a "pale-faced" woman waiting at the pithead.

Worker-writers who contributed to the *UMWJ* and similar union publications were not successful in bridging the space between oral and written discourse, nor were they able to free themselves from the genteel style of their age. None was able to translate—not simply transcribe—oral to written discourse, or communicate performance aspects of orality. Conroy, on the other hand, came eventually to realize the importance of representing in literature the "voices" of working-class experience engendered over time in oral, or near-oral, communities, in what Goody and Watt call the "long chain of interlocking conversations between members of the group through face-to-face contact."[68]

Publications for workers functioned in part as a kind of street literature, embracing oral and written discourse. Zumthor describes the street literature of France in the centuries following the decline of medieval community life: ". . . in the emptiness of their New World they maintained—they tried to maintain, as long as it was socially and technically possible—the breath of that voice, the living word, presence, warmth. . . . In its own way and setting, street literature witnesses that (past) community life. The voice that engendered it and to which it has recourse even today, at every opportunity, constituted the foundation of group consciousness" (translation mine).[69] Conroy followed the oral culture of workers, which included the bawdy songs, sentimental ballads, and tales of his childhood, into railroad shop and factory. His own writing would translate those oral features of workers' lives into an authentic idiom that attracted H. L. Mencken's attention and led to publication in the *American Mercury*. He was what Woody Guthrie called an "ear player," able to recreate what the ear heard into something new yet authentic in its representation of lived experience.[70]

Stanley Aronowitz divides the childhood of workers into two opposing worlds: the hierarchical world of institutions such as school, family, and so forth, and the "noninstrumental" world of play.[71] As we have noted, miner's children enjoyed the latter only briefly. Child labor laws were not enforced until 1938 with the passage of the Fair Labor Standards Act. Play for the working-class child was acted out in a short period of unbounded time in which, through games, he or she learned elements of the natural and social world. This world was circumscribed, as Aronowitz says, by the realm of necessity, in which school played a central role. School introduced class divisions and prepared children for a lifetime of labor. "The very concept of productive labor," Aronowitz adds, "was consonant with human existence."[72]

Moberly schools would not permit free schooling to Monkey Nest children since the coal camp lay outside their district. Undaunted, Eliza walked into Moberly on the railroad tracks to the office of the West Park school principal and through sheer determination persuaded him to accept her four youngest children, Cora, Tom, Jack, and Margaret. However, a great deal of Jack's education occurred at home. Besides their collection of popular fiction and a two-volume dictionary,[73] the Conroys possessed books that one might find in a Victorian middle-class home: Scott, Dickens, Hugo, and so forth. In school, the children memorized texts from Shakespeare, Macaulay, and Longfellow, and moral selections such as "The Old Horse":

> No, children, he shall not be sold;
> Go, lead him home, and dry your tears;
> 'Tis true, he's blind, and lame, and old,
> But he has served us twenty years.[74]

Jack later took this poem as his theme in an autobiographical story, "Charley Was My Darlin'."

Eliza subscribed to popular magazines like *Comfort* and *Hearth and Home*, which carried serialized stories written by Mrs. E. D. E. N. Southworth and by Mary Jane Holmes, who cranked out sentimental novels to divert people in both middle-class and literate working-class homes. These books included romantic tales set in the American South and English "chambermaid" stories, the counterparts of today's televised soap operas. Mrs. Southworth wrote *Self-Raised; or, From the Depths*, a sequel to *Ishmael; Or, In the Depths*. Immensely popular in the 1890s, her novels bore a peculiar trademark: each chapter would begin with a verse inappropriate to the content of the text. Mrs. Holmes's *Homestead on the Hillside*, the story of a genteel young woman's decline, and H. Rider Haggard's *King Solomon's Mines* and *She* were among Eliza's books that Jack later rescued from his mother's library and preserved. Eliza attempted to write in imitation but never got beyond a page or two of manuscript for lack of time. Moreover, she was troubled by the rigid class divisions portrayed in stories about gamekeepers' daughters who have affairs with their masters but cannot marry above their station. She would often sing a song about miners that revealed their weakness for drink, concluding, "It's not the collier's heart that goes astray." Yet she would complain about suggestions in the song that miners were made of "baser clay" than the manor-born.[75] Popular fiction became a staple of a new reading public in the nineteenth century, coinciding with the rise of linotype machines, the extension of railroads, and literacy among workers. This new readership (mainly women) was hungry for "easy" fiction—tightly knit plots, romantic intrigue (within the limits of propriety), and virtuous conclusions.[76] Such literature was part of Jack's "education," as it was in many working-class homes. As a worker-writer, he put it to literary uses, as his mother had hoped to do, and responded to the implicit class divisions to which Eliza had been sensitive.[77]

Photos of Jack's mother in her forties reveal a large-boned woman with deeply creased face and tired eyes, determined, stubborn. Intelligent and resourceful, she nonetheless "had areas of credulity," placing store in dream books and in cure-alls advertised in magazines.[78] Eliza had a discriminating eye for edible plants like the tender shoots of pokeweed; her trips to the butcher proved her skill at dickering. During her frequent shopping trips to town on foot she would stop midway to rest under an elm tree. When Jack accompanied her, he would lie on his back, studying the "small world" of creatures in the tree branches, while Eliza exchanged news with other wayfarers, women like the "loquacious Widow Brewer." "Mother loved to talk," Conroy writes, and "the Widow Brewer was always good for an hour or more."[79] Nothing distracted the two women. Jack recalled the widow's son Edwin tugging at his mother to call her attention to the plight of a worm lodged under her shoe. Her reply was an impatient swat. The worm died.

Monkey Nest camp was close to a hobo "jungle," and tramps often solicited mining families for a meal. Eliza was generous, but when a tramp came looking for food while Tom was in the mine, she naturally felt apprehensive. She would feign his presence, talking to him as if he were sick in bed in an adjoining room, while she fed the tramp in the kitchen.[80] Yet, Eliza believed that hoboes were less dangerous to the family than were the traveling carnivals with their company of "hoochie-coochie dancers, short-change artists, con men and women, and Lord knows what kind of degenerates." Ignoring his mother's warning to stay away, Jack, in the company of his nephews, George, Harvey, and Fred Harrison, sampled the forbidden attractions, which included free-for-all wrestling. The carnival barker would insult the local rubes in order to incite them to get into the ring with one of the professional "carnies," sometimes a woman wrestler. George, the liveliest of the Harrisons, volunteered and was thrown. A strong farm boy could sometimes last a bout with a carnival wrestler. Jack remembered the sideshow with freaks such as the "cigarette fiend," who lay languidly on a couch, his hands and face yellowed with nicotine, cigarette butts scattered about, warning the young boys not to smoke. Another was "the man with the ossified leg" and "the geek," who, kept drunk, would bite the head from a chicken or rat. A black worker from Moberly was recruited to play the part of the "wild man." Dressed in a loincloth, he gurgled and snarled in a pit with harmless snakes. When Jack and the Harrisons saw him several years later in a Des Moines carnival, he revealed his home-sickness for Moberly. The carnival manager told the boys to leave: "You're ruining my show. He's supposed to be wild. He don't speak English!"[81]

Tom, Jack's older brother, confided in Jack that a "morphadite" (localism for "hermaphrodite") had approached him, urging him to join the carnival, an adventure that tempted many a midwestern youngster. Tom was desperate to escape an onerous job cleaning chickens in the Stamper poultry factory. Jack remembered Tom's lice-covered clothes, which Eliza boiled. Tom died several years later, struck by a switch engine at night while returning from work along the Wabash tracks.[82] "Conroys," Jack liked to say, "always had violent and tragic deaths."[83]

Tom's carnival encounter gave Jack occasion to "wonder about the various kinds of morphadites there seemed to be in the world."[84] If the real prospect of adventure and escape attracted Tom, Jack discovered subjects for his literary imagination in marginalized figures like the morphadites, the isolatos, the eccentrics, and the disinherited.

Glimpses of Eliza appear throughout Conroy's autobiographical "Monkey Nest Tales." Perhaps the most memorable image appears in *The Disinherited*, recalling that following the death of Jack's father, she took in washing from the mine superintendent to help support the family: "Her head was enveloped in a cloud of steam all day. The washboard kept her waist frayed, and the front of her dress was always moist with soapy spray. She bobbed up and down, up and down, as tirelessly and as mechanically as an automaton on a peanut roast, pausing only long enough to hang out a batch of clothes, or to stir those in the boiler with a stick."[85] Often her work continued into the night after the children had gone to bed. "I stole to the middle door and watched her standing with arm moving as inexorably as a piston. She pushed her greying hair back from her eyes with her suds-wrinkled hand. Sometimes her eyes were closed as she ironed. Blinding sweat dripped from the tip of her nose and from her chin."[86] "To write of a working-class mother," Richard Hoggart suggests, "is to run peculiar risks." How does one avoid sentimentalizing the self-sacrificing mother about whom the family life revolves?[87] Conroy does not leave the impression that Eliza was a heroic drudge. Prudish, concerned with decorum, she told her daughters, "pretend like you're looking for something, girls," when the horse, pulling them to town in a wagon, let wind loudly. Gender roles in her marriage were such that "Father sat glumly by" while Eliza managed the practical affairs of living. Careworn, preoccupied with everyday concerns, a proud and healthy spirit wounded by harsh circumstances, Eliza worried and fretted. Marriage became insupportable. Divorce was infrequent among the miners; a couple generally agreed to separate. Tom once moved to Bevier nearby where he could continue to work as a miner, but he returned after a month.[88]

* * *

Jack grew up, then, in a working-class subculture whose linguistic features were both oral and literary. The English-speaking miners organized themselves into debating societies.[89] Lecturers would often stop in Moberly since it lay on the main passenger lines of two railroads. Jack's father took him to hear William Jennings Bryan's "Brute or Brother" speech at the Chautauqua tent in Moberly.[90] He remembered Eugene Debs, a thin man with gleaming bald pate and forceful voice, speaking from the rear of the "Red Special" train during the 1908 presidential campaign. Carl Sandburg, whom Jack later knew in Chicago, was aboard. Too young to appreciate Debs's views, Jack nonetheless knew he was in the presence of a great man whose courage and eloquence had singled him out as a working-class leader.[91]

Eloquence was a powerful tool in the struggle of labor leaders to command the attention and to rouse workers to participation in strikes. *The Disinherited* tells the story of a young worker's "education," his appreciation finally of the role of eloquence in empowering labor. Before him is the example of his father. In the harsh, impoverished coal camp, language was empowerment and consolation.

"We were always starved for print in the camp," Conroy once reminisced.[92] The *Indianapolis News* arrived in camp in a package and was distributed by one of the miners. It reported UMW strikes throughout the Midwest and praised Jack London's *The Iron Heel*. Jack savored the wry sayings of Kin Hubbard's "Abe Martin" appearing in the *News*. One of the miners subscribed to the weekly *Appeal to Reason*. In its pages Jack was first introduced to socialist programs and the "culture of political revolt."[93]

The strikes, the material conditions of life in the coal camp, and the immigrant miners themselves were constituents of a radical consciousness in which cooperation, craft autonomy, and collective resistance were the rule rather than the exception. The miners and their wives shared privation, the grief of mining accidents, collective expressions of protest. The rudimentary *Gemeinschaft* character of Monkey Nest derived from their shared memories of strikes, poverty, and disaster and the feeling that they were "a clan apart from the ordinary run of humanity."[94] Bonding them were the common hazards of their occupation, which they loved to recount. Jack heard miners telling about dangerous mining conditions in England, for instance, where tunnels were burrowed beneath the sea. In their discounted profession was the material of legends. A miner's hardiness might consist in little else than being able to drink late and show up the next morning to hew coal all day, but, as Jack knew, there was a great deal more to their lives in Monkey Nest coal camp.

There were periods, usually during strikes, when the miners killed rabbits to make their meals; during one entire winter they had little else but turnips to eat. At Sugar Creek school the teacher asked one of the coal-camp children whether she had had a good lunch. "If you call cold biscuit and lard a good lunch, yes," came the reply. Teacher: "Why are you scratching?" Girl: "I found a louse on my chest."[95] The privation enforced by strikes or periods when demand for coal was slack became associated in Jack's mind with storytelling and conviviality. The strikes were times of excitement for the camp children. When the scabs appeared, the camp children lay in ditches, heaving rocks at them. In the presence of death, insecurity, and material deprivation, Jack grew up among ministering voices, loving presences. These were hardly the circumstances of a dreary, dispirited proletarian childhood. It was, in some essential ways, an ideal childhood for a worker-writer, who, like the miners, lived a separate existence from "the ordinary run of humanity," endured hardship and loss, sought to reconstitute the lost community of Monkey Nest through a shared literary enterprise, and created his own work out of the struggle that existed between his working-class roots and commitment, on the one side, and, on the other, the lure of "escape" through literary recognition and success.

Jack's earliest literary efforts were devoted to "publishing" a one-copy camp newspaper called the *Monkey Nest Monitor*, writing it on butcher paper that Eliza saved for him. The paper contained a comic strip in imitation of the Katzenjammer Kids (in which the principal figures were miners' children), news shared with him by the camp dwellers, and stories based upon the popular romances in Eliza's subscription magazines, but portraying miners in heroic roles, not cap-in-hand subalterns of the type common to *Hearth and Home*.[96] Jack acquired an early reputation of "bookishness," despite his good-natured affability. He was usually reticent in the presence of the miners, listening to their conversation and welcoming their stories and songs. Large for his age, he dropped out of school every spring to help his mother in the garden. It was assumed that he would quit school, probably after eighth grade, and enter work to help support the family. What, after all, was the choice?

The death of Jack's father appeared to seal this "choice" since there was no money for Jack to continue in school—even though Eliza remarried in 1911. What was her alternative? Pip Addis was his name. He had first come to Moberly in a railroad boxcar with a man named Barney. The two rented rooms from Eliza. Barney warned Eliza about Pip, and left shortly thereafter without paying his bill. Pip was what people called a "mean drunk." At the funeral of young Tom, a year after the marriage, he became abusive to the point that Jack's brother-in-law, Henry Harrison, a check weighman at Monkey Nest, was forced to restrain him. Pip was a fantastic figure who spoke with a faint Scots-Irish accent using vivid skid-row language and who lied in extravagant terms about his earlier life as a cowboy and sailor. "O waly, waly," he would sing,

> but love be bonny
>   A little time when it is new;
> But when 'tis auld, it waxeth cauld,
>   And fades awa' like morning dew![97]

His drunken bouts drove the children (and sometimes Eliza) out of the house to hide in a cornfield across the road. Once he took Eliza on a trip to Butte, Montana, where he claimed he had worked. Drunk during most of the return trip, he introduced Eliza as a whore he had picked up in Butte. Margaret, Jack's sister, detested Pip for his abusive behavior toward her mother.[98]

Good men, it seemed, were extremely scarce—or died early. Eliza's brother-in-law, W. H. McKiernan, her first husband's brother, married to Eliza's sister, Cora McCollough, was a mine operator who, descending into a mine shaft to tie a rope around a miner overcome with the lethal "black damp," was himself overcome and killed. For his courage he received posthumously the Carnegie medal and a small lifetime pension, which went to Cora. Jack had known him well.[99]

Death was a familiar presence in the Conroy household. In Jack's later life, the deaths of his wife, son, and daughter perhaps affected him more, but none entered his literary imagination quite like his father's death. Once, before Tom Conroy's death, an aunt had taken Jack into a room where a dead man lay. Forcing Jack to place his hand on the face of the cadaver, whose "lips were glued in a hideous grin," she made

him promise to take his studies seriously.[100] Jack's lively imagination did
most of the prompting for days afterward. He dreamed of being buried
alive, an unconscious feeling of dread, no doubt, of his own uncertain
future. When Tom Conroy was brought to the surface from the mine
explosion, still alive but unconscious, Jack, like the other children, were
left to fend for themselves. He left the house crowded with visitors and
relatives to play in the garden. The sight of his father's tomato plants,
trampled by the mourners' horses, reminded Jack that his father had
taken the hazardous shot firer's job to provide more income for the family so that Jack could continue his schooling. In *The Disinherited*, Conroy portrays his boyhood feelings of guilt in an episode in which Larry
Donovan, seeking atonement, slashes his wrist with broken glass and
daubs "a bloody cross on the altar" to appease "an angry God with prayer
and sacrifice."[101]

The grotesqueness of his father's death, the body laid out on the
kitchen table on a hot July morning, etched itself in Jack's imagination. He heard panting and thought his father had recovered. The panting proved to be from an overheated dog that had sought relief beneath
the temporary bier. Tragic events reveal grotesque shadings in the writings of Conroy and Gorki, to whom Conroy was often compared (I return to this point later). Gorki associated his father's death with the
image of two frogs, which, when the grave was filled in with dirt, were
trapped and buried. In both authors' writings, absurdity, humor, and
pathos are objectified through physical description.[102]

The end of Monkey Nest coal camp signaled Jack's entry into the
world of work and his earliest efforts as a writer. Monkey Nest disappeared finally, leaving a hillock riven with erosion and covered with
scrub trees. Eliza removed Jack (as she would Margaret) from school at
the end of eighth grade. Pip had been hurt in a Monkey Nest mining
accident. He now shoveled concrete for less income than he had earned
in the mine. One morning, Eliza and Jack walked into Moberly along
the railroad tracks. Taking Jack by the hand, she accompanied him into
the Wabash Railroad shops, where it was arranged he would start work
as an apprentice carman. At thirteen he was, if not in physical size or
experience, already a man.

3

The Wabash Shops: Apprenticeship

I knew something epochal was happening to me.
—*The Disinherited*

BECAUSE MINING and the railroads spurred its quick growth in the last decades of the nineteenth century, Moberly, Missouri, a division point on the Wabash railroad, became known as the "Magic City."[1] The roundhouse, repair shops, station, and offices covered some twenty-five acres of Moberly real estate. As in other midwestern railroad towns—Sherwood Anderson's Clyde, Ohio, for instance—the station was centrally located, and individual destinies were regulated by the frequent arrival or departure of passenger trains. The Wabash machine shops, where the railroad cars were repaired, employed over a thousand men when Jack first went to work there. Some four hundred "running men"—train engineers, conductors, and brakemen—lived in Moberly. A railroad junction had created the town, and a railroad president, Colonel William E. Moberly of the Chariton and Randolph Railroad Company, lent it his name.[2] Moberly was a town the railroad made.[3]

* * *

Eliza contacted the superintendent to arrange Jack's apprenticeship in the Wabash railroad car shops.[4] She always took care of such matters, even while Tom was alive. It was customary that an older person would arrange an apprenticeship, "the most important contribution a father could make to his son's future prosperity."[5] A boy of thirteen was usually a docile candidate; a seven-year apprenticeship would give him an occupation and a strong sense of personal identity. Master carmen lived in comfortable brick homes in Moberly. Jack might hope to do the same one day. When Eliza took Jack's hand and walked the two miles along the railroad track to the Wabash shops in 1912, she was taking him across the threshold to the responsibilities of early adulthood, to the enforced routines of work of laboring men in a highly organized, stratified "brotherhood." Despite the fact that Jack continued to live with his family near Monkey Nest, his life now was centered in the town with its busy commercial life, libraries, notorious "levee" district, late Victorian genteel culture, and elegant railroad station where many a young person had set out into the world beyond.[6]

At an age when most boys go to school, play, travel, cast about before applying themselves to some occupation, Jack began a nine-year apprenticeship in the Wabash shops. The workday began at seven in the morning and lasted ten hours, six days a week. On Saturday, the shopmen traditionally walked off the job at five in the afternoon after having cleaned their tools. The railroads continued apprenticeship programs in their shops long after such training had ceased in many other crafts. The factory system caused profound changes in this system. Most workers, apart from skilled tool-and-die makers, could learn their jobs in much shorter periods without formal apprenticeship. Factory workers changed jobs during layoffs or were let go entirely. Apprenticeship was fast becoming an anachronism.[7] The Wabash Railroad was a large-scale organization requiring a variety of skills, "where," according to Walter Licht, "the work was compartmentalized into separate, often geographically dispersed units—work situations, in other words, in which each person occupied a small place in a large complex setting."[8] The companies and the railroad brotherhoods provided the workers with specialized training that would permit them to do their jobs and to advance up the many steps of the promotion pyramid, whose pinnacle was master mechanic or superintendent. The railroads were beginning a period of growth, fired by the war in Europe in 1914. It was a good time to begin one's career with the Wabash. Jack might have spent his entire working life in the shops, lived in a brick house, had things turned out differently. At age thirteen, earning fourteen cents an hour, he had a long ascent before him.

Older men in the shops generally looked after the young apprentices. Eliza's brother, Jim McCollough, was the straw boss in the railroad yards. Jim's son, Russell, an apprentice carpenter in the shops, became Jack's fast friend. Pip Addis found a job in the Wabash shops soon after Jack began his apprenticeship. An older shopman, Jim Whitaker, took a paternal interest in Jack, gave him advice, making things easier for him in the beginning. Family connections had helped Jack obtain the apprenticeship; they continued to assure his success providing he proved himself a steady and competent worker.[9]

Carl Sandburg's father worked as a blacksmith in the Chicago, Burlington, and Quincy railroad shops, and William Z. Foster, Communist party candidate for president in 1932, had been a railroad shopman for the Illinois Central. Foster's autobiography, *Pages from a Worker's Life*, describes the arduous work. Teams of men lifted and carried pieces of a railroad car, such as the long wooden "sill," and moved cast-steel wheels. Such operations required strength and dexterity. Workers protested against the exhausting and dangerous practice of piecework and speed-up forced on them by the company. In his industrial folktale "Greedy-Gut Gus, the Car Toad," written years later while he was on the Illinois Writers' Project, Jack portrays humorously a shop worker's means of protest, which was to cut corners at the company's expense:

> Gus learned how to skimp his work, too. This can be done by putting a whole side on a car with only one nail holding all the boards or by not tightening nuts on drawbar bolts or leaving the nuts off altogether. You can leave an old journal brass in the journal box and put fresh dope around it and get paid for putting in a new one. Of course, it may run a hot box and throw the truck off the rails and play glory hallelujah with a whole train and send the crew to kingdom come, but Gus never bothered his head about that. Just so he was smart enough to make the inspectors believe he was doing the work right.[10]

A thirteen-year-old apprentice was given light tasks. Even so, at first Jack was scarcely able to lift a keg of nails. Despite the rigors, there was space for play in the apprentices' day. Nightfall came early in winter. The apprentices hid behind railroad cars in the yard, dodging the shop foreman, Jim Colley, or Mr. Dacey, the master mechanic. The older men overlooked the apprentices' skylarking. They too had begun their work lives as apprentices.[11]

The Wabash shops formed a close-knit work community, larger, more stratified and regulated than the mines, but offering a young apprentice a sense of identity and companionship. Here was another occupational subculture with its initiation rites and storytelling. It had a union "brotherhood," with its emphasis on self-improvement and mutual assistance, and an identification with an industry that had some of the richest legends and history of any, a site of labor struggle and a symbol of America's growing industrial strength.

Another Missourian, Samuel Clemens, apprenticed in a craft that, had he stayed with it, would have made him virtually autonomous. Riverboat pilots like his master, Mr. Bixby, unlike railroad shopmen, were treated reverentially. By contrast, Jack entered a vast bureaucratized industry in which one's advancement would be based upon one's qualities as a loyal, honest, thrifty, and sober worker. Despite such differences, the experience of apprenticeship was crucial to the literary imaginations of both Clemens and Conroy. They became, in John Seelye's words, "inland prose pilots," master storytellers whose tales drew upon their personal experience, orality, and popular culture. "If peasants and seamen were past masters of storytelling," Walter Benjamin wrote, "the artisan class was its university."[12]

From the beginning, Jack revealed an interest in the social and political structures of his occupation. He learned quickly the distinctions in rank in the shops. An aristocrat among the workers, the "car toad" was one who had finished apprenticeship and journeymanship and was placed in charge of a team of "lumber hustlers," helpers, and "dope pullers."[13] The apprentice carried away the castoff material thrown carelessly to the side by the car toads and ran to the "bolt house" to obtain parts. Among the "privileges" accorded the apprentice was to carry the car toad's toolbox, laden with metal coupling pins. Older workers would nail the toolbox to the floor so that the novice, already unsure of his own strength, would sweat and strain ingloriously to the howls of the shopmen sharing in the prank.

The shops were noisy, dusty, dimly lit places with grime on the windows and tables. Hammers, saws, riveting, men shouting orders and cursing created a constant din. A strong smell of acrid smoke, new paint, and scorched rubber penetrated every recess, and thick dust floated in suspension in the shafts of afternoon light streaming through the dirty clerestory windows. Interludes in the sweaty, busy, monotonous labor were welcomed. A common prank was a variation of the familiar "skyhook" quest. The apprentice was sent to the storeroom to ask for a "whilakaloo brace" or some such nonexistent article.

The dirtiest job belonged to the "dope puller." Waste woolen material soaked in grease was used to pack the wheel journal boxes for lubrication purposes. Occasionally a dope puller had to drop his pants and submit to a ritualistic greasing. Playful sabotage was frequent enough that a more experienced worker would by habit examine the tool he was about to use before picking it up. Sometimes the pranks involved impromptu "dramas," with the foreman's participation, in order to embarrass the novice laborer. A car toad would pretend to be crushed beneath a sill. An unwitting apprentice would rush to help him, lifting the heavy piece. The car toad would leap up and seize the other end of the sill. Just then a foreman would "happen" to pass by. Since, according to the unwritten codes of the shop, a laborer was not permitted to perform the tasks of a carman or his apprentice, the dupe would receive a stern upbraiding for his presumption. Such rituals, besides furnishing entertainment to all but the hapless target, underscored the stratified tasks and hierarchical positions of the workers. Obedience, diligence, loyalty, discipline, and cooperation were values recognized in the shops, not initiative or precociousness.

At fifteen Jack worked in the bolt house, where he no longer had to hustle after lumber to the impatient shouts of the car toads. A year later he was put in charge of a labor gang of lumber hustlers. He had grown very fast and was now bigger than many of the grown men in the shops. Bossing a labor gang was a difficult job. The men quarreled and complained. Jack practiced diplomacy to keep them working. Jack's foreman, Jim Colley, frightened most of the younger men, including Jack, with his belligerent manner of talking. Colley was a formidable boss whose presence alone sent the lumber hustlers and dope pullers scurrying about, feigning activity.[14] Mr. Dacey, the master mechanic, would often ask Jack to show his pockets to see whether he had any tobacco. Like many shop managers, Dacey insisted on abstinence. Shopmen were heavy drinkers, like most miners.[15] Dacey and others, including union officers, linked inefficiency and accidents with alcohol. Smoking was the first step toward perdition and, in Dacey's mind, was equated with bad workmanship.

The Wabash shops teemed with constant interaction among men of all types. Many workers were given nicknames and achieved reputations for this or that eccentricity. "Willie Green" (a.k.a. Joe Kennedy) was peevish and easily exasperated. He hated pranks and turned sour when the men, egged on by his exasperation, made him their target. Some of the repairmen went about their work, taking little part in the pranks. Others were loudmouthed and boastful, like a certain Karl Chapman, who had grown up in Kimberly coal camp, hated blacks, and participated in a violent and clumsy lynching of a black hobo. His boasts in the shops were not welcome. Scoffing at Chapman's swagger and bravado, some older carmen started a rumor that two blacks who had escaped the lynching mob were "Chicago toughs and were returning to avenge the victim of the mob."[16] Chapman regretted his boasting, fearing the reprisals, and made an effort to persuade his fellow shopmen that he had had no part in the lynching.

One of Jack's fellow shopmen was his stepfather, Pip Addis. Jack got along well with Pip, unlike his sister Margaret, who bitterly resented Eliza's marriage to "Mr. Addis," as she called him.[17] Pip and Jack once set out together on railroad passes to visit Pip's childhood home in Coon

Rapids, Iowa; they never made it. In Omaha, Pip started drinking heavily, while Jack stood outside of the bar waiting patiently, listening to strains of muffled music through the closed door. Pip's alcoholic binge lasted two days. Returning home, Pip, in a half-drunken stupor, exclaimed to the other passengers during a stop that a woman was caught beneath the wheels of the train. "I cowered in my seat, sympathized with by some kindly ladies who would exclaim, 'poor boy!' Amid the general uproar, a tall, muscular man grabbed Pip by the shirt front, hoisted him up, and said: 'Shut up, old man, or I'll cave your face in.' Pip subsided into a bitter grumbling until we reached the Moberly station, then lurched from the train vowing to report the conductor and 'get his job.'"[18]

Like Maxim Gorki, Jack was exposed very early to a wide range of human behavior in an adult's world. Both writers were apprentices of life, taking a learner's attitude toward their early experiences and, from these experiences, creating in literature a microworld of society's ignored, crippled, despised, and colorful misfits. Gorki was born into fallen gentry and cruelly booted out of his family home at age eleven to make his way alone. Jack was spared such early misery, yet there exist enough similarities between the two writers—for instance, their literary attraction to the "weeds" of human existence—that more than one critic and editor dubbed Conroy "the American Gorki."[19] Both Gorki and Conroy turned hungrily to books, yet drew their literary sketches directly from life. Both reveal the humanity in ordinary people, raising their perceptions into an affirmative vision that animates their writing, setting them apart from most "proletarian" writers.[20]

Gorki, Conroy, Jack London, and Martin Andersen Nexö were autodidacts whose most influential teachers were the nurturing "good voices" of parents and older workers. Life was their school, together with what they gleaned from their unmonitored, discursive reading. Among their working-class peers they were exceptional people, but then all people are "exceptional" if viewed close up, a perspective that was granted to all four authors. London perceived formal study as a means of escape in order, as Philip Foner says, to sell "the products of his brain."[21] Likewise, Jack determined to better himself through reading and to succeed, despite the fact that he knew of very few examples of working-class people who were able to rise out of their social and economic class.[22] London and Conroy were vigorous, virile young men with strong features and bright blue eyes. Possessing enormous stores of energy, they read compulsively and widely. Jack would read until his head sagged on the table, after ten hours in the shops and the two-mile walk home along the railroad tracks. He bought a nineteen-volume edition of Kip-

ling through subscription.[23] From Moberly's Carnegie Library he borrowed Edward Bellamy's *Looking Backwards*, Ignatius Donnelly's *Caesar's
Column*, Frank Norris's *The Octopus*, Jack London's *People of the Abyss*
and *The Iron Heel*, Upton Sinclair's *The Jungle*, and the monthly *Railway Carmen's Journal*, whose purpose, the editors noted, was to instruct
and to "elevate."[24] Mrs. Bessie Lee, a white-haired and rather majestic
lady, was librarian at the time; her assistant was Mrs. Elsea, whose
daughter, Carolyn Elsea Werkley, became a lifelong friend of Jack's. Perhaps the most active of Moberly's library patrons, Jack would appear in
the library after work, looking like an Irish-American longshoreman in
his soft wool cap, to borrow books and return others.[25] Similarly, a great
deal of Jack London's early education took place in the Oakland Public Library, with the help of Ina Coolbrith, the head librarian.

In Jack's own library were the socialist "Appeal Classics," published
in cheap editions in Girard, Kansas, predecessors of Haldeman-Julius's
"Little Blue Books." One of his favorite books at this time was *Pelle the
Conqueror* by Martin Andersen Nexö, a Swedish immigrant who had
grown up in one of Copenhagen's poorest quarters. Nexö had witnessed
the appearance of early proletarian organizations, had known unemployment and hard winters, and had written of the rise of the enclosure system in Denmark in the late nineteenth century. Jack admired the great
lyrical warmth and conviction of *Pelle*, which reflected Nexö's own experiences as an itinerant worker.[26]

If the sincerity of Nexö's convictions and the humanistic quality of
his compassion for the disadvantaged appealed to Jack, then Jack's attraction to London's work was for quite different reasons. In *People of
the Abyss*, a book that affected Jack powerfully, the author penetrates
into London's East End, not as a Victorian observer, in the manner of
George R. Sim's *How the Poor Live; and, Horrible London* (1889), but
as one who wished to live on equal terms among the poor. London knew
misery from his own youth. Donning a "frayed and out-at-elbows jacket," London dwelled among the destitute in a "doss house," without fa-
voritism.[27] His narrative has the authority of one who has participated
directly in an experience. This narrative authority attracted Conroy,
whose own writing would strive toward the freshness, vitality, and authenticity of lived experience. London makes his case without sentiment, placing telling detail upon detail, faithfully reproducing the voices
of the outcasts and driving his points home with statistical evidence.[28]
Gorki spent most of his early life in pre-revolutionary Russia, in a stat-
ic society of peasants and artisans, without trade unions or a labor movement. London's early experience was much closer to Conroy's, framed
as it was by the contradictions of industrialism, and by the influence of

socialist agitation and populist fervor, the revolt against genteel standards, and the immense vitality of a young nation where jobless young men tramped, along with young men who tramped for the sheer adventure of it.

London and Conroy—to carry the comparison one step further—were large men with a huge appetite for life.[29] At fifteen, Conroy already had developed into a robust young man with an Irish dockworker's booming laughter. With Gorki he could say that he "understood at a very early age that men are created by their resilience to their environment."[30] While London yielded to egoism and primitivist views of racial superiority, Conroy moved toward deeper involvement with the growing labor struggle, cooperative literary enterprises, and identification with the "people of the abyss," the disinherited. Far from rejecting his working-class origins, he found in them the strength and sturdy instincts that nourished him and eventually gave substance to his literary work.

Perhaps because of his patronage of the railroad's own library and his reputation for exceptional literacy, Jack was made recording secretary of his union local, the American Federation of Railway Workers (AFRW). At eighteen he became an apprentice carman, which meant fewer menial tasks and more interesting assignments, such as rolling (and balancing) a five-hundred-pound railroad car wheel. He continued his studies in the evenings through the American Correspondence School, which sent him materials from its offices in Chicago.[31] The carmen heard Jack mumbling what seemed to them strange gibberish; he was practicing Latin pronunciation. People saw him running after butterflies and insects with a net, and gathering leaves and plants; he was fulfilling the requirements of a biology course.[32] A correspondence-school teacher named E. Van Schaik guided Jack through his English lessons. Jack would stay up late at night to complete his assignments for teachers he never met.[33]

Like Hardy's Jude, Jack's obsession with learning approached fervor, often without plan or guidance. Jude suffered crushing disappointment in a class system ill-disposed toward workers' continuing their studies. Trade union and socialist influences, by contrast, endowed Jack's efforts in self-improvement with a larger sense of political interest and historical mission.[34]

The American Federation of Railway Workers was organized on an industrial basis rather than according to individual crafts and was therefore considered by some to be an "outlaw" union. Jack's union, the "Blue Ribbon," existed only in the car shops with which it had a contract. Its goal was to organize all the railway craft unions—including the machinists, the boilermakers, and the powerful Brotherhood of Locomotive Engineers with which Debs, later an advocate of industrial unionism, was associated—into one union. The craft brotherhoods were bitterly opposed to this effort at what they termed dual unionism. Among those arguing against dual unionism, including the Industrial Workers of the World (IWW), was William Z. Foster. As noted earlier, Foster was a shopman at the time (1914) and a member of the Brotherhood Railway Carmen Association (BRCA). In an article he wrote for the July 1914 issue of *Railway Carmen's Journal,* a journal in which Jack would publish his own first essays, Foster cites "dualist folly" as the source of wars between rival unions that result in neglecting labor's basic enemy, the employer.[35] Similarly, the IWW came under the fire of the journal's editors.[36] Jack shrugged off these divisive conflicts within the labor movement as political struggles for power but nevertheless was relieved when the dispute was finally settled.

Jack remembered one triumphant moment, during a giant labor parade celebrating Moberly's fiftieth anniversary on 27 September 1916, when the AFRW rolled a boxcar down Moberly's Reed Street. He also recalled hearing a local attorney, Arthur B. Chamier, who later defended the shopmen in the 1922 strike, deliver an address that day.[37] Not long after, the AFRW yielded its place in the Moberly shops to the Brotherhood Railway Carmen. Jim Whitaker, the grievance man for the AFRW, and Jack simply assumed positions in the brotherhood that were equivalent to their former ones. Jack continued to begin his union letters "Dear Sir and Brother" and to sign them "Fraternally."[38]

The Brotherhood Railway Carmen was all-encompassing, extending its influence beyond the shops to include leisure activities.[39] Following a solemn initiation rite, members were given a badge of fellowship and respect. The motto was "Friendship, Unity, True Brotherly Love."[40] The fraternal function of the brotherhood was strong; for instance, members gave one another advice on problems such as alcoholism, and they offered financial assistance in time of sickness. One purpose of the brotherhood was to gain the respect of the employers and the community. There were reading rooms for "self-improvement" where members could read the brotherhood's journal, with its workers' correspondence. Jack, as recording secretary, periodically sent the magazine his reports on Magic City Lodge 64.[41] As a union officer, Jack made trips to the BRCA headquarters in Kansas City with Whitaker. He was the kind of bright, young, energetic member who was likely to rise quickly in his local.

Moberly, together with its Wabash shops and the Brotherhood Railway Carmen, represented what John Alt calls "an occupational community of early capitalism."[42] Working in the shops in a railroad town like Moberly during the early decades of the century gave the shopmen and their families an exclusive identity in the community and inculcated in them—some more, some less—certain identifiable values and attitudes. Fred Cottrell describes this identity: "Through apprenticeship, the skilled tradesman not only learned the skills involved, but he also was indoctrinated into the subculture supporting it and made part of the system of interpersonal relationships among the men, which were carefully nourished by union organizers and officers. These 'nonoperating' workers maintained closer identity with their fellow craftsmen than with the mixed set of others required to operate the railroad."[43] In a paternalistic industry with delineated rules and standards, the brotherhood protected the worker against exploitation, offered him aid, and fostered a fraternal spirit that extended beyond the workplace. Editorials appearing in the *Railway Carmen's Journal* urge cooperation, fellowship, pride in craft, and solidarity.

The conservative role of the Brotherhood Railway Carmen in the community contrasted with its progressive role in politics before World War I. Indigenous traditions of democratic participation and fellowship mixed in the BRCA with a strong socialist influence voicing complaints against monied interests and strong pacifist views, until the United States entered the war and the railroads came under government administration.[44]

The union supported technical training and the Wabash provided a library where the men could borrow books.[45] While the union scarcely embraced bourgeois values, it nonetheless fostered its members' wish to attain a higher economic status, to live in comfortable brick homes, and to feel themselves respected citizens in the community.[46] Thus, the town's culture, that of the shopkeepers, businessmen, and independent craftspeople, competed for the loyalty of the carmen with their roots deep within the occupational subculture of the shops.[47] The town culture represented respectability, sobriety, and gentility. The children of the carmen went to school with the children of the townspeople; they were "unlikely," as Fred Cottrell writes, "to develop the occupational 'subculture' they once would have grown up in or to maintain any exclusive identity with railroad men."[48]

As a child in elementary school, Jack had identified with the miners of Monkey Nest. Now the shops and the BRCA became his "secondary school."[49] He still lived with his family in the Elvin house near Monkey Nest. Town boys he knew earlier at West Park school, such as Bryan Mead, continued to visit Jack. The Mead brothers—Bryan, George, J. B., and Joe Willie—all were Jack's work colleagues at various times in his life. His other companions were his nephews, the Harrisons, and the Kirby boys. Together they hiked out to inspect train

wrecks and prowl the woods around Monkey Nest, looking for panthers
that were reported living in Happy Hollow. Jack and his friends envied
the Gravitt boys, whose way of life seemed particularly attractive to the
other young boys, most of whom had already begun to work for the
Wabash. The Gravitts came to town with their coonskins, fish, fox skins,
walnuts, and hickory nuts in season to sell. Jack bought their used dime
novels, despite Eliza's proscription. Theirs was an enviable life, indeed.[50]

Jack's status grew in the shops and his work life steadily improved.
By 1916, a minimum hourly wage of fifty-eight cents was mandated.[51]
That year, President Wilson persuaded Congress to enact an eight-hour
day for the railroads, ending a struggle that labor had waged for decades.
The forty-eight-hour work week became the norm.[52] With more mon-
ey in his pocket and feeling restless, Jack began to take more trips on
Sundays to Kansas City. Wabash employees obtained free travel passes
on Wabash passenger trains as "deadheads."

In 1915, when Jack first began his Sunday excursions, Kansas City
still preserved some of the wide-open character of its early frontier era.
From Union Station to the Missouri River, a young man could find the
excitement he sought. The Gillis burlesque theater was one of the rawest
in the country. And beyond the Gillis was the redlight district near the
West Bottoms. In the West Bottoms and to the northeast were the Irish,
Italian, German, Polish, and black communities. On higher ground overlooking the West Bottoms was a tenement area where squatters dwelled
in makeshift tarpaper shacks. The disreputable, even sinister, character
of Kansas City found colorful political expression in the Tom Pendergast era. Years later Conroy would run afoul of the powerful Pendergast machine.

Arriving on the morning train, Jack would catch a show in a vaudeville theater, eat a hearty meal in a restaurant, and return home on the
late afternoon train. At age sixteen, he made brave attempts to gain
admission to the notorious Gillis theater; on occasion he succeeded. The
Gillis was nationally known, especially among railroad travelers, drum-
mers, boomers, businessmen, and workers. There Jack got his "first impressions of female anatomy."[53] Little was held back in the Gillis's bawdy,
slapstick interludes. In one routine, the ladies of a church congregation compare notes concerning their new minister's sexual favors bestowed upon them. The scene changes. A large black teamster is viewed
arguing with a jackass. When the jackass squeals, the teamster warns:
"If you don't quit, I'm going to cut that thing off!" The jackass squeals
louder, at which point the teamster makes a great thwacking noise and
tosses a rubber hose on the stage. The ladies of the congregation appear at that moment, take notice of the severed object, and exclaim:

"Oh, my God, look what's happened to our new minister!"[54] Ernest Hemingway came to Kansas City in the fall of 1917 as a cub reporter for the *Kansas City Star*, seeking to escape his childhood home in Oak Park, Illinois, and its stifling middle-class conventions. It is curious to think that Conroy and Hemingway might have been in the same audience at the Gillis, sampling what Hemingway called the "wonderful and unsavory" life of Kansas City.

Moberly had its own "unsavory" quarter, the "levee," well known by railroad crews and passengers. Many a Moberly youngster had received a stern admonition from a parent: "Don't let me catch you beyond the last block of Reed Street."[55] Next to the Wabash depot was a row of five hotels, including the Baltimore, which dubbed itself the "House of All Nations" by virtue of its international "staff." The Baltimore boasted that it had girls from all corners of the world. A mulatto girl who knew a smattering of Spanish was billed as a red-hot "Mexican chica."

One of the prostitutes, nicknamed "Foot and a Half" because one leg was shorter than the other, initiated countless Moberly youths in sexual knowledge. Her son, who worked with Jack in the Wabash shops, was defensive about his mother's trade. Easily provoked by real or imagined slurs, he was quick to defend her honor with his fists. "Foot and a Half" claimed to have initiated the son of the local junkyard owner, an innocent named Ernie Starr, when she was already quite old, simply, as she said, because she "wanted to keep a hand in it."[56] On a train once between Glasgow, Missouri, and Moberly, a man asked Jack: "Have you been to that sportin' house, the Baltimore?" The question flattered Jack, who at fifteen wished to be thought old enough to be seen as a habitué.[57]

The railroads brought prosperity and culture to Moberly. The pride of a small midwestern town around the turn of the century was its "literary culture," its orchestra, and a new library building furnished by "Mr. Carnegie." "Moberly had a liberal, progressive citizenship, well advanced in moral refinement and literary culture," wrote Forrest G. Ferris in 1904.[58] Touring stock companies stopped in Moberly since it was midway between St. Louis and Kansas City and therefore a welcome layover.[59] The town had its Railroad Literary Club, Halloran Theatre, Union Station with polished brass railings and mosaic tiling, and fifteen miles of bricked streets. An immigrant musician named Professor Johannes Goetze, who claimed to have played under the direction of Johannes Brahms in Cologne, Germany, tutored Moberlyeans, including a young woman who was married to the superintendent of the Wabash shops, W. W. Greenland. The scale of cultural life was balanced between gentility and the notoriety of the "levee," tipping too far, in the eyes of many civic-minded townspeople, toward the latter.

Similarly, two sides to Jack's character and personality seemed to evolve during this apprenticeship period of his life, corresponding to his two names, John Wesley and Jack. John Wesley Conroy was the diligent apprentice who, like Benjamin Franklin, sought to rise, enrolled in correspondence courses, joined an Odd Fellows lodge, voted Republican in one election, and attended the Methodist Church. He became a church deacon in the early 1920s, attending Wednesday night prayer meetings even while writing for radical publications and longing for changes that would assure the worker social justice.[60] Methodism, with its traditions of democratic participation, interest in education, and history of raising "humble men" to positions of leadership seemed comfortable to John Wesley Conroy, who, his grandmother McCollough had assured him, would one day become president. The Protestant concern with sin apparently had a firm hold on Conroy. In *The Disinherited*, Larry Donovan reacts to his father's death, "obsessed with the notion that my own sin had been responsible for what had happened."[61] Likewise, a sense of shame accompanies Larry's sexual awakening. He has difficulty resolving the conflict in his mind between viewing the working-class girl Helen romantically, as a member of the exalted sex to whom he quotes poetry, and seeing her as a purely sexual being who can give him pleasure.

Methodist injunctions against intemperance during Prohibition left some residual feeling in Jack during his entire life. When "demon rum" became too much his friend in the late 1930s, he played the part of "Reverend Conroy" in bars, reciting mock sermons on temperance to besotted habitués.[62] He claimed to be a charter member of the Pilgrim Tract Society, a mail-order evangelistic organization that continues to mail pamphlets inveighing against drink and other forms of intemperance. It has always been assumed that Jack sent these pamphlets to his friends as humorous examples of the human conscience in its eternal struggle against indulgence. His fascination for the street literature of preaching is well represented in his collection *Midland Humor* (1947). Yet one might argue that his fascination had some basis in his curiosity about prohibitions of any kind, and the moral debt that impiety incurs.

Methodism was a religion that attracted working-class people long before the fundamentalist sects of today pitched their mass appeal into homes through the television tube. The Methodist doctrine of perfectionism argues that salvation is accessible to all who seek it. Methodist moral teachings, on the other hand, posed a dilemma for workers for whom the tavern was traditionally a place of fellowship and relief. The heroic Methodism of Edward Eggleston's *Circuit Rider* often slips into fulminations against sin. Jack's Uncle Bill, Eliza's brother-in-law, made a comfortable living preaching his temperance sermon, "From the Gutter to the Pulpit." The Brotherhood Railway Carmen Association, alarmed by the incidence of drunkenness among its members, added its voice to those counseling temperance. E. P. Thompson's remark about English self-educated workers was likely valid for American workers as well: "leaders and chroniclers of the movement . . . raised themselves by efforts of self-discipline which required them to turn their backs upon the happy-go-lucky tavern world."[63]

The "other Conroy," the more familiar Jack, became an intimate of the "tavern world," in fact gathered some of his best stories there. The old commons where workmen had gathered at fairs had retreated into the bar, he discovered. There the "inarticulate" conserved traditional values, what Thompson calls "a spontaneity and capacity for enjoyment and mutual loyalties," in the world of after-work fellowship.[64] The "other Conroy," the charismatic Jack, eventually explored his own way through the West Bottoms, Moberly's levee, hobo jungles, Chicago's North Clark Street—the settings in which he gathered his tales, in the company of the Meads, Fred Harrison, the "Fallonites," Nelson Algren, Jim Light, and many other companions over the years. The Jack that most people knew later in his life was a performer at parties at Green Street, his Chicago home, a comic balladeer of North Clark Street bars, a veteran of boxcar tramping with the Wobblies, cynosure of semi-hoodlums, and storyteller. (Most people knew little about his years as labor radical, strike leader, and migrant worker.) The two Conroys came to exist side by side in the same person. The joining of the two was the dynamic that energized his novels, in which the protagonist ultimately declines both the striving of "John Wesley" and the improvidence of "Jack" in a process of self-definition conditioned by experience.

* * *

Curiosity, his desire to share in others' experiences, made Jack an acute observer with an infallible ear for speech. After work, he frequented the Star Poolroom on Moberly's Reed Street to hear the regulars tell their stories. Chairs were placed on a long bench so that the spectators had a better view of the billiard and pool tables. Jack sat and listened to the men spin their yarns about local happenings and past exploits. Another good locale for stories, he discovered, was the parking lot behind the Merchants Hotel where farmers hitched their horses. The men's stories were full of superstition and odd characters. "Regally they spat and smoked," Jack was fond of quoting (from Kipling) in recalling this time, "And fearsomely they lied." Some men were far better storytellers than others. Storytelling was an entertaining pastime and a deeply communal act in Monkey Nest camp, the Wabash shops, the Star Poolroom, and behind the Merchants Hotel, Jack's favored locales. Linda Degh discovered that among Hungarian peasant people "nearly every kind of work in the fields which is not excessively strenuous can be occasion for storytelling—hacking, weeding, cutting roots, gathering potatoes, planting, sheaving. Storytelling is done during work like this by one of the workers, who sits down near a ditch and entertains the others."[65] Missouri's Randolph County farmers wove tales of legendary animals, weather, hunting, sowing, and harvesting, activities that were intimately connected with the daily life of the listeners.

Some of the storytelling involved patterns of humor and oral delivery that employed repetition, economy of expression, rhythmic speech, farfetched events, and inventive idioms. Others were simple narratives, tales of train wrecks, hardship, or novel occurrences, told without embroidery. In the Wabash shops Jack heard the tale of the fast sooner hound, symbol of worker resistance to mechanization, which he rewrote as an industrial folktale for the Illinois Writers' Project in 1939. Conroy's early interest in storytelling led him to develop a narrative style incorporating a "voice" that creatively transcribed oral storytelling. In *The Disinherited*, the storyteller's voice is one of many voices, all on the same narrative level. His novel is the medium through which the "inarticulate" voices of those who do not write (the workers) are heard.

Jack was also attracted by manifestations of popular and mass culture, rivals of extemporaneous storytelling, such as vaudeville, Chautauqua entertainments, carnivals, and evangelistic preaching. Conroy became a transmitter of oral culture produced in work settings where older traditions of orality were absorbing the newer popular expressions of mass culture. He learned from the miners and farmers how to create verbal performances that draw upon the raw materials of oral and extraliterary narratives. Possessed of a remarkable memory in addition to an ear for spoken language, he eventually forged a literature from both popular and folk sources, and made important contributions to the new field of industrial folklore. His "Monkey Nest tales" and worker narratives capture the worker's cultural and linguistic experience during the period of tumultuous social upheaval when an older order of tradition and rootedness was yielding quickly to a new unstable world of movement and change, represented for the worker by the factory system employing the floating proletariat from farms, mines, and small towns in the Midwest. Jack's task as a storyteller, he would come to realize, was to reproduce the voices of the dispossessed workers and to recover those he had heard as child and apprentice. Like Gorki he wanted people to hear the factory workers and migrants speak, for once people heard them, they could no longer think of them as the "masses," or the "workers," or the "mob."

An early photograph of Jack shows him tall for his age, and robust, with a large, open face and shock of brown hair, sitting on a rock wall reading Kipling. In the car shops, he tucked a book in a pocket, and during idle moments he would read.[66] In another photo he is one of several hundred carmen posing at Moberly's fifty-year celebration, scarcely identifiable from the rest. These photos raise questions: How was Jack able to satisfy his intellectual curiosity and achieve his desire for self-expression, while giving voices to "those who do not write"? And how was he able to declare himself, in Whitman's words, to be "a simple separate person," remain "credentialed" as a worker, accepted on equal terms by his fellow workers, in hyphenated relationship with writer? These questions underlie nearly everything Jack produced as worker-writer.

* * *

As the nation entered war in 1917, the Wabash shops approached a highwater mark. Some 2,700 men were employed, in three shifts, with 900 on each shift. During the years preceding the Great War, the railroads, according to John Stover, "had expanded and developed more rapidly than most segments of the industrial economy."[67] Despite growth in activity, railroad companies experienced financial problems owing to "the steady rise in the costs of railroad operation, without any corresponding increase in the railroad rates and earnings."[68] After foreclosure and reorganization in 1915, the Wabash continued to grow, spreading its great arterial network, making accessible largely undeveloped areas away from major cities in the Midwest. Labor militancy in the railroad shops was on the rise too, even while new social forces were evolving elsewhere, for instance, the public's love affair with the automobile. David Montgomery points out that in the seven years following 1915, throughout the industry at large "the ratio of strikers to all industrial and service employees remained *constantly* on a par with the more famous strike years of 1934 and 1937," despite the effect of World War I.[69] The railroad shops were mainly spared the effect of new machines, which was to remove or debase certain skilled trades. Car repair still required hand labor by skilled workmen. The temporary "nationalization" of railroad management during World War I proved attractive to railroad workers who saw this as an opportunity to gain greater control in the shops.[70] The war drained away many eligible workers from the shops. The brotherhoods asked for pay hikes to keep pace with inflation, taking advantage of wartime de-

mand to pressure management. Management in turn was embittered over
the constant labor demands. Wages in the shops were already high relative to other industries. The stage was being set for a crisis between management and labor in the years following Armistice.[71] The developing
crisis would sweep up all the shopmen in its wake, radically affecting individual destinies.

Jack did not fully appreciate the consequences of this new labor militancy at the time.[72] He had a keen sense of class interests, to be sure,
of labor as a class for itself, as Harry Braverman says, not as a class in
itself.[73] There is no evidence that he felt powerless as an individual
against an oppressive employer or system, or that he was denied, as Jack
London describes in an essay Conroy greatly admired, "The Class Struggle" (1903), "the opportunity to rise from the working class."[74] After
the close of the frontier, with its opportunities for the "strong and capable members of the inferior class," London argues, young, intelligent
workers would be forced to turn their thwarted energies as class leaders
to preaching revolt. But Jack still held on to the notion, implanted by
his father, that through self-improvement he could escape the workers'
world into a white-collar profession. The pay in the shops was enough
that he was able to continue his correspondence studies, and, for a
while, attend night school in Moberly. In the meantime, he was moving up the apprenticeship ladder in the shops. He took part in a small
capitalist venture, investing with other employees in the Wabash Oil
and Gas Company. Jack and another shopman named Turk Wisner traveled to Kentucky to view a producing oil well, staying overnight with
a farmer. There they saw the Ku Klux Klan ride, not to burn a cross
but to warn the farmer not to sell his tobacco, rather wait for the price
to rise. The lesson in capitalist "free enterprise" stung Jack badly. He
subsequently lost several hundred dollars on a dry hole.[75]

The war economy brought boom times to the railroad shops. Management seldom knew where all its workers were, and it became very
easy and tempting for the carmen to take advantage of the relaxed standards.[76] Jack still nourished the hope of success expressed by Larry Donovan in *The Disinherited:* "I had finished one correspondence course and
was on another. When I finished it, I would be an expert accountant.
The school's prospectus had assured me that employers would bid avidly for my services then. There would be a cozy bungalow. I'd sit smoking my pipe, a baby or two at my knee, wife leaning lovingly over my
shoulder. I'd be looking proudly at my bank book."[77] These conventional
aspirations were probably representative among the labor aristocracy, if
not for themselves, then for their children. A whole literature existed,
aimed at working-class families ambitious for their children to "succeed"

in the manner described by William H. Maker's *On the Road to Riches, or How to Succeed in Life* (1895). In the 1920s, however, antilabor legislation and economic restructuring placed such aspirations out of reach of the new proletariat while creating substitute mechanisms of satisfaction through consumer-oriented production. Estrangement from one's hopes is, according to James F. Lea, the "beginning and foundation of politics. . . . Because the human who is estranged by this new self-consciousness seeks to find himself/herself again, to return to the group self."[78] Frequent layoffs and an antiunion Republican administration under Harding were intimations of hard times ahead for labor. Yet the shopmen felt secure in their strong identification with their craft; they had weathered hard times before.[79]

President Wilson called the American people to arms in April 1917 (several months after his election boast that he had kept the nation out of war). Jack registered for the draft at the Randolph County Courthouse in Huntsville. When the medical examination revealed a heart murmur, he was rejected for service. On Christmas Day of that year, the Addises' home burned down. Pip, Eliza, Jack, and Margaret were eating a late breakfast after burning gift wrappings in the fireplace. A fierce flue fire ensued. Neighbors came running to help remove what they could from the house. Jack threw his beloved books from the second floor, but most were badly damaged.[80] The fire destroyed a trunk that Captain Stackpoole, once superintendent of Monkey Nest mine, had left in Eliza's safekeeping. For years the Conroy children had yearned to know its contents; now the "secret" was forever lost. Despite the added financial burden on the family of moving and refurnishing a home, which required his help, Jack attempted once more to enlist in the military. A trip to Kansas City for that purpose was in vain; he was turned down again for health reasons.[81] Moved by the examples of others his age and older enlisting, Jack had sought to join; at the same time, he felt skeptical about the war and the motivations on both sides for waging it.

The carmen's brotherhood had for years expressed antiwar sentiments in its journal, warning, even as Wilson gave his speech, of the exploitation of labor in wartime.[82] Missouri labor in general "had an antimilitaristic bias," according to Gary M. Fink, favoring neutrality. Most unions viewed preparedness, for instance, as a means of putting money in the pockets of munitions makers.[83] The socialist press was saying the same thing, charging that "the war was a capitalists' quarrel, and that America was now fixing bayonets not to make the world safe for democracy, but to redeem the loans made to the Allies by Wall Street bankers."[84] Nonetheless, when war was actually declared, a dramatic turnabout in attitude toward American involvement occurred. A few years earlier the *Carmen's Journal* called on workers to join in peace movements to abolish "the monster, war, capitalism's greatest, bloodiest and most effective means of setting worker against worker. . . ."[85] Yet the editors of the journal called Labor Day 1918 the "greatest of all Labor Days," praising the workers who marched, "not in festive spirit, but in earnest demonstration of their solidarity in the one cause of all humanity."[86] Nonetheless, the BRCA, like most of organized labor at the time, remained deeply distrustful. Previous wars, it was felt, had "developed new opportunities for exploiting wage-earners."[87] If war was to save democracy in the world, then labor at home must enjoy democratic prerogatives as well. "The workers," noted the journal editors, "have suffered much injustice in war times by limitations upon their right to speak freely and to secure publicity for their just grievances."[88]

The fears of organized labor were in large part realized. War hysteria swept the country. The *Nation* was temporarily suppressed for criticizing Samuel Gompers, head of the American Federation of Labor, who gave his support to Wilson. The editors of *Masses*, who brought a blend of comic flippancy and serious commentary to both art and politics, were indicted on the basis of the Espionage Act in 1918 and the magazine's mailing privileges were revoked.[89] Socialists and Wobblies were horsewhipped. Rose Pastor Stokes was sentenced to ten years in prison for her speech on war profiteering.[90] Chauvinistic sentiment was particularly violent in Missouri where vigilantes roughed up pacifists, intimidated less-than-enthusiastic war supporters, and hanged Robert Prager, whose only "crime" was to have been born in Germany.[91] World War I, writes David Kennedy, "effectively stifled serious social criticism for nearly a decade. It broke the backs of radical groups, like the IWW and the Socialist Party, that had been slowly gaining ground for years. . . ."[92]

Conroy recalled the visit of the French War Commission on 7 May 1917. The Moberly Citizens Training Company displayed the American flag and the French *drapeau tricolore* together as a special train, preceded by scouting engines furnished by the Wabash, pulled into Moberly's Union Station. To raise liberty bonds, the Wabash Quartet sang "Just Before the Battle, Mother," and "We Love You, Sammie," in Tannehill Park. Patriotic fervor reached fever pitch when town fathers gave speeches condemning the crimes of the "Prussian War Lords" who had plunged the nation into a bloody war.[93] Edgar Guest's jingoist "War Time Rhymes" were popular at the time:

> I've read about the daring boys that fight up in the sky;
> It seems to me that this must be a splendid way to die.

I'd like to drive an aeroplane and prove my courage grim
And get above a German there and drop a bomb on him.[94]

Jack's own initial patriotic enthusiasm for the war was dampened when he witnessed the tar-and-feathering of a pacifist speaker. The Wabash "running men" who operated the trains returned with tales of vigilante action against the Wobblies. In the boxcars brought into the shops for repair, Jack read Wobbly slogans such as "Sabotage means bending back or breaking the fangs of Capitalism."[95]

Some men, he learned, like Ralph Cheyney, an anarchist, were going to jail for refusing the draft. A few radicals, like Mike Gold, fled to Mexico rather than serve the Wall Street bankers whose interest in the war, the radicals believed, was to profit from interest on loans made to the Allies. Cheyney and Gold were to play significant roles in Conroy's life. Jack read about Oklahoma's "Green Corn Rebellion" in the *Appeal to Reason*. Oklahoma tenant farmers and sharecroppers who participated in the revolt, seeking control over their crop prices, were strongly opposed to the draft. Troops subdued their rebellion in several days. A number of Jack's friends in the railroad shops enlisted enthusiastically in the military. Those who returned were chastened veterans who swore they would never serve in another war. Others veterans joined the American Legion, which prompted Thomas Hickey, one of Jack's fellow workers, to write: "Old Jonny Brennan, who was a sweeper around the shops there just after the war, expressed in his simple manner and with a burr of the brogue, my sentiments regarding the ninety-day wonders, when he said to me one day, 'God dam the dam Laygon—a dhirty bunch o' scab herders.'"[96]

Moberly's levee thrived during the war, when troop trains made overnight or dinner stops. Business was good for prostitutes and tapsters. Jack sampled wartime profiteering when he hired out temporarily to help build cantonments for housing soldiers. Under the "cost-plus" system of contracting, workers were paid whether they actually worked or not. In *The Disinherited* Jack portrayed the jingoism, the intolerance, the violence toward antiwar protesters, the disillusionment of returning soldiers, and the profiteering that he witnessed in Moberly. "I decided that everything about the war was cruel. Behind the Liberty Loan posters, I saw the agitator's bloody, tragic face."[97]

Labor-management conflicts grew very sharp in Kansas City in 1918; during a general strike the National Guard patrolled the streets with bayonet-mounted rifles. Even saloons closed for fear of riots. St. Louis experienced similar conflicts when employers advocated open shop and attempted to block union organization.[98] A violent race riot occurred when St. Louis manufacturers imported black workers to break local trade unions. Following Armistice, the railroads began to make sharp cutbacks. Workers were pleased with William G. McAdoo, director general of the Railroad Administration, who had been instrumental in improving their work conditions. In 1920, the Plumb Plan called on the government to purchase the railroads. Ninety percent of the railroad workers, including the carmen's brotherhood, voted for a strike to urge Congress to adopt the nationalization plan.[99] In place of the plan, however, Congress created the Railroad Labor Board, which exercised jurisdiction over labor disputes and set wages. The board soon lowered wages in the economic downturn following the war.[100] Labor militancy, on the other hand, grew more tense. The Wabash shopmen walked out for a day when a "scab" foreman appeared at the shops.[101] Things were tightening up in the Moberly shops, with frequent layoffs.

Jack continued his plan of self-improvement, finishing high school through correspondence and undertaking a self-directed reading program in the classics appearing in the newly created "People's Pocket Series," published by Haldeman-Julius in Girard, Kansas, later to become the famous "Little Blue Books." Jack was a "charter member" of what Haldeman-Julius would later call his "University in Print," a selection of some five hundred titles in ten-cent pocket-sized editions, read avidly by workers, shop clerks, and professional people all over the nation. Ed Falkowski, the Pennsylvania coal miner and worker-writer who some ten years later joined Conroy's Rebel Poets, recalled their importance in his own education: "The Blue Books were my university curriculum when I worked at the Collieries [mines], for some of the softer jobs I occasionally got enabled me to read a book a day at work—an ideal set-up for the reading and enjoyment of such small lunch-pail editions as came out of Girard, Kansas[,] in those years."[102] Jack still nourished the idea of another career, in accord with his father's wishes. His pay was now seventy-two cents an hour. He had saved his money, staying clear of the saloons. Taking a furlough from the shops, he enrolled at the state university in Columbia, Missouri, thirty miles south of Moberly.

* * *

God help me, I'm in a university,
A lowbrow, a bum, and in college.
I should be working in the mines or out on the section,
Or in the jungles with a lot of crummy stiffs
Singing wobbly songs;
But I'm not—I'm in a university.[103]

At the university in the fall of 1920, Jack signed up for Spanish, French, history, geography, and Latin. Like Jude Fawley, Hardy's worker-protagonist, Jack was proud of his self-taught Latin and eager to display his abilities. He felt particularly gratified when Julia Cauthorn, his Latin teacher, commended him for his pronunciation in reading a selection from Cicero. Jack took a room in the home of a shopman's relative. Walking down College Avenue to his classes, past the Wabash depot, he felt wretchedly homesick for Moberly.

Military training was obligatory at the university. He hated the wraparound leggings he was compelled to wear. The drill sergeant called Jack "big farmer." "You ain't pickin' corn here, big farmer," he said, censuring him for carrying his rifle incorrectly. The whole exercise seemed trivial and onerous to Jack. A number of Japanese were in Columbia at the time, enrolled in the military courses of the Student Army Training Corps (SATC), which they called the "Saturday Afternoon Tea Company." There to study American military practices, they later served as officers in Japan's imperial army in World War II. Jack loved learning but felt uncomfortable at the university. Its institutional values seemed encapsulated in the SATC. The antimilitarist bias of Eugene Debs, the Wobblies, and the *Appeal to Reason* had colored his view of military service.

Feeling estranged from student life, and longing to get home to familiar "woods and fields," Jack returned to the Moberly shops after one semester. He had been a worker since age thirteen. It was not easy to efface that experience in satisfying his father's wish that he succeed as a white-collar professional. The American myth of success had fastened that wish on Tom Conroy, a young immigrant in a new land of unlimited opportunity. Jack, disabused of the success myth, felt more comfortable following the paths of advancement within the working class.[104]

The brief sojourn at the state university forced Jack to deal with his ambivalent position as worker-intellectual. Soon after leaving the university, he made the decision (events partly made the decision for him) to remain in the shops yet not abandon his intellectual ambitions. The traditional path followed by bright, energetic workers was to enter labor politics, to become a class leader.

In 1921, there was a great need for able leaders, given the growing antilabor climate and the backlash against organized labor in the aftermath of wartime labor-capital conflicts. Today, a bright young person has every opportunity to attend college; and being poor and bright incurs special privileges with respect to scholarship aid. But in the 1920s, few such opportunities existed for working-class youth. Labor, like environmental concerns today, seemed poised for cataclysmic transformations. Jack's rejection of social mobility, of success by bourgeois standards, engaged him in new commitments that involved him directly in these transformations and eventually determined the nature of his literary work. The decision was, in effect, a refusal to disjoin worker and intellectual.

* * *

Slow in awakening to sexuality, Jack suddenly became conscious of his urges. He fancied himself a young dandy, but to spare himself the embarrassment of meeting a young woman on the street and having to say hello, he would cross to the other side. Soon after returning from Columbia, Jack developed a romantic interest in a girl named Daisy Bee Gatewood, who lived in Denver, Colorado. He had first "met" her through correspondence after she had written an intelligent letter to a magazine. His romantic interest in Daisy was complicated when his sister Margaret began bringing home a young woman named Gladys Kelly after church. Jack and Gladys had gone to Sugar Creek school together, but Gladys at that time had admired Jack's brother Tom, who could turn somersaults and owned a jackknife. Gladys was a jolly, good-natured, short, slightly plump young woman with pretty brown eyes. Jack was sexually aware but very shy. Gladys, by contrast, displayed her attraction to Jack unashamedly.

The Kellys were poor farmers. Gladys's father, Joseph, who had intellectual aspirations, had gone mad when Gladys was fifteen, and was put away in the "lunatic asylum" in Fulton. Gladys's mother married Dave Bowden soon after; without financial support, she had no choice but to remarry. Bowden turned out to be a violent man and a troublemaker. Gladys left school after eighth grade and became a clerk in Hassem Saub's grocery store. Gladys "had her hooks" in Jack and was fiercely jealous of Daisy Bee Gatewood. Jack had visited Daisy in Denver. Pretty, he thought, but too skinny and not aggressive enough.[105] Gladys and Jack dated for about two years during the time that Gladys worked for the Lebanese grocer, the model for Jack's story "The Siren," published in the *American Mercury*, whose heroine curiously is a shy, bookish young woman. Gladys read a great deal but proved "immune," as Jack's friends often noted, to all of Jack's literary ideas.[106]

After several temporary moves, Pip and Eliza bought a home on Watson Avenue, where Jack and Margaret continued to live with their parents. Further complicating Jack's courtship of Gladys was an enforced furlough at the shops. Layoffs had grown more frequent. Over the Christmas holidays of 1921, five hundred shopmen were laid off. During his furlough, Jack worked as a laborer unloading cement sacks in the construction of a water filtration plant outside Moberly. The job provided the setting of his story "The Cement King," a powerful, poignant account of friendship between races destroyed by prejudice. Over the summer of 1921, he loaded wagons for a hay-baling crew run by the Gutekunst sons, his childhood friends. Jack remembered the heat, the blood sausage meals served in the field, and snakes that the Gutekunst boys mischievously tossed into the wagon.[107]

Jack's courtship of Gladys encountered another obstacle: Dave Bowden, Gladys's step-father, who made it plain that he did not like Jack. One evening when Jack and Gladys were sitting on the Bowdens' front porch, Dave suddenly appeared, saying, "You've got to quit this loving." Bowden's intrusions irritated Jack, who was generally slow to anger. Jack jumped up and hit Bowden, who, carrying a knife, slashed Jack's face near the throat, leaving a large visible scar. It was a nasty episode and Jack would not talk about it. Bowden was given sixty days to cool off in the Huntsville jail, then was released to work for the county. Jack spent a week in a hospital bed. When Jack, who detested violence, saw Bowden on the street several months later, he felt a murderous urge. He bore the scar the rest of his life, refusing to discuss it.[108]

Jack planned to return to his position as journeyman car-repairman after the furlough. He hoped the economy would pick up, since he and Gladys were planning to be married. Before long, he was slated to become a "car toad," as far up the promotion ladder as a worker could advance without entering management. During layoffs Jack continued reporting to the *Railway Carmen's Journal* on Magic City Lodge 64, which was suffering wage cuts and reductions in personnel. These reports, his earliest publications, convey the frustration and anger of the shopmen, questioning the basis of an economic system that casts aside its workers so carelessly.

In 1920, employers had argued before the Railroad Labor Board for lower wages and had won their case.[109] The board released the railroads from paying workers overtime rates during Sunday and holidays. The brotherhoods were extremely upset over the board's concessions to employers. Employers were contracting work to nonorganized shops, or in some cases, transforming their own shops into contract shops to escape labor board regulations. When the labor board finally raised objections in May 1922, Wabash officials refused to listen. The carriers' noncompliance weakened the board's authority. At least one railroad denied unions the right to speak for the workers.[110] The board continued to yield to the carriers' demands for further wage cuts in the shop crafts. By June 1922, a major confrontation was shaping up throughout the country, involving the shop brotherhoods and the railroad companies.

The thirtieth of June 1922 was the date that Gladys and Jack fixed for their wedding, since Jack had received notice that he could begin work again on the first of July. Married in the Methodist parsonage in Moberly, where the Conroys had always gone to church, Jack and Gladys chose Bryan Mead, Jack's childhood playmate at West Park, as best man. Afterward, the newlyweds walked to the Jacobys, Jack's relatives, where they planned to live until they could find their own home. Jack had planned a honeymoon in Denver but Gladys nixed the idea quickly. Jack was affable and impulsive; he might decide to get in touch with Daisy Bee "for old times' sake."[111]

On 1 July, the day following the wedding, Jack reported for work at the shops. At 10:30 A.M., the shopmen walked out, beginning one of the most extensive strikes in American labor history. The Great Railroad Strike of 1922 spread bitterness that scourged many a railroad town like Moberly for years to follow. It also marked the beginning of entirely new commitments for Jack, who, when the strike finally concluded, had few illusions about pursuing the American dream of success. "I knew that the only way for me to rise to something approximating the grandiose ambitions of my youth," the young protagonist says in Jack's first novel, "would be to rise with my class, with the disinherited. . . ." The months ahead sealed his attachment to organized, collective action in place of individual success, the American Dream. The events of the Great Railroad Strike, the defeat of the Moberly strikers, only strengthened his resolve to remain within his class. Beyond all desiring now was the comfortable, secure life of an accountant and middle-class respectability. Was it simply coincidental that Tom Conroy had made a similar choice, that he had taken the shot-firer's job so that Jack might be free to study for a white-collar profession? Was Jack's rejection of middle-class aspirations an act of atonement that he had earlier sought to perform as a child at his father's death? Was this his reason therefore to foreclose finally all possibility of middle-class status, of possible intellectual achievement?

Another course of action appeared, within the turmoil and uncertainty of the ensuing strike: worker and writer/intellectual joined in the same person, posing new contradictions, presenting new choices, offering new possibilities with far-reaching consequences.

Front row (left to right): Jack Conroy (age five), Cora McKiernan (half sister), Tom Conroy (brother), Margaret Conroy (sister, age two), Isabelle McKiernan Harrison (half sister), Tom E Conroy (father); back row (left to right): Joseph McKiernan (half brother), Everett McKiernan (half brother), Eliza McCollough McKiernan Conroy (mother), Henry Harrison (Isabelle's husband). Courtesy of the Conroy family (as are all photos not otherwise credited).

Labor Day, ca. 1918, Wabash Railroad shops in Moberly. Jack Conroy, apprentice carman, stands at right of car, arm raised.

Seated: Eliza Jane Conroy Addis, Jack's mother; standing (left to right): Pip Addis, Jack (in Student Training Corps uniform), Margaret Conroy; 1920.

Conroy, ca. 1918, sitting on the foundation of the Elvin house after fire destroyed it.

Conroy, home from the University of Missouri, with Fred Harrison, his nephew; 1920.

Jack with Gladys Kelly, ca. 1922.

At the Willys-Overland automobile plant, Toledo, Ohio, 1929; (left to right): Fred Harrison, Conroy, Gerald Shinew (foreman), George Harrison (Fred's brother). Courtesy of Don Shinew.

Conroy edited the *Rebel Poet* (1931-32) with Ralph Cheyney.

Newspaper publicity photo of Conroy taken when *The Disinherited* appeared in late 1933. Conroy papers, Newberry Library.

The protagonist of *The Disinherited* as Dan Rico, a newspaper cartoonist, imagined him.

'LARRY DONOVAN'   (Based on Jack Conroy's book "The Disinherited")   by DAN RiCO

'LARRY DONOVAN'   (Based on Jack Conroy's book "The Disinherited")   by DAN RICO

'LARRY DONOVAN'   (Based on Jack Conroy's book "The Disinherited") Part IV   by DAN RICO

Dan Rico serialized *The Disinherited* in cartoon strips appearing in the *Young Worker*.

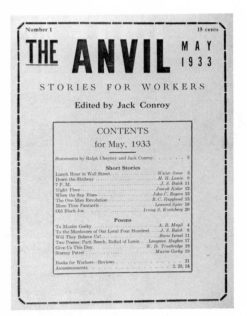

Conroy edited the *Anvil* beginning in May 1933.

Bob Cruden, Scots-born worker-writer, at the Ford River Rouge plant, Detroit, 1929. Courtesy of Robert Cruden.

Joe Kalar, Minnesota mill worker and poet, ca. 1929. Courtesy of Richard Kalar.

H. H. Lewis, farmer-poet, Cape Girardeau, Missouri, ca. 1934. Courtesy of Kent Library, Southeast Missouri State University.

John Rogers, worker-writer and artist, Blue Ridge Mountains, Virginia, ca. 1936. Courtesy of Robin Rogers.

Meridel Le Sueur, literary radical, ca. 1931. Conroy papers, Newberry Library.

4

The Great Railroad Strike of 1922:
The Making of a Worker-Writer

The world broke in two in 1922 or thereabouts. . . .
—Willa Cather

IN THE 1920S, Oscar Ameringer, an independent radical whom Jack greatly admired, published a feisty, humorous, irreverent newspaper, the Oklahoma *Leader*, that attracted Conroy and others with ties to labor. With a felicitous combination of wit and political insight, Ameringer, a German immigrant, tells in his autobiography, *If You Don't Weaken* (1940), how he came to embrace labor's struggle for social justice during the early decades of the twentieth century. Writing from inside the struggle as union organizer and labor journalist, Ameringer encountered disillusionments that he succeeded in mastering by virtue of an instinctive tolerance, reasonableness, and the ability to turn setbacks into humor. Ameringer struck a note of wise honesty and playful shrewdness that resonated in the minds and hearts of young worker-intellectuals like Conroy during a time of upheaval and insecurity.

The 1920s were a tumultuous time for Jack and thousands of other workers left stranded by layoffs, broken strikes, and firings. For the next ten years he followed rumors of job openings, rode the "red ball" (freight train), stood in employment lines, slept in "missions" on skid row, and found occasional work on auto assembly lines and in steel mills. This experience furnished Jack with material for his first worker narratives. In the night, between day shifts, he began to hone his writing skills and make contacts with other writers. His writing would record the profound transformations that affected uprooted workers, the new proletariat, migrating from rural communities to factory cities. His earliest stories portray the demise of work communities and the emergence of new symbolisms in the "communities" of the dispossessed. Like Ameringer's writing, Jack's literary work grows out of what Wallace Stevens called the "intelligence of the soil" and is nourished by midwestern currents of radicalism, the old labor press, and homegrown varieties of populist and socialist culture and politics. Ameringer's skeptical humor and tolerance have antecedents in the folk humor of the German popular stage and satirical publications such as *Simplicissimus*. Conroy's sources are Southwestern humor, vernacular protest, and indigenous radicalism. Continents apart in their early experience and education, both Ameringer and Conroy were part of a small but significant subculture of grass-roots protest in the 1920s, scarcely noticed, until the Great Crash and ensuing events in the early 1930s gave it currency.

*   *   *

"The Depression started early for me," Jack said later in recollecting his experiences as a young journeyman in the Wabash shops and their conclusion in the Great Railroad Strike of 1922 that froze the nation's major railroads. Several years after the strike, one of Jack's old colleagues from the shops wrote how "the railroad strike [had] scattered the old bunch from Moberly, Mo."[1] The hardships following the 1922 strike and the involuntary diaspora of the ex-strikers were decisive factors in Conroy's life and writing. Without the strike Jack might have become a "car toad," enjoyed the respectability that Moberly accorded its labor aristocrats, perhaps assumed leadership in the reorganized union local, as Tom Conroy had been a leader in the UMW local. But things turned out otherwise. Conroy learned a new craft as worker-writer, undertaking his apprenticeship in boxcars, in unemployment lines, and during the short proletarian nights between factory shifts. The Great Railroad Strike of 1922 altered many people's lives in profound ways, bestowing a legacy of conflict that persisted for years afterward. Yet it also produced at least one writer who left an important mark on American letters. Within a decade Jack Conroy was revising *The Disinherited*, his first novel, for publication and starting a literary magazine that would introduce readers to young writers like Richard Wright and Nelson Algren.

Losing a strike, as Melvyn Dubofsky has pointed out, is not necessarily a loss. Strikes serve to raise workers' consciousness of their rights and instill in them the necessity of struggle as the condition of gaining those rights.[2] But the Moberly strike had an indecisive outcome. The Wabash strikers were broken and scattered. Many assumed other names to join union locals in other railroad shops. Few returned to the Wabash shops when the opportunity was given them.

The 1920s proved to be a difficult time for organized labor and workers in certain industries. The typical postwar worker was "a semiskilled machine operator," according to Dubofsky, "who labored for wages in the mass-production industries."[3] The effects of deskilling and a surplus of workers weakened labor's previous gains. Ethnic and racial divisions undermined working-class solidarity. "By 1920 the stage had been set," Dubofsky adds, "for the welfare capitalism and managerial autocracy that would dominate labor relations throughout the 1920s."[4] The Lynds' famous study of Middletown revealed a blue-collar class in Muncie, Indiana, unaware of its collective potential as workers, aspiring rather to middle-class status with little hope ever of attaining it.

Nonetheless a current of worker resistance existed during the 1920s that would join a larger stream of political radicalism in the following decade. Like many workers belonging to the growing army of migrant workers under the administrations of Harding, Coolidge, and Hoover, Conroy drifted from job to job, finding work where he could. There were a few worker-intellectuals like him in their ranks, however, who were teaching themselves a new craft that although economically unsound would prepare them to help create new methods of literary production and shape works of lasting value. Ironically, the 1922 railroad strike that brought the Depression early to Moberly and other railroad towns was a constituent in an emerging consciousness that would soon play a role in creating new expressions of literary radicalism. Labor's defeats would help produce worker-writers who participated in new modes of literary production. Workers in the 1920s shared little in the affluence that the "Jazz Age" represents in the popular mind. They were not among David Potter's "people of plenty."[5] Insecurity and uprootedness shaped their "character." Young worker-writers like Jack Conroy, H. H. Lewis, Ed Falkowski, and Joseph Kalar, eager to share their experiences, made contact with one another through obscure "little magazines" and the Haldeman-Julius publications. There was a need to reach new audiences, to stir in them an awakening consciousness that their experience counted. These early awakenings occurred in the union journals, newspapers, and ephemeral publications appearing in small midwestern towns.

In a sense, the date marking Jack's beginnings as a worker-writer was the day on which the shopmen went out on strike, 1 July 1922. He was not aware of the finality of the rupture with what he had known for the past nine years, the work community of the shops with its routines, frustrations, and rewards. Like most of the some seven hundred shopmen who came out in Moberly with him, Jack thought the strike would soon be settled so that he could resume his life, receiving the weekly paycheck, raising a family, and continuing to write for the labor press. But 1922 was a dismal year for management and labor.

In June of that year, an unarmed union miner was shot near Herrin,

Illinois, inciting a bloody battle in which nineteen nonunion workers were killed. The radical press, such as the *Liberator*, gave a great deal of attention to events of this kind, viewing the Herrin massacre as class warfare.[6] The Great Railroad Strike was viewed as evidence that "Wall Street" ruled America and that government agencies were its lackeys. Robert Minor called for a true labor party representing the worker's interests. Minor remarked that there had been "a day when some tender souls and some tough ones could say that there are no classes in America. Then came the Railroad Labor Board."[7] An antilabor government, the economy, and the general mood of the country did not favor a major strike. The shop craft brotherhoods ignored the lessons driven home bitterly to the miners, namely that "a wise labor leader will avoid a strike on a falling market."[8] Some of the shopmen remembered the ill-timed 1894 strike in Moberly's Wabash shops.[9] The strikers had been in a very weak bargaining position then, with three million unemployed workers hungry for jobs.

Their bargaining power was likewise weak when, in 1922, the shop craft unions issued an ultimatum to the Association of American Railway Executives, demanding that the railroads ignore the labor board's wage-cut order and abolish contract work. Exacerbating the labor-management conflict in the shops was the shopmen's growing frustration at management's ability to extract any concessions it wished. The frustration stemmed in great part from the successes labor had achieved during the period of nationalization in World War I.

Jack's apprenticeship in the shops occurred during a period of great labor militancy in American labor history. The war had brought temporary prosperity to the railroads, stimulating demand for workers and bringing about long-sought changes such as the forty-eight-hour week. By 1920, nearly two million men were working for the government-run railroads. The strike fever that affected so many industries left the railroad brotherhoods largely untouched once the Railroad Administration took control. American labor unions emerged from the war stronger than ever, having won respectability and a place, they assumed, in the national leadership. The hope for government ownership was dashed, however, when the railroads were returned to private ownership. Even while government and employers were still lauding labor's role in Wilson's new industrial democracy, keen resentment toward labor's advances was felt from these same quarters. Employers felt threatened; large strikes in 1919 enhanced their fear of labor's newfound strength and caused them to worry that labor might move in a radical direction. The business depression of 1921 strengthened the employers' hand. Attorney General Palmer was eager to root out potential radical activity, fanning public prejudices against "foreign subversives." Vigilantes broke up socialist meetings and the government prosecuted antiwar socialists such as Eugene Debs. Employers hired blacks as strikebreakers, stoking racial tensions among workers. The propaganda machine that had praised labor's role in winning the war now challenged the right of assembly and free speech.[10]

By 1919 union membership had nearly doubled over the previous five years. There were an unprecedented number of strikes that year. Yet it was also the year the steelworkers, led by William Z. Foster, were defeated, and Seattle's mayor condemned strikers as reds and anarchists. "By 1920," James R. Green writes, "the workers' challenge to manipulation and segregation had been dealt a decisive blow with the defeat of industrial unionism mobilized in the IWW and in the AFL campaigns in the stockyards and the steel mills. It would be a long, terrible fifteen years before a new kind of industrial unionism reemerged to challenge corporate domination of the workers' world."[11] Labor had hoped to win a respected voice in American political life. By 1922, those hopes had dimmed. For many, the failure of the Great Railroad Strike would extinguish them altogether.

In letters to the *Railway Carmen's Journal*, published in the spring of 1921, Jack called attention to the mounting attacks on labor by government, business, and even popular magazines such as *Comfort*, the equivalent then of *Woman's Daily*. The cartoons appearing in Arthur Young's radical periodical, *Good Morning*, Conroy wrote, correctly portrayed the figure of Labor enduring all the woes of the Harding administration.[12] A showdown between labor and capital, he wrote, was approaching.

Jack's letters to the *Carmen's Journal* reveal an earnest young worker with a flair for colorful diction and hyperbole, eager to put a large, bookish vocabulary to use in the cause of labor. The journal, in addition to its burden of union-local news, carried items of literary interest and political commentary, instructing members in the power of effective communication. Its pages were open to worker-correspondents like Jack who, reporting from the locals, were eager to share their thoughts with their fellow workers in a large readership throughout the country. This and other union journals gave them their first opportunity.

The layoff from the shops was longer than Jack had anticipated. By the spring of 1922, the company had reduced its wages for carmen to sixty-four cents per hour. Widespread unemployment made it possible to draw upon unorganized workers (who were often unskilled) should the furloughed shopmen decide not to return. The Moberly local, along with many other locals across the nation, was determined to put up a stiff fight while avoiding a strike. That no longer seemed possible by the end of June when the shopmen voted to walk out. Over 90 percent of the shopmen came out on 1 July, at that time the largest national work stoppage in American labor history.[13] Most of the nation's trains kept running but there were delays owing to faulty equipment and breakdowns.

On the eve of the strike, Jack expressed his contempt of the Harding administration, refuting claims that a business depression and falling foreign orders were to blame for the wage cuts. "During the previous administration," he wrote, "the warm governmental sympathy which now so benignly warms the cockles of the capitalists' hearts was curiously absent or at least passive to the amorous advances of the satraps of privilege. With the change of administration the waning hopes of Big Business revived like the awakening of life in a dead garden, and the accumulated wrath of years burst forth in a veritable Vesuvius of fury."[14] The editor of the journal wondered whether readers would understand Jack's flowery diction and periodic sentence construction. His pride hurt, Jack disregarded the editor's remark. Much later, Jack would listen when H. L. Mencken urged him to develop a more natural idiomatic style. With experience, Jack grew conscious of the humorous potential of ornate diction and farfetched idioms, expressions of his early romance with words.[15]

As the work stoppage took shape, Moberly's newspaper reported that "all the machinists, boilermakers, car repairers, blacksmiths and pipe fitters are out. They left the shops quietly and without disturbance, leaving the sweepers, fire knockers and stationary firemen at work."[16] In the afternoon of the first, a Saturday, the strikers met in the Moberly high school auditorium where they received strike instructions. They were in high spirits; more than seventeen thousand men had come out in Missouri alone. Some nine thousand miners in Missouri had gone on strike several months earlier, 75 percent of all Missouri miners. The spirit of what David Montgomery calls "the new unionism," prevalent during the bullish years up to war's end, carried over into early summer 1922 despite greatly altered circumstances since Harding's election and the actions of the Railroad Labor Board. The Moberly shopmen were in a mood to resist management quietly and patiently, confident that the company would have to yield. The men were ready for the strike. Their resolve bespoke a well-developed consciousness forged during the war years. Labor's bargaining power, as noted earlier, was much weakened in the Harding years. The frustration and disappointment of defeat forged a new radical consciousness that prepared the way for labor's struggles in the 1930s.[17]

The early days of the walkout coincided with Moberly's observance of the Fourth of July, traditionally an important event in Missouri's small towns. Long before the strike a splashy celebration had been planned. L. S. Mounce, a local tenor, traveled around the Midwest singing "When It's Apple-time in Old Missouri" to advertise the event. Holtsinger's National Athletic Carnival erected a tent to hold fifteen thousand spectators. Promoters arranged a wrestling match between Jim Londos and Earl Craddock. Jack Dempsey boxed several exhibition rounds with sparring partners. Sam Langford, a black heavyweight who was never successful in arranging a match with Dempsey, boxed with Jack Taylor. Blind Boone, a black pianist from Columbia, played for the crowd. The Mauldin Aircraft Company of Fulton, Missouri, staged a two-plane flyover coinciding with a parade on Reed Street, a march greatly expanded by the presence of several hundred Wabash strikers. Yet, the American Legion, which had sponsored the program, fell far short of its goal to raise funds for a memorial to Randolph County war veterans. Dempsey generously declined his fee. Despite a poor turnout and subdued spirit of festivity on the fourth, most Moberly residents were confident that the strike would soon be settled.[18]

The strikers were well organized and coolheaded. When it was rumored that sixteen men on the Saturday evening mail-train from Kansas City were company guards, a hundred strikers boarded the train and herded the men into an office of the Wabash station, holding them until the 11:40 P.M. train back to Kansas City arrived. They formed a double line and marched the sixteen to the train. Members of the strikers' families shouted taunts but no violence occurred. Daily meetings were held in Moberly's Fourth Street Theatre where the strikers discussed strategy, adopting a wait-and-see attitude. The striking shopmen issued a statement thanking the people of Moberly for their sympathy and support, pledging no violence or disruption of the mail. Several merchants gave help to the strikers. Hassem Saub, the Lebanese grocer for whom Gladys worked, extended credit during the strike. On at least one occasion he spoke to the strikers at the Fourth Street Theatre, offering them encouragement in broken but expressive English.[19]

By mid-July, however, the strike was bogged down. Rumors circulated that the company planned to hire replacement workers. Worse, it was rumored that the National Guard might be called in. Several of the major railroads had already settled their walkouts, coming to terms with the strikers. Yet shootings had occurred between state guardsmen and strikers in Bloomington, Illinois, where the Missouri, Kansas, and Texas Railroad shopmen were on strike. Moreover, state and government officials were, in several cases, adamantly hostile to the strikers.

Ben W. Hooper, chairman of the Railroad Labor Board, declared that the railroad employees of the American Federation of Labor were outlaws and gave his support to strikebreakers. Chief Edwards of the Kansas City police department charged that "twenty-five I.W.W. radicals" from Chicago had arrived in Kansas City to stir up trouble. Alleging that the railroad centers of Missouri were honeycombed with radicals instructed to "repeat the Herrin massacre," he called for retaliatory action.[20]

Meanwhile the striking miners, who in sympathy with the carmen refused to deliver coal to the railroads, were coming under government scrutiny.[21] President Harding sent an ultimatum to the miners, calling on them to arbitrate or have the mines seized from them. Soon thereafter, Governor Hyde of Missouri pledged to reopen the mines by force if necessary. The first report of violence in Moberly involved a Wabash employee roughed up by a band of men thought to be strikers. Yet greater potential for violence was defused by the strikers' bold action when on the evening of Saturday, 8 July, twenty-seven replacement workers arrived on a Wabash passenger train. The strikers climbed through open windows of the train, removed the men, and marched them over to the old city hall where they questioned their purpose. When the replacements were returned to a later train, again a gauntlet of strikers formed. This time the crowd was angry, having learned that a gun had been discovered on one of the replacement men.

The strike was heating up. The Wabash brought a suit against the strikers, charging that they obstructed people near the station and occupied Wabash property. News arrived that members of the Missouri National Guard and striking shopmen had exchanged shots at New Franklin. Governor Hyde had also ordered the guard to Poplar Bluff, Missouri. By 20 July, all hope for an early settlement was abandoned. Bolstered by the government's support and the settlements obtained by other railroad companies, the Wabash was determined to hold its line. The seniority rights of the shopmen were removed, driving a wedge between labor and management to the point that arbitration seemed impossible. Nonetheless, the striking Federation Shop Crafts continued to press their demands and hope for settlement.

The next day, however, 350 troops of the National Guard arrived in Moberly in a train pulling flatcars, exposing machine guns to public view. Moberly was to be turned into a garrison. It was a grim yet thrilling spectacle that some people would remember for the remainder of their lives.[22] The local Wabash superintendent, W. W. Greenland, had stiffened his refusal to hear the strikers' demands, telling people that "I'll live to see grass growing on Reed Street if the strikers don't give in."[23]

When the first one hundred replacements arrived, they were met by the troops, who pitched a camp in the mill building of the Wabash shops. Governor Hyde justified sending troops without warning, arguing that Sheriff John Milan of Moberly was unable to reassure him that the replacement workers would be protected or violence avoided.[24] The strikebreakers went about firing up the shop boilers, but it was clear to the strikers that they were not actually working; it was simply for show, a device to weaken the strikers' resolve.

An editorial in the Moberly newspaper cited the good behavior of the strikers. "They are a high grade, fine bunch of men," the paper said, "and among them are many of the oldest and most substantial citizens."[25] Noting that Moberly merchants were suffering, the editor encouraged the businessmen nonetheless to continue their support of the strikers. Moberly appeared to be divided into two camps: it was "we," the strikers and their Moberly supporters, against "they," the outsiders, including the "scalies" and the National Guard, whom the strikers unflatteringly labeled "scab herders."[26]

The shopmen continued their game of waiting, and to show their calm resolve they set up a horseshoe-pitching ground along the railroad right-of-way where leisurely games proceeded day and night. The striking shop craftsmen were sitting tight, refusing, according to the chairman of the grievance committee, F. R. Lee, to "rock the boat or violate any laws."[27] When the Wabash placed an ad in the *Kansas City Star*, seeking workers and "guards, those with military experience preferred," Lee replied, "They are willing to bring in the scum of the earth and not only give them good working conditions and free board, . . . [they] also want guards with military experience."[28] Moberly police arrested W. W. Greenland, Wabash superintendent, and W. H. Eckard, division superintendent, charging them with importing men to do the work of the police. Meanwhile, sixty-eight more replacements arrived in Moberly. One of the shops was converted into a dorm. The Baltimore Hotel housed a number of workers. It was said that the men sent their dirty laundry out with the prostitutes, fearing to venture forth themselves without protection.[29] The strikers were having some success in convincing the replacements that they should leave town. Most were not skilled mechanics. Those who did leave said that conditions had been misrepresented to them. It seemed briefly that the balance might be tipping toward the strikers since the replacements appeared unable to do the work in the shops.

No strike benefits were paid; most shopmen looked for temporary work. Gladys's clerking job in Hassem Saub's store helped, but the Conroys needed more income in light of Jack's one-year layoff. A striking carman named Louis Heath had found work in a St. Charles machine shop. Returning to Moberly to wrap up his affairs, he persuaded Jack and another carman, Jesse Hopper, to accompany him back to St. Charles, where Jack and Hopper found a job "bucking rivets" in a railroad car factory. Work in the Moberly shops was slow-paced by contrast. Jack's job was to catch in a small bucket boltlike rivets heated to a cherry red and tossed to him rapid-fire. He would then drive the rivets into place with a heavy hammer. It was dangerous, taxing work, a taste of what lay ahead for him in auto factories. The tempo of the work was machinelike, regulated by time-motion regimens designed to extract the maximum efficiency from a worker's nerves and muscles. After several days, the two men decided to quit. A train conductor permitted them to ride to Moberly in a caboose. The shops in Moberly had allowed time to swap stories, play pranks, even read in fugitive moments. The forced pace of the St. Charles job made them hope the strike would soon be settled. The incident became the basis of Jack's story "High Bridge" and, later, for "Bridge Plant Initiation Ceremonial," one of Jack's industrial folklore contributions to the Illinois Writers' Project in 1939.[30]

In Moberly again, Jack undertook publicity work for the union. One of his tasks was to approach farmers, again asking them to join in the demonstrations. To his chagrin, the farmers, to a man, refused to cooperate. Some of them, in fact, had joined the strikebreakers; they were experiencing economic troubles of their own. Jack lost friends among the farmers, as a consequence. Years later, in the early 1930s, when the left urged a coalition between farmers and workers, Jack, remembering the strike, was skeptical. Farmers viewed themselves as independent businessmen, not employees. The farmers and the Moberly shopmen viewed things differently. However, in a number of sketches written for the Communist paper the *Progressive Weekly* in the late 1930s, Jack, as if to settle an old score, imagined an eccentric, wily farmer named Uncle Ollie who sides with striking workers.[31]

Some of the replacement workers were union members laid off in other railroad towns. A story told in Moberly was of two railroad workers from the same town who changed their names to escape possible union censure when they came to Moberly. Each of the two workers was unaware that the other had chosen to work in Moberly. When they were introduced in the Wabash shops the first day, both men kept up the charade of not knowing one another, blushing all the while in embarrassed silence.[32] The company also enlisted hoboes, no longer booting them off trains but furnishing them with new work clothes, feeding them, and providing them with a grubstake or a free pass on the Wabash. After a few days of work, most left to continue their tramping. It is ironic that the town fathers of Moberly had ordered twenty-four tramps to leave town earlier in the year, listing them as carriers of contagious diseases.[33]

Lee, the general chairman of the grievance committee in Moberly, conferred with other union leaders in the East. The Moberly shopmen had asked only for overtime pay on Sundays and holidays and no wage cuts, demands that possibly could have been settled individually with the Wabash management. Instead, the local had decided to join in the national strike "in justice," as they said, "to other shopmen." The strikers were holding firm. A once-tense situation at the Wabash yards had settled into a humdrum, daily routine. The shopmen pitched their horseshoes and the troops whiled away the time, feeling extremely bored and torpid in the hot August sun. Labor leaders came through Moberly, urging the shopmen to stick it out. The strikers distributed cards to local businesses stating "This Firm 100 Per Cent in Favor of Shop Crafts and Miners." In Emporia, Kansas, William Allen White, a newspaper editor noted for good sense and independent views, was arrested for displaying a similar poster, sympathetic with the strikers in his town, in his window. In Moberly, the word "scab" was painted on the houses of several foremen, including Jim Whitaker, who had mentored Jack when he first began his apprenticeship years before.

The strikers claimed that the replacements were quitting as fast as they arrived. The company brought charges of assault against several shopmen, who were represented by the town's leading attorneys, Oak Hunter and Arthur B. Chamier. The shopmen were anxious to keep their names clean in the face of allegations that they had caused train wrecks and destroyed property. It was crucial that they maintain the support of the townspeople since the strikers were living on credit extended to them by sympathetic merchants. By 14 September, over seventy-five carriers nationwide had signed agreements with shopmen, based on the so-called Willard Plan; a week later, the New York Central settled its differences with striking shopmen. The Wabash, however, sought absolute surrender, refusing to restore seniority rights, which by this time had become the central issue for shopmen anxious to return to work and begin paying off their debts.

The company was emboldened in its confidence that it had mastered the strike when U.S. Attorney General Harry Daugherty successfully sought an injunction from the federal district judge in Chicago, whom he had recommended for appointment. Daugherty charged the strikers with unlawful conspiracy under the Sherman Anti-Trust Act. The vicious injunction forbade officers of the shop crafts from communicating with members or using union funds in pursuance of the strike. It was intended to break the strike at once. The effect was devastating. To many strikers it proved what they had suspected to be true: "that against them were arrayed every power of the financial world, every power of government, every power of capitalistic reactionaries. Hundreds of men were in prison."[34] The Brotherhood Railway Carmen at first attempted to fight the injunction in the courts, then withdrew its attorneys; it could not meet the expense of litigation. Nonetheless strike activities continued despite the injunction. "If anything," Perlman and Taft write, "its sweeping character gained the strikers greater support."[35] Sometime later, the strikers had a moment of sweet revenge: Daugherty was removed from office on corruption charges. The Justice Department thereupon reduced the union's court costs from some $13 million to less than $4,000.

By October, the shopmen's community support was slipping away. Merchants could no longer carry their debts. Sensing a quick kill, Wabash managers sought to sway the businessmen to their side. Eroding the shopmen's base further was an attack on Raymond Stevenson's cafe, not by the shopmen but by strikebreakers. Angered by the assault upon a Wabash employee downtown, a mob of strikebreakers entered Stevenson's cafe near the shops one night at 10:30 P.M. Although Stevenson swore otherwise, many of the members of the mob who smashed his cafe that night claimed that he had refused to serve them on earlier occasions. In another incident, a drunken man wearing a soldier's uniform fired shots in the Wabash yards. The strike was turning nasty. Destruction of property raised fears among businessmen, who were now anxious to be done with the whole costly affair.

To promote their cause, Wabash officials invited 248 businessmen to tour the shops at noon on a mid-November day, after which they were treated to a turkey dinner. Following the meal, T. J. Jones, general superintendent of the Wabash, answered rumors that the shops might be moved away, reassuring the Moberly businessmen that prosperity lay around the corner once the strike was ended. None of the money the Wabash had spent on feeding and clothing the replacements, he reminded the audience, had flowed into Moberly tills; the Wabash had purchased its supplies elsewhere. When one of the guests of the Wabash asked innocently why there were not men at work, Jones replied that it was the noon hour; the men were away taking their meal. Jones was bluffing, but that did not matter. The question that did matter was, where was the strike heading—and how would it end?

At a meeting in the Chamber of Commerce that night, business leaders debated the issue of the strike and the threats to their businesses if they continued to support the shopmen. Lewis Heck, who ran a hat store, defended the strikers. "You must deal with the men," he said, "who were born and raised here . . . who are attending the theatre every morning, and if you would go over and hear their side of the story I feel sure you would have a different feeling."[36] A Wabash agent stood up and replied to Heck, who had spoken to the sympathy still felt by many of the merchants but who had grown exasperated by the length of the strike and its apparent deadlock. "Gentlemen," the agent spoke, "there are I.W.W.'s here. Among the men there are 20 I.W.W.'s in Moberly. They are [sic] sold out the 800 men through false propaganda."[37] No word struck deeper suspicion in the general public's hearts, and, in particular, caused greater alarm among businessmen in the early 1920s than did "IWW" or "Wobblies." The IWW, largely broken after government repression during and following the war, was viewed as a collection of wild-eyed anarchists, agitators, and bomb-throwers, obedient to no law or person.

Word leaked out to the governor's office in Jefferson City that the strike was nearing its conclusion. In late November, the troops on guard in the Wabash shops were reduced to fifty. Then, several days later, it was announced that the troops would go home on 1 December. Hoping to snatch victory from the mouth of defeat, F. R. Lee spoke to a crowd of a thousand in the high school auditorium on the evening of 29 November. His speech began with a history of the strike, from the creation of the Railroad Labor Board under the Transportation Act in February 1920 to the present impasse. Reciting grievances and underscoring the shopmen's patient efforts to reconcile, Lee reminded the crowd how "on July 1, we suspended work peaceably and have endeavored to be peaceable ever since. We are out against forces," he said, "forces of Wall Street, all the forces of the United States Government are against us."[38] The union had sought to negotiate with the company but to no avail. Now the company demanded that the strikers return as new men, joining the company-sponsored union. To add salt to their wounds, the company required that the strikers destroy their old union cards and pay dues to the company union. "We are good citizens," Lee submitted to the gathered listeners. "I want to ask you if you ever saw a better class of men. We have good homes here. Isn't that better than shacks." Citing the property damage done by drunken troops and "scabs," Lee pressed home his point about the strikers' place in the community and their good citizenship. Concluding, he expressed the shopmen's resolve to continue the strike: "This has been the acid test, and we know who are our friends and we are going to pay. But if you drive us out we can't pay."[39]

Most of the strikers must have known that night that they were finished in Moberly. The strike had become a lockout. For a worker, winter was the worst possible time to be unemployed and debt-ridden. What killed the strike finally was the failure of credit, not credibility. Most Moberly citizens, including the business people, still sympathized with the strikers. But new Wabash workers, filling vacated positions, were arriving and it was soon business as usual. Nonetheless, memories would not be buried; resentment burned for years afterward.

In early December, Jack wrote to the Moberly paper, lamenting the fall of community values he knew as a child and apprentice, the familiar ties of trust and mutual regard of coal camp and railroad shops. The Moberly shopmen saw themselves as honorable producers, good citizens, equal in standing to other occupations in the community. They were justifiably proud of their apprenticeship system that controlled access to their trade. Through this system, their informal alliances with other unions, such as the UMW, boycotts, and sympathy strikes, they had developed a strong sense of their rights as a class of artisan-workers.[40] Pride in their skills, independence, a voice in the community, and respect were elements of their workers' culture, which would suffer permanent rupture.

Many other workers across the land felt the burden of degraded work, deskilling, uprooting, and proletarian status, long before the events involving the Moberly strikers. Strikes, won or lost, instill a sense of class awareness. The shopmen had constituted an "island community," to use Dubofsky's term. They could depend upon support from the town during economic downswings. They would have their say again and perhaps win their demands. But in 1922, the Wabash shopmen were broken and scattered. A tragic event marked this fact.

On Saturday night, 1 December 1922, a few days following Lee's speech to the strikers in the high school auditorium, Loring Heddinghaus, a replacement worker, was riding home in the country about three miles south of Moberly. Ahead of him was a parked car with seven or eight men. As he approached the car, the men got out and jerked him off his horse. Heddinghaus, who carried a gun, fired several shots. It was dark but he heard groaning and knew that at least one of the men had been struck. The others ran off into the woods. On Sunday, the Reverend E. V. Lamb conducted services for the dead man, George Comstock, a striker, whose brother had brought him back to Moberly. The news had spread quickly and a huge crowd showed up in the Baptist church, expecting that Lamb's sermon would castigate the Wabash company. Even those who had shown indifference toward the strike felt sympathy for Comstock's widow and child. But Lamb's sermon disappointed the angry strikers. "These are matters of law, not of the church," he concluded. A huge parade to the cemetery rallied the strikers for a while. However, hunger and winter winds drove them away to other towns and cities to find work.

The incident appears in *The Disinherited*, where Jack portrayed it as a stupid and impulsive act on the part of a striker who incited Heddinghaus's violent self-defense. The strike had soured for many people in Moberly. The *Moberly Monitor* editor noted that while violence had been expected before now, it was nonetheless deplorable. "It embarrasses the great majority of the workers," the editorial said, "who are trying to effect an adjustment by peaceable and business-like methods. It makes heavy drafts upon public sympathy. . . . It injures the good name of the community. . . ."[41]

The defeat of the strike scattered the Moberly shopmen like straws in the wind. Some were taken on by other railroad companies and were able to continue in their craft. At least one went to the USSR, along with thousands of other American workers, to build railroads and dams in the Kuzbas.[42] But most drifted into factory cities, joining the masses of workers on the assembly lines, as Jack would eventually do. "Rounding windy corners in distant cities," Jack wrote, "I have collided with shopmen, grasped their hands, crying: 'Well! Well!' striving to capture in a net of words the memories resurrected by the sight of a well-remembered face."[43] The shooting of Comstock had signaled the defeat of the strike in Moberly and presumably an end to the strife, but for years afterward the town was divided. Some of the strikebreakers subsequently joined the re-formed union local, destroying their BRCA cards. "They became good union men," Conroy wrote in his story "That Skinner Bottoms Winter," "and paid their dues to the national shop crafts unions."[44] Most wished to forget the strike. Yet the old bitterness would often bubble up, for instance, when a father would not let a "scab's" son visit his daughter.[45]

Jack was in a mood to exaggerate events following Comstock's death. Something altered terribly for him in the late fall of 1922. He viewed with disgust the drying up of credit, the settling in of the strikebreakers and their acceptance into the community by people other than the strikers and their families. Moberly had changed, he wrote to the editor of the Moberly paper. Quoting Goldsmith, he compared Moberly to once-fair Auburn. "The cold, commercial spirit," he wrote, "and unbridled greed for wealth that brought about the dissolution of the Deserted Village is seething in the hearts of some Moberly men. . . . Surely Moberly's merchants are unwilling to sell the respect and friendship of their patrons for the goblin gold of the Wabash birds of passage."[46]

The Great Railroad Strike of 1922 brought to a temporary close an intense period of labor activism in which Jack, as a young apprentice in the Wabash shops, had taken part. The defeat of the Moberly strikers closed this period abruptly, not only for Local 64, but elsewhere among the leading brotherhoods. What followed during the next several years was nothing that Jack wished to participate in: growing paternalism in labor-management relations, promotion of open shop, and the rise of welfare capitalism.[47]

Industrialism had caught up with Jack and his union "brothers" in the shops. As a child Jack had experienced the destruction of one "island community" of work, Monkey Nest, early signs of which were the importation of strikebreakers, deteriorating safety standards, declining market prices, and more competitive sources of energy. Similarly, in the 1920s, the political and economic power of island communities like the Moberly shops ceded to what David Thelen calls "a new order" devoted to "growth, profits, and higher incomes." Thelen writes: "In the old order individual producers had felt restrained by a concern with reputation in transactions that had been ordered by face-to-face exchanges and personal networks, by their crafts' or professions' traditions, by community moral standards of conduct. The new order burst these restraints, and its ideology exalted competition and encouraged individual producers to discard and ignore anything that prevented them from producing more goods at lower prices."[48] The Wabash shops continued to operate in the old way; but something was broken between the workers and a segment of the community in which the new forces converged. Moberly had always seemed somewhat removed from the larger currents of change. A gap was growing between middle-class businessmen and blue-collar workers. The latter felt less and less sharers in the affluence of the 1920s. The new spirit of boosterism seldom included them. They worried about their futures, given rising prices and the apparent powerlessness of union leadership in the face of open shop. Yet, few workers during this time sought to improve their lot through strengthened trade unionism. Steadily losing ground, the American worker, according to Dubofsky, turned away from protest for a time.[49]

Conroy experienced firsthand this transformed workers' culture in the decade following the Great War; it provided him material for his first stories of workers. The older order of kinship, craft, and community ties, with its preindustrial workers' culture of fraternity and resistance, he perceived, was giving way to a new workers' world of proletarianism. An apprentice car toad at age thirteen, he had now become an uprooted proletarian at twenty-four. When the strike was broken there was little else to do but join the hundreds of thousands of other job-seekers, pursuing rumors of employment openings in distant factory cities.

* * *

What was a young worker to do, possessed of a lively intelligence, an interest in books, and writing ability? The natural course of an ambitious, energetic, and talented young person in America was (and is) to struggle upward, out of the working classes. But Jack had a family to support. Margaret Jean was born in 1923; Tom followed soon after, and Jack, Junior, joined them in 1928. In leaving the university after one semester, Jack had renounced the possibility of a white-collar professional life. Apparently he felt no sense of failure or humiliation at the prospect of a decline in social status as a result of losing his position with the railroad, of slipping lower on the scale, entering the ranks of the proletariat, without hope of advancement in status.[50] The Heddinghaus incident was proof to Jack of the futility of anger. In 1923 new possibilities presented themselves to Jack, who was anxious about putting bread on the table for his family yet eager to begin the next stage of what Gorki termed his "universities."

Apart from short weekend hops to Kansas City and St. Louis, Jack had not traveled far from home. The rebellious Wobbly inscriptions on the inside walls of the freight boxcars in the shops had intrigued him as a young shopworker. On the other hand, the half-frozen hoboes and scrawled notes, advising of railroad "dicks," cautioned him that hopping freights was no easy street. Jack could take care of himself, if he had to. He planned to take the "red ball" to find work in the factory cities where others were headed. In the meantime, however, he found work in Moberly. Gladys and Jack had moved into the Addises' house after Eliza and Pip left for Des Moines, where Pip had found a job in a sawmill.

A new brick road was under construction between Moberly and Huntsville, part of the new federal primary road system. The railroad strike had held up delivery of cement over the summer of 1922,[51] but work resumed later in the summer. In the early spring Jack took a job with the contractor, Lynch McDonald, laying pavement brick. The workers advanced row by row on their knees, placing each brick in a sand bed. Grains of sand ground into Jack's knees and the unused muscles of his back and wrists ached. An older worker, a black called "Old Mose," set the pace for the other workers. Old Mose bent himself to the task with relentless fury while the other workers groaned and cursed. When summer came, the men slowed, but Old Mose continued his furious pace. Late one hot afternoon the pacesetter's eyes rolled back into his head. Slumping over, he struck his head on the concrete curbing. "Well, it was only an old nigger played out," Jack wrote in his sketch "Paving Gang." "That was the way it seemed to the boss and the others. But here was also the death of a life and the setting of a sun."[52] Slowly the road advanced past the city limits about two miles to the Moberly country club, the former site of Stackpoole's house where the Conroys had lived before a fire destroyed the house and its contents. By December, the road had reached Kimberly. Cold weather made it impossible to lay tar between the bricks. The workers' fingers were numb; reluctantly the workers quit, receiving their last pay. Some of them had erected crude shelters out of brush and timber. With winter setting in they took to the road to find work and to look for more substantial shelter.[53]

In late spring, Jack hired on a state surveying crew. He was teamed up with F. Vernon "Swede" Lamson to hold chain and carry the rod for the surveyor. It was an easy job and to pass the time Swede would play pranks, such as placing the rod on Jack's shoe, introducing error in the measurements. Swede was fresh from studies at the state university in Columbia. In Jack he found a companion who would eagerly discuss books they had both read. Students in Columbia, Lamson reported, were reading with delight H. L. Mencken's attacks on the "booboisie." Jack had never heard of Mencken, editor of the famed *Smart Set*. Within a few years, Jack would become one of Mencken's prized contributors to the *American Mercury*.

Swede Lamson recalled Jack's prodigious memory. During their first day together on the surveying job Jack told Swede that the only book he owned was a dictionary and that he had memorized every word in it. After a few days, Swede began to believe it was true. Jack used his dictionary when writing letters and composing submissions to the *Haldeman-Julius Weekly*. Arcane words would appear in his writing, but they were always used correctly. Both Swede and Jack had a fierce ambition to write. The two would bring books to read and discuss at lunchtime. Lamson thought Jack was a member of the Communist party, based on his views; and, he said, Jack "probably thought I was." Their last day on the survey crew, Swede and Jack got into a brouhaha with the boss, who said he was going to fire them both. They said they didn't care.[54]

Swede was a middle-class kid from Moberly whose father was a secretary of the Chamber of Commerce. When Swede finished his studies in Columbia, he headed west where he found a job picking cucumbers. The job had a nightmarish conclusion. Penniless, he hitchhiked back to Kansas City where he holed up, unwilling to ask for a handout from his parents. Jack had kept in touch and knew of Swede's plight. He gave Swede's address to Swede's mother, who promptly sent him money, probably saving his life. Some years later, when Jack was completely broke in Moberly, Swede tried to get Jack to come to New York where Swede was a successful advertising manager with Consolidated Edison Company.[55]

The summer was a brief idyll for the Conroys; with winter approaching, Jack went to work in the drift mines, the shallow shafts in hillsides near Monkey Nest where coal veins lay near the surface. It was dirty, dangerous work, but Margaret Jean had recently been born and Jack was desperate to find income. Henry Harrison, married to Isabelle McKiernan, Jack's half sister, had first gone to work in the mines as a young man. When his son, Fred, turned fifteen, the boy joined his father in the Marriott mine. But, like Monkey Nest, shaft mining in Randolph County was no longer profitable. Most of the mines around Moberly had closed, and only a few miners like Harrison continued to work the drift mines. When Henry, Fred, and Jack heard from a farmer-miner, Lute McDonald, of an abandoned mine in Skinner Bottoms near Happy Hollow, where Jack and Fred had played as children, they were ready to give it a try. Each workday began before daybreak with a long hike through the woods, where they could gather pawpaws ripening after the first frost. In his mind, Jack would always associate that hard winter in the drift mine with the glistening appearance of pawpaw apples, which looked like big avocados and tasted sweeter than persimmons. Some of the drift miners, like Enoch Vaughn, a Spanish-American War veteran who later figured in Jack's tales, lived like hermits year after year, appearing only to assist the teamster in loading a wagon of their coal to sell in town. There was little money in drift mining, but the coal Jack hewed kept the Conroys warm over that winter. Lute quit when the first icy winds blew; his farm provided him with enough to tide him over the winter. The Harrisons and Jack lasted until the spring mud made drift mining unsafe. The mine was a makeshift affair with shaky props and loose soapstone rock. When the roof finally collapsed it was time to quit. Jack and Fred talked about hopping boxcars to Des Moines. Pip Addis worked in a sawmill there; maybe he would help them find work.[56]

Jack and Fred (who was three years younger) were like brothers. Fred admired Jack and would become his constant companion during the next seven years, migrating from one dirty, noisy, dangerous, underpaid job to another. The anxiety of finding work found some compensation in the adventure of riding the rails to new towns. Fred, small, wiry, and feisty, would walk into a bar shouting, "Anyone who wants to leave will have to get past me!" Jack was much bigger than Fred but hated fighting. Fred knew this, of course, so he made the bar taunt into a prank. Fred enjoyed seeing Jack cringe as he issued the challenge.

The drift-mine experience eventually furnished Jack with material for "That Skinner Bottoms Winter" and a worker narrative he wrote for the Illinois Writers' Project, "A Miner's Apprentice," based on an interview with Fred.[57] Riding the "red ball" in search of work provided matter for stories such as "Bull Market" and "They Won't Let Us Birds Roost Nowheres," and a poem entitled "Journey's End."

In the summer of 1924, Fred Harrison and Jack joined the ranks of the proletariat, the growing number of semiskilled, homeless, migratory workers drifting across America, exiles in their own land. Most were headed for factories in Toledo, Detroit, and Chicago, to time clocks, speedup, deskilling, flivver cars, tract houses, homemade beer, and popular entertainment. Craftsmen, artisans, farmers, miners, and mill workers were carried along, like flotsam on small rivulets flowing into one mighty river, the proletariat, the feed stock of industrialism.[58] Jack followed this stream, was swept along by it. Both participant and observer, he survived like an inland Ishmael to trace the appearance of a new oral culture of work whose features he would translate into his own writing.

5

My Universities

Did you any of you get work? I hope so, anyway.
—Gladys Conroy, letter to Jack, 1924

IN THE SUMMER OF 1924, Jack and his nephew Fred Harrison "rode the blinds" (freight trains), "beating their way" across the Midwest. A part of Jack welcomed the opportunity for adventure in new cities. Fred was an ideal companion. Jack had hopped freights before, but now he and Fred were members of an impromptu army of unemployed "working stiffs," pursuing the rumor of a job in some factory town. "Tramping," as it was known then, had evolved its own lore and given rise to a "tramp school" of writers like Josiah Flynt Willard, Walter A. Wyckoff, J. H. Crawford, Jack London, W. H. Davies, William Edge, Harry Kemp, "International Supertramp A–Number 1," and others. "Hobo" tales appeared in the *Liberator* in the early 1920s;[1] by the early 1930s, tales of tramping would constitute a subgenre of the novel, with Kromer's *Waiting for Nothing* and Algren's *Somebody in Boots*. In the popular mind, the vagabond was a romanticized bohemian. Harry Kemp and Jim Tully exploited the armchair vagabond's vicarious fascination.[2] Mrs. Ethel Lynn, dressed as a hobo, tramped across the country, chronicling her "adventures."[3] Mike Gold, editor of *New Masses*, was sure that more education was available in a boxcar odyssey than in a college classroom. The road was a metaphor for flight and discovery. Vagabondage, however, as Jack London points out in "The Tramp," served capitalists' interests by supplying a cheap pool of unorganized migrant workers.[4] The tramping workers Jack knew had little choice but to keep moving. The rails provided free transportation to jobs and carried the down-and-out to skid rows in Los Angeles and Seattle. Not desperate in the way that

Kromer's and Algren's homeless tramps are, the men Jack met in box-cars had expectations of finding work in factories, if not in one city, then another. Tramping cost nothing more than a few cold nights and an occasional knock on the head.[5]

Despite their violent suppression during and following World War I, the Wobblies were still around. Jack "jungled up" and rode with them in boxcars. Both Jack and Fred carried IWW membership cards, an indispensable passport on the rails. A hobo without a card might be thrown off unceremoniously.[6] Riding the rails gave Jack, Algren, Carl Sandburg, and others a close look at "the other America" of the 1920s.[7] Tramping was another way of viewing America, an enterprise that gained a great deal of credibility in the 1930s' "search for America."[8]

For all the romance of the road, there was a tragic element in the displacement of workers to factory cities. The most devastating effect on Jack and many others like him was not primarily economic, for he had always known financial insecurity; it was primarily social and cultural. Karl Polanyi addresses this point in *The Great Transformation:* "To separate labor from other activities of life and to subject it to the laws of the market was to annihilate all organic forms of existence and to replace them by a different type of organization, an atomistic and individualistic one."[9] To render useless one's work skills and to disintegrate family life represents what Polanyi calls a "social calamity [that] is primarily cultural not an economic phenomenon."[10] If the Wabash shop-men, for example, found self-respect and pride in attachment to place and an occupation, then the social realities of factory work to which many of the migrants gravitated degraded those feelings. Urbanization and industrialism substituted new work habits and consumer values for an earlier industrial (and rural) ethos of locality, identity, and tradition.[11]

Resistance to industrialism—to mass production, the monotony of repetitive tasks, and the indifference of bureaucratized management structures—appeared in many forms, Jack observed. Some workers adopted a passive "don't fight it" attitude. Some were simply cast aside, like Conroy's figure of the superannuated worker, "Bun Grady." Some rebelled through subtle forms of work sabotage, such as slowing down or doing faulty work. Despite time-motion studies, machinelike routines, and fatigue, factory life nurtured new folkways. In the new industrial order of time clocks, speedup, and efficiency, human values were expressed through patterns of subversion, usually humor and play, in the face of reductionist forces acting to efface individual difference and self-worth. Conroy's tales of work reflect the changing culture of the worker in response to industrialism. In the steel mill, rubber-heel factory, and auto factories where he worked he found informal work communities, aleatory and fragmented, but no less human than the more traditional forms of community he had known in the mining camp and railroad shops. Illiterate, leaving no written record of their lives, the workers who drifted through his life made lasting impressions on Jack.

* * *

Like the network of rails connecting towns and cities, an invisible network of relatives and friends connected homeless family members. The Addises and several other Moberly families had moved to Des Moines and were living together in an apartment house at 1401 West Locust Street that Jack dubbed "Hotel Fort De Moberly." Pip, Eliza, Henry and Isabelle Harrison and their sons, George and Harvey, and J. B. Mead were all in Des Moines and had jobs. Deciding to join them, Fred and Jack hoboed to Des Moines. Railroad policemen threw them off the train near Moulton, Iowa. As they tumbled in the dirt, the two policemen shot at them, probably to scare them. Dazed and frightened, the two ducked into a woods, later flagging down a bus and riding into Albia. While they were waiting in the passenger terminal for the train to Des Moines, two city policemen came in and asked the ticket agent about something weighing 180 pounds and something else weighing 160 pounds, the weights of Fred and Jack. The two waited in tense expectation of being arrested, but it turned out that the police were looking for two trunks.

Bunking with the Addises at "Hotel Fort De Moberly," Jack and Fred looked for work. Jack stood in line at the employment office of the Pittsburgh–Des Moines Company, which manufactured railroad water tanks, viaducts, girders for bridges, roof trusses, standpipes, and structural steel for buildings. Begun as the Des Moines Bridge and Iron Works, the company had grown rapidly in a few years, producing water tanks that were familiar presences at railroad sidings, and huge bridge trusses for the growing federal highway system. The price of fabricated steel had fallen sharply by 1924, owing to the discontinuation of the so-called "Pittsburgh Plus" system of pricing steel. Chicago's mills now competed favorably with Pittsburgh's, so that the company was forced to shift its production to the Des Moines plant. Increased production in Des Moines accounted for job openings, which had drawn Jack and others there.[12] The company sought young, fit men for the heavy work. Standing in line with Jack was an "old" worker in his late thirties, who when refused because of his age, pleaded and was finally given a job. Jack's thought was, What happens to the "Bun Gradys," men not too old to work but to be hired? Shuddering at the prospect of workers cast aside like refuse, he stepped firmly forward to the employment desk and was hired.

"A novice in the bridge plant [steel fabrication plant]," Jack wrote in an unpublished manuscript for the Illinois Writers' Project, "which prepares the girders and partially assembles steel highway and railway bridges, enters at once into a bedlam of riveting, clanging of steel against steel, shrieking of crane sirens, roaring of oil-burning rivet forges, and an undertone of hoarse and often unintelligible shouts. The old hands become more or less inured to the noise, and also learn to depend a great deal upon gestures. . . . A system of signals almost comparable to the deaf mute's alphabet has been devised, but the newcomer is at a complete loss until he has memorized the gestures."[13] Jack's first job was to attach clamps on heavy steel beams suspended by a crane and guide them to a new location. The crane operator, Jack learned, was an inmate of the state penitentiary who was permitted to work in the steel mill during the day, along with several other inmates, for a token dollar-a-day wage. The news was scarcely comforting to Jack, who pinched his hand while hurrying to attach a clamp. Graduating to a higher-paid task, Jack was sent to operate a steel saw. A foreman, who had taken over the operation of the saw awaiting a replacement worker, gave Jack rudimentary instructions to operate the steel saw, which rotated at high speed and shrieked like a giant dentist's drill. "When the saw struck its mark a tremor assailed me. I winced as the sharp, grating noise probed at the nerves in my teeth."[14]

One of his fellow workers told Jack during a break that the previous operator had been killed when the saw came apart, driving a section of the blade through the operator's chest. Workers had continually to be on the watch as overhead cranes maneuvered dangling steel beams and trusses. One crippled worker named Joe Vash was pointed out as a constant reminder to the workers to be careful. "For weeks he hobbled after us, croaking warnings and prophecies of doom like a dyspeptic raven." Vash recounted grisly stories of industrial accidents, frightening the superannuated worker "Bun Grady," whom the foreman tormented with practical jokes. One day at the lunch hour, a boxer-turned-evangelist performed a pantomime for the mill workers, staging a fight with the devil, "Kid" Satan, and followed by a maudlin testimony of past sins.[15] By that summer Jack had earned enough to bring Gladys, pregnant with their second child, to Des Moines, where she found a job in a cookie factory.

Jack stayed on in the steel mill through the fall of 1924 and into the early spring of the following year. In the fall presidential campaign he heard Robert La Follette, the Progressive candidate, shout his message to a large crowd in Des Moines through an unamplified horn. Gladys wrote her sister, Florence Hardy, in Moberly: "Jack says he is going to order the 'Index' [*Moberly Monitor-Index*]. He is so interested in the election. I'll be glad when he does for I like to get the home news. You will be almost old enough to vote won't you."[16] Jack was attracted to La Follette in part because Senator Burton K. Wheeler was on his ticket. It was Wheeler who had brought down Harry Daugherty, the arch-nemesis of the railroad shopmen. The railroad brotherhoods threw their support to La Follette after it was revealed that the Democratic candidate, William McAdoo, who had operated the railroads during the war, was a special counsel for big oil interests.[17] La Follette attempted to merge the interests of farmers and laborers in a third-party movement and supported many Progressivist aims including antitrust legislation, welfare legislation for working people, and government planning in public projects such as electrification. Despite the fact that La Follette had rejected Communist support (and received stinging rebukes in the *Liberator*), his party was labeled "communistic" in the Republican press and by Coolidge's running mate, Charles "Hell and Maria" Dawes.[18]

La Follette's defeat left workers like Jack little hope that their interests would be represented in government. With the prospect of progressive reform fading, what remained for them? Curiously, the publication of the Workers' Party Platform appeared soon after.[19] Proletarian workers faced a confusing world in 1924. In *The Need for Roots*, Simone Weil observed that workers "are unable to feel themselves at home whether it be in factories, their own dwellings, the parties and trade-unions ostensibly created on their behalf, places of amusement, or in intellectual activities if they attempt to acquire some culture."[20] Her commentary applies with equal validity to conditions among uprooted American workers. The vast migration of workers taking place included southern blacks eager to find better working conditions in northern factory cities, a subject about which Jack would one day write in *They Seek a City* and *Anyplace But Here,* in collaboration with Arna Bontemps. This migration imposed a severe psychic and social tax on the worker. In a time when disillusion and cynicism seemed to affect American intellectuals, La Follette had offered a hopeful vision. His candidacy failed, yet there remained among some intellectuals the aspiration for social justice and compassion for the underdog, while workers longed for representation answering their demands.[21]

In 1924, the Workers' Party, newly organized by the Communist Party of America, neatly divided "workers" and "capitalists" according to their irreconcilable interests, and censured La Follette's moralistic defense of old American ideals that so thrilled the liberal community.[22] Radicalisms of European origin held little attraction for Conroy, who was drawn to the Wisconsin progressive reformer's side, as he was drawn to nativist currents of populism and socialism. By 1930, however, he had joined many intellectuals and members of the artistic community in giving support to the Communist program, for by then the party appeared to offer that dream of greater social justice, which had been defeated in the 1924 election.

Jack was aware of new social forces at work in the workers' world of the later 1920s that proved of greater consequence than the outcome of the 1924 election. In the cities he perceived the tension between urban and rural values among the displaced workers who, coming from traditions in which productiveness was central, were thrust into a world of consumption and spending. "The old virtues of thrift and saving," Merle Curti notes, "now largely gave way to the idea that spending is a virtue, even the highest of all economic virtues."[23] Residential subdivisions like "Rosewood Manor," which Jack describes in *The Disinherited*, sprang up, attracting workers with their low down payments: "Ed and I stepped off the bus at twilight and walked a mile down a dusty road to Rosewood Manor. Two grandiose brick columns supporting a gilded arch marked the entrance, and multi-colored pennants fluttered along the graded earth streets. . . . Only one of the lot purchasers had built a house—the others were living in garages at the rear. The garages of the ready-cut variety. They were identical. . . ."[24] The cult of prosperity generated new aspirations among workers, but their wages lagged far behind their desires. John Kenneth Galbraith points out that while production increased, wages failed to rise comparably. High profits for the rich and lavish spending contributed to the decade's myths of prosperity and easy money. "These profits," he writes, "sustained the spending of the well-to-do, and they also nourished at least some of the expectations behind the stock market boom."[25] The workers Jack knew were easy targets of high-pressure advertisers, the glitz of consumerism. But many also longed for the simpler past they had known.[26] Most people proved indulgent, as Curti says, when confronted with evidence of corruption in high places. "The new acceptance of the philosophy of mass consumption and mass prosperity had overshadowed the older ideology."[27]

On the margins of the 1920s, disillusioned artists and intellectuals gave the decade its reputation for rebellion against genteelism in mores and art. Quite without notice, worker-intellectuals who shaped their ideas on the anvil of experience in factories, mills, and farms would prove influential in earning the epithet "Age of Protest" for the following decade. Jack's experience in the mills and factories of the 1920s had little in common with the popular description of affluence projected by historians such as Frederick Allen Lewis.[28] "The public hatred of wealth has subsided," remarked an observer. "As the years have gone by and

the millionaire era has become the billionaire era, the virus of acquisition has built up its own anti-toxin."[29] Not everyone was infected. In
boxcars, on the factory floor, in city parks where job-seekers and bums
gathered, on skid rows and in employment lines Jack overheard the disgruntled voices of workers who seemed incapable of drawing any larger
conclusions. Resignation, passivity, and weary, cynical humor were more
typical of their responses. "Forget it about making a success by grub-
bing, kid!" the worker-protagonist of *The Disinherited* is advised. "There
ain't any more Alger heroes now. It's the front you put on, doing the
other fellow before he does you. . . . Beat him to it, that's all. You'll find
out I know what I'm talking about."[30] Radicals harangued the workers
in Toledo's Jackson Park, Detroit's Grand Circus Park, and Chicago's
Bughouse Square, but few listened. Hope persisted that if one could
hang on to one's job long enough, there might be a payoff. Henry Ford
placed a new kind of freedom so tantalizingly close to the wage earner
that most workers were willing to accept their tenuous lot.

Jack maintained his intellectual ambitions, but the steel plant had
killed his desire to read at night. Despite the dangers and fatigue of work
he was educating himself in ways that fell outside the curriculum of correspondence schools where he had once hoped to "improve himself."
In the Wabash shops and the steel plant he had perceived new manifestations of a transplanted folk culture, with its strategies of play and
protest. In leftist publications he read about "proletcult" and other programs in the Soviet Union that while giving dignity to the notion of
workers' culture attempted to regiment it. Jack's acquaintance with the
proletariat was entirely experiential and concrete, not ideological, in
contrast to intellectual radicals who exhorted the American worker to
embrace the Soviet example of a workers' republic. He followed the
debates occurring in the pages of the *Liberator*, and later, *New Masses*,
with interest, but these did not touch him in any profound way or indeed relate to his own experience.

The transplanted folk culture in the steel "bridge plant," Jack noticed, preserved many of the formalized conventions—initiation rites,
traditional superstitions, folk naming—of the mining camps and railroad shops. A novice might find a hot rivet in his hip pocket, girders
were electrified, and the crane men were experts in knocking down
stooped workers without causing injury.[31] But factory regimens limited
the "spaces" in the workday for talk and storytelling. The constant
threat of joblessness, of having to move on to find work in another factory city, undermined any organized patterns of worker "subversion" that
Jack had known in the railroad shops. Jack's friend from Moberly, J. B.
Mead, worked in a freight depot, pushing two-wheeled trucks. Jack saw

him one day in a line of men with trucks going as fast as possible to load freight cars.[32] Workers, even those who had lost their jobs several times, still fought to stand in line when rumors of new openings reached them. Some, however, sank into passivity and self-contempt, like Helen in *The Disinherited,* who turns to prostitution.

"The consciousness of everyday life," write the authors of *The Homeless Mind,* "is the web of meanings that allow the individual to navigate his way through the ordinary events and encounters of his life with others."[33] In studying modernization they find links between various structures of consciousness and institutional processes. Of particular interest is their discussion of the effect of technological production on the factory worker. While most workers appeared to accommodate themselves to "human engineering" and "Fordism," Jack maintained the double consciousness of a worker-intellectual who submitted to the routines, demands, and compensation of factory work, yet kept his powers of observation and critical ability alive despite fatigue and anxiousness concerning the welfare of his family. *The Homeless Mind* reveals the perils of factory life for the worker who attempts to remain alive mentally. Technological production requires a new "organization of knowledge" that affects the consciousness of the individual worker. Large-scale work processes, for example, require repetitive machine operations that produce parts which are integrated into larger components through abstract, rational schemes of which the worker is largely ignorant. A worker who might lapse into a craftsman's concretized interest in a single operation or part would interrupt the larger chain of work processes. One's work knowledge is segregated, as a consequence, from "other bodies of knowledge and cognitive styles."[34] Personal relationships on the job compete with anonymous social relations. The purpose of management is "to control the unfortunate intrusions of concrete humanity into the anonymous work process."[35] While face-to-face personal exchanges with other workers characterized Jack's apprenticeship in the Wabash shops, in factories such exchanges proved incompatible with job requirements and staying afloat in the sea of proletarianized labor.

The worker "Lipkin" in *The Disinherited,* who resists openly the new factory regimens, was an exception. More typical of Jack's experience were the "Jasper Collins" figures, victims of false consciousness, or cynical figures like "Ed," who is resigned to his role as an anonymous cog in the machinery yet keeps his personal identity separate from his work. Humor and self-ironization make such a division possible. The danger in such a division, however, is alienation between the two selves and confusion as to which role either identity is playing in any given circumstance.[36] Other strategies Jack observed were indifference toward the larger picture or ways of subverting the rationality of machine work, exposing the machine to damage or feigning injury. Some workers fought back against the values of practicality and rationalization of the work-place with their own improvised values of bad sportsmanship, inefficien-cy, and indolence, not because these would ever succeed but because their anger had settled into a cool logic that matched the coolness of the engineers carrying out the precepts of scientific management. Hot-heads like "Lipkin" rebelled individually, lashing back in vain against a time clock or a surly foreman. Arrested by an unnamed "guard," Lip-kin is fired on the spot by the "employment manager."

Another form of protest available to the worker was simply to quit, a course of action that Jack took in early spring of 1925. J. B. Mead, Fred, and Jack decided to hop a freight to Detroit. Bryan Mead had written, suggesting there might be jobs in the Ford plant. Enroute to Detroit, Jack and Fred "nagged" a freight car carrying coal; J. B. was in another car carrying lumber. Tramping brought one in contact with a great diversity of humankind: hucksters, migrant workers, petty thieves, students on a lark, homeless children, and, of course, the inevitable bum who was running away from something, his existence narrowed to the search for cheap wine and a free meal.

One such hobo was riding in the car with J. B. Partway through Illi-nois, the train stopped to switch cars. When the engine bumped the cars, a pile of stacked lumber tumbled down on J. B. and his boxcar companion. J. B. yelled at the top of his lungs, thinking that he was crushed or soon would be. A brakeman signaled the engineer to stop the train. Swearing that he would strangle the two nonpaying passen-gers if they were still alive, the brakeman had the engineer jerk the car again to push the lumber back. Jack clambered out of the coal car where he had been fast asleep. When he discovered J. B.'s predicament, he gave him his hand and helped him wriggle out from underneath the fallen lumber. J. B. was frightened but not injured. The angry trainmen gathered around the foursome; it was bad moment. The brakeman said to J. B.: "I oughta kick yer ass off this train." J. B. replied. "By God, you or-ter."[37] Relieved that no one was hurt, the trainmen allowed the "hoboes" to continue. The bum revealed himself to be a fast-talking huckster who warned of pitfalls awaiting the unwary in the big city.

An incident that Jack would incorporate in *Anyplace But Here* oc-curred during this trip north on the "red ball." One evening the three Moberly friends camped in the "hobo jungle" near the tracks with three black southern youths who had drifted north, lured by the promise of work in Detroit auto factories. They were cooking their meager dinner when suddenly a railroad detective appeared, brandishing a pistol. Discovering a harmless penknife on one of the black workers, the "bull" marched them away. Later the three returned, angry and frightened. They had been forced to empty a load of hot embers from the steam locomotive tender. Their feet and hands were covered with ugly blisters. Seeing the railroad cop return to hassle the black workers, the Moberly men warned them to hide, then covered their absence. Later the blacks grabbed a freight express despite the Moberlyeans' shouts that the train was headed in the wrong direction. The reply inspired the title of Conroy and Bontemps's book on black migration: "We don't give a damn *where* it goes . . . just so it goes away from *here*. Any place but *here!*" one of them cried.[38]

In the auto factories in Detroit and Toledo, Jack was to discover, black and white met on uneasy terms. In Monkey Nest, blacks worked in the mines on an equal basis with white miners, as noted earlier. The UMW constitution forbade discrimination. Jack had known the racial ugliness of proto-fascists like the Kimberly "toughs." But the immigrant miners from the British Isles generally avoided distinctions based on color. "These boys," Jack wrote of the three black workers he had met on the road, "were from a mining camp where Negro and white workers both belonged to the United Mine Workers' Union. They had been in the habit of descending into the same darkness each workday morning. They lived in the same camp. Black and white children went to school together. This [the railroad cop's action] was something new and terrifying."[39] The Communists made racial solidarity among workers part of its agenda in the 1930s, organizing sharecroppers and defending the "Scottsboro Boys." Jack, who had lived and worked with blacks most of his life, encouraged and published young black writers as editor of *Rebel Poet* and *Anvil*. His collaboration with Arna Bontemps in authoring two important social histories and three popular juvenile books is perhaps the first such collaboration between black and white writers in American literature.

Jack was an observer with a keen ear for idiomatic speech and a remarkable memory, powers sharply honed by the threat of impoverishment. In Monkey Nest and the Wabash shops he had taken part in the fraternal subculture of a work community. On the road he encountered a subculture of bums, pimps, hucksters, runaways, petty criminals, Wobblies, and itinerant workers. But there were also college men on tramping tours of America as their post-graduate education before settling down, and writers looking for adventure and material for their stories. The older Wobblies possessed an independence of spirit and irreverence. Their rudimentary, informal system of networking served Jack later in his editorial work. Vigorous Wobbly idioms and the rebellious spirit of their songs and poems enriched his own repertoire of folk speech. Years later, in Chicago, Carl Sandburg, Nelson Algren, and Jack remembered their separate experiences tramping, "three old Wobblies," Sandburg said.[40] The Wobblies were a tough, resilient, anarchic mix of harvest hands and timber workers. Conroy admired them as the embodiment of the independent rebel, undoctrinaire and nonideological. Most of his boxcar companions, however, were unworthy examples of humankind whose ethic consisted in "doing the other fellow before he does you," as one disreputable hobo told Jack. The romance of the road lay in the popular reader's mind, nourished by "tramp" writers.

There were real dangers "on the road" in addition to the railroad "bulls," mugging, and physical discomfort. After the "jungle" episode, Jack, Fred, and J. B. hopped a freight enroute to Toledo. The boxcars were locked, so Jack clung to a ladder on the outside. The second night out he fell asleep while hanging on. Fred, riding on top, noticed Jack's hold slipping and reached over to grab him by the collar, sparing him from death under the wheels.[41] The close brush with death may have prompted his poem on a tramp who finds no rest in his rambles, which includes this stanza:

> When the bull stamped on your ice-cold fingers,
> And the bellowing darkness sprang between you and the grab-irons,
> The whining wheels ground you, and rolled on, and forgot you.[42]

Mike Gold, an early sponsor of worker-writers in the *Liberator* and early issues of *New Masses,* wrote: "Isn't there more education to be gotten in a year's boxcar trip across America than in a college year? Isn't there more harsh reality in a Ford factory than in a classroom?"[43] Tramping proved to be a school for radicals.[44] A young mill worker from Minnesota named Joe Kalar wrote the Wobbly poet Covington Hall that he had "never met so many worker-intellectuals" as on Seattle's skid row.[45] Worker-writers like H. H. Lewis of Cape Girardeau, Missouri, forged radical convictions in Los Angeles "missions" for the homeless in the 1920s. First-person narratives recounting their experiences would soon appear in *New Masses* and other leftist periodicals, the earliest expressions of a new generation of radical writers. While Greenwich Village bohemians and expatriate writers took deep draughts of Spenglerian world-weariness, a new current of writing, limited in scope but fresh and vigorous, began to appear in little magazines edited by eccentric printer-publishers, whose subject was "the other twenties."[46]

Most popular retrospectives of the 1920s ignore the desperate condition of organized labor and the unemployed "homeless." Better treatments of the period, such as Roderick Nash's *The Nervous Generation,* neglect the masses of workers migrating to find work, focusing rather on popular heroes, popular culture, evangelists, and bigots. Nash justifiably interprets social and political change in the 1920s as evidence of the tension between old and new, between rural and urban values.[47] But he ignores class-specific dimensions of the period: the "people" in his view, and in the view of most commentators, are the undifferentiated masses; intellectuals are urban and university-trained; and artists are those who achieve recognition within the framework of the dominant culture. Yet a new generation of artists and intellectuals was preparing the ground for the 1930s when textile mill workers, factory operatives, and miners would, for better or worse, become subjects of literature and art that was produced in part by those within their ranks. Even as Conroy was riding a boxcar to Toledo, gathering experiences that would enter his writing, Erskine Caldwell, Meridel Le Sueur, and Fielding Burke were beginning to give literary shape to the experience of mill, factory, and farm workers. The "other twenties" included boxcar rambles, southern textile mills, towns, midwestern farms, and Detroit auto factories. These were constituents of a new radical literature with antecedents in literary naturalism, focused on workers as a class rather than as "the other half" who failed in their attainment of the American dream.

Ironically, it was a political conservative, H. L. Mencken, who provided the broadest access to this new current of fresh, vigorous writing drawn from life. Mencken's *American Mercury* printed Jim Tully's "Bull Horrors" (October 1927), Charles Sampson's "Peach Harvest" (October 1928), Henri Tascheraud's "The Art of Bumming a Meal" (June 1925), and Thomas F. Healy's "The Hobo Hits the Highroad" (July 1926). James T. Farrell once remarked that the *American Mercury* writers whom Mencken published—Theodore Dreiser, Sherwood Anderson, Sinclair Lewis—represented the mainstream in 1920s American literature more than did Fitzgerald or Hemingway.[48] This assessment, of course, reflects Farrell's own debt to Mencken, an early mentor. Mencken's "authors" were no less representative of the 1930s: William Faulkner, Zora Neale Hurston, Meridel Le Sueur, Erskine Caldwell, Josephine Herbst, George Milburn, Jack Conroy, and the bricklayers, longshoremen, and taxi drivers who contributed work narratives.[49] The discovery of Mencken's essays in *Prejudices* played a crucial role in Richard Wright's decision to write. Whatever judgment one wishes to make concerning Mencken and "the mainstream," it is evident that these writers owed more to the uniqueness of their experiences in America, involving in certain instances tramping and factory work, than to European literary traditions or café life in Paris, or indeed to the dominant cultural experience of the 1920s.

* * *

Erskine Caldwell described Detroit, "the sometime fourth city of America," as "a one-track city. It eats, sleeps, and breathes automobiles. For that reason it holds a highly selective grip on labor. Unless a worker is capable of fitting into the specialized groove laid out by the manufacturer, his chances of finding employment in Detroit are next to nothing."[50] J. B., Fred, and Jack arrived in the city as paying passengers on the Detroit, Monroe and Toledo Short Line. Tired, dirty, and hungry, they had abandoned their freight train in Toledo and ridden the rest of the way on the interurban railway. Once in Detroit, they set out on foot for Bryan Mead's apartment. Bunking with Bryan for a few days, the men went to one of the many employment agencies to find work. Jack was sent out to a pipe-fitting job, only to discover he was not needed. After several days he was hired as a millwright, paying three dollars to the employment office for the lead. His first task was to repair a pulley high above the factory floor. The foreman ordered Jack to climb up a tall ladder, placed insecurely on the greasy floor. Jack refused and walked out. Bryan had suggested there might be work at the Widman Body Factory, where Jack applied directly and was hired. Fred was hired soon after, and the two found a place to stay, sharing a small room.

In the Widman factory, Jack and Fred encountered "Fordism" for the first time, a term that had come to mean a relentless, near-frantic tempo on the assembly line in which men's arms, hands, and minds were forced like machines to perform repetitive motions dictated by considerations of efficiency and profit. Scientific management, as Gramsci points out, "develop[s] in the worker to the highest degree automatic and mechanical attitudes, breaking up the old psycho-physical nexus of qualified intelligence, fantasy and initiative on the part of the work, and reducing productive operations exclusively to the mechanical, physical aspect."[51] Fordism also meant a surplus of unemployed workers willing to take one's job, no matter how onerous. Workers in the Detroit auto factories told Edmund Wilson, who interviewed them for his documentary book *The American Earthquake*, that any complaint about working conditions or pay was cause to be fired.[52]

Bolting on door sections as they passed by in continuous motion, Jack scrambled and clawed to keep pace with the chain conveyor. The conveyor, he later wrote, was a merciless tyrant.

> I thought its progress was very slow. But the men were chasing about, sweating and cursing, working furiously for a moment, and flying to the next task. . . . I fumbled with screws and let the screwdriver slip out of my nervous fingers, where it caught in the chain

causing it to buck violently. . . . In spite of all my efforts, I fell steadily behind, and at last the boss stopped the chain. I had not worked there long enough to comprehend the enormity of my offense, but the horrified glare of the men imparted some realization of it.[53]

The monotonous repetition of the tasks, speedup, and constant turnover of workers discouraged bonding among the workers.[54] Jack had known personal loyalties and social relationships among the Wabash shopmen. Despite the noise and hazards, small, informal groups of workers formed in the steel mills. But in the Detroit auto factories a robot would have served better than the assembly line worker. Traditional forms of worker resistance did not succeed; a worker could quit, but quitting was of little consequence to the employer. Hundreds more waited for the vacated position, which required little training.

The worker-writer Robert Cruden, an assembly worker in a Ford auto plant during the late 1920s, described the desperation of those seeking work:

> The crowd lurched forward. His companion was torn from him in the rush. Jim banged his elbows into ribs, hit men in the stomach, stepped on their toes, kicked their shins. Curses, cries, grunts, threats rose in quick succession into a roar as the pack mass squeezed itself through the narrow doorway into the office. Jim, caught in the jam, felt elbows in his stomach, work shoes grinding on his toes, hard knuckles cracking on his ribs. He swore, but he could do nothing—his arms were clamped to his sides as effectively as if they were tied with ropes.[55]

Lured by advertisements of nonexistent positions in the factories, workers had come from all parts of the country and abroad to find jobs. The desperate people in this cheap labor pool were easy victims of exploitation.

Beyond the factory gate were the jobless, the drifters, hucksters, petty criminals, prostitutes, pimps, and incompetents, the "subproletariat." Their escape route from starvation was begging, crime, prostitution. Jack and his coworkers knew they were one step removed from this other subculture. Men and women might wait a year between jobs, pawning household goods to pay rent and water bills, walking miles every morning to stand in line for a job at an auto factory, only to be turned away.[56] Those who had lost hope drifted to Grand Circus Park. Better a park bench than facing an anxious spouse and hungry children.[57]

Detroit introduced Jack to mass-production methods and a new industrial workers' culture. Together with Fred he wandered about down-town Detroit in the evenings, craving diversion. The values of the new industrial proletariat were changing fast, Jack noticed, whose own val-ues had been molded in traditional work communities. The family that Jack and Fred visited to buy home brew reflected lower-middle-class as-pirations. Despite the illegality of their home-produced brew, the cou-ple was anxious to preserve the appearance of sobriety and respectabil-ity, ingredients of the "new industrial morality."[58] Proletarian auto workers hoped to share in the new "abundance," enjoying convenienc-es such as indoor plumbing, a "davenport," washing machine, radio, car, all on the installment plan.[59] The Lynds noticed the effect of this new abundance on the lives of workers in "Middletown." Consumption of goods and the decline of the union local's role in their lives acted to disintegrate "the vigorous working-class life that had flourished thirty years before."[60] "It was the material benefits of the here-and-now . . . that reconciled the Middletown worker to the factory grind."[61] Such aspira-tions, together with the mixed nature of the labor force in the auto fac-tories, vitiated the emergence of worker solidarity.[62] Unskilled workers, unfamiliar with labor organization, replaced skilled laborers. Kentucky hill people, conservative and little inclined toward unions, filled many of the openings. Company spies singled out disgruntled workers and potential leaders, firing them on the spot.

Workers invested in homes in cheaply built subdivisions, making their "time payments" from their take-home pay. It was a desperate wa-ger these new property owners made. Failure to make a payment could result in forfeiture of one's investment. Attitudes once characteristic of a worker community were now resolved into a demand for conformity. Mass publications weakened their inhibitions; consumer desire encour-aged them to live beyond their means, without provision for layoffs. "Fun" no longer involved a group of work comrades but activities oc-curring within "a separate sphere of personal life."[63]

The preindustrial artisanal values of Monkey Nest coal camp and the Wabash shops, together with an inbred rural Missouri cultural and eco-nomic conservatism, had not prepared Jack for this new industrial eth-ic. The gospel of borrowing and spending disturbed him; when he was forced to borrow, he rushed to pay back the loan. The disintegration of community life, separation from his home and family, were intolerable conditions of progress, yet the industrious "ants," as he called them, who scraped and saved, then faced foreclosure and repossession, were no better off than the "grasshoppers" like Jack and Fred who sent a part of their paychecks home to their families, and spent the rest.[64] Jack could not forget the sorry spectacle of a mother and her children left stranded on the sidewalk in the rain with their furniture, dispossessed of their home.[65] No new Ford, purchased on time, no tract house and install-ment-plan furniture, no big-city excitement could compensate for the dissatisfaction he felt. Widman still owed him a paycheck. Broke and desperate, Fred and Jack hitched a ride back to Moberly with Henry South, a former Wabash shopman. During three anguishing days, they rode in South's Model T, spending their last pennies for gas shortly be-fore crossing the Illinois River on a ferry. When South stopped at a filling station in Cairo, Missouri, Fred looked at Jack: "Oh, oh," he whispered, "he's going to make us pay for one more tank of gas." But South only wanted to shave in the station's bathroom. The next stop was Moberly, where they could finally eat.[66]

In May of 1925 the Conroys decided to return to Des Moines. Jack's brief proletarian encounter in Detroit made him decide to accept low-er wages. At least his family would be with him. Jack went up with Fred before bringing the family. Of the Moberly contingent in Des Moines only George Mead remained. J. B. had stayed on at Ford in Detroit with Bryan Mead. Jack and Fred moved back into "Hotel Fort De Moberly" on Locust Street and soon after Jack got a job in a sawmill. Within sev-eral weeks, Pip and Eliza Addis came up with Henry and Isabelle Har-rison, soon followed by Harvey and George Harrison. The Moberly clan was back together. The sawmill employed the Harrison boys, and Pip fired a steam boiler in the mill's engine room, a cinch for an old Wa-bash employee. Jack's sister, Margaret, came to visit but found Pip so repellent that after a week she hurried back to Moberly where she found a job in a Woolworth store, running the candy counter.

The Moberly people enjoyed Des Moines. It seemed like a big city to them, yet they were an easy's day drive from home turf. Jack wrote Gladys about the ten-cent theaters and vaudeville shows and the Co-ney Island hot dog "with everything on it." In a couple of weeks she came up with Margaret Jean, who was about to turn three. Jack was happy to have his family together. For the first time in a very long time, it seemed, he felt the leisure and energy to read after work, and to write.

Since leaving the surveying job in 1923, Jack had kept in touch with Swede Lamson. The two old friends still liked to talk about books. Jack owned most of the literary titles Swede mentioned in his letters. For $16.90 in 1923, one could purchase the entire set of 239 booklets, most of them literary titles, of Haldeman-Julius's "Ten Cent Pocket Series." These booklets were widely advertised and distributed. Partly for ideo-logical, partly for business reasons, Haldeman-Julius was determined to bring culture and knowledge to the masses, not merely entertain them.[67]

The ideological inspiration sprang from Emmanuel Julius's associa-tion with the socialist press even before Louis Kopelin, successor to Fred

D. Warren as managing editor of the *Appeal to Reason* in Girard, Kansas, hired him in October 1915. Within a year Julius was married to Anna Marcet Haldeman, daughter of a prominent Girard family and a niece of Jane Addams. By 1919, Haldeman-Julius (he had affixed his wife's name to his own) owned the *Appeal* and its printing press with Kopelin. Before World War I, the *Appeal to Reason,* under the direction of Julius Wayland and Warren, was the mainstay of the socialist press, devoted to the Socialist party's twin goals of "agitation" and education. In the pages of the *Appeal,* for instance, Upton Sinclair first published serially his famous muckraking novel *The Jungle.*[68] Haldeman-Julius used the Party's wish to raise the educational level and social consciousness of the common person as a springboard for his entrepreneurial impulses. A flamboyant man who dressed flashily and drove expensive cars with oversized white-wall tires, Haldeman-Julius was an innovator and shrewd entrepreneur who pioneered many marketing techniques that soon became commonplace not only in publishing but in product sales of all kinds.

One of Haldeman-Julius's mail-order sales techniques utilized questionnaires sent to readers, who responded with astonishing eagerness about their preferences in books. In addition, he solicited correspondence with his subscribers, readers of the Little Blue Books and Haldeman-Julius magazines. Employing an "electrified" system of mass production, he printed 240,000 copies of a book in one day.[69] Keeping an eye on his list of titles, which exceeded 1,100 by 1926 and included many literary classics, Haldeman-Julius employed a triage system to weed out the weak sellers, shunting them over to a department whose task was to provide the classic a racier title. Thus Molière's *Tartuffe* was retitled *A Sinner in Saint's Clothing* and placed in the "passion" category of titles.[70] By 1939, Haldeman-Julius was selling his booklets in vending machines.[71]

"The individual, E. Haldeman-Julius," said the *Baltimore Sun* in 1923, "is doing more to educate the country than any ten universities put together."[72] Employing statistics, surveys, and full-page advertisements, Haldeman-Julius was an active propagandist of good reading. He fancied himself an American Diderot, and indeed some of his writers, like John W. Gunn, thought of him as such. Gunn, in his early study issued as Little Blue Book no. 678, linked him with Diderot's notion that "knowledge was the true and powerful factor, not only in the development of the individual, but in the progress of society."[73] Mencken assailed Haldeman-Julius's publications for their wretched printing quality but extolled his aim in making "excellent books" available at ten cents. An editorialist in the *Minnesota Daily Star* hailed the nickel and dime classics from Girard, Kansas, as harbingers of a new democratic culture.[74] Carl Sandburg in a letter to Haldeman-Julius's literary magazine, *Life and Letters,* wrote: "The Haldeman-Julius hip-pocket library has a fine picked list of the best things men have thought and written. For a five-dollar bill it brings an amazing array of good things to read. It is the brick-layer's hope, the mucker's dream, the wop's wonder of an education."[75]

Haldeman-Julius's detractors objected to booklets devoted to atheism and "sexology." One of his contributors, Louis Adamic, a fervent supporter of the Little Blue Books, complained of the low remuneration Haldeman-Julius provided his writers and the fast-selling potboilers devoted to "sex and love."[76] For every critic, up sprang ten defenders, including Conroy, whose protesting letter to *Outlook and Independent* called Haldeman-Julius the "Ford of literature" and cited his role in making unknown writers, including Adamic, household names.[77]

The Little Blue Books offered a "University in Print" to Adamic, Conroy, Farrell, and many other young writers who were without the means to afford trade editions. In addition to literary classics, Jack purchased ten-cent editions of Clarence Darrow, Dreiser, Mike Gold, Vance Randolph, and others who would figure importantly in his own life as a writer. The Little Blue Books made literature accessible to people living far from libraries and bookstores. Like the earlier English "Cottage Library" they provided an education for those who were able, as Gorki had learned in his youth, to distinguish the worthy from the unworthy. Wendell Johnson, author of *People in Quandaries,* paid homage to Haldeman-Julius, recalling how as a boy on a Kansas farm he had read the classics printed in Girard.[78] In his eighties, Jack still had hundreds of Little Blue Books he had read sixty years before, packed in boxes, a mobile "university in print."

* * *

The sawmill, which produced gun stocks from walnut, was located near the Des Moines River, in bottomland. Jack mentioned his "experience" as a millwright in Detroit and was hired at thirty-five cents an hour to do general carpentry, along with his nephew Harvey Harrison, who was given a more taxing assignment in the mill. In a sketch entitled "For Men Must Work," Jack used Harvey's experience as the basis of the following "apprenticeship narrative," in which the superintendent leads the new worker, "Leo," to learn under the tutelage of a "master artisan":

He stopped beside a band saw. The operator, a concave-cheeked oldster wearing a skull cap, was tinkering with the machine.

"Here's your new disciple, Willie," roared the super. "He's too light for heavy work and too heavy for light work, and too damned lazy, by Christ, to do either. You want to initiate him good. Pour it to him hot and heavy; shove it in him to the red and make him like it or holler 'enough.'"

Willie nodded dourly, baring his tobacco-fouled fangs in a formal smile. Four fingers of one of Willie's hands were gone, and Leo soon discovered that Willie, when in deep thought, had a habit of placing his thumb, standing alone like the lone survivor of battlefield carnage, alongside his nose and resting his chin against the stub of his hand. In the weeks that followed he was to learn more of Willie's idiosyncrasies and ideas than he knew of his own father's, for he was forced to stand near Willie ten hours a day, tied to the machine. By a process of elimination, everything that Willie did or thought became of interest; he was the only living, moving object in a monotony as deadly as that of a prison cell.[79]

The superintendent, a man named Nizer, a salty old millhand who addressed all his workers as "you birds," saw Harvey sitting and eating a sandwich in mid-morning. "What are you doing?" he asked. "Eating a sandwich," Harvey replied dryly, continuing to chew. "By God," Nizer responded sarcastically, "blow the whistle and we'll all eat too!"[80]

A millwright's job in the sawmill permitted a certain freedom and variety. Jack and another millwright, Frank Snider, goofed off on occasion, hiding behind piles of walnut timber in the yard to take a short nap, within sight of a "no loafing" sign. "From the mill building came a steady drone," Jack wrote, recalling the experience, "and intermittently the sharp wail of the saws. At times a log would prove too thick or too tough and the saw would slow down with many a deepening groan and rumbling bass note until it died, sounding like a phonograph record played on a machine that needs winding."[81]

By mid-summer Gladys, pregnant with Tom, had to quit her job in the cookie factory; the smell of freshly baked cookies and burned lard nauseated her. There was no place for Jack to advance in the mill except to harder, more dangerous work. The hours were long and workweeks often stretched to seven days. Jack felt terrible dissatisfaction with such jobs, in the face of which there was seldom any recourse than to quit. His work comrades held grimly on to their jobs, fearing layoffs. However, a windfall occurred that gave him temporary respite.

In early August, the Conroys moved back to Moberly. Gladys was intent on giving birth at home where her mother could help. Fred Harrison, who had met and married a stocking-factory worker named Myrtle, stayed on in Des Moines for a time, moving to Toledo in 1927 to work in the Willys-Overland auto factory, where Jack would eventually go. Pip and Eliza remained in Des Moines, as did Henry and Isabelle. Henry died there the following summer. Harvey told his boss that he wanted to take leave from the job for a short while. The boss told him not to, warning that someone would take his place. When Harvey returned several weeks later, the factory shut down for two months.[82]

The Conroys were in a mood to stay in Moberly after Tom's birth on 16 August 1925. A small inheritance from Gladys's mother, who had died shortly after their return, made it possible to remain there for a while. Jack had no fixed ideas, no "program" for his future. Moberly seemed a comfortable, familiar place to be. Lawyers, tradespeople, and workers had gone to school together and addressed one another by their first names. Settled workers had status in Moberly. Rich and poor belonged to the same Methodist and Baptist congregations. In Detroit, the displaced Moberlyeans were uprooted, anonymous factory workers, members of the industrial proletariat; at home they were someone's neighbor. It seemed that in Moberly one could always find something to do to make ends meet. This wasn't much of a life, but it beat working in a dirty, hazardous mill or on Ford's assembly line.

Together with his friend and early mentor from the Wabash shops, Jim Whitaker, Jack invested the $2,000 inheritance in a grocery story at 222 West Clark Street. A man with a great deal of personal charm, Whitaker was a compulsive gambler who later died in an automobile accident under mysterious circumstances. Some people hinted that he had been murdered for reasons related to his gambling. Jack ran the store; Whitaker, a foreman, stayed on in the Wabash shops. Jack hired Joe Willie, the youngest of the Mead brothers, to run errands. Ruth Jennings, the niece of Whitaker's wife, helped Jack in the store since Gladys, who had retail clerk experience, was home nursing her new baby. Jack, who "knew less about groceries than a hog knows about Sunday," had problems with his partner from the start. Rumor was that Whitaker had run up large gambling debts. Jack's lack of business experience combined disastrously with Whitaker's compulsive gambling. Many of the old Wabash men boycotted the store, viewing Whitaker's earlier role in the strike as betrayal. Jack felt deep loyalty to Whitaker, who had treated him kindly when Jack was a young apprentice. The boycott was unfair, or at least Jack thought so. Technically, as a foreman, Whitaker was exempt from the strike.[83] Whitaker had been the union local's grievance man when Jack was recording secretary for the American Federation of Railway Workers. He had come out in the 1922 strike but after

several weeks decided to return. The union did not count him as a striker in any case since he was a foreman. Nonetheless, he felt bad about
it. Whitaker was another casualty of the 1922 strike but for different
reasons than for most of the strikers. He was bound to suffer either way
the strike went. A sensitive man, he began to drink heavily.[84]

Jack was restless and unhappy as a storekeeper. To relieve the boredom he sent Joe Willie upstairs over the store to see "Cockeyed Rose."
Cockeyed Rose had initiated many a young Moberly boy who, distracted by her truant eye, overcame his shyness and fastened to her ample
bosom.[85] Jack picked up his interrupted correspondence-school education again—he had never received a high school diploma, gaining admission to the state university through examination—and he frequented the Carnegie library, where above the circulation desk a sign read:
"The poorest labourer in the district with his wife and children march
into this library, and members of the highest society of all the world,
without money and without price."[86] Apart from his letter exchanges
with Swede Lamson, Jack had little opportunity to discuss books and
ideas. Seeking intellectual companions, he answered an ad placed in a
little magazine called *Pegasus*, published in Springfield, Ohio, which
offered names of the "intellectually marooned." He received a list from
Merlin Wand, of Ford City, Pennsylvania, whose one-man operation
called "Contacts" was a clearinghouse for isolated book-lovers and neophyte writers. Many of the people who made contact through the organization corresponded for years without ever actually meeting. Several of these early contacts were instrumental in birthing new
expressions of midwestern literary radicalism toward the end of the decade. The constituents of a new consciousness connecting the intellectually marooned found expression in little magazines that had begun
to appear as meshpoints in an expanding network of communication.

After several months as a groceryman, Jack was adrift again. Intellectually, however, he was beginning to take bearings. The years of reading and contacts with others with whom he could exchange ideas in
an ever-widening circle of epistolary acquaintanceship released him
somewhat from his isolation. Little magazines springing up in midwestern towns like Springfield, Ohio, and Holt, Minnesota, provided links
between young, aspiring writers like himself and gave them a chance
to publish their awkward first attempts. In these obscure little journals,
printed on handset presses, a new literature of social content and "crude
vigor" was born without patrons or notice. No one, of course, knew that
the Great Crash of 1929 was just around the corner, although worker-
writers like Jack, Ed Falkowski, and Joseph Kalar, who had suffered layoffs and firings, were persuaded that the "Great Barbecue" could not

continue indefinitely. Yet credit was still available and people continued to spend. Jack decided to abandon shopkeeping and return to factory work in the late summer of 1926, three years before the stock market's "Black Thursday." As the decade wound down, growing worker
dissatisfaction, the years of antilabor legislation, strikes in Gastonia,
South Carolina, and an execution in Boston, Massachusetts, deeply affected a small number of worker-intellectuals who first made contact
with one another through letters and who published their earliest work
in little magazines with titles like *Pegasus*, *Northern Light*, the *Spider*,
and the *Haldeman-Julius Quarterly*. Within a few years, changing expectations in the early Depression years would give obscure "worker-writers" access to the nation's leading publications and presses, and cata-
pult Jack briefly into national prominence.

6

Early Literary Contacts:
Hannibal, 1926–28

To eat dust in their throats and die empty-hearted
For a small handful of pay on a few Saturday nights.
—Carl Sandburg

THE CRAFT-CONSCIOUSNESS that had bonded workers like Jack together under the shelter of trade unionism within a particular work community, such as existed in the Wabash shops, eroded as its members were swept into the proletarian flood of casual labor, without attachment or protection, in the 1920s. Gradually there evolved a new radical consciousness among a few worker-intellectuals who joined with others—anarchist poets, eccentric printers, university-educated liberals, socialists, communists, and independent-minded radicals. These diverse currents flowed together in the pages of little magazines that, lacking any common ground of political conviction, revealed a restless desire for self-expression that prefigured the angry rhetoric of revolt soon to appear in the leftist press. In little magazines, published throughout the Midwest, a new radical critical temper was undergoing formulation. The rebellion was in part against the aesthetic individualism that appeared to characterize *Broom, transition, Secession*, the *Little Review*, the *Fugitive*, and other little magazines. These publications had fought the battles against the establishment along a cultural front that excluded the activist tradition of socialist and Wobbly poets. The new radical temper embraced a group-minded, leftist orientation with a penchant for social content, realism, and reportage.[1] Noah Whitaker's *Pegasus*, for instance, engaged that part of the new radical aesthetic that stressed the activist function of the literary work and the social responsibilities of its author, while assailing the aesthetic's addiction to free verse. The best-known articulation of the new radical aesthetic was Mike Gold's "Go Left, Young Writers!" piece, appearing in the January 1929 issue of *New Masses*, which subsequently published some of Conroy's early worker sketches.[2] The new radical aesthetic represented the convictions of those who were angry, frustrated, and eager to communicate what they felt. Young writers from throughout the Midwest, and sometimes much farther away, made contact with one another through the Haldeman-Julius publications, Merlin Wand's *Contacts Commentary*, and, after 1928, organizations such as the Rebel Poets. Like members of mutual aid organizations that develop in societies undergoing revolutionary transformation, these writers gave one another encouragement, recommending work to editors, offering advice, and so forth—all by mail.

* * *

In the summer of 1926 the Conroys moved to Hannibal, hearing from Gladys's cousin, Josephine Carter, and her husband, Robert, that the International Shoe Company was hiring. The two families shared the Carters' small home. Robert's lungs had been damaged by poisonous gas during the Great War; the heat and fumes of the rubber-heel plant aggravated his poor health. After several months, the Conroys and the Carters moved to another rented house in Hannibal. Soon thereafter, the Carters returned to their farm in Shelbina, Missouri, hoping that Robert's health would improve.[3] Joining the Conroys in Hannibal were Gladys's sister, Florence Hardy, and her husband, Everett. Together they rented a larger, four-room house at 2021 West Gordon Street. Like the Carters the Hardys had fled the impoverishment of farm life.

Applying at the employment office of the rubber-heel plant every day for two weeks, Jack was finally hired. The Conroys had accumulated debts; their money was still tied up in the grocery store, which was not sold until the following year.[4] Gladys and Florence found jobs in the Bluff City Shoe Company factory across from the rubber-heel plant where Jack and Everett worked. Gladys, whom Jack called "Girlie," was a jolly, good-natured, sentimental person, devoted to her family and tolerant of Jack's literary ambitions that kept him up late at night. She was quietly pleased with Jack's epistolary contacts, valuing the correspondents for their human qualities without sharing their literary interests. Margaret Jean, now nearly four, brought her friends home to see her father and have him demonstrate that he could type blindfolded. There was an infectious happiness and audacity about her that won Jack's heart and made him feel very close to her. It was a threadbare time for the Conroys, who were saddled with debts, yet Jack remembered it as a happy time within his family.[5]

Between days filled with acrid smoke and stinking fumes, Jack first essayed writing poems, which bore traces of a bookish, untutored literary apprenticeship, and made literary contacts with other young worker-writers who, like him, struggled to throw off genteel influences. His earliest contacts were with eccentrics like Jo Labadie and Emmanuel Haldeman-Julius. Labadie was surely an American original. Known as the "gentle anarchist," Charles Joseph Antoine Labadie was born of native American and French ancestry. Publishing on his own press in Bubbling Springs, Michigan, Labadie was a printer, editor, and writer. He had been an organizer for the Knights of Labor and at one time the Greenback Labor Party candidate for mayor of Detroit. The Midwest seems to produce odd, unclassifiable hybrid plants every new generation. Perhaps Jack's initial attraction was to Labadie's iconoclastic views expressed in the Haldeman-Julius publications. Labadie's poems appeared in numerous little magazines published by other unclassifiable hybrids like himself.

Jack "met" Labadie through the letters section of the *Haldeman-Julius Weekly*, an indispensable organ of midwestern marginal expression in the 1920s. "I have gathered from your card," Jack wrote Labadie, "that you are a disciple of the radical element in literature and politics, as I am; and I am always delighted to gain the acquaintance of a kindred spirit. This inland hamlet of Moberly is a veritable intellectual Sahara; to my knowledge there being only two communists and less than a dozen socialists in the entire city of more than sixteen thousand population. I am a fervent admirer of Edgar Lee Masters and Arturo Giovannitti but have become apathetic toward Vachel Lindsay."[6] Jack's early writing, including this letter, betrays his early romance with words, reflecting his self-administered course of reading, together with his desire to be taken seriously. The flowery language of his other early letters further reflects Jack's reading tastes at the time. The robust orality of the factory floor, however, was of equal force in shaping his style. Eventually he forged these various levels of language into an idiolect that he employed for comic as well as realistic purposes. The untutored fashion in which he mastered language furnished his writing with a range of expression that exploited the cultural and social function of communication within the bounds of individual experience. H. L. Mencken, whom Jack echoes in his reference to an "intellectual Sahara," was eventually to encourage a simple, forceful, authentic style that was coherent with Jack's experience.[7]

Jack's first literary efforts, together with his prodigious appetite for reading, reveal his irrepressible energy and ambition to find his way into print. In Hannibal he continued the night correspondence study, through the La Salle Business Institute of Chicago, but he abandoned it when his literary contacts began to absorb what little time he had after work. There were only a couple of hours in the evening before he fell exhausted into bed. The contacts began to produce results. Mustering his courage, he sent several poems to Noah Whitaker, editor of *Pegasus*.

Whitaker was an odd blend of rebellion and reaction. His political orientation was socialist and antiwar. His editorial policy, however, was in full rebellion against the "free-rhymers," modern-verse writers represented by Harriet Monroe's *Poetry*. Carl Sandburg received special scorn. Whitaker was fettered to a form of verse making that "was utterly unsuited," as V. F. Calverton wrote in 1927, "to the changing and intransigent drive of the new generation."[8] Calverton believed that "the aristocratic technique which . . . in the nineteenth century had insisted upon the confining metrics of receding decades, *was a contradiction to the demand for a democracy of technique in keeping with the demand for a genuine democracy of social organization.*"[9] By contrast, Calverton wrote, Sandburg's poetry "is a vigorous manifestation of this newer spirit in American letters."[10] At first, Jack engaged in the debate on the side of Whitaker. In 1924 he was writing letters to the *Haldeman-Julius Weekly* defending rhymed verse.

His early poems resemble the efforts of early working-class poets earnest in their desire to match their "betters."[11] Several of his earliest works published in Whitaker's *Pegasus* reveal a self-conscious attention to rhyme and metrics. "Broken Moon," for example, bears the imprint of Whitaker's "schoolmarm" views on poetic composition, as the worker-writer Joseph Kalar pointed out to Jack.[12] The first stanza reads:

> Like yours, my life must ebb, O broken moon
>   Too soon my heart, like yours, grow cold and die,
> O wan and broken moon whose bitter scars
>   Cast pallid shadows o'er a somber sky.[13]

Such poems were jejeune efforts that Jack soon wished to efface. The remedy it seemed, lay in the chastening act of self-criticism and publication. Seeing his first poetic efforts in print embarrassed Jack so much that he turned his hand to freer forms of poetic expression, "unvarnished language," and themes forged on the anvil of experience. These took the place of genteel imitation, what to a young worker had seemed proper to poetry, that is, an elevated subject in refined language.[14]

Sentimental verse and archaic diction were staples of Victorian popular culture. Jack had heard such verse recited in Monkey Nest camp. Years later, he planned an anthology of maudlin verse entitled "Rosewood Casket: A Garland of Rue." The problem in selection, he found, is that often sentimental verse is too good to be considered bad enough, or likewise, too bad to be considered good enough for inclusion. The work of the "Sweet Singer of Michigan," Julia A. Moore, surely belongs; but what about Edgar Guest's?[15] Jack's own "Tragedy," published in Ben Hagglund's *Northern Light*, is a case in point:

> She passed me proudly on the street today.
> Without a word, she looked the other way.
>
> They say that there must dawn a dismal hour
> When the great sun shall burn to ash and die,
> And haggard moons shall hurtle through the sky.
> When from the earth has faded the last flower,
> The stubborn pines upon the barren hill
> Shall know at last that Hope lies cold and still.[16]

Romantic poetry, such as Arthur Davison Ficke's verse, appealed to Jack, who, failing in his first attempts at imitation, turned "that one talent," as Milton said, "which is death to hide" to literary burlesque.

Resonances of early popular influences often have commanding power over the imaginations of apprentice writers. Something had stuck in Jack's mind about propriety in versification; his idea of poetry was shaped by Macaulay and Omar Khayyam. Too, there was the question, soon to preoccupy Jack and other worker-writers, of poetry's appeal to workers, who, it was thought, demanded conventional prosodic elements in poetry. The oral appeal of Joe Hill's Wobbly verse seemed to radical poets like Henry George Weiss to make the case for rhymed verse and regular metrics. Rhymed doggerel had a place in the working-class struggle for social justice. Conversely, Weiss argued, the worker must be educated in new poetic forms so that "you may attract the illiterate working stiff with poems he understands at a glance, and thus lead him by degrees to try and understand the more subtle medium of *vers libre*."[17]

Another worker-poet who was wrestling with questions of poetic form and content was H. H. Lewis, whom Jack would dub "the plowboy poet of the Gumbo," after the thick, sticky soil characteristic of the Missouri boot-heel. Lewis grew up on a farm near Cape Girardeau, and continued to support himself on his parents' farm, "hunkered over the cowdonick," as he wrote,

> *Earning* my one dollar per
> And *realizing*,
> With the goo upon overalls,
>   How environment works up a feller's
>   pant-legs to govern his thought.[18]

Workers would never "get" Lewis's satire, Weiss argued. Lewis, who in 1938 won *Poetry* magazine's prestigious Harriet Monroe Award for Lyric Poetry, was an unclassifiable "weed" in the topography of midwestern literary radicalism. Noah Whitaker first discovered Lewis in New Orleans in 1924 during a time when Lewis was bumming around the country, sleeping in "missions," before returning to his farm work in southeast Missouri. Whitaker had a very high opinion of Lewis's talent, oddly enough since Lewis broke most poetic conventions.[19] Conroy was attracted to Lewis at first, not because he admired Lewis's poems appearing in Whitaker's *Pegasus* (and in Hagglund's *Northern Light*), but for his experiences and eccentric character. "He is an interesting young communist," Jack wrote Labadie in 1926, "having bummed all over the west and witnessed the persecution of the I.W.W. in California; and he sent me an excellent poem of two pages. . . ."[20]

Whitaker helped Lewis set himself up as a part-time printer and publisher. Lewis bought a second-hand press from the Kelsey Company of Meriden, Connecticut, which sold its presses mail-order. He taught himself to set type and began to print a magazine entitled the *Outlander*. Lewis mailed a copy to Jack for his opinion and that is how a very long and interesting (entirely epistolary) contact began between the two worker-writers.

Conroy encouraged Lewis and intervened on his behalf time and again during Lewis's stormy twenty-year affair with both the left and the poetry establishment. The *Outlander* was conceived partly in response to local poetasters whose submissions Lewis mercilessly derided. On one occasion, the fiancé of an aspiring poet wounded by Lewis's attack challenged the editor to a duel. Learning that the fiancé's name was of French origin, Lewis offered to fight with guillotines. The "Plowboy Poet" had aimed "to make a place for every worthy radical" in his little magazine, but ended up in a senseless entanglement with "poetesses."[21]

Noah Whitaker was perhaps as eccentric as Lewis but entirely without Lewis's genius—or his paranoia. Whitaker was the embodiment of the dedicated, self-sacrificing editor and publisher who played an instrumental role in midwestern literary radicalism in the 1920s and the thirties. Supporting his publishing enterprise by house-to-house sales of wire gadgets to hold brooms, which he fabricated in his basement, he accompanied his sales talk with a pitch for his magazine, *Pegasus*. If the sale was made, Whitaker would recite his verse "with all the florid eloquence of an old-time elocutionist."[22] Publishers like Whitaker, working with ancient hand-set presses, gave a start to young worker-writers like Jack, Lewis, and Kalar.

Ben Hagglund, in tiny Holt, Minnesota, was another such one-man operation, both publisher and editor, who supported his literary work by odd jobs. Hagglund advertised his literary little magazine, *Northern Light*, in *Pegasus*. Hagglund and Whitaker, however, shared little beyond their devotion to discovering and encouraging unknown writers. *Northern Light* welcomed free verse and socially committed poetry. Yet much of the verse published in the first issues was of the pallid moon—dead lovers variety, thus in content little different from Whitaker's "mid-Victorian hangover."[23] Hagglund's championing of unconventional verse form began a feud between the two editors. Rhythm, not rhyme, Hagglund argued, distinguishes the new poetry from outworn forms. Carl Sandburg's poetry, despite occasional "blunders," steps to the new rhythms of "the Noise of Industry."[24] In ads that the two placed in one another's magazines, Hagglund cast Whitaker as the "Black Bug" that in buzzing too close to the "New Light" (free verse) would risk injury to its outworn creeds. No need to use its stinger, Whitaker replied, since the "Light" had already gone out. "Dear Bro. Whitaker," Hagglund wrote, "I regret that I could not write you sooner, for I have been as busy as a two-legged dog with the fleas; but permit me to say that the 'Black Bug' advertising has done me good, and it will do you good if you react in the right way to it. Get mad as hops, and they will buy *Pegasus*. . . ."[25] Hagglund had revealed his pecuniary interest in initiating the feud, Whitaker crowed, advising the "keeper of the light" to read Conroy's "Spectra Hoax" article in *Pegasus*. Witter Bynner and Arthur Davison Ficke had parodied the Imagist and Vorticist schools of poetry, publishing their "experimental" poems under pseudonyms in a volume entitled *Spectra* (1916). The *Spectra* hoax expanded into an elaborate joke on the poetry establishment including Alfred Kreymbourg, William Marion Reedy, and John Gould Fletcher, who welcomed the "new and virile tendency" of *Spectra*, before Bynner finally revealed his identity in the hoax. "The ingenius [sic] jokers had deliberately filled the poems," Conroy wrote, "with the most errant nonsense in order to enjoy the antics of the bold and gullible intelligentsia."[26] Hagglund, Whitaker intimated, was similarly capable of humbugging his readers.

The editors' feud placed an erroneous construction on poetic convention as it was practiced by neophytes like Conroy. The free-verse controversy seems mild by today's standards, but it raged at all levels of poetic creation long after Whitman. In fact, Hagglund published both rhymed and unrhymed verse, as did most editors of the little magazines except for holdouts like Whitaker. Despite his admiration for the Springfield publisher, Jack gravitated toward Hagglund's "New Light." Kalar, among others, was unsure of Whitaker's ability to distinguish good poetry from bad.[27] Jack's first attempts at free verse liberated him from the pale imitations with which he began. Natural speech rhythms entered his poetry, such as in "Journey's End" (quoted in Chapter 5) and "Dusky Answer," and became a distinguishing feature of his prose. Moving beyond the stylized patterns garnered from his reading, Jack gained confidence in his ability to hear and reproduce from memory the oral expressions of communal work cultures.

Pegasus and the *Northern Light* helped break the isolation of a new generation of literary radicals west of the Hudson, who were widely separated geographically. Whitaker printed Raymond Kresensky, a Christian-Socialist poet from Iowa; Norman Macleod, a western poet and little-magazine editor; and Kenneth Porter, a Christian-Socialist poet who would one day become poet laureate of Kansas. Conroy, Porter, Kresensky, and H. H. Lewis appeared also in Hagglund's little magazines, along with George Jarrboe (a.k.a. John Ackerson), A. E. Clements, Sanora Babb, W. D. Trowbridge, Joe Kalar, Benjamin Musser, Ralph Cheyney, William Pillin, Lucia Trent, Clement Wood, and Jay Sigmund, most of whom were, after 1929, members of Conroy and Cheyney's Rebel Poet organization, and contributors to Conroy's own little magazines, the *Rebel Poet* and the *Anvil*. Too heterogeneous to be called a school and too loosely connected to constitute a movement—an identification that they would have likely resisted in any case—most of these writers had grown up in small midwestern towns, subscribed to Haldeman-Julius's magazines, were sensitive to contemporary social issues, and most of all were eager to make contact with one another. Joined by worker-writers, anarchists, socialists, and those who remained simply "independents," they expressed the growing rebelliousness of young writers and artists far from bohemian milieus, drawn together by shared perceptions of contemporary social and political realities, which each, in his or her own way, had experienced.

* * *

The International Shoe Company's Hannibal factory, located on Collier Street, was one of the largest shoe manufacturers in the world at the time that Jack worked in the rubber-heel plant. Except for the Widman Body Factory job in Detroit, nothing Jack had previously done prepared him for the tasks he was given. Assigned to a machine with two rollers through which hot rubber passed, Jack was given a hook and told to hack off large slices to be pressed into heels. In an unpublished piece written for the Illinois Writers' Project, he describes the travail of the newcomer:

The bale consists of one or more continuous sheets pressed together while still warm. Thus the sheets become almost welded together so that it requires the services of three men to separate them
for apportioning to the batches of materials mixed for the manufacture of raw heels. Two men fasten lumbermen's canthooks into
opposite sides of the bale and pull against each other until the
sheets begin to divide while a third man stands with a huge knife
to slice the connecting folds. The new man wrestles with the bale
at first furiously and at length hopelessly without making appre-
ciable progress. The men who are mixing the batches dash up at
intervals and feign great anxiety and impatience at the small
amount of work being accomplished. . . .

The calendar is a machine which reduces the "jelly rolls" to
sheets of proper thickness and width for the heel blankers. The
"jelly rolls" are crushed between two horizontal steel cylinders and
emerge on the other side to wrap two or three ply around a drum.
A man standing beside the drum slices the sheet loose, another
grasps the loose end and backs rapidly away with it, while a third
steps up to catch the other end as it is cut free from the drum.
The two men holding the sheet throw it upon a table and it is
cut into proper lengths for the blankers. The new man is assigned
to the end last out of the drum, since this one is harder to catch
and it is also possible for his partner to jerk the sheet vigorously
so that it drops to the floor and becomes soiled and thus useless
until it is re-milled. The new man, naturally, is always blamed. If
he is assigned to the end first cut loose from the drum, a small
pan or wooden block may be placed on the floor behind him. Since
he must back away from the drum and cannot see the obstacle,
he ordinarily finds himself sprawling on the floor with the hot
sheet of rubber piled across his body. The man who is feeding the
jelly rolls into the other side of the calendar cannot see the fun,
but he can assist by speeding the machine so that the rubber reels
onto the drum with great rapidity. The speed, naturally, increases
the panic of the newcomer and also increases the probability of
fumbling or stumbling on his part. When the men on the drum
side feel that a little more speed is desirable, they shout "more
hay!" while the feeder responds with "more corn!" to signify that
he understands and will do his part.[28]

The work was hot, dirty, smelly, and dangerous, like the labor carried
out in the ikon workshop of Gorki's *My Apprenticeship*. Both writers

describe reified work worlds in which diversions from monotonous routines often took cruel and trivial forms.

The workers were a ragtag lot, including drifters and petty crooks as well as displaced rural and small-town workers. One of the workers in the rubber-heel plant at the time was a man named Clarence Earl Gideon. This one-time thief and drifter was suddenly raised from oblivion to historical eminence through circumstances that led to the landmark "Gideon case," which established the public defender system.[29] The *Gemeinschaft* feeling that Jack had known in the Wabash shops was missing entirely in the rubber-heel plant. The workers took little pride in their work; their pay averaged about twenty-five dollars a week. Most hated their work but were glad to have their jobs. A smaller number, like Gideon, felt no such gratitude.

In the rubber-heel plant, Jack met workers like "Jasper," who took pleasure in tormenting his colleagues with trivial pranks and banal humor. The nature of the work seemed to stifle imagination. Jasper was an inconsequential fool whose type Jack encountered in other factory jobs. Another type of worker, the "Nat" of Jack's sketch "Rubber Heels," harbored middle-class aspirations. With his slender wages he bought a flimsy, unpainted wood-frame boxlike house in a new subdivision located below the flood plain. Hating his work, he sought a measure of satisfaction and respectability in becoming a property owner. Other workers saved to buy a radio and afford a weekly movie. Still others, less provident, sought relief in Hannibal's numerous bordellos, located upstairs in the main commercial area of town. One noted brothel, at 111 Bird Street, was run by a "highly respected" madam named Bessie Hoelscher who "paid her bills, bought quality merchandise and didn't cause any trouble."[30] The workers' existence was largely built upon expectation—and fear of losing their jobs. Such an existence, Jack observed, produced workers who could be easily led, offered little resistance toward employers, and were little given to reflection or political action.

A rare figure, then, in the rubber-heel plant was the older worker from Germany on whom Jack based the character "Hans" in "Rubber Heels," enlarging his role in *The Disinherited*. In the sketch, Hans is an enigmatic figure, a socialist who protested against Germany's entry into the war and later participated in the ill-fated Spartakusbund in Berlin, knew Karl Liebknecht and Rosa Luxemburg, and fled when the Räterepublik was violently suppressed by the Freikorps. Hans makes no attempt to hide his contempt toward the "Lumpenproletariat" like Jasper or Nat, with petit bourgeois aspirations. The German radical whom Jack knew in the Hannibal shoe factory becomes in the novel an important vehicle for the ideal of the worker-intellectual who remains within his or her class but seeks "a fuller intellectual life." "We fought on the barricades," Hans tells the young worker, Larry. "Men—and women, too—dying for the Revolution! Do you wonder these dull apes turn my stomach? Don't think you'll escape them if you get a better job."[31] Most of the shoe factory workers in Hannibal are, in the eyes of the one-time comrade of Rosa Luxemburg, victims of false consciousness. No Marxist ideologizing would change that. Hunger alone would open their ears and eyes.

The old German radical that Jack knew was vulnerable, like the other workers, to joblessness. Like the sawmill, rubber-heel factories exacted a toll in human flesh. Workers lost fingers, and a badly mutilated worker would be fired without benefits. The danger was all the greater during the night shift when the monotone whirr of the machinery and the mindless work deadened sensibilities. At such times a loose strip of rubber might pull a hand into the revolving steel cylinders. Jack tended to daydream on the job. He was deathly afraid of the heel-cutting machine with its large cutting arm where more than one worker had lost an arm.[32] The machines made no distinctions among workers; the German lost the use of a hand in a moment of inattention and was fired.

The latter part of 1926 saw heavy blows dealt to workers. Torrential rains burst dams and caused the Mississippi to overrun its banks in September, the month of the Tunney-Dempsey match, flooding the low-lying subdivisions where workers had purchased tract houses. The *Hannibal Courier-Post* told of a drowned woman removed in a rowboat from one of the subdivisions.[33] Jack put the *fait divers* in his story "Rubber Heels." Shortly thereafter, the "flood of years" and heart disease broke the "indomitable will" of Eugene V. Debs, the *Hannibal Courier-Post* reported on 21 October, not long before Debs was to turn seventy-one. Debs had been an inspirational figure to Conroy as to millions of working-class people. The old Socialist party—trade union alliance was moribund in 1926. Whitaker printed Conroy's encomium on Debs in *Pegasus*.[34]

The new year brought some improvement in the Conroys' economic fortunes. Jack decided to secure a chattel mortgage on his house furnishings in order to purchase a new Chevrolet. Jack and Gladys went down to a mortgage company on Broadway. In the windows were clocks indicating the times in different world locations. The manager of the mortgage firm inventoried the Conroy's possessions including a baby carriage. Gladys inquired sweetly, "Don't you want to take the baby too?"[35]

Both of International's Hannibal shoe factories were running at full capacity by early spring 1927.[36] When International announced its decision in March to build a quarter-million-dollar addition to its rubber-heel plant on Collier Street, it seemed to Jack and Gladys that they would be able to stay on in Hannibal indefinitely. Nonetheless, Jack was looking for a less-fatiguing day job that would allow him to invest his main energies in writing. On impulse he took the Civil Service railway postal clerk examination in April, scoring 87 percent in the general tests. However, he never followed up on the opportunity to secure a less-taxing job. By now he seemed welded to labor and laboring people.[37]

The spring brought more flooding. But the main damage of the great Mississippi flood of 1927 occurred further downstream from Hannibal. In May, the newspapers reported Lindbergh's solo flight across the Atlantic. Jack makes no mention of this in his correspondence. Such exploits failed to touch his imagination; he dreamed rather of social justice. Misuses of authority, for example, disturbed him. The newspaper reported that Congress was supporting the corrupt Diaz regime in Nicaragua and that the Hannibal Free Library had decided to ban Sinclair Lewis's *Elmer Gantry* from its shelves. Book banning and abuses of authority were issues of concern to American literary radicals in 1927. The pivotal point for Jack and radicals everywhere on the left came in late summer when Sacco and Vanzetti, after several stays, were finally executed.

Like many radicals, Jack felt a stirring that summer, a shifting of winds that promised relief from years in the political doldrums. His own literary prospects began to improve. Through Hagglund's *Northern Light* Jack made contact with the English publisher E. M. Channing-Renton and, soon after, Arthur Stockwell, who published inexpensive editions. Listing his address as 17-19 rue Venture, Marseilles, Channing-Renton published *Home and Abroad, the English Illustrated Review* for expatriate English on the continent. Eager to expand his "Studies Library," which included biographies, Channing-Renton enlisted Jack to write the life of Mark Twain. The project became a burdensome task; after writing several pages Jack abandoned it. The contact, however, produced a collaboration with Channing-Renton, who published an anthology of rebel verse entitled *Unrest*, edited by Conroy and Ralph Cheyney.

Conroy's network of literary contacts grew, despite his isolation and the demands of factory work. Several of his correspondents were or had been factory workers. Their early poetry, like Jack's first poems, pursued an uncertain course between genteel sentimentality and radical conviction. An early correspondent was Joseph Kalar of International Falls, Minnesota, a papermill worker. Born in Eveleth, Minnesota, on 4 April 1906, Kalar completed teacher training at Bemidji State College at age eighteen. He quickly tired of teaching in remote and sparsely settled Koochiching County. After traveling about the Midwest hoping to get into newspaper work, he returned disillusioned and empty-handed to International Falls, where he took a job as a scaler in a sawmill. Active in organizing the sawmill employees, Kalar was branded a Communist by the company. At the time that he began to correspond with Jack, while Jack was in Hannibal, Kalar had gone to work in a larger papermill in International Falls. During his rambling he had made contact with Olin and Herbert A. Joslin, editors of the *Bohemian; a Journal of Art and Satire,* published in Chicago. Herbert Joslin had also edited the *Gypsy* and *Seed,* magazines that welcomed Kalar's early verse, which had titles like "Tears," "A Fable of Him Who Did Wait," "Moon-Poet," and "In a Grave Yard at Night." Kalar's factory experiences and tramping proved a school in which he was able to advance beyond the jejeune topics of early romantic attachment. By 1928 Kalar was submitting sketches of factory life and radical poems to *New Masses,* having tried unsuccessfully to place them in the *Double Dealer, Poetry,* and the *Dial.*[38]

Other worker-writers soon joined Conroy's growing network of contacts, such as Ed Falkowski, Walter Snow, and H. H. Lewis, whose published works in obscure little magazines eventually attracted the attention of Mike Gold. Gold's sketches in *120 Million* and *New Masses* had provided them with a model and inspiration. In early issues of *New Masses,* Gold (and John Dos Passos) solicited unknown workers from factory, farm, and mill, hoping to develop an intellectual vanguard among the proletariat.[39] In the summer of 1927, these outlanders whose rough hands belied their passion for literature, at least by genteel standards, were committing their deepest reflections to letters circulated among those in small midwestern towns and on farms who, like them, were eager to be heard. For them the twenties had not been a decade of prosperity and Babbittry but one that had witnessed the collapse of work communities, the decline of labor's voice in politics, the spectacle of destitute job-seekers tramping to factory cities, the misery of the homeless on skid rows, and the empty promises of a new society of consumption. By 1927, many workers in mines, mills, and fields had become prisoners of the American dream.

"My head pulsed so strongly," Jack wrote of fitful attempts to sleep, "that it seemed to contract and expand. No more sleep. I raised the shade high enough to admit light, but sufficiently low to keep out the sun's glare. A mudwasp's queer metallic buzz sounded from a ceiling corner; and I watched it while it made many trips through the window after fresh mud to build its cells."[40] Night shifts in the rubber-heel factory forced him to rest during the day when he longed to write, or at least answer a correspondent. Writing was the one skill he maintained now, but where and how was that going to free him from the factory? Attached to his family and with no financial resources, he was not at liberty to experiment. Whatever conflicts Conroy felt, however, he was never lonely or isolated. Kinship, friendships, and literary contacts cast a wide net. There were always visits from Moberly family members, letters from worker-writers and little magazine editors, and contact with the friends that Jack seemed to make everywhere he lived. This irreducible core was the source of great strength and consolation to him.

The evening of 23 August 1927, Jack heard the news of the Sacco and Vanzetti executions from a worker who passed the news through an open window of the shoe factory. His coworkers shrugged and promptly forgot the event. But Jack took the news to heart. He wrote Jo Labadie, the Bubbling Springs anarchist, in October that "I just sit around and cuss the cock-eyed world and every body in it—neglecting my correspondence n' everything."[41] In a similar vein, John Dos Passos's poem "They Are Dead Now—," appearing in *New Masses,* suggested that the event was beyond the scope of poetry. Notwithstanding, poets flooded editors with tributes to the two Italian anarchists. Mike Gold called the Sacco-Vanzetti trials "one of the great proletarian legends—it is a perfect epic of the new America."[42] To the midwestern worker-writers, the execution was a warning signal of capital's renewed attack on labor. While crowds of protesters gathered in Union Square, New York City, and the Boston Commons, Jack's correspondents exchanged letters expressing their anger and disillusionment. The long trial and delays had mobilized sympathizers abroad and touched the consciences of writers and artists, many of whom began to address social themes. Bombs exploded in cities and riots spread in London and Paris. In the Hannibal shoe factories the workers scarcely took notice.

Dos Passos, James T. Farrell, and Nathan Asch, among others, recreated in their novels the emotion felt on the day of the execution. Entire issues of magazines were devoted to the subject.[43] Jack, like many others, committed his feelings to a poem, which appeared in late winter 1928 in the *Spider,* the little magazine published in Columbus, Ohio. Entitled "The Quick and the Dead," it represents Jack's early attempt to graft conventional rhyme and formal diction on to social protest. A few lines indicate the awkwardness such a graft produces:

> How could this puny soul [Judge Thayer], hedged in by bonds and deeds
> And the fat hand that smites as well as feeds—
>> How could he know the glory of their dream,
>> Enthroned on heights above his sordid scheme?[44]

Jack still held steadfastly to the notion that the language of poetry must be divorced from ordinary speech. Angry, disheartened, frustrated, he had hoped to make his feelings about the misconduct of the trial strike home in a direct and feeling manner. He might have found a model in Bartolomeo Vanzetti's statement to Judge Thayer.

The executions inspired the poetry anthology *America Arraigned* (1928), assembled by the poets Ralph Cheyney and Lucia Trent, who viewed the Sacco-Vanzetti trial as proof that the business class was in league with the government against the poor. The anthology led in turn to the founding of the Rebel Poets, whose magazine Jack edited beginning in 1931.

In September, violent weather struck Hannibal again. A tornado blew the roof off Jack's neighbor's home and left a wake of damage enroute to St. Louis, where it capsized a circus tent, releasing the animals. Few people took notice or understood the significance of Trotsky's expulsion from the Committee of the Third International, the arrest of IWW leaders in the Colorado coalfields, or the dispatch of Marines "to clean up outlaw bands headed by General Sandino" in Nicaragua, although these events were duly reported in the *Hannibal Courier-Post*. The public's attention was consumed by scandal, such as Emmanuel and Marcet Haldeman-Julius's announcement of their companionate marriage. To H. H. Lewis the news was simply more evidence that the publisher was basically an unscrupulous entrepreneur and a literary charlatan. The literary radicals were anxious to find new editors. Jack, on the other hand, continued to defend Haldeman-Julius's role in publishing new writers such as James T. Farrell, Erskine Caldwell, Albert Halper, George Milburn, W. D. Trowbridge, George Jarrboe, Bruce Crawford, and others who would subsequently figure importantly in Jack's own literary endeavors.[45]

In the Midwest the Haldeman-Julius publications were a vehicle for extending the older, prewar traditions of protest through the backsliding 1920s.[46] The Haldeman-Julius press published Mike Gold's first book, *The Life of John Brown* (1924). Erskine Caldwell's exposés of injustice and cruelty, wrought by the new industrialism in the South, appeared in the *Haldeman-Julius Monthly*. Farrell contributed an early piece entitled "The Filling Station Racket in Chicago" to Haldeman-Julius's *The Debunker*. Young midwestern literary radicals sent the Girard publisher their realistic sketches of small-town life, often their first publications. Harold Preece assailed street-corner preachers and Albert Halper recounted his experiences in a Chicago post office in Haldeman-Julius publications. Haldeman-Julius published reportage such as Gerald V. Morris's "On the Skidroad, What One Sees on Los Angeles' Street of Forsaken Men." Morris's vivid account of street people and radical organizers lacks the indignation of H. H. Lewis's angry first-person account, "Sidewalks of Los Angeles," appearing in *New Masses* some months later. O. W. Cooley's worker narrative "The Damned Outfit, a Pair of Apple Pickers Fall into a Haywire Dump," prefigures the proletarian sketch of the 1930s. The realistic fiction appearing in Haldeman-Julius's magazines in the 1920s anticipated the new radical fiction of the early 1930s. During embattled times the Girard publisher provided continuity in the tradition that linked the older socialist press of Kerr's *International Socialist Review* and Wayland's *Appeal to Reason* to the new radical press of the 1930s, including Conroy's own *Anvil*. Jack was aware of this and therefore overlooked Haldeman-Julius's commercial motivations. How could one dismiss a publisher who paid young writers like Preece to write Little Blue Books and provided them outlets for their creative work?[47]

Haldeman-Julius's self-ascribed role as "debunker," exposing society behind the glitz of phony "normalcy," attracted young radical writers anxious to portray the "other twenties" based upon their own experiences in small towns, in urban immigrant ghettos, and on the skid rows. It was an easy step for them to move from Haldeman-Julius to Depression-era protest. Moreover, the economic upheaval after 1929 made the controversy surrounding Haldeman-Julius's debunking role seem trivial.

* * *

Jack's initial editing experience began with *Spider, the American College Radical,* which, as Jack soon discovered, was a contradiction of terms. Through Noah Whitaker he had made contact with two Ohioans named Emerson Price and David Webb, both living in Columbus at the time. Price was a bank clerk whose literary aspirations paralleled those of Webb, a friend who had started the magazine in October 1927. Price used the pseudonym Hugh Hanley in order to protect his job at the bank; he felt that he was not fit to do physical labor should he be fired. Price joined the editorial staff of the *Spider* in time for the second issue, which appeared in November 1927. Webb and Price hoped to fan the flames of student unrest at Ohio State University, spreading them to colleges throughout the land. Conroy encouraged Kalar and other worker-poets to submit their work to the *Spider*. Webb was pleased because he sought links between academia and working-class writers. Replying to Kalar's submission of a poem in December, Webb asked whether organized labor would ever again "be worth a dam [sic] in helping our poor working stiffs."[48] Webb hoped to convey the perceptions of the "working stiff" to the college student through poems like Kalar's "War" and Conroy's "The Quick and the Dead." In turn, his magazine would "present to the public the true spirit of the college radical movement."[49]

Jack joined the editorial staff of the *Spider* in March 1928. One of his first contributions as associate editor was to attempt to put the *Spider* on the enemy list of some right-wing organization—he didn't care which—taking his cue from the publicity attending the attacks by reactionary publications on the *Nation* and other liberal weeklies. In an effort to smoke out his reactionary adversaries, Jack claimed that the magazine was receiving "Bolshevik gold" in return for an "effort to convert, pervert, subvert, extravert, intravert, revert, or if necessary, invert, the college youths of this glorious republic."[50] No reactionaries rose to do battle. Rather, the editors of the *Spider* met with suffocating indifference on the part of the collegians, whose minds were on the forthcoming summer vacation. Visionaries the editors may have been in attempting to stir up student radical activity; in 1928, however, the silence was deafening.[51] The magazine ceased publication. "The Vanguard of the Intellectual Revolution" would have to wait. Jack found himself approving Mike Gold's suggestion that worker-poets might learn from their counterparts in the Soviet Union. The working class, not the college radical or the liberal intelligentsia, would furnish the material for a new revolutionary literature.[52]

The *Spider* notwithstanding, literary opportunities seemed promising in Ohio, where Jack had made contacts with Whitaker, Price, and Webb. Thus, when Fred Harrison wrote to the Conroys from Toledo in the spring of 1928 that there might be work in the Willys-Overland plant, Jack was ready. Gladys would wait to see whether things worked out for Jack in Toledo, then join him there with the family. Feeling no regret or apprehension, Jack shook the foul-smelling rubber dust from his clothes for the last time.

7

The Crucible of Experience:
Toledo, 1928–30

Man's dignity is his work, which is a value of a spiritual order.
—Simone Weil

FRED HARRISON had gone to work in the Willys-Overland automobile factory in Toledo after leaving Des Moines in 1926 with his wife, Myrtle, a stocking-factory worker. But Myrtle died in Toledo and now Fred was eager that the Conroys join him. Fred had Myrtle cremated and carried her ashes with him whenever he changed jobs. "Half of those ashes are cigarette ashes," people would say, adding their own cigarette ashes to the pot.[1]

On a weekend in June 1928, Fred drove over to Hannibal in his Willys-Overland Whippet and accompanied Jack, who had given notice to the shoe factory, back to Toledo. Jack traveled in a 1927 Chevrolet he had recently bought, Fred in his Whippet. Sharing Fred's spartan accommodations in a roominghouse, Jack had little difficulty at the Willys-Overland employment office although hundreds of anxious job-seekers stood in line. The prospect of higher wages in the auto factories attracted workers from far and wide. Fred had arranged Jack's job through Gerald Shinew, Fred's "straw boss" at Overland.[2] Jack was twenty-eight, the very figure of a sturdy, experienced worker who could stand the pace of factory work. It mattered a great deal to look young and robust—Jack recalled the "superannuated" worker, Bun Grady, let go from the Des Moines steel plant because he could not keep up the pace of the younger workers. Discrimination was the unwritten rule in hiring and no laws forbade it, or if they did, no one enforced them. In Toledo with Fred, Jack felt that at last he might make a go of it. He wrote Gladys telling her that he would soon have enough money to pay for the family's move.[3]

In moving to Toledo, Jack hoped to become better acquainted with Emerson Price and his other Ohio literary contacts. After day shifts in the Overland plant, Jack pursued his literary interests. New themes, based upon his experiences as a worker, began to appear in his poems, published in *Pegasus*, the *Northern Light*, and the *Morada*. Rejecting pallid imitation, he became a poet of witness and community. He wrote of street preachers, displaced workers, and odd characters like Kurt Leischer, a reclusive German immigrant who lived in the woods near Monkey Nest and sold root beer to the miners.[4] Despite the demands of his job, Jack participated in the founding of the Rebel Poets, edited its mimeographed newsletters, and established a network of writers, animated by a spirit of protest against contemporary social and economic inequities.

His experiences in the Willys-Overland factory furnished primary material for his worker narratives and sketches, beginning with the publication of "Jackson Street: Toledo" in 1930.[5] A winter he spent jobless in Toledo was the subject of his first story published in Mencken's *American Mercury*. The urban proletarian experience of auto workers in Toledo and Detroit fueled Conroy's radical consciousness. Memory kept alive the past devalued in the cultural crisis that accompanied the economic and social devastation of the early 1930s. Through literary expression, Jack affirmed his sense of belonging to generations across time and place who have evolved subcultures in which values—loyalty, kinship, dignity, community—persist despite the irretrievable loss of specific work communities. His literary work reconstructs belief in the face of the devastation of closed factories and desperate families. Always he looked to the vitality and warmth of working-class communities for consolation and hope, even when these communities had ceased virtually to exist.

The rootlessness and alienation of the factory proletariat were subjects experienced directly by worker-writers like Conroy, Kalar, Cruden, and Falkowski. The characters of Conroy's fiction seem confused, wondering, anxious, bearing witness to the tumultuous social circumstances of people caught between older customs and a newer, unstable world of constant movement, change, and insecurity. Jack perceived the cultural struggles of workers for self-expression in their folk sayings, songs, and idioms wherever he worked or tramped. Proletarian workers were ordinary people thrust into extraordinary circumstances by forces over which they had no control, condemned to silence through illiteracy, ignorant of the means to protest, victims of public indifference. Jack's task as a writer, he perceived, was to listen to their voices and to let these voices be heard through his writing. Few writers were so well placed as he, not to speak for workers, but to let them speak for themselves.

* * *

When Jack first hired on, the Overland plant was operating at peak production. The auto industry was booming after years of rapid expansion. By 1925, the Willys-Overland payroll represented 41 percent of Toledo's total payroll. The 1928 Whippet Six coupe, reduced in price, was the first six-cylinder closed car in automobile history to sell for less that seven hundred dollars. During 1928, the Overland plant turned out over 300,000 cars; and employment reached a record high of 23,000.[6] Overland attracted many new workers through radio and newspaper advertisements. Ads lured workers to Toledo from southern textile mills and Kentucky soft-coal regions where jobs had grown scarce. They were men like Jack and Fred who had no resources to fall back on.

Surplus labor acted to keep wages down and check all employed labor at the plant. As early as 1905, Jack London had commented on the economic necessity—from the employer's position—of a surplus labor army. "It is the lash," he wrote in "The Tramp," "by which the masters hold the workers to their tasks, or drive them back to their tasks when they have revolted. . . . There is only one reason under the sun that strikes fail, and that is because there are always plenty of men to take the strikers' places."[7] The Overland workers were not in a position to strike in 1928. Production was up, Overland was open shop, and migrant workers continued to pour into Toledo (and Detroit). Harry Braverman's comment on the ways in which labor power is cheapened describes the situation of the Overland worker. Braverman observed that "for most jobs, the whole of society becomes a labor pool upon which to draw, and this helps to keep the value of labor power at the level of subsistence for the individual or below the level of subsistence for the family."[8]

If ads succeeded in persuading workers to abandon their homes and seek work in northern factory cities, so did word of mouth. Kinship and ethnic networks functioned as a grapevine; one family member would soon be joined by another and immigrant workers followed one another into factory cities.[9] Immigrants would bear exploitation and indignities refused by American workers.[10] Blacks were assigned to menial jobs requiring great physical exertion. Migrants served as a safety valve in the industrial economy of Toledo. They shuttled back and forth between their factory jobs and their homelands, as the economy dictated. Hungarian workers were each saving a thousand dollars to take back to their homeland. One said to George Pfaffenberger, a first-generation American employed in the paint department with Jack: "You come too, George!"[11]

The pay was better than what most of the proletarians had been used to; wages were as much as forty dollars a week for assembly-line work. This was the fabled wage that attracted workers, but the figure was misleading. Layoffs were frequent, with no unemployment compensation. During the difficult winter of 1929–30 many workers were near starvation. Apart from introducing periodic hardship in the lives of the Overland auto workers, the effect was to undermine potential militancy among the workers. Despite the fact that most Toledo auto workers were not actually sharing in the prosperity enjoyed by a relatively small proportion of people in the city, the majority remained uncommitted politically, nurturing dreams of success and modest wealth that were fed by inspirational writers like Orison Swett Marden and Dr. Frank Crane.[12] Protest, when it occurred at Overland, was usually an individual act. The Willys-Overland workers were not organized; nor did Jack anticipate that they might become so. Since the war, trade unions had aligned with business values and management goals; Jack did not look to them for help.[13]

In the early days of Jack's Toledo sojourn, however, the Conroys' lives improved; new possibilities seemed to open up. It was early summer. Fred was, as in the past, a great companion. Good-natured, intelligent, and playful, Fred was devoted to his Uncle Jack, whom he viewed as a close brother. Jack was full of play and mock theatrics. Quick to find humor in the day's commonplace events, he turned a fragment of a conversation overheard in the paint department into an anecdote for telling. Increasingly he turned to subjects close at hand for his writing. His strong, virile features, twinkling blue eyes, and robust laugh must have made a vivid impression on his fellow workers. A consummate observer—without appearing to observe—he had a peculiar habit of avoiding eye contact when listening, of stealing glances, shrewdly studying the other's responses and conduct, without replying. His own response was often disconnected from what had been said, as if his mind were already three steps ahead.

Jack and Fred took the interurban train to Detroit and crossed over to Windsor, Canada, to buy beer, consuming most of it before reaching home once again. The two liked to see stage shows at the Rivoli Theater and visit speakeasies like the Jackson Bar and Hotdog John's near Jackson Street. They soon became familiar with the "scofflaws," merchants who defied prohibition, selling only to people they knew since prohibition agents would pose as customers.[14] At the New Empire The-

ater, Jack saw large "stagey" productions, afterward wandering over to
Courthouse Square, which bordered Jackson Street. Like Bughouse
Square in Chicago, Courthouse Square drew orators, hucksters, intellectual hoboes, radicals, bums, fanatics, and the homeless. A gaunt black
evangelist named Hambone preached whether anyone listened or not.
When he left, an East Indian would sermonize.[15] On Sundays, Jack and
Fred sometimes drove out to Toledo Beach to stroll on the boardwalks
and escape the summer heat. People danced in an open-air hall under
hundreds of electric lights and artificial stars. The sign above the Val-
entine Building boasting that "You Will Do Better in Toledo" had been
removed, but Toledo was still better than anything Jack had previously
experienced.

When Gladys and the family came to Toledo in July, the Conroys
rented a house west of town, near the Chicago Pike, on Byrne Road,
some five miles from downtown Toledo. The Shinew family lived next
door. Gerald Shinew was the foreman who had helped Jack hire on at
Overland. Across the street from the Conroys and the Shinews lived a
farmer named Zacharias whom the Byrne Road denizens dubbed "Farmer
Zack."[16] Bordering Zacharias's land was an insane asylum. Inmates would
often stray away from the asylum into Zacharias's field, where they would
be put to work. Observing this, the asylum guards decided to make some
spending money, hiring the inmates out to Zack, including an occasional
loony who threatened the others, wielding farm tools as he chased them
around the field.[17] About a mile north on Byrne Road was a creosote
plant and a squalid shantytown built by the factory for the black workers, whose job was to dip railroad ties into hot creosote. On the corner
of the Chicago Pike and Byrne Road remains one of the few landmarks
as it was in 1928, the Maplewood Cemetery.[18]

A photo shows Fred, Jack, Gerald Shinew, and George Harrison,
Fred's brother, standing in front of the Byrne Road house in the late
fall of 1928, wearing soft workers' caps and long heavy coats. George
had recently moved to Toledo to work at the Willys-Overland plant,
living with the Conroys and Fred. Gladys's sister, Agnes, visited the
Conroys and the Harrisons for several months. Always there were family ties, a kinship network, and a house full of people.

As long as there was work at Overland the times were good on Byrne
Road. Jason ("Don") Shinew, Gerald's son, remembered Jack sitting at
his typewriter late at night.[19] The house was a three-ring circus. Jack
would continue to peck at his typewriter in a second-floor room, ignoring the noise. The temptation was great to play pranks on Jack. One
evening Fred brought home a box of cream chocolates and took them
to the Shinews, where he filled them with bitter-tasting quinine. Don

and his boyhood friends watched from outside the window in breath-less anticipation while Fred offered Jack the candy. Jack paused from his typing, took a bite, said "quinine" in a factual manner, and returned to his typing, never changing his expression. The unperturbed response was a pose; one prank deserved another.

Jack nicknamed people. George was "Jazzbo," Jack's son Tommy was "Hardhead," and Don was called "Fayah." In the open fields behind the Conroys, Jazzbo and Fred wagered they could throw a baseball bat over the high utility wires. Jack volunteered to hold the wager. At each throw the bat struck a wire so that no one could determine with certainty whether the bat went over or under. Jack kept the wager as payment for his "impartial arbitration," which, he said, consisted in remaining "uncommitted." The Harrison brothers, who had boxed with the "carnies" in Moberly, would put on their gloves at the Conroys and stage "exhibitions." At least once, Jack, who made a practice of avoiding combat, put on the gloves, urged on by the neighborhood children. The "fight" consisted of nothing more than Jack assuming a pose like Jack Johnson and making a few feigned swings. He then handed the gloves grandly to one of the children, briskly brushed the dirt from his hands, and strode away like the champion he was to all children.[20]

Jack drove down to Columbus in late summer to meet Emerson Price. Together the two traveled in Jack's Chevrolet to Springfield to visit Noah Whitaker, the eccentric publisher of *Pegasus* and an outspoken adversary of free verse. Whitaker, who with his long, drooping moustache looked like a character from romantic fiction, was violently opposed to practices such as vivisection. In his basement was his antiquated press, next to a jury-rigged machine he used to manufacture the wire broomholders he peddled from door to door.[21] Editors and publishers such as Whitaker; Hagglund; Norman Macleod, editor of the *Morada*, *Palo Verde*, and the *Front*; Marvin Sanford of Newllano Colony; and Jim Gipson of Caxton Press were instrumental in giving a boost to unknown writers. In these and other little magazines, mainstream book and magazine editors searched for new talent.

Jack edited the April and June issues of the *Spider* when its founder, David Webb, moved back to Chillicothe to start a local historical society and write little chapbooks. Webb had discovered a man in Chillicothe who, he told Jack, could translate any language. Webb hoped to turn the man's talent into a lucrative business. A visit to see Webb made it clear that if the *Spider* was to continue, Jack and Emerson would have to do the work on their own. Jack tried his hand at editorializing. In the April issue he expressed dissatisfaction with the decade's illusion of prosperity when millions of factory workers were being laid off or let go. While corporations continued to make record profits, he wrote, the unemployed were wondering where they would find their next meal.[22] The final issue of the magazine appeared in June 1928. Jack continued his contacts with the English publishers E. M. Channing-Renton and Arthur Stockwell, whom he mentioned in the *Spider*. His work on the Mark Twain biography had scarcely advanced beyond several pages. Biographies for Channing-Renton's "studies" series and magazines for college "radicals" were both blind alleys. There were more pressing subjects close at hand.

The growing crisis in the economy was exacting terrible social costs among desperate migrant workers in the auto plants. The nation staggered toward economic collapse. As recording secretary of the Railway Carmen's local in Moberly, Jack had reported on what was going on inside the shops from the point of view of a worker and representative of his local. Now he felt the urge to communicate what he saw happening inside the Willys-Overland plant and outside, where the jobless formed long lines at the employment office. There was no union in the plant, no communication links with the outside other than word-of-mouth. Jack sought to express what he observed there and in his rambles along Jackson Street. How he was to do this was not yet clear to him in 1928. Gradually he began to see that his task would be to describe the experience of disinherited workers in the immediate and concrete terms of their workday existence. The migrant workers cast adrift in the new factory proletariat were ordinary people deeply individualized in terms of character and the folk experience of their separate pasts. In the factories this folk experience, adapted to the conditions of proletarian existence, appeared in new forms.

The rough palms of Jack's hands proved that he knew this existence first hand. His status as worker made him an intimate of his fellow workers' responses to these conditions. His curiosity, ear for workers' idioms, and powers of observation propelled him toward a new role as informal "recording secretary" of the dispossessed proletariat. But what form would his communications from the factory floor take? Who would publish them? Who would read them?

His first job at Willys-Overland was to remove fenders from the assembly line after they had passed through the enameling oven and place them on handtrucks. The job was not demanding physically, despite the heat of the dryer, and there were intervals during which the workers could talk and joke.[23] Jack's work companions in the paint department were mainly immigrants; Fred and George had been assigned to other jobs. A young Russian nicknamed Kapusta ("cabbage") was sent by the Soviet government to join his father, whom the workers called "Big

Fatty," in order to learn American production methods; after a few months he returned to the Soviet Union. The paint shop inspector was an American worker named Homer Babcock. Homer was an uncouth simpleton whose indecorous sense of humor displayed itself in gross practical jokes. His favorite prank was to unzip his fly and shake his "tool" at Big Fatty. "Don't you want a bite of this, Fatty," he'd say. "Oh, you son of bitch!" the Russian would curse, lumbering like a bear toward his tormentor while flailing his huge hairy arms. As the workers laughed and shouted, Homer would hightail it downstairs to find sanctuary in the foreman's office.[24]

At times the heat in the paint shop was overpowering. The windows were closed to keep dust off the finish of the new fenders. "We were galled to the knees and under the arms; the pungent scent of scorching paint was everywhere," Jack wrote in "Hard Winter." "We sweated abominably. We cursed each other, Prohibition and Hoover."[25] George Pfaffenberger had worked in a brewery plant. "That sort of heat," he remarked to Jack while both were panting for air one August afternoon, "wouldn't last five minutes in the brewery. Not a bottle would have been capped." It was agony to imagine unlimited quantities of uncapped beer.[26]

Overland employed a number of black workers, mainly from southern rural areas, in low-paying, onerous jobs. One of Jack's first "communications" from the factory to be published was a poem entitled "Dusky Answer," which appeared in Norman Macleod's little magazine, the *Morada*, in 1929.

> "Black boy," I said to him, "why do you niggers
> Come all the way from Georgia, take us white men's jobs,
> Work for less pay and stand the gaff they give you?"
>
> It was cold standing in the line that morning;
> Stamping feet rang on the iron ground, and the jobless
> Shivered like hairless hounds, waiting for the gates to open.
>
> He only glanced out of the tail of his chalk-eye,
> Looked at the hole in his worn shoes and snuffled,
> Pocketed his bare hands and give this damn fool answer:
> "Boss, I know a swamp in Georgia
> Where fireflies glimmer thru the trees at dusk—
> Not like these 'lectric lights that shine so cold and hard.
> And steamboats whistle down bayous in Georgia,
> But soft and low—not like these screamin' sirens
> That gimlet in your brain.

Woodpeckers drum on hollow trees in Georgia,
But they don't jar like these air hammers
That 'rat-tat' on your mind.
Boss, I got a wife and kids in Georgia;
I miss them all the time like no one knows!"
Something in the droop of his thick blue lip,
Something in the glint of his chalk-eye,
Give me the answer better than his damn fool words:

Something must be rotten down in Georgia![27]

"Dusky Answer" is an early expression of Jack's interest in workers' sociolects, an interest that would later become manifest in the speech rhythms and generic forms of his workers' tales appearing in the *American Mercury*, *Pagany*, and elsewhere. In a definition of "rough art," Goethe wrote: "Now this characteristic art is the only true art. When it acts on what lies round it from inward, single, individual, original, independent feeling, careless and even ignorant of all that is alien to it, then, whether born of rude savagery or of cultivated sensibility, it is whole and living."[28] In Toledo, Jack made his first attempts to create a "rough art" that like the subjects of his worker narratives was "whole and living."

White migrant workers from Kentucky resented the black auto workers sharing their workspace. Racial tension, Jack observed, absorbed a great deal of energy that the workers might have invested in improving their own situation. Literary radicals, including Conroy, Erskine Caldwell, Langston Hughes, I. L. Kissen, and Frank Yerby (to name those Jack published in his little magazines), made the impoverished migrant workers, black and white, in southern rural areas and northern factory cities subjects of their writing in the 1930s. Jack's experiences among migrant workers in Toledo and Detroit later became the focus of his research funded by a Guggenheim grant and the subject of two books coauthored with Arna Bontemps.

Mike Gold's role as editor of *New Masses*, beginning with the June 1928 issue, proved crucial for worker-writers like Conroy, Kalar, Lewis, and Falkowski, who, impatient with conditions in the factories and rural areas, were searching for guidance and a mentor. Founded in May 1926, the magazine was initially cast in the mold of the *Masses* (1911–17) and the *Liberator* (1918–24), "the pre-Bolshevik mold of the bohemian left," as David Peck observes.[29] Under Gold's editorship, however, *New Masses* began to solicit submissions by worker-writers and other radicals who had only a passing acquaintance with Marx. Among those who sent contributions were midwestern radicals who, lacking in Marxist understanding, knew by heart their Whitman, Dreiser, Sandburg, Masters, and Anderson.[30] Gold hoped that these new proletarian voices might be harbingers of an impending revolution. Jack was familiar with Gold's own early writings, including his description of the unemployed who had "abandoned the benches and were standing in doorways and under the sheltered entrance to the Cooper Union library. They were in the reading room, scores of them, gazing like slow-witted kine through the endless pages of the meadow-wide newspapers; they did not read with intelligence, as do men of brains and perception such as ourselves, they were thinking of the coming night, when they would have to go out to find a bed and a crust somehow."[31] Such scenes, Gold said, were symptomatic of "this mysterious plague of unemployment that breaks out every seven years in the capitalist world." "How clean and brave it is in Russia!" Gold mused. "How much better to starve and die there! There no one hides the hunger of millions behind the folds of a flag! There no one feasts while his brother starves! There misery is inevitable, it is the cruelty of nature, which can be borne, not the cruelty of man to man!"[32] Most questions of verifiability were put aside in the rhetoric of revolution; Gold made a very persuasive argument to the young worker-writers.

By 1928, the midwestern radicals were taking a closer look at the Soviet Experiment, persuaded that the American economic system had failed to provide adequately for its workers. However, few radicals, with the exception of Ed Falkowski and H. H. Lewis, were willing to swap places with the Soviet worker. Revolutionary belief among the midwestern radicals was more sentiment than abstract theory. Nonetheless, they had done a great deal more thinking about contemporary affairs than had the ordinary worker, who seemed predisposed to passivity and despair. Neither worker nor worker-intellectual, however, had thought out fully the consequences of their convictions (or loss of belief).

It was the fate of worker-intellectuals like Conroy and Kalar to be caught between two worlds, the actual quotidian workers' world in which they labored and the community of thinking, literate people to which they aspired and their intellectual ambitions drew them.[33] The greater separation lay between the worker-intellectual and his fellow worker. Kalar alludes to this division in a letter to Jack in late 1928. "It is easy," he wrote, "to be radical in an ivory tower—it is much harder to be honestly radical when one is in direct contact with the proletariat. There is such swinish indifference to ideas. . . ."[34] Kalar was disgusted with the recent November election in which workers helped Hoover succeed in winning another term in office. Yet he, like Conroy, remained firmly committed to his working-class roots. Detached by virtue of his intellectual aspirations, he nonetheless felt at home affectively within the ranks of his fellow laborers.

In the summer of 1928, Kalar tramped west on a pilgrimage to the Boise state prison where Joe Hill, the martyred Wobbly poet, was executed, and from there to the *bas-fonds* of Seattle, Los Angeles, and Tijuana, an odyssey other young radicals had made or were planning to make. The ferment and freedom of ideas on Seattle's skid row, he observed in a letter to Covington Hall, contrasted with the passivity of unemployed workers on Denver's Larimer Street, indeed with the complacency of employed factory workers. "I never met so many worker-intellectuals before in my life," Kalar wrote Hall, an older rebel poet whose poems had appeared widely in Wobbly and socialist publications. "Many of the ideas floating in the air were crazy and startlingly absurd—but at least there were ideas, which is much more than one can say of many another industrial center."[35] Kalar felt keenly the separation, the ethnological gap (*coupure ethnologique*), to use Jacques Rancière's expression, that sets a worker-writer apart from his or her worker comrades. Rancière writes: "In order for the artisans' protests to be heard . . . they had to make themselves over in such a manner that they lived as workers and talked like the bourgeois, i.e., a double, irremediable exclusion" (translation mine).[36] Literacy, articulateness, introduces ambivalences in the worker-intellectual's life with respect both to his trade and to his companions.

The ability to express one's thoughts well is, of course, a necessary condition to become a working-class leader. An aspiring writer seeks acceptance among other writers and intellectuals, a desire that in itself presumes a separation, an alienation from the workplace. Rancière argues that the distinctive quality of worker-writing (workers writing for workers principally) lies precisely in the ambiguity occasioned by the conflicts of unmediated expression of working-class existence. The worker-writer mediates the complex interrelationships existing between himself or herself and workers' culture, and between the workers' and the dominant culture.[37]

The ambivalences engendered in the act of writing as a worker mark uniquely the discourse of the worker-writer. Circumscribed by the complex interrelationships involving pride in identification with one's fellow workers and the perception that one's productive labor is exploited, the worker-writer's creativity occurs in the marginalized space between two cultures, working-class and bourgeois. Within this space Jack (and Joe Kalar) attempted to conciliate the division between his status as worker and his intellectual aspirations.

* * *

America Arraigned! (1928), the anthology of protest poetry published by Lucia and Ralph Cheyney, offered the prospect of a new poetry in harmony with diverse revolutionary forces in the making. Married to poet Lucia Trent, Ralph Cheyney was the son of the distinguished historian Edward Potts Cheyney. A philosophical anarchist and pacifist, Ralph spent most of World War I in Fort Leavenworth federal prison for refusing to be drafted. Another "distinguished alumnus" of Fort Leavenworth was the Wobbly poet Ralph Chaplin. Editors of *Contemporary Verse*, the "second-oldest poetry magazine in the United States, the only poetry weekly in the world," they claimed, Lucia and Ralph Cheyney operated a correspondence school of verse in Chicago.[38] Ralph supported their poetry enterprises by working as a secretary for the Izaak Walton League in Chicago's loop. *Contemporary Verse*'s third editor was Benjamin Musser of Atlantic City, New Jersey, a close friend of the Cheyneys. The contents of *America Arraigned!* led Mark Van Doren to comment that while an occasion such as the Sacco-Vanzetti executions does not guarantee a good poem, as the weaker poems in the anthology show, the best writers have, at times, written "the best propaganda, even when they were writers not accustomed to such a task."[39] To most radicals the Cheyneys' anthology was tougher, more in tune with social reality than Genevieve Taggard's *May Days* (1926), which gathered verse from the old *Masses* and the *Liberator*. *America Arraigned!* was a sign to many that the tonic of anger in the wake of the executions had finally cured poets on the left of what Mike Gold called the "hangover of the esthetic 1890's."[40]

The anthology prompted Jack to contact the Cheyneys and to recommend the collection to all of his correspondents including Kalar, who promised "to get a copy of the Sacco-Vanzetti anthology this payday" despite his mounting debts.[41] Jack sensed in the Cheyneys' collection a new wind of rebellious fervor. His own awkward imitations of English poets, such as "Cornwall: A Memory," published by Fowler Wright's *Verse & Song*, seemed now hopelessly irrelevant.[42] Kalar remarked to Jack in a letter: "Cornwall may be good poetry—but it makes no impression on me."[43] Similar anthologies of protest verse, including Upton Sinclair's *The Cry for Justice* (1915), Thomas Curtis Clark's *Poems of Justice*, Vincent Burns's *Red Harvest*, and the soon-to-appear *Anthology of Revolutionary Poetry*, edited by the anarchist Marcus Graham (1929), were a fresh wind that filled the sails of a new generation of rebel poets in the late 1920s.[44]

Seeking to gather the scattered poets of protest under a single umbrella organization, Cheyney and Conroy together agreed to cooperate in founding the Rebel Poets. The idea for the organization was Cheyney's; Jack's part in its inception was to share his contacts and the labors of editing a newsletter and an annual anthology to be called *Unrest*. Cheyney was named the organization's first president, Jack the first secretary. All contacts between Cheyney and Conroy were epistolary—the two founders never met. From the beginning there were significant differences between them: Jack admired Cheyney's convictions that won him a prison sentence during the war for resisting the draft, but Cheyney's political views seemed vague and soft-headed. Cheyney preferred the term "social vision" to "revolutionary." To Jack the term "rebel" meant people like Arturo Giovannitti and Covington Hall, two Wobbly poets of the preceding generation. In Jack's mind the Wobblies represented the true rebel spirit with their vigorous protest and irreverent humor. Pre–World War I radicals, like Floyd Dell, likewise felt a kinship with the Wobblies.[45] Romantic symbols of rebellion and bohemian freewheeling spirit, the Wobblies had drifted into Greenwich Village, where they found enthusiastic acceptance among Dell and other Village radicals.[46] But Jack's contacts with the Wobblies had been in boxcars and city parks, not in Village "coffeepots." The Wobblies did not split intellectual hairs or erect rigid political orthodoxies. They were independent rebels; Jack hoped to find more like them for his organization.[47]

Cheyney had protested the arrests of Giovannitti and others in an article on the IWW, published in 1917.[48] But in their poetic judgments, he and his wife suffered from a "Victorian hangover," preferring measured cadences and stylistic elegance to more robust examples of rebel verse such as the Wobbly poets produced. Here, for example, is one of Trent's "Banners of Rebellion":

> I have grown weary of these stunted trees,
> The irritating regularities
> Of buildings and the staid and patterned streets
> Where small drab houses "set" and where one meets
> Women with baby carriages who chat
> Across the snow-patched grass of this or that.
> I have grown weary of this ashen sky,
> The ominous factory smoke that straggles by,
> The grim monotony of lives that pass
> Like weak, thin spurts of wind through withered grass.[49]

Trent's "rebellion" is largely on aesthetic grounds.

The Rebel Poets organization represented no single political agenda, movement, or artistic credo. It seemed to spring up spontaneously near the end of a decade that witnessed the persecution of radicals and labor activists, scandals in high public office, setbacks for organized labor, and finally the long, tragic spectacle of the Sacco-Vanzetti trial. The words "rebellion" and "humanity" were sufficient to rally members scattered thinly over the country. Tiny Rebel Poet chapters were formed and memberships were recorded in England, Germany, France, and Japan. Joining the Rebel Poets were anarchists, liberals, Communists, Christian Socialists, Wobblies, populists, and the expatriate poet Harry Crosby, editor of the Black Sun Press, nephew and godson of J. P. Morgan, and notorious *enfant terrible*. The wave of radical indignation of the late 1920s lifted up and carried the Rebel Poets along into the early years of the Great Depression until the organization foundered on sectarian shoals.

The Rebel Poets' first project was a poetry anthology, entitled *Unrest: The Rebel Poets Anthology of 1929*, edited by Cheyney and Conroy. Manuscripts were solicited starting in the summer of 1928, soon after the birth of the organization. Jack wrote most of the letters, willing at this point, out of deference to Cheyney's greater experience, to do most of the work. The beginnings were rudimentary; Jack typed and sent out carbon copies as descriptive flyers to prospective contributors. Poems in *Unrest*, he wrote a member, "will be collected from *Poetry, Dial, New Masses, Bozart, Contemporary Verse, Spur*, and journals of such calibre." They will be "conspicuously free from the piffle which infests the commercialized anthologies."[50] Cheyney's list of contributors and subscribers to his little magazine, *Contemporary Verse*, Jack's contacts, and poems appearing in a selection of little magazines provided candidates for inclusion in the anthology. One of those candidates was a poet from Kansas named Kenneth Porter whom Jack had contacted after reading his poetry in *New Masses*.

Born in Sterling, Kansas, of Scots-Irish and Covenanting stock, Porter put himself through Sterling College, working summers in the wheat harvest and at a dozen other manual occupations. Porter was a graduate student at Harvard when Jack first contacted him. Deeply religious, he was also a committed socialist. "I had been a socialist, intellectually, since 1925," Porter, Kansas's poet laureate, wrote shortly before his death in 1981, "arriving at that position via the La Follette Progressive campaign of 1924, and in Boston I soon joined the Yipsels (Young People's Socialist League) but for some reason or reasons did not join the Party until 1932, when I became quite active, assisted Jack Wheelwright in organizing what was at one time a good-sized Cambridge Local [of the Rebel Poets], soap-boxed, contributed to the *Socialist Call, Arise!*, and *The American Guardian.*"⁵¹ Porter's lifelong literary career was sandwiched in between activist work and a scholarly profession.⁵² Jack had admired Porter's poems in the *Christian*, the *Christian Century*, *Unity*, *World Tomorrow*, and *New Masses*, all magazines of liberal or radical content. Porter agreed to let Jack reprint "Undefeated" in the first *Unrest* anthology. He was surprised and dismayed to learn that *Unrest* required a three dollar fee for inclusion, a "contribution" that Cheyney, who held that poetic production should be based upon good business principles, imposed. Porter, as a historian of business, should understand.

The editors made many mistakes in publishing the first *Unrest* volume but gained a great deal of useful experience. Attracted by his offer to publish the anthology at low expense, the editors chose the London publisher Arthur Stockwell. Revealing further their naiveté, Cheyney and Conroy asked contributors to select their own poems, the effect of which was to tempt them to submit orphans that had never found a home elsewhere. Another problem lay in the divided aims of the anthology. Paragraphs of the introduction were written alternately by Conroy and Cheyney. One paragraph complains of "anthologies vomited from the stolid presses by trainloads . . . [with] poems of every hue except red" (Conroy). The succeeding paragraph reads in part: "Poetry is the fruit of passion and the flower of compassion . . ." (Cheyney).⁵³ Protégés of the Cheyneys and students of their correspondence school of poetry submitted their work to Cheyney, who felt obliged to publish it. Jack, on the other hand, saw fit to include Keene Wallis, a Wobbly who had appeared in the old *Masses*, Giovannitti, Kalar, Jim Waters, George Jarrboe, and other radical poets. A curious product, the anthology included six poems by the expatriate Harry Crosby. Cheyney's "schooled" poets wrote imitations of Shelley's rebel verse of the kind that Joe Kalar, in his review of the anthology, said was "culled and blue-pencilled heavily."⁵⁴ Several poems, including Kalar's "They Blow Whistles for the New Year," Herman Spector's "Anarchist Nightsong," James Rorty's "Address to a Great Public Servant," Norman Macleod's "Blind Baggage," George Jarrboe's "The Unknown Soldier Speaks," and Conroy's "Journey's End," reveal a freshness and vitality that to editors and reviewers like Kalar portended a new rebel spirit rising.

The anthology was promised for 15 February 1929 but by June it had not appeared. Stockwell was known in publishing circles as an inferior vanity press, Jack learned—too late to change—from Channing-Renton, who would not carry through his promise to distribute copies. Conroy should have asked Channing-Renton to submit a bid in the first place, he was advised, instead of relying on an unknown.[55] To make things worse, when the first copies finally arrived in Toledo in the summer, W. K. Fudge of the Mitre Press in London notified Jack that "big circulating libraries and bookshops absolutely refuse to take Stockwell's books."[56] Porter complained of the uneven quality of the first *Unrest* and received a reply from Cheyney reminding him that the anthology "was run on a pay-as-you-enter basis, which explains much."[57] In the future, however, a committee representing the interests of the Rebel Poets would pass on all submitted material.

To promote sales of the first volume, the editors placed ads emblazoned with this arresting exclamation: "Bombshells for complacency, stagnation, reaction and respectability! *Unrest, The Rebel Poets Anthology for 1929.*" Despite the uneven quality of the contributions and the problems with Stockwell, Jack was pleased with the result of his efforts to build a network of corresponding poets. The critical reception, however, was less than enthusiastic; rather than a bombshell, most readers found a fizzled firecracker. Nonetheless, the first *Unrest* was better, said Joe Kalar, than the pale imitations divorced of "robust actuality." "The vast horde of american [sic] 'little' poets still warble sweetly of roses, divinely blind to the incongruity of it, while factories belch smoke and suffocate all the roses, and in North Carolina awakened slaves are shot down callously, beaten, and jailed. . . ."[58] Kalar himself had "warbled" a few years before, and, like Jack, had since kicked over the traces, so that his derision directed toward the poetic "purists" was in some part a rejection of his own early work. In Kalar and Conroy, the tendency to write of "sadness, frustration, sunsets, and love" had been all too compelling.

Kalar was in an uncompromising mood that winter of 1928–29, scorning the publications that had helped the literary radicals get their start. Of *Pegasus* he wrote to Lewis: "Whitaker is the Daddy Browning of poetry, embracing 'poetry' with the ardor of an old eunnch [sic]."[59] And to Jack: "Haldeman-Julius and his Holy Church of Ranting Atheists needs a thorough bastinado. I despise Haldeman-Julius so thoroughly that the thought of him and what he stands for makes my mouth taste of piss."[60] But his choicest invective was reserved for the middle-class liberal poet whom he addressed in an unpublished "Insolent Query," which he sent to Jack, Lewis, Kenneth Porter, and other writer-correspondents. Kalar wondered why literary radicals (viz. "midwestern radicals") feel gratitude toward the "literati," such as Edna St. Vincent Millay, John Gould Fletcher, and others, for their "spasmodic literary revolt" expressed in poems honoring the martyrs, Sacco and Vanzetti. "And why," Kalar queried, "exactly does the radical press box the cautious praise of bourgeois dilletants [sic] after a visit to Soviet Russia?" (Kalar referred to visits by Dreiser, numerous journalists, "schoolmams," "*Dial* literati," and others to the Soviet Union.) "Do the writers and the creative artists of the radical movement suffer from an inferiority complex?"[61]

Kalar, along with other literary radicals, was emboldened by Gold's sponsorship of worker-writers, beginning in the July 1928 issue of *New Masses*, which appeared to signal a new trend on the cultural left. The sponsorship, however, proved premature. "The late Boom period," as Michael Folsom writes, "was unpropitious for radicalism, for the working-class Muse, and for middle-class intellectual sympathy towards such a blunt leftist approach to the arts. It took a new generation of radical professional writers in the Thirties to make *The New Masses* again a force in American cultural life, and by then Gold was no great force in the magazine."[62] Poetry, Kalar wrote elsewhere, "is a handmaiden of the bourgeoisie." But the work of a new generation of rebel poets—Herman Spector, Norman Macleod, Kenneth Porter, Keene Wallis, H. H. Lewis, Conroy, Henry George Weiss, Kalar, George Jarrboe, and others—would herald a "proletarian literature of revolt."[63]

The midwestern radicals found a vigorous sponsor in Mike Gold, who announced in the July 1928 issue that henceforth under his editorship *New Masses* was to be devoted to "the world of revolutionary labor"; its pages would be written by "the working men, women, and children of America. . . . The product may be crude, but it will be truth."[64] With one stroke, the magazine's cover abandoned the satirical, expressionist caricatures of Hugo Gellert, Art Young, and Louis Lozowick (they would soon return). The June cover featured a stylized worker, glorified in the Soviet manner soon to be associated with Socialist Realism. Subtitled "A Magazine for Rebels," its first issues under Gold published a backlog of pieces by John Dos Passos, Ezra Pound, and Dorothy Day, characteristic of earlier issues when Joseph Freeman, Hugo Gellert, and others were the contributing editors. The July issue was subtitled "A Magazine of Art and Labor," headlining the "Poems and Tales by Miners, Sailors, Clerks, Carpenters, Etc." Gold solicited manuscripts from the midwestern radicals, publishing Kalar, Porter, and Lewis, together with Rebel Poets such as Ed Falkowski, Walter Snow, Spector, Macleod, Raymond Kresensky, Jarrboe, Weiss, Waters, and others who later appeared in Jack's own magazines. Following Gold's announcement Ed Falkowski wrote Gold: "Hurrah for the new *New Masses*! It makes me want to write to you. I've got a lot of coal dust in my system that I have a choice of writing or sweating out." And from Kalar Gold heard: "By God! if *New Masses* is to be the voice of the low-brow failure, rebel, boy worker, ditch digger, I am yours to a cinder, indeed. Don't try to be respectable—we can always get the *Dial, New Republic*, and the *Na-*

tion when we hunger for the clean white pants of respectability."[65] But several months later, Kalar, perhaps having scrutinized the new format and contents of *New Masses*, reminded the editors that considerations of poetic quality apply to revolutionary poems as well.[66]

Most of the contributions Gold received in response to his appeal were in sketch form and poems, reflecting the personal experience of the writer. The poet Stanley Burnshaw, a *New Masses* contributor at the time who had worked as "a white-collar man in [a] steel mill," described in a letter what was probably representative of submissions received by Gold from the worker-writers: "I would write the very same night that I had been working. I have taken ages to pare down the proletarian stuff to its gray, bare, wistful threnody; and the bareness, grimness, the aridity (if you will) is retained in the solid, monolithic life-feeling."[67]

The brief period of enthusiastic sponsorship under Gold (and soon Walt Carmon) was a curious episode given the Communist party's ambivalent commitment to "proletarian" fiction and worker-writers early in the next decade. Peck argues that Mike Gold's editorship of *New Masses* provided guidance and encouragement to these new writers, who anticipated new trends in fiction and documentary writing appearing in the 1930s. "The alteration in the basic character of American literature after 1930, in other words, the sudden emergence of an American proletarian literature in both creative and critical forms, was largely the achievement of the editorial policies of the *New Masses*, particularly in this period before 1930, when workers were urged to write of their lives and writers were urged to turn to the lives of workers for their subjects and their themes."[68] An irony is the fact that Jack's own writing was not among the worker-writers' submissions to *New Masses* following Gold's call. His first publication in *New Masses*, "Whistling Past a Graveyard: Toledo," appeared in March 1930, nearly two years later. Gold's own sketches in Mencken's *American Mercury* made a greater impact on Jack than did Gold's exhortations in *New Masses*.[69] Without question, Gold had played a powerful inspirational role in the early "careers" of the worker-writers. His collection of essays and sketches, *120 Million* (1929), and the autobiographical account of growing up in the Jewish ghetto of New York's Lower East Side, *Jews without Money* (1930), were literary beacons toward which they set their own courses. But Jack felt a closer kinship with Walt Carmon, another midwesterner, who by early 1929 had become the silent hand at *New Masses*, encouraging the worker-writers and offering them criticism.

Little has been written detailing Carmon's contributions or those of the *New Masses* business manager, Frances Strauss. Gold, more inter-

ested in writing and talking than in the detail work of running a magazine, turned over most of the editorial tasks to his managing editor,
Bernard Smith, and to Walter Carmon, who succeeded Smith early in
1929. According to Norman Macleod, Erskine Caldwell, and others who
made visits to the editorial office at the time, Walt Carmon, by then
managing editor, was the real workhorse at *New Masses* along with
Strauss.[70] Carmon had a special affinity with the worker-writers and
midwestern radicals, a point I explore in a later chapter, and continued to function as their spokesman and go-between when he was in
Moscow. The period of *New Masses*, marked in considerable part by the
writings of worker-writers, ended effectively when Walt Carmon left the
magazine several years later, first to dry out in Florida (he had a drinking problem), then to travel to the Soviet Union to work for the *Moscow Daily News*. By late 1933 *New Masses* had become a "weekly political magazine." At that point most of the midwestern literary radicals
had grown weary of the relentless scrutiny of orthodox Party critics who,
they felt, were content to count the number of Marxian angels that
could dance on the point of a pin.[71]

The midwestern literary radicals felt closer in spirit to Walt Carmon,
a shrewd, down-to-earth former professional baseball player from Ohio,
than to Gold, and closer to Gold than to the eastern radical intellectuals. Most of the midwesterners felt that the nature of class struggle
and alienated labor was best learned through the everyday experience
of factory work. It was possible epistemologically to come to Marx's
views on alienated labor through experience, without special study, yet
the majority of workers did not.[72] Moreover, there was nothing resembling a radical consensus among the midwesterners. H. H. Lewis revealed an almost religious devotion to Stalin and Lenin while kicking
back like a Missouri mule at the Party's apparent indifference to his idiosyncratic expressions of fealty to the workers' republic. Kalar always
cast a jaundiced eye on life and theory. He liked to discuss communism
with his work colleagues in the paper mill, who mainly listened because
they liked him; yet his correspondence frequently reveals his dissatisfaction with the Party. He owed a debt to *New Masses*, he said. "*New
Masses* kept me on the road, in this period, when the hallucinative fog
of egotism . . . would ebb and I would write." Yet he chafed at the magazine's ideological bit: "it is impossible, nay, it is suicidal, to expect us
to write affirmatively when the roof of the old world is cracking and
the flames of the new lick maddeningly distant. I have come to a more
or less complete ideological break with *New Masses*."[73] In fact, the midwestern radicals had very little actual contact with the Party or the
opportunity to discuss Marx, John Dewey, or any thinker.

Kalar, for example, knew no workers of Communist leanings in the paper mill. A "cell meeting" in International Falls was unlikely to attract more than three or four people. Kalar was regarded as something of an oddity among his fellow workers for his intellectual interests and radical convictions. "Whatever virtues communism may have," Kalar wrote his friend, Warren Huddlestone, "does not bother or intrigue [the coworkers] or appeal to loyalty; they just sense in some dim woozy way that Kalar is an interesting person, and that it would be just like him to spout communism and declare feverishly that he is of the faith."[74] None of the midwesterners had any close familiarity with Marxist thought, either through schooling or discussion such as was likely to occur in eastern radical circles. Conroy claimed years later that to see *Das Kapital* on the shelf was enough to give him a headache. Yet it was true that experience knocks lessons into the heads of a few thinking individuals who do a great deal of reading.

If Marxism can be said to have had any important appeal to the midwestern literary radicals, then it was an "Americanized" version adapted to local circumstances rather than any European transplant. Midwestern indigenous radicalism has appeared in numerous varieties: anarchists, atheists, populists, Debsian socialists, and right-wing survivalists. If there can be said to exist any underlying pattern, it is probably antiauthoritarianism. An anti-ideological current runs through the various radicalisms, as if the midwestern mind functions according to contingency and not principle. The ideological sources of midwestern literary radicals like Kalar, Le Sueur, Conroy, Lewis, Corey, Kresensky, and Porter derive from indigenous traditions of protest—expressed in earlier manifestations such as the Farmers' Alliance, the People's Party, the Non-Partisan League, the IWW, certain unions, and various infusions of immigrant liberalism such as the free-thinking Forty-Eighters.[75] Their legacy was grass-roots democratic expression, a spirit of egalitarianism and individualism-neighborliness that seemed at times at odds with the demand for revolutionary change.

The Depression spawned new social realities and responses. A new spirit of social protest required new forms of cultural expression. The Communist party's cultural apparatus clasped the midwestern radicals to its bosom for a while, gave them space in its magazines, and provided them forums like the John Reed clubs in St. Louis and Chicago. The party seemed to be doing something worthy—sponsoring magazines, lectures, clubs, organizing the unemployed, defending the rights of blacks. The pragmatic midwesterners were impressed by actual results. Publication in radical journals often led to access to major publications, in certain cases, to a book contract. Publishers like Alfred Knopf and Pascal Covici were likely to read the little magazines, both conservative and radical, scouting new writers.

The midwestern literary radicals of Conroy's generation found their subjects in the social-political upheaval that was beginning to spread like a prairie grass fire. Their literary response followed in part in the tradition of midwestern forbears—Hamlin Garland, Herbert Quick, Ruth Suckow, Sherwood Anderson—who revealed the essential dignity and value of "ordinary people," confronted with tumultuous social and economic realities. Ray Billington makes this point: "During the last decades of the 19th century, when the industrialization process was at its height, scores of Midwestern writers protested vehemently against a civilization which rewarded farm toil with debt and factory labor with misery."[76] *New Masses,* under Gold's editorship, was one of the catalysts of a chemical reaction in which the reagents—Lewis, Conroy, Kalar, Corey, Le Sueur, Josephine Herbst, Edward Dahlberg, and others—formed new compounds uniquely midwestern. Less well known (or documented) is the role of editors like Whitaker, Hagglund, Haldeman-Julius, Macleod, Conroy, and a dozen others in midwestern small towns who joined them in catalyzing the turbulent reaction.

* * *

Several days before the new year of 1929, Fred Harrison tied bottles of home-brewed beer to a long rope and lowered them into a well near the Conroys' home on Byrne Road, planning to retrieve them intact to celebrate New Year's Day. Donning his long woolen underwear, Fred descended into the well to recover the chilled bottles. The celebrants gathered eagerly at the wellhead, anticipating the arrival of the beer. The new year began with great fits of laughter when Fred emerged, crestfallen, holding the necks of bottles that had been smashed on the bottom in lowering. No one present would forget that day or the new year.[77]

The bull market continued into the early months of 1929. Willys-Overland's payroll reached twenty-eight thousand employees in March. Most workers had purchased a car and many were paying installments on cheaply constructed homes in subdivisions, as the shoe factory workers had done in Hannibal. The auto worker helped bring about the automobile revolution in the 1920s, which would ultimately affect most people's lives more than any political revolution envisioned by radical poets. Unions remained embattled; labor conflicts were soon forgotten except for the bitterness left behind among the participants. But the automobile remained a permanent feature of the American landscape and a focal point of people's lives. Workers were able to live in suburbs like "Rosewood Manor" and commute to the Overland plant on South

Cove. Eventually suburbs absorbed Byrne Road and spread two miles beyond. The suburbs, like the cars, wrought enormous changes in the way people lived. A taste of autonomous mobility and suburban spaciousness made the ensuing years all the more difficult for the millions who lost their jobs, their homes, and their cars. No longer an instrument of convenience, the car became a instrument of survival.

Warning signs of imminent economic chaos abounded in 1928–29, but most of the Overland workers were too preoccupied with holding on to what they had to pay attention. "Men everywhere! 'NO HELP WANTED' is all you can see around the factories. Men on the street corners. Men at the factory gates. They turned the hose on 30,000 of them at Ford's in Detroit the other day."[78] Most auto workers had experienced seasonal layoffs, living precariously on the edge of repossession and hunger. Their fear of unemployment caused greater desperation among those, like the southern textile workers, who had faced hard times and were making the best of what little was left them now.

Strikes in Elizabethton, Tennessee, and Gastonia, North Carolina, in March and April of 1929 were bloody preludes to the great wave of labor activism of the 1930s. The 1930s would see terrible labor strife and great victories, radical social legislation, and a change of heart toward the common worker evident in artistic work—Aaron Copland's music, John Steinbeck's novels, John Ford's films. Early literary harbingers were the flood of expression in the wake of the Sacco-Vanzetti executions, the Gastonia strike novels, the new radical magazines, and the Rebel Poets. Auto workers seemed passive in the face of signs promising trouble, like the nemesis of over-production. "The acquisition of money was the main objective of life," Irving Bernstein writes, "and people were measured by the externals money bought—where they lived, the make of the car they drove. In the shops, workers were more concerned with maximizing income than with learning skills or gaining leisure by shorter hours."[79] A menacing calm lay above the factory haze, a gathering storm. Millions of people would soon be driven from their homes, unprotected before the raging elements.

At the keys of his battered typewriter during proletarian nights on Byrne Road, Conroy began to give testimony of the growing number of "disinherited." To many of the radicals, Jack was their "great stimulator," writing them encouraging letters, suggesting their names to editors, serving as a clearinghouse. Kalar remembered him as "a big bastard with an Irish mug and a wife and genuinely generous and with lots of energy. . . . It was Conroy who pulled me out of my funky hole after I had sworn solemnly never again to write."[80] Gold presented a generalized portrait of worker-writers like Jack undertaking the challenging

task of writing from within the experience of the disinherited, threatened themselves by unemployment and dispossession. In his call "Go
Left, Young Writers!" published in the January 1929 *New Masses*, Gold
called for "a knowledge of working-class life in America gained from
contacts, and a hard precise philosophy of 1929 based on economics,
not verbalisms." The worker-writer, he intimated, would play a key role
in the coming revolution. "A new writer has been appearing," he offered,

> a wild youth of about twenty-two, the son of working-class par-
> ents, who himself works in the lumber camps, coal mines, steel
> mills, harvest fields and mountain camps of America. He is sensi-
> tive and impatient. He writes in jets of exasperated feeling and
> has not time to polish his work. He is violent and sentimental by
> turns. He lacks self-confidence but writes because he must—and
> because he has a real talent. He is a Red but has few theories. It
> is all instinct with him. His writing is no conscious straining af-
> ter proletarian art, but the natural flower of his environment. . . . A
> Jack London or a Walt Whitman will come of this new crop of
> young workers who write in the *New Masses*.[81]

Few rhetoricians on the left could match the vitality of Gold's horta-
tory writing, despite its obvious hyperbole and occasional bathos. His
attack on Thornton Wilder, for instance, animated a wild letter exchange for months in the *New Republic*.

Gold's rhetoric tickled the imaginations of midwestern radicals, who
were generally cool toward theoretical disquisitions such as appeared in
New Masses' editorials and essays next to reports by Kalar and Lewis
on skid rows and Falkowski on his experiences as a miner in Pennsylvania and Germany. Kalar expressed his impatience with theory in a
series of letters to the editors in the fall of 1929: "the *New Masses* is
publishing far too many manifestoes on the desirability and significance
of proletarian art—thus dissipating energies and space which probably
could have been more profitably used in actually *creating* proletarian art,
or, to put it more humbly a proletarian mirroring of life. . . . What I
would like to see is a *New Masses* that would be read by lumberjacks,
hoboes, miners, clerks, sectionhands, machinists, harvesthands, wait-
ers—the people who should count more to us than paid scribblers."[82]
Without suggesting influence it is arguable that the midwestern radicals took a Deweyean approach to the uses of theory in art, for instance,
as expressed in *Art as Experience* (1934), in which Dewey denies a distinction between aesthetic and other experiences of heightened vitality, and in the pragmatic claim that intellect is not separate from its social context.

*　*　*

Jack was carrying the main editorial and secretarial burden of the Rebel Poets by the spring of 1929 while the Cheyneys were occupied with *Contemporary Verse*, their "Bureau of Criticism," and newborn twins.[83] There were signs that Ralph Cheyney was feeling uncomfortable in the company of the leftward-turning rebels whom Jack enlisted.[84] Yet he was very excited about the forthcoming *Unrest* and gave Jack full credit for expanding the Rebel Poets' mailing list.[85] "Conroy's the boy to keep track of memberships," Cheyney wrote enthusiastically to Porter, "—and the broth of a boy he is! If there were more of him in the world, it would be a better and far more interesting spot in which to pass one's time."[86] Jack had already begun soliciting submissions to the 1930 *Unrest*, negotiating with Channing-Renton on publication terms. Channing-Renton asked that Rebel Poets pay fifty English pounds for the first edition of a thousand copies to help bear the risk should sales not cover costs. The binding would be greatly improved, the publisher promised, and he would place ads at his own expense in English publications.[87] "I am determined to make a good show of 'Unrest 1930,'" Jack wrote to Emerson Price, whom he had made the Rebel Poets' business manager.

Price cranked out the monthly Rebel Poets newsletter on a leaky, blue-ink hectograph, contributing to the expenses from his slender wages as a bank clerk. Jack had learned a costly lesson in dealing with Stockwell about the importance of promotion and distribution (and careful editing). "I saw a splendid duplicating device advertised in *Popular Mechanics*," he wrote Emerson, "$36.00, on monthly terms. We'll need one of these in the book business, of course."[88] Emerson had agreed to become Channing-Renton's book distributor in the United States, promoting and selling the "Studies" series. Channing-Renton, who sent three thousand "two-coloured prospectuses" to the *New Masses* Book Service, was teaching the two Rebel Poets about the value of self-advertisement.[89] Another mentor in publishing was the old anarchist poet Jo Labadie, who printed inexpensive booklets on a hand press. Jack and Emerson drove to Bubbling Springs, near Detroit, in the summer of 1929 to pay him a visit.

Pinned to the interior walls of Labadie's house were various letters he had received. When Jack introduced himself, the anarchist quietly pointed to Jack's letters. Labadie possessed an extraordinary collection of little magazines and letters, which later formed the basis of the Labadie Collection of Radical Literature at the University of Michigan.[90] Labadie was an extraordinary fellow in the eyes of the two Rebel Poets, a model for struggling radical publishers. His example was quite simple in theory but seldom realized: it required a printer and an editor who would work for virtually nothing, sustained by goodwill and conviction. Jack's genius as an editor lay in enlisting such people's help and winning their trust.

Jack hoped to provide an alternative radical magazine, undoctrinaire, eclectic, independent. When *New Masses* rejected some of Jack's reviews and his first worker narrative, "Jackson Street: Toledo," he wrote to Emerson: "One must almost have a communistic slant before he can get in." In the same letter he noted that Walt Carmon, who had become managing editor of *New Masses*, replacing Bernard Smith, had rejected Jack's review of Harry Crosby's poems, "because it seemed to admire the Paris expatriates. He [Carmon] is orthodox when it comes to form, while Mike Gold leans to the modernistic forms. Between the two, however, Carmon is much the better editor."[91]

The rejection of "Jackson Street: Toledo" was ironic since Jack seemed to have Gold's sketches, such as appeared in *120 Million*, in mind when he penned his portrayal of Toledo's soapbox corner. Jack admired Gold's vigorous prose rhythms, vivid scenes of street life, and colorful idioms.[92] "Jackson Street: Toledo" appeared in the *Earth-Pamantul*, whose claim to be "The Only Publication in the Roumanian and English Language on the Planet" was surely indisputable. Published in east Chicago by a Rumanian-American named Theodore Sitea, the *Earth-Pamantul* attracted a number of worker-writers and Rebel Poet contributors, including John Rogers, H. H. Lewis, Hugh Hanley (a.k.a. Emerson Price), Henry George Weiss, Cheyney, and Trent. Following like pigeons the suggestions of a fellow Rebel Poet (usually Jack), Rebel Poets would land on a new publication that was looking for contributors. Price had taken on the English-language editorship for the bilingual magazine in addition to his responsibilities as American agent for Channing-Renton and his trials with the Rebel Poets' leaking hectograph. Jack's review of Crosby's poetry was welcomed by Macleod's *Morada*, published in Albuquerque, where "Dusky Answer" had appeared.

Gold's own writing was often at odds with his exhortations to others. His East Side sketches, for instance, lacked the partisan slant familiar to *New Masses*. Behind Gold's posturing, his habit of wearing worker's clothing and chewing on a cigar, Jack sensed a genuineness, a *Menschlichkeit*. Gold's proposals were often cockeyed, such as his "national corps of writers." Gold had in mind Ed Falkowski, textile worker Martin Russak, H. H. Lewis, and Joe Kalar, but "there are others," he assured his readers. "Instead of having a board of contributing editors made up of those vague, rootless people known as writers, we will have a staff of industrial correspondents, whose function will be to report each month, in prose, poetry, plays and satire, what is happening in each part of industrial America."[93] This was the very antithesis of what Jack had in mind for the Rebel Poets, which was to be a loose-knit, voluntary, diverse group of writers organized into local chapters to "serve as cultural oases where radicals may congregate for discussion of revolutionary art and other activities. In this way, the otherwise isolated proletarian should be made to feel that he is not fighting alone in his assaults against the citadels of capitalism."[94] Kalar replied to Gold's proposal, citing the difficulties of writing after an exhausting day of labor in the paper mill: "ten hours spent on the job would hardly give one the enthusiasm to write about it—for ten [hours] irons out even the bitterness and hate—leaving only an arid apathy and a desire for 'escape.' . . . The casual proletarian—the floater, to whom it doesn't matter so much what he works at—and to whom, of necessity, all jobs are in his province, can probably get and report a truer picture of a steel plant than a real steelworker—in two weeks. The brutality of it, the cruelty of it, are undoubtedly more apparent to one 'fresh' than to one hardened to the grind, for the years can make even injustice seem commonplace."[95] The midwestern worker-writers grew skeptical of similar "proposals" divorced from workplace reality, emanating from Union Square radical circles. Westerner Norman Macleod's vignette of Mike Gold expresses how the midwesterners regarded "East of the Hudson" radicals vis-à-vis their grasp of actual industrial conditions.[96] In a letter to Jack, Macleod recalled "Mike Gold with cigar, spitting out of tough guy side of mouth, debating with Heywood Broun, who was getting drunk from a pitcher of water laced with gin placed on top of the grand piano he insisted be hoisted up to the floor of the John Reed Club meeting place on 14th street, NYC."[97]

* * *

As 1929 progressed, conditions steadily worsened for Jack and his workmates at Willys-Overland. There was now a third Conroy child, Jack, Junior, born on 18 June. The doctor was having financial problems and charged Jack twenty-five dollars; Margaret Jean and Tom had cost only fifteen. Pressed to bring home a higher wage, Jack told Fred to turn in his (Jack's) timecard at Overland, for he intended to sign on at the Ford plant in Detroit, an act that curiously resembled his father's decision to become a shot-firer. Ford had incorporated efficiency methods in its assembly line. Efficiency experts measured the motions of workers with a stopwatch, looking for wasted time or motion. Jack knew speedup methods at the Widman body plant several years earlier. A new component was the terrible monotony. In the paint department at Overland, Jack could daydream; he felt nothing but numbness at the drill press in the Ford plant. He was robotized. "When the shift is over," wrote a contemporary labor historian, "the workers tumble half-dead with fatigue into buses, trolleys, or their own cars, mainly secondhand. Some acquire nervous twitchings popularly called 'the shakes.' They get home 'too tired to do anything but eat and go to bed.'"[98] Jack satirized Ford's efficiency methods in an industrial folktale written some ten years later:

> When Highpockets first came into the mill room, he was walking like a man stepping over cornstalks. We knew he was a hillbilly from way back at the forks of the crick. Them guys raised on punkins and yaller crick water is anxious to work and get ahead; a jitney looks as big as a grindstone to them.
>
> The time-study man had made it hard enough on us before Highpockets come, but afterwards—oh, mama!—afterwards, boys, it was hell on wheels. The time-study man, that mother-robbin' creeper that watches you from behind dolly trucks and stock boxes, he's always trying to figger a way to get more work out of you at the same pay. He'll even ask you if they ain't some way you could do a little more than you are. He never expects you should say yes, and that's why it almost knocked him off the Christmas tree when Highpockets told him he reckoned he could do a sight more than he was. . . .[99]

An extended hyperbole (and metonymy), the tale ends with Highpockets employing all his limbs to oblige the time-motion expert, who continues to load tasks on him. "Highpockets" caricatures scientific management, the robotization of the assembly-line worker. A folktale subverts technological practice through the playfulness of language.[100] "I flared up and quit the job over some sarcasm of the boss," Jack wrote in "Bull Market," "but I found that I had not escaped by quitting. Other factories had the same conveyors, the same scientific methods for extracting the last ounce of energy. The same neon tubes pulsing with blue fire and the same automatons toiling frantically beneath the ghastly rays that etched dark shadows under their eyes and blackened their lips to resemble those of a cadaver."[101] After several days in Detroit, Jack decided that he preferred to chance layoffs from the Willys-Overland paint department than to be a robot on Ford's assembly line.

With heavy heart Jack made his way to the interurban station to return empty-handed to his family in Toledo. He worried that since he had resigned Overland might not hire him back. At the station was Fred, who had come up from Toledo after work. Together they rode back home, Fred teasing Jack for acting so impulsively. Jack, however, would not be teased out of his dispirited frame of mind. Finally, as they approached Toledo, Fred confessed that he had not turned in Jack's card as instructed. Sensing that Jack might regret his impulse, Fred had reported to Overland that Jack was sick. Jack had been convinced that he might have to return to the filthy rubber-heel plant in Hannibal, or perhaps face standing in job lines. Now Overland seemed like a good job.[102]

Twice now Jack had struck out in Detroit auto factories. Worse even than in Toledo, Detroit workers were submerged in conditions of want and insecurity, preoccupied with material needs.[103] Police patrolled Grand Circus Park, forcing the unemployed to keep moving and arresting those who dared talk while standing. Many of the auto workers were in debt, gambling that they would remain employed. A Brookings Institution study, *America's Capacity to Consume* (1934), revealed that in 1929, 78 percent of the population had family incomes of less than $3,000; 40 percent less than $1,500. Still the big auto manufacturers continued to advertise for workers; few, however, were actually hiring. Robert Cruden describes in *Conveyor* (1935) the terrible competition in which the auto companies were "swept into the struggle for control of the automobile markets of the world. Higher production, lower cost, reduced prices—the orders from headquarters flashed through to the factories, to the superintendent, to the foremen, to the straw-bosses, to the workers."[104] Cruden, who wrote under the pen name James Steele, was working in Ford's River Rouge plant at the time of Jack's "impulsive" employment.[105] One of his early worker narratives, "No Loitering: Get Out of Production," describing conditions in the Detroit auto factories, appeared in the *Nation* in the early summer of 1929. Jack wrote Walt Carmon at *New Masses*, admiring Cruden's letter report "1930 Model: Detroit," which Carmon published. The report described the deteriorating economy and the rise of crime in the motor city.[106]

The stock market climbed to all-time highs in the summer of 1929.[107] Unemployed women turned to prostitution while wealthy Toledoans danced at the Commodore Perry Hotel. Maurice Chevalier and Claudette Colbert were playing in Ernst Lubitsch's *The Smiling Lieutenant* in the recently opened Paramount Theatre on the corner of Adams and Huron streets. The speakeasies on St. Clair Street were thriving. Hucksters and con men worked Jackson Street, where a young Harvard graduate declaimed the Communist cause to an indifferent audience of drifters, jobless workers, and the curious. "Yeah! He's a smart kind," says a huckster in Conroy's "Jackson Street: Toledo," "got a good line . . . but he won't get nowhere. He's makin' hisself enemies when he might be pullin' down big jack, with his gift. In my racket now, he could clean up."[108] The hot weather held through 3 September, the day when the great bull market, as Galbraith notes, simultaneously reached its peak and ended.[109] Within a week the first cool nights of autumn knifed through empty streets. No one had any idea what lay ahead in the hard winter to come.

8

Exiles in Their Native Land:
The Rebel Phase

Prosperity this winter is going to be enjoyed by everybody that is fortunate enough to get into the poor house.

—Will Rogers

BY THE FALL OF 1929, the auto factories had built too many cars for a slack market. The response of workers was to hunker down and hope that the inevitable layoffs would bypass them. To Jack the approaching season of layoffs, besides introducing the usual hardships, was an impediment to his literary work. "The Overland is uncertain," he wrote Emerson Price, "can't tell what they'll do next. It's useless to look for work elsewhere this time of year. This keeps my mind unsettled and I can't get much done."[1] The possibility of an extended layoff threatened the Conroys as much as it did other workers at Overland since Jack earned nothing from his writing or editorial activities. Yet there seemed to be growing interest among editors, both conservative and radical, in the experience of workers. Moreover, the growing number of Rebel Poet contacts convinced him that the organization needed its own magazine.

Gladys encouraged his literary ambitions, despite the uncertainty of the family's finances. The Conroys lived cheaply and Gladys accepted cheerfully their impecunious life; she had never really known anything else. She was a worker herself, on a "leave" to care for her small children. She would soon return to factory work. Should everything else fail, the family could always go back to her mother's farm in Moberly, where they could plant vegetables and survive. This was their security. As things evolved in the early Depression, millions of jobless people counted themselves very lucky to have as much.

Despite the hardship, the early Depression years created new possibilities for worker-intellectuals like Jack. Economic turmoil furnished opportunities for change—perhaps a change in consciousness, the midwestern radicals hoped—among the masses of jobless workers. The Piedmont revolts seemed to presage it. The Gastonia mill strike caused astonishment in 1928; but labor revolt would soon become commonplace, the midwesterners said. In the meantime, they faced a hard winter, harder than anyone had anticipated or experienced. Still the spring might fulfill their revolutionary hope. Joe Kalar was fond of quoting Zola's *Germinal*, which concludes in just such hope following the defeat of a mine strike: "a black avenging host was slowly germinating in the furrows" and "soon their germination would crack the earth asunder."[2] When April finally arrived, however, the discharged factory workers were in no mood for rebellion. Instead they dragged their ravaged belongings along the Chicago Pike, past Byrne Road, in broken-down flivvers "creaking under burdens of furniture, bedding, lares and penates, children, and even Kentucky hound dogs, their long ears flying like banners in the breeze."[3] These were not workers poised for revolutionary action but dispirited families fleeing the factory cities following closings and dispossession, exiles in their native land.

*   *   *

In August 1929, Jack made a brief trip back to "his native Missouri wilds," mulling over in his mind all the while the future of the Rebel Poets.[4] His idea was to establish autonomous local chapters, syndicating the members' work to the labor press and helping to arrange for the publication and promotion of their books. A chapter in New York was forming. Despite continuing problems with Stockwell (late shipments, split bindings), Jack was gratified with the organization's progress.

Mike Gold commended Jack on the 1929 edition of *Unrest* in a letter that Jack shared with Emerson Price. "Like Kalar he [Gold] deplored the multiplicity of lyrical and saccharine poetry. 'What are these shrinking gazelles doing in a munitions factory? Who let them in?'"[5] The Wobbly poet Covington Hall praised the Rebel Poet anthology and orders were received from as far away as New Zealand. A hectographed letter sent by Rebel Poets glowed: "No one may measure the number of spirits that can be kindled by this red flame of revolt!"[6] Ads in *New Masses* were getting results. Orders for *Unrest* arrived from New York City's Rand Store and from Gale's in Washington, D.C. Walt Carmon of *New Masses* promised to promote *Unrest* and give a boost to the Rebel Poets.[7] For the second Rebel Poets anthology, the editors chose Channing-Renton over two other English publishers, Bill Fudge and S.

Fowler-Wright. Stockwell was slow in returning the preface and type-script of the 1930 *Unrest*, which Conroy and Cheyney had foolishly sent him before deciding on a publisher. Jack and Emerson were talking about opening a radical bookstore in Columbus, but they dropped the idea when Overland began sending workers home several times a week be-fore they had punched in.

The left was fragmented into diverse radicalisms on the eve of the Great Crash. In 1919, the Socialist party had split, one faction even-tually coalescing into the Communist Party of America; the remaining faction warred incessantly with the Communists, who in turn vilified the Socialists as bourgeois opportunists. The CPA had little experience with or comprehension of indigenous radicalisms in the Midwest. Most of its early members were foreign born; meetings, according to some accounts, required a great deal of translation. After 1925, the CPA looked to the Third International for leadership. These facts alone were enough to make the CPA unattractive to most midwestern radicals. One, however, who embraced the Soviet example enthusiastically was the Missouri farmer-poet H. H. Lewis, who dedicated his first collec-tion of poems, *Red Renaissance* (1930), to the Bolsheviks: "Written by a Missouri Farmhand and Dedicated to Soviet Russia." In seeking to provide the broadest possible forum for the diverse strains of radical conviction on the left, Jack solicited Lewis's contributions to *Rebel Poets*.

Isolated on his eighty-acre farm in Missouri's boot-heel, Lewis pos-sessed the fierce sincerity of an Old Testament prophet and looked like Blake's sketches of God. His eyes stabbed at you and a wild shock of hair made him seem even taller than he was. Lewis's parents were 100 percent old-stock Americans. His lineal ancestors were charter mem-bers of the Old Bethel Baptist church in 1806, the first Protestant church west of the Mississippi. Nicknamed "Bug" by his schoolmates for his habit of becoming intensely absorbed in observing nature rath-er than joining in games, Lewis was a loner who attended high school for three years and left without a diploma. He was a great reader, sail-ing through high-school equivalency and Civil Service exams with high scores. After a cold winter as a postal clerk in Chicago, Lewis asked to be transferred to St. Louis. He saved his pay, announcing to his par-ents that he had decided to live in New Orleans and become a writer. After an unexpectedly cold winter in New Orleans (1920–21 or 1921–22), he tramped west to California where he nearly starved on Los Angeles's "stem."[8] The experience was radicalizing. Returning to the boot-heel farm of his parents, where he labored to earn his keep, Lewis wrote his first sketches and poems. Noah Whitaker, whom he had met in New Orleans, published Lewis's early writing in *Pegasus* and put him in contact with Conroy. Jack prompted Lewis to write of the hardships he had experienced tramping and submit them to *New Masses*. After Gold became editor, Lewis was named a contributing editor of *New Masses*, an honorary position that imposed no duties.

Gold admired Lewis's vigorous writing and worker's pedigree. "You certainly have the goods—vigor, slanguage, experience et al—" Gold wrote Lewis after reading his satirical poems on "aesthetes" and his narratives of life on the stem in Los Angeles. Lewis's "Sidewalks of Los Angeles" testifies graphically to the fact that homeless people were dying of hunger on the streets.[9] It was a shocking experience for the sensitive young farmboy, who "soured on life," according to his father, as a result.[10] Skid rows were seedbeds of radicalism in the 1920s, as noted earlier. A few days among society's outcasts cut deeply in the social consciousness of sensitive young midwesterners like Lewis and Kalar, who felt lonely and estranged in Seattle, Los Angeles, and Tijuana.[11]

Joe Kalar was put off by the strange behavior exhibited in Lewis's letters, mentioning his reservations in a letter to Jack: "I am glad that Lewis has carved a niche for himself in *New Masses*, he really doesn't deserve it: yet. His 'Midnight Mission' has guts but is so poorly written in parts it nearly makes me vomit. . . . But I've got a feeling that Lewis will make a greater appeal with the working stiff than either you or I or Cheyney. . . . I can understand Mike Gold's liking it: for Mike too has a subconscious suspicion that art is bunk, tho he would be the last to admit it."[12] Neither was Norman Macleod, a Rebel Poet and the editor of *Palo Verde* and the *Morada*, sure how to take Lewis. "Who and what is H. H. Lewis?" he asked Kalar. "I have had some curious letters from him."[13]

Eager to locate "proletarian" poets who would herald the coming revolution, Gold made Lewis one of his *New Masses* vanguard of writers. Gold was anxious to show that conditions in the hinterlands would produce revolutionary peasant poets, as Russia had produced Nikolai Kljuev.[14] Lewis was no "heav'n-taught ploughman" (Robert Burns) to be sure; nor would he ever fit comfortably in any Party-assigned category. Yet he was the genuine article, a worker-poet, something that could not be said about Slim Martin and other "worker-writers" whom *New Masses* had published in its early issues.[15] A ferocious satirist, easily offended, Lewis would eventually prove to be an embarrassment to the Party. Notwithstanding, his talent was sufficient to earn him a prestigious poetry prize and the admiration of William Carlos Williams.

Harold Lewis was Jefferson's agrarian yeoman gone sour. Alienated and lonely, he searched for a secular faith in a fallen world. Communism appeared to offer Lewis the promise of a better hand than the one the poor gumbo farmers had been dealt. The radical socialist-populist spirit that swept across rural southeastern Missouri around the turn of the century had virtually disappeared following World War I, emerging again in the sharecroppers' strike of the late 1930s.[16] In the late 1920s, the small boot-heel farmer was caught up in changes brought about by mechanization, falling farm prices, and debt. Lewis was tired, as he wrote, of "looking up a mule's pratt," and of the dung on his overalls. Yet he was attached to the home that his parents, and later his brother, continued to provide him in exchange for his help on the farm. When Mencken published one of his stories, his family began to believe that he was indeed a writer.

Critics on the left began to take notice of Lewis, including V. F. Calverton, editor of *Modern Quarterly*, who hailed him as a rising star of proletarian literature.[17] The *New Republic* allowed that the Missouri gumbo poet "might well be the red-starred laureate, the Joe Hill of the Communist movement."[18] William Rose Benet, in his *Saturday Review of Literature* column, on the other hand, held Lewis's earthy vigor in contempt. Jack, who admired Lewis's feisty, irreverent humor, often came to his defense, as in his reply to Benet. Lewis's verse, he wrote, is bad "for Ivory Tower aesthetes who browse undisturbed in the sedentary confines of the library, while outside millions of desperate men are starving," a defense that the midwestern radicals often made, underscoring a putative division between the Midwest and the East that was not only ideological but aesthetic.[19]

Nonetheless, the spirit of the Rebel Poets was collaborative, not based upon any consensus other than what was implicit in the organization's slogan, "Art for Humanity's Sake." Jack attempted to accommodate all socially conscious convictions and unclassifiable individuals on the left in one independent radical movement. But divisiveness on the left and the divergences of aesthetic aims were too great ultimately to fit comfortably into one scheme. Even Cheyney and Conroy, the inspiration for Rebel Poets, would eventually part ways.

* * *

All communication, Nietzsche declared, begins in duress; as an endangered animal, man needed his peers.[20] Erich Fromm and others argue that communication is a means to break the isolation endemic in modern society, especially in times of distress. Conroy's literary contacts constituted a communication network for radical writers. Rebel Poet members, eager to share news, sent the letters they received on to others in round-robin fashion. "The correspondence of some Rebel Poet,"

Walter Snow wrote Kalar, "has almost as wide circulation as our poverty-stricken magazine."[21] Books were also shared by mail, to spare the cost of purchase. The letters enabled the corresponding Rebel Poets to share their experiences and thus gain a sense of empowerment in the face of growing frustration and anger.[22]

It was tempting to feel oneself part of an epic revolt of the oppressed that would soon take place in America in which the figure of humanity would rise up against the evil god capitalism. Correspondence, the Rebel Poets' newsletters, and the little magazines were the main instruments serving this early phase in the evolution of midwestern literary radicalism. The rhetorical terms of the revolt were expressed in anthologies like Marcus Graham's *Anthology of Revolutionary Poetry* and the *Unrest* collections of rebel verse.

Growing consciousness demands symbols and language. Graham's anthology was particularly influential in the mutual aid phase. Born in Rumania of Orthodox Jewish parents, Graham immigrated at age fourteen to Philadelphia where he apprenticed first as an egg-candler, then as a garment cutter. Graham was introduced to socialism through Wayland's *Appeal to Reason*, which circulated in the cutting shop. His reading led him to anarchist publications, including Hippolyte Havel's *Revolt*. Fleeing conscription in World War I, and, as a consequence, experiencing the first of many troubles with U.S. immigration officials, Graham eventually found his way to London where in the British Museum he began to gather material for his book. Working again as a cutter in New York, he paid for the publication of his *Anthology*, which appeared in 1929, expensively bound, with a dust cover showing a red militant, arm upraised and fist clenched, and an introduction by Cheyney and Trent. The dedication was by Carl Sandburg, "I Am The People, The Mob," from his *Chicago Poems* (1916).[23] The anthology brought together rebels in a single volume of poetry, from Crabbe to Giovannitti, some four hundred poets in all, including well-known poets like Emerson and lesser-knowns such as Ralph Chaplin.

Graham was a rude and demanding individual who nonetheless commanded great respect in radical circles. H. H. Lewis recalled meeting Graham in a Los Angeles roominghouse, surrounded by a group of devoted "disciples" sitting cross-legged on the floor. His anthology was very influential among Rebel Poets, who later came to Graham's defense in the summer of 1930 when he was jailed in Yuma, Arizona, on charges of possessing seditious literature (copies of his own *Anthology*). Protests by the Marcus Graham Defense Committee thwarted the government's attempt to deport Graham to Mexico. It was a show of strength by the

Rebel Poets, who discovered that letters had a powerful influence, even if, as they maintained, democracy was corrupted by the "plutes."[24]

Conroy and Cheyney hoped that their second *Unrest* collection would meet the standard Graham had set in his anthology, and to that end they were selecting mainly poems that had been published during 1929 and reviewed by a Rebel Poets' committee. Still clinging to the ideal that such a collection could appeal broadly to a coalition of all radicalisms—"communists, anarchists, religious modernists, socialists, birth control advocates, or any of the many sects of radicalism and liberalism"—the two editors decided to dedicate their second *Unrest* to Upton Sinclair. "He is the only individual who is admired by all liberal and radical factions," Conroy proffered.[25] Jack held tenaciously to his purpose that Rebel Poets should remain nonpartisan, singling out Harry Crosby as an example whose credentials for inclusion in *Unrest 1929* (and the subsequent collection) were simply that he "despised the sordid life of polite society."[26] Crosby was dead, the victim of a macabre death pact from which his wife, Caresse, ultimately withdrew. "Too aristocratic to embrace a proletarian ideology and too fundamentally a lover of truth to enjoy a world of lies," Norman Macleod wrote in the *Morada*, "he found the only way out."[27] Harry Crosby, Conroy hoped, would provide a bridge from the Rebel Poets to expatriate and avant-garde writers, attracting them to the organization. Jack was naively certain that the spirit of revolt against capitalism would infuse all thinking people's consciousness regardless of class, education, or artistic creed.

Thinking people sometimes had other axes to grind, Jack discovered. A feud erupted between Cheyney and his former editor of *Contemporary Verse*, Benjamin Musser. Without warning to his coeditors, Cheyney and Trent, Musser delivered the control of the magazine (which he owned) to his friend Ernest Hartsock, editor of *Bozart* and founder of Bozart Press, whose name was "a daring retort to the redoubtable H. L. Mencken, who in the *Mercury* had delivered a playful but pointed thrust at the literary South by calling it the 'Sahara of Bozart.'"[28] The gift, and thus the removal of the Cheyneys from the magazine, occasioned bitter feeling. Musser had created a slight stir in a *Poetry World* article by suggesting that it "is nearly impossible for a woman to be a great poet."[29] Moreover, his faith in the power of poetry to incite an insurrection was a great deal less secure than was Conroy's or the Cheyneys'. He made this clear in an article appearing in the December issue of *Poetry World*, to the consternation of Emerson Price, who published a blistering rejoinder on his inky hectograph. There was simply no room in Rebel Poets, Price said, for such "sad young men." Indeed,

Musser, in a letter to Porter, disclosed his reservations concerning the inevitability of revolution: "I see no glorious dawn just ahead of us, no bright tomorrow for the worker and the downtrodden. . . ."[30] The first crack had appeared in the scaffolding that was to serve for the erection of a full-scale organization complete with its own magazine.

There was some truth to Musser's contentions that Cheyney and Trent relaxed their standards when patrons submitted their poems for publication. Jack sensed this and yet knew that without "Rowlfandloozie," Rebel Poets would collapse.[31] A poet named Louise Burton Laidlaw, who happened to possess a million dollars, appeared in the 1929 volume of *Unrest*, to Conroy's chagrin; he marked her, among several other contributors, for exclusion from the subsequent *Unrest*, given that "the spark of revolt in them was extremely faint."[32] It appeared that Rebel Poet Louis Ginsberg, father of Allen Ginsberg, might have relaxed his standards also in judging Laidlaw in his review of *Unrest*. He had been a guest at a party thrown by the Laidlaws, according to *Poetry World*.[33] Conroy wished to tighten his own standards of acceptability in the 1930 edition of *Unrest*, in excluding not only weak imitators of English Lake Poets but also the "Musser school of radicals." The public, he wrote Cheyney, wants "strong red meat. Apostrophes to 'harlots and hunted' and rhapsodies over poets' boundless souls can be found in almost any anthology."[34]

The two Rebel Poet founders were pleased at the sales of the 1929 edition of *Unrest* despite the split bindings and Stockwell's "criminally slow" filling of orders.[35] Rebel Poet membership now cost $2.50 for those who could not afford the "active membership" fee.[36] Cheyney was angry that Mike Gold had not put either *Unrest* editor on the *New Masses* editorial board, a courtesy among little-magazine editors who exchanged issues and ads. A succession of irritations such as this gradually alienated Cheyney from the radical movement represented by Gold and, to Cheyney's growing dismay, Conroy.

* * *

Autumn of 1929 brought the usual layoffs at Overland. Jack sensed deeper trouble than usual. I. A. Miller, president of Willys-Overland, warned the auto companies against "the evils of overproduction" following a directors' meeting in October.[37] By late October, stocks were being dumped. Five days after Black Thursday, 24 October, Overland stock had plunged twenty-eight points to six. Yet many business leaders in Toledo were still optimistic, not ready to concede that the great Hoover bull market had finally gone bust. Some were predicting the end of the recession by spring.[38] By November, however, the Overland payroll was down from 28,000 of the previous March to 4,000. Temperatures dipped in mid-November while unemployed workers rose before dawn to stand in line at Overland like men separated from their regiment forming up out of habit. Announcements that some workers would be hired back fueled their hope. "The Overland is not doing anything," Jack reported to Emerson. "One day's work in two weeks. It's hell, and if you've never been through it you can't begin to appreciate it."[39] In December, Jazzbo's foreman came down to the enamel department and said that the entire Overland plant would close until late in January. Jack was unable to sleep at night wondering what would become of his family. "You can't know the dumb despair that sweeps over me," he wrote Price, "when I encounter the very real and important prospect of my children and wife without food. . . . She hasn't lived the vagabond life that I have . . . desperate men are walking the pavement."[40] Jack picked up his paycheck one day convinced that it was his last day of work. Instead the foreman transferred him to another department, one of four workers out of several thousand who were to be kept on. "I suppose I should be thankful, but such incidents keep me . . . in an eternal hesitation waltz, vacillating between life and death. . . ."

The optimism of Toledo's Chamber of Commerce did not square in Jack's eyes with what he saw actually happening on the streets. "I saw a poor bastard with two flat tires," Jack described to Price, "a decrepit car that looked as though another mile could not be coaxed out of it, and a wife and three children, ill-clad and blue with the cold, vainly attempting to repair two inner bulges. . . . He was a thousand miles from home, absolutely broke . . . and all he wanted was a chance to work."[41] Jack remained with a skeleton work crew in the plant one or two days a week. There were approximately 75,000 employable male wage-earners of Toledo's total population of about 320,000. Of these, 30,000— some 40 percent—were out of work by January 1930. More than the usual winter slump, this amounted to devastation. The Overland plant, a city within a city, with thirteen miles of railroad, eleven miles of freight docks, and large structures of concrete and glass windows, felt like a ghost town to one reporter who visited there.[42]

In this hard winter of 1929–30, Jack sensed the fear of starvation all about him in the stricken city. "Christmas," he told Price, "finds the Conroy fortunes at the lowest ebb ever. . . ." Yet Jack was still drawing a few dollars' pay. At the Hotel Commodore Perry the wealthy again gathered to celebrate the New Year. Down the street from the hotel was a soup kitchen provided by Addison Q. Thatcher in an abandoned warehouse. Ad Thatcher was one of Toledo's most colorful characters. A former marine engineer turned boxing promoter, he had brought Willard and Dempsey to town for an exhibition match. Ad's surplus food kitchen used stale bread from bakeries and wilting vegetables from grocery suppliers to feed the poor. Elected mayor in 1932, he was defeated two years later.

The *Toledo Blade* began to feature stories of misfortune, tales of "victims of cruel fate," such as one worker who, desperate to feed his family, tramped the streets for work, turned to begging, then "died of hunger and weariness on a downtown corner Thursday as the crowds went to lunch."[43] In Cleveland the unemployed rioted in front of city hall demanding "work or food," until they were driven away by police using clubs and threatening them with freezing water from fire trucks. Workers were starting to flee the city as though it were some pestilence-ridden place. Down the Chicago Pike they came, in their cars, some on foot pulling coaster wagons loaded with suitcases. The auto workers had lost their nerve and were heading home, trusting that their relatives would take them in. "I saw a middle-aged man," Jack wrote in "Hard Winter," "seemingly petrified by the side of the highway. He stood like a statue, one arm extended toward the west. His face was set and hopeless like a stone mask. Begging a ride, he did so proudly; no energetic thumbing and appealing. A battered suitcase rested between his legs. Nobody heeded him. The cars whizzed along the grey concrete and the winter dusk settled down."[44] A smart "speedster" with youths going home from college slowed to take the hitchhiker. "Are you tired of walking?" the boys inquired of the old man. To his eager affirmative reply they responded "Then run a while!" and roared off with peals of laughter.

"The air is full of nervous expectation, for every worker knows his time card may be numbered," Jack wrote in *New Masses*. "Southern Ishmaels who sought the bright gold of the rainbow's end, pack their suitcases and clear out of town."[45] Many auto workers had cars and could migrate to other jobs or find refuge among relatives over winter. They were mobile yet powerless. The cheap subdivisions with their unpainted boxlike homes were abandoned, the half-finished brick columns marking the entrance to "Sunset Meadows" a pathetic monument to their aspirations.

Two cultures remained in conflict in the 1920s, as Warren Susman argues: "an older Puritan-republican, producer-capitalist culture based on a vision of limits and restraint, sacrifice and savings, and a newer culture based on the possibilities of abundance and the virtues of fulfillment and gratification, which emerged in the late nineteenth century."[46] In the older culture, workers had sought to reshape their free time within the distinctive working-class institutions of "the extended home, the lodge or fraternal order, and the saloon." A distinctive, autonomous working-class culture existed, according to John Alt, "which was valuable for the celebration and enjoyment of life on the one hand (however minimal this was in fact), and the class struggle on the other."[47] Raised in the ethic of the older work culture, Jack felt himself an alien in the newer consumer-oriented workers' world and seemed unable to adapt to its values. Ford became the symbol of this new workers' world; the auto industry created the first large-scale proletariat in America. "The promise of Fordism," James R. Green writes, "was to reward high levels of production with new kinds of consumption for the masses."[48] Jack observed this conflict and began to make it an important subject of his writing. He rued the manipulative features of mass culture without sharing the fear of certain critics that the bad would drive out the good.[49] Working-class culture had never been "pure" of popular and commercial influences.

Within the "new culture" of commodity relations and consumer spending, Jack and other midwestern radicals saw the possibility of creating a new workers' culture that would restore community and solidarity. New modes of literary and cultural production were called for. Such a project required artists and editors on the margins who without rejecting entirely what Stanley Aronowitz calls the "norms of dominant consensus" would offer an alternative.[50] The dispossessed worker might not be able to participate in avant-garde culture, or indeed in mass culture, but in 1930 as Botkin was publishing his first *Folk-Say*, Zora Neale Hurston was gathering folk material on Polk County lumber and turpentine camp workers, and Constance Rourke was completing her study of American humor, there was hope that the experience of the migratory workers, the dispossessed, the assembly line stiffs, mill workers, and farmhands might serve to reintegrate culture into everyday life. This would require finding what Simone Weil called "modes of transcription suitable for transmitting culture to the people."[51]

Robert Penn Warren, in his introduction to the 1963 edition of Elizabeth Madox Roberts's *The Time of Man*, first published in 1926, notes that Roberts's novel, initially received with acclaim, fell out of fashion in the ensuing decade. *The Time of Man* "presents Ellen Chesser not in active protest against the deprivation and alienation of the life of the sharecropper, but in the process of coming to terms, in a personal sense, with the tragic aspect of life."[52] "The agenda of the 1930s," Warren continues, "carried many items bearing an urgent need to change the social and economic environment but none bearing on the need to explore the soul's relation to fate. Any literary work that was concerned with an inward victory was, in certain influential quarters, taken as subtle propaganda against any effort directed toward outward victory. It was as though one had to choose between the 'inner' and the 'outer.'" Rather than explore the inner landscape of the soul, Warren contends, "the tendency was to accept the graph, the statistic, the report of a commission, the mystique of 'collectivism,' as the final reality."[53] In joining the inner with the outer in a voyage that is both metaphysical and concrete, exploring the soul's relation to fate and the ugliness and misery of human existence, Roberts's novel might have served as a blueprint for the 1930s. Such was Warren's conclusion in retrospect.

For the worker-writers, however, physical deprivation and a driving sense of urgency made such a balance difficult to achieve, quite apart from the question whether they were striving for it. In some instances, cultural agendas were set for them; in others, the writers were simply not up to the task, through lack of time, resources, or literary sophistication. At the American Writers' Congress in May 1935, Jack attempted to explain the obstacles facing the worker-writer. "Everything is confusing," he concluded, "and we have so little in the way of precedent or example, we are hampered by cultural deficiencies, we are harried by the fear of unemployment when working and by bodily and mental fatigue. But we have something vital and new to communicate. Our first duty is to attempt an interpretation of those aspects of American life important to the masses, and the next duty is to communicate this material as simply and clearly as we are able to the largest body of readers we can command."[54]

The terms of the cultural transcription Conroy contemplated were to be essentially social, occurring not within the solitude of the individual soul but through communication with others, something akin to Dewey's notion of "conjoint communicated experience."[55] The project Jack set for himself in the midst of human suffering during the hard winter of 1929–30 was to reconstruct through writing a polyphonic community of workers' voices, now fragmented and disjoined.[56] Such a project grew from within the workers' world he knew in which the voices he overheard existed dialogically on the same level as his own. This was not the material of best-sellers, he discovered. To look for metaphysical connections, "the soul's relation to fate," in the firing of workers from their jobs would be a philosophical exercise in essentialist thinking. Unemployment is not some unalterable "human condition." There exists in collective action the power to resist, to alter human conditions. The inner victory portrayed in Conroy's *The Disinherited* occurs in the awakening consciousness of the protagonist, in conflict with fear, ignorance, prejudice, self-delusion. The worker-writer's task, as Jack perceived it, was to be a witness to his time, and to record the inner *and* outer struggles.

What he saw were hungry, desperate people with no place to turn. "Their tragic patience, their incessant betrayal and exploitation by the predatory powers," Jack wrote Kenneth Porter, "all sweep me with a poignant emotion. . . .

> I hope you were reared in happier surroundings than those I have always known. My father was killed when I was ten. The mine owners insisted upon two men firing all the shots in the mine, and he was blown to bits trying to make the rounds. My fourteen year old brother quit school and struggled to support a family of seven. A freight train ran him down in the dark as he came wearily home from work one night. I saw my mother work her life away to keep her brood together. I half educated myself by performing menial tasks; and since then I have known the life of a bo, a migratory worker, a bindlestiff. Now all of this usually transforms a man into a cynic, but it made me so only in the case of those who seem to me to be enemies of the working class. . . . The cause of the laborers is my religion, and it is holy to me. I can imagine the horror of the Russian peasants when the Soviets ruthlessly tear down the sacred ikons.[57]

Jack was skeptical of the Communists, their "aloof attitude and their continually 'throwing' somebody out for insubordination." Yet the Party was organizing workers in Detroit and Toledo. When the police intervened violently against the demonstrating workers in Detroit, Jack and many others moved toward the Communist camp. Such were the passions of the time that Jack, an independent-minded radical who felt spiritually bound to the Wobblies, was moved to confide in Emerson Price: "I now feel that I am more in accord with the communists than any other group. I believe the police brutality in these demonstrations will drive thousands into the Communist Party."[58]

Jack and Fred lingered in Toledo during the late winter and early spring of 1930 in the belief that once fear and want had reduced the number of job-seekers they would be able to stay on should Overland resume production. The skeleton crew to which Jack belonged was now working only one day a week. At Farmer Zack's they picked carrots from the frozen ground until their fingers were stiff and useless.

Hard times increased the Rebel Poets membership list. Ben Hagglund, editor of *Northern Light*—now called *Western Poetry*—joined, giving the Rebels a promotional boost in the January issue of his little magazine. Hagglund was the kind of self-sacrificing printer Jack needed for a Rebel Poets magazine, despite Ben's seasonal caesuras in the spring when he joined an itinerant threshing crew in Clermont, Iowa, taking him away from Holt, Minnesota, and "Old Ironsides," his antiquated press. With his earnings Hagglund hoped to make "a *real* radical out of *Western Poetry* . . . and to hell with art!"[59] Another new member was Raymond Kresensky, a Presbyterian minister in Algona, Iowa, who had published in *New Masses* as well as in Christian publications. A young artist named John C. Rogers, who had appeared in *Earth-Pamantul* along with Jack, Kalar, and Lewis, sent Conroy a letter with hand-drawn cartoons in the margins, illustrating himself at work as a "tree surgeon." No one embodied the spirit of the Rebel Poets (or the *Anvil*) better than Jack Rogers, Conroy said later.[60]

Cheyney lost his job in Chicago, forcing Lucia and Ralph to move back with his parents in Philadelphia. As a consequence, Jack was burdened with the main editorial work, including the correspondence, which had grown rapidly since plans for *Unrest 1930* were announced. Jack and Emerson were using Channing-Renton's letterhead, "'Studies' Publications," as his American representatives. Emerson helped Jack with the secretarial work involved in putting together the new *Unrest* collection of Rebel Poetry, paying some of the expense from his bank clerk's job. Jack continued to defend the Cheyneys against Musser's insinuations that they truckled to wealthy "poetesses."[61] Cheyney's egotism, on the other hand, was wearing on Jack. Ralph liked to "blow his own horn" in the Rebel Poet *Newsletter* and was upset when his name was not mentioned in reviews.[62] An additional burden continued to be the English publisher, Stockwell, who had frustrated sales of *Unrest 1929* by delaying shipments. Prospects looked bright, nonetheless, for the second anthology.

In April, Louis Lozowick, the gifted *New Masses* artist, sent Jack a jacket design for *Unrest 1930* at no cost. Rebel Poets was making significant gains in cutting across geographical and ideological demarcations. A number of Rebel Poets, for instance, were contributing editors of *New Masses* and other radical publications of the left. It appeared that Kenneth Porter, with Jack's urging, might start a Rebel Poet chapter in Cambridge, Massachusetts. The organization was gaining momentum, increasing the prospects for the publication of a Rebel Poet magazine. Jack and Emerson sent out invitations to join. The text read: "If you are tired of literary societies full of 'stuffed shirts and tea-drinking friends of the sky-lark' and if you want to help serve the labor, feminist, anti-imperialist, and anti-militarist movements, you belong among the Rebel Poets—and the Rebel Poets need you."[63] The words in quotation were Mike Gold's but the appeal to a broad spectrum of radical interests reflected entirely the idealism of the Rebel Poets in 1930.

The house on Byrne Road was to be refurbished and sold, the landlord announced to the Conroys one day in late winter. The family moved to a "light housekeeping room" on Wayne Avenue, described in "Hard Winter": "Cribbed, cabined and confined in a diminutive 'living room' and a microscopic kitchenette, the walls press on their [occupants'] minds. Decaying relics of a pristine gentility, the rooming houses are unsanitary, dark, and fetid. When you stumble up the sudden stairs and snap on an unshaded bulb, a million cockroaches scamper for the shelter of a dank and rusty sink. The wall paper is damp and bilious with liver spots. The children have no place to play."[64] The Conroys had reached a deadend. In desperation, Jack and Fred found jobs as "stack monkeys" in a sugar-beet warehouse near Toledo, loading beet pulp into railroad cars for cattle feed. "This job," Jack wrote, "had gathered the disinherited from many a closed and crippled factory: and the cruel competition for bare existence made rats of them."[65]

Six feet tall, weighing two hundred pounds, Jack could take the heavy work. But the other stack monkeys made life hell for the newcomers, raising the conveyor so that the 150-pound sacks came crashing down on their shoulders. They were ready to quit after about a month; when Fred was knocked off a stack one day, that did it. It was June; they had made it through the hard winter. There was money enough to buy gas. In a two-car caravan, the Conroys and Harrisons headed back to Missouri. They had held on longer than the "Kentucky hillbillies," but the end effect was the same: no job, no prospect of a job, but at least a "home" to go back to where they could plant a garden and decide what to do next.

* * *

In 1930, unemployment rose from 2,500,000 to 4,000,000; by 1933, it would reach 12,000,000 (in round figures).[66] People were being evicted from their homes for failing to pay rent and more were subsisting on near-starvation diets.[67] The plant closings and uprooting of families created a new social frontier. Failure impelled people to leave their homes and move on, not because of new opportunities elsewhere but to survive. For some this meant returning to childhood family homes; for others, it meant keeping in motion, as Warren Huddlestone, a midwestern literary radical, discovered.

Huddlestone was born in Kokomo, Indiana, a factory town where two auto companies, Haines Automobile and Apperson Automobile, had gone under before the Great Crash. Huddlestone, like many young workers in Kokomo, grew up certain they would never find jobs. Living at home Warren had time on his hands, which he spent in the Kokomo library. Reading Sherwood Anderson's "I'm a Fool" convinced him that he too could become a writer if an "ordinary person" like Anderson was able to. Determined to make a virtue of adversity, he tramped around the country early in the Depression, gathering experiences he hoped would furnish material for his writing.

Tramping for the sake of experience seemed a great luxury when several years later, in 1931, his father lost his job as a carpenter and could no longer keep his son at home. Warren was given five dollars and sent off to make his way in the world. On the road were other job-seekers aimlessly drifting. The drifters waited at both ends of towns for rides, without fixed destination. Towns had no funds to feed them. Police in small towns kept the drifters moving, escorting them to the city limits with instructions to keep going. Life on the road forced Warren to concentrate on the essentials: a meal, a place to sleep, staying clean. The experience was like living in a tunnel, he recalled: nothing on either side, only ahead and behind. Huddlestone slept in courthouse basements and in the open, washing himself in service stations when permitted. The drifters seldom traveled together or talked to one another. When he later wrote of this time there was no landscape in his description and little consciousness of others.[68]

The new "social frontier" opened by the early Depression is curiously predicted in Frederick Jackson Turner's famous frontier thesis according to which the closing of the western frontier posed unanswered challenges to society in dealing with a new social world of cities and capitalist finance.[69] Turner's western frontiersman with his "coarseness and strength," his "buoyancy and exuberance," had by 1930 become a defeated, quiescent drifter, like Warren Huddlestone, Tom Kromer, and countless other jobless men.[70]

If the early Depression created the conditions of a new social frontier, characterized more by "savagery" than "promise," then it also forced many midwestern radicals to stay at home, one effect of which was to focus their subject matter.[71] If you had a home to go to, you dug in there. Travel was scarcely an option. Despite the fact that they lived in the same state, H. H. Lewis and Conroy didn't meet until 1936. Letter writing continued to connect people widely separated.

The enforced "idleness" of the Depression produced writers and provided them with subjects drawn from their experiences and immediate surroundings. Self-expression "could not be downed," Dale Kramer said of the early Depression era, "even if we had to do our revolting at home, more often than not right on Main Street itself." Editor of *Hinterland,* published in Cedar Rapids, Iowa, beginning in 1934, Kramer contributed substantially to helping young writers, many of them midwestern literary radicals, get their work into print.[72] Instances of social inequity offended the midwestern radicals—hungry people, ostentatious wealth, special privilege—as their radical forebears had protested "vehemently against a civilization which rewarded farm toil with debt and factory labor with misery."[73] Early signs of a new spirit of revolt appeared in the midlands: the Cow War in Iowa, the nutpickers' strike in St. Louis, the penny auctions.

The new spirit of revolt bore the characteristic marks of an older midwestern literary radical tradition: an intimate familiarity with one's surroundings, a sensitivity toward the unyielding limitations of small-town life and the hardships imposed by change. In terms characteristically midwestern, the desire for equality and social justice remained unabated among this new generation of radicals; suspicious of ideologies and abstractions, they took a firm, pragmatic view of life. These things had not changed from the previous generation. But their subject matter, contemporary social reality, posed staggering challenges. Paralysis gripped people used to mobility and progress. The radicals were doubly marginalized: economically and as writers. Mainstream publications and channels of literary communication, for instance, were, with few exceptions, closed to them. Publishers themselves were suffering financial loses and consequently their editors were not willing to take risks on unknown writers on unpopular subjects. The midwesterners created their own channels of communication. Little magazines continued to spring up throughout the Midwest like dandelions after a spring rain. The desire to "witness" was strong. The stories often read like personal narratives. The authors felt they were creating a new culture from the bottom upward.

No one of the radicals attained the celebrity status or achieved the lasting national reputation of the expatriate writers. The early years of the Depression produced no great writer in the Midwest by the standards of the dominant culture. Reality was too overpowering somehow, the terrible social drama of dispossession and failure too consuming. Writing from the margins, but not as bystanders, since most of them were directly engaged in the experience of dispossession, the radicals touched on aspirations and concerns central to the lives of large numbers of people. Their writing testifies to the courage and resourcefulness of the "disinherited," but few of the multitudes actually read it. Their political naiveté, journalistic attachment to contemporary events, and simple, direct writing styles won them little mainstream critical approval. Their names are scarcely household words. How then shall we assess their work?

Any assessment, I believe, should take into account the political, economic, social, and cultural circumstances within which their work was created, the dominant systems of literary recognition/reputation that pose formidable obstacles to unknowns, and the climate of reception that is generally unfavorable to radical literature. Within the experience of a terrible social drama, the midwestern radicals expressed the collective anguish and suffering of dispossessed people. They focused on the "outer victory," as Robert Penn Warren says, hoping for sweeping changes in society's economic structure. Their real "victory," however, was an inner one: their struggle to write and publish on the margins of the dominant culture, their generous exchanges (the "networks" of communication), their audacity, one might say, in breaking the silence when it was maintained that "prosperity was just around the corner"—and most people, even the dispossessed, were predisposed to believe it.

* * *

Not all the midwestern literary radicals went home to survive the Depression or were driven from their homes to join the multitudes of drifters. Some had gravitated east to New York City in the 1920s, not because they were "revolting from the village"—the constraining mores and cultural limitations of small-town life in the Midwest—but simply to make literary contacts with other writers and with editors. Among these were Paul Corey and Ruth Lechlitner.

Born and raised on a farm in Shelby County, Iowa, Corey attended the University of Iowa, where campus radicals supported La Follette and discussed "the feminist revolt of the twenties."[74] During a summer job in a California lumber camp, Paul became acquainted with a worker who dressed carefully and had carefully formed opinions about solidarity and community, quite in contrast with the other lumber workers. When Corey returned to Iowa City at the end of the summer he carried with him a deep impression of this man, a Wobbly. Little wonder Wobblies incited such violent reaction, Corey mused: they posed a threat to the status quo much greater than did the downtrodden, grey masses, the so-called "proletariat."[75]

Ruth Lechlitner was a graduate student at the university, working part-time for John T. Frederick's the *Midland*. Frederick promoted midwestern regionalist writers like Ruth Suckow while steering clear of radical commitments. Paul and Ruth became friends, later marrying. Aspiring to become a writer, Corey headed for Greenwich Village with a friend. One of his odd jobs was to compile names for the Brooklyn telephone directory. Released with "a good recommendation" when the work was finished, the incident furnished the subject of a short story Corey wrote for Conroy's *Anvil* in 1933. Meanwhile, Ruth had come to New York City where she worked for Mark Van Doren of the *Nation* magazine during the time of the Sacco-Vanzetti executions.

On their slender savings, the two embarked for France, taking up residence in Bandol-sur-mer in the south, where they became acquainted with Frieda and D. H. Lawrence. Returning from Europe in 1929, Paul and Ruth put down roots near Cold Spring-on-Hudson, living cheaply in a stone house built by Paul, an accomplished mason. For a time, the Coreys rented a New York apartment, Ruth writing book reviews and Paul reporting for a real-estate guidebook. The stone house at Cold Spring became a refuge during the Depression since the two midwesterners could live cheaply by growing vegetables and selling eggs. The Coreys began to place their writing through the little-magazine circuit. Ruth's poetry and Paul's farm sketches appeared in the *Anvil; Hinterland; Kosmos; 1933: A Year Magazine; Poetry;* and others. Several of these stories became the basis of three novels, called the "Mantz trilogy."[76] Ruth Lechlitner, who wrote poetry reviews for Irita Van Doren's *New York Herald Tribune Books Section,* became a widely published poet of radical verse, such as the following stanza from "The Last Frontiers":

> We slept apart from the earth; we knew hunger
> Not of the flesh, and we set our feet upon the highways
> Toward those frontiers of shining glass and stone—.

The poem makes reference to a new social frontier, not one of opportunity but of despair.[77]

Harboring deep reservations about political orthodoxies on the left or right, Corey wrote Jack in the early 1930s that the country needed a "program indiginous [sic] to America," not communism or any other "ism."[78] He felt a great attraction to Oscar Ameringer's *American Guardian:* "It was a great little sheet pushing left-wing ideas and cutting down the reactionaries and right wingers. But above everything the paper had a great sense of humor. I could never swallow the deadly seriousness of Marxist philosophy."[79]

The Coreys were midwestern radicals who believed deeply in self-sufficiency and individual enterprise, and just as firmly in cooperation and in "conjoint communicated experience." When Paul needed something for his house, he would make it himself, often innovating out of indigenous materials.[80] Their home became a favorite weekend retreat for writers and editors from the city, such as Richard Wright and Willard Maas. Independent-minded, the Coreys met censure for not adjusting their sights to publishers' demands. Eastern publishers were often looking for writers they could "build up." *Reader's Digest* considered Corey for such a role, but quickly dropped him when he expressed his support of labor unions. Ruth was excluded from the Trotskyist crowd in New York who gained considerable influence in publishing circles after 1935.[81]

Mainstream editors were reluctant to publish writing with a strong regionalist texture. Drab sketches of farm life, reminiscent of Ruth Suckow's work, were no longer welcomed. To be labeled "farm fiction could stop any story dead in a magazine slushpile."[82] On the other hand, Corey's sketches lacked sufficient revolutionary hope to qualify them for publication in the eyes of some radical editors. The breakthrough for Paul occurred when he sent a parody of farm life to editor Jack Stoll of *1933: A Year Magazine*, entitled "Land O' Love," inspired by the strong sex angle in Erskine Caldwell's sharecropper tales. The story later became the basis for his novel *Three Miles Square*, which carried to its logical conclusion the assumption that anything as outrageous as Caldwell describes could be found within any three-mile square of Iowa farmland. Humor required no compromise of radical conviction or independent thought. The Coreys were active with the League of American Writers after 1936. Later in the decade, Paul Corey joined the New York Writers' Project.[83]

In Greenwich Village, and later at their Cold Spring home, Ruth wrote reviews for *New Masses*, and she and Paul were friends of other writers active in the left—John Herrman and Josephine Herbst (who was from Iowa), Stanley Burnshaw, Willard Maas, and others—but in general the two midwesterners were little involved with the New York radical cultural "scene." Paul's radical roots were firmly planted in Iowa soil: populism and progressive ideals.[84] The Party-sponsored proletarian movement would never succeed in America, he felt. No one would admit to being a "proletarian"; the American myth was much too powerful. Corey often found himself in disagreement with eastern radical intellectuals on such questions.[85]

In the 1920s, literary "rebellion" had come to mean the "revolt from the village," the rejection of middle-class mores, of philistinism, genteel literary standards, and prudery. After the demise of the old *Masses* and the *Liberator*, John Herrman argued, literary aesthetics was divorced from radicalism. "In those dear good charming lovely wellworthwhile boisterous human etc days of the *Masses* and the *Liberator* there were radicals who were literateurs and literateurs who were radicals."[86] But neither exists now (in 1927), he said; only the two isolated categories: "artists" and "revolutionists." The "artists" fled to Paris to write; the "revolutionists" moved down to Union Square in New York City. Each group had its own publications: in Paris, the "artists" published in *This Quarter, transition*, and other expatriate magazines.[87] The "revolutionists" had their *New Masses*. What a magnificent thing it would be, Herrman suggested, if the literary quality of *This Quarter* were infused with "social background"—social and political content—of the radicals.

The rebellion of the "artists"—the literary experimentalists who "revolutionized" the word, the expatriate writers who violated sexual taboos in literature—had altered the climate of reception when the new generation of literary radicals began to publish. The expatriates and literary modernists had fought their own battles to gain recognition, publishing first in little magazines open to experimentation. With recognition came critical attention and mainstream publication.[88] The literary radicals had found no such acceptance by the early 1930s. Mainstream editors received them coolly, unwilling to take risks on unknowns whose subjects were politically sensitive. Most established critics ignored their work. Expatriate writers like Edmund Wilson, Malcolm Cowley, Matthew Josephson, and Robert McAlmon, however, began to respond to signals sent by the radicals about the social and economic crisis. Admiring the literary experimentalism of the modernists but assailing their shallow imitators, the midwestern radicals reasserted the social-political content of rebellion, looking to earlier models such as appeared in socialist and Wobbly publications.[89] What was called in Eugene Jolas's *transition* "the revolution of the word" inspired debate among literary radicals without marking their work in any significant way. The "artists," on the other hand, were excluded from the close-up familiarity with working-class subjects, condemned as it were to remain observers despite the attempts by some in the 1930s to espouse ideals of collective identity. The reintegration of the "revolutionists" and the "artists" never came to pass in the proletarian literature movement that was just beginning to pick up speed following the appearance of the so-called Gastonia strike novels, Gold's exhortations in *New Masses*, and the emergence of a new generation of worker-writers, rebels, and radicals.[90] Literary radicals like Conroy, Le Sueur, Lewis, Spector, and others were "experimentalists," but their experiments consisted of adapting and transforming nonliterary, collective sources drawing upon orality, popular culture, folklore, and personal narrative.[91]

In her essay "Verse-Drama for Radio: A New Direction," published by James Laughlin's New Directions press, Ruth Lechlitner wrote: "Stein, Joyce, Proust, Cocteau may be known to few students of language; but the small-time gangster, or the factory worker . . . may do more to vitalize a language than any dozen big-time cultish 'experimental' writers."[92] Lechlitner and others cautioned the radicals about accepting the literary moderns as models for their own writing. The danger was, they said, that the experimental quality of the "revolution of the word" would undermine their purpose, which was the revolution of the world—they believed that a fascination with form and language detracted from the social purpose of writing. Conroy decried the phony imitations of literary modernism in little magazines: "The freakishness displayed by some 'lower case' and 'expatriate' journals too often connotes lunacy rather than genius. Eccentricity is not an inevitable corollary of merit. Fidelity to life is always the final and only trustworthy touchstone."[93] Herman Spector, a New York Rebel Poet, expressed the radicals' disdain of "esoteric" verse without social concern, a quality associated with the expatriates and literary modernists, yet admired their achievement. Gertrude Stein, James Joyce, E. E. Cummings, the "famous esoterics" are great artists, he said. But "it is the colloquial influence they exert, and the general 'esotericizing' end of their Method-over-literature that we find so odious."[94]

"Esoterics" and "obscurity" were evidence of what Walter Snow, in a letter to Conroy, referred to as the "cult of unintelligibility," a term Max Eastman had coined earlier in a *Harper's* magazine essay.[95] The charge against the literary modernists was not that they dared innovate but that they were communicating to a very few, the intellectual cognoscenti. Perhaps one of the most damning self-indictments, from the radicals' perspective, was Eugene Jolas's "proclamation" published in *transition* (1929), one declaration of which read: "The writer expresses. He does not communicate," and another: "The plain reader be damned."[96] Linguistic difficulty was characteristic of literary coteries, which, in the economic chaos of the early 1930s, had ceased to justify their existence and were viewed by the radicals as dying gasps of the bourgeoisie.[97] Spector, Kalar, Conroy, and others called for a literature of commitment that addressed the concerns of working people, in a language they understood.[98] The "highly sophisticated verse" of fellow Rebel Poets H. H. Lewis and Herman Spector, published in *New Masses*, was too experimental for Henry George Weiss, who urged them to follow the example of the Wobbly poets Joe Hill and Ralph Chaplin. Of what use is Gertrude Stein and E. E. Cummings to workers? he asked.[99]

The radicals' differences with Jolas's avant-garde *transition* magazine sharpened when Joseph Vogel, prose editor of Charles Henri Ford's *Blues* magazine, a journal devoted to experimental verse, blasted *transition*'s "evil influence on young writers."[100] Vogel, who later contributed to Conroy's *Anvil*, accepted a story by an unknown from Chicago named James T. Farrell. Vogel resigned from the magazine when Farrell's story was published—Ford had changed the capitalizations to lowercase. Such forms of bogus "modernism" disgusted Vogel.[101] Overreacting, he wrote Mike Gold at *New Masses*, in protest, singling out Ezra Pound, who had advised Ford with *Blues* in its first year. Curiously, Vogel had written flatteringly of the expatriates in a satire on the domestic publishing scene in the 1920s, published in *This Quarter* two years earlier.[102] Vogel, who had tried his own hand at experimental forms and styles, and who admired Joyce and Eliot, regretted, in the letter to Gold, Pound's influence on Louis Zukofsky and others who "had worshipped at his [Pound's] throne."[103]

Earlier, Zukofsky, acting as Pound's agent, had visited Vogel and Spector to organize a group of young writers to promote Pound's work in America. Vogel and Spector, however, refused to be recruited. Moreover, the example of *transition* had done little else, Vogel alleged, but spread "a contagion" of new "experimental magazines throughout the land," like *Blues*, "a washy imitation of its mama in Paris."[104] Joe Vogel was an independent radical who did not think of the little-magazine movement in terms of left or right, modernist or traditional, but as a springboard for young writers eager to get a start when mainstream publications would not accept their work. A man of quick wit and gentle humor, his novel *Man's Courage* (1938) "come[s] to terms," to use Robert Penn Warren's criterion, "in a personal sense, with the tragic aspect of life," yet deeply engages contemporary social reality.[105]

The "debate" was more colorful than substantive, in large part because of Ezra Pound's involvement and the response Pound provoked from Kalar, Gold, and others. Norman Macleod and Pound made contact through Macleod's coeditor, Donal McKenzie, and began to exchange letters. One of these was published in Macleod's *Morada* with Joe Kalar's reply.[106] In it Pound defines the proletariat "as that part of the population engaged solely in reproduction of the human species," and dismisses efforts of the radicals to "have an 'advance' in social organization in the U.S.A. among a population too grovelling servile to maintain the status of organism bequeathed it by his forbears. . . ." Kalar, whom Macleod enlisted for the task, responded that the force of events under capitalism would inevitably produce a proletariat, for there alone lies "sanity, purpose, or direction" while artists like Pound have "retreated into classicist isolation, absorbed in color and music and words to the exclusion of life and reality. . . ." In fact, Kalar argued, Pound "has partially stated our aims." The passage Kalar cited appeared in Pound's concluding remarks: "It is all very well to print writing by 'farmers, plumbers, teamsters . . .' and excellent that they shd. confine their expression to subjects with which they are familiar, but it is a sign of nothing save obfuscation and laziness on the part of intellectuals 'with leanings toward . . .' that they utterly refuse to examine or describe either the actual working conditions of American society. . . ." Kalar was triumphant that Pound had concurred on the one essential point. Expanding on the point, Kalar added that the "new proletarian literature" must be "direct," "pinned down to specific instances," "honest."[107]

For the last issue of the *Morada*, Macleod teamed up with Donal McKenzie, a former student colleague at the University of New Mexico. McKenzie had gone to Lago di Garda, Italy, for an eczema cure. There he met Pound, and there the final number of the magazine was published.[108] The editors were listed as McKenzie and Macleod, "european & expatriate" and "american" respectively, suggesting that exiles on both sides of the Atlantic had joined hands. Contributors included Eugene Jolas, Ezra Pound, Louis Zukofsky, Robert McAlmon, Kay Boyle, Joe Kalar, and John Rogers; in addition, Jolas, Kalar, and Cheyney were listed among the contributing editors. It appeared that the "revolutionists" and the "artists" were finally reintegrated, as John Herrman said they had been in the old *Masses*.[109] There was in fact no actual integration of the two groups, only coexistence in the pages of Macleod's magazine.[110] There were, however, several interactions, the most prominent being Ezra Pound's response to Mike Gold. The connection occurred in a most lively way.

Gold's essays and "Notes of the Month" in *New Masses* attracted Pound's attention in Rapallo. In a friendly but scolding letter to Gold, reprinted in *New Masses* (October 1930), Pound, who was apparently offended by a remark Gold had made about Mussolini's Italy, challenged the notion that Marx had any special authority or infallibility. "Does a communist membership card confer literary genius on its holder?" he asked. Gold liked Pound's spiritedness and replied in kind, attacking Pound's defense of Mussolini's "co-operative state." The left had studied Mussolini's state and it smelled of fascism, the direction Hoover's America was heading: "Big Business on the throne, Labor in the ditch." "It won't work, Ezra. In the first depression the bosses begin cutting wages and throwing men on the streets to starve."[111]

In an "open letter" to Pound the following September, Gold continued the debate. There is no need to explain Marxism, Gold wrote, but since fascism in Italy had so few interpreters, Pound should provide an explanation. "Write for the world, Ezra, your exact program of Fascism. Tell us, not in literary hocus-pocus rhetoric, but in precise formulas, what Fascism means to do." Recruits are rife in America, Gold added. "You may yet return triumphantly, Ezra, to a Fascist America, and lead a squad that will mystically, rhetorically but effectively bump off your old friends, the artists and writers of the *New Masses*." The letter concluded: "Always ready, but hoping to see you in hell first."[112] The Pound-Gold debate continued in the same quirky manner in Macleod's *Morada* and *Front* magazines.[113]

The literary radicals attacked the expatriates' unwillingness to engage in the workers' cause at home and their self-constituted sovereignty, which lacked social cohesion.[114] T. S. Eliot became the whipping boy of leftist critics, particularly as his views grew more conservative. Nothing like the debate between Brecht and Lukács over modernism occurred; there was no American equivalent of the Frankfurt School of Social Theory, which saw in modernism a genuine artistic challenge to the alienating and reifying trends underlying capitalism and mass culture (and Stalinism). The American left's critical response to the "revolution of the word" rarely surpassed Gold's eccentric remarks. The real issues lay deeper, however, in questions involving access to publishers, the nature of reception, horizons of expectation, alternative systems of literary production, and cultural politics.[115]

On the question of obscurity the radicals were joined by a growing number of converts. One of the earliest of the expatriates to "break ranks" was Malcolm Cowley, demanding communicability in art in place of "Rosicrucian" aesthetics.[116] Many of the expatriates had returned home by the early 1930s. Edmund Wilson turned his hand to reportage, writing of the factory worker in Ford's River Rouge plant in *American Jitters* (1932) and suggesting that most American writers would do better to write propaganda for communism than to continue writing it for capitalism.[117] In his conclusion to the first edition of *Axel's Castle* (1931) Wilson called for a break with the world of the private imagination. By 1932, Wilson was in Pineville, Kentucky, publicizing a miners' strike. "Looking backwards," Cowley wrote in the fall of 1932, "I feel that our whole training was involuntarily directed toward destroying whatever roots we had in the soil, toward eradicating our local and regional peculiarities, toward making us homeless citizens of the world."[118] In the 1934 edition of *Exile's Return* Cowley embraced the workers' cause.[119] The climate of reception appeared to improve for the rebels with the leftward turn of intellectuals and artists.

With this shift, new influences, including those by the modernists and returned literary exiles, seemed likely to make their way into the radicals' work at home. Joe Kalar was open to these influences, more so than was Conroy, who drew upon sources closer at hand. The anthology *We Gather Strength* (1933), edited by Kalar, Spector, Edwin Rolfe, and S. Funaroff, for example, reveals modernist influences. But the Rebel Poets seemed anchored in earlier traditions of versified social protest. The organization was too diverse to constitute a movement directed toward experiments in form and technique appropriate for new social conditions. Rather it acted as a telephone switchboard connecting isolated writers, making them aware of one another's existence and exposing them to one another's versified views. The group's publication, the *Rebel Poet*, was more a speaker's platform than a chorus of poetic voices orchestrated according to an artistic score. Rebel Poets never entered the cultural mainstream nor left any permanent mark on the evolution of American poetry. Nonetheless, in the early phases of 1930s literary radicalism, it offered sanctuary and encouragement, and an experimental basis of cooperative, nonhierarchical forms of literary production.

Joseph Vogel, author of *Man's Courage*, 1939. Courtesy of Joseph Vogel.

Paul Corey and Ruth Lechlitner, Cold Spring-on-Hudson, New York, ca. 1932. Courtesy of Paul Corey.

W. W. ("Wallie") Wharton, business manager of the *Anvil*, ca. 1928. Courtesy of Alexandra Wharton Grannis.

Sanora Babb, author of *An Owl on Every Post*, ca. 1938. Courtesy of Sanora Babb.

Walter Snow, coeditor of the *Anvil* during its last issues, ca. 1931. Courtesy of Maurice Isserman.

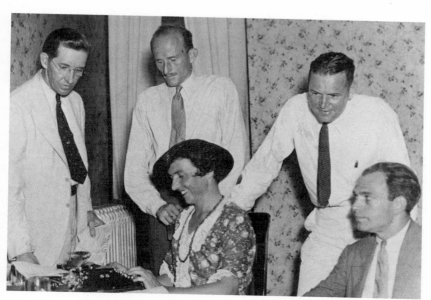

Left to right: Bruce Crawford, Emmett Gowen, Shirley Hopkins, Conroy, and Al Hirsch. The group demonstrated for free-speech protection in Alabama in July 1935. Conroy papers, Newberry Library.

STEEL WORKERS

Hear
JACK CONROY

Noted Author and Lecturer — Winner of
Guggenheim Prize

SPEAK

Thursday Evening, Feb. 11
7:30 O'CLOCK

LABOR TEMPLE GRANITE CITY

Mr. Conroy, author of "Disinherited" and "World to
Win" whose wide experience and extensive travels
make him a most sought after speaker. He will speak
on problems that are of immediate interest to steel
workers.

| ADMISSION FREE! | EVERYONE INVITED! | ADMISSION FREE! |

Under Auspices of
Educational Committee of A. A. of I. S. & T. W.

Handbill advertising Conroy's speech to mill workers in Granite City, Illinois, 11 February 1936.

In Des Moines, Iowa, to speak to the Farmers' Holiday Association, May 1936, Conroy (second from right) met with (left to right) Carroll Norling (*Hinterland* magazine), Jay Du Von (Iowa Writers' Project), Ruth Stewart (IWP), and Joe Jones. Conroy papers, Newberry Library.

A party at the Conroys' Green Street home, Chicago; (left to right): Jack, Gladys, Leo Lipp (*Anvil* contributor), Studs Terkel, Win Stracke. Conroy papers, Newberry Library.

Nelson Algren and Conroy, Chicago, ca. 1947.

Tom Conroy with Jack's friends from the Illinois Writers' Project and the Southside Community Center, Chicago; seated (left to right): Margaret Brundage, Tom Conroy, Ferne Gayden, Gwendolyn Brooks, Margaret Burroughs; standing (left to right): Marion Perkins, Vernon Jarrett, Robert Lucas. Conroy papers, Newberry Library.

Gwendolyn Brooks presents the Literary Times Award to Conroy, 1967. Conroy papers, Newberry Library.

Conroy (right) with his printer, Ben Hagglund, ca. 1970.

Conroy swapping stories with Bruz Williams, roustabout, in Moberly, early 1970s. Photo by Leland Payton.

Conroy, 1982. Photo by David Eppelsheimer.

Studs Terkel interviewing Conroy, 1987. Photo by the *Moberly Monitor-Index*.

Jack at the Sugar Creek graveyard, burial site of the Conroys. Photo by Bob Black. © 1973 by the *Chicago Sun-Times*. Reprinted with permission.

9

Worker-Writers and Editors:
1930–31

> For the experience of each new age requires a new
> confession, and the world seems always waiting for
> its new poet.
>
> —Emerson

DESTITUTE FAMILIES IN St. Louis had erected a makeshift shantytown
between the Terminal Railroad tracks and the Mississippi River, a few
hundred yards south of the present site of Saarinen's arch. St. Louis's
"Hooverville" was the largest of all the *pis aller* "cities" that since 1929
had grown like mushrooms on a rotting log. Most of the inhabitants
were dispossessed St. Louisans, forced to improvise shelter from river
jettison, metal scrap, and packing crates. On their return to Moberly
from Toledo, Fred and Jack stopped at Hooverville, where men spent
the day "rustling" up any kind of odd job. Black workers were hired as
"sandhogs," burrowing beneath the river. The foreman had stopped hiring white workers since they would not tolerate the conditions; only
blacks were desperate enough—a curious example of "reverse discrimination." Hooverville was a self-contained community with its own "city
government." A home might consist of a single packing crate, yet it
possessed a neat picket fence.[1] Hooverville may seem now an inspiring
model of grass-roots ingenuity, but to Jack and Fred it symbolized terrible devastation in people's lives.

By mid-July 1930, the Conroys had found a two-room apartment on
Hurley Avenue in Moberly, sharing the monthly eight-dollar rent with
Harvey Harrison, Fred's brother.[2] Bill Wisdom, married to Jack's sister
Margaret and owner of a small construction company, hired Jack when-

ever work materialized. Within several weeks of his return to Moberly, Jack was pushing a wheelbarrow and shoveling sand to build a new Shell Oil Company station. Laid off from the shoe factory in Moberly, Harvey came down to the construction site and helped Jack shovel. The two families shared the household expenses and pooled their incomes. At the end of the summer Wisdom sent Jack and Fred to an old river town, Boonville, Missouri, to construct a building for the telephone company. At night Fred and Jack slept beneath the stars on a sandpile. When the frost came, Fred was hired at the Brown Company shoe factory with Harvey. Gladys soon joined the Harrisons when the factory, having received a large government order for boots, called back its laid-off workers.[3]

Jack liked working with his nephews and felt lonesome in Boonville when Fred left. The Conroys moved into a shack on Collins Avenue belonging to Jack's mother, paying four dollars a month rent. In the shack, Jack edited the *Rebel Poet* and wrote his stories that would be published in Mencken's *American Mercury*. He was now a "pick and shovel stiff," Jack wrote Walter Snow, "gnawed by ants and lashed by rain."[4]

Snow, who played an instrumental role in Jack's editorial work, was born in Gardner, Massachusetts, in 1905. His father, a Dartmouth College graduate from a working-class background, was forced into factory work following World War I. Lacking financial means to continue, Walt quit high school in Willimantic, Connecticut, and accepted a laborer's position in a local thread mill. He had just turned sixteen. Like Jack, Kalar, Lewis, and Falkowski, Snow absorbed Balzac, Swinburne, and Shelley during his free hours. He tramped with the Wobblies (in 1924), worked as a stagehand one theater season for the Provincetown Players in New York City, finally turning to journalism. Moved by the Sacco-Vanzetti executions in 1927, Snow joined the Communist party through the Newspaper Guild's fraction. A nucleus organizer and part-time reporter for the *Daily Worker*, he was for a time what the Communists call a "good element." Several of his poems appeared in *New Masses* after Gold appealed for submissions in the June 1928 issue.[5] To support himself he wrote for pulp magazines while working on more serious subjects, for example, a "Communist-Balzacian study" of a bull-market banker.[6]

Snow was representative of literary radicals who as a result of "tough luck, lost opportunities, continuous poverty, and catastrophic misadventures" were adrift ideologically, searching for political commitment. Revolution to them seemed imminent, yet by temperament they were rebels, capable only of individual acts of protest. Typically they were given to citing the Russian Revolution without having thought through the possible consequences of a similar revolution at home.[7]

Isolated radicals like Snow, who maintained contact with other radicals through correspondence, could read about the Soviet Experiment in *New Masses*, which published Dos Passos on his 1928 trip to the Soviet Union, Hallie Flanagan on Soviet theater, and Ed Falkowski on what it was like to work in a mine in the Caucasus. A *New Masses* contributor wrote from Moscow in the summer of 1930: "I wish I could transmit to you one-hundredth part of the thrill of living in the midst of all this. You in America need it, and need it badly."[8] Travel to the Soviet Union was cheap, but, apart from Falkowski, Macleod, Ben Field, and Walt Carmon, few of the radicals in touch with Jack through Rebel Poets actually made the trip. Therefore, most of the radicals eager for eyewitness accounts welcomed the publication of Joseph Freeman, Louis Lozowick, and Joshua Kunitz's *Voices in October*, appearing that summer. There they could read of *rabkor* (workers' correspondence), proletcult, workers' literary groups, and innovations in form and style for the purpose of creating "the foundations of Communist culture."[9] Art, they learned, might have a new social basis, which was part of an all-embracing culture.

In the autumn of 1930, a delegation of Americans, representing *New Masses* and the New York John Reed Club, attended the Kharkov Conference (Second World Plenum of the International Bureau of Revolutionary Literature). The Pennsylvania coal miner Ed Falkowski, who was working in the Artema anthracite mine in the southern Caucasus at the time, joined "J. Q. Neets" (a.k.a. Joshua Kunitz) in Moscow to form the "New Masses Moscow Reception Committee" greeting Gold, William Gropper, Josephine Herbst, A. B. Magil, and others arriving from the United States for the conference in Kharkov.[10] Neets was impressed with the Soviet Experiment; in a letter to *New Masses* he wrote: "I am now in Moscow: Never in my wildest dreams have I imagined myself capable of such intense yet sustained joy as I feel here."[11] Falkowski's experiences working in Soviet mines sobered his view of conditions in the workers' paradise; nonetheless he remained convinced.[12]

Coming straight from a pick-and-shovel job, Falkowski had more in common with his fellow miners in the Caucasus than with intellectuals like Joshua Kunitz who shared his admiration for the Soviets. Kunitz, Joseph Freeman, Harry Alan Potamkin, and others were *New Masses* critics, intellectuals who had made common cause with worker-writers like Falkowski during the proletarian phase of the left. During these early years the real differences between the intellectual radicals (for lack of a better term) and the worker-writers were glossed over, despite discussions over the importance of literary quality and so forth (Gold minimizing the importance of technique).[13] Falkowski's knowledge of the worker was experiential, not ideological. The Party's cultural functionaries and critics, however, overlooked at first such differences in the interest of building "a world of revolutionary labor." Supportive of the Party's defense of workers' rights, its interventions on behalf of the hungry and jobless, the worker-writers tended to ignore the Party's efforts to bring them in line ideologically, to make them "Party-minded."[14]

Thus the ten points of the Kharkov conference, reported by the American delegates, intended as a "concrete program of action for the United States," had the familiar smell of the "coffeepot" (New York cafés where intellectual radicals met and discussed ideas) to the midwestern radicals. Underlying the program were initiatives calling for "discussion groups," the study of Marxist classics, and, most important, the strengthening of the role of the Party ideologues at the center.[15] The John Reed clubs and *New Masses* would implement such a program. The worker-writers paid such initiatives little heed; Gold's vision of a worker-correspondence movement better represented their interests and temperaments: a new literature from the ground up, not a "program" from the top down that emanated from a "center" located east of the Hudson River.[16] Yet there were significant differences between, on the one hand, the decentered Rebel Poets organization and the various grass-roots radicalisms of the Midwest, and, on the other hand, the centripetal tendencies of the Party's cultural programs and the emergence of a radical intelligentsia anxious to distance itself from the "vulgarisms" of the proletarian movement. These differences were not to surface until sometime in late 1932, after which deep splits in the cultural left began to appear.

There were other signal events occurring in 1930 that pulled the midwesterners toward the Communists. Most of the midwestern radicals had renounced genteel literature in favor of vigorous new styles and subjects suitable for expressing contemporary social reality. Thus Mike Gold's bastinados directed against the "aesthetes," the exponents of art for art's sake, echoed the midwesterners' own animus toward genteelism. A notorious expression of this animus occurred when Gold attacked Thornton Wilder's *The Woman of Andros* in *New Masses*. Gold's critical writing made little logical sense, since, as Edmund Wilson pointed out, Gold himself shared Wilder's "sensitiveness to human contacts, a love of picturesque detail, a gift for molding firm prose into short comprehensive units, and even a touch of sentimentality."[17] Moreover, Gold's rhetoric was closer to the spirit of midwestern protest, the "raise less corn and more hell" kind from populist speechmaking, than to the dreary solemnizing of Party ideologues. Gold's vigorous interventions counterbalanced the "coffeepot" intellectualizing in the Party. Gold and Walt Carmon created a space for the midwestern radicals close to Party cultural activities, making them feel they were part of the movement. East Coast radicals often ignored the midwestern radicals or criticized them for their lack of theoretical acumen—their "bohemianism."

The Party won support from the midwestern radicals in its defense against a special congressional committee, headed by Hamilton Fish, assigned to investigate Communist activities. For months during the summer and fall the committee listened to testimony about the CP's aims, alarmed that the Soviet trading corporation's office in New York City, Amtorg, might be spreading Communist propaganda. Implicated in the attempt to bring the public's contempt down upon the heads of the left was Grover Whalen, police commissioner of New York City, whose testimony ultimately proved false. Finally, the mounting evidence of massive unemployment, including riots, which the Hoover administration continued to ignore or treat as an aberration, drove the midwesterners into the Communist fold. "Bleeding heads," Bernstein records, "converts unemployment from a little-notice to a page-one problem in every important city in the United States. No one could any longer afford to ignore it."[18]

As 1930 gave way to 1931, multitudes were feeling the brunt of what Dos Passos called the "two nations." Appearing in magazines were advertisements for ocean sailings showing wealthy travelers in white-duck pants and furs. The spectacle of a few benefiting from the increased value of the dollar while the majority were scraping by infuriated the radicals at home, who were persuaded by such perceptions rather than by "discussion groups" and the study of Marxist classics. Langston Hughes's poem on the recently opened Waldorf-Astoria hotel, "Advertisement for the Waldorf-Astoria," is representative of the radicals' emotional response to what they perceived as flagrant social inequity. One verse reads:

> Look! See what *Vanity Fair* says about the
>   new Waldorf-Astoria:
> "All the luxuries of a private home. . . ."
> Now, won't that be charming when the last flop-
>   house has turned you down this winter?[19]

The cultural left resurrected the top-hatted caricatures of capitalists, familiar to readers of the old *Masses* and the socialist press. Wall Street and the dollar sign were symbols of corrupt power, as they had been for the populists. Traditional notions of the "people" were endowed with

new meanings: the common person in aggregate, the folk with its native good sense, generosity, and instinct for democratic life. Key words
like "people," "brotherhood," "the worker" were mythicized in the invented traditions of the left.[20] Such abstractions continue to nurture
the cultural left today. Yet an alternative, authentic tradition coexisted within the Party's invented traditions, I argue, in the writing of midwestern radicals like Sanora Babb, Meridel Le Sueur, and Paul Corey
and in the literary productions of worker-writers like Conroy and Kalar.
Party rhetoric, Conroy perceived, would not salvage the destruction of
a communal past, a workers' culture that had once existed, at least as
he had known it. Any authentic tradition on the left must reflect actual experience, not wishful thinking, and serve to reproduce the cultural memory of shared values lost with the destruction of older work
communities and the emergence of a new consumer-oriented mass culture. By the fall of 1930, Jack's ideas on how to achieve this were beginning to crystallize.

*   *   *

In Conroy's early "tales of work," subliterary and popular genres—
folk tales, dime novels, popular ballads, worker narratives—are creatively transformed into "hybrid genres" that preserve the accents of
working-class communities and reflect the attitudes and values of individual workers.[21] H. L. Mencken, editor of the *American Mercury,*
was Jack's earliest mentor in producing sketches and short stories that
represent an important evolution in his development as a writer. In
the course of this development, Conroy learned to combine folk
knowledge, work experience, and the popular genres with traditions
of worker narratives in a narrative effort to situate the "I" with respect to the "other" in the relationship of participant-witness.[22] Jack's
earliest writing had consisted of worker's correspondence (letters to
union journals and magazines) and romantic poetry. He later turned
to reviews, occasional essays, and worker narratives such as "Jackson
Street: Toledo" and "Whistling Past a Graveyard: Toledo." Mencken's
acceptance of Jack's earliest stories validated these converging genres.
Conroy was a fresh, new voice. Mencken searched out such voices
regardless of their politics.[23]

Jack's initial contacts with Mencken began while Jack was still on
the Boonville construction job, sleeping on the sandpile at night. By
October the nights had turned cool. Shortly before Thanksgiving something miraculous relieved him of the necessity of continuing in Boonville, away from his family: Mencken had asked him to submit a story;
and Alfred Knopf, the publisher, had written a personal note encour-

aging Jack to turn his experiences into an autobiography.[24] Jack had written Mencken about H. H. Lewis; like Pocahontas, Mencken replied, saying, why don't you submit something yourself. He would pay $135 for a story, more than a month's wages for Jack in his current job.

Walter Lippman had called Mencken "the most powerful personal influence on this whole generation of educated people," but by the mid-1920s his influence on young writers was waning.[25] Some readers, like E. Haldeman-Julius, detected an antidemocratic, snobbish attitude in the Sage of Baltimore.[26] Singleton explains Mencken's attraction to political radicals: "Essays by radicals appeared in the monthly even before the Depression, not so much because of the editor's belief in freedom of speech, but because of his agreement with certain small areas of leftist thought—notably in the anticlericalism shared by both parties—and because such contributors were apparently willing to tone down the worst of their didacticism and militancy for a chance to appear in the magazine."[27] If Mencken's satire was directed toward Coolidge's America, it was pointed just as fiercely at the American hinterland; yet he published short stories with midwestern settings by Ruth Suckow, Meridel Le Sueur, James T. Farrell, and others.[28] But counterbalancing such prejudices was his appreciation of fresh, vigorous writing, the idiolects of uncommon experience. Mencken praised Dreiser, Sherwood Anderson, and Sinclair Lewis but had little good to say about Henry James.[29] In the early Depression, vigorous writing also won over other editors who had no strong commitment to the left's cultural movement. Richard Johns's *Pagany*, for example, in its first issue, January 1930, welcomed a broad diversity of contemporary writing, including modernist and realist, then turned away from aesthetic experimentation to make room for "newer and lesser-known writers, who . . . had something more vital to say" as the economic crisis worsened.[30]

Long before his interest in Jack's worker-writing, Mencken had solicited new voices, publishing "slices of life" by Jim Tully (on hoboing), the black writer George S. Schulyer's "Memories of a Pearl Diver" (on dishwashing), Mike Gold's East Side reminiscences, Charles Sampson's "Peach Harvest" (on drifters), Ernest Booth's "We Rob a Bank," and H. L. Davis's "Team Bells Woke Me." One of the first "pure" worker narratives to appear in the *Mercury* was M. L. Batey's "One American's Story," in September 1929. Batey, a former textile-mill worker, had never before appeared in print. "It is printed exactly as he wrote it," Mencken explained, "with only a few small changes. He is representative, save in his unusual articulateness, of the thousands of other workers in the textile mills of the New South."[31] Was it "representativeness" that Mencken was after or the discovery of some fresh, new talent? My hunch is that Mencken's interest in the diversity of American speech drew him to first-person narratives. Mencken's interest in language was at least as strong as his ethnographic interest in experience. Personal experience furnished the living speech he was after: Gold relating his early life in a New York immigrant ghetto; J. Frank Dobie describing an unbroken horse in Texas.

Jack sent H. H. Lewis's sketch "School Days" to Mencken in the early fall of 1930. Retitling the sketch, Mencken published "School Days in the Gumbo" in the January 1931 issue of the *Mercury*. Lewis's breaking into a major publication gave a great boost to the worker-writers. Mencken was put off by Lewis's "socialistic fulminations." "After all," he wrote Jack, "suckers would still be suckers under Bolshevism."[32] In Mencken's eyes, Lewis's earthy humor and linguistic originality (or better, eccentricity) redeemed the political values. His patience with the gumbo poet, however, was not limitless. He turned down another of Lewis's submissions, a story of mail-order fraud involving a man who rolled a peanut around with his nose.[33] Mencken was interested in actuality, but Lewis's capricious humor pushed too far even if, indeed, there had been such a figure like Lewis's subject in the American scene.

Jack was successful in his role as midwife, placing others' work, but Mencken wished to see what Jack could write of his previous hungry winter in Toledo. By late December, Jack had sent the sketch "Hard Winter" to Mencken, who published it in the February 1931 issue. Between Thanksgiving and Christmas, Jack proofread the 1930 *Unrest* galleys. He continued to encourage Lewis, writing an introduction to Lewis's first collection of poetry, *Red Renaissance* (1930).

Lewis's volume of poems was the first to appear in a series of Rebel Poet pamphlets published on Ben Hagglund's "Old Ironsides" press in Holt, Minnesota. The *New Masses* reviewer noted that Lewis "writes without a lot of skill, but with the power and fury that comes from sincerity and convictions of the things that make a worker's life: hunger, Sacco-Vanzetti and the hope of workers in the Soviet Union."[34] After some initial disagreement on the aims of the magazine, the muskeg printer and the Moberly editor came to terms on publishing the *Rebel Poet* magazine. Hagglund, ever the iconoclast, held to an obscure political faith called "Equitism" while Jack declared that his sympathies lay with the Soviet Experiment. "You are just as damned obstinate and bullheaded that *you* are right as I am that *I* am right," wrote Hagglund. "But we are both rebels—on that ground we meet."[35] Jack assured Hagglund that his organization's magazine, the *Rebel Poet*, would be open to "every voice that cries out in the wilderness of this Age of Steel." People, Hagglund said, need a good jolting to wake them up to "this damnable thing that is strangling us all."[36] For instance, both Hagglund and Conroy liked Lewis's verse because, they said, it spoke to workers in their own language. (This is not altogether true, since only Lewis's plainspokenness and earthy diction resemble workers' speech; the rest is Lewis's own.) Lewis brandishes his low humor, Jack wrote in the introduction to the volume, on the tines of "an odorous manure fork" in the cause of the outcast. Lewis was a man with a hoe, but he was no longer content to lean on it "in dumb despair."[37]

Ben Hagglund was a poor man's patron of writing. Whatever faults he possessed as a printer—these would soon become apparent—he was a selfless, generous person. Both editor and printer were hard-pressed for cash. Ben hired himself out to bale hay; Jack contributed some of his fee from Mencken and his wages as a construction laborer. It was a fortuitous pairing of editor and printer: both Hagglund and Conroy believed deeply in making their publication accessible to unknown radical writers of merit, at the lowest possible cost. Without Hagglund it is unlikely that *Rebel Poet* (or later, the *Anvil*) might have existed. With the new year, 1931, there was reason to feel optimistic: Jack had published his first short story, found a printer for *Rebel Poet*, and received the first copies of the new *Unrest* from the English publisher, Channing-Renton. Jack sensed a growing interest in writing that expressed the anger and frustration of the dispossessed.

The jobless drifted through Moberly. One group, looking for refuge at the city hall, was sure that the Depression was a result of prohibition, woman suffrage, and foreign immigration. Several of the older workers in the group attributed the crisis to overproduction. City officials remarked on the character of the group; unlike the "bums" and drifters of the past, these itinerants sought work.[38] An impromptu "Bums" hotel opened to house the seekers. In the nation's capital, the jobless petitioned Hoover for aid, raising fear among some people that the petition was led by communists. In England, Arkansas, people were actually starving.

Like small-town newspapers elsewhere, the Moberly paper was eager to report on suspected "red" activities. In Oklahoma a group of "reds" had insulted the secretary of war. Demonstrations of the unemployed were called "Communist inspired." "Communist agitators" staged riots and conspired, in one instance, to sabotage a dirigible, the paper diligently reported. In Oklahoma and Arkansas, people were rioting over lack of food; a "near state of revolution" was observed in the stricken areas.[39]

Jack's own radical activities brought him under the scrutiny of his hometown paper. In announcing Mencken's acceptance of Jack's story, the Moberly newspaper called Jack a "self-styled radical." "Jack Conroy," Goetze Jeter, the paper's young reporter, wrote, "is perhaps Moberly's principal contribution to the ranks of those who hold radical views on governmental and social conditions in the United States."[40] Conroy was happy to fill the role of the town radical, hoping that the effect of the sensationalist "red" report would publicize the plight of the hungry. Mencken's own notoriety was part reaction to his outspoken views, part admiration for his word power. When Mencken attacked Arkansas on the occasion of the famine, suggesting that charity might not be sufficient, the governor grudgingly admitted Mencken's skill in writing.[41]

In these early days of the decade, when fascist mobs were smashing shop windows on Potsdamerplatz in Berlin, provoking the Communists in the shadow of the Reichstag, it appeared to Jack and the midwestern radicals that America would soon be faced with choices too. Hoover's relief commissions had made little visible effect on reducing hunger and homelessness, while Communist organizers in Minnesota, New York, Oklahoma, and elsewhere seemed to meet success. If Gold represented the vigorous, atheoretical side of the Party's cultural movement, then the Midwest's John Reed clubs showed that writers could cooperate in learning their craft as radical writers. Jack lent his support to the Communist movement while pursuing democratic ideals in his own work as writer and editor. In the *Rebel Poet* he was interested in stirring workers and writers from their apathy; later, in the *Anvil*, his aim was to empower them, through their own words, to gain and ultimately take control of the higher ground of democratic life.

Lewis and several others looked to the Party as needful people look to the church for solace and leadership; others, like Jack, were attracted by the Party's effectiveness on behalf of the disinherited.[42] Communist organizers *were* effective in making the misery of the black sharecropper and white factory worker known.[43] Thoughtful workers found no satisfaction after a while in attributing tattered clothes and hungry bellies to woman suffrage. Protests and demonstrations restored their dignity. In Jack's view, the purpose of "agitation" had to do with shoring up the shaken self-image of individuals accustomed to bending their heads further with each new blow. "I have not yet been quizzed by the Fish Committee," he wrote about himself in the editorial notes accompanying "Hard Winter," when it appeared in February 1931, "nor proscribed by the D.A.R., nor listed in 'The Enemy within Our Gates' section of the *National Republic*, but I am hopeful."[44]

The world was feeling the effects of the Depression by early 1931; attenuated shock waves from the Great Crash finally reached small towns like Moberly, insulated by their localized economies. The Moberly paper carried reports of the Marines' landing in Nicaragua; of mine wars in Harlan County, Kentucky, and the suspicion of a Communist plot; of Spain's decision to become a republic and the rise of gangsterism in the United States; of "society aviatrixes" setting new records, the construction of the Hoover Dam, hunger demonstrations in Arkansas, floods in China, and soup lines at home. By the summer of 1931, the *Monitor-Index* implied, everyone was flying around the world, or planned to. Yet, in adjacent columns were reports of rising unemployment and hunger marches—the contrasts could not fail to catch readers' attention. The brunt of the Depression came late to Moberly; people were beginning to feel the humiliation of joblessness and anxiety concerning the depleted city funds. Itinerancy had grown quickly. A great diaspora was in motion. As a rail center, Moberly saw many of the homeless pass through.

Newspapers and the radio avoided reporting the worst. "In those years," Malcolm Cowley writes, "the press was afflicted with a lofty sense of its own responsibilities. Its function of telling people what happened was being subordinated to the apparently greater function of saving the nation's business."[45] Jack had his sources of information. The Rebel Poets continued to exchange letters, some with correspondents as far away as Moscow and Tokyo. Letter writing connected isolated writers like Joe Kalar and Warren Huddlestone, who continued their correspondence for years, scarcely knowing one another apart from their writing. Hud, as he was called, wrote Kalar of the period he had spent on the road, forced to leave his parents' home when his father, a self-employed carpenter, could no longer find work. After a year on the road, sleeping in flophouses and eating "one square" per day, Hud hitched back to Kokomo in May 1931, wondering what he would do next. In the meantime, however, his father discovered that people would pay for small repair jobs. Hud joined him, and in this manner the family survived the worst years.[46]

Hud could scarcely afford any luxury, but he had money for postage. Letter writing permitted him to hang onto his aspirations to write. Adversity brought the radical writers together in letters that gave one another confidence to continue. Editors of new little magazines were looking for narratives describing the Depression based upon individual experience.[47] If some of the radicals were not direct participants in the hardships suffered by Hud and others, they observed what was occurring, sharing their observations with other Rebel Poets and readers of little magazines. Raymond Kresensky, the Presbyterian minister from Algona, Iowa, visited hobo jungles and witnessed farmers' revolts, writing of these to Kenneth Porter, the Presbyterian from Sterling, Kansas, who was studying history at Harvard. Both were Rebel Poets and contributors to little magazines. By 1932, Kresensky was sure that "Some thing [sic] radical has to happen."[48]

"It is no longer a physical wilderness that has to be wrestled with," John Dewey commented in 1930. "Our problems grow out of social conditions: they concern human relations rather than man's direct relationship to physical nature."[49] On the social frontier of the 1930s "coarseness and strength" were not sufficient to deal with foreclosed opportunity; heroism seldom involved physical exploits, rather perseverance, endurance. Hard times struck Moberly but it was not the same feeling that the city proletariat experienced, the despair that infects so much proletarian literature. The Conroys grew vegetables. Gladys had her job at the shoe factory. With the money from the *American Mercury* stories the Conroys were able to see a movie at the Grand Theatre and buy shoes for the children. In nearby Higbee, Italian miners sold nonalcoholic "Choctaw" beer that imbibers mixed with grain alcohol. Still, hunger's specter lingered at the Conroys' door. Jack depended upon his brother-in-law to give him work each time there was a new contract. "God! It is pitiable to see the men hanging about the contractor like hungry wolves," Jack wrote to Emerson Price, "timidly approaching him, and accosting him with a sickly and despairing smile."[50] The Conroys were making it through the bad years. Slack times between jobs permitted Jack time to pursue his writing and editorial work.

The 1930 *Unrest* appeared shortly after Christmas, a much-improved volume of rebel poetry in contrast to Stockwell's vanity production.[51] Yet the mixed quality of the contributions reflected still the divided aims of the editors. Falkowski complained in the *Moscow Daily News* that too many of the poems echoed the "lyric pain" of fledgling writers and that American poets had a long way to go to match the German proletarian poets who wrote more knowledgeably.[52] Porter praised the collection's proud commitment to propaganda without doctrinaire attitudes.[53] The editors had made an effort to identify their anthology with such high-minded propagandists as Percy Bysshe Shelley, who had written pamphlets and distributed them. It was not enough, the editors judged, to inscribe *Unrest* in the tradition of political verse; it must contain explosives. "This book," Conroy and Cheyney boldly proclaimed, "should be suppressed because it is full of mental T.N.T. for blowing up Capitalism."[54] The *New Masses* reviewer doubted whether rebel poets could live up to such a claim. The better writers among the contributors, he counseled, "should seriously reconsider their affiliation with men and women who apparently believe that the Chase National Bank trembles a little every time a poet writes a tetrameter."[55] *New Masses* was so humorless. The Wobblies employed comic bombast. Ameringer used humor to get his message across. There was a killjoy quality about Party intellectuals, Jack noted, and a suspicious attitude toward literary uses of the imagination.

Besides the killjoys there were those like Mencken who saw humor where it was not intended. Mike Gold's contribution to the 1930 *Unrest*, "A Strange Funeral in Braddock," Mencken wrote, "tells very effectively of a Bohemian puddler who was overtaken by a burst of molten metal, and had to be buried by a derrick, encased in three tons of steel. But why this episode should reflect upon the capitalistic system," Mencken mused, "does not appear. Precisely the same accident might have happened in a Soviet steel-mill, and there is no reason to believe that the Bosheviki would have been more successful in separating the corpse from the steel than Charlie Schwab's hirelings were at Braddock."[56] U.S. Customs found the volume neither amusing nor lacking revolutionary explosiveness. "Don't you think this sounds a little bit socialistic?" an officer queried Emerson Price. But Price would concede nothing and was finally given Channing-Renton's shipment from London.[57]

Jack was convinced that laughter was a means to reach the worker, and for this reason, he was persuaded that H. H. Lewis was on the right track. It was easy to run afoul of Lewis's "peasant wit," he wrote in the introduction to *Red Renaissance*. Lewis spared no one, not even his benefactors. When the cantankerous gumbo firebrand heard that Walt Carmon of *New Masses* objected to "School Days in the Gumbo," Lewis wrote Kalar that the magazine "is a clique—controlled by the gang which loiters around its office and the John Reed Club."[58] The Cape Girardeau farmer-poet had first attracted Gold's attention with his irreverent satires on religion and middle-class mores. "We'll take a chance with the postal authorities," Gold wrote, "and publish your poems."[59]

Jack enjoyed Lewis's antics and shut an eye to his occasional fits of megalomania, for instance, when Lewis attacked V. F. Calverton in a letter, published in Calvert's *Open Road*, for his "menshevik" liberalism. "I am an *American Mercury* author now. Please remove me from your mailing list." Jack liked to quote such Lewisisms to friends. Nonetheless, he thought Lewis had a talent for comic satire and hoped that he might eventually win an audience of workers, if not intellectuals. Lewis ironized his situation, as in "In All Hell," a poem Jack published in the first number of *Rebel Poet*:

> I am the boor that rises in the
> middle of a concert and stumbles

toward the aisle. As the soft fingers
of the violinists quaver upon the
whining strings, as the conductor
and the audience lean to taut
attention. . . . at the very raptest
moment I get up and stalk out.[60]

When Lewis read Kresensky's poem "50 cent Flophouse" in *Unrest*, he
wrote Conroy: "Hell, that's no flophouse, that's a hotel. A flophouse
costs 10 cents!"[61] Jack prized Lewis's humor, remaining his supporter long
after others, stung by his unpredictable satire and wary of his mercurial
temperament, abandoned him.

Jack attributed the slow sales of the 1930 *Unrest* to the sour *New
Masses* review. "It is the opinion of some," he wrote to Porter, "that *New
Masses* is becoming a Mutual Admiration Society piloted by a rapidly
narrowing clique of metropolitan writers."[62] Jack felt distant from the
New York coffeepot "provincials" and said so in a letter to *New Masses*. Praising H. H. Lewis and Joe Corrie, a Scots worker-poet, Jack reminded the editors that "all proletarians cannot be garment workers or
live east of Philadelphia." He was beginning to question whether the
"clique of metropolitan writers" would make room for the midwestern
radicals. The East dominated publishing, as it had in Twain's and Howells's time. Gold's editorship of *New Masses* had improved access to radical publication. Nonetheless the midwesterners thought that by organizing their own publication circuits they might attract the attention
of eastern publishers.

Jack's sketch "High Bridge," published in the April 1931 issue of *New
Masses*, caught the attention of the New York literary agent Maxim Lieber, who contacted Walt Carmon at the *New Masses* office. Carmon
arranged for Lieber to become Jack's agent.[63] Lieber's office was at 545
Fifth Avenue, within easy walking distance from publishers' offices. He
had been a publisher himself in the 1920s and later worked for Brentano's, a publisher, until it shut down in the spring of 1930. Harry Hansen, literary editor of the *New York World-Telegram*, suggested that Lieber, with his publishing contacts, become a literary agent. Lieber's first
client was Louis Adamic, who recommended Carey McWilliams.
McWilliams brought William Saroyan, who would soon establish his
reputation, and before long Lieber's list of clients included Erskine Caldwell, James T. Farrell, Josephine Herbst, Meridel Le Sueur, Albert Halper, and many other young radical writers in the early 1930s, when the
prospects looked bright for writing that engaged social themes.

If Max Lieber liked a manuscript he would walk it to a publisher and present it himself. He took a personal interest in his clients' work, keeping after a publisher if he was convinced that a manuscript had merit. Moreover, he knew what kinds of stories certain publishers preferred. This did not stop him from pushing a story when the chances of acceptance were slim. An Alfred Knopf editor saw Lieber approaching one day with a sheaf of manuscripts. "Are you bringing me another communist?" he asked. Times were hard for publishers, who suffered from the financial crisis as well. Yet many were open to new voices, and critics like Harry Hansen were drawing their attention to new writers appearing in the little magazines. Lieber's connections and perseverance were an essential element in the early careers of writers, some of whom, like Caldwell and Saroyan, found mainstream publishers. It is difficult to exaggerate the importance of Lieber's role as their literary agent and spokesperson.[64]

Jack sent his manuscripts to Lieber except for those he sent directly to Mencken, an arrangement he had with Mencken before engaging Lieber. Nonetheless, Jack paid Lieber his 10 percent commission on stories Mencken published, which Lieber accepted "weakly."[65] Mencken's imprimatur raised Jack's hopes and perhaps induced Lieber to "smell some profit." But Caldwell was Lieber's money-maker, not the Monkey Nest worker-writer. A few commercial successes permitted Lieber to risk worker-writers such as Kalar and Conroy. Kalar wrote to Huddlestone that Lieber "is the only agent that will take stuff without an advance payment. . . . No initial payment, no payment until a story is sold. That's a boon to we bastards without even stamps. . . ."[66]

Kalar, Falkowski, Cruden, Rogers, Lewis, and Snow were worker-writers or writers who had been workers and were now engaged in other trades—the distinction is crucial. The Soviets had given the term worker-writer currency, as early as proletcult days. There had always been workers who wrote in America, for example, the Lowell textile-mill operatives in the previous century. The question was, Who published them? For whom did they write? There was no identifiable worker-correspondent movement in the United States, no workers' circles in factories devoted to self-expression through writing. Beyond a small group of intellectuals and editors associated with *New Masses* there was nothing resembling the various movements in the Soviet Union—Proletcult, Smithy, the Onguardists, VAPP, RAPP—that promoted workers' writing.

The American worker-writers had no formalized relationship with the Communists or the Party's cultural movement; rather they depended upon the patronage and encouragement of editors like Gold and Carmon. The worker-writers were exceptional individuals impelled by some

inner desire to write of their experience, in the margins of their workday lives, carrying home the echoes and accents of the work world each
day. Their first efforts were poor imitations. Example and maturity taught
them to write from their own experience. At their best, their writing
was spare, direct, unpretentious. They wrote in short breaths, at night
after work, occupying two selves, as it were: worker and writer.

No better example of this double role, the hyphenated worker-writer
(and its complexities), was Ed Falkowski. Jack "met" Ed through Merlin
Wand's organization Contacts as early as 1926. Ed was a third-genera-
tion miner in Shenandoah, Pennsylvania, where English was only one
among several languages spoken.[67] His grandfather was a Polish immigrant who attended the St. Stanislaus Polish church and played in a small
orchestra after shifts in the mine. His father, a Debsian socialist and leader
in the union local, had taken part in the 1902 anthracite strike. The el-
der Falkowski was an imaginative, well-read man with a passion for theater. Enlisting fellow miners and the Falkowski children, he recreated
figures like Bibus and Wrobel of the popular Polish stage in dramas staged
for the Polish-speaking miners in Shenandoah.

Like Jack, Ed had left school early, to go to work. Ed was sent to the
Ellen Gowen mine (called "Lanigans") until he was twenty-five. Like Jack
too he carried a Latin primer in his lunchpail, studying hungrily during
stolen moments. Both were made recording secretaries of their locals while
still in their teens, probably because of their "bookworm" reputations. The
union furnished the means by which Jack and Ed first became writers.
Ed's reports on union meetings appeared in the *Shenandoah Herald*. Jack
and Ed did not meet until much later, in Chicago, but their correspondence sustained Ed's hopes of advancing his writing into a career. Year's
later, Ed remembered how much it had meant to come home from the
mine to find Jack's letter discussing books and offering encouragement.
"[W]e had a close worker-kinship in our endeavors."[68]

Ed's literacy prompted a fellow miner to suggest that he apply for a
two-year scholarship at Brookwood Labor College in Katonah, New
York. By chance, the president of Falkowski's mine district, Christ Gold-
en, was a member of Brookwood's executive committee. Recommended by his mine local, the mine board, and Golden, Ed left Shenandoah
in October 1926 to pursue his "dreams of something beyond the mountains that girded the town."[69]

At Brookwood, Falkowski received an education in trade union history and tactics taught by the school's head, A. J. Muste, and faculty,
Arthur Calhoun, David Saposs, Helen Norton, Polly Colby, Jasper
Deeter, and others.[70] They were a distinguished group of labor scholars
and teachers. Deeter, for instance, later founded the Hedgerow Theater near Philadelphia where Falkowski's play *Quitting Time* was pro-

duced in 1938. At Brookwood, Ed played the part of Hallemeier in
Capek's *R.U.R.*, and he toured with a dramatic troupe from Brookwood
to play in union locals throughout the East. Drama (street theater and
impromptu skits) was an important cultural element of organized labor's
struggle for political power in the 1930s. Falkowski studied journalism
and read a great deal of literature, hoping for greater involvement in
his own local when he returned home. But in 1928 the mines were letting men go. Ed's old job was gone, and so was Lanigans mine. "In
Shenandoah," he wrote in a short piece published in *New Masses* in
December 1928, "a certain colliery hasn't moved a wheel for months.
The miners are as rusty as its whistles from idleness."[71]

Ed helped raise funds for miners striking in the soft-coal region of
Pennsylvania, in the course of which he was sent to speak at the Church
of All Nations on Second Avenue in New York City. The chairman of
the meeting, Cecil Hedrick, a student at Union Theological Seminary,
suggested that Ed accompany him to Germany where they could find
jobs arranged by the German-American Work-study Exchange. Shipping out as a dishwasher on the luxury liner S.S. *Deutschland*, Ed landed at Hamburg, and from there went immediately to Dresden where his
money promptly ran out. A representative of the Studentenarbeitsdienst
in Dresden assigned Ed to the brown-coal fields of Niederlausitz in Lower Saxony, near Leipzig.[72] For eight months Ed was given apprentice-
type tasks in the mine, timbering and the like.

The following two years were an intense period of immersion in German work life and language, leaving Ed time to write only short occasional pieces for *New Masses* such as "Notes of a Ruhr Miner" (July
1929), a description of speedup that threatened to incite revolt among
the miners; "In the German Bambus" (September 1929), a portrayal of
impoverishment in the soft-coal district; "In a German Mining Town"
(November 1929); and "Mine Funeral—Germany" (January 1930). It
was a remarkable effort given the demands of work and those of making one's way in a new culture and language.

After Niederlausitz, Ed was sent to Osterfelde in the Ruhr, near
Rheinhausen, another soft-coal mine. When the job ran out at Osterfelde, Ed went into a pit near Bottrop, a job arranged through the Christian Miners Union. After eight months he went to work in the steel
mills near Krefeld. Ed, who had acquired a good command of spoken
and written German, was warmly received by his fellow miners. Feeling guilty that he had clung to his work-student status too long, he considered going home. But letters from home were discouraging; Ed was
advised to stay in Germany. Things had gone from bad to worse in the
Pennsylvania coalfields.

If he could not return to America, then he would go to Poland,

the next best thing. There a trade union representative told Ed that
no foreigners would be hired. The economic crisis was closing Polish
mines as well. Just when all doors seem to shut, he received a letter
from Mike Gold urging him to proceed to the Soviet Union; in the
letter Gold included fifty dollars. Together with another fifty he received from an article on mining conditions in Upper Silesia, published in the New York *Bookman,* Ed set out for Berlin to obtain a
work visa. In Berlin he became acquainted with literary radicals who
were giving a great deal of attention to the figure of the worker-writer. Gold's one-man promotion of the American worker-writer seemed
a straw in the wind by comparison.

German worker-writers like Hans Marchwitza and Willi Bredel were
gaining recognition and acceptance in the early 1930s, before the Nazi
period. The German worker-writer traced his lineage back at least as
far as Hans Sachs. Nineteenth-century worker-writers such as Georg
Herweg, Georg Weerth, and Heinrich Kaempchen, never popular authors, nonetheless had won the admiration of well-known writers such
as Theodor Fontane, Gerhart Hauptmann, Richard Dehmel, Arno Holz,
and others.[73] Ed met Otto Biha, editor of *Linkskurve,* who urged him
to write for his magazine, the leading periodical of the German literary
radicals. "In those days," Ed recalled, "I needed very little persuasion.
Articles flowed from my typewriter—I never made two versions of anything I wrote—and never kept a carbon copy since carbon paper was
not easy to get."[74]

Falkowski was probably the only American to write directly for the
German periodical, in German. In his report from Berlin, entitled
"Rebel Poets in Germany," dated 31 July 1931 and published in *Rebel
Poet* (August–September 1931), Falkowski shared some of his impressions of German radical colleagues. *Die Linkskurve,* the magazine of the
Association of Proletarian Revolutionary Writers of Germany, was located in Berlin during the waning years of the Weimar Republic, a period best associated in the popular mind with romanticized decadence.[75]
Linkskurve "constituted the concluding chapter," writes Werner T. Angress, "of a proud German intellectual tradition of revolutionary literature"[76] with roots as far back as Walter von der Vogelweide. Ed contributed several essays, including a portrayal of mining conditions in
Germany entitled "Das Land der guten Hoffnung."[77] Conceived in a
spirit roughly similar to the Rebel Poets, that is, to join writers of diverse origins—worker-writers, middle-class intellectuals, older radicals—
in common cause in order to promote a new revolutionary workers' cultural movement and provide a forum for its literature, *Linkskurve* lost
its momentum finally in its casual dismissal of National Socialism and
its irrelevant attacks on bourgeois literary figures.[78]

Falkowski had an astonishing ability to make contacts and penetrate the revolutionary cultural milieus of Berlin, perhaps on account of his sturdy worker credentials and fluency in German.[79] His essay "Amerika wendet sich nach Links," published in *Die Linkskurve,* provided an overview of American literature from a radical's perspective.[80] In Wedding, the proletarian heart of Berlin, Ed visited the offices of the revolutionary magazine *Rote Fahne* where he made the acquaintance of Willi Munzenberg, editor of *Welt am Abend.* Through Kurt Klaeber he met Egon Erwin Kisch, whom he saw later in Moscow, Johannes Becher, Ludwig Renn, Erwin Piscator, and others active in the literary left.[81] As Klaeber's friend and houseguest, Ed gained entrance to revolutionary circles, where he was warmly greeted—an American worker-writer, a *Kumpel* (pitman) in German mines.

Falkowski was Conroy's main Rebel Poet contact in Germany. Through his dispatches from Germany (and later the USSR), American radicals learned of European revolutionary activity. "Being a 'rebel poet' in Germany," Ed wrote in *Rebel Poet,* "does not mean evoking rhythms out of a profound inkwell. . . . a poet must be something more. He must be an agitator. . . . If America is a-political, Germany is its precise antipode."[82]

This dual focus in Falkowski's reportage shaped his *New Masses* contributions too. In one issue he described both a German mining community and workers' art.[83] The young man who had labored in a Pennsylvania mine until he was twenty-five now reported knowledgeably on revolutionary theater, German radical milieus, and Berlin street life.[84] In addition, Ed sent dispatches to Carl Haessler's Federated Press just as Haessler had once had done for the *Liberator* in covering the 1922 Herrin coal strike. Germany had provided Ed with work, sharpened his linguistic and writing abilities, and furnished contacts with German literary radicals. Convinced that a revolution was in the making in Germany, Falkowski became acquainted with leading revolutionary writers in Berlin. It is fantastic to think that Falkowski's perceptions differ so radically from, say, Christopher Isherwood's in *Goodbye to Berlin.* Isherwood penetrated the twilight world of Berlin's demimonde only minutes from the offices of *Linkskurve.* Yet, in retrospect, the misplaced zeal of revolutionary ambition is a strange but fitting bedfellow of Kurfuerstendammer decadence: both made ready subjects for fascist propaganda. If Falkowski viewed events from a narrow perspective, Isherwood remained on the surface of things. A few writers such as Brecht and Ödön von Horváth were able to grasp the contradictions of the late Weimar Republic through their art. The value of Falkowski's writing, by contrast, lies in its immediacy, its reportage style, and its radical perspective.

Again Ed thought of returning home, and again his mother urged him to find something to do in Europe. Acting on Gold's suggestion, Ed left for the USSR. He would not accept a tourist visa; after a month he was granted a work visa. His destination was ultimately the Donets Basin coal mines—the Donbas.

Arriving in Moscow in the summer of 1930, Ed looked up Sergei Dinamov, a Soviet critic, Americanist, and soon-to-be editor of *Literature of the World Revolution* (later *International Literature*), a Soviet magazine that did much to publicize American worker-writers through its multilingual editions. American writers and intellectuals in Moscow were isolated from the workers' republic that Ed wished to discover. Not content to observe as a journalist, Ed wished to work alongside Soviet miners.

Pat Touhy, whom he had met in Pittsburgh during the Pennsylvania coal strikes of 1928–29 (Touhy had organized the Progressive Miners), introduced Ed to Lozovsky, the head of Profitern (professional workers union), who assigned him an interpreter named Stelman and sent them to Gorlovka, a soft-coal mine in the Ukraine. Preferring anthracite mining, Falkowksi left for the Donbas, the hard-coal region. Impatient and needing income, he searched out the editor of an industrial newspaper in Rostov-on-Don, who advised him to apply at the Artiem mine in the northern Caucasus. Recruited from U.S. factory cities hit by layoffs, as many as fifty thousand Americans were engaged in the construction of the Nadezhdinsk steel mills, the Dnieprostroi dam project, in building other dams and auto plants. Many had worked in the Soviet Union since the early 1920s.

Arriving at the Shachty-Artiem mines, Ed was put to work immediately. Ed learned Russian, living in the home of a Party functionary and attending meetings of the theater-writers' union in off-hours. Reports of his experiences were published in *New Masses*, revealing again his dual interest in working-class conditions and artistic activity.[85]

Hearing that Ed was visiting in Moscow, Anna Louise Strong asked him to become a roving reporter for the *Moscow Daily News*, interviewing American "specialists" (*spez*) in the Soviet Union. In the offices of the *Moscow Daily News*, located on Strastnoi Boulevard (later in the Julius Hammer office building at Petrovksy 8), Ed met with Mikhail Borodin, who had been instrumental in arranging for Bill Haywood, the legendary Wobbly, to come to the Soviet Union. It was an exciting time to be in Moscow for a young American worker-writer who was learning Russian painfully but with success. It was tempting to accept Strong's offer. Moscow theater life gave Ed a further reason. Ed attended plays directed by Meyerhold and Tairoff, and when a troupe of American actors, including Langston Hughes, came to Moscow, he went to their hotel to greet them. In Moscow, various restaurants were designated for separate unions: the newspaper union, engineers' union, writers' union, and so forth, all of which he was a member. In the bar at the Hotel Metropol, Ed came in contact with the *valuta spez*, as they were known, the technical specialists who came to the Soviet Union to earn high wages rather than for ideological reasons.

As a reporter for the *Moscow Daily News* Ed visited sites where the *spez* were engaged. Some years earlier, Lenin had placed Bill Haywood on a committee to establish a colony of foreign workers in the Kuznetsk Basin of western Siberia. Haywood had fled the United States, indicted under the new "criminal syndicalism" laws designed to snuff out IWW opposition to the war. Arriving in Moscow in May 1921, he was met by Borodin, who subsequently introduced him to Lenin. The enthusiasm for the Kuzbas project felt by American workers, engineers, and their families, some of whom were Wobblies, belonged to the earlier period of Soviet industrial development by the time Ed began his trips to Kemerovo, the Dnieprostroi dam, Gorki, and the Donets Basin.[86] At the Gorki auto plant Ed met Walter Reuther, later United Auto Workers' head, who, like Ed, had attended Brookwood Labor College. The Russians had built bungalows for the Americans, many of whom were Hungarian, Irish, German, and Italian by origin. Unemployed in the United States, they had emigrated to Russia with no idea of returning. Some, like Falkowski, learned Russian, married Russians, and raised families. Others made no contacts outside their foreign-worker communities, killing time between shifts in poker games, counting the days until they had enough money to leave. At dance night in Ruthenberg village, established for the American workers in Gorki, Ed observed the cosmopolitan mixture of Hungarians, Irish, Germans, and Italians, "all from the workshops of Detroit. Many are advanced in years, and know the bitterness of unemployment. Anchored at the Molotov auto plant, they have abandoned dreams of return."[87]

The Soviets treated the American *spez* well, providing them with special foods and entertainment. After seeing a production of Langston Hughes's *Scottsboro Limited* in Ruthenberg village, Ed thought about organizing a "suitcase theater," a traveling minstrel show, like the Soviet "blue-blouse" street theater, to dramatize the problems of Soviet socialist construction for the American *spez* to help them adjust to life in the USSR and deal with their prejudices. Nothing came of the idea. The American engineers tended to remain outside of Russian political life, afraid of "infection," while efforts to initiate an equivalent of *rabkor* (workers' correspondence) fell on sterile ground. American workers were accustomed to keeping their complaints to themselves, fearing reprisals should they return to the United States.

Eager to extend his network of revolutionary writers, Jack wrote

Falkowski urging him to draw the attention of Soviet critics and writers to the work of the Rebel Poets. Ed had reservations about Conroy's
accommodationist position, admitting anarchists, Wobblies, Christian
socialists, and so forth as members. Reviewing the 1930 *Unrest* for the
Moscow Daily News, Ed criticized the eclecticism of Conroy's revolutionary "movement." Moreover, Bruno Jassiensky, a member of MORP,
the Soviet bureau that passed judgment on proletarian writing, complained of the "many anarchic tendencies that seem unhealthy" in the
Rebel Poet, predicting that Rebel Poet members were unlikely to "take
those leftward steps that may be demanded by future exigencies."[88] A
chapter of Rebel Poets in Moscow, Ed intimated, was ill-advised. Russian publications were mainly interested in Russian poetry on Russian
problems, addressed to Russian workers, a fact that, Ed admitted, resulted in "flat and ranting" verse. Of interest to the Soviets, on the other
hand, were sketches by American workers describing conditions in the
States. Indeed, Soviet magazines such as *International Literature* were
beginning to pay attention to writers like Jack, H. H. Lewis, Joe Kalar,
and Robert Cruden, largely as result of Walt Carmon's interventions.
Rose and Walt Carmon had come to the Soviet Union following Walt's
departure from *New Masses*, living in a room near Bolshoi Dimitrovka
Street, where Ed often visited.

Falkowski made plans to remain in the Soviet Union. He had married, was a father, and was earning his living as a roving labor journalist. He had befriended influential people in RAPP (the proletarian writers' association), including Bruno Jassiensky, Tretyakov, Bezimenski, Bela
Illes, and others. In 1931, Ed covered the Promparty trials in Moscow
for the *Moscow Daily News*.[89] His hard-won fluency in Russian and familiarity with Soviet mines and factories took him beyond the island
communities of the American *spez*. Jack published several of Ed's reportages in the *Anvil*. His descriptions of industrial villages such as
Stechenkino and Sverdlov evoked for American readers the omnipres-
ent mud, picket fences, sturdy people, and bright faith of the Soviet
Experiment as it affected the Russian worker only one remove from
Tolstoy's peasants.[90]

If there was such a thing as an American emigré literature in the
Soviet Union during the early 1930s, Alan Calmer wrote in the *Daily Worker*, Falkowski must be counted among its members.[91] Journalist and novelist Myra Page would belong too. Alone among the Americans Falkowski was able to write with a certain authority about the
experience of the Russian worker. Investing his future in the Soviet
Experiment, Ed devoted his writing skills to reportage in the interest
of communicating the experience of Soviet workers to their Ameri-

can counterparts. In the ensuing purges, however, he left the Soviet Union, leaving behind his family and his career as a writer.

"Terrible things happened then," Ed later reminisced. "Wonderful people went up in smoke."[92] His boss at the *Moscow Daily News*, Charles Ashleigh, an Englishman who had traveled with the Wobblies in the United States and spent time with Bill Haywood in Fort Leavenworth prison as a political prisoner, was suddenly "purged" in a Party *chistka* (literally, "cleaning"). Crushed by his sudden dismissal, Ashleigh left immediately for London. Untouched by Stalin's purges in 1937, Ed stood by helplessly when comrades lost their jobs, or worse, disappeared. Convinced that the purges were a brief, unfortunate episode, unrepresentative of the underlying spirit of Soviet socialism, Ed decided to ride out the Stalinist *chistka* in the United States. He fully expected to return soon to his Russian wife and his son, George.[93]

His parents meanwhile had settled in Toledo, where Ed joined them, looking for journalism work on one of the two local papers. The editors were not interested in his Soviet credentials. Just when all doors seemed closed, he received Claude Williams's invitation to teach at Commonwealth College, a labor school in Mena, Arkansas. Drafted in World War II, Falkowski was released to work in a defense plant. Ed never returned to the Soviet Union. After the war he reached an amicable agreement with his Soviet wife to divorce. The odyssey of an American worker-writer who had labored in the mines of three nations terminated in a nursing home near Columbia University where I finally located him in 1982. Harassed by the FBI during the Cold War years, Ed had drifted from one trivial occupation to another, supported in increasing measure by his second wife, Helen, who had visited the USSR as a young student in the late 1930s. Aged, frail, yet still nourishing the hope of returning to the Soviet Union, where, he claimed, old people received better treatment than in the United States, Ed Falkowski told me his tale. Its proudest chapter was the role he played in Poland's admission to the United Nations, a favor he wished to return to his grandfather, a Polish peasant who had entered the United States without a passport and supported his family by picking slate at Miller's colliery (the English term for mine, which Ed favored) in Shenandoah, Pennsylvania.[94]

My meetings with Ed Falkowski helped me refine the notion of the worker-writer in an American setting. The term "proletarian writer" is ideological, detached from any comprehensible basis in social relations and experience. Worker-writer, on the other hand, has an analyzable basis in the lives and work of individual writers. Both Jack and Ed had grown up in close-knit, ethnically diverse work communities and attended public school through the eighth grade. Jack apprenticed at age thirteen; Ed's mother signed a certificate so that he could enter the mines at fifteen. Their mothers used family contacts to place Ed and Jack in apprentice-type jobs and accompanied them to work the first day. Both fathers were literate miners who had their own private libraries, admired Eugene Debs, and were leaders in their union locals. Jack and Ed were autodidacts whose hunger for books commanded the respect of their fellow workers. Each was a familiar patron of the public library (Ed had to travel to nearby Hazelton), and each expressed an early desire to write. Both read the *Appeal to Reason* and the Haldeman-Julius Little Blue Books, and both found their way into writing through union journals.

Gold named Falkowski among the new worker-poets whom he heralded in taking over the editorship of *New Masses* in 1928, a group that included Joe Kalar, the silk weaver Martin Russak, H. H. Lewis, Herman Spector, and Keene Wallis ("an old Wobbly").[95] Like Jack, Falkowski began writing poems but discovered that his strength lay in close observation and autobiographical reminiscence. Ed's earliest prose pieces, "A Miner's Good Morning" and "Coal Miners' Children," appeared in *New Masses*, followed by a number of reportages. His most effective writing occurs in passages describing the feel of work and the faces of workers. Gold had been influential in Falkowski's finding his way as a worker-writer. Whether it was his close identification with the revolutionary movement or a penchant toward fixed convictions, Ed's talents seem, in retrospect, to have been largely wasted. He seldom exceeded the narrow limits of revolutionary reportage; his wind was sufficient for the length of a sketch, not for the demands of a novel or book-length study. Yet he was alert to important figures and currents in radical cultural movements, here and abroad. His significance lies in the possibilities that his cosmopolitanism suggest, not in his actual literary production.[96]

"In America," he wrote to H. H. Lewis from Moscow, "too few workers are writing. Proletarian literature is still mainly in the hands of intellectuals."[97] Yet it is this tendency to sacrifice art to ideology, to begin a narrative with a feeling for particularity and mood, then to refuse further organic development, that ultimately aligns Falkowski's work with the "proletarian intellectuals" whom he criticized. Falkowski sought recognition as a writer while attempting to maintain his ties to working-class experience in the Soviet Union through labor journalism. There were many observers, literary and journalistic, who had written sensitively and knowledgeably about the world of work. But the source and uniqueness of the worker-writer's special contributions lay in the nature of the hyphenation. When worker and writer disjoined, Ed

Falkowski could no longer claim that uniqueness nor did it continue to nurture his writing.

10

Proletarian Night:
The Sources of Conroy's Art
in Worker Narrative and Folklore

> I have no idea what kind of a compromise be-
> tween manual work and authorship has produced
> Jack Conroy.
>
> —Dorothy Canfield

IN EARLY 1931 Jack joined a large crew of workmen laying pipe connecting Moberly to a natural gas pipeline south of town. Hired by a
local contractor, Jack dug trenches for the pipe lying along a survey line.
Skilled workers welded the pipe; Jack was part of a locally recruited
workforce.[1] The Conroys enjoyed temporary relief from their usual money woes. The Brown Shoe Company factory on Carpenter Street in
Moberly, where Gladys was employed as a trimmer, was operating five
days of every week—people were walking more in the Great Depression. Moreover, the Army had placed orders for a service shoe.[2] The
largest among the fourteen Brown shoe factories, the plant was (is) a
classic red-brick three-story industrial structure with eyebrow window
arches, situated next to the railroad tracks on a quiet residential street.
Directly across, a tavern prepared lunches for the workers, who received
them by means of an improvised rope hoist, through windows on the
upper floors.[3] The Conroys continued to live in a house—a shack, really—belonging to Pip and Eliza at 130 Collins Street in Moberly. The
house had no indoor plumbing, no running water, and large cracks in
the wall.[4]

Work as a ditchdigger exacted a heavy toll physically from Jack but left his mind free to think and imagine. Forsaking the sleep of the ordinary laborer, he continued to pursue his literary ambitions at night. The paradox of his situation was that unskilled labor left his mind fresh, yet bodily fatigue demanded that he rest. During feverish nights, the brief interstices permitting literary activity, the worker-writer is released to his imagination. This liminal space, the "proletarian night," the correlative of sacrifice and ambition, distinguishes worker-writers from their fellow work companions, introducing ambivalences inherent in their amphibious status.[5] The exceptionality of the worker who labors by day and writes at night is defined in part by what Jacques Rancière calls "a symbolic rupture which is constituted by the entry into writing, that is, into the domain of the literate."[6] Figuratively, proletarian night is the consciousness of difference within sameness. Jack shared the tasks, risks, and working-class education of his fellow workers. So long as he continued to write in his in-between hours, while shouldering family responsibilities, knowing that there was little chance he would escape his situation, he felt divided. This is the particular nature of worker-writer, to be joined and divided at the same time. Yet this division/joining yields a perspective particular to the worker-writer. The coupling of worker and writer was not for Jack simply a virtue made of necessity. If Jack had a chance to succeed as a writer, then it was in the house of labor, as participant and "witness," with a certain angle of vision.

The hyphenation joining worker and writer engenders ambivalences within which creativity takes place. More familiar to the general reader are the ambivalences incurred when working-class subjects cross class boundaries, such as occurs in the work of D. H. Lawrence, Jack London, and Alan Sillitoe. Literature has generally treated labor as a prison-house from which the bright youngster seeks escape through intellectual achievement.[7] Escape, whether through formal education or white-collar occupations, means turning away from but never really divesting oneself of one's class origins.[8] The situation of the worker-writer, however, engenders ambivalences of another kind, reconciled in the uneasy balance between the two statuses, worker and writer.[9] Jack felt comfortable in the familiarity of working-class existence, which he was loath to exchange for something uncertain, an *éspace désert*, as Rancière says.[10] Both Kalar and Conroy felt this. What promise was there, after all, for a better life? In the streets were jobless white-collar professionals along with dispossessed factory workers. And yet the worker-writers craved recognition. Recognition, however, would introduce new ambivalences, the loss of the hyphenated status, separation from the worker's world. In such choices and constraints lay the creative tensions that energized their writing.[11]

* * *

"We saw them in the streets," recalled Granville Hicks,

> the unemployed who were getting by, wandering hopelessly in
> search of work, or standing dazed and bewildered on street cor-
> ners. Those who were not getting by we saw sleeping on the stairs
> of subway entrances, covered with salvaged newspapers. . . . I was
> one of the lucky ones, for I had a job in the bad years, but my
> father lost his job and he and my mother moved in with us. Ev-
> eryone in the middle class, however lucky he may have been him-
> self, knew someone, and if he had any compassion, was helping
> someone who was less fortunate.[12]

Fear and shame seized the jobless white-collar worker; among the workers appeared a new subproletariat of vagrants, beggars, and hustlers.[13]
Wage levels for those still employed were set by what the most desperate would accept, in cruel verification of Ricardo's Iron Law of Wages.
Most workers had little political experience.[14] The rank and file seemed
apathetic, seized by a disabling anxiety that would, in the course of a
few years, erupt in waves of labor militancy.[15] The worker-writers played
a limited role as activists in the labor struggles of the 1930s, yet as "un-
acknowledged legislators" they expressed the buried stirrings of consciousness in the laboring masses and unemployed, anticipating the
spontaneous revolts and organized protests that brought sweeping political changes.[16] Labor's struggle to achieve a voice, to be heard in
American life, was the single most important political involvement of
Jack's life.

   In the proletarian night when other workers enjoyed the sleep of
those whose jobs did not require them to think (in Rancière's phrase,
"que leur métier n'oblige point à penser"),[17] Conroy and other exceptional worker-writers were reconstructing a world of work in their writing, drawing upon the materials of the day's experiences, the fugitive
exchanges between workers, the small and grand strokes of workers'
existences, searching for and recovering the "folk" in transformed work
settings. In the fitful nights between days of labor, the worker-writer
"dreams" the work world. The proletarian night is another name for the
worker-writer's dual consciousness.[18] The feverish dream-state of the
exhausted worker-writer is described in Joseph Kalar's poem:

> Now that work is done, the whistle blows,
> its scream harsh as laughter out of steel,
> piercing through the fat, pushing aside

the fur, the sleep, the dream,
finding each sad little cringing nerve
twitching in its cell of tired flesh,
while from the stack and the round mouths
of black dripping pipes, smoke puffs,
puffs, and sound dies, and giant wheels
cease their grinding, and pistons find rest
in the slimy clutch of oil and grease.
Now that work is done, the mill no longer
with a drone grinds gold out of flesh,
but with the night and its quiet dark
and sleep that presses on the eyes,
the tumult and the drive persist, and we find
remembrance in each nerve and bone and cell
of the grating sharp insistence of each wheel,
the slap of belts, tumultuous din of steel,
the insolent commands, the curses and the sneers
(with humility such a poor veil to hide
the hate that flames electric into the eyes);
though the body cries for rest, writhing
with aching flesh throughout the night,
and sleep descends with its blind crazy dreams,
stuffing the mind with rags that dull,
conviction, still inviolate, remains,
that sleep will not hail victory in,
remove the steel thumbs of the mill
that gouge into the temples (here and here),
return one beam of lost forgotten day,
or drive one foe into the avenging street.[19]

It is a *formidable épreuve*, as Rancière says, to sell one's labor without alienating one's thoughts.[20]

In the late winter of 1931, the pipeline job played out, Jack suddenly had more time than he was able to use constructively. His hope lay in selling another story to Mencken, who wrote after "Hard Winter" appeared: "I hope you have something under way that will fit into the scheme of *The American Mercury*."[21] A reprieve came when *Reader's Digest* paid a hundred dollars for permission to reprint the story in its March issue. "Hard Winter" gave Jack the boost he needed to start a series of stories based upon his experiences as a factory worker, the experiences that in a sense rounded off his "education," the period of self-fashioning, of coming to awareness, that had begun in Monkey Nest when he first copied out the "news" on butcher's paper for the miners. The progress of his growing consciousness, shaped by historical and social conditions, is the subject of his tales of work, the subtexts of *The Disinherited*. The struggle in his mind between the desire for success in conventional terms and a deeper identification with the "disinherited" is the connecting strand in his first novel, which is interlaced with a thick web of work narratives, folk legends, anecdotes, workers' sociolects, grotesque incident, and historical allusion.

A worker narrative is a form of personal narrative centering on some experience such as initiation to a new job, a humorous occurrence, one's relation to one's boss and fellow workers, eccentric characters, loss of work—in sum, incidents from a worker's life whose telling, at the very least, represents a desire to communicate and offer empirical evidence useful in social history and ethnography. Beyond that, however, worker narratives are often entertaining, humanistic expressions of cultural values and social priorities related by a privileged "insider" in the idiom of a collective experience.[22] Personal narratives are stories we tell one another, as David H. Stanley says, about everyday experience, "stories which center themselves in decision-making, conflict, ethical ambiguity, and danger, so that the personal narrative is more often than not a tale about the teller as much as it is about his experiences."[23] Worker narratives achieve full significance through the narrator's identification with an historical epoch, most commonly in a context of political resistance.[24] "Only the practice of action, political and union engagement," argues Philip Lejeune, "enables the life of a worker to achieve identity, that is, structure and value . . ." (translation mine).[25] Or the worker narrative furnishes an episode in one's life, a preface to ascend the economic/social ladder, to become a class leader.[26]

Recent collections of worker narratives, such as *Brass Valley* and *Alone in a Crowd*, reflect new methods in historical documentation.[27] Few authentic worker narratives are extant today that were written before, say, 1920—a fact that reflects upon the conditions of literary production at the time. What we commonly know about American workers in the preindustrial and early industrial eras was mediated by the "champions of the workers": Horace Greeley, William Henry Channing, and others—and novelists such as Sarah Savage, Rebecca Harding Davis, Elizabeth S. Phelps Ward, Hamlin Garland, Theodore Dreiser, and Upton Sinclair. The best-known labor novel today is still Sinclair's *The Jungle* (1906), in which a worker is the central figure throughout. We celebrate Sinclair's account of a Chicago packinghouse not for the portrait of Jurgis Rudkus, the beleaguered immigrant packinghouse worker, but for the novel's exposé of unsanitary practices in the preparation of meat.[28] On the other hand, worker narratives have long been available to the contemporary reader, usually a worker, in union journals and trade publications. Early union journals, such as the *United Mine Workers' Journal*, which came regularly to the Conroy house, published worker narratives, such as one entitled "A Miner's Story" (3 July 1902), a realistic account in the first person by a Pennsylvania miner who complains that his life is scarcely better off than when he first entered the mine as a boy. His children will have to go into the mine too because there is no money to educate them. Such narratives, of course, were addressed to other miners; there was little chance that they would ever touch a broader readership. Occasionally worker narratives turn up unexpectedly in official documents ordinarily devoted to statistical data. A model of the kind appears in the annual *Missouri State Mine Inspector's Report* for 1902 by Charles Evans (mentioned in chapter 1), an immigrant Welsh miner who in his position as state mine inspector did not lose touch with miners and their needs. In prefacing his report Evans chronicles his life, employing many of the "tropes" characteristic of the genre, including a brief but happy childhood, initiation to disaster and death, attachment to family, apprenticeship, union association, worker solidarity, growth of consciousness, identification with labor's struggle for rights, and his rise as a miner to leadership roles.

Traditionally, workers have appeared as subjects of folklore more often than they have written of themselves. The best-known tales, derived from the stories that workers traditionally have told one another, exist in popularized versions about figures such as John Henry, Paul Bunyan, Mike Fink, and Joe Magarac, all linked with specific occupations, performing superhuman feats like pagan gods of labor. Countless anonymous ballads and chanties recount the representative lives of various tradesmen. Early in this century ghost-written and heavily edited "life stories" were published, such as *Letters from a Workman* "by an American Mechanic" (1908) and the "life stories of undistinguished Americans" appearing in Hamilton Holt's *Independent* (between 1906 and 1920). The latter, based upon first-person narratives, were recast into standard English with improprieties removed for a genteel readership.[29]

The lack of published worker narratives from this period has more to do with the conditions of reception and the prevailing systems of literary production than with questions of literacy and desire. On the other hand, "worker narratives" provided the subtexts of important autobiographies and novels that we value today, not for the same reasons that we appreciate worker narratives—as historical documentation and humanistic expression—but for their literary value and, in most cases, illustration of the hero's social and professional advancement. Franklin's *Autobiography,* Twain's *Life on the Mississippi,* and Howells's *A Boy's Life* are an elaboration of workers' apprenticeship tales. Reflecting the aspiration to learn a trade, apprenticeship is a significant stage in the narrator's life, representing the growth of practical wisdom through experience. But the long-term goal is to free oneself from the trade, implied in the relationship between the author and his subject (himself as a young apprentice).[30]

Other forms of "worker narrative" exist in songs and poems, written and oral.[31] Among miners, balladry was especially abundant.[32] Miners' poems were published in the *UMW Journal,* such as "Pick Coal Rhythm" by Lou Parrelle and Andy Lucas, who mined bituminous coal. The first stanza reads:

> If you look for job I tell you true,
> The coal mine he no place for you;
> If you listen while I tell,
> He some place just like hell.[33]

Such regularly cadenced verse is easily memorized, a quality that favors its continued existence through oral transmission. In the composition of Conroy's tales of work, such "simple forms" of expression function as subtexts, preliterary forms of expression, just as slave narrative and folklore constitute subgenres of black literature, transformed and recast.[34] Jack noted the resemblance: "Some of the ex-slaves managed to acquire enough learning to tell their own stories with eloquence and force. In all cases, the inherent drama of the material lent a strength and immediacy resembling that which distinguished the better proletarian novels of the 1930's—recording the human agonies of the Great Depression."[35] In Conroy's own writing, popular ballad and folklore function metonymically and intertextually, echoing oral performances he had witnessed in work communities, rudimentary expressions of protest, sorrow, humor, and dignity.[36]

Worker narratives embrace a wide variety of expression. Whether dreary accounts of oppressive circumstances, instruments in the process of self-fashioning and, by extension, the empowerment of one's class, or merely anecdotal, they serve to give meaning to the author's life. Worker narratives express the human need to be heard, to penetrate the silence surrounding areas of human experience located in laboring occupations. The writer is not content to be viewed as a "folk character" or eccentric. Underlying the narrative is a self-validating desire for recognition, identity. Worker narratives are testimonies of individual conscience, a witnessing to one's time. This is what it is like to do such-and-such in a particular place and time, they tell us.[37]

"Who ever heard of a bad autobiography?" Mencken wrote. "That is, a bad *honest* one."[38] "Honesty" meant a number of things to the *Mercury*'s editor. To authenticate his narratives written by workers (and by hoboes like Jim Tully), Mencken printed the author's credentials in short note-portraits. His interest was not in the fact that the writer was a worker; anyone who had a good story to tell from personal experience and wrote it in a fresh, vigorous manner attracted his attention. Mencken had a scholar's love of ethnographic difference and linguistic variety, evident in his three-volume study *The American Language* (1919–48). Publishing "birds of passage" like Tully and M. L. Batey, Mencken was more interested in defining the national culture in terms of its diversity than in promoting individual contributors' reputations.[39] Mencken rejected contributions by James Thurber, Kay Boyle, and, until 1934, Thomas Wolfe—not on literary grounds but because, as Singleton remarks, of his "growing interest in presenting a lively show at the expense of refinement of thought and expression."[40] Mencken's delight in "a pungent and irreverent phrase" drew him to the "shanty-Irishman," Jim Tully, whose first-person tales of tramping, hobo "jungle" adventures, and prison life appeared in numerous issues of the *Mercury*. Freshness of telling, not pungency, probably accounted for the publication of Batey's "One American's Story" in the September 1929 issue. The story is a pure worker narrative, the first story that the textile-mill worker had written. Mencken published it as it was written, in simple, declarative style with no embroidering.

Mencken exhibited a bias against literary experimentalists. No reflex action, however, guided his exploration of the obscure and unconventional reaches of American life, rather an unorthodox devotion to stirring up something fresh and new in American culture, a culture that, to his mind, had grown stale, fussy, and prudish.[41] If Mencken hoped to discover the authentic "low-down Americano" reality of democratic life as it is actually lived, publishing bricklayers, sawmill hands, convicts, and Wobblies, alongside stories by Josephine Herbst, Zona Gale, William Faulkner, and Elizabeth Madox Roberts, then, according to Mike Gold, Mencken's influence could also be a corrupting one. In his review of Tully's *Shanty Irish*, portions of which first appeared in the *Mercury*, Gold assailed America's premier debunker for encouraging a fake swagger in Tully, a true proletarian on par with Gorki. The main point, Gold wrote of *Shanty Irish*, "is to glorify and romanticize the amount of hard drinking an old Irishman can do. . . . Deep in his [Tully's] heart he must have other things to say of his grandfather and family, rebel things he was ashamed to say because Mencken and Hollywood might smile at his naive sincerity."[42] So much for Tully (and

Mencken's notion of authenticity), who had kicked around America, "done all the dirty work . . . been hammered to steel on the road," and written at least one honest book before "they got him, I mean Hollywood and Mencken."[43]

While he assailed Mencken for tempting a true proletarian to stray from the just and upright path of literary rebellion, Gold's own "East Side Memories," one of several sketches that formed *Jews without Money*, appeared in the September 1929 issue of the *Mercury* (in the same issue with Batey's worker narrative). Gold's sketches were a model of working-class autobiography: warm, intimate pictures of life in an immigrant ghetto, as memorable as Lewis Hine's famous photos. There is little in them, however, that prefigures Gold's call for a new proletarian literary movement. Indeed, revolution intrudes only at the conclusion of *Jews without Money*.[44] Jack was deeply impressed by Gold's sketches and his first (autobiographical) novel. "Where is there another writer so tender and bitter, so simple and profound?" he wrote in a review. "If he has faults I am too blind to see them, too utterly swept away by its graphic power."[45] More than Gold's passionate rhetoric on proletarian literature, the simple, sensuous, passionate believability of *Jews without Money* and *120 Million* influenced Jack and other worker-writers.[46] Literary radicals bashed Mencken in the early 1930s for his conservative political views (Mencken's rejoinder appeared in 1934), yet many of them—Gold, Conroy, Farrell, Le Sueur, Caldwell, Herbst, and others—found new readers through the *Mercury* who refused to read *New Masses* or were unaware of the obscure little magazines in which radicals were published.[47]

Mencken was perhaps attracted to Jack for the same reasons he liked both Tully and Batey. Times had changed, however, and neither Tully nor Batey reflected new realities. Hard times, for instance, had tempered the romantic appeal of tramping. Mencken was holding up George Milburn as a model to young writers like Jack. Milburn's "Tales from Oklahoma" in the *Mercury* were sketches of colorful eccentrics, "locals," that presaged the focus on folk elements, authentic idiom, experience, and humor characterizing some of the best radical writing in the 1930s. Not their political alignments, however, but the vigorous, fresh use of the vernacular and the flavor of lived experience attracted Mencken to Conroy, Milburn, and H. L. Davis.[48] It was ironic that early intimations of new currents in literary radicalism would appear first in the *Mercury*, for instance, worker narrative, linguistic localisms, and occupational lore.

The sources of Jack's literary art, beginning with his sketches for Mencken, lay closer to traditional worker narratives and scholarly explorations of folklore and ethnography than to the orthodox formulations of the cultural left. While Gold was exhorting radical writers to forge literature into weapons for the working classes, persuaded that art would arouse the sleeping masses, scholars like Constance Rourke, Benjamin A. Botkin, Ruth Benedict, Margaret Mead, Robert Redfield, J. Frank Dobie, Zora Neale Hurston, and others were exploring folkways, ethnography, and folklore, concerns that would distinguish some of the best writing of the 1930s, including Conroy's own.

* * *

What Richard Pells terms an "extraordinary interest in folk cultures, agrarian communities, and peasant life that sprang up in the early 1930s" paralleled a renewed interest in vernacular expression and an attraction to lived experience faithfully retold.[49] Intellectuals, as Pells says, traveled to far-flung villages in New Guinea, Mexico, and New Mexico to study primitive cultures close up. The purpose of observers like Stuart Chase and Waldo Frank was to "launch a serious cultural critique of existing conditions in the United States."[50] Benedict's studies of native Americans in New Mexico, for example, suggest a peaceful way of organizing society free of dominating hierarchical structures—a kind of countercultural alternative to power relations and authoritarian institutions.[51] In place of institutions and structures within society that isolate and alienate, reducing human relationships to a profit-and-loss balance, ethnologists and sociologists found in regional experience and primitive cultures expressions of commonality and human dignity.

Monolithic views and dominant notions of culture that ignored native sources of folklore and popular culture found a powerful challenger in Constance Rourke. Rourke refuted Van Wyck Brooks's contention that a "usable past" must be found, or invented, despite the divisions in a society preoccupied with externals and neglectful of intellectual life. Such a "past" could not be "created."[52] Rourke argued that the constituents of a unique American culture lay close at hand. Borrowing a chapter from the German folklorist Johann Gottfried Herder (1744–1803), Rourke looked to popular and folk forms of expression that were central to communal groups, adducing their relationship to broader manifestations of culture. Rourke found the connection she sought in humor. In her influential study *American Humor, a Study of the National Character* (1931), Rourke traces figures like the ring-tailed roarer, the minstrel, and the acerbic Yankee from native sources in popular culture and folklore to their appearance in literature. In 1931, *American Humor* was a cultural declaration of independence and self-affirmation.[53] This same affirmative spirit seemed to infuse new interpretations of regional experience as well. Conroy's Monkey Nest tales are striking evidence of this infusion of folklore into work narratives and autobiographical fiction, but in fact folk humor is an essential element of his narratives almost from the start.[54]

New currents were stirring: social protest, interest in ethnographic difference, and, in some cases, the uses of humor and sex. Erskine Caldwell's work popularized these new currents, but they were widely evident in the work of other literary radicals, for instance Paul Corey's sketches and Ben Field's short stories.[55] Ben Botkin and John T. Frederick were influential in affirming folk values and promoting an interest in regional difference, Botkin as editor of *Folk-Say* (where H. H. Lewis and other midwestern radicals appeared) and Frederick as editor of the *Midland*.[56] Both played instrumental roles in Conroy's industrial folklore work in 1938 through 1941 when he was a member of the Illinois Writers' Project. Botkin and Frederick published young writers whose subjects were drawn from material immediately at hand, an enormous boon to writers stranded in one place. An important model for Jack's *Anvil*, Frederick's *Midland* "grew out of a fundamental belief in the diversity of the country," providing an alternative to the centralized publishing enterprises of New York.[57]

John T. Frederick blazed the trail for midwestern little-magazine editors like Conroy and Dale Kramer. Anxious to correct the stereotyping of the Midwest, Frederick sought to counterbalance the eastern bias in publishing.[58] Independent in his editorial policy, like St. Louis's William Marion Reedy before him (*Reedy's Mirror*), Frederick urged a new note of social realism. Frederick "helped to keep young writers active and interested," Loren Eiseley recalled, ". . . when it was almost impossible to get attention elsewhere."[59] Frederick, a political conservative, did not feel as kindly toward the midwestern radicals as they did toward his magazine.[60] The noncommercial spirit and devotion with which Frederick carried out his editorial duties inspired young writers and editors like Conroy, Paul Corey, Ruth Lechlitner, and many other literary radicals. Conroy corresponded with Frederick, steering writers like Ben Field his way. Field, a New Yorker who worked on Frederick's farm in Michigan in order to learn about midwestern rural life firsthand, played a fateful role when Conroy's *Anvil* merged with *Partisan Review* in 1936.

Without Frederick's bias against urbanization, industrialization, and profit making, a young University of Oklahoma professor named Benjamin A. Botkin was equally devoted to encouraging young writers like H. L. Davis, George Milburn, William Cunningham, J. Frank Dobie, and Lynn Riggs in delineating local difference through speech and lore.

Traditionally folklore study assumed certain governing conditions such as homogeneity, isolation, and stability. Botkin challenged these assumptions, putting the stress on adaptation and showing the process of acculturation, for instance in industrial settings. Diversity and heterogeneity, he showed, were more characteristic of folk custom and behavior than homogeneity. "Centers" of liminal stability exist within larger instabilities caused by economic hardship and uprootedness.[61] In his *Folk-Say* volumes (1929–32) Botkin sponsored a regionalism more aligned with new currents in literary radicalism than was Frederick's *Midland* (which ceased publication in 1933).[62] Botkin published occupational lore from farms, oil fields, and chain gangs, heralding a "progressive" folklore in which the emphasis was on the expressions of work communities. Folklore, in Botkin's view, not only responds to the social dynamics of contemporary life but provides the ground in which literature takes root and replenishes itself. The "folklore of the present," he wrote, "the product of social change and cultural conflict and adaptation, throws valuable light on actual social conditions and problems realistically portrayed."[63]

"Folk" and "folklore" meant different things to different people when Botkin's initial *Folk-Say* appeared in 1929. The two terms were commonly associated with past rural experience or isolated pockets of folk culture sheltered from twentieth-century urbanization and modernity. The novels of Harold Bell Wright and Henry Ford's Greenfield Village reinforced the antiquarian view of folk tradition in the popular mind.[64] During its first years, the Museum of Modern Art refused to exhibit folk artifacts made after 1900. Yet avant-garde artists were attracted to folk art, deriving inspiration from simple forms and primitivistic freshness while ignoring the context in which it was produced.[65] Preservationists fostered the notion of folk art as artifact, frozen in time; in some instances, attempts were made to restore lost customs or inculcate traditions that were actually inappropriate, such as morris dancing in the southern Appalachians.[66] Such notions of folk expression observed class lines, idealizing the lives of its subjects while neglecting the preference of their native subjects for commercialized music rather than Child's ballads.

Carl Sandburg, Vachel Lindsay, and Stephen Vincent Benét provided an important connection between the older legacy of the southwest humorists and the social realities of the 1930s. The native elements of American art had its defenders among the avant-garde, but many, like Robert Coady, editor of the *Soil*, focused on the surface of American life, as Tashjian says, "espous[ing] an aesthetic primitivism" of jackhammers and jazz.[67] Folk and folklore were topics of debates in the 1920s

among avant-garde artists and writers searching for literary uses of machine-age technology and structures. These debates focused on formal
problems, ignoring the social and political contexts in which folk art
is produced, particularly with reference to black Americans.[68]

Matthew Josephson, influenced by his exposure to Dada in Paris, welcomed the new symbolisms and tempos of machine-age life, rather oddly
discovering in technological structures "folk-elements" possessing aesthetic value. Greenwich Village intellectuals and avant-garde artists
admired the formal properties of industrial structures but expressed an
uneasiness regarding technology itself.[69] In his paintings of locomotives
and his photos of the Ford Motor Company's River Rouge plant (1927),
Charles Sheeler abstracted the sheer lines of power and the smooth,
slow curves of machine technology while attending to realistic detail
with photographic accuracy in his painting. Sheeler was, as Rebecca
Nemser says, "master of the industrial sublime." Yet, she notes, "it is
striking how both the paintings and the photographs of River Rouge
are almost entirely empty of people, despite the fact that tens of thousands worked there. The few who do appear in Sheeler's vision of the
Rouge are tiny, bent figures dwarfed by the great machines."[70] Modernists painters in their search for purity of line missed the human machines
inside the plant. The impending crisis in the economy that put factory
laborers out on the street, making them all too visible, produced an
ideological crisis in artistic circles: How to make an art that reflects
democratic beliefs (which grant, among other things, artistic freedom)
without compromising artistic standards?

Machine culture preoccupied intellectuals, artists, and writers in the
1920s. Some, like Waldo Frank, saw nothing but spiritual deprivation
in the industrial landscape.[71] Others, like Thomas Hart Benton, embraced technology with enthusiasm, selecting with discrimination symbols and images for their art. Ugliness was more often cited as a reason
for condemning industrialism than was the spectacle of men and wom-
en laboring in unsafe conditions for low pay. Sandburg knew intimately the sweat, smoke, and grime of industrialism, but his aim was intensely nationalist in spirit, as Roderick Nash points out.[72] Industrialism was
a permanent part of the landscape and woven into the fabric of society. Factory closings made this much painfully clear. The 1930s called
for new myths, symbols, and subjects answerable to the immediate needs
of a nation that had temporarily lost its nerve.

If modernity had come to mean disruptive change, alienation, discarding the past, breaking with convention and tradition, and a kind
of metaphysical condition of homelessness, then Botkin, Rourke, Alain
Locke, and a growing number of writers, artists, filmmakers, musicians,

intellectuals, little-magazine editors, and activists sought to restore a sense of community and reaffirm democratic practices. Their numbers soon included Aaron Copland, Pare Lorentz, Thomas Hart Benton, Dos Passos, Steinbeck, Williams, Lewis Mumford, Reinhold Niebuhr, as well as members of the Federal Art, Theater, Music, and Writers' Projects. For a time, the worker became a subject of art and literature. The left talked of building a workers' cultural movement; establishment publishers grew interested in radical subjects, although few hazarded the financial risks involved in publishing unknowns.

The emergence of this new cultural attention to industrial subjects was welcomed by Botkin, who in his *Folk-Say* volumes rejected the Paul Bunyan kind of occupational folklore popular among nationalists in the 1920s. Such folklore was "rooted," as he said, "in the myth of pure national cultures and pure races, that is, folklore as the expression of the soul of a race or nation."[73] At worst the nationalist view of folklore might degrade into a regressive folk dogma, a racist *Volksgeist*. Botkin, as Hirsch notes, "was one of the first American folklorists who did not view the modern world as a threat to the existence of folklore."[74] Industrialization destroyed traditional patterns of folklore but gave life to transformations in the aleatory, unstable communities of the factory. While nostalgic preservationists like Henry Ford attempted to preserve the past, Botkin and others looked for new manifestations of folk expression in urban and industrial settings. The Southern Agrarians' regressive view of regionalism, Botkin argued, ignored the industrial and occupational social structures that furnish the conditions for folklore.[75] Marxist critics were just as negligent of the circumstances that produce folklore, according to Constance Rourke, who took them to task for ignoring the significance of regional difference. Rourke argued that to understand class struggle in America one must give attention to the industrial and rural character of regions. Not in some abstract "intellectual synthesis," she said, is it possible to uncover the potential for revolution but in the "obscure but essential phases of the native character," which differ according to local differences. It is an error to make proletariat and folk separate categories. Industrialization standardizes ways of life, but differences remain. Calverton and other Marxists ignore these differences.[76]

This new emphasis on regional difference, cultural pluralism, and a broadened view of "folk" that included the dispossessed factory worker raised howls of protest from some quarters.[77] Missouri's Thomas Hart Benton antagonized eastern critics who were quick to see evidence of provincialism, if not mediocrity, in the work of the American Scene school.[78] Henry Nash Smith, in Botkin's *Folk-Say, A Regional Miscella-*

ny: 1930, replied to the charge of parochialism arguing that "provincialism is not a bondage, but a freedom."[79] Writers could hope to find impetus for creative activity by absorbing themselves in the place where they happened to be. In fact, many had no other choice.[80]

Regional difference, social content, and "labor lore" were elements of a new democratic myth of concern constructed by the radicals, who resurrected traditional values such as community and cooperation and reasserted others such as the right to live without want, from the fruit of one's labor, and the right to take exception in open assembly.[81] In the social distress of the early Depression such values constituted a new democratic myth of concern that could serve as a foundation for a new society. The existence of such a myth of concern, however, had to compete for the worker's attention with the escapist fictions of mass culture. The Hollywood dream merchants, popular fiction writers, and commercial designers were tough competitors for the democratic myth-makers. The promise of a new consumer world, not revolutionary rhetoric or schemes for a workers' America, would succeed in winning people's attention. Yet a small number of artists and writers ignored the odds against their success, feeling that somehow they were responsible for reconstructing a democratic culture, as if the people possessed the raw ingredients but had lost the recipes. For Conroy, this responsibility was shaped by the curve of his own experience and conscience. His work as writer and editor was an acting out of the radicals' version of the democratic myth.[82]

The resources of orality, folk expression, and regional difference furnished Conroy's writing with the material to elaborate this version of the democratic mythos. His tales of workers describe the breakup of older, organic forms of community, tracing the dispossessed into the factory cities where they attempt perilously to reconnect, and offer, in isolated instances, rudimentary expressions of resistance.[83] Working with the materials he gathered in the course of his experience as a worker, Conroy helped shape a new subject matter in American literature that reflected the social forces and indigenous cultural traditions representative of dispossessed workers in the decades following World War I.

Several currents that would alter American literature flowed together in the early 1930s. New figures began to appear in stories and novels—migrant workers, Georgia sharecroppers, Southside Chicago gang members, "bottom dogs," hucksters, panhandlers, gangsters, strikers, Communist organizers, desperate visionaries, dispossessed black workers, abandoned women, runaway children—all evidence that some terrible calamity had shredded the social fabric. Long before labor's collective voice wrought fundamental changes in the workplace, the literary radicals gave literary expression to the unheard voices of these marginalized people, to "those who do not write."

In the early Depression, people had time to talk; talking was a consolation to them. The new social frontier provided opportunities for writers to listen to the people talking and to record impressions. "Talking" appeared in the titles of stories and documentary narratives such as Meridel Le Sueur's "I Hear Men Talking" and Benjamin Appel's *The People Talk,* both writers whom Jack published. Little-magazine editors were interested in the "people talking" represented in the fictions of young writers like Le Sueur, Conroy, Algren, and Caldwell, ethnologists of the dispossessed. Trained in ethnography, Zora Neale Hurston made studies of the speech patterns and lore of southern black communities, including her native Eatonville, Florida. Hopping freight cars, Algren jotted down in a notebook peculiar speech locutions of fellow migrants. Regional dialects were no longer synonymous with the provincial novel. In Oxford, Mississippi, Faulkner "discovered that my own little postage stamp of native soil was worth writing about and that I would never live long enough to exhaust it . . . so I created a cosmos of my own." The appearance of "road books" by James Rorty, Nathan Asch, and Erskine Caldwell attested to the interest of readers in regional difference.

Conroy transformed the material of oral expression and occupational folklore—subliterary texts—into the generic forms of autobiographical fiction. Attuned to speech genres, to the rhythms and syntax of workers' speech in their social context, Jack conveyed more than the curiosity of ethnographic difference or historical fact. Inscribed in his writing are the accents of workers' sociolects as well as intertextual echoes from folkloric and popular expression. His tales of work transcribe the "unofficial poetry" of experience that comprises the speech acts of the workplace. Autonomous social discourse weaves his texts together in an egalitarian balance, distributing them horizontally on the level of the subject. The narrator is subsumed within the inner dialogism of voices playing against one another. Words interact with words of "the other," the interaction taking place, as if overheard in the imagination of the worker-author. Jack possessed an ear for spoken language, an uncanny memory, and an irrepressible sense of humor that set him apart from most of the proletarian novelists. First-hand experience, realism leavened by folk humor, and the creative transcriptions of workers' speech genres—"novelized" in Bakhtin's sense—are literary ingredients of Conroy's writing that first attracted Mencken's attention. They distinguish his work from the proletarian "formulas" that diminish so much

1930s radical fiction.[84] Another characteristic of his work has to do with
what Gramsci calls the "common sense" element of folklore wedded to
timeless strategies of survival and resistance.

According to Gramsci, dominant views of folklore tend toward the
naive, nonthreatening conceptions of the folk in accordance with the
"'official' conceptions of the world . . . that have succeeded one another in the historical process."[85] Folklore, Gramsci wrote, should be studied "as a 'conception of the world and life' implicit to a large extent in
determinate (in time and space) strata of society and in opposition (also
for the most part implicit, mechanical and objective) to 'official' conceptions of the world. . . ."[86] Mass culture, by contrast, is consensual,
"an important factor in the encouragement of counter-hegemonic practices."[87] Folklore—genuine expression, not "fakelore"—presents an alternate value system expressing patterns of resistance, cooperation, commonality, subversion. Such a value system is implicit in the folklore of
marginalized peoples, such as the Uncle Remus tales.[88] In his industrial
folktales, like "The Fast Sooner Hound" and "Slappy Hooper," Conroy
discloses similar patterns of vernacular protest among factory workers
and artisans in which cunning and subterfuge are marginal strategies
of survival and resistance.[89] Jack, of Jack and the Beanstalk, was "the
great-grandfather of all folk heroes," according to Ben Botkin, for these
reasons.[90]

Conroy's tales of work portray a folk consciousness in crisis. If irony
and paradox represent a modernist mode of consciousness, a perceptual
response to an absurd and fragmented world, as Alan Wilde argues, then
a counterpart in the workers' world, as viewed in Conroy's stories, is earthy
humor and stoical fatalism.[91] In the early 1930s, the cultural authority of
modernism implied, according to Alfred Kazin, "the reversal of the 'century of hope,'" initiated by Emerson "in an age of faith."[92] Such a reversal was in Mike Gold's eyes defeatist. In response to the Party's demand
for affirmation, proletarian novelists forced their material into formulaic
narrative patterns. Conroy's tales of work, by contrast, derive their "affirmation" through the perception that fundamental to the folk consciousness is the will to endure.[93] In his "Soviet phase," Jack moved closer, at
least in his critical essays, to accepting the Party's attitude toward affirmation, evaluating literature on its quotient of "social awareness."[94] Yet,
even during the time that he felt closest to the Party and supportive of
its aims, Conroy wrote stories like "The Weed King" and "The Cement
King" whose "affirmation" lies in fundamental qualities he associates with
timeless folk characteristics (such as stoic endurance) rather than in as-
criptive proletarian formulas.[95]

Jack was interested in promoting a working-class ethos by creating a new literature drawn upon the traditional materials of indigenous folk expression and worker narrative, placing his stories in settings familiar to uprooted workers: the factory floor, railroad yards, mining camps, skid rows, and so forth. His tales of workers, written in the period 1930–35, bear witness to the tumultuous social circumstances of industrial workers and farmers who, caught between an older traditional order and a newer, unstable world of movement and change, seem confused, wondering, anxious. Conroy's tone, Daniel Aaron remarks in his introduction to the 1963 edition of *The Disinherited,* "is bemused and wondering rather than protesting and declamatory."[96] A storyteller, not a fiction writer, Jack drew upon the resources of memory, orality, and observation in his attempt to render the texture of experience. Jack transcribed creatively the speech, gestures, attitudes, folkways, and antics of workers he had known, preserving the blunt, unpolished artlessness and comic realism of the original. This was a far cry from the genre of contemporary folk plays made popular by Paul Green and Lynn Riggs, or the spirit of John Gould Fletcher's folklore researches into balladry, yet in a sense it was a tougher assignment because Conroy did not rely upon literary conventions familiar to middle-class readers. Like African-American writing—the work of Langston Hughes or Zora Neale Hurston—Jack's storytelling borrows performance-oriented conventions from oral tradition, places language in specific work settings, and integrates folk consciousness into an alternative value system that interprets specific cultural and social circumstances of marginalized peoples.[97]

Conroy's work shares too with the writing of Ignazio Silone, the Italian author of *Fontamara* and *Bread and Wine,* in employing language that corresponds to the harsh existence of their subjects—Silone's *brutto stil nuovo* and Conroy's "crude vigor." In *Fontamara* (1930), Silone uses forms and idioms drawn from and familiar to the hapless *cafoni,* peasants of the Abruzzi. There is less need to invent than to encounter directly in one's art the immediacy of their existence. Both authors portray the droll manner in which people turn oppression and suffering into humor and dwell unsentimentally upon the grotesque aspects of human conduct. Moreover, both represent a new comic realism, a carnival spirit of alterity rather than alienation, affirming the self as subject, humanizing, exploring the space between oneself and the other rather than withdrawing into the self. In this space between lay a communicable experience to deliver in its own accents, idioms, and modalities.

Communicable experience grounded in orality was, as pointed out earlier, a constituent of Jack's early education and preparation as a writer. Humorous storytelling and bawdy songs were a staple of the Irish and Italian miners in Monkey Nest. From the time he first apprenticed, Jack gravitated to storytelling locales. The farmers who gathered behind the Merchant's Hotel on Saturdays told of superstitions like the "horsehair snake" omen, a motif employed in telling the story of an ostracized miner crushed to death in a drift mine ("Down in Happy Hollow"). In the Wabash shops Jack heard of wonder dogs and the tricks of legendary "car toads," material that he used in his stories and industrial folktales.

The direct, vivid speech of Wobbly storytellers in the hobo jungles, boxcars, and union halls impressed Jack during his tramping days. The Wobblies created a kind of performance art defined by its own genres, loosely knit peculiarities of expression, drawing upon gritty experience, humor, folklore, and idiomatic speech. It is interesting to compare their writing with Conroy's. The Wobblies' Joe Hill: "As a rule a fellow don't bother his head much about unions and theories of the class struggle when his belly is flapping up against his spine. Getting the wrinkles out is then the main issue and everything else, side issues."[98] Conroy: "Boys, I'm here to say and state that that piece-working merry-go-around will make a man slap his own dear baby brother square in the mouth and pick his pockets or steal his sugartitty when he ain't looking. It's dog eat dog and the devil take the hindmost. A man had better get him a tin bill and pick horse apples with the chickens. He'd better let somebody punch out his eyes and get him some blue glasses and a cup and a sign 'Please Help the Blind' and sit on the corner the rest of his natural days."[99] Similarities lie in the heavily stressed beat of the prose rhythms and the flavoring of speech with vivid localisms. The language is direct, economical, forceful, yet "philosophical." The Wobblies' anarchic, independent spirit colored Jack's own political "porkchop" philosophy.[100]

"The storyteller," Walter Benjamin writes, "takes what he tells from experience—his own or that reported by others. And he in turn makes it the experience of those who are listening to his tale. The novelist has isolated himself. The birthplace of the novel is the solitary individual, who is no longer able to express himself by giving examples of his most important concerns, is himself uncounseled, and cannot counsel others."[101] Storytelling, Benjamin argues, grows out of "the milieu of work" and the storyteller "will always be rooted in the people, primarily in a milieu of craftsmen."[102] Orality, craftsmanship, and wisdom identify Conroy's best work.

Oral thinker and prophet of the concrete, to use E. A. Havelock's terms, Conroy drew upon popular, vernacular, and literary sources, improvising like a folk storyteller, discovering in forms of expression forms of experience.[103] His task was to orchestrate his chorus of worker narratives into a many-voiced novel representing the reality of the worker's world, as he knew it, in which the narrator would serve more as a listener than as an active protagonist in the action. The folk spirit survived under the conditions of industrialism and the crisis of the economic depression. It was better to create stories from within these patterns than to impose some schema of ideological origin. The worker-writer's role, as Conroy conceived it, was to reproduce from the fragmented evidence of a confused and broken reality a coherent narrative that remains true to the heterogeneous cultural diversity and irregular textures of the original experience.

Mencken pushed him to expand his storytelling into a novel. In a fury of expectation and hope he assembled a montage of stories into the first draft of *The Disinherited*. In longing for success as a writer, which would free himself and his family from the economic uncertainties that had bedeviled his working life, however, Jack encountered a different set of contradictions. The very conditions of recognition, of literary prominence, were antithetical to the editorial enterprise he would soon initiate. In the model of Rebel Poet networking and later in the example of the *Anvil*, Jack participated in creating a rhizomatous system of literary production that was at odds with the arborescent structures of literary prominence characteristic of the dominant culture. As an editor, he was opposed to the author system, to literary cliques and the "making" of a writer's reputation, yet in order to achieve recognition his own writing must ascend the hierarchical scale of literary reputation within an unfamiliar system of production and publication. Literature as a vocation might free Jack from manual labor, but entry into the dominant literary system generated other contradictions. Increasingly, Jack grew dependent upon the Party's cultural apparatus, not only for the material support it offered his magazines through its distribution agency but because it helped establish his reputation without forcing him to choose between the twin statuses essential to his creative life, worker and writer. Such contradictions ultimately cost him both the *Anvil* and his recognition.

11

The Gathering Storm: 1931

The American public does not like to read about the life of toil. . . . if our writers were to begin telling us on any extended scale of how mill hands, or miners, or farmers, or iron-puddlers really live, we should very soon let them know that we did not care to meet such vulgar and commonplace people.
—William Dean Howells (1891)

ACROSS THE BROAD CORNLANDS and in isolated mining communities in 1931, farmers, miners, and unemployed factory workers manifested their discontent, foreshadowing organized strike activity in the cities. Even small midwestern towns like Moberly, where rebellion was a privilege reluctantly accorded youngsters, witnessed street demonstrations. A favorite metaphor on the left was the "gathering storm," an expression that Myra Page borrowed to title her novel of black-white tensions in the South. "Reds"—outsiders always in the minds of small-town denizens—were behind the small demonstrations (a brace of participants at most) in Moberly's Tannehill Park, according to the local newspaper.[1] In the spring, Iowa farmers forcibly resisted state veterinarians commissioned to inoculate dairy cattle against tuberculosis and marched on the state capitol in Des Moines. Faced with foreclosure, other farmers staged direct actions, spilling milk in the notorious "cow wars," seizing and threatening to hang a judge, and organizing themselves into the Farmers' Holiday Association.[2] These were spontaneous, nonideological, grass-roots demonstrations of anger and frustration. The nature of the farmers' rebelliousness was more conservative than radical, in line with Jacksonian independence, demanding individual rights, like the earlier populist movement.[3] Mainly property owners, the rebellious farmers felt little solidarity with miners and factory workers. Nonetheless, Conroy hoped that worsening conditions would introduce a new consciousness among the farmers, whose best interests lay in collective action and solidarity with workers.

It was a time of foreclosure and shutdown, but it was also a time of breathless possibility. To the literary radicals the political climate seemed poised like a midwestern summer afternoon, tense and foreboding, ready to produce a mighty storm. Raymond Kresensky, the Presbyterian minister now living in Bellevue, Iowa, wrote to fellow Rebel Poet Kenneth Porter of his travels through Illinois, Indiana, Tennessee, and Missouri:

> Obviously I was impressed with the numbers of boomers on the road but then we have had the unemployed going by day in and day out on the freights. I saw an unemployment parade in St. Louis and left just one day before the riots. In Evansville it seemed like thousands sleeping out in the parks but Nashville looked comfortable. The people in the mountains of East Tennessee have plenty of food and looked prosperous to me—but then they never had anything and they never speculated. I dare say the depression has hit Iowa farmers pretty hard but prosperity hit them hard too. Now in one county there are 54 foreclosures in the Fall term of court—in Iowa.[4]

To Kresensky, revolution seemed near, but how it would begin was not yet clear. Unemployed councils, largely upon the initiative of the Communist party, were organizing the jobless and homeless. On the other side, counterrevolutionary forces had begun to clash with the radical left in a number of notorious cases, including the Scottsboro Boys affair, when, in the spring of 1931, eight black youths in Alabama were arrested for allegedly raping two white girls, who, like themselves, had bummed a free lift on a freight. Tensions were mounting, tensions that, the midwestern radicals hoped, would charge a new rhetoric of revolt and supply revolutionary subject matter.

* * *

In the summer and fall of 1931, the Conroys were still living in the Addises' shack on Collins Avenue. Jack's brother-in-law, Charlie Kelly, remembers the conviviality of the Conroy home, the evenings when Jack made chili in a "thunder mug"; it seems that penury drew the family together.[5] Jack returned to digging ditches, an experience that he shaped into the sketch "Pipe Line," published in the *American Mercury*.

Walt Carmon, who, as noted earlier, moved to the Soviet Union to join a number of foreign journalists on the *Moscow Daily News*, drew the attention of the International Union of Revolutionary Writers (IURW) to Conroy's literary work, both as editor and writer. Jack returned the favor with a glowing notice in *Rebel Poet* of the IURW's magazine, the English-language edition of *Literature of the World Revolution* (later, *International Literature*), which first appeared in June 1931.[6]

Anxious to expand contacts abroad, Jack solicited exchanges with German and French revolutionary writers. In France the Association des Écrivains et Artistes Révolutionnaires (AEAR) named Conroy a member in absentia and published an anthology of American radical writers, *Poèmes d'Ouvriers Américains*, which, as Jack noted in a *New Masses* review, oddly left out Kalar, Herman Spector, Frank Thibault (and Conroy himself), who better represented American worker-writers than did Ralph Cheyney or Miriam Allen deFord, who were included.[7]

As mentioned in an earlier chapter, Ed Falkowski had made contacts in the spring of 1930 with German proletarian writers and editors in Berlin after quitting mine work in the Ruhr and, on Mike Gold's suggestion, heading for the Soviet Union to take up similar employment and to write of his experiences as an American worker in Soviet mines. Falkowski's contacts with Johannes Becher, Erich Weinert, Kurt Klaeber, and other German revolutionary writers inspired reflections on their rebel counterparts in America, to the disadvantage of the latter. Conroy published Falkowski's essay "Rebel Poets in Germany" in the August–September 1931 issue of *Rebel Poet*, in which the Pennsylvania miner's son decried poems of the lyrical variety dedicated to revolutionary causes, works lacking evidence of the author's personal engagement (the criticism sounds suspiciously like that frequently leveled against Ralph Cheyney, Conroy's coeditor of *Unrest*). Despite bars to free expression in Germany, Falkowski wrote, German rebel poets speak out to workers in their own rhythms and accents, a far cry from the "inkwell" variety appearing in American magazines of the left.

Conroy himself was striking a more strident revolutionary tone in his *Rebel Poet* editorials; certainly no one, least of all Falkowski, would have suggested that Jack was not personally involved in the struggle or did not speak directly to fellow workers. Yet the old tendency toward florid language, a weakness Mencken had pointed out, cropped up in Jack's occasional rhetorical excesses. In the same issue in which Falkowski's assessment of the German rebel poets appeared, Jack fulminated on capitalism's moribund extravagances, concluding that "the American worker is not the clod he seems to be. He has begun to think; when he gets into his full stride his footsteps will shake the earth and tumble down many a gaudy and gilded temple."[8]

As loose and slight as they were, connections with editors and literary functionaries in the Soviet Union, through the intervention of Falkowski, Carmon, and later Norman Macleod, occasioned Conroy's more outspoken support of the workers' paradise, as evidenced by the appearance of Soviet poets in the *Rebel Poet* and by Conroy's polemical editorializing. Jack published translations of the Soviet experimental lyricist V. V. Mayakovsky, who committed suicide in 1930; the peasant poet Demian Bedni; and the German revolutionary Johannes Becher. The translator for the Becher poem was a brash, outspoken immigrant named Philip Rahv who would figure large in events affecting the fate of the Rebel Poets and later Conroy's *Anvil*. In the double issue of *Rebel Poet* (June–July 1931), Cheyney and Morris Spiegel speculated on the emergence of a new intelligentsia in the Soviet Union, created from the proletariat. Topics and commentaries reflecting favorably on the Soviet Experiment multiplied during the brief existence of the *Rebel Poet* (just under two years). There were poems anticipating a revolutionary future along Soviet lines (John Rogers's "Someone," in number 4), a woodcut print of Lenin in the fall 1931 issue, and a surplus of very bad poems, including one entitled "Karl Marx Started It," beginning, "All hail to Marx, the champion of mankind!"[9]

In retrospect, it seems uncharacteristic that Jack would defend the Soviet Union against charges of religious persecution and liquidation of the kulaks; he would have resisted mightily any such incursions against his own freedom and personal welfare. Yet in letters to his friends Conroy seemed impervious to criticism of the Soviet Experiment.[10] After all, it was a time when intellectuals and artists were inclined to look the other way in viewing reports of Stalin's brutality. No less than Lincoln Steffens, celebrated for his truthful exposure of urban corruption, claimed that he had seen the future during his visit to the Soviet Union and suggested that America would do well to emulate it.[11] Steffens's *Autobiography*, published in 1931, impressed Jack deeply. He noted Steffens's preference for communism over capitalism as a modernizing system for backward countries but apparently overlooked the fact that Steffens expressed no desire actually to live under communist rule.[12]

Conroy's political judgments were often colored by feeling rather than cool analysis, understandable when one reviews the menace that impoverishment posed for him and his family and the anger he felt toward a seemingly indifferent Hoover administration. Indeed, the John Reed clubs and the CPA encouraged the idea among writers that the capitalist economy was at fault for the workers' plight, not any shortcomings on the part of the workers themselves. The figure of Theodore Dreiser, who visited the Soviet Union in 1927–28 and returned as an impromptu spokesman of the Revolution's aftermath, was invoked as a model for writers, at least until charges of anti-Semitism threw into question his moral authority.[13] The USSR, beyond its borders, had become for many an alienated writer and artist what Simone Weil called "the spiritual home of the working class, their 'country.'"[14]

Jack had entered his "Soviet phase" by the summer and fall of 1931, a period of conflicting claims on his intelligence and attitudes, as we shall examine. Ready to refer readers to works that would give "the correct revolutionary interpretation of international events," he nonetheless bolted from Party strictures and institutionalized vanguard organizations; these were deeply at odds with his independent radicalism, which like the anarchic, detached rebelliousness of the IWW resisted rigid, top-down Party structures. Even in periods when to some radicals the Soviet system seemed the only alternative to despair and defeatism in America, Jack would not go so far as to pledge unflagging loyalty to the hammer and sickle; yet it delighted Jack to see H. H. Lewis's rude attempts to "épater la bourgeoisie" with verses such as:

> I'm always thinking of Russia,
> I can't keep her out of my head,
> I don't give a damn for Uncle Sham,
> I'm a left-wing radical Red.[15]

Events were such in 1931 and 1932 that Conroy was forced into an ever-deeper dilemma between his sentiments and his deeper instincts. His editorship of the *Rebel Poet* is a case in point. Begun as an eclectic organ, accommodating all stripes of rebel activity provided they promoted the magazine's putative aim, "Art for Humanity's Sake," the *Rebel Poet* was pulled in different directions when factions formed and tensions mounted during the early Depression years.[16] Cheyney and Conroy had begun the Rebel Poets as an independent radical organization in the wake of the Sacco-Vanzetti executions; both were anxious to represent the myriad of radical convictions, from eccentric vegetarian-pacifist to mainline groups such as the Socialist party. One steady conviction united all members: revulsion toward instances of social inequity, ascribed vaguely to "big-money power," and the decade of post–World War I political reaction. Conroy and Cheyney supported in a general way the fragmented revolutionary program of the left but remained cautiously independent of affiliation with any political party, electing rather to follow their own eclectic cultural program. Nonetheless, the coexistence of competing idealisms, characteristic of the early Rebel Poets, soon dissolved; the 1930s called for declaration and engagement. Moreover, Cheyney and Conroy discovered fundamental differences between their own attitudes and aims, which eventually led Cheyney to disclaim any links with Jack's editorial program.

Raised in genteel circumstances, drawn to liberalism by his father's influence, Ralph Cheyney believed, along with Shelley, that poetry might change the world. Jack was a worker-intellectual, a veteran of strikes and homelessness, whose commitment to a tradition of cooperative, fraternal resistance was forged through action and example. Cheyney grew evermore distant from Jack, who openly welcomed Communist causes in the pages of the *Rebel Poet,* eventually breaking with his editorial policies altogether. Friends had warned Conroy for years that the Cheyneys were opportunists whose main concern was to turn poetry writing into a money-making enterprise by enticing aspirants to subscribe to their courses. There was desperate little money in peddling poetry as a trade, as the Cheyneys discovered in their soon-defunct venture to run a correspondence school of poetry.

Some of Jack's correspondents urged him to improve the *Rebel Poet,* suggesting that he turn the magazine leftward and dump the Cheyneys. Walt Carmon, managing editor of *New Masses,* complained of the low quality of the verse printed and promised support.[17] "You need not be a party member, but one simply can't keep out of the main stream of the movement," he wrote.[18] Walt Snow, former mill worker and chief Rebel Poet contact in New York City, pressed Jack even more than did Carmon. It appeared that Snow judged poetry solely on its radical content. When Snow sent his choice of best poets appearing in the 1930 *Unrest,* Jack scribbled in the margins of Snow's letter: "At least 1/3 of these are out-and-out Communists."[19] Take a stand, Snow told Conroy: "Personally I think you are more of a Bolshevik. . . . But remember, Conroy, that if one tries to appeal to all branches of the so-called liberal-radical movements at this stage of the class struggle he will be left out in the cold." Conroy's marginal comment reads: "We can be most effective by being inclusive. How many of these rebel social vision poets or poetry-readers are narrow communists? A small minority!"[20] Jack wished to incite revolt in his publications without endorsing any party or orthodoxy.[21]

The most outspoken correspondent on the subject of the *Rebel Poet* and the Cheyneys' editorial influence was Joe Kalar, the Minnesota worker-writer. "Log-rollers," he called the Cheyneys, "labor racketeers" who "are exhibiting the labor and revolutionary movement for the satisfaction of their egos." What was needed in the Rebel Poets was more "lumberjack robustness" in place of a "literary odor" that Kalar identified as an attribute of the eastern radical crowd.[22] Jack himself wrote Cheyney, advising him to stop patronizing "fat girls" with money whom

Ralph solicited for his correspondence poetry courses; yet, at the same time, he knew the Cheyneys were hard up and needed cash.[23]

Meanwhile Conroy's editorial work was beginning to receive attention in Moscow, owing to Falkowski's promotion. Leaving his mining job in the Caucasus, Ed had gone to Moscow in the spring of 1931 for a visit and to investigate a longer stay there. On Jack's insistence, he took issues of the *Rebel Poet* to the IURW people, who promised to consider it for official recognition, which Jack felt would increase the magazine's distribution.[24] In so doing, Jack was cutting into the territory already established by *New Masses* and the John Reed clubs, the main communication links and impetus for the revolutionary cultural movement in America.

There is no reason to assume that Jack's aim was to undermine the CPA's efforts toward consolidating its literary activities; *New Masses* had cooperated in distributing *Unrest 1930* and was publishing Jack's sketches. "Paving Gang—On a Job in Missouri" was accepted for publication early in 1932. Yet the midwestern worker-writers—Kalar, Lewis, Conroy—were generally critical of *New Masses*. In their view its editorial policies were aligned with the New York radical crowd who showed little interest in and even less understanding of what was happening west of the Hudson River. The midwestern radicals expressed their dissatisfaction with *New Masses* (and suspicions regarding Union Square radicals) in letters to one another. In a letter to the editors, Jack criticized the magazine's eastern bias and its muddled notions of proletarian literature, suggesting, for example, that abandoning capitalization and difficult syntax would do little to further the workers' struggle. Admiring Gold and Carmon, Jack nonetheless expressed his belief, in a letter to Kenneth Porter, that the *New Masses* was "becoming a Mutual Admiration Society piloted by a rapidly narrowing clique of metropolitan writers."[25] Other midwesterners were feeling likewise: Jack's old publisher, Noah Whitaker, wrote that the *New Masses* was "a pitiful exhibit of in-growing conceits of New York coteries."[26]

The general gripe among the midwestern radicals seemed to be that *New Masses* had ceased to write to and for the worker. Nonetheless, the *Rebel Poet* was growing evermore dependent upon the New York comrades, and indeed Jack himself would soon be looking anxiously toward the East in his efforts to find a publisher for his first novel. However, the extent to which Jack actually took part in the "movement" was limited by his isolation. His participation consisted almost exclusively of editorializing; he continued to remain unaffiliated with any political party, as he said he would in the *Rebel Poet* manifesto. Yet even this position would, in 1933, yield to a more explicit declaration in favor of "the only Workers' and Farmers' government in the world" when, in the first issue of the *Anvil*, Jack finally openly declared his departure from the earlier accommodationist position of the Rebel Poets.[27] As Cheyney suggested in his counter-statement, Jack's drift away from accommodation and toward affirmation of the Communist movement was "an inevitable development."[28] The inevitability Cheyney mentions probably refers to the fact that events seemed to be taking a course independent of the *Rebel Poet* editors. Falkowski was in Moscow presenting the Rebel Poets' case to the Soviet literary bureaucrats, and in New York a splinter group of Rebel Poets would soon determine the fate of the magazine.

Falkowski was eager that the *Rebel Poet* gain recognition in the Soviet Union and pressed the *Moscow News* to review it. While still with *New Masses* in New York, Walt Carmon likewise had sought to attract the Soviet press to the American worker-writers, sending Jack's "High Bridge" to the IURW in Moscow together with a photo and Jack's biography. "After all," Carmon wrote Jack, "I know of no other piece that gives as fine a view of midwest proletarian life in a mining burg. And they go nuts for that kind of stuff abroad."[29] Similarly, Carmon promoted Lewis, Kalar, Rogers, and others, acting as a voluntary go-between, a role that he performed *sur place* in Moscow. The IURW's approval offered the prospect of better distribution for the *Rebel Poet* and a wider readership for Jack's work.

The Rebel Poets themselves were by no means of one mind in seeking closer ties with the Soviet Union. One of the most "red" of the Rebel Poets west of the Hudson was Henry George Weiss. Weiss was an autodidact, an ex-Wobbly who had written for the workers' press in the 1920s and various CP magazines, and who preferred conventional verse forms for his poems. Suffering from tuberculosis, Weiss lived in a desert shack in Arizona, corresponding with literary friends like H. H. Lewis, writing science fiction for *Weird Tales*, and sending lengthy Marxist analyses to Isidor Schneider.[30] A longtime contributor of militant poems to radical magazines, Weiss, along with W. S. Stacy and Lewis, brooked no accommodation of liberal reform. Lewis, for instance, impaled the "liberal" on his pitchfork:

> While social temblors rock the scene
> And sift us, man from man,
> He rides the bounding fence between
> —As only a eununch can.[31]

Opposing the militants like Weiss was Covington Hall, whose poetry had in fact served as inspiration for the Rebel Poets. Hall represented a living connection with the older radical movement associated with the Wobblies and the old *Masses*. The term "rebel" in Conroy's mind came closest to embodiment in the figures of Hall, Arturo Giovannitti, Jo Labadie, Joe Hill, and Ralph Chaplin, in brief the previous generation of fervent radicals who opposed war and oppression in lyrical, spirited cris de coeur and rousing, irreverent attacks that raised public ire. They provoked furor in a manner that the Rebel Poets hoped to recreate but, owing mainly to the uneven quality of the *Rebel Poet* contributions and its unsteady purposes, never attained. A reviewer had called H. H. Lewis the Joe Hill of the revolutionary movement, but Lewis, despite his robust talent, was too quirky and unpredictable to step into Joe Hill's role as workers' bard.[32] Perhaps it was premature to expect a political culture like that of the Wobblies. Nonetheless, apart from Kenneth Patchen and several others, Rebel Poets failed to turn up any Arturo Giovannittis or Covington Halls.

Covington Hall warned Jack against Weiss and the militants. Henry George Weiss, he wrote Jack in the fall of 1931, "is dogmatic with Communistic ideas. . . . I am not one of those who believes that the revolution in this country can be duplicated after the Russian Revolution. . . ."[33] There were others, like Thomas O'Flaherty, editor of the *Wasp* in Chicago, who echoed Hall's admonitions. To David Webb, Jack's former coeditor of the *Spider*, O'Flaherty confessed dissatisfaction with Party orthodoxy. (Webb sent the letter to Jack.) The Party, he wrote Webb, "would like me to hitch it [the *Wasp*] to one of their stars. But that would kill it since it would be disciplined into sectarianism."[34] Jack seemed to be of two minds: eager to remain independent in his editorial judgments he nonetheless was attracted to the literary movement identified with the CPA, persuaded that it showed more vigor and promise than the Socialist party, whose adherents Michael Gold called "tea-drinking friends of the skylark."[35] Too, the internationalist nature of the CP appealed to Jack, who was anxious to establish Rebel Poet chapters abroad, for instance, in Japan, where he had contacts with revolutionary writers Masaki Ikeda and Masaki Fujio. Finally, the Kharkov conference of 1930 called upon American writers to declare themselves as partisans of the Soviet Union in its struggle against internal economic crisis and the external threat of fascism. Rivalries and power struggles within the Rebel Poets and the prospect of censorship, however, soon made unquestioning obedience to the Party impossible.

It was one thing for the U.S. Post Office to ban the mailing of the *Rebel Poet*, which it did the second issue for printing an objectionable poem, "Rally to Battle." But Jack balked at Soviet criticism. The post-office censorship was proof to Jack that his magazine was having an effect, and furthermore it was good promotion for further issues.[36] And when in the fall of 1931 the third *Unrest* anthology of rebel poetry appeared, he was delighted to see it assailed in Gastonia, South Carolina, site of textile-mill strikes a few years earlier. "The *Gastonia Gazette* says that Cheyney and I should be jailed," Jack wrote to Kenneth Porter; it "calls the book filthy, indecent."[37] On the other hand, Jack had reason to suspect that the IURW had begun to scrutinize the Rebel Poets, although there is no evidence he became suspicious until at least a year later, when the question of editorial freedom became critical to the continuation of his magazine.

The first clues that Conroy could not seek Party patronage and approval without giving up the editorial freedom he so valued came at year's end, from Falkowski in a letter. Ed had discussed the Rebel Poets with Bruno Jassiensky, an MORP literary functionary. To the Soviet literary bureau, it appeared that the Rebel Poets "manifested many anarchistic tendencies that seem unhealthy, and that a large number at present connected with the group will eventually flounder out of it being by disposition indisposed to take those leftward steps that may be demanded by future exigencies."[38] Jack objected to Jassiensky's characterization of the Rebel Poets in his reply to Falkowski. Ed wrote back from Moscow that Jack should not be dismayed by the criticism since Soviet criticism was based upon insufficient understanding of American conditions, for example, the broad range of interests and political divisions. Nonetheless, he advised Jack to publish poems that are "concrete instead of aesthetic revolts" and eventually most of the half-committed would shake loose after "indulging in sprees of red rhetoric."[39] In the winter of 1931, Jack was lending his prose talent to building socialism: in the March 1932 issue his editorial, "Art Above the Battle?," called upon writers to support the John Reed clubs, *New Masses,* and the *Rebel Poet* in response to "the fascist dictatorship [that] is in almost full control of the press, the screen, and the radio, particularly the latter."[40]

At home in Moberly, Jack consolidated his reputation as a "red communist," from the local paper's perspective at least, when hunger marchers came to town in October 1931. A young reporter named Goetze Jeter, who had attached "self-styled radical" to Conroy's name the previous January, was largely responsible for the characterization in the newspaper. This was a journalistic warm-up, it turned out, for subsequent efforts in dramatizing Moberly labor troubles when the shoe-factory workers, including Gladys Conroy, went out on strike in 1934. Close on the heels of a drive to provide "charity" to hungry workers in Moberly came a representative of the Unemployed Council, openly declaring himself to be Communist and announcing a hunger march for

26 October. The *Moberly Monitor-Index* covered the demonstration held
in Tannehill Park, noting that "most of the group appeared to be of foreign birth or lineage," an old saw about radicals that was often heard
during the Palmer raids after World War I. Moreover, the paper reported, marchers were selling the *Daily Worker,* "a Communistic publication printed in New York."[41] "Conspicuous among the local sympathizers was Jack Conroy, local writer and self-styled radical," Jeter wrote.
"Conroy, who has had articles to appear in H. L. Mencken's *American
Mercury,* nodded vigorous approval of certain statements and like the
shouter in old fashioned church services at times burst forth with cries
of 'Yes, Capitalism is doomed,' and other like expressions of approval."
   Jack objected in a letter to the editor, which was printed on the front
page. The letter "expresses Conroy's disgust," the editor noted, "in most
entertaining and positive style." The reporter was keeping an eye on
Moberly's notorious radical, but Jack was even more keen-eyed. "The
ubiquitous youth," Jack wrote, "dodged here and there, cocking an in-
quisitive ear at every private conversation, evidently hopeful of unearthing a dastardly 'red' plot to overthrow the government." Jack reported
that he had submitted Jeter's name to Congressman J. Hamilton Fish, the
leading red-baiter. Moreover, the foreigner was actually a man named Mr.
Smith; and Karl Marx was not to be confused with Groucho, Zeppo, Bep-
po, or Harpo. "Now there are cracks in the shining armor of Prosperity,"
Jack concluded, "no 'chicken in every pot,' and many garages still lack
the two cars envisioned by the Great Engineer in the rosy dawn of his
reign."[42] Conroy's rejoinder delighted the editor, who gave front-page attention to the "reds" when they appeared in the state capital on the eve
of May Day. Theodore Dreiser, the Moberly paper's headline reported,
"Makes $35,000 Yearly But Gives Nothing to Charity."[43]
   Jack perceived the need for an alternative press that would reach
small towns like Moberly, but he overestimated the influence of small-
town newspapers as opinion makers. Most Moberlyeans were on the side
of labor; a railroad and mining town, Moberly had lived with dissension and known plenty of labor radicals—and more were to follow soon
when the Brown shoe factory went on strike in 1934. Few if any people in Randolph County voted the Communist ticket in 1932; yet no
one would have taken seriously the suggestion that Jack be run out of
town for having urged them to vote it.[44] In any case, it seemed unlikely to Jack that the revolution would begin in places like Moberly with
a long tradition of organized labor and collective action; in Detroit,
maybe, but not in Moberly, where blue-collar children went to school
with the middle class and you were judged on your achievements, not
on how much money you had. Lacking intellectual companionship in

Moberly, particularly for radical thought, Jack took the train into St. Louis—when he could afford it—to attend meetings of the Union of St. Louis Artists and Writers, later the John Reed Club of St. Louis, and to frequent, along with other artists and writers, the Blue Lantern on the riverfront.

There wasn't money in the Conroy home to send Jack to New York City; he had hoped to help straighten out the personal conflicts developing in the Rebel Poet chapter there and to meet Carmon and Gold at the *New Masses* office. His first trip to New York, however, was to attend the American Writers' Congress in the spring of 1935; and by that time he had lost his *Rebel Poet* and was about to lose the *Anvil;* in both cases, because of distance, Jack's creations were claimed by others.[45] Those who represented his interests were proved ultimately ineffectual against opportunistic individuals and interest groups thriving in the confusion and ambivalence of leftist cultural politics. Jack's sincerity and openness proved his undoing in more than one instance.

Struggling to maintain his family and to keep the *Rebel Poet* coming out (irregularly), Jack sold his 1927 Chevrolet. He had kept the car mainly to ferry Pip Addis between his two sewage disposal jobs. Pip's job was to pour sewage out on a bed to let it dry, a job that, apparently, no one else in town was desperate enough to want. The dried sewage was sold as fertilizer. Pip would return home in stinking clothes; Eliza's attempts to kill the smell with lime was of little avail. Here was a character and a tale for Jack: a "weed" that grew on ravaged soil, deserving a storyteller's art; but the tale was too close to Jack, involving his mother. Pip was a continual embarrassment to the family. Margaret, Jack's sister, still hated Pip with a fury. Jack did what he could to make the strain easier on his mother, nursing the sick automobile between the two sewage disposal sites until essential repairs could no longer be put off. The car sold for thirty-five dollars, enough for a month's groceries, but Jack put some of it back to buy books and pay for printing costs.[46] It was the last car Jack ever owned (or drove).

The winter of 1931 saw little economic improvement in Moberly. While the Lindberghs were in China, sympathizing with the famine-plagued victims of floods late in the fall of 1931, towns like Moberly gave refuge to transients in "Hoosier Hotels." One hundred and two Wabash shopmen were let go and the rest given a pay cut. Farmers hunted rabbits and gave them to schools for lunches. Railroad men appealed to older hoboes to look after homeless youngsters who were appearing in greater numbers in the boxcars. Jack wrote a sketch for *New Masses,* "They Won't Let Us Birds Roost Nowheres," portraying the plight of the American *bezprizorni* (homeless).[47]

Max Lieber peddled Jack's stories to *Scribner's, Harper's* and other mainline magazines in 1931. The editors liked his stories but balked at accepting them.[48] Mencken, on the other hand, admired Jack's vigorous observations of working-class existence and urged him to submit more stories. After publishing "Boyhood in a Coal Town," in the May issue of the *American Mercury,* the Baltimore iconoclast wrote Jack: "What is to be next? I'd certainly like to print you again."[49] "High Bridge," published in the April issue of *New Masses,* marked the addition of robust humor and comic realism to Jack's worker narratives and sketches. The *New Masses* editors were moving toward political commentary, giving increasingly less space to the worker-writers, indeed to literature, despite the demand on the part of readers for more sketches like "High Bridge."[50] In a note accompanying Jack's story the editors announced that Conroy had embarked on a novel, soon to appear, incorporating his *New Masses* sketches.[51] In 1931 the future seemed bright for Jack, who despite the demands of his work as a laborer (and the desperate periods without employment), looked forward at the end of the day to his literary activities. Digging ditches or shoveling sand, he was a long way from the fervent radicalisms of Union Square; yet it was at least possible to express in words for others to read the anguish and small victories of his day, together with his hope for a better future.

Jack, like many who yearned for a better life for the worker in America, felt that conditions made revolution imminent. In this revolutionary moment lay the possibility of a new literature. Writers on the left connected literary evolution with political change; their role was to portray the present crisis as sharply as they could, and let events take their own inevitable course toward revolution. Cruden, Kalar, and Robert Minor eventually abandoned their literary/artistic ambitions for active engagement. Writers spurned the romantic ideal of the lonely, isolated artist, the credo of art for art's sake, and in its place attempted to forge a literature of commitment. The critic Granville Hicks asked his radical colleagues what he could do to help Communism.[52] Even writers who in the previous decade had distanced themselves from American political life were moving leftward, including Robert McAlmon, Archibald MacLeish, John Dos Passos, Kay Boyle, Edmund Wilson, and Malcolm Cowley. However variously committed to leftist causes, they shared an unequivocal antifascist bias. Former expatriates like McAlmon had little difficulty, remembered his close friend Norman Macleod, in making such a transition to political commitment in the early 1930s. Heralded by the Gastonia mill strikes, the Sacco-Vanzetti executions, the farmers' revolts, and the devastating conditions affecting the unemployed, the "new literature" was in broadest terms a literature of social consciousness. The "malaise of the twenties" that affected the expatriates was put aside in the face of demanding social reality.[53] In a burst of energy the new writers of the 1930s examined the native scene with a sociological lens. Nothing was as certain as the need for change.

Dos Passos's *The 42nd Parallel*, published in 1930, the first in his *U.S.A.* trilogy, was arguably the first important novel signaling the emergence of a new social consciousness among Depression-era writers.[54] Dos Passos's novel reflected an awakening interest in rediscovering America and searching for its meanings among its people. Constance Rourke, looking to folklore for clues to American life, showcased American creativity in the great "Index of American Design," which she directed.[55] A new regionalism, as mentioned earlier, "more authentic and less sentimental than that of the 1880's," according to Henry Steele Commager, "celebrated every section of the country."[56] Every region produced its interpreters: J. Frank Dobie in Texas, Vardis Fisher in Idaho, Erskine Caldwell in Georgia, Mari Sandoz in Nebraska, William Faulkner in Mississippi, H. L. Davis in Oregon, John Steinbeck in California, James Hearst in Iowa, Louis Bromfield in Ohio, all drawing upon their intimate knowledge of place. As Commager points out, Mencken's debunking and Sinclair Lewis's gouging satires gave way to the search for national character, involving specialists in many fields, like Howard Odum, a sociologist at Chapel Hill. Mencken validated American idiomatic speech, and artists like Thomas Hart Benton, John Steuart Curry, and Grant Wood were experimenting with new American forms to portray their American subjects. Critics like Vernon Parrington prepared the way for a harder look at American realities through literature; to Mike Gold and Granville Hicks the New Humanism of Irving Babbitt seemed as remote and irrelevant as the real San Luis Rey fictionalized in Thornton Wilder's 1929 novel.

Hard times awakened an interest in the lot of common people; in increasing numbers, writers hitchhiked and hoboed, or drove a car if they had a sponsor, to listen to the voices of the people and record impressions of the American scene. Granville Hicks, hoping to raise the general reader's consciousness, urged novelists to visit farms and stand in breadlines and record what they saw.[57] "Road books" appeared, some conceived as travelogues cast in a social context, such as James Rorty's *Where Life Is Better: An Unsentimental American Journey*, Nathan Asch's *The Road: In Search of America*, Robert Whitcomb's *Talk U.S.*, Sherwood Anderson's *Puzzled America*, and Erskine Caldwell and Margaret Bourke-White's *Say Is This the U.S.A.*, while others, like Tom Kromer's *Waiting for Nothing*, recorded personal travail.[58] Like their literary counterparts, the picaresque novels of sixteenth-century Spain, all of these informally documented the experience of uprooted people searching for work. The implications of this new attention to the "blue highways" of America were profound in American literature. Lewis Mumford wrote at the time that "this apprenticeship, this seeing of the American scene, this listening to the American voice may mean more for literature than any sudden forcing of stories and poems."[59] A new expression was born, "flivver tramps," and the automobile came to mean not only mobility but survival.[60] The focus of this "new literature," which strove to preserve the authentic accents of common people, was experience. Edmund Wilson published his observations of American life across the economic scale in *The American Jitters* (1932). Nelson Algren, barely out of college, rode freight trains to Texas, recording impressions and conversations, which he sent to Conroy and other little-magazine editors.

Jack's own observations of the American scene were made as a worker-writer, not as a journalist. He admired the naturalism of Dreiser and Zola, but his own writing was a vernacular hybrid of realism, personal narrative, and folklore. He perceived—or chose to view, for artistic purposes—industrial workers as a folk group, focusing on their speech, humor, lore, and storytelling, all features of an oral culture that survived in the workplace despite "speedup" and specialization. "There exists among all industrial workers," he said, "a sort of free masonry, figures of speech, psychological characteristics, etc., which is universal among them. Writers of the white collar class and from the bourgeoisie sometimes catch flashes of the inner workings of factory hands, miners, etc., but rarely anything resembling a full-dimensional picture."[61] His stories during this period portray human creativity in inhumane settings, through the idioms and gestures of his factory workers, creatively transformed, as I discuss in a later chapter, yet vividly realistic. His tales of workers, remolded into his first novel, *The Disinherited*, are rooted in history and an objective physical world yet preserve characteristics of older, traditional folk cultures. Like Gorki and Nexö, Conroy was both a folk artist wedded to labor's cause and a realist writer whose work is of ethnographic and social historical interest.

Gorki, for instance, identified folklore as the oral art of the people, of workers. Oral lore functions, he said, as an organizer of experience.[62] In his speech before the First All-Union Congress of Soviet Writers in 1934, Gorki set great store by folklore, which he said expresses the realities and aspirations of the working classes. Partly in response to this address, the Soviets began encouraging the collecting and socialist interpretation of folklore. In the United States, the left began to assimilate folklore into its political culture in the Popular Front period. Conroy's "Uncle Ollie" tales, published in the Party's *Sunday Worker Magazine* and *Progressive*

Weekly, reflect the Popular Front interest in folklore expressing "the realities and aspirations of the working classes."[63]

As members of a disenfranchised folk group, Conroy's workers display a "folk" view of experience through language, behavior, and attitudes. Vernacular in origin also are the images and metaphors. Folklore, Conroy shows, compensates for, or at least is a response to, alienation, isolation, humiliation, boredom, in brief, the experience of factory workers during the low-water mark of industrial capitalism. Worker resistance, for instance, takes many forms in Conroy's writing: play, indifference, diversion, pranks, storytelling, jokes, and subversion.[64] Visible to the "insider," the worker accepted by his mates, are informal structures of protest expressed in the language of resistance. Jack had been privy to these informal expressions since a child in Monkey Nest; he had endured the usual greenhorn pranks in the Wabash shops, hunkered shoulder to shoulder with Wobblies in boxcars, stood in picket and unemployment lines. Workers' language—the jokes, anecdotes, storytelling, verbal pranks—often masked subtle displays of resistance. The most flamboyant uses of language as a gesture of resistance, Jack observed, occurred among the Wobblies, as mentioned earlier. Wobs were often eccentric characters, like "Pirate" Larsen who later took part in the San Francisco dock strike, and their speech was just as colorful as their manner.[65] Jack was a privileged insider to the industrial workplace who, like Joel Chandler Harris, retold stories by people with whom his readers had no direct contact. Heralded as one of the rising stars of the new proletarian school, Jack violated nearly every tenet of proletarian realism.

Mike Gold, for instance, complained that Jack's characters were not typical enough of workers, "that too many of them are social sports and eccentrics."[66] But Jack, who preferred true versions of workers' lives to false ones and was keenly aware of the difference, dealt with workers as he knew them. Workers, he perceived, evolve their own ways of dealing with their exploited condition quite apart from socialist solutions. A tireless advocate of "proletarian writing," nonetheless Jack had greater interest in exploring the folk character of his workers than in creating fiction that would pass muster with Marxist critics. In the idioms and lore of workers he hoped to discover suitable metaphors for their experience, as Zora Neale Hurston, Richard Wright, and Langston Hughes looked to black folk culture for suitable metaphors.[67] Realism alone was insufficient for Jack's purposes in conveying the "exceptional ordinary" through his worker narratives, which frequently incorporate the grotesque alongside the commonplace. Conroy's anarchic, utopian worldview expresses itself through humor and folk expression, undermining "the serious man" of proletarian realism.[68] By temperament Jack felt greater attachment to the freewheeling autonomy and simple humanity of the Wobblies than to Party disciplines. Yet, his "He Is Thousands," published in *New Masses*, reveals Conroy's ambivalence on the question of "correct" ideological context in his writing; his second novel, *A World to Win*, even more so. In both instances, Jack desired to provide the correct revolutionary context and affirmative mood while remaining true to his subject matter. On the other hand, his texts, with a few exceptions, evade the ideological content that frequently attaches to slice-of-life portrayals.[69] The same instinct that steered Jack away from realist aesthetics in his writing spares his work from the doctrinaire character that mars inferior proletarian literature such as Clara Weatherwax's *Marching! Marching!* (1935). When, as in Gorki's work, Jack's art succumbs to the appeals of orthodoxy, then these are the more noticeable for being exceptions.

Yet Jack's position on proletarian literature was never made entirely explicit; the confusing stances taken by the Party on the question of point of view, form, and subject matter were hardly of any help to young worker-writers. Jack followed the twists and turns of proletarian theorizing; there is no evidence, however, that it had much effect on his writing, certainly in the early period. No one questioned Jack's proletarian credentials.[70] Yet even Kalar criticized his writing when it revealed a "romantic individualistic point of view," a charge later made by a number of critics concerning Jack's characterization of his young worker-protagonist, Larry Donovan, in *The Disinherited*.[71] The worker-writers' knowledge of the "proletariat" was experiential, practical, not theoretical or ideological. There was some posturing on the left: in New York, proletarian costume balls were staged to raise funds, and Mike Gold dressed in worker's garb with a soft, billed cap, consciously cultivating a proletarian appearance. The left invented its traditions in part, exhuming figures like Joe Hill to create legends for a new heroic era of labor radicalism.[72] Such "invented traditions" nettled Kalar and amused Jack. Gold was perhaps sincere in seeking to present Jack as the genuine article; others, however, exploited the proletarian boom, including the media who covered it, those who were looking for the man with a hoe, a country rube who penned verse, a Shakespeare in overalls.

The worker-writers entered the lists of the left when the Party was fresh with restored legends and martyrs like Sacco and Vanzetti, Tom Mooney, and the Scottsboro Boys. Little magazines solicited their work; major presses scouted their writing (but seldom took the financial risk of publishing it). Swept along by the progress of events—the deepening economic crisis, the demands on the part of Party critics, Gold's exhortations, the crop of new little magazines—still worker-writers had little example to go by and no clear sense where their work was going. In a letter to Warren Huddlestone, Kalar wrote: ". . . we have not yet had a clear formulation of what proletarian esthetics is. A new wind, perhaps, is first felt by those most sensitive, that is, the 'intellectuals,' which probably explains why so many writers have turned to communism when the mass of the proletarians is still swathed in bourgeois buncombe. Somebody has said that we have no proletarian literature, we have only revolutionary literature."[73] On the other hand, Jack, Kalar, and H. H. Lewis were called upon to defend their writing at times. In the letter quoted above, Kalar complained of a rejection by *New Masses*, which charged him with holding defeatist sentiments for portraying his worker-protagonist on the verge of tears. "I had a battle," he wrote Huddlestone, "with someone over my phrase 'God how he did want to cry.' Defeatism! The piece is autobiographical, it is honest, it is objective, and if an unemployed worker does not sometimes feel like 'crying,' then I'm an asshole."[74]

The early 1930s witnessed endless debates on proletarian literary theory; from the worker-writers' perspective most commentaries on the subject were confusing, sententious, or vague. If proletarian literary theory was confusing, then Jack's own commentaries scarcely shed much light on the subject. Nor do they clarify his own writing—or have much relation to it except in the most general way. In a review of Bob Reed's "Flat Tire," he called for "social direction and awareness" in the proletarian short story; there must be, he said, a "clash of social forces, the undertones of battle."[75] Answering a questionnaire concerning the trend of the proletarian literary movement, Conroy noted the "unmistakable social awareness that occasionally creeps into even such staid journals as *The Atlantic Monthly*."[76] What he meant by "social direction" and "awareness" was usually summed up in the example of the Plowboy Poet, H. H. Lewis, whose verse thumbed its nose at traditional poetics, establishment critics, and even *New Masses* on occasion. Sincerity, honesty of expression, truth to experience, these seem to be the basis of Conroy's "proletarian" aesthetics. It was more important to Jack that real workers recognize themselves in Jack's writing than that it win critical praise from Gold and Hicks.

Loyal to proletarian literature as an ideal and to proletarianism as a social fact, Jack remained apart from sectarian factions debating interpretations. He had a workingman's impatience with theory and theoreticians. Rather than an intellectual debate he preferred a performance, a good story, the company of workers or artists. When he turned his hand to writing social history, he told stories of individuals who made the history. He avoided formulations and abstractions; when they do appear in his polemical writings they sound forced. An insightful literary critic, a brilliant editor, a memorable storyteller, Jack possessed intellectual abilities that were instinctual, intuitive, discursive. He would have felt cramped by any formalized system of thought; proletarian theory was a closed system, continually shifting its bounds, grounded in what Joan Wallach Scott, in a discussion of gender, terms "binary opposition."[77] Trapped in a dualism that excluded "bourgeois fiction" as worthy of the revolutionary struggle, such an artificial construct placed constraints on creativity in the interest of the "politically correct" message. Any such "system" was bound to conflict with Jack's boundaryless curiosity and openness to new experience. Yet, as I say, he tirelessly advocated its cause while breaking its "rules." He was certainly not alone in this; another rising star in the proletarian sky at the time was Erskine Caldwell. Both writers were interested in workers as members of a particularized folk group, not as proletarian heroes in labor's struggle for social justice. Consequently, the dreariness that pervades most proletarian fiction is absent in their fiction.

When Conroy's writing violates his own informal tenets, it is usually not for having forced ideology upon content but is evidence of conflicts within himself. It bespeaks the ambivalence he felt, for instance, toward intellectuals and the resentment he perhaps felt toward never having had the opportunity for formal education beyond eighth grade, night school, and one unhappy semester at the state college. He quoted approvingly Donal McKenzie's poem, published in *Unrest 1931*, entitled "Proletarian Student," which expresses the resentment of a steelworker in night school toward his teacher:

> It's hard—when the fires still reel
> in a man's brain, raw for sleep,
> to key a mind for pedantry—and then
> to snap back answers like I handle grates.

If, Conroy argued, workers haven't the leisure to study literary theory or satisfy the plot demands of mainline publishers, then they scarcely have time to educate themselves in Marxist theory.[78] Yet, Conroy, in his "A Note on the Proletarian Novel," pointed to the success of writers like Robert Cantwell, Agnes Smedley, and Robert Cruden, proletarian writers who "labor under great difficulties." Whatever faults lie in their writing, he argued, can be attributed to "the necessity of leading a dual life. Back of it all, there's always the struggle to live, the impediments of fatigue from the daily job and the difficulties imposed by lack of education and facilities for publication."[79] Nowhere does he mention the necessity of studying proletarian theory.

Conroy was no formal theoretician, yet he showed himself to be a forceful propagandist, in command of a vivid revolutionary rhetoric when the occasion called for it. Employing images of decay and putre-faction, he describes in a *Rebel Poet* essay the imminent collapse of cap-italism: "Just as the tumblebug rolls its egg so that the larvae may eat through and destroy the shell, so has the capitalist implanted in the social structure the germ of his own destruction. Greedy grubs have eat-en away the retaining walls; the whole structure crumbles visibly be-fore the aghast eyes of its architects."[80] In "Art Above the Battle," Jack avowed that "capitalism is cracking fast these days." "It is our task," he urged, "to divert the thoughts of these befogged individualists toward the building of a Socialist Society."[81] The task would be made difficult owing to the fascist control of the press and media. Some bookstores, for instance, refused to stock *Unrest 1931*. The wealthy donated to *Po-etry* magazine but not to revolutionary publications. "O but my DEAH, you rawlly cawn't mix puah aht with beastly propaganda! O let us gather pansies while we may, for Youth is fleet and skips away."[82] (Conroy's mimicry of the rich was always a crude parody of upper-class English, probably the effect of reading popular romances in his mother's library.) The *Rebel Poet*, under Jack's editorship, published wood-block and li-noleum-print cartoons of top-hatted capitalists carrying fat money-bags, muscled workers, and portraits of Lenin and Gorki.[83] A dual-valued per-spective underlies references to bourgeois culture throughout all issues of the *Rebel Poet*. Art is viewed as a tool of the leisured class; its sub-ject is beauty, the purity of art. Rebel poetry, on the other hand, deals with actual conditions with little regard for niceties such as the aes-thetic qualities of verse; sincerity is more important. Conroy suggested that H. H. Lewis's poems were very bad "for Ivory Tower aesthetes who browse undisturbed in the sedentary confines of the library, while out-side millions of desperate men are starving."[84] Granaries are full of rot-ting grain while men starve. Capitalism casts aside its discards, or toss-es them scraps under the title of charity. Workers are passive and ignorant of the real issues, but tomorrow will begin to bring change. A new literature, using Soviet models, is evolving, sketching in that rev-olutionary tomorrow. Such are the general themes of the *Rebel Poet* dur-ing its brief run of seventeen issues.

Previous generations, to be sure, had produced revolutionary rheto-ric, during the American Revolution and abolitionist times, for in-stance.[85] *Rebel Poet* picked up the fallen banner of the socialist left, the militancy of Jack London's *The Iron Heel*, speeches like "The Class Struggle" and "Revolution," for example, and revived radical art for po-litical purposes, cruder than the *Masses* but in the same spirit. Art joined with propaganda spoke to the needs of the *Rebel Poet* readers. Anger, frustration, and irrational feelings required a vent. Expressing these emotions on paper was undoubtedly therapeutic for the contributors; and new readers were drawn into the fold of the revolutionary movement, among them Ray B. West, Jr., whose contributions later were made in Western history and as editor of the *Rocky Mountain Review*.[86] It was the temper of the times to couple art and politics, and no apologies for propaganda were made on the left.[87] The *New Republic* offered a prize of twenty-five dollars for the best political poem on the Reichstag fire trial in Germany. Proletarian literature was *Tendenzliteratur*, as Lukács termed it. Nonetheless, its practitioners were by no means of one mind concerning how to write it.

Conroy probably broke every "affirmation" of the proletarian line in the course of his literary work; admired for its realism, it is in fact a homegrown hybrid of folklore, southwestern humor, social history, transcribed orality, and personal and work narrative. Highly intertextual, it bears the imprint of speech genres from many sources: his reading, the workplace, and memory. Jack sought connections in a disconnected time. He put the resources of folklore, orality, personal narrative, humor, and so forth to use in dealing with the loss of traditional culture as he knew it and in an effort to reconstitute the values of the work community he had known in Monkey Nest, which was oral, performative, *solidaire*. In the factories and wherever he had worked, Jack viewed a transplanted work/folk culture, an older order in unsteady transformation, lacking direction and concerned with survival; it was appealed to by mass culture, which offered diversion, and consumer culture, which promised to make life easier. If there were parallels between his own work and the desultory prescriptions of proletarian theory, then they had to do with the fact that he was more interested in the exchanges and interactions among individuals in a work group then in individual character development. Moreover, he was persuaded that class origin and conflict were essential forces governing workers' lives. Few workers had come as far as he in their perceptions. There is nothing in his writing that suggests that most workers would evolve similar radical convictions. Larry Donovan, the protagonist of *The Disinherited*, is, like Jack, an exception; when he decides finally to join the ex-Sparticist, Hans, in organizing, presumably, for the coming revolution, no one else joins him except Ed, whose attachment is to Larry, not to any political cause.

The question of proletarian consciousness among American workers was in fact the subject of much debate and conjecture (and inflated expectation) in the early 1930s. Jack knew that there was no eager readership among workers for his writing, that he had to build an audience, educate his readers, participate in labor's struggle to raise consciousness. What European radical intellectuals conceived for the proletariat was entirely inappropriate to the American experience, as Ed Falkowski seems to have sensed in his contacts with the Bund der Proletarisch-Revolutionären Schriftsteller (BPRS) in Berlin and in his work for the *Moscow Daily News*. Not only was the German working class far more advanced politically than the American; the revolutionary movement was sufficiently powerful to maintain writers, something the American radical movement could not promise. On the other hand, Falkowski had difficulty explaining American conditions to the Soviets, how different, for example, the American situation was in comparison with the Soviet.[88]

The question whether radical belief could be imposed upon the American worker, or whether it would evolve out of circumstances of the individual worker's life, was critical to the revolutionary movement and a subject of much discussion. It was the topic of at least one memorable discussion, on a weekend when John Herrman visited his friends Paul and Ruth Lechlitner Corey at the Coreys' farmhouse in Cold Spring, New York, in the early 1930s. Herrman was estranged from his wife, Josephine Herbst, the author of a successful novelette, "The Big Short Trip," published in *Scribner's Magazine* (August 1932). He had been a "guest delegate" in Kharkov at the 1930 Conference of Revolutionary Writers along with Josephine. Herrman represented the view of eastern radical intellectuals, the expectation that a proletarian spirit might be fostered in the United States, and out of this, the impulse for revolution, ideas whose origin, in Corey's view, lay in middle-European ideology and were inappropriate to the American situation. Corey challenged the notion, arguing that proletarian ideas were forced transplants, requiring generations of serfdom such as the Russian people had endured. Yes, there were uprooted workers in America, but most held on to the American dream; the American myth that they or their children would succeed was greater than any collective proletarian consciousness. No one, in any case, was calling himself or herself a proletarian except Mike Gold; only the New York intellectuals were fostering the notion. It was possible to foster a union spirit among workers, perhaps even a socialist spirit among a segment of the people, but never a proletarian consciousness. The rhetoric of the eastern intellectuals was all wrong on this score, Corey concluded; but Herrman was not persuaded.[89] Certainly there are few radicals among Conroy's workers; the figure Lipkin, for instance, is a hot-headed worker, ineffectual in his protest. Fundamentalist preaching and the success myth appear to make a stronger appeal to workers than does revolutionary rhetoric. Yet the penchant for individual choice can fuse spontaneously into collective protest in special instances, such as Jack depicts in the penny-auction episode of *The Disinherited,* or in the conclusion of *A World to Win.*[90]

While radicals debated such questions at length in the "coffeepots" around Union Square, historical forces were at work, which, if not successful in fostering a proletarian spirit among American workers, nonetheless were reducing the worker to a defenseless migrant, destroying pride in labor and traditional bonds among workers, breaking up families and creating a permanent pool of homeless, including children. The collapse of American democracy seemed imminent with or without a proletarian revolution. Nonetheless, the majority of workers, Jack wrote, were still content to find "intellectual relaxation and mental stimulus" in popular-culture ikons like Amos 'n' Andy and Mutt and Jeff. A "cultural anomie" seemed to grip the masses.[91]

* * *

Jack set his own writing aside momentarily to help his old friend from Toledo days, Emerson Price, submitting Price's "Ohio Town" to Mencken, who published it in the *American Mercury* that fall, under Price's pen name, Hugh Hanley. Mencken was turning out to be the worker-writer's best friend; nevertheless, the rambunctious Missouri gumbo poet, H. H. Lewis, persisted in calling Mencken "an intellectual pervert," standing to lose a great deal by alienating the Baltimore Sage.[92] Mencken liked Lewis's rawbone "slanguage," as Mike Gold called it, but was gradually put off by Lewis's aggressive pro-Soviet attitudes.[93]

Persuaded that talent lay behind Lewis's impulsive, even reckless antics, Jack answered detractors such as William Rose Benet.[94] Not easily shocked by rough-hewn satire, Walt Carmon, however, drew the line with Lewis. In a Lewis poem entitled "Poof, No Chance to be President," which later appeared in the collection *Road to Utterly* (1935), published on Hagglund's press, the following stanza appeared:

> Oh how can I struggle
> And win through strife,
> Looking up a mule's pratt
> All of my life?[95]

There are no "revolutionary implications," Carmon finally retorted, "in a dung pile."[96] Despite his cranky, quirky behavior, Lewis received praise from critics like V. F. Calverton who considered Lewis and Conroy to be the rising stars of proletarian literature.[97] A *New Republic* reviewer implied that he was to be taken seriously.[98] And *New Masses* continued to print Lewis's poems even when he wrote angry letters critical of the editors and their magazine.

Lewis was in some ways a liability to Conroy, the Rebel Poets, and later the *Anvil* group. Apart from his reputation of crudeness, his detractors resented his contentious outspokenness. Suspicions grew that he might be paranoid. More "Stalinist" than Stalin, Lewis embarrassed the Party, which viewed him as an unguided missile. Lewis had a penchant for addressing his remonstrances directly to Stalin, for instance, although there is no evidence that he ever received a reply. In one letter to Stalin, Lewis complained that the CPA ignored Stalin's teachings and were straying from the path of Party orthodoxy.[99] His quarrelsome behavior tended to isolate the farmer-poet even more than did geography; yet opinion remained divided on Lewis's importance in the movement.

Communism extended to Lewis a belief, a promise of heaven in the here and now, or at least a better hand than most poor gumbo farmers in southeastern Missouri had been dealt. The effects of his trip west, mentioned earlier, and encounters with Los Angeles flophouses clearly were factors in his "conversion" to the idolatry he expressed toward the Soviet Experiment. The tall, large-boned farmer-poet with fierce prophet's eyes was in reality a lonely, impressionable young man who exteriorized his feelings of self-abasement through humor and vituperation.[100] Hailing him as the Demian Bedni of American letters, Henry George Weiss suggested to Lewis that "you get the *Daily Worker* more often."[101] Lewis's fierce, mischievous, ironic humor would scarcely have sat well, in any case, with the Party press for long. "Gumbo Jake"—his own ironical sobriquet—possessed an exuberance of language that spilled out of the narrow confines of his handcrafted Sovietism, winning critical praise eventually, following a long self-administered apprenticeship from the early idolatry of "Example-Song":

> Russia, Russia, righting wrong,
> Russia, Russia, Russia!
> That unified one sovereign throng,
> That hundred and sixty million strong,—
> Russia!
> America's loud EXAMPLE-SONG,
> Russia, Russia, Russia![102]

Temperamental, quick to take offense, Lewis nonetheless never wavered in his admiration of "honest old Jack," to whom he would send letters he received with comments scrawled in the margins. Jack in turn saw Lewis as an innovator, a leader in experimentation in working-class poetry. Evidence of this was the fact that his poems were being read and quoted by factory workers, always a touchstone for Jack. Lewis was a touchstone of cultural politics in the 1930s; the history of his literary reception reveals the shifts in literary politics on the left. An old-stock American whose ancestors had first set plow to the land, a "wild jack-ass" speaking out in protest as populist tenant farmers had done the generation before him, Lewis protested against the hideous inhumanity of capitalist economics.[103] Lewis seemed ideally suited for those seeking a rural bard of the revolution; yet the very character of the man, translated into the erratic beat and outrageous idiom of his verse, collided with those who would champion him. His originality, marred by bumptious excess, refused to be bridled. Promises were made to Lewis; but finally he came into active disfavor among the left's cultural doyens. In one exchange with the editors of *Partisan Review*, before it melded with Conroy's *Anvil*, Lewis was labeled a "necrophilic son of a cretin." He responded by calling the editors "horses' rectums."[104] Purged in the Popular Front, Lewis continued a running feud with the CP hierarchy, which, in his eyes, had strayed from the correct line.

One day, long before gaining notoriety in leftist cultural circles, H. H. Lewis had stopped his plow in midfield, shaken an angry fist at God, and sworn an oath to the Red Star.[105] Apart from his eccentric behavior, or perhaps because of it, Lewis was the very figure of a midwestern independent radical, scorning hierarchies of any kind, yet willing to attach himself to a quixotic quest.[106]

If Lewis met resistance to his brand of radicalism from the left (he was ignored by conservative critics), his reception in the Soviet Union was warm and inviting. Soviet literary functionaries were eager to promote American worker-writers, including Conroy, Lewis, and Kalar. When Lewis's collection *Salvation* appeared in 1934, a reviewer in *International Literature* wrote that the gumbo poet "is the original, vivid, if undisciplined worker-poet. . . . The verse in this book is militant, richly satirical, often hilarious and often beautiful."[107] The *Moscow News* wrote that Lewis was "the only one [American revolutionary poet] of his kind in America; and for that matter, perhaps the only one of his kind in any country."[108] In December 1931, Lewis scribbled a note to Jack in the margin of a letter from Ed Falkowski, who suggested that Lewis come to the Soviet Union, work on a state farm, and that in preparation he should learn Russian. "Let's go!" Lewis wrote Jack, ". . . But who will finance the getting of us over there and getting us back. . . ."

Jack was anxious to send a Rebel Poet representative to Moscow but had no plans to go there himself. He had his hands full already; he could make his contribution as an editor. It heartened Jack that the Soviet press was eager to receive correspondence from American workers about conditions in the States from a worker's perspective. Perhaps there was a chance of creating an audience for worker-writing in the United States; what was going on in the Soviet Union in organizations like RAPP might serve as an example. Jack made a note on the letter: "We must have some of our members send some sketches."[109] But problems beset the Rebel Poets. The Cheyneys were off on another scheme to raise money for their literary endeavors, this time by publishing the photos of poetasters in their magazine in exchange for money.[110]

Jack encountered increasing difficulty in accommodating the diversity that he had originally sought for the *Rebel Poet*.[111] Falkowski's reports from Moscow indicated too that the Soviet bureau (MORP) was withholding its approval of Jack's little magazine on account of its "anarchistic tendencies."[112] The original revolutionary spirit of the magazine had grown thin and divisive by the end of its first year of publication. Conroy's internationalist aims for the Rebel Poets, to initiate chapters worldwide, had only very limited success. Members of the Japanese proletarian group wrote back, saying that a Rebel Poet chapter in Japan would conflict with their own efforts. Falkowski approached the Soviets about a Moscow chapter and was told that the Russian press was hungry for poems but not those published abroad—or at least they must be written about Russian problems for Russians. A handful of writers and poets in England might have been termed a Rebel Poet chapter, but they themselves were too scattered to hold meetings. Indeed, Jack had never attended meetings of Rebel Poet chapters in New York and Boston. From Boston, Kenneth Porter reported on Rebel Poet activities whose participants included John Wheelwright and Seymour Link.[113] Walter Snow was Jack's key link to the New York chapter, and the news from there was that factions had begun to form, slowing down the work.

The new year was to be a turning point for Jack, who began to believe that what was needed was a publication that would speak to workers and perhaps ferret out new writers from among their ranks.[114] Playing an ever more prominent role in this new attitude was the attention that Jack was receiving in the Soviet Union, the growing recognition, for instance, in the Soviet press of American worker-writing.

12

Comrade Jack:
The Soviet Phase

In regard to your work it would be well for you all
to remember that you are making history. . . .
—Agnes Inglis to Conroy

IN THE WINTER OF 1931–32, the Salvation Army was serving two hundred meals a week to hungry people in Moberly, Missouri, a town of some eight thousand inhabitants. The community was so short of shelter that the homeless were turned out after two nights and told to move on. The number of homeless had increased to a floating army who walked, bummed rides, or rode freights from town to town. Ex-servicemen, members of the Bonus Army, rode freight trains through Moberly in the early spring.[1] Throughout the Midwest, the middle class was beginning to feel the effects of the Depression. Some Moberly stores closed and the city reported it was without funds. A Kiwanis Club speaker ascribed the Depression to lack of ambition and to failure.[2] Two thousand jobless, organized by the Party's Unemployed Council, rioted in St. Louis, and in July troops were called in to quell a Bonus Marchers' riot in Washington, D.C.[3] Three thousand workers marched on the Ford River Rouge factory demanding jobs; four people were killed when the police opened fire. While the police looked for Communist agitators, thousands of Detroit auto workers marched in the victims' funeral parade carrying a red banner with the slogan "Ford Gave Us Bullets for Bread." Police placed the New York financial district under heavy police guard, fearing a "Red" attack.[4] In 1932, Iowa farmers blocked roads to withhold farm goods from going to market and protested when President Hoover visited Des Moines. The Party initiated a series of hungry people's dem-

onstrations in Washington, D.C. In southern Illinois when the Progressive Miners of America sponsored a demonstration, riots ensued. By
year's end, it appeared to many that the country's political system might
not remain intact. When the newly elected president, Franklin Delano
Roosevelt, first spoke to the nation, however, it was to counsel against
giving into such fears.

The nation's hardships and anxieties showed up in the harder, more
militant tone of submissions to the *Rebel Poet*, inveighing against capitalism. Miriam Allen deFord wrote of workers who don't see the larger
picture:

> Starvin' to death
> For 'most a week—
> Thank Gawd I ain't
> No Bolshevik.[5]

One poet revised his poem after it had been submitted because, he said,
the original version was too mild; it needed more propaganda. Poets
were moving to the left so fast that they felt obliged to revise the content of their poems to keep abreast.[6] Raymond Kresensky, who had defended Norman Thomas's Socialist party a year earlier, began to revise
his own political position in reply to Jack's espousal of the Soviet cause;
Kresensky wondered out loud to Kenneth Porter and Conroy where the
effects of land erosion, a depressed economy, and a growing insurgency
among farmers would eventually lead. The Communists were doing more
than anyone else to help the jobless, Jack wrote to his Rebel Poet
friends. He had seen the Party's work in organizing Unemployed Councils in St. Louis. And when he saw police and hired company guards
beat up the unemployed demonstrators, he realized how uneven the
struggle between labor and capital had become.[7] Such events, not conspiracy or control, influenced writers and intellectuals in their move
leftward early in the 1930s, as Matthew Josephson suggests in *Infidel in
the Temple*. It is evident from their correspondence that Kalar, Jack,
Huddlestone, Kresensky, Cruden, Rogers, and Snow thought the contemporary situation through carefully and that their convictions were
deeply felt. Their approval of the Party's defense of blacks and radicals
in the courts, its organizing of the unemployed, suggests that they were
not dupes but thoughtful individuals who participated sensitively in the
experience of their generation.

While approving the Party's interventions on behalf of the unemployed and blacks, Conroy nonetheless ignored Party dictates and didactic tendencies among its orthodox ideologues.[8] In *The Disinherited* a
character says: "That's why them soapboxers never get anywheres. Why

don't they talk about beans and potatoes, lard and bacon instead of 'ideology,' 'agrarian crisis,' and 'rationalization.'" As 1932 wore on, however, Jack entered deeper into a never-never land with respect to political commitment. He was beginning to receive attention from the Soviets, yet at home the Communists admonished him for his independent attitudes and behavior, particularly in his capacity as editor of the *Anvil*. Temporarily setting aside whatever ambivalence he felt toward Party discipline and "correct" ideology, he wrote, under a Rebel Poet letterhead in March 1932, that "Our attitude is that of the John Reed Club and the International Union of Revolutionary Writers."[9] Moreover, his *Rebel Poet* essays and editorials made heavy use of the Communists' revolutionary rhetoric: capitalism was dying, the American worker "has begun to think; when he gets into his full stride his footsteps will shake the earth and tumble down many a gaudy and gilded temple," and so forth.[10]

Revolutionary rhetoric thrived in the early 1930s, going hand in hand with a general impoverishment in the realm of thoughtful political writing among American critics and writers closely associated with the left. John Strachey's lectures on dialectical materialism in 1934 were an exception. (Strachey was a visiting Englishman.) There was a tendency on the left to attitudinize rather than to probe deeply into theory; political debates in John Reed Club meetings often became occasions for fault finding. Jack kept his own counsel in the meetings; he shared his thoughts afterward, quoting a verse or remarking on something humorous someone had said, committing it to memory and telling it in anecdotal fashion again and again to friends. Walter Snow's letters kept Jack abreast of the New York John Reed Club where the stakes were a great deal higher than in the St. Louis club.

The western poet and editor Norman Macleod remembered the jealousies and backbiting among writers and critics at *New Masses*, where he served as a fill-in editor for one issue, and in the John Reed Club meetings. Arriving in New York after a drive across the country from Hollywood (where he helped found a John Reed Club) in the car of an English writer named Dorothy Fletcher, chauffeured by a black homosexual lifeguard named Willie, Macleod was welcomed warmly by the *New Masses* staff, who knew him through his reportages on Alabama steel workers and San Francisco dockworkers. Several New York comrades were critical of Macleod's articles and poems on the American West. "What does this have to do with workers?" someone asked him at a John Reed Club meeting in New York soon after his arrival, referring to a poem on the Grand Canyon.[11]

Macleod walked into an atmosphere of dissension and angry invective unfamiliar to him. He recalled years later one particular exchange between Mike Gold and Charles Yale Harrison, author of *Generals Die in Bed,* at a John Reed Club meeting. Something the flamboyant Gold said infuriated Harrison, who jumped up from his chair, flailing his arms around exasperatedly. In doing so he accidentally struck an Irishman sitting next to him. Harrison then retreated sullenly to the side of the room, where he stood next to the wall with arms folded and a grim expression. The Irish Communist, who was well into his cups, wandered absently around the room without his eyeglasses, then returned to his seat. Besides such mock-burlesque events, meetings were frequently the scene of shouting matches and explosions of temper.[12] At the center often was Gold, who seemed to thrive in fierce debate and who sustained his readers through a vigorous contestatory style such as in his "Open Letter to the Young Men of Wall Street." He attacked Floyd Dell, who dropped out of the radical movement to embrace family life, for signing a letter, "Yours for the Revolution!" (Gold knew that Dell meant the sexual revolution.) Behind all the half-comic gesturing, however, were power struggles that in the coming summer of 1932 would affect Jack in faraway Moberly, Missouri.

Differences continued to exist between the convictions of East Coast radicals and Jack's own political habits of thought. Jack viewed his workers as more subject to the enticements of mass culture and consumerism than to slogans like "workers unite!" or abstract lessons drawing upon Marxist analysis. Sentiment, not reason, attracted him (and many others) to the Communists. While midwestern literary radicals viewed the CP as a "bright star of hope in the sky," as Jack wrote John Rogers years later, most played no active role in the movement.[13] Jack attended meetings of the John Reed Club in St. Louis, which had recently been organized with the help of the Chicago club.[14] These meetings put him in contact with Orrick Johns, Joe Jones, Wallie Wharton, Jack Balch, and several Party district organizers who began to figure importantly in his life after the publication of *The Disinherited.* If, as Coser and Howe allege, some zealous fellow travelers drove themselves to rites of self-humiliation and fanaticism, Jack was not one of them.[15] He approved of the manner in which the CP, through its Unemployed Councils, attempted to accord dignity to the unemployed worker, black or white, yet he pursued his own "cultural program" independently as editor of the *Rebel Poet* and later the *Anvil.* Supporting the Party's aims while following his own private agenda—fundamentally democratic, autonomous, and decentralized—placed him in equivocal situations intellectually and represented a basic contradiction between his editorial positions and his actual practice.[16]

To be active in the CP at that time meant Party discipline and self-sacrifice, sacrifice even of one's family life, for the Party was a larger family; one owed it devotion and loyalty.[17] Impatient with hierarchical structures of authority of any kind, Conroy could make no such commitment. Encounters with kangaroo-court denunciations in the St. Louis John Reed Club meetings only bolstered this conviction. Present but not an active participant in the nutpickers' and the gas-house workers' strikes in St. Louis, Jack felt a greater kinship with these examples of grass-roots radicalism than with top-down structures of institutionalized radicalism known as vanguard grouping in which a small cadre of people was in charge of theory and tactics.[18] Fundamental to the vanguard notion was the substitution idea, namely that a party substituted for a class (Lenin), and eventually a single individual substituted for a class (Stalin).

By year's end, the *Rebel Poet* would fall victim to a form of the substitution notion. Jack's imperfect knowledge of Marxist theory belied the tacit dimensions of his political convictions. In a *Rebel Poet* essay he writes of "materialist dialecticism." His grasp of leftist history proved somewhat faulty too; the Sparticists are referred to in *The Disinherited* as the "Spartacides." He was reluctant, as pointed out earlier, to take Marx as his text. Yet the actual details of American workers' conditions, the misery of working-class existence in factory cities, the helplessness of the unemployed taught him what he needed to know about *Klassenkampf* and *Verfremdung*. He was a rebel on humanitarian grounds, reluctant to temporize or cast issues in political theory. Jack would quickly lose interest in anything expressed in abstract terms, not in the immediate, concrete human terms of human existence. He admired the Soviet Experiment, praised the Party's work, at times even called himself a Communist, but in the same breath he would turn solemnity to humor, backing off in the spirit that made it difficult for him to accept any authority in ideas. He was too far removed, as he liked to say, from New York's Union Square where ideas were discussed fervently.[19] His increasing independence from and resistance to eastern hegemony and Party authority earned him the label of "bohemian" and eventually cost him the support of the Party cultural apparatus.

Contradictions in Jack's attitude toward the Party expanded with time. At the same time that he supported in editorials and essays the aims of the Soviets, his own actual practice grew evermore counterhegemonic and decentralized. There were other contradictions, based less on praxis than on ideology and cultural differences. The regional basis of art came under Party fire, as the Missouri painter Thomas Hart Benton, living in New York and closely associated with the Party, discovered to his dismay.[20] To Marxist critics the strong regional bias of midwestern writing and art was backward and reactionary.[21] Similarly, evidence of "individuality" was considered antiprogressive.[22] On these issues affecting literature Jack was fundamentally at odds with contemporary Marxist critics. Nonetheless Jack continued his steadfast support of the Party. By contemporary standards, this aligned him with the Stalinists—strange when one considers Jack's repugnance toward what Trotsky called "the stifling pressure of the apparatus" and "witless bureaucratic command."[23] Yet to American radicals like Conroy, "Stalinist" meant loyalty to the main cause despite errors and "Trotskyist" meant renegade disruption. Similarly, other Soviet figures and terms received American meanings in their translations to American experience, often quite divorced from the original. Midwestern radicals were always hopelessly behind in following developments in Soviet literary theory and politics.[24]

Conroy's views on proletarian literature and the "cultural front," appearing in *Rebel Poet* editorials and elsewhere, were not consistent with his actual literary practice, except on one main point: the centrality of the worker. The question of Soviet influence on his writing and attitudes is not easy to summarize. Rather than the equivocation toward political commitments that Eric Homberger views as characteristic of American radical writers, Jack appears in retrospect to have given unqualified support to the Soviet Experiment in his editorializing while pursuing a course as writer and editor relatively independent of the Party. What he chose to overlook, as evidenced in his defense of Stalin's purge of the kulaks, was, in Simone Weil's words, the "cold brutality which permeates the politics of a State, especially a totalitarian one; while at the same it has all the prestige attaching to a champion of justice."[25] Impressive to Jack was the absence of unemployment in the Soviet Union, as Gold reported after returning from Kharkov in early 1931, and the respect and dignity it accorded the worker. In the *Rebel Poet*, Conroy quoted approvingly from Waldo Frank's recent Soviet travelogue, *Dawn in Russia* (1932): "What is taking place in Russian today is the most precious social event, the most precious social life, of our crucial epoch. . . . We must defend the Soviet Union with our spirit; if need be, we must defend it with our bodies." At the same time he ignored Frank's apprehensions about Stalin's dictatorship and his warning that Americans should remain loyal to their own traditions and institutions.[26] Welcoming the attention of Soviet critics, nevertheless Jack must have felt uneasiness toward Soviet censures of American little magazines like the *Left* and *Front* appearing in the IURW's *International Literature*. American radicals followed developments in the Soviet

Union through *Literature of the World Revolution* and its successor, *International Literature*. Jack read these journals, as well as the *Moscow News*, available in the workers' bookshops that he frequented in St. Louis, Kansas City, and Chicago.

Jack knew vaguely about RAPP, the Soviet revolutionary group of proletarian writers, and had read in *New Masses* the report of the American delegation to the 1930 Kharkov Conference. The background of Soviet literary politics, the power struggles between rival groups, the dissenting opinions at Kharkov were, however, unfamiliar material to him; moreover, he had little interest in the intrigues and counterintrigues among ideologues. Nonetheless, what came out of Russia gave him heart to continue his own work and in significant ways parallels his own efforts. American industry was scarcely ready for "shock brigades" of writers within its factories, as urged by RAPP, yet Jack hoped his magazine would elicit submissions from worker-writers, like himself veterans of the assembly line.

RAPP was a product of the Sixth Comintern Congress strategy, grounded in the conviction that an imminent proletarian revolution, following economic crisis and war, in the capitalist nations would take place with the Party in a leadership role vis-à-vis the working class. While the sectarianism and dogmatisms of RAPP, which placed literature in the service of the Five-Year Plan, were insupportable to Conroy's mind, he nonetheless shared RAPP's interest in improving the literary quality of worker-writing. RAPP, and its successor, VOAPP (All-Union Federation of Associations of Proletarian Writers), which dominated Soviet literary politics until the Party disbanded it in April 1932, continued to influence radical writing, in the Soviet Union, in Germany (until the Nazi dictatorship), and to a far lesser extent in the United States, for instance, in its encouragement of the short, journalistic sketch.[27]

American radical circles were slow to respond to changes in Soviet literary politics, namely, the disbanding of RAPP in 1932 and the appearance of Socialist Realism, made official at the First All-Union Soviet Writers' Congress in 1934. Jack's praise of *Those Who Built Stalingrad*, a collective writing project, in his 1935 American Writers' Congress speech, reflected the RAPP focus on encouraging writers from the laboring class of factory workers and farmhands. It was characteristic that Jack would take what he found useful and ignore the rest, such as the stifling conformity of RAPP's attempt to dominate Soviet writing. Similarly, Gold and other American Marxists selected what they wished to champion from the confusing and shifting changes in Soviet literary theory and politics. Changes in Soviet policy occurred so quickly that even while RAPP went on the offensive in promoting its version of worker-correspondence, the Party, acting on Gorki's suggestion, had already decided to do away with RAPP (and other literary partisans) in order to consolidate all writers, regardless of social origin, in a single organization.[28] In place of worker-poets like Demian Bedni, Mikhail Sholokhov became the model of the Soviet writer. Jack joined other reviewers in praising Sholokhov's *And Quiet Flows the Don* and *Virgin Soil*.[29]

If the cultural revolution was intended to bring about a Soviet America, ruled by the proletariat, Jack devoted most of his efforts as editor of *Rebel Poet*, and later the *Anvil*, to promoting a democratic, rhizomatous culture, closer to indigenous models found in Girard, Kansas; Holt, Minnesota; and Oklahoma City than in Moscow. The discrepancy, then, between some of the poetry appearing in the *Rebel Poet*, calling for a revolution along Bolshevik lines, and his editorial practices mirrored the contradictions mentioned earlier having to do with his support for the Soviet Experiment and his own "deviancy" as an independent-minded rebel who felt more comfortable with the folk spirit and humor of Oscar Ameringer's *Guardian* than with the CPA's feverish efforts to keep abreast of the Comintern line. Ameringer, who previously had edited the Milwaukee *Leader*, the *Illinois Miner*, and the Oklahoma *Leader*, viewed socialism in the Southwest as more populist than Marxist. His column "Adam Coaldigger," which Conroy knew from the *Railway Carmen's Journal*, was famous among miners. (The name was a play on "a damn coal digger.") Ameringer typified a type of independent radical who turned things to humor yet had trenchant words about the Herrin, Illinois, massacre and the condition of workers in southern textile mills. The Party did not welcome Ameringer's humor always and generally ignored his work.

* * *

Editor of *Rebel Poet*, contributor to *American Mercury* and other magazines, coeditor of three *Unrest* anthologies, Jack had reason to be optimistic that Mencken's connections would help him find a publisher for his book manuscript. Publishers, looking closely at their declining book sales, were reluctant to take a risk on an unknown worker-writer. The manuscript of his first novel was still a loose collection of sketches, scarcely recommending itself to experienced book editors. Largely unfamiliar with the expectations of mainstream publishers, Jack left the job of peddling his manuscript to Max Lieber. Moreover, his own practice as editor—taking risks on unknowns, relying on voluntary help, minimizing printing costs—ran counter to those of most publishers. He was not prepared for the rejections of his book manuscript he would soon receive, nor was he certain how to revise in order to make it acceptable.

The *Rebel Poet* was running on a shoestring budget, largely dependent upon Hagglund's balky press and volunteers (including John Reed clubs) to which Hagglund sent bundles for distribution. Moreover, Jack was unhappy with the Soviet critic Bruno Jassiensky's response to the magazine, reported by Falkowski in Moscow. Jassiensky predicted that based upon the evidence of the organization's magazine, most Rebel Poets would duck out after "indulging in sprees of red rhetoric."[30] Jack had counted on the Soviets' support; recognition from Moscow would mean promotion through its influential *International Literature*. Falkowski advised Jack to look for poems that were more concretely linked to contemporary subjects, rejecting submissions that were merely "aesthetic revolts." Don't be dismayed by Soviet criticism, he added, which is often based upon insufficient understanding of American conditions. The Soviets sought specific platforms and closer ties with Party objectives; Jack hoped to create a Wobbly-like world federation, broad in scope and providing access at all levels.

Jack's disappointment extended to *New Masses*, whose selection of short stories (he particularly liked those of Whittaker Chambers and Mike Gold) was diminishing with each issue.[31] Anxious to fill a gap he perceived, Jack began to accept sketches for the *Rebel Poet*. The first to appear (and the first Jack ever published as an editor) was "Beyond the Mountain," by John C. Rogers. Rogers, a Virginian, soon became one of Jack's hopefuls for a new literature centered on the worker. Rogers was a triple threat on the cultural front, an artist, poet, and short-story writer. Born in Alexandria, he left high school early, supporting himself at laborer jobs, experience that became material for his writing. He attended an art academy, afterward producing linoleum cuts and woodblock prints for little magazines, jobs he solicited through a *New Masses* ad that read: "Art Work done by proletarian Artist—Estimates—Sketches. Prices Proletarian."[32] His story "Beyond the Mountain" is set in the Virginia hills where Rogers spent his summers as a youth on his grandfather's farm. The story is a sketch in its simplest form, without the artifice of plot, an exercise in first-person journalistic reporting concerning unemployed workers who spend the night in jail on vagrancy charges, then move on "beyond the mountain," witnesses to poverty among the hill folk. Earlier, *Unrest* had drawn Rogers's attention to Jack, and both contributed some of their earliest material to Theodore Sitea's bilingual *Earth-Pamantul*. In portraying their childhoods, both writers blended idyllic evocation with growing radical awareness, sharing an interest in dialect and folklife. Rogers's interest in Virginia hill people attracted the attention of B. A. Botkin, who published two of Rogers's stories in his fourth *Folk-Say* collection.[33]

The historian Dee Brown remembered Rogers as a gracious person of aristocratic bearing, a bohemian artist whom Brown and his wife, Sally, met frequently at a bookstore in Washington, D.C., and later at a hangout called Romany Marie's Tavern in Greenwich Village.[34] Rogers was secretary of the John Reed Club in Washington, D.C., having helped organize it. To Conroy, looking back years later, Rogers embodied perhaps better than anyone else the spirit of the radical 1930s.[35] Rogers joined Conroy, Kalar, Lewis, Falkowski, Snow, Le Sueur, Algren, and others like them (in Jack's eyes) as the radical, literary avant-garde in bringing about a cultural revolution, polycentric, nonhierarchical, and progressive. Working independently of one another in scattered locales, from Moberly to Moscow, each would write the unembellished truth about contemporary America for a broad audience of white- and blue-collar workers. Such was the notion taking shape in Jack's mind in 1932.

Rebel Poet was printed on low-quality paper, in clear, bold print. The first five issues were a single signature, four 8-by-11-inch pages, with no artwork, ads, or cover. Subsequent issues were twelve pages in length and included simple but effective linoleum-block prints, exchange ads, and a book page.[36] Early issues of *Rebel Poet* addressed contemporary social issues such as unemployment and hunger. The bulk of the poems are angry protests against wealth and privilege, humanitarian appeals to bring about social justice. The familiar images of earlier radical publications, for instance, *Masses* and the *Liberator,* are evoked: the obese capitalist, the oppressed worker. Hope is found in "tomorrow" with its (undefined) promise of a revolutionary future. The naive faith in the role of poetry in the cause of revolutionary change prompted one contributor to charge the Rebel Poets with taking in one another's washing: "Rebel poets read rebel poetry, rebel poets write rebel poetry for rebel poets to read."[37] The proletariat, he allowed, prefer Edgar Guest, if they read poetry at all. Much of this faith in the revolutionary potential of poetry sprang from Cheyney's breast; in an essay in the same issue, he expressed hope that American workers would learn to respond to poetry as Russian workers do. Jack, on the other hand, worried about the small subscription list, leaving Cheyney to his virgin speculations on poetry's role in the revolutionary tomorrow. Three doubled issues were followed by a triple issue in the fall of 1931, signaling the financial plight of the organization and Hagglund's wayward printing schedule. (Hagglund contributed money from Rebel Poet booklet earnings to at least one issue.)

Rebel Poet skipped an issue, appearing again in March 1932, its thirteenth number, with an entirely new emphasis. Departing from the humanitarian protests and faith in poetry's revolutionary potential, characteristic of the early issues (and Cheyney's own poetry), number 13 laid heavy stress on the Soviet Experiment, reflecting the RAPP-dominated program that Magil, Gold, and other members of the American delegation to Kharkov had brought home a year earlier and spelled out in *New Masses*. The cover carried a Rogers poem and a woodcut print showing workers with upraised fists and flags. Jack's essay "Art Above the Battle?" called for dedication on the part of artists and writers to the cultural revolution. Fascist practices, he wrote, are in control of "the press, the screen, and the radio."[38] Demian Bedni, the Soviet peasant poet, was a significant presence in this issue (in Fania Kruger's translation), evidence that Jack was sensitive to RAPP's proletarian models. Falkowski, the Rebel Poet's "man in Moscow," continued to commend the realistic attitude of Soviet writers, citing the factory brigades of writer-correspondents. "The poems are almost skeletal in form, telegraphic jottings, electric words compressing the gist of their thoughts, which run parallel to throb of factory and guffaw of steel mill and backfire of tractor-squadrons plowing up oceanic state farms."[39] To produce such a thing, Falkowski implied, it was necessary to "sleep on springless bunks" and write on "constructive" themes. Demian Bedni's "roaring ballads," he wrote, have spurred "other warrior-voices," urging the worker to further effort. Bedni's worthy American counterpart, Falkowski remarked elsewhere, echoing Henry George Weiss, was the Missouri gumbo poet, H. H. Lewis. Lewis's volume of poems, *Thinking of Russia* (1932), shared Bedni's virulent antireligious bias and propagandist animus but little else. Bedni reveals nothing of Lewis's quixotic humor and pungent satire.[40] Jack himself seemed to take his cues directly from the RAPP platform in calling for a "militant affirmation and tendency to 'materialistic dialectic' [sic]."[41]

The thirteenth number of *Rebel Poet* revealed the editor's growing attention to the Soviet Union. The Rebel Poet's organizational structure had begun also to favor the Soviets, revealing centripetal tendencies, departing from the loose polycentric eclecticism Cheyney and Conroy had introduced. The hard fact was that *Rebel Poet* had its largest circulation in New York City where alone five hundred copies of the March issue had sold. Leonard Spier handled the New York subscriptions at his home on Seventy-fourth Street with the consequence that the New York Rebel Poet chapter began to dominate the organization. Among the active members in New York City was Walter Snow, who hoped to get the Party to distribute *Rebel Poet*, as it did *New Masses*. Since Hagglund was making up deficits from his own pocket (Jack earned nothing from the publication), the shift to New York was necessary to keep the magazine afloat. Conroy appointed an editorial board, following Snow's suggestions, which supervised the Rebel Poets. All the board members, apart from Conroy, lived in or near New York City. Board meetings were disputatious; tensions were growing and there was little Jack could do about it. Cheyney was absorbed with his poetry correspondence school and had little say in the actual running of Rebel Poets.

The story of *Unrest 1931*, the Rebel Poets' third anthology, was likewise problematic. The subjects were revolutionary heroes and martyrs—Sacco and Vanzetti, Tom Mooney, Debs, Lenin, the working masses. Sherwood Anderson's long poem "Machine Song: Automobile" embraced the machine age, casting aside the "old self . . . that self in me, that would not live in my own age." "Will you take a new age? Will you give yourself to a new age? / Will you love factory girls as you love automobiles?" the poem asks, sounding vaguely like a Soviet ode to tractor brigades.[42] William Rose Benet, in his *Saturday Review of Literature* column, "Round About Parnassus," called Anderson's "Machine Song" "bad prose, boringly repetitive," and panned Cheyney's poetic tribute to Eugene Debs.[43] The reviewer for *Nation* magazine was kinder: "Most of the poems are proudly 'propaganda,' and a few are artistically right."[44] Particularly galling to Conroy was the review in Abernethy's *Contempo*, published in Chapel Hill, North Carolina. In his response, "Sweet Are the Uses of Criticism," which Abernethy would not publish, Jack wrote: "To hell with you, stuffed-shirt gentlemen and lily-fingered, pink tea ladies! We're going to seek our audiences among the inarticulate masses to whom and for whom we speak!"[45] His new audience would be among the members of the Workers' Cultural Federation and John Reed clubs. "There's even a John Reed Club at Chapel Hill!" was Jack's rejoinder to the *Contempo* editors, who, he accused, promoted an apolitical Faulkner in place of Dreiser.

The question of readership worried Jack, who perceived that workers were attracted to popular radio shows and comic strips, not rebellious verse. With all good intent, Conroy hoped to rouse the sleeping masses. The principal readership of *Rebel Poet*, in fact, was comprised of the contributors themselves and like-minded rebels—the magazine made few conversions to the cultural revolution. It is likewise unlikely that *Unrest 1931* converted anyone to revolutionary causes; it spoke mainly to those who viewed social problems in class terms, citing the Sacco-Vanzetti executions. "This book," Cheyney and Conroy wrote in their introduction to the anthology of Rebel Poet verse, "is not for those who find no poetry or beauty in the lives and deeds of men like these. For such we have nothing to say." Here was an admission that rebels were writing for other rebels, or at least people halfway there. *Rebel Poet* notions of social injustice were too ill-defined to attract the ordinary reader, who had a great deal of difficulty connecting his own experience with the Soviet worker's or finding solace in a "World brotherhood."[46]

The American publisher of *Unrest 1931*, Henry Harrison, ran a vanity press, printing books of mixed quality, including a volume of his own poetry entitled *Myself Limited*. Walt Carmon called him "a racketeer."[47] Several contributors, including Harry Roskolenkier, complained about paying to have one's poem reprinted in *Unrest*, a criticism that Kenneth Porter had raised in earlier volumes. A major weakness of *Unrest 1931* was its lack of focus. A good revolutionary poem required more than well-founded convictions. The anthology included a number of effective poems, most critics agreed, but on the whole it was a weak performance. Jack was consoled by the fact that the *Gastonia Gazette* (South Carolina), published in the town where the labor balladeer Ella May Wiggins was murdered during the textile mill strikes, "flayed us."[48] Cheyney should be jailed, the *Gazette* editors concluded. To be assailed by a reactionary newspaper was a sign that rebel verse energized its detractors. The same paper kept a close watch on radicals in Chapel Hill, North Carolina, attacking *Contempo's* Abernethy, who it claimed had been expelled by the state university for his ultraliberal convictions.[49] *Unrest* was not making converts, perhaps, but it was at least successful in goading certain reactionary elements in society.

Jack's own short stories, on the other hand, were finding an appreciative audience. Mencken accepted Jack's story of his job in a Hannibal, Missouri, shoe factory, entitled "Rubber Heels," for the April *Mercury*. "It's capital stuff," Mencken wrote, "and I'll be delighted to take it."[50] He sent a sheaf of Jack's stories to Alfred Knopf, the publisher, calling Jack a new Zola.[51] Carmon wrote Jack, praising "Paving Gang," which appeared in *New Masses*. Lieber was peddling Conroy's "Little Stranger" at *Pagany* and *Hound and Horn*. Jack was doing his own promoting of new writers, sending Ben Field's (a.k.a. Moe Bragin) "Farm Sketches" to Mencken. In March, Mencken accepted another Conroy story of work, "Pipe Line"; in his reply to Jack he wrote: "It is reported on all sides, in this part of the country, that the end of the world is at hand, and thousands of people seem to believe it."[52] Mencken never took such talk of impending revolution seriously.

When in March, Henry Ford's private police beat up workers participating in a march protesting unemployment, Jack was outraged. He wrote to Representative Ralph F. Lozier in Washington, D.C.: "The men who fought with stones at Detroit yesterday may return tomorrow or next year with guns. This country will shake from the tramp of their feet. You gentlemen who sit in Congress are in a position to prevent much bloodshed. . . ."[53] The Depression had become an intrusive reality in many people's lives and would not be pushed aside. The *American Guardian's* editor, Oscar Ameringer, visited twenty states in 1932 to observe conditions, reporting his findings in hearings before a House of Representatives subcommittee studying unemployment. He told of overproduction, waste, and hunger existing side by side. Apples, he said, were left rotting on the ground because of low prices while the homeless searched for scraps of food in refuse piles.[54] Companies placed signs on their doors: "Do Not Ask For Work. There Is No Work. This Means U." The paper mill in International Falls where Joe Kalar worked reduced its work schedule to two days every two weeks.

"Something radical has to happen," Ray Kresensky wrote Kenneth Porter, both Christian ministers. "And since men are naturally fighters, we are nothing more than fighting, struggling beings trying to get along[;] we might as well exaggerate that struggle between the classes and have it out."[55] Several months later, after a trip through the South, he wrote to Porter again: "Everywhere along the way I noticed the people getting together in parks and arguing, discussing, conversing freely. The conditions are ripe for Revolution but who's going to start it? As yet we haven't the men, nor the brains for anything so drastic."[56] Announcing to Jack his plan to form a Rebel Poet chapter in Boston, along with Seymour Link and John Wheelwright, Porter received Jack's reply: "We have to build our movement from within, as has been done in Germany."[57] After a bad fall while trimming trees, a profoundly discouraged John Rogers considered taking his own life, then made up his mind that as an artist he might contribute something to the revolution.[58]

Confident that the *Rebel Poet* might play a role in raising the revolutionary consciousness of its readers, Conroy urged his friends and readers to abandon all the "four and seventy jarring sects" of radicalism and join behind the CP in the fall elections.[59] Bill Jordan of the Workers' Cultural Federation in Chicago was urging his readers to do the same, in a flyer announcing a conference for April to which Jack was invited but could not attend. The desperate spectacle of hungry people, Henry Ford's hired goons, and the farmers' riots in Iowa were pushing liberal intellectuals further left. In Philadelphia alone, a quarter of a million people were near starvation and over a quarter of the schoolchildren were profoundly undernourished, according to estimates by Pennsylvania's governor.[60] In its September issue, *Fortune* magazine reported that with over ten million unemployed, "it is conservative to estimate that the problem of next winter's relief is a problem of caring for approximately 25,000,000 souls." Prominent intellectuals and writers, including John Dos Passos, Edmund Wilson, Sherwood Anderson, Sidney Hook, Waldo Frank, and others, signed a manifesto in the summer of 1932 supporting the Foster-Ford Communist party ticket, not because they agreed altogether with Party ideals, but because the Party at least provided a vision of a better life.[61] Despite the growing desperation, the *Fortune* editors were surprised to find very little unrest among the masses of people. Communist hunger marches turned out relatively few supporters. Demonstrations, with exceptions (the march on the Ford plant at Dearborn in 1932), were widespread but generally bloodless. Nonetheless, there was "a limit," the editors of the business magazine concluded, "beyond which hunger and misery become violent."[62] Under such circumstances, Jack wrote the editors of *Earth,* a little magazine published in Wheaton, Illinois, fascism is a possibility, and therefore there is no point in trying to "save" the country from communism.[63]

Max Lieber sensed a demand among certain editors for stronger stuff with more revolutionary content, and when H. H. Lewis sent him a satirical sketch called "The Great Corn-Husking Derby," Lieber wrote Jack: "God beams on the Communists."[64] However, he cautioned that mainline publishers like Knopf were reluctant to take financial risks and therefore Jack should not to be too optimistic about his manuscript. He should get to know Granville Hicks, Lieber advised, who scouted for Macmillan. Lieber had heard from Bob Cruden, who was finishing a novel based upon his experiences as a Ford assembly worker in Detroit. Mainstream editors had read with interest the worker-writers' stories in the little magazines. Would mainstream publishers give these unknown "proletarians" the opportunity to reach a wider readership? The stakes were very high for both writer and publisher in 1932.

"The proletarian bull market," as Jack later called it, had begun. Recognition of Jack's work would benefit other worker-writers like Cruden, Lewis, Kalar, and Falkowski. Moscow critics were taking notice of American worker-writers. Quality magazines like *Pagany* accepted proletarian stories. *New Masses* published Moe Bragin's farm sketches and Cruden's reports from inside the Ford Motor plant. Momentum seemed to be building; Jack looked happily at the growing prospect of a cultural revolution in which his Rebel Poets would play an active role. "In regard to your work," wrote the Labadie Collection librarian, Agnes Inglis, at the University of Michigan, "it would be well for you all to remember that you are making history, and so do not forget to register your work in libraries."[65]

Whittaker Chambers, later notorious for his role in the Alger Hiss conspiracy case, warned Jack against premature elation, the "fulsome praise" by friends in place of "Bolschevik self-criticism."[66] At *New Masses*, "self-criticism" had produced a shakeup, including Carmon's dismissal as editor, much to Jack's dismay. Jack had a great deal of trust in Carmon's judgment, viewing him as one of the few among the New York radical groups who understood the midwesterners. In a precious, condescending tone Chambers replied to Conroy's objections to the direction *New Masses* appeared to be taking, ignoring Lewis's work, for instance. Lewis's reception was a measuring stick for Conroy; those who were put off by Lewis's "crude vigor" were likely to be stiff-necked, orthodox Party-line types. Jack fumed for weeks.

When *Pagany* accepted his "Bun Grady," about a superannuated worker, Jack wrote triumphantly to its editor, Richard Johns, that the story would be a chapter in his first book.[67] The fact that Mencken had published so much of the contents ensured, he felt, that the book would find a publisher. In the May issue of *New Masses* appeared Conroy's "He Is Thousands," a story of company "bulls" beating up workers seeking jobs. Conroy expanded the death of one worker to represent all workers who are victims of class oppression. It is a simple but powerful piece of politicized narrative. Along with Meridel Le Sueur's "Women On the Breadlines," published a few months earlier, it is probably the best example of revolutionary writing to appear in *New Masses* up to that time—as good as Gold's "A Damned Agitator," a story Conroy had admired in *120 Million* (1929).

In the spring of 1932, Jack seemed committed to Party aims, rejecting milder alternatives such as Norman Thomas's socialists offered. He wrote Kenneth Porter: ". . . so I, like a primitive Baptist, plant my number tens [shoes] on the solid rock of Lenin and refuse to compromise with the world and the flesh by traipsing off to another 'united front.' . . ."[68] Jack was too broke to attend the First National Conference of John Reed Clubs in Chicago in late May, despite Bill Jordan's urging that it would be an opportunity to make contacts and push for the Party's endorsement of Rebel Poets. Oakley Johnson, executive secretary of the John Reed clubs, suggested that Jack sponsor a contest for anti-imperialist war poems in the *Rebel Poet*.[69] Jack responded with an entire issue devoted to "anti-imperialism. "All those," he wrote in an editorial note, "who desire the correct revolutionary interpretation of international events, especially those of coloniel and semi-coloniel [*sic*] countries, should read and study the 'Anti-Imperialist Review.' . . ."[70] John Rogers provided a woodcut print on imperialist war especially for the issue. The word "correct," part of the language of orthodoxy, had crept into Jack's editorial language and format of the magazine.

At the national conference in May, a struggle for turf was engaged of which Jack could scarcely be aware. Outside the actual meetings in Lincoln Auditorium, delegates maneuvered for control of the cultural front, the effect of which was to consolidate the power in the East, since, according to Daniel Aaron, "probably only the New York delegates were aware of these background maneuverings."[71] Certainly nothing was intimated in Bill Jordan's letter to Jack that this was so, although he did point out the ascendancy of the New York John Reed Club among the ten clubs represented at the meeting.[72] It was only natural, after all, that the New York club would play a central role since the national headquarters were at 63 West Fifteenth Street (the offices of *New Masses*). At a subsequent meeting in 1934, however, eastern radical intellectuals attempted quite openly to impose their views, as we shall see, infuriating the midwesterners. Sectarianism had become sectionalism, it seemed. In 1932, such incipient divisions were masked by the JRC national agenda's call for unity against "imperialist war" and defense of the Soviets' peaceful intent.[73]

Jack was eager to do his share, ignorant of shifting political winds projected on the Party's weather map. Jordan asked Jack to write a skit for a "truck theater," a traveling group of actors that the John Reed clubs were going to send out to small midwestern communities over the summer. Jack was to create a skit illustrating the plight of farmers; Lewis would do a satire on the two major parties, as well as on the Socialist party.[74] Soon after, the St. Louis John Reed Club asked Jack to work up a one-act play for the Workers Theatre in St. Louis.[75] If Jack came out squarely for the "red front" in the spring of 1932, events over the summer soon chastened his growing commitment to the Party. The first concerned Walt Carmon's "retirement" from *New Masses*, probably in part because of his addiction to alcohol, but also because Party men like Whittaker Chambers were shifting the magazine's focus to political commentary. Noticeable by their absence from *New Masses* were Kalar, Lewis, Henry George Weiss, and others whom Carmon had promoted.

Carmon spent several months in Florida taking a rest cure, then left for Moscow in late summer to work for the English-language edition of *International Literature* and *Soviet Travel*. There he fell in with "Ed Falkowksi and the *Moscow News* crowd."[76] Carmon had promoted the midwestern radicals; his leaving confirmed in Jack's mind that the Party was anxious to shed itself of worker-writing and "bohemian" midwesterners who did not keep abreast of the Party's changing line. Carmon expressed something of this feeling in Moscow when he wrote Jack that after the dissolution of RAPP in April 1932, writers felt more freedom.[77] The Party dispensed with rival literary groups to form a single union of writers and began to promote Socialist Realism. Unaware at this point that the Party's new program for literature would introduce new restrictions on subject matter, both Conroy and Carmon welcomed what appeared to be a hands-off policy toward literary endeavor. Jack hoped for Party support in matters of promotion and distribution, but he insisted on maintaining control over his editorial functions.

Thus, in late May, when Rebel Poet Philip Rahv wrote "Comrade Conroy" that the New York Rebel Poet group had met and was drawing up a manifesto for the purpose of making more precise the concept of proletarian literature, Jack was apprehensive. Too many writers are on the fence, Rahv wrote, and need direction. Praising H. H. Lewis's *Thinking of Russia*, Rahv excoriated the Worker's Bookstore for refusing to sell it (ostensibly because it lacked propaganda value). "His writing is racy, agile, muscular, and sparkling with wit," Rahv wrote Jack.[78] But Rahv's actual target was Jack's eclectic editorship. Rahv sought to polemicize the magazine, turn it into a keen-edged axe in the proletarian struggle against class exploitation.[79]

The summer of 1932 was the highwater mark of Rahv's Stalinist orthodoxy. In the August issue of *Rebel Poet*, devoted to black writers, Rahv reviewed Langston Hughes's "Scottsboro Limited." "There is no metaphysical religiosity, no futile psychologising about it," he wrote; "it is a genuine example of the new literature whose theme is the collective, not some mythical *individualists* who only exist in the fog-soaked brains of petit-bourgeois rationalizers of capitalism."[80] In the subsequent "anti-imperialist issue," Rahv strove to exceed his previous effort, attacking bourgeois critics, "these sleek gentlemen, in the beatitude of their esthetic Nirvana," and addressing his readers:

> We, the young writers, working in offices, mills, factories, on the farms, or trudging the streets in search of employment; we who are intent on a literary career . . . are now faced with a key decision that will undoubtedly determine the entire course of our literary existence. Shall we take on the coloration of the bourgeois environment, mutilating ourselves, prostituting our creativeness in the service of a superannuated ruling class, or are we going to unfurl the banner of revolt, thus enhancing our spiritual strength by identifying ourselves with the only progressive class, the vigorous, youthful giant now stepping into the arena of battle, the class-conscious proletariat?[81]

Jack printed Rahv's tumid polemic, fascinated by its excessive rhetorical dimensions, like the sermons of hardshell Baptists he had heard as a youth. In his first contacts with him, Jack felt that Rahv might become a valuable addition to the New York Rebel Poet chapter. Jack was impressed with Rahv's intellectual credentials, his ability to translate Russian, and his connections with the New York radical intelligentsia. By attracting New York radicals to the Rebel Poet cause, Jack hoped to place the distribution of his magazine on a more secure footing, yet maintain his inclusionary editorial policy. Rahv, it soon appeared, had other plans for the Rebel Poet organization.

Cheyney, calling himself alternatively a philosophical anarchist and a Socialist, had already seceded from the Rebel Poets, unwilling to move closer to what he perceived to be the magazine's hardening stance. In fact, according to Walter Snow, Cheyney was miffed that his protégés ("subscribers to his racketeer poetry-in-six-lessons courses") were not welcome in *Rebel Poet*, in light of the New York group's ascendancy in the organization.[82]

Cheyney was correct about the narrowing of the magazine's acceptance policy, for which he blamed Jack. The truth was that after the June meeting of the New York Rebel Poets, Rahv announced to Jack that henceforth Jack's eclectic editorial policy must give way to a consistent militant line and critical analysis. It was not enough to think like a proletarian; one must "feel it organically."[83] To ensure that his point of view would prevail, Rahv gathered together a faction of loyalists within the chapter, including Walt Stacy, Fred Miller, and later, V. J. Jerome. With Stacy as newly elected secretary, the group began right away to proscribe submissions that the majority considered to be liberal and socialist. Different hands submitted drafts of a manifesto. The ideological content of *Rebel Poet*, the New York group agreed, must be more consistent; henceforth, poems of questionable ideology would fall under group scrutiny. The magazine, it was agreed, was not an organ "for encouraging possible rebels."[84]

Rahv, who later would champion European modernism, was eager in 1932 to prove his abilities as the Sainte-Beuve of proletarian literature. Rahv attacked "unintelligibility," mentioning the poet Louis Zukofsky as a model to avoid. "The new proletarian expression needs criticism badly," he wrote Jack, "not only taking the form of attacks on the enemy writers ['bourgeois intellectuals' like T. S. Eliot], but also clearcut discussion of our own work as well as lucid analysis of the creative potentialities in our frontrank [*sic*] writers, such as Kalar, Lewis, Gold, etc."[85] To begin with, Rahv proposed an analysis of Joe Kalar's work. "He is one of the few," Rahv opined, "in whom the philosophical background of dialectic materialism can be clearly discerned. Of course, you understand that I don't consider him a *genius*: I don't suffer from any propensity to go into raptures, especially in the case of a writer who has not as yet attempted . . . to master the major forms of literary ex-

pression." Praising a Kalar sketch, Rahv conceded, "our NY intellectuals would have to go far before they could duplicate it."[86]

As Rahv tightened his grip on the Rebel Poets, choking off anti-
Marxist interlopers, Leonard Spier, a Conroy loyalist in the New York
group, confessed to Jack the group's failings. At a special reading of poetry, called "Red Poets" night, Miller and Stacy of the Rebel Poets got
cold feet and did not show up. "That's the way it goes," Spier lament-
ed to Jack. "They talk and they write letters and manifestoes, but when
it comes to doing something, they leave it to the 'other fellow.' I'm quite
disgusted. If it wasn't for yourself and a few others, I'd throw the whole
thing up in the air."[87]

In Holt, Minnesota, Ben Hagglund decided he might have to work
night shifts in order to continue publishing *Rebel Poet*. Jack knew Hagglund's worth to the magazine: "Our printer tightens his belt and matches every dollar with redoubled energy," Jack wrote in the August issue.
"His steady diet is turnips; he shares his printshop with a cow. He, like
a camel, is able to exist for long periods without food or drink. . . . he'll
continue to use his antiquated hand-press . . . to agitate for bread and
freedom."[88] Responses to Jack's appeal for help brought in enough dollars to permit monthly publication of *Rebel Poet* into the fall. In the
meantime, hoping to attract direct Party aid through its distribution
agency, Jack named V. J. Jerome, a Party functionary, to the New York
group's board. Jack was desperate to keep *Rebel Poet* afloat, but in fact
the decision emboldened the "Rahvites," who within months announced
their intention to scrap the magazine as it was, give it a new title, and
impose their own editorial policy. How factionalism succeeded in splitting the Rebel Poets is worth examining from the perspective of radical literary politics in the early 1930s.

* * *

In distant Moberly, Jack remained curiously optimistic about the outcome of the New York group's infighting and factionalism reported by
Snow and Spier—or perhaps he chose to ignore it. Eager that the Party become involved in the magazine's distribution, Jack had approved
the decision to place Jerome on the editorial board; Jerome, he thought,
would help sell the idea to the Party's Central Committee. A power
struggle for control of the magazine was taking place, however, pitting
Rahv against Spier, each with his supporters. Conroy felt (or hoped)
that the factionalism and contention in the group would eventually
cease, but instead it continued to grow.

In a letter, Walter Snow took pains to describe to Jack a typical Rebel
Poet meeting that took place in Spier's Bronx apartment. Present were

Rahv, Herman Spector, Miller, Jack Kainen (the artist), Snow, Spier, and John Ackerson (whose pen name was George Jarrboe). "The Rebel Poets meeting was dominated by Rahv," wrote Snow, "who talked almost continually and insisted that his brief Manifesto was infallible, and that the final Manifesto must include the names of Charles Henri Ford and Zukofsky, even though E. E. Cummings might escape censure because he was the translator of 'Red Front.'" The group voted on names of other poets to castigate in their manifesto. Among those suggested were William Carlos Williams, Gertrude Stein, T. S. Eliot, and Ezra Pound, promulgators of the "cult of unintelligibility." No need to mention Stein, Eliot, and Pound, Rahv averred; their day of influence had passed and they were no longer important. *Rebel Poet* should march under the Third Internationale's banner. It was wrong to mention William Z. Foster, the CP candidate in the forthcoming election. "For all you know," said Rahv, "a cablegram might suddenly come from Moscow stating that Foster was no longer kosher and Jay Lovestone or somebody else would be back in power again." Summing up the meeting, Snow wrote: "Rahv really is quite a brainy fellow and a very persuasive talker, and therefore doubly dangerous. . . . He tried to overwhelm the boys with a bewildering flow of suggestions and showed off his knowledge of German." After the meeting broke up, Spier expressed his fear to Snow, who had traveled down from Willimantic, Connecticut, that rival factions might divide the Rebel Poets.[89]

Jack, in his reply to Snow, seemed unalarmed, willing to give latitude to individual differences among the New York members. Rahv, he said, "is an egoist, but properly handled, can do a lot of good." Spier, he added, is a complainer, but a good worker. The main task, he concluded, was "to keep them all working as harmoniously as possibly."[90] Jack was pleased with the September "anti-imperialist" issue of *Rebel Poet*. There was even some hope of publishing an *Unrest 1932*, using Hagglund's press.

Conroy was lending all his support to the Communists in anticipation of the forthcoming elections in November, to the point that John Wheelwright, a member of the Boston Rebel Poets and the "leading spirit" of the newly formed Poetry Forum of Cambridge,[91] felt obliged to scold him in a most amusing manner. Conroy had turned down several of Wheelwright's poems because they lacked the "forthright simplicity which we are now trying to cultivate."[92] Maintaining that morals were an important question in assessing the working class, Wheelwright announced that he planned to write poems on the "greed of the American workingman, that is, his preoccupation with wages rather than power." At the same time he rejected the use of violence in the revolutionary struggle. Conroy's political judgment was "unsound," Wheelwright charged. One must appeal to workers on moral grounds. Conroy's militancy, he suggested, owed to an excess of emotional energy. "You are an Irishman, I think. Take full account of the fact, if you are."[93] To underscore his message, Wheelwright dashed off a poem and sent it to Jack. Entitled "1932," it began:

> Conroy, brave Irishman, remember Erin! Condemn slave
> drivers no more than their slaves.
> Longshoremen, lumber jacks, and Bogus Armies,
> hitch-hikers, tramps, the ropes of sandwich
> hand-me-out bread lines, cooperative
> squatters, dispossessed dupes of thrift stamps
> or get-rich-quick Insurance Policies
> cannot beat Uncle Sam in '32!
> Conroy, brave Irishman, remember Erin!
> And above all don't wet your pants with anger.
> The Daughters of the American Revolution,
> the Grand Old Army and the Ku Klux Klan,
> the Order of Cincinnatus, Tribe of Tammany,
> strike-breaking cops, strong-arm men, fighting cock
> marines, gobs, buddies, firemen,
> won't lose their jobs in 1932![94]

After several more such stanzas, the conclusion urges Conroy to take a long view toward revolution, comparing the evolution of present events with those revolutionary landmarks of the nineteenth century: 1832, 1848 (März-Revolution), and beyond that, 1870 (the Paris Commune).

Wheelwright's advice must have had some effect on Jack's attitudes toward the forthcoming November elections. In a letter to Kenneth Porter in early August, Jack said he would give some thought to arguments favoring Norman Thomas, the SP candidate, although he was skeptical. When a delegation from the St. Louis John Reed Club, "boys and girls, all graduated from Washington University this year," came to Moberly that summer to visit Jack, they called him a defeatist for maintaining that the masses of people were as yet untouched by radical propaganda and would vote for Roosevelt—in other words, for echoing Wheelwright's notion.

Others were also attempting to caution Jack about the Party. From Commonwealth College in Mena, Arkansas—a labor school in Arkansas's Ouachita Mountains—came a letter from the school's executive secretary, Charlotte Moskowitz, who remarked that the "selling" of the Party to people in the area was not working. "Most of us down here," she wrote, "consider ourselves pretty good communists, you know, but we can't work with the party. It's the old question of tactics again." Ameringer's *American Guardian* is much more successful than the *Daily Worker*, Moskowitz noted; "it drives things home to them in a way which does not ruffle all of their prejudices the first minute, and with a sense of humor, which immediately disarms them. . . . Most of the 'movement'—what there is of one—is all sewed up in a bundle of stereotypes and home-made ethics which don't seem to hit the spot with anyone but a neurotic. The sound, sane, sensible people that we want to draft into the movement won't bite on that kind of bait."[95] A year or two before, "Chucky" Moskowitz had left the Party without abandoning her support for its aims. Its methods, she complained to Jack, were offbase: "you see I don't think the party is doing much—it's getting all excited and smashing everything else, and not realizing that it's thereby smashing itself, and it's certainly not taking advantage of getting in some real groundwork at this time when time means so darned much." There wasn't a great deal, however, Jack could change at this point. Burdened with his own writing, working as a day laborer digging ditches, worried as ever about financial problems, he scarcely had time to read manuscripts, keep up his correspondence, and contribute editorials to *Rebel Poet*.

Jack sensed that the magazine was slipping out of his editorial hands and took measures to save it. He discussed with Ben Hagglund the idea of moving Ben's printshop to Avery, Iowa, an abandoned mining community, where Jack and Ben talked about establishing a community of artists and writers. Axel Peterson published his idiosyncratic paper, *Boomer*, in Avery. Hagglund would start a local weekly, modeled after Sherwood Anderson's paper in Marion, Virginia, and *Crawford's Weekly* in Norton, Virginia, publications that had national circulations.[96] With Jack and Hagglund together in Avery, perhaps H. H. Lewis and other midwestern radicals might join them. Something had to be done to resist the shift of the magazine's center of gravity to the East, returning it to where it properly belonged, under the direct supervision of its editor and printer. Should Avery not be possible, Jack considered Commonwealth College, where several years later Frederick Maxham would move *Windsor Quarterly*. But lack of money killed the scheme. Jack had little choice but to continue to work with the New York comrades (and hope that the factions would make peace) if he wished his magazine further life.

Spier continued to do the legwork, distributing *Rebel Poet* to newsstands and the Party's workers' bookstores. In his apartment on Franklin Avenue he set up "Repot" to sell radical books, including Rebel Poet booklets. A clerk for Baker and Taylor, wholesale booksellers, Spier sandwiched in his Rebel Poet work after hours. If the magazine was to grow, however, it would need a more solid foundation than Spier's tireless dedication.

At the 13 July meeting, the New York group decided to approach the Central Committee of the Party directly, urging it to take over the distribution work. Snow reported a "cordial reception" when Rahv, Miller, and Snow appeared at Party headquarters.[97] Rahv wrote Jack after the 21 July Rebel Poets meeting, assuring him that "the group is coalescing into an harmonious working organization. The antipodal attitudes of Spier and Miller," Rahv said, "are gradually being submerged in the stress of new tasks and ideas." Rahv anticipated Party financial support for the magazine and welcomed the publication's improved quality. "As I have written you once, lowbrow and proletarian are synonymous to the bourgeoisie, but not to us." He promised to help get *Unrest 1932* off the ground and suggested to Jack the topic "Is Bourgeois Literature Dead?" for a fall symposium to raise money. Rahv heaped praise on Jack's story of coal miners appearing in the August number of the *American Mercury*.[98]

Jack was in a mood to accept Rahv's assurances that things could be worked out among the New York Rebels. The shakeup at *New Masses* and the deposal of Carmon signaled the left's increasing attention to political rather than literary concerns. Jack, on the other hand, hoped to provide a forum for radical literature through his Rebel Poets organization on a worldwide scale. Seeking reconciliation among warring elements, he chose to downplay indications that a coup was in the making within the New York chapter.

In a letter following his acceptance of "Pipe Line" for the September issue of *American Mercury*, Mencken asked Jack to keep sending him stories.[99] After "Pipe Line" appeared, Emerson Price wrote Conroy, "I think you are made as a writer,"[100] while Jim Rorty cautioned, "don't let that beer keg Mencken take the bite out of your style."[101] Jack was counting a great deal on Max Lieber to place his stories with magazines like *Pagany*, the *Hound and Horn*, and other unaligned magazines opening their pages to proletarian stories. Carmon wrote from Moscow that one of Jack's stories would soon appear in Russian translation, in a collection entitled *Miners Speak*, along with a Kalar story.[102] Alfred Knopf was evaluating Jack's book manuscript; already Jack had a second novel in mind, to be entitled "Little Stranger," an expansion of a short story of the same title. Despite the fact that Jack was selling his stories, Snow cautioned him not to give up his job digging ditches. Snow, Weiss, and other Rebel Poets who produced hack work for the pulp press admired the fact that Jack continued to do manual labor to support his family. Writing for the pulps was anathema, Snow warned, to creative writers.[103]

The news from the publication front was encouraging, but Jack was dismayed to receive a disturbing "round robin" letter in late August from the Rahv faction. The authors claimed that Spier had assumed "dictatorial powers over the New York Chapter." Spier, a poor judge of poetry, had made several bad editorial decisions, the letter said. He had botched the "Call to Negro Poets and Writers" in the August issue, for example. As to reports of his legwork: grossly exaggerated, the letter claimed. As proof of Spier's ineptitude, the letter cited the fact that Edwin Rolfe, Sol Funaroff, and Herman Spector had stopped coming to the Rebel Poets meetings.[104] The letter concluded with a set of demands: expand the editorial board to six to include Jerome and Rolfe while maintaining Conroy as editor in chief. Weathering the first storm of angry dissent, Spier held on to his position as managing editor at the 29 August Rebel Poets meeting, leading the discussion in planning the November issue, to be devoted to "The World Revolutionary Literary Movement." Nonetheless, it was agreed that the editorial board would decide on all manuscripts.

Rahv blustered, demanding Spier's resignation, but the agent of the coup that soon wrested *Rebel Poet* from Jack's loose, accommodationist control was V. J. Jerome, the Party functionary who had been added to the editorial board in the hope of persuading the Party to help with the distribution of the magazine.[105] Soon after joining the *Rebel Poet* board, Jerome had gone to work carefully dissecting the magazine's manifesto and questioning its slogan, "The Internationale of Song." These were hardly representative of the group, he advised; henceforth, expressions of ideology would be left up to the New York group.[106] Jerome's appointment to the editorial board proved to be crucial. At first it appeared that the authority implied by his position in the Party's cultural hierarchy would act to smooth out differences between the rival factions. He humbled "Ring Leader Rahv," Snow wrote Conroy, with his Party credentials. Moreover, Jerome would assure a correct ideological line, excluding reviews, for example, of V. F. Calverton, who had recently offended Moscow. Jerome's quiet, authoritative presence, Snow told Conroy, seemed to work miracles in the Rebel Poets meetings. Rahv jockeyed to sit next to him in Spier's cramped apartment. When Jerome decreed that only a Party member versed in Marxism should review Calverton's new book, *The Liberation of American Literature* (1932), Rahv nominated himself.[107]

With Jerome's ascendancy in the Rebel Poet chapter, "the boys had their eyes opened to new glorious vistas," Snow wrote. Decimating Rahv in the discussions of correct ideology, Jerome proceeded to call for Communist love songs and class-struggle lyrics in future issues of *Rebel Poet*. Jerome's presence would checkmate Rahv, John Ackerson felt, and provide the necessary balance of power in the meetings to keep things going.

Jack grew increasingly frustrated with the New York Rebels, sensing that a great deal of their activity was talk with little action to show for it.[108] He hated rancor among peers; he felt that one should join in fighting against oppressive bosses, not with one another. The East Coast radicals, on the other hand, seemed to have a great tolerance for dissension. Jack received reports of contention and debate raging in the offices and pages of *New Masses* among those who, like Rahv, were eager to gain credibility as Marxist critics. The contentiousness soon spilled over onto the New York Rebel Poet meetings. In the August issue of *New Masses*, Rahv enforced distinctions between bourgeois and proletarian writers, prompting a scathing response by A. B. Magil in the December number of *New Masses*. Magil's rebuttal represented orthodox Party views that downplayed differences between the IURW and fellow travelers.[109] Some of this discussion was the aftermath of the liquidation of RAPP the previous April, which fueled the confusion that existed among American Marxist critics.[110] "The shakeup in the literary circles in Russia," Joe Kalar wrote Warren Huddlestone shortly before Christmas, "has its repercussion, in a smaller way, here. *Rebel Poet* was taken over by the strictly communist group in New York who knew just what proletarian art is and as a result the whole thing is 'done fer.'"[111]

The controversies and feuding absorbed energy, from Jack's point of view, that could be better spent in doing actual work, such as distributing the *Rebel Poet*. There were, he discovered, few self-sacrificing people around, such as the Minnesota muskeg printer, Ben Hagglund, who was willing, if necessary, to repair his press with baling wire. It appeared that "workhorse Spier" was one of those indispensables Jack needed to keep the magazine going; but Spier's insistent manner alienated the other members. Spier displayed a "Mussolini attitude," according to Snow, who was beginning to think that Rahv and Miller might be correct in their assessment of Spier. It appeared that Spier was deciding who should be allowed to attend Rebel Poet meetings.[112] Soon thereafter, however, Snow again swung around to support Spier. Spier might not have sound literary judgment, Snow concluded, but he was a more decent, reliable fellow than any of the Rahv group.[113] Moreover, despite Jerome's presence, the Party showed no interest in taking over the tasks of distributing *Rebel Poet*. And the Rebel Poets board rejected Spier's suggestion that every board member would guarantee the sale of twenty copies. Rahv's idea, which was to hire people on commission to distribute copies of *Rebel Poet*, likewise met rejection.[114]

Disputes within the New York group grew evermore intense in the fall of 1932. The conflict between Rahv and Spier had degenerated into a struggle of wills. "Hell, wotta mess!" Snow wrote. "It seems that both Rahv and Spier are liars and looking out only for Mr. Number One."[115] Rahv was incensed that Spier withheld a telegram from Snow that gave Spier a bargaining edge in the dispute over potential publishers for *Unrest 1932*. Spier was "under-handed," Snow wrote Jack; Rahv, on the other hand, was acting more reasonably, presumably under Jerome's influence.[116]

Conroy's hold on Rebel Poets weakened as the board took on new powers, owing mainly to Jerome's presence. Jerome was impressive with his command of Marxist doctrine and his position as instructor at the Workers' School. "Jerome's analysis of Calvertonianism was so lucid," Snow reported to Conroy, "that even Rahv realized that he was a tyro listening to a trained Marxian."[117] No one objected to Jerome's insistence that in return for distributing the magazine, *Rebel Poet* must "maintain a correct ideological line on controversial questions that may arise, such as reviews of books by anti-party, although self-professing Communists, like the Lovestoneites, Trotskyites (Max Eastman) and the free lance Calvertonians."[118] The editorial board no longer acted on Conroy's recommendations in every case but decided on submissions to the magazine. The Rahvites were ready to trade Hagglund in on a New York publisher with a better address. There was even talk about changing the magazine's name to "Pen and Gun," or "Red Dynamo"; Rahv preferred "Class Front." Spier, concerned about losing readers who objected to the poor quality of some of *Rebel Poet*, suggested "Red Express."

Despite the concessions Conroy made in order to save his magazine, the hoped-for Party commitment to assume the tasks of distribution was never made. Furthermore, contradictions within the New York Rebel Poets group, split by rival factions and riven with conflict, became apparent when a symposium, scheduled for October to raise funds for *Unrest 1932*, was suddenly canceled despite the fact that the event was advertised and Malcolm Cowley, Max Lieber, and James Rorty had accepted invitations to speak and prepared their talks. It was decided to replace the symposium with a series of "Gorki evenings." The New York Rebel Poets changed their minds again because another group, the Revolutionary Writers' Federation, was planning a Gorki event; the Rebel Poets reverted to the symposium idea, but the invited speakers declined. The embarrassment of fumbling an important opportunity to promote the fourth Rebel Poet anthology fueled Jack's disappointment with the New York group.

In a burst of anger, Spier's wife, Olga Monus, wrote Jack, charging the Rahvites with bungling the symposium plan. Moreover, Olga reported Rahv's plan to unseat Conroy as editor in chief.[119] Months of internal tremors within the New York chapter weakened, then tumbled the house of the Rebel Poets.

The final issue, number 17, appeared in October, ironically, with a cover designed by Olga, a talented artist. The content and scope of the magazine's concluding number was almost entirely dictated by the New York group and reflected the group's dominance in editorial matters; Conroy's mark is seen mainly in the presence of H. H. Lewis's poems. Over its brief life of twenty-two months, *Rebel Poet* had moved from a little magazine of scattershot social protest, printing poems of frustration and anger against injustice and inhumanity, to one centered in New York, glorifying Soviet achievements.

Within weeks after the publication of the October issue, Jack made up his mind to disband the editorial board. The rivalries had reached out to embrace him in Moberly: Rahv and Stacy were fed up with Conroy having any editorial say, Snow warned. When Rahv, Stacy, and Miller demanded censorship authority in return for money they raised for *Unrest 1932*, Jack, in an editorial fiat, dissolved the Rebel Poet organization. His plans now were to start a new magazine, profiting from the experience of *Rebel Poet*. Kalar wrote to Warren Huddlestone in December that because the New York Rebel Poets had fallen under the sway of a "strictly communist group," Conroy had dissolved his connections and was planning to launch, "the first of the year or thereabouts, a quarterly (also definitely communist) called *The Anvil*. We belong there. *New Masses* is in the hands of the theorecticians [sic] but not for long—let us hope."[120]

Exhausted, broke, and discouraged, Jack dreaded winter's arrival when construction work came to a halt. How was he to pay the heating bills and have enough for a few gifts at Christmas? The Rebel Poets affair had gnawed away his conviction that an umbrella organization of left-leaning and anarchist members might exist. His last job in the fall of 1932 was to move a filling station; he grew increasingly anxious to find a publisher for *The Disinherited*, sensing that time was running out.

As the November elections neared, Jack solicited votes for the Communist candidates, Foster and Ford, as did many prominent writers such as John Dos Passos, Sherwood Anderson, Erskine Caldwell, Edmund Wilson, Sidney Hook, Matthew Josephson, Langston Hughes, Horace Gregory, Malcolm Cowley, and James T. Farrell, all joined in an organization called the League of Professional Groups for Foster and Ford.[121] "Am busy trying to scare up some Communist votes in this benighted section," Conroy wrote Paul Romaine in Chicago. "Some hope. Three or four years ago Communists were regarded here as shaggy, sub-human beasts. Now they think they're a little woolly, but not so bad, after all."[122] Some people declared outright that they would not vote for a "nigger" (Ford), no matter what party he represented.[123] The effort to recruit voters was not entirely quixotic despite the fact that only 6 votes were cast for Foster in Randolph County (34 were cast for the Socialist candidate, Norman Thomas; nationally, the CP received 103,000 votes in 1932).[124] Jack complained to Porter that many who had promised to vote the Party ticket stayed home or changed their minds. Jack had no illusions that Foster/Ford might win; he wished simply to register dissatisfaction with the two major parties.

At home, Jack's problems were doubled when his youngest son, Tom, came down with pneumonia. Tom had gone to school in a thin coat on an early winter day. When he returned at the end of the day, he was wearing a heavier coat donated by a charity. Angered, Jack sent the coat back, borrowed money from his stepfather, Pip Addis, who was still employed at the Moberly sewage plant, and bought a new coat for Tom.[125] Laid off from construction work, he had to depend upon Gladys's shoe factory salary and the income from stories sold to the *American Mercury*. Living expenses were low. To economize further, the Conroys moved to a shack on the Kellys' farm. "I live here like Thoreau beside his pond," he wrote Harry Hansen, the book columnist for the *New York World-Telegram*, "and you can throw a cat through the walls of my shack in a dozen places."[126]

To compound Jack's problems, news arrived from Lieber that Knopf had finally decided to decline *The Disinherited* manuscript after months of deliberation. Lieber took the manuscript to Harcourt Brace, without success, then carried it over to Viking Press, with the same result. Next he sent the manuscript to Macmillan notwithstanding Macmillan's reputation for making conservative choices. Macmillan's reader, Granville Hicks, sent in an unfavorable report in December 1932, killing the book's chances. Some of the sketches were good, Hicks said, but overall it lacked unity; the climax, he argued, should "be held together by the note of revolt." The question of unity, he conceded, was problematic in a collection of sketches. "I hope you are going to try a novel one of these days. . . ."[127]

Jack was still smarting over the Knopf rejection. Why hadn't Knopf read the sketches in Mencken's *Mercury* instead of asking for the manuscript, he wondered in a letter to Lieber. Lieber boosted Jack's spirits, reminding him that Bartlett Cormack, who wrote "The Racket" for a Broadway production, was trying to sell Jack's "Pipe Line" to Hollywood. Calverton wrote Jack, offering to take the manuscript to Scribner's or Long and Smith's,[128] but Lieber made Jack promise not to take him up on it. Meanwhile, the spring book lists were filling, and book sales were down. The National Association of Book Publishers reported that publishers had reduced their budgets for new titles drastically. People were going to libraries to read rather than buying new books.[129] Jack had grown to depend upon the $135 he received for each *Mercury* story, but since September, none of his submissions had met Mencken's approval. On the back of an envelope he sketched out the substance of a new story titled "The Rise and Fall of the Siren," hoping this time to connect with Mencken.

The job layoff in December offered one compensation: Jack could begin to catch up with correspondence and plan his new magazine. In International Falls, Kalar had gone back to the sawmill; Rogers was ill from absorbing herbicides while cutting trees for the USDA.[130] Lewis's farm chores eased up as winter arrived. Kalar wrote Snow: "Not the work, but the hours, militate against my ever creating as I would like to create—I have always been caught in the trap of long hours and small pay, which meant that what I wrote had to be done on the fly, with little or no time for revision. Fred Miller put the matter neatly when he wondered how proletarians could write at all."[131] Snow's own progress from factory work to professional writing hardly offered a satisfactory response.

Writing for pulp magazines, an income-producing activity he had turned to, deadened his creative energies, Snow complained. How could he produce something of worth? Worker-writers, he declared to Jack, would succeed as writers *because* of their laboring jobs; the honesty of physical work would strengthen their writing. It was difficult, he said, to believe in what one was doing, turning out the mechanically contrived plots for adventure and mystery publications. Other writers expressed similar admiration for the worker-writers. Rorty praised the vigor and actuality that came from Conroy's direct involvement in the world of labor.[132] Grace Wellington, a Philadelphia writer, expressed similar admiration for Jack's style: "it is simple and direct without any affectation of the staccato method which becomes so wearisome with its everlasting repetition . . . he knows his miners with his heart, as well as with his mind. . . ."[133]

To suggest to Conroy, however, that manual labor made one a better writer, or that he *preferred* low-paying, tiring, dirty, monotonous occupations, was an example of the muddleheadedness among nostalgists who idealized workers. He had been a worker all his life and was not prepared to do anything else. In the Depression one was lucky to have any kind of work. As I discussed in an earlier chapter, Jack had once aspired to formal learning and a white-collar profession, much as his father had wished him to do. But the events of the Great Railroad Strike, a growing consciousness nurtured by his reading, union associations, and years of migratory labor persuaded him to remain a worker. He felt more "comfortable" among workers, he once suggested to me.[134] Jack was not one to make claims about his intentions, to suggest, for instance, that he consciously remained within his class in order to work to better the worker's lot. Family responsibilities made it virtually impossible to change his mind, even supposing he had wanted to. Finally, his writing sealed his identification with labor and reflected the circumstances of his work-existence. Nonetheless, Jack found some consolation in the unskilled labor he was compelled to accept in the early Depression years; there was a certain virtue, he mused, in writing about hunger rather than sexual needs. A moralist at heart, but never a moralizer, he usually followed up such a remark with a comic music-hall verse or lines from the "plowboy poet," H. H. Lewis: "Though village bards still toot the erotic fife, / An erection's not the highest thing in life."[135]

In the Soviet Union one escaped a toiler's life through study or Party work. What was different about the American experience was the middle class. Jack's conscious choice to remain a worker, made somewhere along the line, was in a sense a rejection of white-collar status. The choice raised the possibility of a worker achieving intellectual distinction. Little in America served as a model. Jack was interested in Soviet efforts to create intellectual opportunities for workers. For this reason, he had looked to the Soviets. Yet there was a great deal more to it than Soviet-worship. Deep-lying cultural factors constituting Jack's emotional and intellectual satisfactions had to do with his status as worker-writer—the union struggles, the miners' solidarity in Monkey Nest, the richness of workers' orality and humor, his perception that the "true intellectual life" (Hans's expression in *The Disinherited*) lay in forms of labor activism. Jack's identification with working-class people involved renunciations at certain times in his life—for the very reason that, given his abilities, other opportunities existed for him.

The nature of the renunciations in turn defined his role as a "proletarian" writer and spokesman for the worker. One renunciation was his decision not to continue through formal study the pursuit of a white-collar profession; another was his engagement as worker-writer (as opposed to seeking bourgeois writer status). These renunciations in turn generated other paradoxes and conflicts. One important paradox, treated in an earlier chapter, involved his status as worker-intellectual, which granted him a certain distance, a perspective, since he was at the point of a division, at the same time within and outside his class.[136] It was inevitable, then, that such a division introduced tensions in his life.

Worker-writers and artists—exceptional individuals like Jack—attempted to resolve such tensions in various ways. Robert Minor left his profession as artist to enter Party work. Bob Cruden, Abe Aaron, and others abandoned their aspirations as writers to become involved in labor organization. Aaron, a contributor to Conroy's *Anvil*, was actively discouraged by the Party from continuing his writing.[137] The Party made it clear that it was not particularly interested in literature as a form of labor activism. "Now I must make my decision," Aaron wrote Jack in early 1934. "Will I write, or will I continue as an active section functionary? When I told the committee how I felt, saying, was it a question of writing or of the section committee, I must choose writing, I was accused of individualistic tendencies. Hell, I tried to explain, it's not a question of giving up party work but, rather, of giving up one type of party work. It didn't go over so well. Now, in a case like this, what is one to do? I wonder if Mike Gold ever faced this problem."[138] The Party by no means singled Aaron out for neglect of duty. Its own cultural arm, the John Reed Club, was given little support. "I find in the party," Aaron continued, "that the J.R.C. is regarded disdainfully and with tolerant amusement by a great number of comrades. Now, of course, I understand that trade union, basic work is of prime importance. But, also, I contend that writing is what I think I am fitted for and is what I want to do, and that the problem is to find how, *as a writer,* I can aid in basic work." Aaron turned to Conroy for advice. "Jack, I mean to write. But what am I going to do about the party?"[139] Jack had run into similar conflicts in distributing *Rebel Poet*. The Party's International Labor Defense representative in Portland, Oregon, told Spier not to send issues of the magazine, that there was no time for revolutionary-cultural ventures, and in any case, there was no hope in attempting to attract bourgeois intellectuals to the magazine since they were not interested in class struggle.[140]

A major Hollywood studio's acceptance of Jack's "Pipe Line" as a movie script would have introduced further tensions in his status as worker-writer, but no such acceptance was forthcoming. Lieber kept Jack's hope alive, writing that David Selznick, RKO's producer, would make the final decision, but soon after, in early January 1933, Lieber wrote again with the studio's decision against the script. It was "too good and too important a story to use as a program feature for William Boyd,"

Lieber said.[141] In the same letter was another rejection of *The Disinherited* manuscript, this one from Covici-Friede, who invoked the familiar rationale that such a book would not sell in today's market. By this time, however, Jack was full of plans for a new little magazine to be called the *Anvil*. He had emerged from the emotional slump of a month earlier and was busy lining up his new editorial board, convinced that a nonsectarian, independent approach, allowing more space for sketches and short stories, would catch hold. The radical movement had grown out of its early rebellious phase; now it needed a more mature magazine focusing on how people actually lived and felt.

Changes in Soviet literary policy (following the creation of the All-Soviet Writers Union in April 1932) appeared to vindicate Jack's early nonsectarian intent with the Rebel Poets; at least, that was the conclusion Jack reached after hearing from Walt Carmon in Moscow. Carmon wrote that he had "attended the plenum of the All-Union outfit of writers. General atmosphere wonderful. Since the 'COR-R-R-ECT' boys were landed on their tails in April, all writers including nonparty are working more freely and everybody happy. Object: include all writers possible, criticize 'em but show that they are ours. None of this holier than thou goes and they mean it."[142] The letter prompted Jack to exclaim in a letter to Kenneth Porter: "The comrades have cleaned house over there with their usual thoroness [sic], and the ideas I have been trying to inculcate in *The Rebel Poet*—sniped at both from the Left and the Right—will be dominant in radical literature from now on."[143] Boosted by what appeared to be the new spirit on the left, which sought backing from all who lent their support to the leftist movement, including bourgeois writers, Jack announced his plans for a new magazine to be called the *Anvil*. The announcement was made in late December at the John Reed Club in St. Louis, where he met with H. H. Lewis to give a reading. Mencken was publishing stories of work without inquiring into the politics of the author; similarly, Jack would call for submissions on the basis of literary quality, works written in vigorous prose and addressed to the contemporary crisis.

The revolutionary situation had changed considerably over the three years of the Rebel Poets. The early enthusiasms had led to excesses and a loss of restraint; strident sloganizing undermined the effectiveness of the organization and its magazine, alienating sympathizers less committed to the struggle, and incurred criticism from several important contributors. Conroy himself had come under fire from the Party, which accused him of "bohemianism," of tolerating unorthodox positions, courting apostates and "social fascists," and of revealing an undisciplined independence. He issued a special invitation to workers and made public his support of the Communists without placing these as editorial restrictions. *Anvil* would fill the gap left by *New Masses*, which, as Snow wrote to Jack, was becoming too theoretical.[144] The last few months had exhausted Jack; he was experiencing splitting headaches and had difficulty pushing himself to write. Yet he was determined to continue his magazine editing, profiting from the lessons learned from the Rebel Poets experience without abandoning the basic formulas that had inspired the organization's magazine, for example, its rhizomatous system of literary production.

Jack shared Whitman's belief in the binding power of literature to draw people divided by race, class, sex, and occupation together in society, not along the lines of Michael Gold's naive vision in which farmers pen sonnets and factory workers perform impromptu skits, but by focusing the magazine on humanitarian issues and resisting parochialism, either genteel or radical.[145] *Rebel Poet* fell far short of this aim. It began in a spirit of social protest against injustice and inhumanity, moving finally to an agenda that seemed dictated by the IURW: editorials in praise of the Soviet Union; the rhymed journalism of the "RAPP" issue (number 13); the "Negro number" (number 15); the anti-imperialist issue (number 16).[146] *Rebel Poet* had published some of the earliest poems of Kenneth Patchen, born in a family of steel workers and coal miners; introduced American readers to Joe Corrie, a Scots miner, and the German radical Johannes Becher; and devoted an issue to black writers. Apart from the inclusion of several H. H. Lewis poems, *Rebel Poet* had in its last issues become an organ of the New York chapter. The youthful rebellion of early contributions yielded to awkward appropriations of half-digested Marxist discourse; the shock value of manifestoes and pungent imagery had worn thin. With V. J. Jerome and the Rahv faction in control of the editorial board, "dialectics of learning" replaced Conroy and Cheyney's initial "Art for Humanity's Sake," the loose, anarchic, humanitarian vision of the magazine's opening manifesto. Conroy's Whitmanesque faith in poets as a social force, those who, to use Whitman's words, are "marked for generosity and affection and encouraging competitors," was bound to conflict with Jerome's (and Rahv's) heavy-handed interventions.[147]

Of inconsistent literary quality, given to excessive sloganizing, and swayed by emotional commitments to the Soviet Experiment, *Rebel Poet*, at its best, gave voice to a wide diversity of poets who shared a common sympathy in the plight of the underdog and spoke out against the powerful interests and institutions in society, unveiled by the Sacco-Vanzetti executions, which continued to ignore human suffering during the early years of the Depression. The medium was the quick topi-

cal poem or letter-like reportage—immediate, direct, vital, like field
reports, expressions of a rebel consciousness.[148] Among the Rebel Poets are names familiar still: Louis Ginsberg, whose own work was eventually overshadowed by that of his son, Allen Ginsberg; Kenneth Fearing, best known for his detective novel (and movie) *The Big Clock;*
Kenneth Patchen, who experimented in setting poetry to jazz music and
was popular among college students in the 1950s and 1960s; Harry Crosby, expatriate and editor of the Black Sun Press; Sherwood Anderson;
and Langston Hughes.

If it was not intended to aid young poets in achieving reputation, to
produce famous names, what then was the importance of the Rebel
Poets? The Rebel Poet organization was an early experiment in establishing networks of writers, informal communication circuits, challenging the hegemony of mainstream and avant-garde magazines. Conroy
and Cheyney set up a rudimentary corresponding society, as in the early phase of European workers' movements. The key ingredients, as I've
noted, were cheap publication and wide distribution. In the 1930s, these
represented counterhegemonic cultural trends in a field—publishing—
that, as a rule, narrowly constricted entry and imposed narrow aesthetic standards. The Rebel Poet enterprise was fundamentally centrifugal,
at least in its inception, an effort to establish a corresponding network
of separate, autonomous epicenters, usually individual poets isolated in
small towns, or the chapters in Boston and New York (before the Rahv
clique and the Miller-Spier conflict), who kept in touch and helped in
the distribution of the magazine.

To maintain the centrifugal nature of the enterprise, to avoid stiff-
ening into doctrinaire positions, Jack planned to choose the editorial
board of his new magazine carefully. The Rebel Poets lacked an animating vision, but *Anvil* would make its purpose clear. Jack expressed
this purpose in a phrase extolling "crude vigor," a choice of terms that
revealed his innocence in how to win to his side those who are indifferent or unsympathetic. It was another instance in which "innocence"
(or perhaps mischievous humor) would ultimately lead to fateful misunderstandings.

13

Proletarian Bull Market: 1933

Rude and coarse nursing-beds . . . but only from
such beginnings and stocks, indigenous here, may
haply arrive, be grafted, and sprout in time, flowers
of genuine American aroma. . . .
—Walt Whitman, "Democratic Vistas"

AN OLD FRIEND from Jack's Toledo days, Norman Dopher, came to
Moberly over the Christmas holidays. Dopher, who had been a foreman in the Willys-Overland factory where Jack, Ed, and George Harrison worked, drove Jack to Kansas City, where they spent New Year's
Eve in a taxi dance hall. Both were well in their cups when they headed back to Moberly in the early morning hours. Confusing the roads
that led away from Kansas City, the two workers ended up near Springfield, in the Ozarks. Gladys was always complacent about Jack's nights
out on the town; there were few enough of them, to be sure.[1] Gladys
was still working at the shoe factory, providing most of the income during the winter of 1932–33. The family was in debt, still owing real-estate
taxes on their former Collins Avenue home. In the shack on the Kellys'
farm, Jack revised the manuscript of his novel and edited the first issues of the *Anvil*. The shack was a publicist's dream and when *The Disinherited* finally appeared in late 1933, much was made of it.

Almost fourteen million workers—a quarter of the civilian labor
force—were unemployed when Roosevelt took office early in 1933; by
the following winter, seventeen million would be on relief.[2] Car and
truck production had fallen by 75 percent between 1929 and 1932.
Freight-car loadings were off by one-half. Yet there was plenty in the

midst of the poverty. If one had money, it went a long way in the 1930s. The *American Mercury* advertised luxury ocean crossings to Europe in the same issue with Jack's chronicles of the disinherited. The contrasts were bitter. In Moberly, hunters staged a contest to bag rabbits, which were given to the Welfare Society for distribution to the poor.[3] In Jack's "Bull Market," four workers, crouching at the side of the tracks, waiting to hitch a ride on a freight, look up to see a passenger train pass: "complacent swells wielding silver cutlery and dabbing at their mouths with linen napkins reminded us that we had not eaten since noon, twelve hours before."[4]

Not simply the hard times but the spectacle of deprivation in the midst of plenty radicalized some exceptional workers who might otherwise have chalked things up to bad luck or blamed themselves. The majority of workers, on the other hand, felt shame and fear, according to the celebrated studies by Stephen Bakke, beginning with *The Unemployed Man: A Social Study* (1933), at Yale's Institute of Human Relations. Jack witnessed the humiliating spectacle of families on foot, pulling coaster wagons with their belongings along busy roadways. The detail appeared in "Hard Winter"; later a Farm Security Administration photographer would record the scene in a remarkable black-and-white image. You kept moving on—or you starved to death, Jack remembered years later.[5] "Nothing impairs morale," Jack wrote, "like the dissolution of a last pair of shoes."[6] Middle-class accountants made weak efforts to avoid recognition as they stood in soup lines. Yet, a new feeling emerged within the dislocations of the economic hard times, a shift away from individual preoccupation, paradoxically, as Richard Pells explains: "The depression itself encouraged the conviction that human problems would never be solved by the individual alone—indeed that an emphasis on personal liberation and self-expression might be positively harmful in the context of a national disaster."[7] The "plowboy poet," H. H. Lewis, saw the trend:

> Well, here we are, ha! bumping fate again,
> Millions, millions, millions of idle men!
> There's no escaping *now*: from shore to shore
> That individual trend can move no more. . . .[8]

The social frontier of the 1930s needed interpreters and reporters—had not the western frontier produced storytellers like Bret Harte and Mark Twain who told of lawless mining camps and illusions that men substitute for thought and vision? The *Anvil* would serve such a purpose. Hunger forced most people to shed illusions; the task was to find reason to hope. Fear, deprivation, despair, acts of courage, and resolve—

these were the common denominators of the 1930s social frontier. This was a time, Jack said later, when "more concern was given to the belly and its needs than to the fevers of the organs just below."[9] "Belly" and nether organs—how characteristic of the 1930s to erect such an opposition. There were no ambiguities about hunger, Jack argued, no irony in dispossession, no relativism in social injustice. The temper of the times enforced a two-valued system of judgment and a demand that one choose.[10] Ordinary people were suddenly thrust into extraordinary circumstances. What choices had you when you lost your home, were on the street with no job, had no prospect of one and no safety net? In the 1930s, choices were constructed in opposing pairs: flamboyant outlawry and threadbare decency, bitterness and compassion, pride and defeatism.

If opposing terms characterized a great deal of what people experienced and how they had come to view things in the 1930s—rich/poor, worker/boss, inside/outside, justice/injustice, prosperity/deprivation—then writers were similarly polarized, the division most familiar to them being proletarian/bourgeois. The two-page cartoon of Theodore Scheel's "Book Revue of 1933," appearing in the New York World-Telegram, grouped contemporary writers in such a manner. Portrayed on the left page were Conroy, John Dos Passos, Theodore Dreiser, Sherwood Anderson, Erskine Caldwell, Michael Gold, Dorothy Parker, and others; on the facing page were Ernest Hemingway, Thomas Wolfe, Eugene O'Neill, Willa Cather, H. L. Mencken, Dorothy Canfield, and others. The identifying symbols on the left were workers' overalls and paint buckets beneath a silhouette of a factory; identifying the "bourgeois" writers were the silhouette of an urban skyline, a dollar sign, coats, tails, and top hats.[11] The interesting fact here was that a mainstream newspaper accorded recognition to a radical perspective. The division along class lines, of course, did not account for shades of difference within the groupings. What, after all, did Mencken have in common with Hemingway—or Conroy with Dorothy Parker, except that the latter had expressed her sympathy for the worker's plight?

Scheel's cartoon underscored the extent to which the worker had become a subject in American letters, for better or worse, and how two-valued views were gaining respectability. New Deal mural art produced other kinds of distortions by idealizing the figure of the worker.[12] Jack was critical of simplistic views of working-class experience, the assumption, for instance, of homogeneity. The worker figures of his stories are as highly individualized as any other class of people. As editor of the Anvil, Jack sought individual portraits of working-class experience framed in a social context. The hour when the worker's voice would

finally be heard, he believed, was approaching. Brecht asked the essential questions (Jack said later) in his poem "Questions from a Worker
Who Reads":

> Who built Thebes of the seven gates?
> In the books you will find the names of kings.
> Did the kings haul up the lumps of rock?
>
> . . . .
>
> Where, the evening that the Wall of China was finished,
> Did the masons go?[13]

In the *Anvil* and his own writing Jack's aim was to let the masons speak
for themselves.

Jack's frequent visits to St. Louis during this time persuaded him that
labor lacked the means to communicate its unique experience. By 1932,
the Communist Party's Unemployed Council was organizing jobless workers—unemployment in St. Louis hovered near 25 percent. Wage cuts at
the Funsten Nut Company and discriminatory practices against blacks
brought workers out in May 1933.[14] The strike brought to prominence
Bill Sentner, a former architect and artist, who had joined the St. Louis
John Reed Club earlier in the year. Sentner, with whom Jack had frequent contact over the next few years, emerged a leader from the nutpickers' strike and a Party district organizer. During this particular strike,
Jack witnessed mass demonstrations, including a large gathering at the
Labor Lyceum where black and white workers mingled and "Solidarity
Forever" was sung. The nutpickers' strike was a successful demonstration
of labor's newfound strength; it was like the old days for Jack, when the
unions had a voice. He had not seen anything like it since his Wabash
Railroad days.[15] The nutpickers' strike furnished material for Jack's sec-
ond novel, *A World to Win*, as did St. Louis's "Hooverville."

Hooverville was to Jack a peculiar mix of despair and resourcefulness. Living conditions were lamentable. Yet there was a primitive form
of organization among the inhabitants. A church was built from scrap
metal. In the mornings, people would go on foraging expeditions in the
city, looking for castoffs. In *The Disinherited*, Hooverville is contrasted
with the squalor of a squatter's camp in which the apathetic dwellers
have given up. It was far better, Jack concluded after his stay in St.
Louis's "colony of the dispossessed," for people to stick together in hard
times.[16] The growing resolve of workers in St. Louis, the resourcefulness of the Hooverville denizens, reinforced Jack's own determination
that the *Anvil* would approach working-class existence affirmatively,
avoiding the gloom of defeatist proletarian writing.

On his visits to St. Louis, where he spoke to Washington Universi-

ty's National Student League and the John Reed Club, Jack sought out
his artist and writer friends in the cafes and bars of the Mississippi levee.
The bohemian milieu still bore traces of the period immediately before
and after World War I when the eccentric Harry Turner, editor of *Much
Ado,* and his friends were regulars in the Rock House saloon on Chest-
nut and Wharf streets.[17] In the Blue Lantern Inn at 22 Commercial
Alley (near where the Rock House had been), long a favorite hangout
for artists and writers, Jack met with Orrick Johns, a poet and the former
drama critic for *Reedy's Mirror,* and Joe Jones, a housepainter turned
artist.[18] Wharf workers and artists mixed in an atmosphere thick with
cigarette smoke, jazz music, and the smell of bootleg gin. One young
habitué wrote in tribute to the Blue Lantern:

> So lift up your glasses
> And drink to the lasses
> Who sometimes have courage to sin,
> And laugh at the masses
> Of consummate asses
> Who know not the taste of gin
> Nor the soul of the Blue Lantern Inn![19]

Jack Balch, who later shared in the editorial work of the *Anvil* and
joined Conroy on the Missouri Writers' Project, rubbed shoulders with
the literary and artistic crowd at Hogarth Riverune's Blue Lantern. Riverune (a.k.a. Jack Walter) published a literary magazine called *Vagaries.* Contributors were Balch and "bohemians" like Frank Sullivan; Guy
Golterman, Jr. (author of the tribute); Harry Niemeyer, Jr.; and others
now forgotten. In Conroy's *A World to Win* (1935), the Blue Lantern
is a setting for the young protagonist, Robert Hurley, who has (misbe-
gotten) aspirations to become a writer.

   Joe Jones, the ex-housepainter, lived on a houseboat on the Mississippi levee that offered a good vantage point from which to sketch workers on the docks and riverboats. With Jack and Orrick Johns, Jones
motored downriver in a small boat, cruising slowly by Hooverville,
which stretched a mile along the Mississippi River's western shore.
Jones, later Conroy's roommate in St. Louis, won notoriety when he
formed an art class for the unemployed in the old St. Louis Courthouse.
On one occasion, Jones and Johns drove over to Moberly to visit Jack.
"We found him in a small cottage," Johns writes in *Time of Our Lives,*
"tending three young children who frequently got tangled up in the busy
typewriter. His wife worked all day in a Moberly shoe factory."[20]

   In his second novel, *A World to Win,* Jack dramatizes the situation
of a young writer who, drawn toward bohemian milieus in St. Louis, is

repelled by the "clever people," yet finds unauthentic people in radical circles as well.[21] Instead of following some artistic creed or political ideology, the novel suggests, young writers should devote themselves to subjects drawn from their own experience rather than imitate and fail. Robert Hurley, the aspiring writer, is advised to open his eyes and report what he sees.[22] Young factory workers who aspire to write should drop their yearnings to write like Hemingway of distant places and make use of material at hand, of factory life and employment lines.[23]

It was a formidable task Jack set himself. He hoped to wean workers away from romance and escapist fiction that bore no relation to their lives. He envisioned a workers' literature of short sketches, like pulp fiction but attuned to contemporary social problems affecting working-class existence. Such a literature should ask disturbing questions; its language itself should challenge prevailing dominant norms. Plato had written in *The Republic* that those who have seen the light must return to the darkness and share.[24] From Jack's perspective, the task was to do just the opposite.

✳ ✳ ✳

Demonstration marches, strikes, and other manifestations of worker militancy in Gastonia, Minneapolis, San Francisco, Dearborn, St. Louis, and elsewhere charged the literary imaginations of writers, from proletarian to established writers like Dos Passos and Steinbeck. When Orrick Johns left for New York soon after visiting Jack in Moberly, he sensed something radically different among writers and artists in contrast to some ten years earlier when he had lived in Greenwich Village. "Gone the bohemianism and cynicism," he wrote, "the concern with sex and aesthetics that I remembered. Most of the people I knew had been hit hard by the depression. They were beginning to see that their professional lives depended on forms of organizations. They were joining artists' unions and writers' unions, picketing in strikes of publishers and newspapers, and even walking in the ranks of department store strikers."[25] Many were profoundly affected by the threat of fascism in Italy and Germany. There appeared to be a new market for writers responding to these concerns. Mainstream novelists had little experience directly with the main subjects of the early 1930s: factory layoffs, breadlines, hunger, dispossession, strikes. Jack hoped to find and encourage a new generation of young writers who could communicate vividly and forcefully from experience, the "young writers," he wrote in the *New Masses* notice of the *Anvil*, "from the mills, mines, forests, factories and offices of America who are forging a new literary tradition. . . . We will endeavor to publish the best fiction and verse available."[26] John "Jack" Rogers, Joe Kalar, H. H. Lewis, Meridel Le Sueur,

Bob Cruden, Ed Falkowski, and soon a host of others were proof that such writers existed.

Mike Gold had provided a model several years earlier in *New Masses*, calling for "Poems and Tales by Miners, Sailors, Clerks, Carpenters, Etc."[27] "Every other magazine," Gold wrote in 1928, "is always hunting for 'big names.' But we want the working men, women, and children of America to do most of the writing in the *New Masses*. The product may be crude, but it will be truth. And truth, though she slay us, is the most beautiful of gods in the pantheon."[28] But *New Masses* no longer bore Gold's particular imprint, particularly since Walt Carmon had left it. Throughout 1932, Jack had expressed his desire in letters to Carmon, Kalar, and Lieber that *New Masses* continue to seek out and publish new writers, especially those from the "hinterland." *New Masses* appeared to be moving away from literary matters to criticism and politics. There were still strong examples of the proletarian narrative in *New Masses*, such as Whittaker Chambers's "Can You Make Out their Voices," and works by Meridel Le Sueur ("Women on the Breadline"), Moe Bragin (who contributed to the *Anvil* under the pen name Ben Field), Dos Passos, Gold, H. H. Lewis, Myra Page, and John Rogers. Two of Jack's stories were published there in 1932 and one in 1933. Yet Jack sensed that correct ideology was increasing its hold on the *New Masses* office, and he knew that could not be a good sign for the midwestern radicals.

Herman Spector, who earned his living driving a cab in New York City, articulated what troubled Jack and the midwestern radicals in the revolutionary movement. Spector wrote Snow, who sent a copy to Jack: "We need poets and creators rather than the manifesto-shooters, finale hoppers, and ash-flickers who abound in the purlieus of the proletarian cultural movement."[29] The "manifesto-shooters, finale hoppers, and ash-flickers" had gotten control of *New Masses*. What Jack had in mind drew inspiration from the early *New Masses* under Mike Gold, with Carmon's active collaboration as managing editor, and H. L. Mencken's *American Mercury*. It bears repeating, in underscoring Conroy's own editorial purpose, that Gold had urged young unknowns like Kalar, Lewis, and Spector to share their experiences in lively personal narratives, for which his own "East Side stories" might provide a model. While Gold's influence was mainly inspirational, Walt Carmon offered practical editorial assistance; from 1929 on he looked after his "boys," as he called the worker-writers, including Jack, Kalar, Lewis, and Falkowski, all of whom (except Falkowski) were, like himself, from the Midwest.[30] Jack also looked to Mencken as an example of an editor who valued freshness and vitality among new writers. Like Gold and Mencken, he was determined to seek out unknowns with talent who were able to communicate their experience in an authentic and vigorous American idiom, an enterprise that, he knew, would depend upon the dedicated cooperation of contributors, printer, and editorial staff.

Most of the midwestern radicals' early writing attempts had been instinctive affairs, unstructured and impressionistic; now Kalar was beginning to formalize the ideas behind those first stories appearing in *New Masses*. He talked about the "sketch" form "into which I blundered in the heyday of enthusiasm. . . . I had no conception of the potentialities of the sketch. . . ."[31] Jack was thinking along the same lines. The proletarian sketch was the form best suited for new writers with fresh viewpoints, writing out of "what life gives us in the form of experience," as Richard Wright later said.[32]

In the attempt to define a proletarian aesthetic, American radical critics often borrowed—sometimes inaccurately—from the Soviets. The word *Ocherkism*, a virtually untranslatable term meaning the making of stories or sketches, appeared in a *New Masses* essay written by Leon Dennen, an American living in Moscow.[33] Among the forms available to the proletarian writer was the "sketch" (the sort of prose narrative that *New Masses* was printing less and less). In the Soviet Union, the sketch form—*skaz*—had served an important literary purpose during the first Five Year Plan; Gorki defended it vigorously against critics who viewed it as a lower form of art.[34] Actually "sketch" stories were a very old form in Russian literature: in Gogol's "The Overcoat," plot is reduced to the minimum and personal tone is correspondingly stressed, signaling "the transfer of focus from the narrative plane to the discourse plane."[35] The Russian formalists Shklovsky and Eichenbaum studied the sketch form in order to illuminate techniques of plot construction in the short story and the novel.[36] Mikhail Bakhtin underscored the oral quality of the sketch, "a socially or individually defined manner of storytelling" in contrast to literary professionalism. The storyteller is not a literary man, Bakhtin wrote; "he usually belongs to a lower social strata, to the common people . . . and he brings with him oral speech."[37] The plotless nature, the personal-narrative quality of the sketch, preserving accents and idioms, was a form suited to the needs of the nonprofessional writer in the Soviet Union of the RAPP period, according to Katerina Clark. Straddling journalism and literature, the sketch is within the grasp of the novice writer. The sketch can be written quickly; it answers the need for quick production and timeliness.[38] The proletarian *skaz* and the worker-correspondence movement grew out of specific historical moments—the industrialization of the Kuznetsk Basin, for example.[39]

The proletarian sketch appeared to be ideally suited for the factory workers, who, as Conroy said, "have something vital and new to communicate."[40] Apart from the limitations of time that hampered the worker-writer, there was a suggestion that too much attention to art deprived the subject matter, drawn from life, of its vigor and authenticity. Kalar scolded Huddlestone: "Jesus Christ, Huddlestone, don't be a hangover from the Jazz Age. Go out in the street and get real filthily dirty. Forget the plots. Grab a chunk of life and chew it and spew it out again. Life isn't a plot, it just goes on and on and is not culminated by a trick ending, very often."[41] The use of conscious artifice was at issue; at what point does the writer "distort" his subject matter in the interest of art? The great realist writers like Balzac had made their writing *seem* real, concealing their art. Literary realism, however, had become conventional, losing "a quality of authenticity," which William Carlos Williams, John Dos Passos, and painters like Charles Sheeler hoped to recover by detaching familiar things from ordinary experience, estranging the senses to achieve "a fresh perception of reality."[42] Similarly, Conroy, Lewis, and, to a lesser extent, Joe Kalar eschewed verisimilitude, transforming the materials of oral and extraliterary narrative to create verbal performances that call upon the reader's imaginative participation. They gave their attention to language and the manner of telling in portraying events and people, to the point that Mencken urged Kalar "to inject a little more dramatics in the episodes."[43]

It is a simplification to suggest that the worker-writers borrowed the idea of the sketch entirely from the Soviets. Sherwood Anderson, after all, wrote "plotless" stories, corresponding to his notion that life does not furnish plots. Haldeman-Julius penned sketches of working-class life for socialist publications like the *Milwaukee Leader* and the *Western Comrade*. Most *Anvil* contributors were familiar with Jack London's sketches of working-class life on the bum and with Gold's *120 Million*. The sketch form is a close relative to reportage. Kalar's and Conroy's early prose writing embraced both forms. H. H. Lewis's prose narratives perhaps represent best the early proletarian sketch in their subjective evaluation of events and in communicating the personality of the writer through the telling. They are scenes, really, not fully developed narratives.[44] Conroy's "Jackson Street" and Kalar's "Midnight Mission," on the other hand, tend more toward reportage. It was inevitable, given the immediacy and authenticity that Jack sought for the *Anvil*, that the sketch form would predominate. It was a form that most fiction writers begin with; it need not be an amateur effort, however, as Gogol's work had shown. It seemed eminently suited for Jack's purposes and the time.[45]

One could follow discussions of the proletarian sketch form in *New Masses* as theoreticians made rudimentary attempts to devise an aesthetic for the proletarian short story. The Soviet critic Sergei Dinamov's young protégé Anna Elistratova (who would champion Jack's work) scrutinized American examples of the proletarian sketch and found them wanting. Acknowledging that the sketch had become the leading form, she pointed out the shortcomings of *New Masses*, critiquing Robert Cruden's "Layoff: Ford Factory" and "Men Wanted."[46] Kalar was infuriated at the presumption of the Soviet critic, but other aspiring writers tended to read such critiques carefully, including Abe Aaron, who worked in the Chicago Post Office with Richard Wright, both of whose work appeared in the *Anvil*. But most *Anvil* contributors, such as Nelson Algren, had little use for such discussions and critiques, American or Soviet.[47]

At the same time that the worker-writers evolved the sketch form for their own purposes, *New Masses* was drifting away from Gold's (editorial) commitment to the writings of "miners, sailors, clerks, carpenters, etc." as first announced in the July 1928 issue. In place of Gold's emphasis on developing an intellectual vanguard from the proletariat, reporting from factory, farm, and mill, the editors of *New Masses* solicited better-known writers and addressed contemporary political questions on the left. The midwestern worker-writers began to sour on *New Masses*. "Who killed proletarian art?" wrote Kalar to Huddlestone in December 1932. "I, said Cock Masses, I killed proletarian art, with my little thesis and theory, I killed proletarian art."[48] Kalar, Lewis, and others were all the more bitter because early issues had held out for them such high promise. *New Masses* had given them their start. "*New Masses* kept me on the road, in this period [1928–29]," Kalar wrote Huddlestone, "when the halluncinative fog of egotism . . . would ebb and I would write. Thru *New Masses* I became acquainted with a number of fine fellows, Jack Conroy, H. H. Lewis, Walt Carmon, and others."[49] In a follow-up letter Kalar wrote, "*New Masses* started something and only incredible obtuseness prevented it from being carried to its logical goal. I refer to the days when it printed poems by a shoe worker, coal miner, oil-digger, clerk, benzine worker, etc. etc. . . ."[50] Max Lieber, who as literary agent worked directly within New York's publishing world, wrote Jack: "I have had the feeling all along that the *New Masses* was becoming entirely too dialectical, and at the same time losing its virility. But if something isn't done very soon about this, *New Masses* will die of inanition."[51] The suspicion that midwestern radicals felt toward the *New Masses* editors (apart from Walt Carmon) might have derived in part from regional differences and the old populist animus against the East.

"No wonder the New York literary guys are always wrangling," Jack wrote Kenneth Porter, suggesting that there were profound cultural differences between the two regions of the country.[52] Further, there was a feeling among the midwestern radicals that the revolutionary movement which *New Masses* was promoting encouraged exclusivity and cliques, and that its recent efforts to solicit bourgeois writers meant the abandonment of worker-writing altogether.

Conroy must have communicated some of this suspicion to the ex–New York Rebel Poets because Fred Miller, who had served on the RP board, mentioned to H. H. Lewis in February that Jack had been criticizing Rahv, Miller, and Walt Stacy in regard to the defunct organization. "Is Friend Jack adopting Spier's tactics, I wonder? . . . It shouldn't be very hard," Miller continued, "for *The Anvil* to 'make everything east of the Hudson look sick' at this stage of the game—what've we got here beside the *New Masses?*"[53] Again, the midwesterners turned to Carmon for approval (and protection?). Snow had a tendency to add fuel to the fire in his eagerness to defend Jack, Kalar, and the others. In a letter to Carmon, dated 27 March, Snow spelled out the story of the Rahvites and Rebel Poets; and now, he said, Rahv "is going to try to attack and wreck *The Anvil*." For instance, Snow claimed that Rahv was "the Big Gong" behind a new magazine to be published by the New York John Reed Club, yet noted that he was unable to launch an earlier project for a new magazine to be called *Proletfolio*.[54]

Fred Miller too planned a proletarian competitor of *Anvil*, which first appeared in the fall of 1933. Subtitled "a magazine of proletarian short stories," *Blast* ran five issues (September 1933 through November 1934), publishing a number of short stories by William Carlos Williams (who served as advisory editor) and writers like Paul Corey, Ray Kresensky, Joseph Vogel, and H. H. Lewis whose work was also appearing in the *Anvil*. Miller, whom William Carlos Williams described as "a tool designer living precariously over a garage in Brooklyn," claimed that the first issue of *Anvil* was not up to snuff; as a consequence, he was impelled to bring out *Blast*.[55] (Subsequent issues of *Anvil* were much improved, he conceded.)[56] In spite of any rivalries that might have existed (in Miller's mind at least), both editors were of one mind in their desire to provide an alternative to *New Masses*.[57] By 1933, the proletarian literary front, heretofore almost exclusively defended by *New Masses*, was taken over by *Anvil* and *Blast*, soon to be joined by *Dynamo*, *Partisan Review*, and several other precariously funded magazines.

Apart from Fred Miller, Jack had to deal with several other potential critics of the *Anvil* in producing the first issue, which appeared in May 1933. He still had not cleared accounts with Ralph Cheyney fol-

lowing the demise of *Rebel Poet*. There was misunderstanding, perhaps
even bad feeling between the two founders of Rebel Poets. Snow had
even suggested that Cheyney planned to sue Jack over *Unrest*.[58] Moreover, Cheyney loyalists like Benjamin Musser had withdrawn support
from Rebel Poets toward the end.[59] The reckoning of accounts occurred
quite politely in the first issue of *Anvil*.

Cheyney prepared a "statement" when he heard of Jack's plans to start
a new magazine. Without having seen the first issue, he placed the *Anvil* squarely in the Communist camp, expressing regret that Jack had
departed from the early eclectic spirit of the Rebel Poets. "I am not a
Communist," Cheyney wrote. "Neither is Lucia Trent. Both of us are
left-wing Socialists. As such, we reach a parting of the ways. . . . though
Jack Conroy may regard me as a double-dyed villain, I admire him as a
gifted author and self-sacrificing rebel who should have the utmost loyalty of Communists."[60] Jack replied that while Cheyney seemed determined "to warn everybody that I am a wicked Communist . . . I've never
attempted to disguise my belief that the literary movement revolving
around *The New Masses* is the only one in this country possessing any
degree of vitality." All the other leftist movements, he said, were of little
consequence by comparison. Contributors need not be Party members,
he added, but, on the other hand, he could not support anyone or any
organization that "joins in the wolf pack yelps against the only Workers' and Farmers' government in the world." Cheyney had retreated from
the struggle, Jack concluded. "It is perhaps inevitable that, with the
sharpening of the crisis, some will travel in one direction—to the
right—while others will veer left."[61]

As indicated by his choice of associate editors, Jack had decided to
steer a course between the RP leftists who had taken a "militant Communist stand" and the loose grouping of Socialists, anarchists, and others
represented by the Cheyneys.[62] The "centrists" included Carmon, A. E.
Clements, Hagglund, Hugh Hanley, George Jarrboe, Kalar, Lewis, Rogers, Edwin Rolfe, Snow, Spier, and Henry George Weiss. More accurately, they were Conroy supporters. Of these only Spier, Rolfe, and
Snow had been members of the *Rebel Poet* editorial board during its last
issues. The Rahvites—Rahv, Walt Stacy, Fred Miller—were noticeably
absent, as was V. J. Jerome. The Rahvites' plans to launch a new magazine never materialized; ironically, members of the Rahv faction later
played decisive roles in the ultimate fate of the *Anvil*.

Jack marked time in the early months of 1933, gathering manuscripts
for the first issue and fussing at Hagglund's customary slowness in getting the type set on his antique press. Help came from many of the
former Rebel Poets. One of the first public announcements of the proposed *Anvil* appeared in the Sunday books section of the *New York Her-*

ald Tribune. Conroy's *Anvil* "will consider realistic prose (no criticisms or manifestoes desired). . . . Tut, tut, why not? What is the Left Wing coming to?"[63] Rogers succeeded in attracting the attention of a humorless *Richmond* (Virginia) *Times-Dispatch* writer to the *Anvil*: "Ben Hagglund, the printer, will publish the new journal in a barn that he shares with a lowly proletarian cow—just how Mr. Rogers knows that the cow is a proletarian is beyond me, but that's what he says."[64] Fania Kruger, a poet from Wichita Falls, Texas, who had published in *Rebel Poet* (and contributed money), passed through Moberly, regaling Jack with stories of life in prerevolutionary Russia. She bore scars still from her childhood there. "Inasmuch as her husband was along," Jack wrote Snow, "I didn't ask to see the scars."[65]

A worker-writer whom Conroy hoped would submit his work to the *Anvil* was Bob Cruden, an auto worker and union activist. In a letter to Walt Carmon several years earlier, Jack had expressed his admiration for Cruden's reportages and sketches appearing in *New Masses*, the *Nation*, and the *New Republic*.[66] Cruden had come to Detroit from Scotland with his parents at age thirteen when, following World War I, declining shipbuilding dried up Glasgow's economy. His father, a hairdresser in Scotland, struggled to learn a new trade as an auto worker in Detroit. Living in Detroit's immigrant quarter on the east side, Bob delivered newspapers, earning more than his father's factory wage. In high school Cruden received high marks and encouragement for his writing. He enrolled at Detroit City College, where he fell in with a group of progressive-minded activist students and teachers (and met his wife, Janet). After three years, Cruden was forced to abandon his studies when factory layoffs cost his parents their home.

In 1928, working as an auto assembly-line worker first for Packard, then Ford, Cruden struggled to find time to pursue his ambition to write. One of Cruden's earliest publications, a worker's view of conditions in the Packard plant, appeared in the *Nation*. At City College he had already begun to submit journalistic articles to Federated Press, portraying, from a worker's perspective, deteriorating labor conditions in Detroit. When a John Reed Club was organized in Detroit in April 1931, Cruden became its secretary. Drawing from his experiences and Janet's (she had gone to work as a punch press operator), Cruden penned worker narratives for *New Masses* and the *New Republic*.[67] Cruden's portrayal of unemployed auto workers in Detroit's Grand Circus park, titled "When the Snow Came," published in the February 1933 issue of *New Masses*, finds a counterpart in Conroy's "Bull Market," published soon after in the *Outlander* (summer 1933). Cruden's narrative is grey-toned naturalism; Conroy colors his narrative with expressionist, bitter-ironic hues.

A short while before he accepted Cruden's sketch "Own Your Own

Home" for the *Anvil* (September–October 1934), Jack cited Cruden's unpublished novel as an example of the difficulty that worker-writers encountered (Conroy was experiencing similar difficulties) finding publishers who would "stomach the revolutionary implications of the conclusion."[68] By 1933, Cruden, whom Karl Radek would mention in his keynote speech at the 1934 Soviet Writers' Congress, had left creative writing for labor journalism in Ohio. Like other young radical writers impatient with the restraints of publication and the frustrations of literary creation, Cruden addressed what seemed to be more pressing needs, accepting an activist role in the labor movement. By the time Cruden's novel, *Conveyor*, found a publisher in 1935, the proletarian "bull market" had turned bearish. Revolutionary dreams were exchanged for sit-down strikes in the labor movement, to which Cruden made his contribution as a publicity writer and editor for an Akron rubber union.[69]

* * *

Jack saw some financial relief when *Common Sense* accepted his story "Covered Wagon—Modern Style," paying him a much-needed forty dollars. Mencken accepted "The Siren" for the *Mercury* provided Jack make changes, including eliminating the ending in which the main character, a Syrian immigrant, returns to his native land and is executed for his part in a revolution. Pressed for money during the winter months, Jack did not contest the suggested changes.

Of larger consequence to him was the possibility in early spring of 1933 that the manuscript for *The Disinherited* might finally have a publisher. Upton Sinclair wrote a note to the publisher John Farrar recommending Jack's manuscript.[70] Ogden Nash, reader for Farrar and Rinehart, read and liked it, but the third reader said no.[71] Ever persistent, Lieber turned back to Covici-Friede, who had refused the manuscript already, persuading Pascal Covici to look at the manuscript another time. After all, Lieber argued, the episodic structure of William March's *Company K* had not detracted from its sales. With the proviso that Jack make revisions, integrating the material, Covici-Friede accepted the manuscript in early March for publication, advancing Jack $125. A bank closing tied up the money had Jack received for "The Siren"; the money would not be available until at least September. The near brush with impoverishment subdued much of the joy the Conroys ordinarily might have felt at the news of the acceptance. Of more concern to Jack at the moment was Hagglund's delay in getting out the *Anvil*.[72] Mencken's letter, nonetheless, picked up his spirits: "I am delighted to hear that Covici is to do your book. At the moment the publishing business is completely paralyzed, but there are already signs of a picking up and by September business should be fairly good again."[73] Accepted during one of the worst years publishers had known, Jack's first novel would likely appear in time for the Christmas-market reviewers. It was an enormous piece of luck, but Jack faced making substantial revisions. The *Anvil* made heavy demands on his time; somehow he had to make more room for his editorial work. The task of recasting *The Disinherited* in the form suggested by Covici-Friede seemed insuperable.

* * *

The title *Anvil* Jack borrowed from a Bulgarian publication of the same name; Jack had read a description of the Bulgarian *Anvil* (founded in 1926 by George Dimitrov, later famous for his part in the Popular Front and the Reichstag trial) appearing in the June 1931 issue of the IURW publication, *Literature of the World Revolution*.[74] The title suggested a number of things: the world of work, obviously; firmness of purpose, as expressed in Sandburg's "The People, Yes": "This old anvil laughs at many broken hammers. / There are men who can't be bought."[75] Most important, the title underscored the notion of raw material hammered into shape, befitting the magazine's slogan: "We prefer crude vigor to polished banality."

Mencken had demonstrated the value of writing that, if lacking cleverness, communicated experience in a fresh and compelling manner. But to extend an open invitation to anyone who had something vital to tell was like opening the Tour de France to anyone who rides a bicycle. Jack was flooded with submissions of low quality. He spent days bringing contributions up to scratch. Joe Hoffman, a one-armed St. Louis radical, sent in a badly written short story that nonetheless offered some possibility. Hoffman, desperate to prove himself as a writer, made it clear to Jack that rejection would destroy all hope. "After much painful correspondence" with Hoffman (who would later edit a little magazine called *Span*), Jack rewrote the story for publication.[76] Jack spent countless hours offering editorial advice to prospective contributors.[77] Frank Nipp remembered that when Jack rejected his poem on John Brown, he accompanied the rejection note with a two-and-one-half page, single-spaced letter explaining the purpose of the *Anvil* and so forth.[78]

A note addressed to "Camrad Jack" arrived from an Indiana coal miner announcing that since unemployment had provided him time to write he was planning to submit a story. "I believe I am best fitted to write storys [sic] on conditions as they actually exist and not in a fictious [sic] form. There is so many fakers watching for suckers like me," he confessed.[79] Despite his weak writing skills, the miner might have had an interesting story to tell; Jack did not rule out the possibility. In a very few cases, with a great deal of editing, Jack published such submissions. Then there were the proletarian sympathizers who made awkward attempts to imitate working-class speech. "I truckses into the tentses and flangs my armses around his neckses," one aspiring author wrote. Another was anxious to get into his story quickly. He began: "It was evening. Men were going in and out of the brothels."[80] It was necessary to *create* the new proletarian literature; it did not exist already. New writers would have to be found, their efforts encouraged and their work edited. Conroy's role as editor required this kind of nurturing. A new literature of "rude and untutored vigor"—de Tocqueville's term for what he felt a heterogeneous American folk might one day produce—would not simply spring spontaneously out of the earth. It required editors and publishers willing to take risks to plant the seed and make it grow.

Disappointed with early submissions, Jack decided to publish the work of old standbys, many of whom had helped him in launching the magazine. Thanks to Lieber, Maxim Gorki's literary agent in the United States, the Russian writer gave permission to Jack to print a translation of the famous "Stormy Petrel" for the first issue. But on the whole the issue was of very mixed quality. Snow attempted to justify the poor quality of many of the submissions: workers, he said, "were still duped by the entertainment narcotics provided by the bourgeoisie." It was necessary for writers like himself to rid themselves of "a bourgeois hangover" and then educate an American audience to read the proletarian short story as it developed.[81]

In the first issue of *Anvil* appeared Snow, Lewis, Rogers, Kalar, Hagglund, and Spier, all Rebel Poets and veterans of the proletarian writers' brigade. Snow's story was a chapter from a novel-in-progress (some 200,000 words in length, never published). Snow had let Jack know that he hoped to be represented in the first issue.[82] One of Conroy's St. Louis acquaintances from the John Reed Club and the Blue Lantern, Jack Balch, scored with both a short story and a poem. The poem, entitled "To the manlovers of our local Four Hundred," referring to St. Louis's bluebloods, began this way:

> Ladies & gentlemen:
> I wish to inform your excellencies
> that this afternoon, wednesday, twothirtythree,
> the northeast corner seventh, twothirtythree,
> the northeast corner seventh & market sts., a hand—
> to repeat: (

the repetition, both parentheses, all are mine)
an anonymous hand withdrew itself from a blocklong
limousine
and bestowed twentyfive cents in a one quarter coin
on the first poor
snotnosed syphilitic crumblybutted fatboyjazzing
son of a sonofabitch's degenerate workhating bastard's son
who had enough strength wit virility charm foresight
& quite generally speaking remnants of industry left
to beat the Next Man to it.[83]

The poem's stylistic pretense (an imitation of E. E. Cummings?) amused Jack and appalled H. H. Lewis, who wondered outloud about Jack's editorial judgment in printing the work.

Apart from the self-abasing, earthy humor of H. H. Lewis's "Down the Skidway," most of the contents of the first issue, including Langston Hughes's poem praising Lenin, were weakened by heavy-handed political point-making. Snow's manuscript was too wordy and had to be pruned. Rogers must have sensed the shortcomings in his own sketch; he wrote Snow that it was "written in a hurry and in an overheated kitchen, it should be close to the soil, altho I am not the dyed-in-the-wool proletarian that Lewis is."[84] Jack was optimistic: Erskine Caldwell had written that he planned to send something to *Anvil*; Granville Hicks (*New Masses*), Dinamov (of the IURW), and Walt Carmon (with *Moscow News* and *International Literature*) promised to help.[85] Hicks liked *Anvil* 1 and hoped that Jack would publish "stories about the daily struggles of workers. . . . Chambers did one or two good stories of this type for the *New Masses*, but he's almost the only person who has tried it."[86] Carmon enjoined Kalar to "prod Jack Conroy into making the *Anvil* a real thing—not the amateur job the *Rebel Poet* was. Jack has a weakness: he's too dang good-hearted and that doesn't make an editor. So pick his tail up."[87] Carmon was convinced that American proletarian literature would overshadow its bigger brother in the Soviet Union. His several months in the Soviet Union had made him chauvinistic. On the Soviets he wrote: "Sometimes they're so cocksurely smug they get my goat. Of course the bastards have a lot to brag about, I can't deny. *What* have we done? That's why I tell you to tell Jack to do a *good job*. We have more *it*—they know what to do with it." A great deal appeared to be riding on whether *Anvil* would succeed. People must have sensed this because help came from a variety of sources.

Jack counted on his associate editors to do a great deal of the distribution work and fund-raising. He had picked them because they were workers, not talkers, he told Snow.[88] A. E. Clements pinched 500 stamped envelopes from the bank where he worked and sent them to Jack for *Anvil* correspondence. Hagglund affirmed his commitment as publisher while hinting that he would soon be looking for another site for his press. *Anvil* "will last," he wrote. "It is a durable commodity."[89] Ben contracted to print 1,000 copies of the first issue, 24 pages in length, measuring 8 1/2 by 11 inches, with a cover, for $50, absorbing $25 of the cost. Snow sent $18, a considerable sum in those days, and disclosed ambitious plans for a Proletarian Writers' League, headed by Conroy, to finance *Anvil*. Spier distributed 300 copies of *Anvil* in New York City, but urged Snow, who assisted Conroy, to remove his name as associate editor for fear he might lose his job.[90]

Help took a number of forms. Mike Gold sent encouragement and advice: "make it [*Anvil*] middle west, full of gumbo mud local color and hhlewis and chicago detroit etc. etc. [*sic*]—you will achieve a character that way. . . . rural notes from Moberly is what I want, local stuff with the bark on."[91] From Cold Spring-on-Hudson, Paul Corey sent addresses of potential subscribers, along with a note expressing his view that *Anvil*'s literary and political programs should draw upon traditions and material indigenous to America. "I don't belong to any political party; I'm an observer. . . . Communism in this country, it seems to me, is like trying to superimpose the diet of an eskimo upon an equatorian."[92] Corey and others offered their views on contemporary politics, perhaps hoping to temper Jack's own. To midwestern radicals like Corey, one of the attractive features of the *Anvil* was its independence, its promise to be free of sectarian attitudes and ideologies.

Conroy welcomed dialogue with his contributors and readers; *Anvil* belonged to them, after all. *Rebel Poet* had become monologic in the end, unrepresentative of the diversity of views on the left. Writers exchanged opinions in their letters, and Jack heard them, for the letters were often passed around. Hagglund wrote Jack, dispelling the notion that farmers were in a mood for revolutionary change. They are "all bourgeois-minded," he said, and "not motivated by a lofty desire to demonstrate the class-struggle." Roosevelt and Floyd B. Olson of the Farmer-Labor Party attracted the farmers because they appealed to their individualism.[93] Once farmers had maintained their hold on their land it would be business as usual. Hagglund was wearying of his neighbors in Holt, Minnesota, and their "lunatic" prejudices. He thought of moving his press to Commonwealth College in Mena, Arkansas, but changed his mind and left for the Newllano Colony in Louisiana.

Anvil's subscription list by May had reached 250—a year's subscription was $1.00, or $2.00 with a membership to the Proletarian Writers'

League. Two hundred copies were exchanged with other magazines. The remainder would be sold at 10 cents each. The results were pleasing to Conroy, Snow, and Hagglund. Little magazines exerted influence well beyond what their circulation would suggest. Spier alone placed 100 copies in the first week. By 22 May the first issue of 1,000 had sold out; the editors were eager to get the second number out soon. It was important to reassure readers who had seen so many little magazines die after the first issue.

Anvil received national attention when Heywood Broun, noted columnist of the *New York World-Telegram*, addressed his column, "It Seems to Me," to it. "I have pretty nearly decided," Broun wrote after seeing the first issue, "not to make my new book a proletarian novel. In this decision I have been very largely influenced by reading a magazine called *The Anvil*, which carries the descriptive subhead, 'Stories for Workers.'"[94] Snow, who had taken on a great deal of *Anvil*'s correspondence for Jack (who was busy with revisions), chided Broun in a letter for judging the magazine on the basis of one story, Kalar's "Night Piece." Broun had posed the question in his column whether Kalar's language was suitable for workers, quoting a passage that began: "All the week stealthily through dark alleys and sombre side streets and proud, sneering, vacant lots. Arms interlocked, thinking how blackly in the room the shuddering crescendo of it had palpitated." Proletarian literature failed, he concluded, because proletarians were not writing it. Walter Snow replied that worker-writers like Kalar (who *was* a true proletarian) did not dare write like radical Harold Bell Wright lest they be condemned for crudity and boorishness. Proletarians had no easy task; they were criticized from both sides, Snow said, from aesthetic critics and propagandists. He drew Broun's attention to other stories in the issue, challenging him to make a try himself if he thought he could do any better.[95] Nonetheless, the charge of stylistic vulgarity implied in Broun's review would dog Conroy's proletarians—hadn't he lauded crudeness in the slogan "We prefer crude vigor to polished urbanity"? This was rather like waving a red flag in the faces of those who cherished stylistic elegance in the leading magazines; actually it was a restatement of the old conflict between genteel literature and an indigenous American art that admitted the grime and idioms of the working world.[96]

Snow and Willard Maas, alert to the promotional opportunities provided by Broun's column, urged Clements, Spier, and others to place it in prominent locations. Spier got the Workers' Bookshop and the Rand School to post the column with an inscription in bright colors: "Do you agree with Heywood Broun? The much-talked-of 'Anvil' is on sale here!"[97] Erskine Caldwell wrote Jack advising him to tell the critics to go to hell; he would help *Anvil* all he could. When John T. Frederick, editor of *Midland*, wrote that he was going broke and was faced with suspending publication of his magazine, Jack offered to help with what little cash he had. The influential *Midland* ceased soon thereafter, and in a sense Jack felt that he must now also carry on Frederick's work in discovering new writers in the hinterland.

The tasks that Jack had set himself—editing a magazine and preparing a novel for publication—would have overwhelmed someone of less energy and resolve. The conditions set by Covici-Friede meant recasting *The Disinherited* manuscript in fundamental ways. He had no time for the Broun affair; his mind was entirely preoccupied with the revisions. When Jack wrote Lieber in March that he felt "unequal to the task of recasting [the] material within the frame suggested by Covici Friede," Lieber suggested enlisting the help of Edwin Seaver, the associate editor of *New Masses* in its early days and the author of *The Company*. Seaver's role in the revisions would be kept confidential, Lieber assured Jack. Seaver's fee of thirty-five dollars came out of Jack's stipend from Covici-Friede. By 7 April, Lieber had Seaver's report on the manuscript, which he forwarded to Conroy.

The letter-supplement to the Covici-Friede contract stipulated that Jack's manuscript undergo fundamental structural changes. These included threading the sketches on a single narrative line, following the progress of the central character from childhood to the present time; showing his relationship to women; and recasting the material into a form of a novel.[98] The intention of these changes was, of course, to make a novel out of a book of sketches. Seaver, on the other hand, hoped to make Jack into "a revolutionary writer," a notion he was spelling out in essays published in *New Masses* and *International Literature*.[99] Several of Seaver's suggestions were structural. Jack accepted Seaver's tripartite sectioning of the chapters: "Monkey Nest," "Bull Market," "The Hard Winter." As to the question of narrative development, Seaver suggested giving the narrator "increasing and predominant interest as the book goes along." But, here Seaver invoked a Kharkov tenet. The real hero was not the protagonist-narrator, Seaver argued, but the disinherited, and for that reason the narrator should through the course of the book emerge as more than an observer; "he emerges not only as a participant in the mass but as the conscience of the mass. At present, the narrator is only the bystander and the participant, which is OK for H. L. Mencken but not for Jack Conroy."[100]

Jack followed the general outline of Seaver's advice quite religiously. Its main features were both stylistic and political: provide narrative development through the narrator's growing consciousness; shift verb tenses within paragraphs to increase "vividness"; rework individual chapters to achieve unity; portray the narrator's sexual contacts with women. The last proved especially difficult for Jack; not that he was prudish in any way—he was a married man, after all, with three children. In describing sexual behavior, however, he retained from youth a certain shyness with regard to women, a natural forbearance that had characterized his earliest contacts. Finally, Seaver asked him to eliminate the "reminiscent, autobiographical strain," a revision he found nearly impossible to make. *The Disinherited*, after all, was quite personal, particularly the "Monkey Nest" episodes; Jack had lived nearly everything in the book.

By the time he set about making revisions, Jack had come to accept Granville Hicks's verdict on the manuscript of *The Disinherited*. In his reader's report the previous December, Hicks pointed out its lack of unity; however, his advice had been to leave it as it was, try to publish it that way, and start to work on his next book, a novel.[101] After all, Gold's *Jews without Money* had found a publisher. Listening to Hicks, Jack had concluded that he was unwilling to make further revisions; a publisher would eventually take the manuscript in its present form.[102] It turned out to be very bad advice. Ignoring both Conroy's and Hicks's opinions concerning the further disposition of the manuscript, acting rather on his own intuition, Max Lieber probably made publication possible. (The previous year Jack had scolded Lieber for calling *The Disinherited* a novel. "Forgive me," Lieber replied, "for alluding to your autobiography as a novel.")[103] Credit therefore must be accorded Lieber for *not* listening—and to the editors at Covici-Friede, who took a second look at the manuscript. If both were "heroes," then the unknown soldier was Edwin Seaver.[104]

Pascal Covici and Donald Friede were what were known in the trade as blue-pencil editors; they encouraged authors to make their own changes. Covici, for instance, had a great deal to do with John Steinbeck's success, publishing first *Tortilla Flat* in 1935, and later (as Viking editor) *The Grapes of Wrath*. Covici was persuaded that a book must meet the tastes, needs, and mood of the times, and that when those changed, no amount of craft would make a book sell. He was known also for sticking by his authors, as he did in accepting Jack's second novel (in 1935), even when the market for proletarian writing had lost what little momentum it had from previous years.[105]

In 1933, Covici-Friede apparently sensed a market for proletarian literature; other publishers likewise expressed interest in publishing proletarian novels but few were actually takers.[106] Jack was sure that publishers were hostile to proletarian writers and stories of the underdog.

"Pray for better days when purblind editors will realize that honest stuff is relished as much as or more than the conveyor-belt, cellophane-wrapped, untouched-by-humanity sophistry which clutters up the pages of magazines absurdly afraid of the new and vital."[107] Although Viking brought out Albert Halper's *Union Square*, which Gold viewed as a vicious attack on the revolutionary movement, in early 1933, indications were that publishers were in no mood for taking risks on books about the revolutionary movement. Publishers were cutting salaries of employees and asking stencil cleaners to double up as readers in novel contests.[108] Jack was puzzled, therefore, when Macmillan accepted Arnold B. Armstrong's *Parched Earth*; it was in his view "too propagandistic."[109] Publishers' ways were strange to the worker-writers, whose best hope in attracting mainstream publishers' attention, most felt, was through the little magazines, not direct solicitation.[110]

Seaver had a direct hand in shaping Jack's first novel in two principal ways: suggesting that Jack show the narrator's rise to political consciousness and that he add sexual interest. (These subsequently turned out to be the most criticized aspects of the book when it was published.) Covici-Friede outlined the changes that would have to made and Seaver suggested how to make them, but Jack undertook the revisions himself with no assistance; *The Disinherited* remained entirely his book. On several points, in fact, he departed from Seaver's framework of suggested revisions. Jack complied when Seaver urged him to add scenes of "illicit pleasure."[111] "Nothing is more despicable," Seaver wrote, "I agree with you, than literary cockteasing for sales appeal. On the other hand, the making and breaking of love is after all a normal part of the pattern of our existence. . . ."[112] Hardly erotic, the scenes of "illicit pleasure" that Jack added collapse within the narrator's consciousness into anger and disgust—disgust with himself for having sex with a "chippie," anger at the degradation of a female worker (for whom he had felt a romantic attachment) turned prostitute to survive.

Moreover, Jack was unable to fit the progress of his narrator's growing sociopolitical awareness into a formulaic mode that satisfied Seaver's notions about revolutionary writing. For example, Seaver proposed concluding the narrator's rise to consciousness in an emotional climax: "why not have him join the Communist Party?" Fortunately, Jack refused the suggestion, choosing rather to send the narrator off with two other workers in an open-ended commitment to the cause of workers. Jack's own political education had occurred by fits and starts, and he was unwilling to violate the truth of that fact for ideological reasons. Rather than the "conversion" ending of inferior proletarian writing, then, Jack has Larry Donovan stumble into the act of engagement con-

cluding the story, as if the circumstances motivating the decision finally are irrefutable.

As contemporary events turned out, Larry Donovan's decision to join
in labor's struggle for social justice prefigured actual successes for the
industrial worker: the formation of the Committee for Industrial Organization (later the Congress of Industrial Organizations [CIO]), the establishment of social security and workman's compensation, the rights
granted labor to organize, and so forth. The conclusion of *The Disinherited* may have appeared revolutionary to some at the time of its publication, but in light of subsequent struggles for economic and social
justice, for example, during the civil rights era, it proved to be quite
reasonable—scarcely the emotional climax that Seaver, a Party faithful, had hoped to see.

Seaver expressed other reservations about Jack's narrator. Like a number of critics following publication of *The Disinherited*, Seaver was mys-
tified that a worker (Jack's narrator) would quote poetry.[113] Seaver's conventional view of workers—as to what they should or should not
know—was shared by critics and readers who expected a certain standard of boorishness and illiteracy on the part of the worker. For a worker
to like poetry was evidence of a "bourgeois hangover." Fortunately, Jack
left his characterizations of workers intact. On the other hand, Seaver's suggestion to tie the loose episodes together in the manner of an
Entwicklungsroman imparted a unity (despite numerous remaining loose
ends) that the original lacked. Lieber swore Seaver to secrecy concerning his involvement in the revisions; the secret was apparently kept all
these years.

It must be admitted that without the kind of help Seaver furnished,
The Disinherited as we know it today would not exist. Jack's strength as
a writer lay in short breaths; he lacked the long-distance runner's endurance necessary to stay the entire course of a novel to the conclusion. Revising was painful; he was sick with exhaustion, a "sort of general collapse after the strain," when on 10 June he mailed the revisions
to Jean Helfrich, the wife of his old friend from Ohio days, Emerson
Price, who typed the manuscript.[114] With relief he turned his attention
back to neglected *Anvil* affairs. Snow had helped with the correspondence during the previous several months and Jack was anxious to provide him a break.

Jack accepted a Seaver story for *Anvil* 2, doubtless in return for Seaver's help with *The Disinherited*, since it was not up to the standards Jack
hoped to achieve. In return for Leonard Spier's help on behalf of *Rebel
Poet*, Jack wrote the foreword to Spier's small poetry collection, *When
the Sirens Blow*, printed on Hagglund's press. The tireless Spier had car-

ried bundles of *Rebel Poet* to newsstands and now volunteered to assist with the *Anvil*. Wishing to put the distribution of the *Anvil* in more professional hands than the *Rebel Poet* "bundle brigade," however, Jack enlisted the Party's Central Distribution Agency. Despite Jack's "bohemian" independence, the Party cooperated, meaning that *Anvil* would be sold through the Workers' Bookshops and other distribution outlets. The hitch was, of course, that Party cooperation could be withdrawn at any time—if Jack should fall into disfavor. He felt little apprehension about the arrangement in the beginning; after all, wasn't the CP the workers' party? Subscriptions, moreover, would eventually free him from the Party's patronage.

Jack was working a lot "smarter" now, building a network of connections, enlisting the help of his many contacts. When Erskine Caldwell called him "a genius of an editor," he must have been thinking of his ability to get others involved in making the magazine a common enterprise. There was nothing manipulative in this; people wanted to help Jack, including those who had never met him—nearly all his contacts in regard to the *Anvil* continued to be epistolary. Perhaps his enormous energy infected people with a desire to help. His little-magazine colleagues were impressed; a note appeared in the *Windsor Quarterly*: "Editor Jack Conroy's own vigorous personality can be felt through *The Anvil* which he has directed to a position well at the fore of the proletarian magazines."[115]

Little magazines were springing up in midwestern towns like Dubuque, Cedar Rapids, Davenport, and Peoria. The contributors were mainly unknowns, scattered far and wide. Stranded by the economic crisis, they hoped to establish contact with other writers and editors through publication. In response to the fact that the commercial press seldom published little-known writers, particularly if the writing was political in content, leftist magazines like *Anvil*, the *Dubuque Dial*, the Cedar Rapids *Hub*, *Hinterland*, *Left*, and others attempted to create a space outside the hegemonic literary system within which a literature of renewal might be produced.

Radical literary magazines of the 1930s were, in the main, forms of cultural response to crisis. In the minds of many leftist writers the economic crisis had been long in arriving; for them the political crisis had begun a decade before. The "Red Scare," the near eclipse of the radical movement following World War I, the decline of organized labor's influence, indeed the paper prosperity of the 1920s—all these weakened literary radicalism but by no means eliminated it in the postwar period before the great stock tumble. The new midwestern literary radicalism was born during the 1920s in Haldeman-Julius's magazines, where young writers like J. T. Farrell, Albert Halper, George Milburn, Conroy, Erskine Caldwell, H. H. Lewis, and W. D. Trowbridge were appearing in print, usually for the first time.[116]

Grass-roots publishing ventures such as Haldeman-Julius's publications, Wayland's socialist press, and Oscar Ameringer's Oklahoma *Leader* had demonstrated that cheap printing, wide distribution, social content, and popular readership might combine in a successful publishing enterprise. These publications, as noted, served to inform and educate a generation of young midwestern writers—miners and railroad workers like Jack Conroy—and aspiring middle-class authors from isolated, culturally undernourished small towns. Publications like the *Haldeman-Julius Weekly* and the Little Blue Books were intended to create a democratic culture on the plains: a literature sprung from indigenous roots furnishing low-cost books and magazines. From the perspective of Girard, Kansas, avant-garde literary magazines such as the *Dial, Contact, S4N,* and *transition* were not meant to "communicate" with the common reader. At least one Haldeman-Julius writer saw it as a case of Girard versus Concord (Massachusetts). The Girard "group" was diffuse; there were few big names, apart from Upton Sinclair. Contributors sent in their material from all over the country, united "in a common stream of cultural influence that spreads itself throughout the whole country."[117] Concord, on the other hand, had not provided the material for popular movements. The Girard group genuinely admired Emerson, Thoreau, and Hawthorne; but to the Girard socialist-populists, "Concord" represented a culture of the educated few, despite Emerson's faith in the common people.

The widely dispersed Girard group offered mutual support and made editorial contacts—all by mail. As mentioned earlier, many of these writers would correspond for years, never actually meeting. During this period in the evolution of midwestern literary radicalism, the mutual aid phase, writers made contact with one another, emerging from their isolation in small communities, exploring the possibilities of publication, evolving a shared consciousness of their isolation and, in some cases, their dispossession.

The catalyzing impulse of this emerging consciousness was, as discussed in an earlier chapter, the Sacco-Vanzetti executions. The continuing excitement of the Soviet Experiment fueled the perception that literature would play a role in bringing about revolutionary change. Marcus Graham's *Anthology of Revolutionary Poetry* and the Cheyneys' *America Arraigned* led in 1928 to the organization of the Rebel Poets, whose adherents, like Shelley, Yeats, and, more recently, MacDiarmid, held that politics was compatible with poetic expression. This new literary radicalism was still in its "communication phase" at this stage of its evolution. During the early years of the Depression, writers felt anger, frustration, and a need to communicate their feelings, as well as to experiment on paper with solutions to the crisis.

Poetry, Nietzsche argued, frees language from distress, delineating consciousness, which is not tied to immediate needs. It was just such a liberation of consciousness through language that, I believe, motivated a great number of young men and women, remotely isolated from one another, to share their stories and poems, usually based on experiences, in the pages of the little magazines of the early 1930s. Communication brought them closer together, broke the isolation, empowered them. The communication "phase" was not limited to the little magazines of the late 1920s and early 1930s; it may also be observed in the art of the period, for example, in Thomas Hart Benton's New School for Social Research mural (1930). Writers and artists in the little magazines of the 1930s explored experience—their own and others'—attempting to unveil the social and political forces they believed operated in people's lives.

Some writers suggested that these forces might be changed to improve the lives and destinies of suffering toilers, out of work and out of luck. Some thought they could be controlled. The *Left,* published in Davenport, Iowa, plunged into the revolutionary phase of radical evolution, following the example of *New Masses.* Its editors were a group of young writers—Jay Du Von, George Redfield, Marvin Klein (a.k.a. Mark Marvin), Robert C. Lorenz, and Willis ("Bill") K. Jordan—all from middle-class homes (Jordan and Lorenz had been University of Illinois school chums). Davenport had earlier been a pocket of Socialist strength, electing a Socialist mayor in 1920; Floyd Dell, Susan Glaspell, George Cram Cook, Arthur Davison Ficke, and Alice French were all from the river city.[118] The *Left* was edited in a windowless room above Lorenz's bookstore.[119] Joining the Davenport radicals was Alroy Mosenfelder (a.k.a. John Alroy), whose parents owned a furniture store, a probable source of the meager funding that kept the *Left* alive for two issues.[120] Inspired by Mike Gold's call "Go Left, Young Writer," not the populist Girard program of slow growth of consciousness through education and communication, the young Davenport firebrands saw harbingers of the coming revolution in the struggle between the CP, which strove to organize a local Unemployed Council, and the manufacturers' association that opposed its efforts.[121]

Billed as "A Quarterly Review of Revolutionary and Proletarian Art," the *Left* was intended for "export"; experimental in its aim, it had little basis in the regionalism of, say, Frederick's *Midland,* which influenced

Conroy's editorial perspective. The first issue, appearing in the spring of 1931, included criticism, short stories, poetry, and essays on cinema. The latter was an innovation in radical little magazines of the time. Seymour Stern and others discussed alternatives to Hollywood mass fare and reviewed Soviet revolutionary cinema. Rebel Poets—Norman Macleod, John Rogers, Joe Kalar, H. H. Lewis, and Leonard Spier—were represented in the first issue, along with east-of-the-Hudson radicals Sherry Mangan, Harry Roskolenkier, Horace Gregory, Edwin Seaver, Alan Calmer, and Louis Zukofsky. Conroy's sketch of an incident from the 1922 railroad strike appeared in the second issue, along with stories and poems by Bob Cruden, Albert Halper, Kalar, Ed Falkowski, Edwin Rolfe, Herman Spector—and "Jon" Cheever (the same John Cheever who turned to genteel fiction, the author of *The Wapshot Chronicle*).[122] Surveying hundreds of workers to discover "what the proletariat reads," Louis Adamic, the Serbo-American novelist, concluded that "the overwhelming majority" of the working class in America read only newspapers and pulp magazines.[123] Such surveys indicated to radical editors like Conroy and to the Davenport radicals the need to attract readers away from pulp magazines—for example, the pernicious *Saturday Evening Post*—in order to focus their attention on the contemporary dislocations and suffering imposed by economic crisis under capitalism. The inspiration for little magazines like the *Left*, the *Anvil*, *Left Front* (Chicago John Reed Club), *Hub*, the *Dubuque Dial*, the *New Quarterly* (Rock Island, Illinois), and *Hinterland* (Des Moines) drew in great part from the conviction that a new radical consciousness, distinctively midwestern in character, was in the making.

There were basically two schools of thought among the midwestern radicals as to how this rise in consciousness among the toiling classes and disaffected intellectuals might occur. The one, represented by Conroy's new magazine, the *Anvil*, argued in effect that change would take place from the ground up; the other, reflected in the editorship of the *Left*, cultivated top-down ideological views that, the editors felt, might, given proper expression, sift to the bottom and spread out like fine sand. In both cases, the editors were devoted to the discovery of new writers, the breakdown of the author system characteristic of the establishment press, and wide readership.

More revolutionary than the writing or ideology were the *form* of distribution, the conditions of literary production, and the nature of the little magazine themselves. The *Anvil* and the *Left*, and many other magazines growing like milkweed on midwestern soil, challenged the old order of centralized, hegemonic literary expression, "the Concord group," what midwesterners conceived of as the eastern literary establishment. Unfortunately, many of the radical little magazines replaced one kind of literary politics with another. In this connection it is important to consider questions of distribution and patronage, which are essentially economic considerations.

Years earlier, J. A. Wayland had his "Appeal Army," volunteers who distributed the *Appeal to Reason* without pay. One issue ran to four million circulation; thus a Socialist publication was once the largest-selling newspaper in the world.[124] The Rebel Poets had attempted to build a network of correspondents and contributors, assuring a small but widespread distribution. The contributors, acknowledging their stake in the magazine, accepted the task of selling two or three copies. Building on his RP list of correspondents, Jack hoped for a similar participatory feeling among *Anvil* contributors and supporters. Meridel Le Sueur distributed the *Anvil* at factory gates; Abe Aaron in Chicago and Leonard Spier in New York City placed copies in bookstores and newspaper kiosks. The voluntary spirit was one element of a program to make *Anvil* a democratic medium, idealistic to be sure, but not without precedent in the Chartist era and in various forms of street literature, including religious tracts and chapbooks.[125] Copies and ads were exchanged with other little magazines. Jack and Walter Snow nurtured the subscription list like a new-born flower, yet subscriptions never exceeded a thousand. Direct sales accounted for the major part of the growing circulation, which by 1935 reached almost five thousand, a number that did not, however, accurately reflect the number of readers. Many readers were not able to afford the cost of an individual issue; little magazines continued to be passed around a great deal and read in libraries.

The voluntary efforts of contributors and supporters, along with cheap production costs, would be instrumental if the *Anvil* were to succeed. *Anvil* was distributed through bookstores such as Gotham's in New York City, Brentano's in Washington, D.C., the Stanley Rose Book Shop in Hollywood, Jake Zeitlin's in Los Angeles, and the Workers' Bookstores in St. Louis, Chicago, Detroit, and other large cities.[126]

Despite the willingness of some major bookstores to carry radical magazines, the *Anvil* and the *Left* had to depend mainly upon the Party's Central Distribution Agency. In 1935, when the CDA accepted some 3,000 copies for distribution, *Anvil*'s peak circulation reached some 4,500 subscribers and buyers, an astounding figure for a radical little magazine that published stories and poems of unknown writers on contemporary social issues.[127] A key figure in the Party's distribution agency was William Browder, the brother of the CP secretary, Earl Browder, both native Kansans. Failing to penetrate the American News Company's subway and railroad terminal stands, Browder's CDA displayed *Anvil* prominently in hundreds of newspaper kiosks throughout New York City, next to subway entrances and elevated railroad stairways.[128] *Anvil's* newsstand success impressed William Phillips and Philip Rahv, who within a year were editing *Partisan Review*, first as the organ of the John Reed Club of New York in 1934. *Anvil's* considerable success, ironically, raised concern within the Party's cultural circles. The *Left* had submitted to Party criticisms. Jack, on the other hand, revealed his editorial independence time and time again and was therefore viewed by Party orthodoxists as unreliable.[129]

The *Left* came under the scrutiny of the International Union of Revolutionary Writers in Moscow, as did most leftist little magazines and writers of the era. Despite its rejection of capitalism and acceptance of the revolutionary movement, the *Left* was found wanting by IURW on several counts. A simple declaration of faith to the cause is insufficient, a reviewer wrote in *Literature of the World Revolution*, the organ of the IURW; one must prove one's convictions on the firing line of daily revolutionary tasks.[130] The editors of the *Left* had committed several serious "errors" in their first issue, printing, for instance, an essay by the heretical V. F. Calverton, editor of *Modern Quarterly*, who among other deviations held that "Revolutionary art has to be good art first before it can have deep meaning."[131]

In a remorseful letter to the IURW, *Left* editors Du Von and Redfield apologized for their blunders and promised to make the necessary corrections in the next issue, including removing Calverton's name as associate editor from the masthead. The revolutionary phase had, for the *Left*, devolved into an authoritarian phase; moribundity was close by. In a follow-up critique a year later, another IURW reviewer praised Redfield and Du Von's "healthy self-criticism," publishing their letter along with lengthy analyses of theoretical errors in the second issue of the *Left*. "We must be prepared," the reviewer concluded, "to do everything possible to help them cope with these difficulties . . . to safeguard them in advance from repeating the same mistakes that have already been overcome in the process of the Soviet proletarian literary organization. . . ."[132] The *Left's* abject genuflecting to the Soviet star added nothing to its depleted financial coffers. The planned third number never appeared. The faith of the editors in the revolutionary movement was strong; their faith in the Soviet cultural bureaucracy was even greater.[133] The *Left* had shown promise in its two issues. Marvin Klein was in touch with Henri Poulaille's Nouvel Age group in France and planned an essay for the third issue on the French radicals. In the heartland of America, the Davenport radicals pointed out new directions for the radical movement, internationalist in scope and Marxist in principle.[134]

The *Left* plotted its bearing from the Red Star, erring into the treacherous waters of Ideology and foundering on the shoals of Finance. Conroy planted his *Anvil* in Missouri soil; it spread its connections horizontally throughout the cartography of American social experience. Emboldened by the example of Frederick's *Midland*, Haldeman-Julius's publications, and the attention suddenly accorded expressions of folk experience and workers' reality, Jack hoped to cultivate a new radical literary movement by drawing together the interests of the writer, worker, and reader. Mainstream publishing practices "created" best-selling writers and erected arborescent scales of literary value. To make literature accessible, cheap and accessible printing was, of course, necessary. The main ingredient, however, was the people who made personal sacrifices as an act of faith—the printers in their garages, the editors in their homes, the writers peddling the issues, the readers paying what they could. Writers received no pay, printers spent their own money, and editors advised new writers where they might be published and offered constructive criticism. Jack converted a faith in community and cooperation (Monkey Nest) into a system of literary production in which the writer was a craftsperson in touch with the needs of his or her readers. In contrast to such a system, the dominant culture industry creates tastes in readers, affirming the hegemony of capitalism; rather than taking an active role in the production of art, audiences are manipulatable, passive objects in a commodity culture.[135] The cultural elite, on the other hand, acts as if people can get along without art.

Producers and consumers of literature were, in Jack's view, far apart. The proletarian magazine competed with a gigantic culture industry for the worker's attention. (Many of Jack's *Anvil* contributors wrote for the pulps out of economic necessity.) In his essay "What If You Don't Want to Write for Money," Jack wrote bitterly about the trade press and the obstacles to publication, counseling young writers to submit their work to the little magazines even when they did not pay. These, he said, offered the only hope for the writer intent on publishing something of worth.[136] Jack wished fervently that his *Anvil* would turn up unknown writers with talent. His magazine would prepare the soil for the emergence of a new literature that, he hoped, would be in closer contact with the people and the American experience than was the dominant culture with its devotion to prominence and literary personality.

Like the great Jewish intellectual Walter Benjamin, who in the 1930s fled into exile from Nazi Germany, Jack viewed literature as a transforming *praxis*; the old bourgeois apparatus of production and publication, with its assimilative practice, must be countered by a new "production aesthetic" of critical consciousness and participation aimed at working people, writers, and artists. Such a process of literary production corresponded to a new democratic culture, just as the publishing practices of the mainstream press, with its blockbuster mentality, and the hierarchical scale of literary values cherished by critics reflected capitalism.[137] The experiment lasted a relatively short time; already, new arborescent structures were appearing on the left to cashier the independent little magazines. Indeed, there was some doubt in Jack's mind over the summer of 1933 whether his magazine would make it beyond the first issue.

* * *

Exhausted from the labors of revising *The Disinherited* and launching the *Anvil*, Jack found little respite over the summer of 1933. Doctors discovered cancer in his mother while operating for gallstones, sewed her up, and left her to die. Money problems continued to assail the Conroys. Gladys and her fellow workers at the Brown Shoe Company factory faced pay cuts. Jack had depended upon the small remuneration he earned for his stories, but now Mencken wrote that payment for "The Siren" would be delayed until September. Lieber as a rule tried the paying magazines, like *Scribner's*, first when seeking to place Jack's stories. Jack continued to send stories to magazines like *New Masses* that did not pay. Joe Freeman, editor of *New Masses*, was anxious to publish stories of America's homeless children, inviting Jack to submit, which he did.[138] When the story ("They Won't Let Us Birds Roost Nowheres") appeared in the June issue, however, Jack expressed his disgust with the editorial cuts. A "timorous" editor, Jack wrote Howard Wolf, deleted two off-color anecdotes told by one of the homeless boys, substituting "Then he told two dirty stories." "Keerist! That's the kind of stuff that makes outlanders like me hesitant about sending things to *New Masses*."[139] The *Anvil* would not be fastidious. In Jack's mind, it was a question of truthfulness to experience—boy tramps *do* tell dirty stories. In 1933, the question of obscenity in literature found an intelligent response in the famous *Ulysses* test case; Judge Woolsey decided against the prudish censors, who sought to limit free expression. The question was by no means settled, however; magazine editors rejected manuscripts submitted by Erskine Caldwell, for instance, which Jack then accepted for *Anvil*.

Homelessness was also the subject of Jack's story "Hoover City," published in the English-language edition of the IURW publication *International Literature*, in Moscow. Carmon, who had arranged for its publication, subtitled the sketch "A Story of the Unemployed by an American Worker-Writer," in line with his effort to promote the "boys" from the Midwest—Conroy, Kalar, "Humpy" Lewis. This sketch, like "They Won't Let Us Birds Roost Nowheres," was based upon Jack's experiences riding the rails with his nephew Fred Harrison, Jack's nonliterary counterpart and the one figure that binds together many of Jack's proletarian sketches from this period. What was popularly viewed as an interlude of anarchic freedom in the 1920s—tramping on freights—now in 1933 was an act of despair on the part of the homeless. Several years earlier, Mike Gold had viewed tramping as a learning experience for apprentice writers.[140] No one was making the choice between college and a boxcar trip now; boxcars contained desperate people, not adventurers. Few writers, other than an occasional Algren or Kromer or Loren Eiseley, hazarded the experience. Survival, not the desire for anarchic freedom, drew the floating subproletariat that Algren and Conroy describe to railroad yards to hazard nonpaying traveler's status on freight trains, leading nowhere and never returning.

Nelson Algren bummed south on freights to Texas in the fall of 1933, recording in a notebook scraps of dialogue and impressions of his homeless companions. Algren measured himself against Conroy at this time, according to Bettina Drew, "believing he would wrest from Jack Conroy the title of 'American Gorky.'"[141] Algren knew Jack's work through the *American Mercury* and *New Masses;* his own writing, like Jack's, appeared first as sketches in little magazines, including *Anvil,* which were then refashioned into his first novel, *Somebody in Boots* (1935). Synthesizing short pieces into a longer narrative had as much to do with the physical circumstances of his life—on the edge of poverty—as with his inexperience as a novelist. Indirectly, Jack played another role in Algren's early writing career through a poetry collection called *We Gather Strength,* published earlier in the year, with Gold's enthusiastic introduction. The four contributors—Herman Spector, Joe Kalar, Edwin Rolfe, and Sol Funaroff—had been active Rebel Poets, all, apart from Kalar, members of the New York chapter. The collection was important enough to Algren that he hitchhiked to New York to meet Spector and Funaroff. The trip was providential; Algren landed a book contract from Vanguard Press for his first novel.

Jack had become a cultural hero for young radical writers like Algren. "Every radical who heads Westward," Snow wrote Granville Hicks, "makes hundred-mile detours to see him."[142] Algren, who by the fall had drifted to Alpine, Texas, was talking about Conroy to students at Sul Ross College there, and planned to come through Moberly on his way north after Christmas.[143] Mordecai Gorelik and his wife, Frances Strauss, business manager of *New Masses,* visited Jack in Moberly. When Dale Kramer, who was both a printer and writer, came through Moberly in

1934, Jack sent him to the Newllano Colony in Louisiana to help Marvin Sanford, whom Jack had selected to replace Hagglund as publisher of the *Anvil*.

Snow continued to push for a New York printer but Jack had already contracted with Sanford, a printer with the Llano Cooperative Colony in Newllano, Louisiana. First begun as a socialist colony in 1914 near Los Angeles (Antelope Valley) in response to industrial capitalism with its sweatshops and city slums, in 1917 Llano was moved to Louisiana, where an attempt was made to build Llano's communitarian ideals into a self-sufficient community, which would include a day-care center and a newspaper. Many a famous socialist lived in or passed through Newllano at one time or another, including Kate Richards O'Hare, Covington Hall, and William Edward Zeuch.[144] Sanford, who had earlier published a socialist paper in Everett, Washington, during World War I, joined his father, "Dad Sanford," to print the *Llano Colonist* and to contract for occasional printing jobs.[145] Moving *Anvil* to Newllano delayed the second issue almost four months. The next nine issues appeared in bimonthly editions without interruption.

Earlier *New Masses* had welcomed proletarian writing, but by late 1933 the editors had turned almost entirely to political and theoretical matters, leaving a vacuum largely filled by *Anvil* and *Blast*, soon to be joined by *Dynamo* and *Scope*.[146] There were other little magazines calling themselves "proletarian," but these were the main ones. And of these, *Anvil* led the others by several lengths. Few little magazines printed more than 500 copies each issue. Even the much-respected *Pagany*, financed privately, did not achieve a circulation greater than 1,000. *Blast* at its peak never exceeded that number. And *Partisan Review* was printing around 2,000 copies in its early days while *Anvil* doubled that figure. Jack's publishing formula—low printing costs, voluntary help, cooperation on the part of the Party's distribution agency, accessibility to new writing and writers, networking, and the imprint of Jack's energetic personality in each issue—seemed to work favorably. The next nine issues appeared without interruptions from Sanford's linotype. Other magazines like *Blast* and *Scope* turned their printing over to Sanford, who now called his sideline printing business the Anvil Press, using the Llano colony's equipment.

After Christmas, Hagglund joined Sanford in Newllano. There was no pay, the meals were often fried potatoes mixed with peanut butter, but it gave Hagglund a chance to learn the linotype machine and stay in touch with *Anvil*. Despite privations, these were heady days for literary activists on the left. There were many like "Bensk" Hagglund (his sobriquet at Newllano), who made considerable personal sacrifices to

help *Anvil* on its way. Jack had a way of getting others to work for him
without remuneration. There was something great-spirited about the
man; it touched those who had any contact with him. Often when he
refused a poem or story for publication in the *Anvil* he would send it
on to another editor, paying for the postage out of his meager cash reserves. This was the sort of thing that won people's loyalty and made
them want to help Jack. He was discriminating and for that reason his
instinctive generosity carried weight; you valued it. A large-spirited man
with an inexhaustible capacity for friendship, Conroy revealed a peculiar vulnerability: he placed friendship before interests and personal gain
yet longed for recognition of his work. This ambivalence toward literary success marked him for the remainder of his long life. When *The
Disinherited* appeared in November of 1933, however, it seemed that
recognition had finally come his way.

14

"Something Great Has Begun": Reception and Recognition

> I should demand a programme of culture, drawn
> out, not for a single class alone, or for the parlors or
> lecture rooms, but with an eye to practical life, the
> west, the working-men, the facts of farms and jack-
> planes and engineers. . . .
> —Walt Whitman, "Democratic Vistas"

> How many mute and inglorious Richard Wrights
> and Albert Maltzes are hidden in the ranks of
> union labor in the factories, mines and on ship-
> board.
> —Jack Conroy,
> "Young Writers Need Elbow Room"

THE PUBLICATION OF Jack's first book in November 1933 received attention out of proportion to the number of books actually sold. Reviewed in all the major newspapers and in small-town newspapers
throughout the country, *The Disinherited* was greeted with wonder, curiosity, and interest by both conservative and leftist critics.[1] Almost
overnight Conroy was propelled into the public's attention both in the
United States and abroad. The country had experienced the Depression for nearly four years; reviewers welcomed a book that gave an insider's view of its effects on working-class people. Their curiosity extended beyond the content of the book to its author. Who was this
worker who wrote and how was he able to do it? seemed to be the question on many reviewers' minds.

"I have no idea," Dorothy Canfield wrote in *Book-of-the-Month Club*

News, "what kind of a compromise between manual work and author-ship has produced Jack Conroy. But his account of the hard, but by no means always gloomy, life of the vigorous son of a coal miner has the very ring of truth."[2] Reporters came to Moberly to discover for their readers an authentic backwoods bard. One photo, widely circulated, shows Jack posed in a field, tethering a cow with one hand and hold-ing a pitchfork with the other.[3] Jack, ever-obliging, humorously con-sented. The cow belonged to a neighbor; Jack knew next to nothing about farm work. If one examines the newspaper photo carefully, the phoniness of the pose is apparent: the cow was already tethered to a post, and no farmer holds a pitchfork with the tines pointing upward.[4] No matter. Readers had their Shakespeare in overalls.[5]

By 1934, prolonged hard times had awakened in the public's mind sympathy for the worker; and if sympathy was not forthcoming, then the outbreak of violent strikes that year forced the country's attention on the plight of the laborer. Roosevelt, who had won the recent elec-tion in a landslide, had promised, after all, to give consideration to the "forgotten man at the bottom of the economic pyramid." The chang-ing temper of the country altered the horizon of expectations—the set of unconsciously held assumptions at the moment in history when a text is read. Readers were perhaps now ready to acknowledge the existence, if not the importance, of realistic accounts of working-class life; and the appearance of books like *The Disinherited* prepared the way for the reception of ultimately better-known novels such as Steinbeck's *The Grapes of Wrath.* The "success" of Jack's first novel, then, must encom-pass its effect in shaping the consciousness of both its critics and read-ers, given the considerable attention it received. The significance of *The Disinherited* derives from the novel's figuration of its author-worker, who managed to break the silence imposed upon working-class expression by the dominant culture. Finally, it is revealing to study the history of the reception of *The Disinherited,* for it underscores the fact that chang-ing ideologies and institutions affect the reception of a literary work over time, a point I plan to return to in examining both the history of Jack's recognition and the reception of his writing.[6]

The Disinherited was hardly a runaway best-seller when it first came out. In 1933 appeared a romance called *Anthony Adverse* by a little-known author, Hervey Allen, which sold 275,000 copies the first year despite its hefty cost (in Depression dollars) and length of a thousand pages. Jack's first novel, by contrast, had sold only 2,700 copies by April of 1935. These figures do not tell all, however. Books like *The Disinherited,* like maga-zines, were passed around a great deal because the readers they attracted could not afford to buy them; and of course readers borrowed copies from libraries.[7] After all, Sherwood Anderson's *Winesburg, Ohio* sold fewer than 5,000 copies in its first issue, and Jean Toomer's *Cane* sold less than 500; yet these were two novels that eventually became classics of American literature. Erskine Caldwell, who had an advance copy of Jack's book, wrote Jack encouragingly: "I'm convinced that 'The Disinherited' will live a long life. . . . it is a book of the people. . . . That's the kind of book I'd like to write. . . ."[8] The timing of publication had seemed perfect; and the great strikes of 1934 bore witness to the conclusion of *The Disinherited*, in which a farmer-labor alliance seems near. Yet Jack was discouraged, convinced that people did not want to read about hard times in the midst of the worst Depression the country had ever known. In *The Disinherited* two starving men spend their last pennies on "soda pop." People indulged in delusion and sought to escape through popular forms of entertainment. Exhibiting an early manifestation of a self-ascribed condition he later called "only a bridesmaid, never the bride," Jack felt sure that impediments of some kind or another would deny his work the larger audiences it deserved. He criticized Covici-Friede for not marketing the book sufficiently.[9] Pulling him the other way was a "refusal to succeed," a conviction that to remain on the margin was the way things had to be for a working-class author. Pausing after such a thought, and raising one hand like an old-fashioned orator, Jack liked to quote the stanza from Sheamus O'Sheel that begins:

> They went forth to battle, but they always fell;
> Their eyes were fixed above the sullen shields;
> Nobly they fought and bravely but not well,
> And sank heart-wounded by a subtle spell.[10]

On the one hand, the dominant literary system promoted its own values and ideology with no space for worker-writers; on the other, literary success posed risks for the worker-writer who strove to remain true to the continuity of radical convictions.

For the left, the publication of *The Disinherited* was viewed as an event important to the cultural movement, despite reservations on the part of critics disappointed by its neglect of certain proletarian conventions and the protagonist's fondness for romantic poetry. Neither of these "flaws" appeared in Dan Rico's comic-strip version of *The Disinherited* appearing in the Communist paper the *Daily Worker*. The left promoted Jack as an example of the indigenous American radical, a protoproletarian, a WASP worker. They might have used Meridel Le Sueur, "but she was a woman," Jack said, referring to the Party's "male orientation."[11] Conroy seemed like a left-leaning publicist's dream come true: an Irish immigrant's son in the Midwest, born in a mining camp, a veteran of union struggles at factory gates and unemployment lines. Most proletarian writing had come from urban ghettos. Here was proof that proletarian literature could be created by real rank-and-file workers. Moreover, Jack looked entirely the part of the heroic proletarian with his solid build, square jaw, bright eyes, and shock of brown hair. The name "Jack" had a working-class ring to it, like Vince, Gus, or Harry. Michael Gold wrote an ecstatic "love letter" to "Dear Friend and Comrade Jack," published in *New Masses*, in which he praised Jack as a leader of the proletarian literary movement; "graduates of steel mills like yourself begin to write novels and poems, something great has begun. . . . You know this life, Jack, as well as a Hemingway knows the atmosphere of fifty Paris bistros. . . . I can smell your rubber mill, and have been bored to madness by the work-sodden people in your rooming houses."[12] Several weeks later he was wondering outloud in the *Daily Worker* whether Jack might fear criticism from the establishment. What mainline critics were saying, however, about Jack's first novel gave no reason for fear or, as Gold suggested, feelings of inferiority such as Jack London experienced vis-à-vis the bourgeoisie.

Conservative and radical reviewers both embraced *The Disinherited* enthusiastically. John Dos Passos praised the honesty of Jack's writing: "an absolutely solid, unfaked piece of narrative." Dorothy Canfield drew attention to the authenticity of workers' speech in Conroy's first book: "The talk of working men, chatting idly together, is wonderfully vivid and sounds truer than any we have had till now." Conroy had avoided "the taint of propagandism," wrote Margaret Wallace in the *New York Times Book Review*.[13] Clifton Fadiman in the *New Yorker* echoed Wallace's comment: "The book has no particular form, being in this respect closely imitative of the life of the migratory worker who is its hero. But the atmosphere rings true. There is no forced proletarianism about it, nor is there that youthful Hemingway romanticism which sees the depressed worker merely as a picturesque tough."[14] Mencken cited the vividness of workplace detail, allowing that Conroy was "less successful when he comes to deal with the more complicated relationships and the more complex individuals."[15] Whit Burnett, editor of *Story*, called Jack "an American Gorky," as did several other reviewers, including J. Hoptner of the *Philadelphia Record*. The *Los Angeles Post-Record* reviewer said that Conroy "speaks for a people who are inarticulate as a rule; whose voice is only heard in times of desperation."[16] And Granville Hicks offered an explanation: "There is no question why it is so good a book: it grows out of Conroy's own experience as a worker."[17] In the minds of most reviewers, the book's strengths lay in honesty, authenticity, the value of first-hand experience, and the feeling that Jack had faithfully rendered his workers through their own characteristic idioms and attitudes. Criticism that the plot was weak was answered by the observation that worker's lives are not plotted in any way; it is characteristic of the work world that figures appear then disappear; the continuity lies in the shared fortunes of workers faced with economic distress and personal misfortune.

Most of the reviewers, both mainstream and leftist, seemed confused in judging *The Disinherited* according to traditional novelistic criteria. The disjointed quality of the narrative, the uneven characterizations, the different levels of language spoken by the narrator were viewed as the rough edges of a first novel that, because of its fresh and vigorous portrayal of working-class subjects, deserved to be read. Evident in most of the reviews was an unfamiliarity in dealing with narratives that fall outside traditional novelistic boundaries, for example, those that exist on the margins of literature and nonliterature. Overblown praise of inferior proletarian novels affected the reception of novels on working-class subjects. Standards of evaluation were constantly debated. Gold's own views were scarcely consistent since returning from Kharkov. Viewed in terms of either dominant or proletarian models, *The Disinherited* eluded categories. Unfamiliarity and confusion led, in some cases, to wrongheaded judgments. Mike Gold scolded Jack for what Gold considered to be an unacceptable transgression of class distinctions: allowing his protagonist to quote romantic poetry was an indication that he felt inferior to the bourgeois world.[18] In the minds of most proletarian critics, the boundaries between worker's and middle-class worlds should be clearly drawn. That Jack seemed to transgress these borders confused Gold and others who apparently did not perceive that the ambivalent status of the worker-writer was in fact one of his main subjects.

The largely positive reception of his novel and his sudden national recognition intensified certain fundamental contradictions at this point in Conroy's literary career. For the first time in his life, Jack was presented with the opportunity, it seemed, to become a literary personage, a professional man of letters. Success beckoned. The dilemma was not whether to abandon his day labor jobs and live from the earnings of his writings—he would have welcomed that. The contradictions lay in the question of status. Recognition meant disjoining worker from writer, the status that up to this point in Jack's life had been undeniably his. Now a different choice lay before him; to become a professional man of letters would mean abandoning this status, and in a more fundamental sense, it would mean trading the intimate terms on which he lived as a worker with other workers for some kind of disreputable success.

The dilemma was this: economic need dictated that he spend most of his waking hours in laboring jobs—or preoccupied with finding work. The prospect of becoming a professional writer, on the other hand, offered escape from manual labor. But to accede to the status of professional writer was to abandon his dream of a workers' culture in favor of a literary career ruled by vertical structures of prominence in which writers strive for reputation by producing best-sellers. Yet the worker's culture he envisioned rejected these very notions. The *Anvil* was a forum for new writing and writers characterized by diversity and by horizontality, returning the power, as it were, to the producer. As editor, he hoped to create an alternative literary system that would circumvent the arborescent structures of the dominant culture. Embracing success, on the other hand, would engage him in an literary system ruled by publishers and critics who, as authority figures, had the power to make or break a writer. Their approval would engender competitiveness among his fellow writer-friends. And one's writing would become simply a commodity sold to the publisher, as independent artisans sell their products in the marketplace. Jack knew all too well the vulnerability of the individual artisan; power, security, and social justice lay in collectivity, not in individualist cottage labor. His experience with publishers in attempting to place *The Disinherited* convinced him that writing was no different from any other laboring trade in this respect. Bosses had the power and could dictate terms as arbitrarily as did the absentee Smith heirs whose invisible hand ruled Monkey Nest coal camp. But the miners had organized and fought back.

Jack had a horror of the isolated individual exposed to ruthless capitalist interest. Writing was a vocation that might free him of money problems; yet he had little taste for the jealous competitiveness that seemed to characterize the writer's existence. It was a dilemma that Jack never quite resolved in his mind. Writers need to help one another, like the Monkey Nest miners, for their own mutual benefit. Proletarian and radical writers must seek mutual acceptance among themselves given their relative isolation from the dominant systems of literary production. Comradeship, not rivalry, was the basis of any proletarian culture worth its name. Departures from this standard struck Jack very hard, as if the offenders had committed acts of disloyalty. He expected such behavior from the bosses but found it unacceptable among fellow toilers in the writing trade.

Thus, James T. Farrell's hostile review in *Nation* magazine appeared to him as a kind of perfidy. Jack felt that Farrell, a fellow journeyman writer, misappropriated the review forum in order to display his merits as a critic and thereby elevate his own status at Jack's expense. If so, it was a reputation cheaply purchased. Farrell wrote that the "younger American writers" valued "sincerity" over art. "Literature," he said, "demands re-creation, which is an arduous process; it demands characters that are human beings and not mere fictions."[19] "Mr. Conroy," he continued, "is extremely careless, if not slapdash, in his method and in his characterizations. . . . [He] has acquired many facts, and his American idiom is authentic. He has chosen a field of American life that is rich in literary possibilities. As reporting, his work is satisfactory. As a novel, it is superficial. He has described a number of things. He has re-created almost nothing." Farrell's churlish tone and his pretense in lecturing to his readers annoyed Jack. The two midwesterners at the start of their careers as writers had much in common and good reason to give one another encouragement and support, but Farrell had made them *frères-enemis*.

Conroy and Farrell did not actually meet until 1934, but each knew the other's work since both were midwesterners who had come up through the same little-magazine circuit. Like Jack, Farrell had first published in the Haldeman-Julius publications.[20] In his correspondence with Henry Haldeman, son of E. Haldeman-Julius, Farrell told how he had been brought up on the "Little Blue Books," an admission that revealed the impecunious circumstances of his youth as well as his love of reading. He did not mention that he had gone to the University of Chicago. Abe Aaron, a post-office worker and John Reed Club member in Chicago, had known Farrell as a student colleague at the university. Aaron wrote Jack attempting to explain Farrell's behavior soon after the review appeared. Farrell, Aaron said, was an eccentric, a "bohemian" who was "a little off his nut as regarded the C.P." "'I am an aesthete,' Aaron recalled Farrell saying as a student, "'I don't believe the C.P. speaks the language of the American worker. . . .'"[21] Conroy's and Farrell's earliest critical exercises appeared in *Earth* magazine in 1930.[22] Both published in the *American Mercury* and their stories appeared in the same issue of *Pagany* in 1932. Farrell's story is of a boxer who dies after a fight; Jack's is of a worker who, judged too old to continue in his job, is discharged and slips quietly from life. Their first novels were displayed side by side in a Brentano's bookstore in 1934, where Dee Brown noticed them.[23]

Both were Irish-Americans (Farrell was slightly younger) from poor families, the one from an urban lower-middle-class Irish milieu in Chicago, the other the son of a miner, a lapsed Catholic. Temperamentally, Farrell was feisty, contentious, fiercely independent, egoistic, and devoted to the writer's craft. Conroy was sanguine, at times melancholic, equally devoted to the writer's craft, and generous of his time as an editor. The decisive experience for Farrell had been urbanization with its tenements, street gangs, and thwarted ambitions; for Conroy it was factory life, a difficult but happy childhood in a mining community, union activity, and migratory labor. Each author portrayed as his central figure a young man growing into consciousness; yet while Farrell saw political implications in rape fantasies and violence, Conroy combed the broken fragments of proletarian existence to reconstruct a lost community. Both writers possessed unusual gifts of observation and an ear for the rhythms of working-class speech. And both portrayed without embellishment the drab, self-deluded existence of unskilled workers. But while Farrell's characters, stifled in their will to power, move consistently and inevitably toward some failed purpose, Conroy's figures, like Brueghel's peasants, are scattered over the canvas, their common lot, scarcely grasped by the inarticulate, unawakened workers, providing the thematic unity. Conroy's "reporting," to use Farrell's expression, is a form of literary ethnography, a creative transcription of orality, folklore, and workplace local knowledge. Farrell disliked proletarian fiction and said so in his talks with Nathanael West.[24] Conroy was cast as the standard-bearer of the proletarian novel when *The Disinherited* appeared; perhaps that had something to do with Farrell's response. Or perhaps, as Herbert Klein (a Davenport radical who had gone to New York to edit *New Theatre*) wrote Jack, it had more to do with the fact that Farrell did not want to do the review in the first place but gave in finally when the *Nation* editor insisted. This would explain the edginess and cavilling of Farrell's review.[25] Ironically, George Milburn, an Oklahoma writer and frequent contributor to the *American Mercury* who drew upon orality and folklore in his own writing, had wanted to do the review for the *Nation*. For some reason, however, the editors gave the review to the reluctant Farrell.[26] In short, a bad editorial decision may have precipitated the famous literary feud.

Friends came to Jack's defense; Jack always seemed to attract people who wanted to help or protect him. Erskine Caldwell wrote after the new year, "Farrell swung a sledgehammer at me several months ago, too. What's wrong with that guy?"[27] Grace Wellington, a former *Rebel Poet* contributor, commiserated: "The review isn't really vicious—but pointless and contradictory. One is forced to recall that Farrell also writes of the proletariat! Perhaps a new lance in the field cannot be borne with tranquility, eh? I still am inclined to believe that the wish to be 'different' and therefore 'profound' had much to do with the general tenor of the review in question."[28] Walt Carmon, who had helped Farrell get his first novel published at Vanguard, wrote Jack that politically Farrell seemed to be moving in the wrong direction. Hearing that Horace Gregory offered faint praise in his review of *The Disinherited*, Carmon commented: "What prizearses they both turned out to be."[29] He then wrote Farrell and told him so.

When another young midwestern writer, Edward Dahlberg, made a gratuitous remark about Jack in a review of Farrell's new book, Jack smelled a rat. In the review, Dahlberg wrote: "Unlike Jack Conroy's prose, which is the remnants of writing that has been done in the past five to seven years, Farrell's Americanese is enormously skillful and deeply fused."[30] This from a young novelist who called James Joyce a "counterfeit titan," dismissed the writing of Dreiser, Caldwell, and Dos Passos (and Conroy), and called a Waldo Frank novel a "major novel of our times."[31] What had Dahlberg in his craw?

On the heels of the Dahlberg review of Farrell, Farrell responded with an overwritten, flattering review of a Dahlberg novel, praising its technique and imagery. Jack suspected a mutual admiration society; rumor was that Farrell and Dahlberg were good friends. The Farrells had spent Thanksgiving day with Dahlberg in his New York apartment after their return from Europe in 1932.[32] Farrell and Dahlberg seemed resolved to nettle Jack. Granville Hicks wrote Jack pointing out Dahlberg's "habit of using reviews as a vehicle for nasty cracks."[33] Stanley Burnshaw of *New Masses* suggested that Orrick Johns start a letter-writing campaign in *New Masses* protesting the two disobliging reviews.[34] The first sally in the counterattack against Farrell and Dahlberg came from Henry George Weiss, an ex–Rebel Poet suffering from tuberculosis in the Arizona desert, in a long apologia for Jack in *New Masses*.[35] Dee Brown, later famous for his American Indian chronicles, seconded Weiss's letter.

Jack struck back at Farrell in a review, appearing in *Partisan Review* in early summer 1934, of Robert Cantwell's *Land of Plenty*. Responding to Farrell's criticism in his review of *The Disinherited* that "younger American writers" were not creating characters who lived (Dahlberg made a similar claim, naming Dos Passos and others), Conroy wrote facetiously that modern critics (that is, Farrell and Dahlberg) were somewhat more liberal-minded than in Shakespeare's time when workers were depicted either as "fools or rogues." "Poolroom bums and budding gangsters planning 'gang shaggings' and yearning after the anatomical projections and crevices of 'bitches' and 'pigs' may pass muster as legitimate guinea pigs for the scalpel of an 'artist' [an obvious reference to Farrell]. But let a writer venture into the affirmative side of the class struggle, portray a heroic Communist or worker, try to catch the atmosphere of a strike or a factory, or the revolt of the oppressed, and anguished howls immediately arise, briny tears flow over the violated canons of 'art.'"[36] Jack's broadside struck its intended target. When Farrell told Dahlberg of the "personal and slanderous attack," Dahlberg complained that the New York John Reed Club comrades were responsible for printing the review. Farrell and Dahlberg were not going to reply to it.[37]

Alan Wald in his biography of Farrell suggests that Stalinists in the Party had an active hand in the feud from the start.[38] Conroy's correspondence supports this assertion, but with an important qualification: personal differences initiated the feuding, evolving into ideological side-taking, rather than the other way around.[39] True, Orrick Johns, in the Stalinist camp at the time, assured Jack that he would not lack support in the fight with Dahlberg and Farrell.[40] Yet, Erskine Caldwell and others who rushed to Jack's side had no Stalinist axe to grind in the matter. Granville Hicks made an attempt to downplay the affair. "Farrell, by the way," he wrote Jack, "isn't a bad guy. I've seen him twice in recent weeks, and on the whole I like him. I doubt, however, if he has much critical ability."[41] Moreover, by the end of May, Stanley Burnshaw of *New Masses* wrote to Jack cautioning him to forget the whole thing.[42] Such feuding served only to undermine the movement. Despite his criticisms of the Party's cultural policies, Farrell contributed to *New Masses,* the *Daily Worker,* and *Partisan Review* and was an active collaborator in the movement.[43] Furthermore, Farrell had helped the Party in its efforts to win over talented writers and intellectuals. Weiss's supportive letter to *New Masses* had made important points, but additional letters in defense of Jack would give the appearance of "logrolling," Burnshaw wrote Conroy.[44]

Burnshaw's letter irritated Jack, particularly the reference to logrolling. Miffed too because Burnshaw had unjustly accused him of sending on to John Alroy (one of the Davenport radicals) a letter he had received from Burnshaw, Jack replied indignantly that the controversy lay deeper than partisanship within the movement. "It is the difference between an exotic, imported from the Left Bank of the Seine, literary style [Dahlberg], a negative, defeatist one, as typified by Farrell and Dahlberg, and an affirmative one, expressed by writers who are invariably belittled by both Farrell and Dahlberg."[45] The misunderstanding ended when Alroy wrote Burnshaw suggesting that he apologize to Jack for the wrongful allegation concerning the letter, pointing out that Burnshaw after all had invited letters to *New Masses* in defense of Conroy. Burnshaw, anxious to repair any damage to the movement, obliged. There were indications, after all, that Dahlberg was now moving left. His new novel, *Those Who Perish,* was revolutionary fiction, Burnshaw reported in a review several months later; Dahlberg, who had previously belittled proletarian fiction, might be experiencing a change of heart. The important thing, Burnshaw felt, was to avoid "expense of spirit" on the left.[46]

Farrell's independent attitude in the face of leftist currents in the Party was in these years not a great deal different in substance from Jack's own; both supported Party aims but balked at attempts to impose orthodox standards. Farrell was outspoken at times in asserting his independence; Jack kept his reservations about Party discipline and policies to himself while going his own way. Conroy's independence as editor was a factor in the loss of the *Anvil;* yet he never openly blamed the Stalinist wing of the Party. Farrell, on the other hand, openly broke with Stalinists in the Party, garnering Mike Gold's censure for his review of Odets's *Paradise Lost* in *Partisan Review.*[47] When the William Phillips–Philip Rahv axis of the early *Partisan Review*—Rahv and Phillips had earlier been ardent participants in the Stalinist wing of the Party—made known their new-found conversion to Trotskyist ideals and admiration for modernist literary technique, Farrell provided them a working paper (*A Note on Literary Criticism*) for their change of heart.

Tensions from the feuding carried over into the American Writers' Congress in April 1935. Farrell sensed that Conroy's supporters composed "a kind of anti-Farrell gallery." Farrell enjoyed poking fun at them, goading them to react.[48] Farrell's mischievous antics, such as prompting the premature closing of a session by leading the audience in singing "The Internationale," did not soften the antagonism. The publication of Farrell's *A Note on Literary Criticism* in May 1936 signaled an ideological rupture between Conroy and Farrell, whose differences up to this time had seemed more like a donnybrook between two headstrong Irishmen. The feud continued for years.

How then do we explain the appearance of Farrell's story in the final issue of *Anvil,* in the fall of 1935? While I treat this question later, it is sufficient to note here that Walter Snow had taken over most of the editorial duties by that point and was anxious to publish well-known writers. Jack had little part in the decision.

The Chicago bookseller Stuart Brent recalled Nelson Algren and Jack in Chicago in the 1940s mimicking Farrell. "Nelson Algren and Jack Conroy could perform a remarkable duet on the subject of James T. Farrell, Conroy in a broad Irish accent, Algren in a clipped, half-muttering manner. I never learned the personal source of their animosity, but the name of Farrell had the magic to channel all their hostilities and frustrations into a fountain of pure malice. It was wonderful."[49] Algren remembered Farrell's negative report to the publisher of Algren's first novel.[50] The feud became an extraliterary enterprise involving satire and hoaxes. Farrell caricatured Conroy as Pat Devlin in *Yet Other Waters,* misquoting Jack's American Writers' speech; Jack featured Farrell as a drunken, child-beating father in a melodrama staged in Chicago, and he orchestrated a bogus letter published in the *New Republic.*

The Farrell-Dahlberg-Conroy affair sent Jack on a *fausse piste,* absorbing energies that might have been better spent elsewhere. Hadn't Erskine Caldwell and Josephine Herbst told him to dismiss criticism and go his own way? It seems now, with the advantage time and reflection give, that Farrell's and Dahlberg's remarks were merely random sparks thrown off by colliding views on proletarian fiction, a debate without clearly drawn issues. The fact that Conroy's name and work figured in the debate deeply textured (and distorted) the reception and interpretation of *The Disinherited.*[51]

* * *

To the midwestern radicals the so-called "proletarian debate" was a confused and confusing *dialogue de sourds.* Little magazines abounded with articles theorizing, extolling, or criticizing proletarian literature. Yet the term remained open, a monkey wrench to shore up or dismantle the coming cultural revolution. No one was able to give the term a satisfactory definition; as a movement, proletarian literature never attained unity of purpose or aim; as an ideology it was confusing to radicals like Jack who were impatient with word slinging; they associated it with the eastern radicals ignorant of how things really were in the heartland. The midwesterners tended to look to works of the past when praising what was good for proletarian literature. Zola, Nexö, London, and Rolland were ill-suited, however, as models for a proletarian literature that, according to early IURW directives, "ordered" writers to "depart for the provinces to work under the command of the regional headquarters. . . ."[52] Snow and Kalar, for instance, thought that Zola's *Germinal* was quite simply the best proletarian novel ever written.[53] Conroy admired Gorki, Zola, Dreiser, and Nexö, not for any "proletarian" qualities but because they dealt truthfully with subjects that touched the lives of common people.

As editor, it was sometimes painful to Jack to read the submissions in response to his call for a worker's literature. Jack distinguished between good and bad writing, no matter by what title it went, proletarian or otherwise. The main issues, he felt, concerning proletarian fiction were two-fold: its truthfulness to working-class experience, and the question of readership. In an essay intended to encourage new writers, Jack cited James Rorty, who said that *Uncle Tom's Cabin* "would have been a great deal more effective if it had been written by a slave able to transform into words what he actually *felt* and *knew*."[54] "The 'Uncle Tom's Cabin' of American industry is yet to be written," Conroy added. "I venture to predict that it will be written by a worker or ex-worker rather than by a sympathetic observer like Miss Brody [author of *Nobody Starves*], who, despite her compassion, cannot achieve a full-dimensioned portraiture possible for one more intimately acquainted with the sub- ject."[55] The great transformative novel of the American worker must differ from the rags-to-riches model of a Horatio Alger success story; it must not end in bourgeois respectability. American Marxist critics in the early 1930s were exploring along similar lines, arguing the question of authorship. Few proletarian authors possessed working-class creden- tials. Were proletarian novels to be written by nonproletarians?

Critical standards for proletarian literature were subjects of consid- erable debate and discussion in the John Reed clubs and in publica- tions of the left. Hazards lay in the path of those who defined proletar- ian fiction as antonymous to bourgeois literature, posing a duality of binary opposites. According to Jane Caplan (in another context), such an opposition "works only because each term's identity has been artifi- cially stabilized by repressing what it actually has in common with the other."[56] Such a duality neglects commonalities and similarities, setting one against the other by suppressing what one has in common with the other. This fallacy deeply affected the debate on proletarian literature that consumed so much time and magazine space in the early 1930s. In the ideologically driven debates, novels of inferior literary quality sometimes received overblown praise from the left. Brody's *Nobody Starves* is a dreary chronicle of hard luck and bad times in Detroit auto factories that turns compassion for the worker's plight into quirky melo- drama. The sales of most proletarian fiction never matched the claims of sympathetic critics and promoters. Clara Weatherwax's *Marching! Marching!*, awarded the prize for best novel by *New Masses* in 1935, was an easy target for detractors like Farrell, who said in a *New York Her- ald-Tribune* review that the title should have been "Stumbling, Stum- bling."[57] Mary McCarthy roasted Weatherwax's awkward novel of class struggle "with her damnable impudence."[58] The Weatherwax novel nonetheless represented much of what most of its sympathetic readers found acceptable in proletarian fiction by 1935: the desire to shape read- ing tastes and to attribute workers' suffering to "the system." But no proletarian novel ignited the aspirations of an oppressed class; no war was fought to raise exploited workers from wage slavery. In the *Satur- day Review of Literature*, Mencken dismissed the whole lot of proletari- an writers, suggesting that someone outside the proletarian movement would have to write the "great proletarian novel." "There are, of course, some among them who actually issue from the one-crop farms and steel mills, and thus come by their esthetic theory honestly, but they are not numerous. . . ."[59] By 1934, it was clear to Conroy, Robert Cantwell, and Louis Adamic, among others, that the central question in revolutionary and proletarian writing was not so much who wrote it, or even how it was told, but who would read it. At least one magazine queried authors: "For whom do you write?"

For authors such as Cantwell and Adamic, as well as for a number of communication statisticians, the question of readership revolved around claims about working-class readership. Adamic concluded that workers read *True Romance*, not *Nobody Starves*. Cantwell countered Adamic's claim, arguing that the issue was what books American workers were *not* reading (and why), concluding that a large potential audience of working-class readers existed.[60] But the discussion of readership in terms of numbers or potential numbers hit wide of the mark. The real problem facing worker-writers, Conroy suggested in a Socialist magazine called *Call of Youth*, was that "worker-writers are hampered and stultified by the strictures of publishers, who almost invariably demand certain elements, such as 'sex interest,' and exciting plot, no vital criticism of the social order, 'suspense,' and the other conventional appurtenances of fiction. . . ."[61] Hampered by publishers' demands for fiction that will sell, worker-writers must also face critics who "emphasize their faults—faults often due to the necessity of leading a dual life."[62] The question of publication, critical acceptance, and readership, then, were contradictions linked to a worker-writer's "dual life." What he meant by this, he wrote, were the actual material conditions in which working-writing is produced.

But a further consideration involves the general reader and the literary marketplace. The general reader's attraction to fiction issuing from working-class experience derives not from political sympathy necessarily but from its testimonial value, its "witnessing" of human conflict and response. Such was traditionally the case for worker narratives, tales of rural life, and exposés of the "other half."[63] The problems of proletarian literature were framed by the reception of literature of testimonial character. For literature to possess authentic testimonial value, it must preserve the accents and character of the "witness" writing it or furnishing the content to the writer. Workers or farmers as a class do not ordinarily produce literature; but they have their own collective memory that is expressed orally.[64] Documentary writing involving first-person narratives—as we know it today, for example, in Studs Terkel's *Race* (1992)—scarcely existed in the early 1930s or before. To attract a publisher such literature required rewriting, recasting the material into an acceptable format and language; in short, it implied literary techniques. Such transformations diminished the value of its testimony in order to inscribe it in the dominant literary system. Its readership consisted principally of educated readers, not workers and the poor. Publication within the dominant literary system exposes a work to criticism that tends to judge it according to traditional novelistic standards, ignoring unfamiliar cultural coding inscribed in the text. The worker-writer is pulled between the desire for testimonial authenticity and the demands made to satisfy publication within the dominant channels of communication. Such contradictions were not resolved during proletarian fiction's brief tenure in the 1930s. Nonetheless, they lay at the heart of Conroy's literary enterprise as worker-writer and editor. Making the thirteen sketches and short stories that constituted the *Urtext* of *The Disinherited* into a novel was not only a concession to narrative interest but a requirement to fit literary (and ideological) norms, construed variously by Seaver, the Covici-Friede editors, and Granville Hicks. There were many "faults" in the result. "Back of it all," Jack wrote, "there's always the impediments of fatigue from the daily job and the difficulties imposed by lack of education and facilities for publication."[65]

The Disinherited immediately attracted readers and drew praise from critics despite its departure from traditional practice in the novel form. At least one critic tried to justify praising Jack's first novel despite its lapses in literary technique. "The strength and sincerity of the effort," Selden Rodman wrote, "as well as the experience and hardship unfolded in the tale, must give to more than one critic an inferiority complex, a feeling that he is quibbling over aesthetic abstractions."[66] A number of critics seemed perplexed in deciding whether to view the rough edges of *The Disinherited* as literary flaws or as compelling, realistic evidence of the untidyness of the experience portrayed. Robert Forsythe, a critic for *New Masses*, counseled proletarian writers to forget the novel form altogether, arguing that a forthright story of proletarian life needs no embroidered literary treatment.[67] The implication was that proletarian literature might evolve from the varieties of first-person narrative and simple forms within the reach of the untrained, unlettered worker. It was a form of condescension, perhaps unintended, implying nonetheless that between traditional literary practice and simple forms of narrative nothing existed.

Jack had no intention of abandoning literary form and precedents. In praising Robert Cantwell's *Land of Plenty* (1934), for instance, he acknowledged its effectiveness in employing traditional novelistic practice to tell the story of a plywood-factory strike. It was just such a novel that would win workers to fiction dwelling on social issues. "I know

Robert Cantwell's factory," he wrote. "I can smell and see it, and every character in *The Land of Plenty* will be recognized as an old friend by anyone who has learned about workers by being one, who felt the itch that sweat and sawdust bring, who has hated a high-balling foreman or thrown a brick at a scab."[68] In Jack's view, Cantwell's achievement was rare. The domain of worker literature was largely unexplored and full of pitfalls. "The problem of writing about factory work from personal and deep-seated knowledge," he said in a lecture several years after the publication of *The Disinherited*, "seems almost an insoluble one. Even sympathetic writers of the bourgeoisie or white collar class frequently get a distorted picture. They picture a worker as a man ten feet tall and five feet broad, devouring whole sheep at a gulp and lustily guzzling oceans of beer and other liquids. . . . It is better," he offered, "for middle class writers, perhaps, to idealize the worker than to burlesque him or pity him." But the best hope for an "authentic working-class portrait," he concluded, was the "worker who remained at his job and writes about it in his leisure time, providing he has the inherent talent. . . . But such combinations are not ordinarily found. Factory workers with the will to write and the ability dream of escape rather than mirroring their jobs and shop mates in literature."[69]

To learn to write, Cantwell had read the prefaces of Henry James while working in a lumber mill. Jack's method of composition in writing *The Disinherited* involved the montage of separate pieces that had their basis in orality, folklore, popular culture, and worker narrative. The essential elements of literature about workers, Jack reasoned, was "insight and feeling" and a sensitivity toward language. One who is able to write from inside the worker's experience, who possesses insight and feeling concerning workers' experience, their characteristic attitudes and locutions, presumably might, through the use of the first-person point of view, produce an authentic picture. The primacy of work, the resources of collective memory and orality, the folk view of experience rendered through workers' sociolect, and the linguistic features of working-class life creatively transcribed were characteristics of Jack's writing that he referred to as "vivifying the contemporary fact"[70] and being a "witness to the times."[71] They represented a renewal of realism, a conscious rejection of the determinism of naturalistic fiction, and an attempt to reproduce the feeling of working-class life as Jack knew it without embellishment or sentimentality.[72]

* * *

The early draft of *The Disinherited* was assembled from its thirteen constituent pieces into a literary montage.[73] Jack lined his stories up and had each recite like a proletarian *Chorus Line*. After many rejections, however, it became apparent that his task was to orchestrate the voices, tracing the progress through a narrator-self in discovering his own "voice." Certain structural and aesthetic problems presented themselves in undertaking this task, and it soon became clear, through publishers' rejections, that Jack had not solved them adequately.

Montage was a structural feature of Dos Passos's *1919* (1930). Carl Sandburg's *The People, Yes* (1936) assembles slang sayings, jokes, proverbs, and so forth in a long poem. The documentaries and "living newspapers" that soon appeared with WPA sponsorship employed versions of *Stationentechnik*. In a sense, Conroy's *Anvil* is a single montage of worker narratives and sketches unified by its editorial aims, a composite expression of Depression hopes and failures. The modern novel had its origins in the episodic picaresque novel, which grew out of conditions of economic turmoil, the breakdown of community, and the deprivation of lower classes in society. The picaresque novel raises questions of narrative reliability, however, quite inappropriate to the "tradition"—worker narrative, orality—in which *The Disinherited* was written.[74] There are picaresque elements in *The Disinherited*—social commentary, the loss of the father, the good and bad "masters," mobility, the question of "rising" on the economic scale—but these are likewise elements of worker autobiography and worker narrative, which constitute the subtexts of Conroy's novel.[75] One of the main points I wish to make here is that any analysis of Conroy's writing must acknowledge the subliterary traditions of orality and worker expression from which it derives.[76] So much binds Conroy's storytelling to Walter Benjamin's description of Leskov. There is no individual subject; *The Disinherited* is composed of tales reflecting their collective origin in the workplace. "The storyteller," Benjamin argues, "takes what he tells from experience—his own or that reported by others."[77] "A great storyteller will always be rooted in the people, primarily in a milieu of craftsmen."[78] The notion of the traditional storyteller as artisan, a collector, drawing from others' experiences and his own, possessed of aural memory, describes Conroy better than any conventional literary classification. To understand *The Disinherited* we must take into account the nature and origins of its subtexts, which are uniquely related to working-class experience and history. Similarly, black literature draws upon preliterary, vernacular forms of expression such as slave narratives and oral tales.[79]

For instance, "Boyhood in a Coal Town," one of the pieces that Jack reworked into *The Disinherited*, is a starting-out-to-work type of worker narrative familiar in stories of apprenticeship, including those of Benjamin Franklin and Samuel Clemens.[80] A narrative account of a young worker's introduction to the world of work is nearly *de rigeur* in worker autobiography. Characteristic of worker autobiography in general, according to David Vincent, is a desire to communicate experience circumscribed by political and social realities that, in the process of change, threaten to obliterate the past.[81] Worker autobiography grows out of the collective experience of a group, expressed through oral recollections that, unless they are transcribed, will eventually disappear.[82] Worker autobiography shares with other "autobiographical acts"[83] the perception of life as a process. But process in worker autobiography seldom has to do with personal development as such, that is, the introspective search for selfhood. Rather it records the author's desire to communicate a life lived, the struggle for dignity and social justice, the joys seized despite hardship, all this within a communal setting. It involves a description of distance traveled rather than a quest for meaning. Historical events are narrowly circumscribed for the worker-autobiographer, having to do mainly with the struggle to find (or keep) one's job, memorable instances of labor conflict such as strikes, and in the case of labor militants, the story of one's involvement in labor's struggle for social and political emancipation.

If autobiography typically poses itself in oppositional terms, confronting the self with society, with the aim of emancipating the autonomous self, then worker autobiography inscribes this struggle in much narrower terms, usually in the conflict between labor and capital. Of course, the type of autobiographical expression is varied among workers, and for every militant worker who got into print, there is at least one account of the rise from humble origins to respectability through diligence, abstinence, thrift, and piety.

In America, autobiographies of working-class leaders, such as John Brophy and John L. Lewis, have found mainstream publishers on the basis of their participation in events that, in retrospect, were deemed significant in labor history rather than because their stories had intrinsic value as such. For the same reason, militant worker-intellectuals, such as William Z. Foster and James Boggs, are published by leftist presses. The heavily edited "Life Stories of Undistinguished Americans," published by Hamilton Holt in his *Independent* magazine at the beginning of the century, selected narratives for their story value, not for their historical worth; as a consequence, they are what Lejeune terms "stories excluded from and co-opted by those who control literature" (translation mine).[84] Evidence of an entrepreneurial spirit and the ambition to rise economically, such as appear in George W. Swartz's *Autobiography of an American Mechanic* (1895), were more likely to recommend an American worker's autobiography to a mainstream publisher than alliance with working-class values or labor's cause. On the other hand, the publication of Theresa Malkiel's *Diary of a Shirtwaist Worker* (1910) signals an interest in progressive reform. In general, the main concerns of worker narrative are historical and social, not linguistic or aesthetic. Such narratives are valued more for the perspective of the author than for any intrinsic literary worth.

Worker autobiographies are subject to institutional constraints, raising questions concerning authenticity and comprehensiveness. The conditions of publication disclose the purpose and nature of the individual autobiographical narrative. Moreover, personal narrative (of which the worker narrative is a less flexible subgenre) "always involves," according to Sandra Stahl, "some manipulation of the truth of the experience." Telling one's story involves contradictory requirements in which the author negotiates the conflicting demands of truth and "aesthetically dramatic structure."[85] An additional consideration is the "teller's identity," which becomes increasingly ambiguous to the extent that the narrative is embellished with dramatic elements.[86] Lejeune discusses the question of authenticity in worker narrative, noting historians' "suspicion regarding writing" since writing implies editing and therefore tailoring one's story for publication.[87] Burnett argues for written autobiography without "intermediary reporter or observer to change the situation."[88] Frequently, worker life histories claim to tell "a true factual story." Like the teller in the personal narrative, Conroy claimed "truth" for his novel; yet factual truth is not meant here but rather truth to the author's perceptions: cultural truths.[89] A worker's life in all its everydayness—the day-by-day small defeats and frustrations and triumphs of working-class existence—has never made popular reading matter. Stories of success or sensation usually find publishers; ordinary worker narratives, on the other hand, traditionally have been written for other workers and published in trade and union journals (or not published at all).[90] The Federal Writers' Project in the 1930s pioneered the collection of worker narratives (transcribed) in a systematic manner.[91] In the last twenty years, increasing value has been placed on worker narrative and oral history in the study of labor history. As a consequence, a number of collections, such as Nancy Seifer's *Nobody Speaks for Me!* and Jean Reith Schroedel's *Alone in the Crowd* have appeared from mainstream and university presses.[92]

Worker narrative and autobiography reflect a variety of aims and interests. In a few instances, actual accounts of work are passed over. Some express hope for change; others, resignation. For labor militants, engagement in political action imparts structure and value to their lives, which are closely identified with the labor movement.[93] All worker autobiographies resemble one another in certain significant ways. The worker's family is preeminent since typically family members depend upon one another, not only economically but for emotional support. Friends are important, all the more when work is unsatisfactory and opportunities limited. The death of a parent is viewed not only as a personal loss but an economic catastrophe, as in the death of Tom Conroy, which forced Jack to abandon formal school after eighth grade and enter apprenticeship. Childhood is a privileged time before the obligations of family and work intercede; memories of childhood are therefore vivid in that they are associated with settings in which happiness is wrested from hardship, coarseness, and need. Books are remembered because they are scarce. (Workers who write their own lives generally are readers.) Imagination serves in the absence of ready-made entertainment. In our time when children—perhaps working-class and ghetto children more than others—spend eight hours and more before a television, how can we claim that an exceptional working-class child like Gorki, Nexö, or Conroy was culturally deprived?

Childhood in worker autobiographies is lived in close quarters with the adult world; death, hardship, danger, suffering, sex, all intrude, unlike the world of Rousseau's *Emile* in which childhood and adulthood are separate and autonomous, or the Bildungsroman in which growing up is a gradual passage from innocence to experience.[94] Attitudes toward early sorrow and work vary greatly in worker autobiography. Resignation, conciliation with the hard facts of existence, and an unwillingness to write in any detail of their sexual or emotional lives characterize many workers' life histories. Exceptional workers, "articulate workingmen," like Conroy, for whom language was a liberating vehicle more than a means of social or economic advancement, were, by contrast, eager to record their lives in the concreteness of everyday existence, yet they preserved the same reticence concerning their emotional and sexual experience. The best autobiographical writing offers models for seeing and understanding in which hunger or despair becomes recognizable beyond the scope of the text. It creates "situations" (in the Sartrean sense) that are not permitted, however, to expand into larger, transcendent truths but remain as "relationships," a situation in the process of development, inviting the reader to take part in some unfinished business.[95]

The structure of worker autobiographies is episodic, not because of chronological development so much as the material circumstances of work; each episode characteristically focuses on a particular job or the change (or loss) of job. The narrator meets a variety of figures, appearing, then disappearing, as jobs are changed and so forth, so that there is no continuous development of any one figure apart from the narrator. Each job provides occasions for encountering other workers engaged in similar tasks, but who are widely divergent in temperament, attitudes, personality, moral sense, knowledge, consciousness, and appearance, offering material for a novelist's exploration of individual difference. Through such occasions, the narrator confronts his or her own existence, each adding to the evolution of what Muenchow calls *Geschichtsdenken*.[96] These then are the elements of worker autobiography that underlie Conroy's own "life writing" in his tales of work and *The Disinherited*.

The thirteen shorter pieces are tied together by the figure of the narrator, Larry Donovan. Larry tells the story of his childhood in a coal-mining camp and the growth of a rich imaginative life in the nearby wooded hollows despite his family's privation. His childhood, bounded on one side by the presence of violence and on the other by examples of communal solidarity (the miners) and selflessness (his mother), comes to an abrupt end upon the death of his father in a mine accident. At age thirteen, he begins an apprenticeship in the railroad shops and an exhausting program of correspondence courses, eventually abandoning the latter. The remainder of the narrative follows fairly closely—apart from the romantic episodes—the events of Jack's life to 1932. Conroy adapts his experience, however, to the demands of storytelling in framing the conclusion. Almost by chance, Larry Donovan stumbles into an open-ended political commitment—unlike the protagonist of conventional proletarian novels in which all preceding events of the story point to the inescapable conversion ending.

In *The Disinherited* many voices compete for attention. It is the life history not of an individual alone but of a group of workers, or workers drawn from an entire class, the disinherited. The narrator is one of these, more thoughtful than the others, but not set apart, rather placed on the same level with the others. Jack's first novel tells more about workers who accept their lot passively than it does about the revolutionary harbingers of change the Communists wished to find in proletarian fiction. Jack supported Party aims but was unable to align his own observations on working-class life and attitudes with Party ideology. A storyteller, Jack was also a social historian with a sense of irony, quick to see the humor in events and the quirks of human character. Coal mines, the Wabash shops, a rubber-heel factory, a steel mill, and auto assembly plants had been his university. His experience ranged widely; he had known an ordinary lifetime's share of experience in his first thirty years. Like Maxim Gorki, the intensity and range of the experience had made him compassionate, tolerant of human foible, an observer with an infallible ear for speech and storytelling.

Both Conroy and Gorki (in the trilogy) present workers as sharply delineated, vivid figures (Yakov, the stoker, Bun Grady, the superannuated worker) who, because they pass briefly through the narrator's life, lack further development. The variety of characters without continuous development—in common with the picaresque novel—presents a problem compositionally to the worker-writer concerned with the forward movement of his narrative. Conroy solved this narrative problem in a very special way.

The sketches that Jack reworked in making *The Disinherited* can be divided into two groups: the tales of workers and the autobiographical Monkey Nest tales. Each of them bears the imprint of the material conditions in which they were produced (proletarian nights, between shifts of work, and during periods of anxious job-seeking), and each derives—at least in thematic content, structure, and links with labor history—from a tradition of worker narrative and autobiography, which is to say, a desire to communicate one's uniqueness while representing the shared experience of a group (and class).[97] Jack's uses of folklore, vernacular speech, popular culture, folk locution, humor, orality, and other manifestations of subcultures are the materials and tools in creatively rewriting worker narrative and autobiography. They are the special trademarks identifying his writing. Conroy's art consists then in creatively transforming these "simple forms" in literary narrative. Such "simple forms," Jauss argues, derive from preliterary expression associated with subcultures, and "lie in advance of the historically realized manifestations of a literary culture, but not as archetypes . . . rather as possibilities which can be selected, realized, or also not realized according to cultural codes and social conditions."[98]

Worker narrative and the proletarian sketch derive from specific historical moments, reflecting the growing consciousness of the worker-writer as it evolved through life experiences in working-class situations. An implicit element of this consciousness is a series of ruptures. There exists, first of all, a symbolic rupture, described by Jacques Rancière, between two mental states: the one that "writes itself" into narratives and the other that "sees itself living in the everyday context of the workshop." The rupture is "constituted by the entry into writing, that is, into the domain of the literate."[99] Secondly, there exists an actual rupture, represented by the hyphenated condition of the worker-writer. Jack felt a deep solidarity with other workers but did not always share their attitudes and values. Joe Kalar complained to Jack about his fellow workers' "swinish indifference,"[100] yet confessed on several occasions to Huddlestone that he would rather remain in his job than occupy an office chair.[101] Observing the unemployed lumberjacks during a strike in International Falls in 1932, he wrote acidly to Huddlestone: "they sit around on chairs, corpses sitting on chairs attending their own Irish Wake . . . forgotten men . . . instead of fighting back."[102] Kalar grew increasingly cynical and turned inward, weary of fighting back and being defeated.[103] On the other hand, he was keenly aware that his work life provided him material and inspiration for his writing, and he complained mainly of the lack of time to write. "Not the work," he wrote Walter Snow, "but the hours, militate against my ever creating as I would like to create—I have always been caught in the trap of long hours and small pay."[104] In *The Disinherited* these ruptures—discordances between the narrator's aspirations and quotidian reality—are reflected in the double-voiced discourse of the characters. In these, modes of discourse intersect, evidence of heterogeneous cultural and social practices rather than what Rancière calls "cultural homogeneity."[105]

Conroy drew upon living speech patterns, yet his art lies in selection, stylization, and what Bakhtin calls "doubly oriented discourse."[106] The double orientation implies a type of discourse that aims at the "referential object of speech," according to Bakhtin, "as in ordinary discourse, and simultaneously at a second context of discourse, a second speech act by another addresser."[107] The stylization of Conroy's writing in the sketches, *The Disinherited*, folktales, and stories like "The Weed King"—stylization is one of that story's most interesting features—derives from what Bakhtin calls the "dialogic relationships among texts and within the text."[108] Words, phrases, and references point to other speech acts from which, as Bakhtin says, they are borrowed or after which they are patterned. The double-voiced quality of expression, in which voices play off one another, within and among separate addressers, serves to underscore the author's role as both listener and evaluator, as well as his special sensibility as worker-writer. In place of strong authorial discourse and carefully delineated psychological characterization, Conroy's writing in this period explores the intertextual relations of his experience and reading, crossing the line repeatedly between oral and literary, folk vision and social history, autoportrait and memoir. The diverse voices represented in the text have equal authority and words speak across the bounds of the text to other "texts," including oral discourse. We discern a special sensibility in these sketches and *The Disinherited*, one that is aural and intertextual.

More than simply a transcription of factory life, or the product of a journalist's sojourn among dispossessed workers, Conroy's narratives convey the feeling and texture of his workers' linguistic world. Drawing from the stockpile of actual workers' speech, the rejoinders of ordinary exchange, Conroy fashioned his sketches of factory life, giving voice to those who do not write their own lives. It was a collective enterprise between author and the figures who comprise his tales.[109] The role of the worker-writer is to mediate the cultural significance of his subject matter by attending to the contradictions inherent in the speech acts he records. The credibility of the narrator is an essential problem in such transpositions of worker narrative/autobiography (the collective activity of those who furnish the discourse). Jack solved it in two ways. The first consists of identifying his narratives as forms of *vécu*, the testimony of one who had actually lived the experiences described ("a witness to my time"). Secondly, he represented the figure of the worker-writer—not necessarily himself—in the story as a first-person narrator. Lejeune calls this a "contrat de lecture," an implicit contract that the author proposes to the reader having to do with the ways the text is read (and received).[110]

Conroy dialogizes fragments and vestiges of workers' speech genres, weaving them together horizontally, placing the voices on level with his own in a democratic, egalitarian balance. Dialogic relations are preserved; they remain vital and actual in light of subsequent social history; one can still "polemicize" with them. His art is collaborative; workers contribute their speech and experiences to the writer, who preserves their voices in texts that belie the notion that because workers have left few written records they are inarticulate. Conroy discovered what V. S. Pritchett calls the "original and despised sources which have often been fruitful to novelists" in the folk experience of factory and mine workers.[111] Not one language but many "languages," a diversity of individual voices, shape Conroy's writing, the heteroglossia, to use Bakhtin's term, of working-class experience as Jack knew it. His work presents not fully fleshed out characters, then, or psychological insights into individual personality, but characterization through voices speaking in diverse, individualized accents and socio-idiolects. Actual meanings (again to borrow from Bakhtin) are constituted "against the background of other concrete utterances."[112] In this "verbal-ideological world" the narrator finds his own voice.[113]

Drawing from the heteroglossia of living utterance, then, Conroy fashioned texts incorporating the low genres of folk humor, popular literature, anecdote, worker narrative, and orality. In the life histories of the nineteenth and early twentieth centuries, workers' speech is edited, grammar is imposed, like indigenous folk music choreographed for a Broadway musical. In Conroy's writing, however, actual locutions he had heard are echoed in the texts, representing the speech genres of factory life. His characters function simultaneously on two levels: as personages who bump up against the concreteness of an everyday world

and as folk characters. In the rootless, proletarian world of early industrialism, Conroy discovers and portrays in his writing a pervading folk
sensibility moving deeply, like an underground stream, in the experience and speech of the workers he knew.

The task that lay before Jack and his generation of writers was to
articulate the voices of broken communities and to enlarge sympathies
by engaging the reader, not primarily in the personal tragedy of a single individual, but through the evocation of a people's consciousness,
reflecting deep-lying feelings toward community, injustice, adversity,
uncertainty, and loss. The workers and common folk of Conroy's writings are not the grey working masses of early industrial realism, those,
for example of Lewis Hine's photos or Dreiser's portrayals of Chicago
"wage-seekers." But neither are they the fully realized characters of Tolstoy or Stendhal. They occupy a third ground, one that employs comic
techniques—for example, dialect and literary burlesque—as vernacular
protest. In the Steamboat Mose passage of *The Disinherited,* for example, we feel the pressure of being pushed on a job, the withering heat,
and the poignancy of wasted life. Rather than transcribing speech, as
some proletarian writers attempted to do, usually without success, Conroy transformed it, concentrating on the humorous and characteristic
locutions of folk speech, yet focusing on his main subject, which was
to show that human values could exist in settings hostile to them: in
the factory, in soup kitchens, among the dispossessed.[114]

It was a staggering task. The compromises that he was forced to make
to provide for himself and his family placed severe constraints on his
literary ambitions. The evolving climate of reception, structured in part
by the programmatic literary politics of the left, in part by mainstream
editors' and critics' newly awakened interest in the Depression as a subject, affected the difficult job of making *The Disinherited,* finding a publisher, winning a readership. Sustaining him was the excitement felt by
his generation of writers, who, as Jack declared, had "something vital
and new to communicate" and publications that were open to their
work.

* * *

The *Anvil* and *Blast,* edited by Fred Miller at 55 Mt. Hope Place in
Brooklyn, were soon joined by *Dynamo, Partisan Review, Scope, Partisan,* the *Dubuque Dial, Windsor Quarterly,* and others publishing proletarian poetry and fiction. A *New Republic* editorialist compared them
to the little magazines of the avant-garde following World War I—
Broom, the *Little Review*—which likewise promoted new, unknown writers in the face of established publishers unwilling to take risks. "The

little magazines had an influence out of proportion to their circulation; they launched writers who afterwards came to dominate a good part of the literary scene; they trained editors and educated the audience. . . . The advance-guard magazines of the twenties, railing against American civilization primarily from an esthetic point of view, were edited in Rome, Paris, Vienna and half the capitals of Europe. These new arrivals [for example, the *Anvil*], preaching the international revolution, hail from such plain American addresses as Mount Hope Place, Brooklyn, and Moberly, Missouri."[115] *Dynamo, a Journal of Revolutionary Poetry*, edited by Sol Funaroff, Herman Spector, Joseph Vogel, and Nicholas Wirth in New York City, first appeared in January 1934. Vogel and Spector, who were good friends, recall thinking up the idea of the magazine while taking walks near the Metropolitan Museum of Art.[116] They were persuaded that most young writers faced impossible odds trying to publish in *Collier's, Atlantic Monthly, Scribner's*, and other large-circulation magazines. *Dynamo* was born in Spector's apartment on 125th Street, with an initial contribution of twenty-five dollars from the sale of a Spector story to the *American Mercury*.[117] Spector wrote Snow for the *Rebel Poet* mailing list. Unable to afford office space, the editors met informally in people's homes where they discussed manuscripts, tossing bad submissions across the room.[118] Stanley Burnshaw, Kenneth Fearing, Isidor Schneider, Joseph Freeman, Mike Gold, Edwin Rolfe—all appeared in *Dynamo* during its brief life of four issues.

Twice a contributor to *Anvil*, Joe Vogel was another young writer whose early career was nurtured by little-magazine editors like Conroy. Moreover, he is proof that there were no "typical" revolutionary writers, nor was Conroy as editor seeking any for his magazine. A 1926 graduate of Hamilton College, Vogel had already contributed an essay on dialect to *American Speech* and a piece written for a college course to *New Masses* before shipping out on a cattle boat to Italy after college. On returning he took a written log of his experiences to the *New Masses* editors, who promptly accepted it. Before joining *Dynamo*, Vogel had published in the prestigious *American Cavalcade* as well as in *Pagany, Anvil*, the *Left*, and *Blast*, and he had helped edit *Blues* with Charles Henri Ford (although Vogel resigned when Ford changed the typescript of a Farrell story to lowercase type). Devoted to writing about "matters of contemporary interest," he said, Vogel nonetheless refused to be bound by avant-garde or leftist aesthetic doctrines.[119] He was interested in modernist literature, carrying on a lengthy correspondence with Ezra Pound (they had both studied Provençal under the same professor at Hamilton), and was adept at both satire and serious writing. However, he bolted from Pound's influence when he perceived a literary clique forming under Louis Zukofsky. Vogel's novel *Man's Courage* (1938), acclaimed when it first appeared and recently republished after languishing in obscurity, is a kind of nonpartisan political fable. Like many other talented literary radicals from the 1930s, Vogel was "disappeared" with the ascendancy of Europe-oriented modernist literature and the cautiousness of publishers toward writing of social content during the Cold War years.[120]

In early 1934, *New Masses* switched from monthly to weekly publication and altered its scope. Granville Hicks, now literary editor, had written Jack several months earlier of the change: "I believe that the decision to make the *New Masses* a weekly, primarily political and critical in orientation, is a step in the right direction. But it puts an added responsibility on such magazines as *Blast, Dynamo,* and *Anvil.* You are now responsible for encouraging and first publishing the rising poets and story writers. I hope that we can have the fullest cooperation between the *New Masses* and the proletarian quarterlies."[121] Joining the three journals "responsible" for proletarian writing was *Partisan Review,* under the wing of the New York John Reed Club. In the first issue, appearing in February 1934, Philip Rahv and Wallace Phelps (a.k.a. William Phillips) pledged their editorial loyalty to "the revolutionary working class." Rahv was the ex–Rebel Poet who had earlier advised severing "all ideological ties with this lunatic civilization known as capitalism"[122] and who had led the splinter faction that attempted to wrest *Rebel Poet* away from Conroy's editorship in order to turn it into a militant organ. After failing to start his own magazine (*Proletfolio*), Rahv joined with Phelps and the members of the John Reed Club in turning the mimeographed JRC newsletter into *Partisan Review.* Like Rahv, Phelps displayed a fondness for Stalinist rhetoric in 1934. In a review of Joyce's *Ulysses,* Phelps complained that the Dublin author's "method could hardly be used to portray social conflict or human conflict against a background of class struggle."[123] In 1934, both Phelps and Rahv regarded *The Disinherited* as one of the few revolutionary novels in which, they said, "we get a sense of thematic exploration that suggests the immense possibilities ahead of us."[124]

In the first nine issues, Rahv and Phelps, who at that time considered proletarian writing "a form of avant-garde literature,"[125] published authors like Meridel Le Sueur, Ben Field, Nelson Algren, Edwin Rolfe, Jack Balch, Herman Spector, and Richard Wright, that is, contributors whose writings were just as likely to appear in *Anvil.* Eager to establish *Partisan Review* as an intellectual forum of revolutionary literature and criticism, the editors included critical essays and European writers and critics, such as André Malraux, Louis Aragon, and Georg Lukács. The early *Partisan Review,* engaged like the *Anvil* in creating a cultural space for literature of social content, assumed the role of literary arbiter on the left. Rahv and Phelps soon emerged as spokesmen of a revolutionary intelligentsia, animating discussions and contributing critical essays on the development of Marxist literary theory. "On the pages of the *Partisan Review,*" an ad proclaimed, "the leftward moving professional writers and the young revolutionary writers from factory and mill meet in a common effort to forge new literary values."[126] Raising the standards apparently meant no welcome for unknown writers, for none appeared in *Partisan Review;* most contributors were already well known in the little-magazine circuit.

The New York radical intelligentsia—which now included Rahv and Phelps—were eager to make contact with the proletariat. Most remained isolated, however, from the workers' world. "If," as Orwell wrote in *Road to Wigan Pier,* "a real working man, a miner dirty from the pit, . . had suddenly walked into their midst, they would have been embarrassed, angry, and disgusted. . . ."[127] There were fundamental differences between the *Anvil* and *Partisan Review* almost from the beginning; Rahv and Phelps's ascension solidified them. Reflecting the editors' own temperament, *Partisan Review* was open to stylistic experimentation, internationalist in perspective, and wedded to theoretical discussion.[128] The *Anvil,* by contrast, represented a radical temper nonideological in disposition, grass-roots in orientation, and grounded in the immediacy of personal experience. Conroy sought out unknowns, hit home on occasion, and made many near-misses. The two magazines might have coexisted harmoniously, since each fulfilled a separate need. However, this was not to be.

The half-life of a little magazine in the early 1930s was short. *Left Front,* the magazine of the Chicago John Reed Club, had ambitions to expand into a fiction magazine like *Anvil* but died after the fourth number (May–June 1934). Four magazines of the left that were publishing fiction and poetry—*Anvil, Partisan Review, Blast,* and *Dynamo*—seemed to have the best chance of surviving longer. Alan Calmer in the *Daily Worker* wrote that these four were breaking with the tradition of "arty" magazines, moving into the streets to confront social issues that mainstream editors had avoided.[129] On the street, confrontations occurred in odd ways. Some communities had laws against "seditious" literature. Suspicious police apprehended the novelist Frederick Manfred, who was carrying copies of *Anvil* and *Blast.* Manfred thought for a moment, then told the officers that he was a blacksmith—the magazines, he said, were trade publications.

In a speech before the International Labor Defense organization in early 1935, Walter Snow described the difficulties the *Anvil* had faced and its successes. A few years earlier, he said, there was little place for young revolutionary writers to publish their work. "But today every young author is trying to write proletarian short stories. During the past two months, the *Anvil*, the pioneering proletarian fiction magazine, has received more than two hundred would-be proletarian stories. The majority, of course, have been rather feeble efforts."[130] At first, *Anvil* was slow in receiving good submissions. "We were writing for our muddled selves," Snow admitted. It was not easy to wean workers away from their *Police Gazette* and Fannie Hurst stories. Gangster tales, he said, might reveal how crooked businessmen and politicians are, but they assist in poisoning the minds of workers. "We must appeal to people to break the mood of intellectual resignation," Snow concluded, a task that he optimistically assigned to *Anvil*. Conroy himself was convinced of the need to build a workers' culture; *Anvil* was one such cultural activity, along with theater, that could be instrumental in constructing links among working-class people. It was necessary to remove the isolation of writers from the masses of people and to avoid obscurantism. The forms of a new literature would include "personal narratives, stories of the underdog, and vital sketches," narrative types that were within the reach of writers with a vital story to tell.[131]

The working-class culture Jack envisaged would constitute, in Stanley Aronowitz's words, "a new horizontal organization of communications within which all 'receivers' would also be 'transmitters,'" as opposed to capitalist modes of literary production in which "'culture' is disseminated from above through a pyramidally structured communications apparatus."[132] Much depended upon voluntary help, such as Sanford's Anvil Press in Newllano, and the charismatic energy of the editor himself. *Anvil* was uneven in quality, both in content and in the material composition of the magazine. Commenting on the poetry in one issue, Kalar wrote Huddlestone: "I suppose Conroy can't help it; after all, he can print only what is submitted him."[133] Some issues brought a flood of appreciative letters and inspired comments such as Williams Carlos Williams's: "For some time I have maintained that the 'radical magazine' is not a series of failures, always dying, but one continuous success, impossible to kill. . . . I'd like to know more about 'Anvil.'"[134] Among the new talent that Jack fostered were blacks, convicts, women, and post office workers. Jack accepted racially sensitive stories in *Anvil* when other editors declined to publish them because of their content. The civil-rights struggles of the 1950s and 1960s, feminist issues of the 1970s and 1980s are prefigured in *Anvil*; yesterday's radicalisms became today's mainstream concerns.

Erskine Caldwell's short story "Daughter" is tame by today's standards, but Maxim Lieber refused it on grounds that it could prove offensive even to *Anvil* readers. Caldwell sent the story directly to Jack, who printed it.[135] Too much proletarian writing, Jack felt, was defeatist, unnecessarily pessimistic, an attempt to mirror a collapsing world while ignoring the humor and poetry of common life even in times of distress. Caldwell's story tells of an impoverished black sharecropper who shoots his starving daughter to release her suffering and, in ironic counterplay to the typical lynching story, is released by the sympathetic mob. For Conroy, the piece struck a note of affirmation that was needed to balance the despairing, angry proletarian writing that filled his mailbox. To certain critics, "affirmation" was too much like the heavy-handed didactic quality of Socialist Realism. Edward Dahlberg recalled bitterly that writers "were often attacked for producing petit-bourgeois and 'defeatist' literature."[136] Caldwell was unflinching in his portrayal of sharecropping's terrible human costs; rather than dwelling on the degraded circumstances, however, he portrayed the awakening conscience of the townspeople who learn of the sharecropper's plight. Jack rejected Huddlestone's stories of tramping as too resigned, quietist. Similarly, in refusing Willard Maas's bleak sketch "Cannery Mothers," Jack wrote the author: "I have to preserve a kind of balance between the negative (workers beaten and oppressed but not rebellious), the militant phases, and humor, satire, etc. It happens that the bulk of our material is in the vein of your sketch."[137]

Jack's criticism of capitalism was not merely economic. Proletarian existence robs one of life. Workers die spiritually before their bodies play out. John Ruskin and other nineteenth-century English writers were appalled at the devitalizing effects of industrialism. "There is no wealth but life," Ruskin wrote in *Unto This Last*. Gorki, suffocating among dispirited workers living in a basement, read to them to cheer them up. It was Jack's nature to prefer life-affirming stories to gloomy tales of a dehumanized subproletariat.[138] Like Tolstoy, he preferred natural, spontaneous expression to mere cleverness. Expressions of dignity and protest have occurred in folk art throughout history, which, as Benjamin argues, functions as a locus of remembrance.[139] Mass culture denigrates the individual, dehumanizes.[140] Jack's "affirmative" view of proletarian life was akin to earlier forms of folk art in which human resourcefulness and endurance prevail. Workers, he said, deserve better than what the commercial press provides. "Crude vigor" was a term much scorned by critics ready to see in proletarian literature a new version of pastoralism—or an attempt to substitute vulgarity for literary standards.[141]

Principal among Jack's aims as editor was discovering and nurturing

new talent. Established writers had a publishing market, but few opportunities existed for young, untried writers. Jack was a facilitator by
nature, deriving great pleasure in helping others get into print, even
when it cost him time for his own writing. The *Anvil* enterprise embodied something fundamental about the 1930s, Ben Hagglund said, a
"collective spirit." "The collective spirit had us enthralled briefly; then
when things eased up a bit, the old individualistic spirit got us again,
and we were right back at each other's throat."[142] Nurturing was strong
in Jack—a characteristic that according to traditional gender roles is
assigned to women—and indeed had been strong in his mother. In his
first contacts with Mencken, he had talked not about his own writing
but about H. H. Lewis's. He knew how much writers were indebted to
editors. "In all this big land," recalled Sanora Babb, a novelist and an
Anvil contributor, "Jack Conroy was a voice and a heart, and a definitely non-organizational individual, but a concerned individual."[143]
Erskine Caldwell wrote in 1934: "I'd rather have you publish a story in
The Anvil than to get it in anywhere else."[144] The Japanese proletarian
writer Masaki Fujio exclaimed to Jack after receiving *Anvil* 2, "You are
making ahead!"—adding that he was using *Anvil* "in stimulating our
young workmen writers here."[145] Agnes Smedley, author of *Daughter of
Earth*, on her return to China in 1934, wrote Jack asking that he help
her brother, a construction worker in California, who needed Jack's
encouragement and guidance in writing a story about the terrible conditions of his job: "I'd like to see my brother become one of the workers on the job who learned to write." Send him the *Anvil*, she requested; ". . . all the men he works with are moved by bitter resentment,
but they see no way out. The C.P. has done no work at all amongst
them and most of the pamphlets produced by the Party are for intellectuals or workers who have become intellectuals of a sort. They certainly aren't for the ordinary native western workers. They appeal to
the *New Yorker* chiefly."[146] From Abe Aaron came news of a young black,
a fellow worker on the night shift, who was writing poetry. "He intends
to send some of it to you."[147] Smedley's brother never published in the
Anvil, nor did many other workers who, with persistence and editorial
help, might have told a good tale. Yet some workers did, among them
a young black post-office worker named Richard Wright.

15

The Road to Mecca Temple

How do I know that I give a damn for people in
general, the generality of people . . . their suffering?
. . . it may be all bunk
—Sherwood Anderson, *Beyond Desire*

SOME FORTY YEARS AFTER the *Anvil* first appeared, a group of writers,
disturbed by the increasing number of publishing conglomerates, gathered to discuss alternate ways to publish their work. Accustomed to paternal relationships with their editors and publishers, the writers had
trouble establishing fraternal relationships with one another. Since most
were used to publishing with commercial houses, "we soon realized that
emotionally our sanction as writers still came from the publishers." In
other words, writers are like independent artisans without a craft guild;
for them the publisher is "the boss." "[W]e were just playing the game,
providing the boss with a product to sell if and when he thought it
would be worth money to him."[1] This view of artistic creativity as a
specialized form of production, "subject to much the same conditions
as general production," is, according to Raymond Williams, associated
with the "significance of the Industrial Revolution."[2] With the rise of
a large middle-class reading public, Williams argues, literature became
a commodity created by professionals in a market arrangement between
writer and public. The artist was viewed as a special kind of person,
imbued with genius (a notion borrowed from the Romantics), and art
itself was considered to be a "superior reality." The artist, in turn, dis-
dained the public, or at the very least felt alienated from it.

It is of course absurd to suggest that the *Anvil* unseated the commodity relationships governing literary production or modified in any per-

manent way the role of art and the artist in society. Nonetheless, the availability of cheap means of mechanical reproduction, the coopera- tion of self-sacrificing printers, and a limited demand for the writing of social concern that generated so much excitement among young writ- ers in the 1930s made it possible for Jack and others associated with the *Anvil* to free literature, within a very limited domain, from pure market considerations and alter competitive relations among writers. That this democratization of literary production, however inconsistent and precarious, occurred at a crucial moment, coinciding with the ris- ing power of the working class (as evidenced in the labor struggles just beginning), was not accidental. By 1934, continued hard times had awakened sympathy toward workers; and if sympathy was not felt, then the outbreak of violent strikes in Toledo, San Francisco, and Minneap- olis, involving the rank and file in militant action, forced the country's attention on the plight of the worker. Malcolm Cowley, in the 1934 edition of *Exile's Return*, describes the returned expatriate writers as "alien observers" in their native land.[3] The decline of the dollar's val- ue abroad had brought them home, where they encountered breadlines and men standing in the snow wearing threadbare coats. In perceiving the deprivation and no longer secure in the belief that society could provide the material means for life, they abandoned their faith in the religion of art. Skeptical now of the function of art, artists had no choice but to participate in the class struggle, Cowley wrote.[4] In taking the side of the workers they stood to gain "a sense of comradeship and par- ticipation in a historical process vastly bigger than the individual."[5] Ironically, the exiles would absorb space in the better-known magazines, making it more difficult for writers with working-class topics but less name recognition to publish.

The absence of a locally constituted hierarchy of precedents, the sense of being free to experiment pragmatically, and the lack of "walls" were elements in what Michael Gold would later denote as the "fuzzy 'democracy' of the midwest school."[6] By 1934, *New Masses* had become representative of the centralizing trend in the left's cultural programs, a centripetal site of literary production that sought to attract writers of reputation, including Cowley, Ernest Hemingway, Matthew Josephson, and others who had been "exiles" during the previous decade. The mid- western radicals, on the other hand, resisted the centralizing tendency, which they associated with the locus of power in the East. John T. Fre- derick's *Midland* and William Marion Reedy's *Reedy's Mirror*, for in- stance, were two literary magazines that had attempted to provide pub- lishing outlets in the Midwest. It was a very old animus, that felt by midwesterners toward easterners. One hears it in the attitude of

Melville's Missouri Bachelor (*The Confidence Man*): "As for Intelligence Offices, I've lived in the East, and know 'em. Swindling concerns kept by low-born cynics, under a fawning exterior wreaking their cynic malice upon mankind."[7] Erling Larsen, a young aspiring writer in the 1930s, remembers "how much we in the hinterlands thought . . . about what was going on in the effete East. We had absorbed pretty thoroughly the Nick Carraway doctrine [of Fitzgerald's *The Great Gatsby*] that the yellow cars of the Milwaukee Road ran through the heart of honesty and that Manhattan was inhabited by that famous drunken woman wearing a white evening gown and lying on the stretcher and by editors who cared about money but not about what we knew was the truth."[8] Grant Wood and Thomas Hart Benton, American Scene painters of the 1930s and spokesmen for an aesthetic in revolt against what they perceived to be Eastern art cliques and orthodoxy on the left, engaged in becoming better acquainted with "native materials" at home.[9]

Part of the animus expressed against the East was prejudicial, ingrained suspicion toward urban dwellers; but real differences were thought to exist. Whitman in "Democratic Vistas," Frederick Jackson Turner in "The Frontier in American History," the Progressive historians Charles A. Beard and Vernon L. Parrington, and others held that democratic aspirations were most likely to be fulfilled in the midlands and farther west. Aligned against such aspirations were vested interests in the East, the locus of privilege and power.[10]

One who articulated eloquently the differences felt by midwestern radicals, the uniqueness of their place, culture, and history, was Meridel Le Sueur, born in February 1900, in Murray, Iowa. Le Sueur's depictions of working-class women, appearing in the *Anvil*, the *Dial*, *American Mercury*, *New Masses*, and elsewhere, wed a feminist consciousness to progressive ideals in midwestern settings.[11] Daughter of crusading midwestern radicals (her strong-willed grandmother was active in the temperance movement; her stepfather, Arthur Le Sueur, was Socialist mayor of Minot, North Dakota; Arthur and her mother, Marian, helped found the People's College in Fort Scott, Kansas), Le Sueur remembered visits by Debs, Emma Goldman, and Alexander Berkman to her childhood home. Trained as a dancer and actress, a stand-in for Pearl White, Meridel grew disgusted with Hollywood's entertainment world and turned to factory and restaurant work to support her writing. Diverse influences—D. H. Lawrence, Zona Gale, Vachel Lindsay, Kate Richards O'Hare—shaped her writing, which covers a broad range of expression, including lyrical humanism ("Persephone"), journalistic realism ("Women on the Breadlines"), and worker narrative ("Sequel to Love," published in the *Anvil*).

Like Conroy, Le Sueur recast fragments of overheard conversation and people's stories into literary narrative. A single event in which Le Sueur participated, the Minneapolis truckers' strike of 1934, became the setting for portraying the feelings of a young middle-class woman drawn into a group of militant workers. "I Was Marching," published in *New Masses* in September 1934, is an example of effective radical expression: personal feeling is conveyed without sacrificing wider historical implications; the propagandist intent is not imposed but springs from carefully motivated narrative action. In clean, spare prose, forceful yet sensitive, Le Sueur's narrative action accelerates quickly, proceeding to a conclusion in which the growing momentum of feeling spills over suddenly and convincingly into physical expression. Le Sueur's writing defines, perhaps as well as that of any of her contemporaries, what was "different" about midwestern literary radicalism: narrative vigor coupled with social content, an honesty to the subject matter that Conroy sought—and sometimes achieved—for the *Anvil*.

Addressing the American Writers' Congress in 1935, Meridel Le Sueur heralded the birth of a new culture in the Midwest, profoundly different from the veneer of genteel culture transplanted by exploiting profit-seekers. "We have never, in the Middle West," Le Sueur said, "had ease or an indigenous culture. We have been starved since our birth. . . . Now we know where to put down our roots, that have never been put down, that have been waiting through a bad season. . . . The idealistic duality of the New England culture never did us much good. . . . We, of the petty bourgeois and the working class, have been dissenters, individual madmen, anarchists against the machine; but now the Middle Western mind is finding a place. . . ."[12] This new culture, Le Sueur proclaimed, will come out of revolutionary ferment, the joining in the common perception of danger by "the farmer, the industrial worker, the brain worker, the writer, the artist." The communal basis of art, the role of experience, the valorization of indigenous traditions— these were to form the foundation of a midwestern culture worthy of its name. These were ambitious claims, and resonant with the rhetorical fervor for which Le Sueur was known. Yet she was not alone in making them; it appeared in mid-decade that a coalition of midwestern radicals were intent on their realization.

The perception that the channels of communication are controlled by eastern publishers and that, as a consequence, midwestern writers, like Hamlin Garland, have traditionally written for eastern readers was central to the Midwest Writers' Conference, meeting in Chicago, 13– 14 June 1936. Among the signatories to "A Call to All Midwest Writers" were Le Sueur, Conroy, Algren, Richard Wright, Jack Balch, Dale

Kramer, and H. H. Lewis. The threat of fascism and the difficulties of publication headed the agenda. The new generation of writers in the Midwest, the call read, "publish wherever possible, but mainly in those magazines edited by closed groups in the eastern centers, or in some far country; and they learn of each other's work through these channels, though they may be neighbors. New York City itself seems closer, more available, than Des Moines. . . ."[13] The call was a manifesto of cultural independence from the East. In William Dean Howells's lifetime, according to Irving Howe,

> one of the vivid cultural incursions came from the Midwest, by writers like Dreiser and Anderson, but by others too, whose work embodied the pathos of a struggle for articulation, a grasping for the sounds of heightened consciousness. Each breakthrough was seen as a threat to established standards by the genteel culture establishment of the East, and so in truth it was. Inevitably there followed a roughening of language and a coarsening of taste, but also an enlargement of sympathies and the emergence in our literature of figures, themes, and settings previously unseen. . . . Democratic cultures move ahead, or perhaps only move along, through internal struggle. . . ."[14]

But Le Sueur, Conroy, and the other midwesterners were proposing cultural independence, not further "incursions."

* * *

"I have some good news for you, Jack," wrote Abe Aaron from Chicago in late 1933. "I have sort of a gang, friends I acquired at the post-office. One of them is a Negro lad about my age. He is writing blank verse. He intends to send some of it to you. . . . I imagine you'll be as wild over it as I am. It's the real thing. You sent my gang to the J.R.C. [John Reed Club] when you sent me there, Jack. I doubt that there will be cause for regret from any quarter."[15] Jack was admired by literary aspirants who were touched by what Van Wyck Brooks called, in reference to William Morris, his "contagious personality."[16] In spreading his editorial net wide, Jack had landed a big catch: Richard Wright. Jack encouraged Aaron to attend a meeting of the John Reed Club at 1475 South Michigan Avenue, where the former editors from Davenport of the *Left*, Bill Jordan and Herbert and Marvin Klein, were members of the editorial committee of the club's new publication, *Left Front*. Aaron had worked part-time at the Chicago central post office several years earlier while a student at the University of Chicago. A fellow post-office worker was Richard Wright, who had come to Chicago from Mississippi by way of Memphis in late 1927, passed the post-office examination, and become a substitute worker. Good opportunities existed for blacks in the post office; a fourth of all positions were filled by black workers.[17] Aaron and Wright struck up a friendship when they discovered they both wanted to write. Together with Harry Bernstein and Sam Gaspar, Aaron and Wright formed what Conroy later called "the Chicago Post Office school." All were or had been clerks or substitute clerks at the post office and all eventually became contributors to the *Anvil*.

Murray Kempton in *Part of Our Time* claims that the *Anvil* fueled Wright's determination to become a writer.[18] Much has been written about Wright's early literary career—his own retrospective account is biased by his revision of earlier views regarding the role of the Communist Party in his development as a writer.[19] Aaron recalls suggesting to Wright that he read the *Anvil*, which Aaron had discovered by chance in the University of Chicago library. When Wright had left the South for Chicago he was, according to Jean Bethke Elshtain, "a prime candidate for despair, degradation, 'negative self-identity,' 'false consciousness,' oppression, exploitation and victimization."[20] Influenced by Mencken, Wright read American realist writers, which provided him, as Fabre says, "with the means to analyze the society he lived in."[21] Perhaps the *Anvil* played a role in steering him away from what Kinnamon calls the "puerilities" of his early sketches; at the very least it offered, as did Dreiser and Mencken earlier, a critical analysis of social conditions. *Anvil* stories seemed accessible and close to actual experience.[22] In the fall of 1933, on Jack's suggestion, Aaron brought Wright with him to a John Reed Club meeting, where he received a warm and uncondescending welcome.[23] His contacts with the Party and the John Reed Club were catalysts in his transformation into a poet of revolutionary verse.[24] His first two published poems appeared in the January–February 1934 issue of the John Reed Club's *Left Front*, along with a sketch by Tom Butler (a.k.a. Abe Aaron), Kalar's review of *The Disinherited*, Orrick John's review of the *Anvil*, and a drawing of Conroy, by now prominent in the club's pantheon of cultural heroes.[25] After Wright's initial success, Aaron sent his poems to Jack. It is correct to claim then that Jack published Wright's first writings in a magazine of national circulation. "Strength" and "Child of the Dead and Forgotten Gods," which appeared in the *Anvil* (March–April 1934), blazon their leftist convictions. Marxism, as Kinnamon points out, was the match that lit the fuse of Wright's literary imagination.[26]

The emergence of a black writer of such great talent from total obscurity was a great success story for the *Anvil*, not because Jack set literary prominence as his goal (with the exception of Erskine Caldwell, none of the *Anvil*-ites achieved literary fame during the tenure of the magazine), but because it gave evidence that the *Anvil's* method of literary production would yield a harvest of unknown talent. The expanding network of contacts had paid off, as Jack hoped it would. If there was hope for a vital culture in the hinterland, then it meant making connections among isolated writers from Butler, Pennsylvania (Abe Aaron), and Virginia's Piedmont (John Rogers) to Alpine, Texas (Nelson Algren), and Caldwell, Idaho (Vardis Fisher), tracing a literary communications system that, like the Wobblies, sought to create its own machinery of production and distribution independent of the establishment press and the dominant culture, and whose forms were mediated by the shared interests of the literary community that it helped define.[27] This was a thoroughly human project in which writers' work and lives intersected, touched by Conroy's "vigorous personality."[28] Dependent so much upon the vision and efforts of its editor and printer, however, it was a highly vulnerable enterprise. The life of a little magazine was very short as a rule; the generativity of this evanescent literary phenomenon nonetheless reassured Jack that even when *Anvil* went under, other little magazines would search out new writers and address contemporary social issues. This was the nature of the little magazine, as he pointed out time and again.[29] Yet *Anvil* was deeply involved with aspirations indissolubly bound to both its editor and its time. These two characteristics—its project of discovery and its mediation through a literary community of writers—joined in a unique cultural enterprise.

Conroy viewed literary creation not as specialized kind of production but as a human activity like other forms of labor, a collective enterprise. Like many other little-magazine editors he was concerned about the influence of the marketplace in shaping literature, indeed in directing its course. James L. W. West III describes the rise of a literary system of production since 1900 dominated by commercial interests with its stable of authors, blockbuster mentality, publishing conglomerates, and market studies.[30] With the invention of the press, it was inevitable that books too would be treated as commodities. "Printed books," Marshall McLuhan writes, "themselves the first uniform, repeatable, and mass-produced items in the world, provided endless paradigms of uniform commodity culture for the sixteenth and succeeding centuries."[31] Radical editors over the centuries resisted the commodifying of literature, printing cheap editions and giving space to dissident voices. The mechanical reproduction of forms and images made the book a commodity at the same time that it permitted the democratization of art, opening access to cultural production. Jack viewed art as a practical means of transformation, a way of empowering the individual and re-

storing the essential dignity of uprooted people, disenfranchised by economic circumstance and social alienation, through cooperative solutions
and human solidarity. The bourgeois literary system, as Walter Benjamin
argues in "The Author as Producer," served to create divisions between
writer and reader, and assigned writing itself to specialists.[32] The evolution of the novel reflects the history of the bourgeoisie. "Its world,"
as Alan Swingewood says, paraphrasing Benjamin, "is industrial and
bourgeois and its reader individualistic and privatised."[33] Moreover, the
bourgeois press has an astounding capacity, Benjamin claims, to assimilate and publish revolutionary topics without altering its own status
or that of the possessing class.[34] It was this system of commodity relationships between authors and publishers and the vertical structures of
publication that Jack opposed in the *Anvil*, whose purpose was to so-
cialize literary production, wresting its control from the guardians of
culture and the conglomerates.

In retrospect, the *Anvil* project seems hopelessly utopian: substitute
a rhizomatous system of horizontal connection for one of arborescence,
hierarchy and prominence; resist the growing power of the mass media
that, in Joachim Schulte-Sasse's words, "tend to destroy and expropri-
ate individual 'languages' in the interests of domination."[35] Deeply influenced by the cheap editions of popular literature he had read as a
youth in Monkey Nest and by the mail-order Haldeman-Julius Little
Blue Books, Jack was convinced that the key to the production of a
workers' literature lay in using the simplest and least costly resources
and employing distribution networks for the widest possible availability. The project was built on goodwill and personal dedication, an aleatory foundation: the people who made personal sacrifices as an act of
faith—printers working in their garages for expenses, writers who received no pay for their contributions, editors with offices in their homes
advising new writers where they might be published and offering constructive criticism. Such a system of literary production revealed social
impulses involving rituals of camaraderie and expressions of personal
dignity in place of competitiveness, profit motive, and personal ambition. The *Anvil*-ites—more broadly, the literary radicals who contributed to the little magazines of the 1930s—anticipated the subsequent
achievements of "dominated social groups"—blacks, Hispanics, and
women—who, as Schulte-Sasse says, "reappropriate language, allowing
it once again to become a medium for expressing the needs and material, concrete experiences of individuals and groups."[36]

Jack's editorial aims touched the desires and needs of isolated writers who as unknowns had no hope of breaking into the establishment
press. The *Anvil* was an attempt to initiate a new relationship with the

writer and reader, as opposed to the market relationship of commercial publication; the distance between writer and reader was narrowed—the reader with enough skill might become a contributor. The writer was not a special person possessing a higher kind of truth; writing was an act of communication. Isolated writers felt joined through publication in little magazines. Malcolm Cowley recalls how in the 1930s "writers of this time were trying to escape from a feeling of isolation and ineffectuality," not in searching for personal fulfillment and identity, as in the previous decade, but through expression of social ideals.[37] In searching for "the poetic metaphor" whose goal "would be a society in which the participant aspect of action attained its maximum expression," Kenneth Burke expressed a similar purpose.[38]

These desires and needs of isolated writers in the 1930s are expressed throughout the editorial correspondence of the *Anvil*. Feelings ran strong. Disputes were taken seriously and fought hard. Passionate people were struggling with their own personal conflicts as well as with political causes. It was by most accounts a decade of anger, high emotions, faith, dedication, generosity, and moral blindness. While financial insecurity and disappointment dogged Jack's own efforts, his work as editor pulled him into others' personal struggles. Nelson Algren wrote Jack in early March 1934, soon after his release from jail in Alpine, Texas, regretting that he had not been able to stop to see Jack in Moberly. He had ridden freights back to Chicago and was broke. Jack returned a short story of Algren's entitled "Buffalo Sun," remarking that it was "not so near to *The Anvil* policy," and urging him to submit it to a new little magazine, *Calithump*, published by Wailes Gray and his wife in Austin, Texas.

Algren's early short stories anticipated the terrible anger and bitterness of his first novel, in which he wrote of dehumanized people, the Lumpen, losers, and scum, without hope of betterment or promise of wisdom. Jack accepted two Algren stories, including "A Holiday in Texas," which appeared in the May–June issue of the *Anvil*. It was a piece intended for "a forthcoming novel" (*Somebody in Boots*), but for some reason Algren left it out when he began composing his first novel. Sensing a terrible loneliness and bitterness in Algren's writing and letters, Jack encouraged him to get in touch with Bill Jordan of the John Reed Club, Abe Aaron, and Sam Gaspar, hoping that their company might help remove the loneliness and improve Algren's spirits.[39] Algren sent three more stories ("Kewpie Doll," "Winter in Chicago," "Within the City") to Jack, portions of *Somebody in Boots*. The fierce realism and grotesqueness of Algren's writing—to the point of being funny at times—gave promise that he would become an important force in the midwestern radical culture movement signaled by Meridel Le Sueur and promoted by Jack's editorial work. Algren's stories cried out in pain, registering the protests of the human spirit on the bottom rung of the economic and social ladder. Jack's encouragement and example played an important role in Algren's early literary development. He gained great satisfaction from nurturing other writers' talent—and felt great anguish at times in contemplating the status of his own writing. The two activities continued to be at odds.

The time he devoted to editorial work was of course time away from his own writing. Editing the *Anvil* was part of a larger cultural aspiration: he hoped for the recreation of communities involving structures of solidarity and cooperation within working-class milieus and saw literature as one means to this end. Yet, writing is fundamentally a solitary enterprise. Contributions to the *Anvil* came from a wide diversity of individuals, including from minorities and marginalized groups. If the *Anvil*-ites constituted a community, then it was what Randolph Bourne, referring to an earlier generation of radicals, called a "community of sentiment."[40] Jack spoke of the *Anvil*'s "group spirit."[41] This "community," which had no basis other than mutual goodwill and shared purpose, was pluralistic in a time when society was sharply divided along lines of gender and race. Langston Hughes, Richard Wright, and a "black poet named Desmond O'Neill . . . from Kansas City [who] vanished from sight,"[42] published in the *Anvil*. Blacks' experience in contemporary America was the focus of stories by Erskine Caldwell, I. L. Kissen, and others. Meridel Le Sueur, Sanora Babb, Josephine Johnson—all of whom went on to distinguished writing careers—were among the women contributors.[43] "I started *The Girl* in *The Anvil*," Meridel Le Sueur recalled much later. "I probably wouldn't have written it without *The Anvil*. You'd send what you wrote to Jack—and whether he published it or not you'd feel a part of it."[44] There was at least one Yiddish poet among the contributors, Moishe Nadir. A submission came from the Wisconsin State Penitentiary, from the pen of Leon McCauley, who taught himself to write in prison. The material for his story came from an ex-Wobbly, James Kilrane, one of several Wobblies who contributed to the *Anvil*.[45]

The quality of the stories varied greatly. A short story by Boris Israel, who later became an organizer in the South and was murdered, rages in barely concealed contempt for humankind.[46] Algren accused Conroy of ruining people's lives by encouraging them to become writers. People should never give up things to try writing, he said, after reading a manuscript with the title "Life, Death and Winter's End."[47] Jack missed publishing one of Tennessee Williams's early short stories through an editorial misjudgment. He accepted Williams's manuscript, but when subsequently he relinquished some of the editorial responsibilities to Walter Snow, it was not published.[48]

The all-around *Anvil* contributor who in Jack's mind best embodied the radical spirit of the 1930s was the ex–Rebel Poet John Rogers.[49] Both artist and writer, Rogers carved roughhewn printing blocks from wood and linoleum, creating prints for the *Anvil* and other little magazines such as *Hinterland*. The rudimentary physicality and boldness of Rogers's prints, reminiscent of the style of the 1920s Mexican movement El Taller de Grafica Popular, were visual counterparts of the "crude vigor" Conroy sought in submissions to his magazine. Rogers turned sharply leftward after witnessing the government's violent suppression of the Bonus Army in 1932.[50] Rogers's letters to Conroy, signed "Jack II," contained hand-drawn, colored sketches in the margins, like the letters of the Western illustrator Charles Russell. No more "proletarian" than most of the *Anvil* contributors, Rogers took a number of manual-labor jobs in order to support himself, fashioning his block prints in off-hours. Two of Rogers's best literary sketches, "Heart of My Grandfather" and "South," appeared in Botkin's *Folk-Say IV* (1932). Rogers left his tree-trimming job to join the Civilian Conservation Corps in 1935, became a member of the Federal Writers' Project, and served in the Air Force during World War II.[51] Despite exhibitions of his work in Washington, D.C., galleries, Rogers attracted only slender critical recognition. The bold images, the iconography of social justice, were out of place and out of sync with postwar America. Shortly before he died, he wrote in the *North Country Anvil*, a magazine inspired by Conroy's *Anvil*:

> As an old man, or an older one . . . the thing that saddens me the most are the number of my former friends and associates who have repudiated the past—have become soft, conservative and apologetic about their life during the lean years of the 1930s. I never repudiated them. I rejoiced in such a life. One government investigator wrote that I was not only not ashamed of my past I seemed to be proud of it. Yes, I would live the same life over again, only I would be more radical—if I were black I would be a Black Panther, if I were white I would be a Communist. I would not be a tired liberal who doesn't know which way to go or which way to jump in a crisis. . . . I recall talking to the late Floyd Dell, novelist and author of *Moon-Calf* and *Love in Greenwich Village*—a former editor of the old *Masses*—Dell told me that he didn't think as he did in the old days, he had mellowed. I think both he and

his wife worked for the Public Library system in Washington—I felt as though Thomas Jefferson had told me he no longer believed in democracy. I felt let down and lost. I also felt like saying: why you old s.o.b., you gave your best years for democracy and freedom for art and literature, you can't repudiate it all now. I didn't say anything—I let him autograph a copy of one of his books and left. . . . I am an old man now, but I am happy and proud that I went out and distributed leaflets that protested the execution of Sacco and Vanzetti. In my small way I had tried to stop injustice. I know now, I did not fail: the Establishment failed, and is still failing. The younger generation must correct this failing. It is not an old man's job.[52]

Many had embraced radical causes in their youth and later abandoned them; others like Rogers, Conroy, and Le Sueur, on the other hand, were rebels throughout their lives, not alone in the convictions they held but in the risks they took and choices they made. Noteworthy in retrospect is the number of former *Anvil* contributors who remained "unreconstructed rebels" throughout their lives.

The *Anvil* showed that a literary magazine could emphasize proletarian content without holding to any programmatic ideological line. Joseph Vogel's satire "Violets Are Blue," published in the sixth number of the *Anvil*, drew attention to the factionalism of the left, which amounted to a chorus of the deaf. The *Anvil*-ites were united (but not of one mind) in their compassionate response to contemporary experience—homelessness, unemployment, economic and social inequities, racism—but as individuals they represented various American brands. Most displayed a sturdy Emersonian self-reliance and independence of mind characteristic of people who, long after the anger and emotions of an earlier day are past, do not regret the "indiscretions" and passions of their youth.

Norman Macleod in his eighties, stricken with five major diseases, continued to write protest poetry from his nursing-home bed. Paul Corey built his own home from hand-crafted rock and wood and cared for his wife, the poet Ruth Lechlitner, for years after she became a stroke victim. Meridel Le Sueur, her work essentially blacklisted, wrote children's stories during the McCarthy years, and lived to see much of her early work reprinted with the rise of the feminist movement in the 1970s. At age ninety-three, she still spoke passionately in favor of social justice, like the Kansas Populist, Mary Elizabeth Lease. Joseph Vogel lived to see his work emerge from obscurity. In 1989, Syracuse University Press reprinted *Man's Courage*, honoring his achievement as a writer. Edwin Rolfe, a Rebel Poet board member, went to Spain as an American volunteer in the Civil War and served in World War II. In poor health, disappointed and angry at the spectacle of old friends like Clifford Odets betraying themselves in face of HUAC inquisitors, Rolfe died in 1954, long before his work would receive the attention it deserves.[53] One *Anvil* contributor who did not stay a rebel course, however, was Howard Rushmore. Rushmore, who as a cub reporter on the Mexico, Missouri, *Intelligencer* in 1934 had looked in admiration to Conroy as a model, turned his involvement in the left's cultural movement into a paying career exposing Party connections for Westbrook Peglar, writing for confessional magazines, and serving as a consultant to the McCarthy committee in the anticommunist crusade of the 1950s. The dramatic (and bathetic) finale occurred when Rushmore killed his wife, then himself.[54]

* * *

During his frequent visits to St. Louis in 1934, bunking in the home of Gladys's brother, Charlie, and his wife, Jack made contacts with Bill Sentner and other labor organizers, who enlisted his help in writing strike bulletins. Labor seemed to be on the move finally; the nutpickers' strike was followed by the Amalgamated Clothing Workers' strike, the bakers' union strike, the Fisher Body Company strike, the gas house workers' strike, demonstrations of the unemployed in Hooverville, and several years later, the electrical workers' strike against Emerson Electric in which Sentner played a central role. The strike bulletin, introduced by Miles Dunne, leader in the Minneapolis truckers' strike in 1934, who came down to St. Louis to help launch the *Gas House Worker*, proved to be an important instrument of communication. Jack perceived that St. Louis workers were reluctant to accept radical proselytizing; unions urged organizers to tone down the rhetoric and encouraged the grass-roots nature of strikes like that of the gas-house workers. Nonetheless, radicals like Sentner, a Communist district organizer, played important roles in educating workers in running an effective strike.[55] The strike bulletin, Jack noted, was the lifeline of a strike. The role of the strike bulletin in the St. Louis and Minneapolis strikes stuck in his mind; in his address before the American Writers' Congress in 1935 he cited it as a model of clarity and simplicity worthy of emulation by worker-writers. His remark was misinterpreted, however, and became grist for the mill of detractors for whom worker-writing was a rude interloper in the sanctuary of canonical literature.

The focus of radical-artistic activity in St. Louis at the time was a once-elegant mansion nicknamed the "Kremlin," located on the corner of Franklin and Grand. Ray Koch, a labor activist and writer who moved there from Commonwealth College with his wife, Charlotte Moskowitz, in 1937, remembers it as a "crossing of two major streetcar lines. A half block of business and living space along the south side of Franklin. Anchored on the corner was a drug store and eating place. Across the street was a huge clock that couldn't always be read because of the heavy mix of coal smoke and fog called smog. The lode was not the artists but the Vanguard Bookstore, which made it a junction of cross currents, a meeting place, a gathering at the well of intellect and culture, a place open to and used by people from every segment of St. Louis society. . . ."[56] Frequent visitors were Jean Winkler and Wallie Wharton, who served as St. Louis editors of the *Anvil*. The artist Joe Jones occupied a studio-apartment in the old mansion, which housed the leftist Vanguard Bookstore on the ground floor. (Jack shared an apartment in the "Kremlin" with Jones in 1936 when Jack worked on the Missouri Writers' Project.) Joe Jones had gained considerable notoriety in the winter of 1933–34 when he taught art classes to the unemployed (mainly black) in the Old Courthouse where the Dred Scott case had been argued. Jones, a devoted Communist at the time, fought and won, with the help of the John Reed Club and with permission from the St. Louis Art League, the landlords of the building, to hold the class there. The Art League soon regretted its decision: Jones hung Soviet posters and with his students, including several from the Washington University art school, constructed a giant mural in chalk entitled "Social Unrest in St. Louis," which occupied an entire second-floor courtroom.[57] The provocative nature of the posters and mural created a stir in the newspapers and occasioned a break-in by the American Fascist League, whose members tore down the posters and left a threatening letter behind. Despite his eviction, Jones continued to hold classes on the sidewalk in front of the building, causing a near riot when police interceded. Jack enlisted Jones to do the linoleum-print cover for *Anvil* 4 (January–February 1934), which depicted black and white workers looking to a leader figure for guidance against an urban background symbolizing progress, a crude imitation of Soviet political graphics.

This was the Comintern's Third Period, a highly sectarian time on the left before the Popular Front appeared with its accommodationist programs. To step out of line meant Party censure. A gadfly on the hide of the Art League, Jones walked the straight and narrow on Party matters. Jack, on the other hand, strengthened the impression of his "bohemian" unreliability in the eyes of the CP cultural commissars and local Party district organizers like Sentner and Pete Chaunt. He attended John Reed Club meetings in St. Louis infrequently—it is hard to imag-

ine Jack sitting solemnly in a meeting listening to a discussion of Marx's
"The Eighteenth Brumaire of Louis Bonaparte." Granville Hicks rebuked
him for deficiency in Marxist understanding; Mike Gold saw "dangerous bohemian tendencies in Larry Donovan," the narrator of *The Disinherited*.[58] Yet when Erskine Caldwell visited Moscow in early 1934,
there was talk that Jack would be invited to the Soviet Congress, to be
held later in the year.[59] Jack's reputation in the Soviet Union remained
strong. In April of 1934, a flattering portrait appeared in the IURW's
International Literature.[60]

     Spurring Jack to support the Communists were events such as the
violent repression of the Socialist workers' rebellion in Vienna and the
nascent fascist movement at home. In Melrose Park, near Chicago, reactionaries broke up a demonstration by workers. In St. Louis, when
extremists attacked Joe Jones and his unemployed workers learning to
paint in front of the Old Courthouse, Orrick Johns wrote Jack: "We've
got a grand fight on over [at] the old courthouse. Lining up in true po-
litical-fascist style. We had a Ku Klux warning yesterday, from NABA
(National American Bands of Action), a lynch-crew, and they tore up
some Soviet posters while they were there."[61] *Dune Forum* editor Chester Arthur, grandson of an American president, remarked in his review
of *The Disinherited* that "the very people you are trying to enlighten turn
against you and kick your teeth out, calling you a damned red...."[62]
At one memorable John Reed Club meeting that Jack attended, the
English writer John Strachey spoke on the terrible brutality of fascism
in Europe. In the United States, literary radicals were, in some cases,
victims of police oppression, like Tillie Lerner (Olsen), who had to go
into hiding when subjected to an attack on suspicion of being a "red."[63]
In a speech to the Kansas City Workers Modern Library in March, Jack
criticized Dahlberg, who praised Farrell for portraying protofascist hoo-
ligans in his novels. "This seems to be the most specious sort of reasoning," Jack told his Kansas City audience. "We don't need to be looking for Fascists as much as we need to be perfecting means to combat
them."[64] The possibility that fascist elements might attempt to gain
power in the United States loomed like some hideous specter before
Conroy (and other radical writers), who portrayed fears of the threat
in his second novel, *A World to Win*, which, in 1934, he had begun to
write.

     The menace of fascism, the social distress of the unemployed, the
growing resolve of labor—all impelled Jack to express support for the
Party's general line without, however, any "surrender of the will."[65]
When the Party attempted to dictate his behavior, he balked, as the
following incident reveals.

Jack, Joe Jones, Orrick Johns, and Jack Balch were scheduled to give a talk on "Art and the Class Struggle" at the Workers Modern Library, 1621 1/2 Grand, in Kansas City the evening of 5 May. Jack had made several trips to Kansas City to give talks at the Workers Theatre and the Workers Modern Library. He stayed with ex-Wobbly Jeff Ralls and several jobless workers in a "flea-bitten flat" overlooking the odoriferous stockyards, where they made beer in the bathtub and ate canned hominy from the relief office. To Ralls, Jack was a "second Jack London."[66] At the Workers Bookstore Jack met Harold Gunn, a printer and the brother of John Gunn, who had been an editor and writer for the Haldeman-Julius press in Kansas, and Aldine Matteson, secretary of the library, who later married Harold. Conroy's friendship with the Gunns continued in Chicago some years later. Like Jack, Harold loved to talk about books, recite, and drink.[67] Printers, Wobblies, college students, workers, and scions of wealthy Kansas City families frequented the Workers Modern Library and the Workers Theatre, some dressing in overalls to look "proletarian." When the organizer of the forum in Kansas City wrote Pete Chaunt, the Party's district organizer in St. Louis, that the Workers Modern Library allowed Trotskyists to speak, Chaunt told Jones not to attend a "symposium . . . for the benefit of a degenerate Trozkyist [sic] outfit."[68] Jones left a message for Balch that the forum was off, and let Orrick Johns know of Chaunt's decision.[69] Orrick Johns "crawfished," then decided to stay home. Jones sent Conroy a telegram: "We decided to cancel Saturday symposium after having learned anti-labor political factors in your forum. We refuse to support unprincipled political enemies of Soviet Union and of Communist International leader of world struggle for bread and freedom."[70]

Conroy went alone to Kansas City, angry that anyone should be "ordered" not to speak and lose an opportunity to make one's views known. Jack wrote Joe Jones saying that workers who attended the meeting "will now be persuaded by the Trotskite [sic] elements in Kansas City that the Communist Party and the St. Louis John Reed Club have sabotaged a meeting at an open forum to which the Party is always turning for both moral and financial assistance." Jack added, "As long as we remain cloistered in obscure halls, hair-splitting over minor points, the revolutionary cultural movement of the Midwest is likely to remain where it is."[71] Orrick Johns made a lame attempt to justify his not showing for the Kansas City forum, saying he had already declined the invitation several weeks earlier despite that fact that he allowed his name to remain on the program.[72] Balch felt bad about the way things had been handled; "if these people are as bad as Chaunt says, *all of them*, then how is it that Conroy, who had once written me about the swell reception he had there, did not know it?"[73] Jones, Balch, Johns, and Stanley Burnshaw of *New Masses,* who was in town for a visit shortly after the "affair," "had it out," agreeing that the response to the invitation had been muffed. To help set things right, Balch sent Jack a dollar to help pay for a Hagglund edition of H. G. Weiss's poetry.

In his letter to Joe Jones, Jack said that he would "abide by the decisions of the John Reed Clubs and the Communist Party when they are by somebody seasoned and well-balanced," but in this and other instances, his actions belied such declarations. Privately, Jack enjoyed parodying Party organizers like Pete Chaunt. Assuming a gloomy mien, Jack would mimic: "this is no time for long faces, comrades, we've had long faces too long." Organizers like Chaunt and Sentner replied in kind, disparaging the cultural work of the John Reed Club. Sentner loved to bait Wallie Wharton with contemptuous remarks such as, "You and your James Joyce and his Dublineers [sic]."[74]

Wharton, active in the John Reed Club and its successor, the Union of St. Louis Artists and Writers, seldom missed an opportunity to satirize Party functionaries, showing up at fraction meetings to raise troublesome, needling questions. Party cultural commissars, like Alexander Trachtenberg, tolerated reports of such antics with indulgent humor. Jack enjoyed the sandy-haired Scots-Irishman's wit and his organizational ability, enlisting his help with the business end of the *Anvil.* Sensing the degeneration of Party ideals into orthodoxy, represented by the policy of "Democratic Centrism," Wharton's wit turned caustic (and often bawdy).[75] He recited for his friends:

> I've got a leanin' toward Lenin these days,
> They tell me a leanin' like that really pays,
>
> . . .
>
> Tho Lincoln and Landon are grand names to utter
> It's lays about Lenin that earn bread and butter.[76]

* * *

Jack went up to Chicago in late May to give a talk on "Revolution and the Novel," at the invitation of Bill Jordan of the John Reed Club. Jack's energy reserves appeared inexhaustible, but the burden of editing the *Anvil* and writing a second novel, tentatively titled "Little Stranger," was beginning to demand its toll. Sanford, *Anvil's* printer at the Llano Co-Operative Colony printshop, worried him with funding and staffing problems. Sanford was about to lose Hagglund, who, tired of peanut butter and fried potatoes, planned to return to Holt, Minnesota. "It seems to me," Ben wrote Jack, "that, in the light of the class struggle, it really matters very little whether the *Anvil* continues or not, for it reaches only the bastard intellectual class (of which I am one), who dangle, as Joe Kalar has it, 'between the legs of capital like deflated testicles.'"[77] Jack too wondered at times whether it was worth all the effort. Robert Cantwell, whose novel *Land of Plenty* (1934) Jack admired, urged him to continue publishing the *Anvil*: "there is no place where the young people can get a hearing, and this at a time when the world is giving them more to say."[78] The editor of *Trend*, E. Ely-Estorick, wrote: "I've always admired you, Jack. . . . I've always been aware of the pioneer work you are doing. You see, you're down to earth, and when the decisive days come the breath of the soil will be within you . . . and where will the bleating jackasses be, oh probably where they spend many of their inspirational hours, having their balls scratched in the bohemian studios of some muchly married amarosa. Most of these literary bastards need a big city like New York in which to burden their pathological natures."[79]

Sanford indicated his willingness to continue printing *Anvil*, charging only for the materials, but he pleaded with Jack to find a trained helper for him in the printshop.[80] Sanford enlisted colony members, including his father, "Dad" Sanford, to help in the shop. Sanford indicated that with a linotype operator and one hundred dollars per issue for materials and postage he could continue publishing *Anvil*, to which he was devoted. Hagglund left Newllano but remained ardently interested in *Anvil*, urging Jack to stick with newsprint stock to keep production costs down.[81] Sanford was using both book stock and newspaper stock, as the slender finances permitted. Numbers six and eight compensated for the cheap paper with book-stock covers and colored ink. But the increased weight of book stock shot mailing costs upward. Willing to take the risk of higher production costs, however, was Walter Snow in New York, who hoped to find a New York printer for *Anvil*. Distressed at the use of cheap paper, Snow lobbied Jack to improve the magazine's appearance with (expensive) eggshell. Also dismaying to Snow was the lack of "big names" displayed prominently on the cover.

In early summer 1934, Dale Kramer, then an unemployed linotype operator who subsequently edited the midwestern little magazine *Hinterland* in Cedar Rapids, Iowa, came through Moberly to visit Jack. Seeing an opportunity, Jack persuaded Kramer to join Sanford in Newllano. Kramer later recalled that Jack "sold me into slavery."[82] Jack remembered Kramer's visit because it occurred during the strike at Moberly's Brown Shoe Company factory where Gladys worked as a shoe stitcher for four dollars a day.[83]

The strike was an economic catastrophe for the Conroys since the family had little other source of income. The $135 paychecks from Mencken had ceased since he left the *Mercury*. The Moberly shoe factory struck on 9 May, led by Clarence Gullion, who, with his wife, were workers in the four-story brick plant on Carpenter Street. With nearly 100 percent participation, the first strike lasted three weeks. Gladys and her sister Agnes Hickman stood picket duty, arranged so that one of the strikers could go fishing. There was a small-town familiarity among the strikers that made the strike different from the violent strikes in Toledo and Detroit. Goode's Tavern across from the factory gave food and coffee to picketing workers who prevented angry strikers from breaking factory windows.[84]

Goetze Jeter, "the ubiquitous youth" who reported for the Moberly *Monitor-Index*, "hopeful of unearthing a dastardly 'red' plot to overthrow the government,"[85] portrayed the events of the Moberly shoe-factory strike in *The Strikers*, published in 1937. In Jeter's fictional portrayal, the strikers are sheeplike *racaille* who tell dirty stories, pick on weaklings, and imbibe freely. The town politicians are in bed with company officials, and ultimately the strikers turn on their leader, "Farland" (Clarence Gullion), lynching him in an angry mob scene. The happy worker, Jeter's novel concludes, is the one who stays clear of labor disputes, hoping for recognition by paternalistic employers. Gullion protested to the *Monitor-Index* editor and Conroy panned the book in a *Post-Dispatch* review. Jeter was sore at Jack for years afterward.[86]

The spring of 1934 bore the promise of revolution for poets Orrick Johns and Muriel Rukeyser,[87] but in the Midwest the violence of gangsterism was closer at hand. Bonnie and Clyde died in a police shootout in May; in July, Dillinger lay bullet-ridden in a Chicago street. Spring yielded quickly to summer and relentless, suffocating heat. By 27 July, 412 Missourians had died from the heat, more than in any other state. Jack moved a table outside beneath the shade of a tree to write his second novel. Gladys poured water over his head, but even the water was warm. Covici-Friede had given him a contract for a second book, and expectations were high. "*The Disinherited* is a trumpet call," wrote the editors of *The Writers 1934 Year Book*, "setting the stage for the great novel we hope will come from Conroy's pen."[88] Moberlyean Bob Goddard, reporter for the *St. Louis Post-Dispatch*, visited Jack. Goddard's article was entitled "Missouri Writers Writes in Overalls," calling attention to Jack's working-class status. His table, Goddard observed, was piled high with manuscripts and letters. "He has a well-filled file of newspapers which contain dramatic situations," the reporter revealed. "He uses this file in plot construction."[89] The manuscript of the new novel was moving slowly. Jack worked at odd jobs for Bill Wisdom's construction company, tearing down buildings and laying pavement. These were heavy demands on his time, and for that reason he turned increasingly to Walter Snow, Wharton, and others to handle editorial responsibilities for the *Anvil*. Even as Jack received glowing letters from Erskine Caldwell and Joseph North praising his editorial work, and as Walt Snow made ambitious plans to expand the *Anvil*, forces were gathering from diverse directions which would cut short the *Anvil* enterprise at the peak of its fortunes.

*   *   *

The story of Jack's loss of the *Anvil* has been told by Fabre, Gilbert, Aaron, and Conroy himself. On the basis of extensive interviews with people directly involved in the *Partisan Review*'s takeover of the *Anvil*, including William Phillips (Wallace Phelps), together with letters that have finally been made accessible, I offer my own version.

Jack had come under Party fire in the past for having permitted *Common Sense* and Calverton's *Modern Monthly* to publish his stories. The fault of *Common Sense* from the Party's perspective was to be a liberal journal; the charge against Calverton was more serious. Calverton, who had broken with the Stalinists in 1932, and printed Max Eastman, whose *Artists in Uniform* report on the Soviet Union was viewed by many on the left as high treason, was branded "the official corrupter of the left intelligentsia."[90] The charges were spelled out in a lengthy article appearing in the January 1933 issue of *New Masses*, written by David Ramsey and Alan Calmer. Jack thought the article was unjust to Calverton and said so.[91] Calverton had been after Jack since the summer of 1932 to submit a short story to *Modern Monthly*. Following the *New Masses* attack, Calverton wrote Jack saying that he was opposed to the Stalinist "fight against democracy in the party which resulted in Trotsky's expulsion from the party."[92] To suggest anything less than revulsion against Trotsky was considered as outright apostasy by the Party, but apparently Jack felt otherwise. He submitted "A Coal Miner's Widow" to Calverton, who published it in the August 1933 issue of his magazine.

Jack angered orthodox Party ideologues further when he printed an advertisement for Calverton's magazine in the *Anvil*—an act not calculated to wave a red flag in front of the bull but achieving that effect nonetheless.[93] Such things weakened the Party's support of *Anvil* over time, not that the Party had a strong commitment to it or any other literary magazine. Literary activism, as pointed out earlier, ranked low on the Party's agenda. The Party's cultural apparatus respected Conroy's achievements in proletarian fiction but, as noted earlier, disapproved of what they considered to be individualist-anarchist tendencies in his personality.[94]

The publication history of the *Anvil* reveals how political Jack's editorial role had become in 1934. Shortly after the business with Calverton, Jack committed another offense in the eyes of the Party by running an ad in the *Anvil* for Brown's *Toward a Bloodless Revolution*, a pamphlet printed by the Anvil Press in Newllano. The passions of the time were such that a small infraction could stir up a tempest. Brown, the former editor of the old *Masses*, who had fled to Mexico during World War I, was considered a counterrevolutionary, a heretic. Giving space to Brown in the *Anvil* created problems for Jack, but his most grievous transgression was to print Robert Whitcomb—even Snow threatened to disavow Jack.

Whitcomb was an organizer of the Unemployed Writers Association, which petitioned Congress and the Civil Works Administration (CWA, the forerunner of the Works Progress Administration [WPA]) to provide work for writers. The notion of the government providing employment for writers was, of course, formalized by the Federal Writers' Project in 1935.[95] Whitcomb, who had been bumming around the country to gather material for a book entitled *Talk United States!*, was a dissident from the Party's perspective, a "Trotskyite snake" who had been expelled from the John Reed Club in New York. In contact with the Party's cultural apparatus, Snow served as the *Anvil's* go-between in New York, faithfully reporting news to Sanford and Jack. Without consulting Jack, however, Snow, who was worried that the magazine might lose the support of the Party's distribution network, apologized to Party cultural commissars for the Brown ad. Soon after, Jack printed Whitcomb's extract "from a forthcoming novel," "On the Sea," emblazoning Whitcomb's name on the magazine cover of *Anvil* 9 (January–February 1935). A Party reporter, Philip Sterling, gasped in recounting to Snow Conroy's apostasy. To worsen matters, Wallace Phelps and Philip Rahv, editors of the *Partisan Review*, hinted that Snow, as Conroy's representative, might be brought up on charges before John Reed Club members. Deeply anguished, Snow wrote a scalding letter to Jack. Jack was too far away, he said, to know about "the war-to-death waged against Lovestoneites, Trotskyites and other renegades. . . . How can I impress this fact on you strongly enough? Maybe in this way: If Whitcomb or any other known renegade ever appears again in *Anvil*, I will be compelled to sever all connections with the magazine and publicly disassociate myself from you—even you!"[96]

In the same issue, Conroy (or perhaps Sanford) had deleted a passage from Snow's announcement of the Anvil League of Writers that asked that members "must pledge also to defend the Soviet Union and to take no action hostile to the Communist Party, U.S.A."[97] Rumors,

Snow said, were abroad that *Anvil* was renegade. While Snow hastened to patch things up with the Central Committee of the Party, there were other indications that *Anvil* was coming under attack from several sides. Ignoring the warning signs, Jack was determined to unburden some of the load of editing so that he could finish "Little Stranger." Max Lieber wrote him: "So many of your friends who have been rooting for you ever since the publication of *The Disinherited* would be terribly let down if you don't follow it up with a first rate book."[98] Tired and upset, staring at impoverishment again, Jack was despondent that his second novel might not fulfill such expectations. He worried too that Snow might desert him. Snow wrote back immediately, in a better frame of mine, assuring Jack that he would stick by him, and accepted a larger share of the editorial duties.[99]

The Party cultural commissars' growing annoyance with Jack's *Anvil* signaled a division in the making between the Party cultural functionaries, located in the East, and the midwestern literary radicals. This division—or perhaps it was simply a misunderstanding—was underscored at the national conference of John Reed clubs convened in Chicago in October 1934. Meridel Le Sueur, who had come from the Minneapolis truckers' strike, felt called upon, for instance, to defend against allegations that the midwesterners were hopelessly parochial and nonideological. Orthodox Party critics had in the past attacked the centrifugal tendencies of regionalism; the implication was that the midwestern radicals were unwilling to conform to, or were simply ignorant of, the correct ideological basis of art. Sanora Babb recalls that "'Regional' was the stinging word used by certain influential New York groups to try to keep writers outside NY in their places. It was a patronizing put-down, but I don't think any real writers were stopped by it. Just annoyed. It still goes on in various ways to all points West. One answer has been the rise of many small publishers in the West, not vanity presses either."[100]

The Party seemed ambivalent on the regional basis of art. The John Reed clubs were an expression of the Party's interest in a geographically diversified culture; however, even as little magazines of the Midwest were praised in the *Daily Worker*, plans were underway to abolish the JRC.[101] Party ideology regarding literature took a right turn with the All-Union Soviet Writers' Congress in August and with the Popular Front. Andrei Zhdanov, later Stalin's minister of culture, called upon writers to utilize the literary techniques of realism to portray new socialist man. Karl Radek stressed the importance of attracting writers, including those of bourgeois origin, over to "our side" in the struggle against fascism. Gorki argued that folklore was the ground of literature, yet he repeated Zhdanov's demand that the proletarian state educate "engineers of the soul."[102] Socialist Realism meant in effect that a vanguard group would be charged with the cultural instruction of the working class. The production of literature was henceforth to follow Party prescripts under the scrutiny of the All-Union Soviet Writers. The cultural apparatus would be centralized, organized roughly along the lines of the Party's pyramidal structure called "democratic centralism." Paralleling the shift to greater centralized control, yet a broader, less sectarian approach to literary expression in the Soviet Union, were similar tendencies in the CPA's cultural programs, announced (or intimated) at the Chicago JRC national conference in late September.

The Chicago Convention of John Reed Clubs signaled important shifts in the Party's cultural policies with implications for the *Anvil* that Jack did not fully realize at the time. Underlying the changes were certain contradictions surfacing in the Party's ambivalent attitude toward the John Reed clubs and their purpose—which was presumably to discover and foster new literary and artistic talent. In St. Louis, Party organizers like Chaunt and Sentner disparaged the efforts of the local John Reed Club. Party people in Chicago were known to be especially severe with JRC writers, demanding that they devote more time to Party work and less to fulfilling their literary aspirations.[103] The struggle between artistic expression and Party discipline appeared to find relief, however, when Alexander Trachtenberg, Party cultural commissar from New York, spoke before the convention, assuring the writers that the Party did not wish "to interfere with the free exercise of talents, or to absorb talented people in other work."[104] But at a fraction meeting in a hotel room, Trachtenberg, an ebullient little man with a moustache and a disarming sense of humor, announced that the John Reed clubs would soon be disbanded in favor of a unified organization of credentialed writers. The announcement stunned Richard Wright, who was there: "I asked what was to become of the young writers whom the Communist Party had implored to join the clubs and who were ineligible for the new group, and there was no answer. . . ."[105] The midwestern radicals were confused and angry, ascribing the policy shift to the growing consolidation of power among radicals east of the Hudson. It was further indication that literary production sites must continue in the Midwest.

Little magazines like the *Anvil, Hinterland, Left Front,* and *New Quarterly* had helped foster the idea of a radical culture attuned to the needs and interests of midwesterners, based in great part upon cooperation and goodwill.[106] Jack's editorial work was, of course, an instrumental part of this cultural project. Meridel Le Sueur and other midwesterners felt involved in the *Anvil*; authors promoted it and helped, in some cases, with distribution. They were the "conduits," as Meridel Le Sueur said, just as the Wobblies had participated in the production and distribution of their own publications.[107] These were small but significant achievements in decentering literary production in the 1930s. To the dismay of Le Sueur, Conroy, and other midwesterners, these achievements came under attack at the conference, a sign that an agenda was being enacted without their knowledge or consent.

Jack had made the trip to Chicago with three companions from Moberly in Charles Waterfield's Model A Ford. (Waterfield was married to Jack's niece Zella Harrison; the other travelers were Harvey Harrison, his nephew, and a man named Frost, who went along for the adventure.) The foursome stayed in a cheap hotel on State Street in which, as Jack recalled, rooms were

> plasterboard cubicles[s] just big enough for a one-man cot. Chickenwire was stretched across the top which gave a measure of privacy, but didn't keep out sounds or smells. . . . There was a black and tan burlesque show hard by with well-stacked Negro and white girls dexterously bumping and grinding in separate but equal formations. A kind of segregation prevailed, as white girls and black girls never danced together. The comedians and straight men were white. These and other cultural divertissements beguiled my travelling companions while I repaired to the upstairs headquarters of the John Reed Club, just down the street.[108]

Jack's companions prowled the bars and burlesque shows on South State Street while Jack attended meetings at the JRC national convention, returning in the early morning hours. While the accommodations were deplorable, they were within their budget. They felt lucky; many of the convention participants had arrived by boxcar.

At the Chicago convention, Jack first met Richard Wright, Meridel Le Sueur, Nelson Algren, Abe Aaron, Sam Gaspar, and other *Anvil*-ites. Later, in an apartment party, he talked to Wright, who, he later recalled, was "a good-looking and pleasant-mannered young man but abstracted and aloof from the alcoholically induced merriment about him."[109] Algren and Jack became friends immediately. Joe Jones, Jack Balch, Walter Snow, and Paul Romaine (from Milwaukee) were there, and Orrick Johns reported the event for *New Masses*.

Jack discussed the problems of writing about factory work in his talk to the conference. Pity or idealizations, he said, often distort the efforts of middle-class writers in describing factory life, while few workers possess the literary skills or desire to write of their experience. Robert Cantwell's *Land of Plenty* (1934) was the "best novel of factory life yet written by an American."[110] Walter Snow told of efforts to provide sep-

arate groups within the John Reed clubs for writers and artists, and commented optimistically on the prospects of proletarian literature after its
difficult gestation period in the face of hostile bourgeois critics and indifferent readers. New audiences were interested in proletarian writing,
he claimed, pointing to recent sales. Snow's impulse was to be upbeat
and positive, and he called upon his listeners to act likewise in their
own work.[111] Snow's optimistic heralding of proletarian writing, his tendency to ignore trends that spoke otherwise, was to play a fateful role
in the evolution of the *Anvil*.

The poet Alfred Hayes sounded the keynote of the Chicago convention: sectarianism would be put aside to make room for a broad cultural front to include all fellow-traveling intellectuals and artists in the
struggle against fascism. Alexander Trachtenberg, who spoke in the
name of the Party's Central Committee, reinforced the Popular Front
position that accommodation with bourgeois writers was to replace the
old hardline leftist desire to enlist literature in the class struggle.[112]
Wallace Phelps and Philip Rahv of *Partisan Review* explained the role
of leftist magazines in the movement. "The worker-writers," said A. B.
Magil in his lecture to the some forty delegates, "are the buried trea-
sure hidden away by centuries of capitalism. To reach them, to help
them find themselves is our task."[113]

For Le Sueur, the emotional moment of the conference occurred
when Philip Rahv spoke in criticism of the midwestern radicals.
"Phelps and Rahv both were there. They made these real brilliant
speeches. That was the first time that I ever entered a political arena. They made this awful speech about Jack's writing and my writing,
and in the middle of this, that the farmer was already a capitalist, that
. . . there's no use writing about the farmer, that he didn't love the
land—that was just romanticism. And oh, [their speeches were] on
the highest intellectual level. . . . I was offended by the fact that they
said that we didn't love the land . . . and that we deliberately gave over
to the mortgage and the high interest." Le Sueur said, "And so I made
my first speech, and I wept, which I think was good because an intellectual type doesn't like weeping at all. And I . . . told them about the
exploitation of the land, the seizure of mortgages, and the bank.
. . . And the rebuttal said I was just a romantic, my work, my writing
was romantic and sentimental, and so I didn't know how to answer
to that. But Trachtenberg . . . rose to my defense. And said that, quoting Marx [*sic*]—and he was accused of being emotional—, and he said
something like, everything that's human is my concern. . . ." Rahv's
reply was, "How can you love the land under capitalism?"[114] Jack sat
near the back of the room, half-listening to the speeches, talking to

Richard Wright. The "easterners," he recalled much later, quoted Marx "chapter and verse," dazzling the midwesterners who "had been raised on Sockless Jerry Simpson."[115] Awed and intimidated by the rhetorical displays of ideology on the part of the New York radical intelligentsia, the midwesterners were unaware that, despite the speechmaking at the conference, cultural functionaries of the Party had decided to abandon worker-writing as a liability and to eliminate the term "proletarian literature" itself from their publications.

In retrospect, both Meridel and Jack were persuaded that Rahv and Phelps had executed a swift power play at the Chicago conference, in collaboration with the Party cultural commissars. Le Sueur recalled,

> So they came in under the guise of splitting [the cultural movement] ideologically. You know, when you want power. So they came to this meeting, and had this whole ideological thing . . . [they] even brought up nativism and the thing in the Soviet Union where they had agrarian radicals, you know, in the 1905 revolution, and they had some, what were they called? . . . they loved the land. Something like that now, when they're going back to the land. They had a whole thing in Russia, in the 1905 revolution . . . the something-niks [Narodniks] they were called. But there was a whole Tolstoyean movement, a political movement to go back to the land . . . so they compared us to them and you know, they had been analyzed to death by them. It was really highly ideological, that's what got us. And everyone thought, well, maybe we're wrong. And they called my midwesternism, regionalism, you know, all kinds of Marxist terms. What is regionalism?, you know. They attacked all of them, [including] Jack Conroy, and then after they did that, they split the conference.[116]

It was a power play familiar to politicians, left or right: one interest group deliberately divides the larger group along ideological lines and in the ensuing instability consolidates its position. As editors of the New York John Reed Club's *Partisan Review*, Rahv and Phelps were interested in raising the discourse of proletarian literature and criticism to a higher level of regard. The Party appeared to approve—not because it was concerned about literary quality but because it hoped to attract established writers to its fold.

When Granville Hicks, in an article entitled "Our Magazines and Their Functions" appearing in the 18 December *New Masses*, called for the reduction in number and the limiting of scope of magazines on the left, he said there was a place for *Partisan Review* as long as it was "primarily devoted to long, theoretical critical essays." *Dynamo* should be folded into *Partisan Review,* and *Blast* should yield to *Anvil* as the principal medium for publishing proletarian short stories. There was no more room, he said, for the autonomous radical literary magazines that seemed to proliferate throughout the land; "such Bohemian individualism and irresponsibility are entirely incompatible with the serious tasks of revolution and the intelligent discipline of revolutionaries."[117] Hick's program for the little magazines on the left should have warned Conroy and Snow that something was afoot within the Party's inner cultural circle, but neither perceived it. Snow, who had taken over the main tasks of managing *Anvil's* daily editorial tasks while Jack finished his novel, was in fact feeling quite pleased with the attention he was receiving from Party's cultural functionaries like Alexander Trachtenberg and William Browder.

Snow enjoyed meeting with the wily, dynamic Trachtenberg, the Central Committee's representative in charge of the cultural front. He felt like a "bigshot," he said, to be invited to "an exclusive affair in honor of the tenth anniversary of International Publishers to be attended only by persons prominent in publishing circles."[118] Rumors abounded, Snow reported, that he (Snow) was in cahoots with Whitcomb. Another rumor was that "*Anvil* was out to knife *Partisan Review.*" Clearly, *Anvil* was on probation, Snow cautioned. No more Whitcomb or ads for Lovestoneite publications. One of *Anvil's* stories showed cops fraternizing with workers, giving advice "on revolutionary tactics." The CP policy, Snow reminded Sanford, was that cops were rats, agent-provocateurs. In the future, such stories should be censored, but Snow would seek Trachtenberg's verdict on this matter. To make sure Sanford complied, Snow wrote Wharton, *Anvil's* business manager, asking him not to send any more money to Sanford; Snow was planning to find a New York publisher.

Snow returned from a meeting with Trachtenberg and Browder on 15 December, feeling satisfaction that he had stabilized *Anvil's* future. "*Anvil* henceforth," he wrote proudly to Jack, "will be the official fiction magazine of the Communist literary movement." Willner, of the Party's Central Distribution Agency (CDA), would accept all remaindered issues and "boom" *Anvil.* Furthermore, Rahv, he said, "has been *ordered* to cease his old feud with me and to work with me in the most friendly fashion to boom *Anvil.* All rumors against the *Anvil* must be spiked, declares Trachtenberg. . . . *Partisan Review* must carry more detailed and friendly notices of *Anvil.* . . ." Finally, Snow announced to Jack that "we must print only the best stories available and not regard *Anvil* as a 'tryout' for beginners."[119] Crude vigor was out.

Jack could scarcely question Snow's sincere purpose in promoting the

Anvil, given that Snow was contributing funds from his own meager newspaper salary. Moreover, *Anvil's* finances were not sufficient to continue without the Party's distribution network—the newspaper kiosks, bookstores, and so forth. Too many unsold copies of *Anvil* 9 had languished on the Party's bookstore shelves to satisfy Willner. Jack was in a jam, yet he was deeply disturbed and fumed to Snow about evidence of orthodoxy holding sway. Snow said not to worry, that Jack was burned out by *Anvil* work and other responsibilities, and that he should leave *Anvil* to Snow, who would provide Jack with temporary respite from editorial worries.[120] Clinton Simpson in New York would aid Snow. When Erskine Caldwell heard of Jack's plans to turn over the main editorial duties to Snow, he wrote: "Don't tell me you are retiring from *The Anvil's* editorial chair. I hope not, for the magazine, but if you need the time for your own work, naturally it is the only sensible thing to do." Write those great things you have in you, he urged Jack.[121]

It soon became evident that Snow had plans to make *Anvil* "bigtime," increasing its circulation and improving its literary and production quality. This meant in effect abandoning its main commitment—to discover new talent, to take a chance on untested writers' "juvenile junk" (Trachtenberg's term) in hopes that they would develop and flourish as writers. Snow seemed to have yielded to a "bigness" complex, mimicking the language of literary prominence, of arborescence, quite opposed to *Anvil's* devotion to horizontality, or rhizomatous development. Trachtenberg, Snow noted, "asserted that you [Jack] were debasing your name and lowering your own deserved reputation by sponsoring, as an editor, more than half of the stories in the current *Anvil*."[122] For this reason, Snow said, he hoped that Jack wouldn't be angry when he (Snow) dumped several stories, including one by Tennessee Williams, that Jack had accepted for the magazine (there was still a large backlog of manuscripts that Jack had accepted, which continued to make *Anvil* Jack's magazine in content, despite Snow's cuts). In a separate letter to Sanford, Snow insisted that Sanford print the tenth issue (March–April 1935) on expensive eggshell, in keeping with the magazine's newly acquired status.[123]

By the early winter of 1934, Jack had slumped into one of his seasonal low spells, depressed by the blows he had received from Snow, Sanford (complaints about costs and lack of help), Covici-Friede (anxious to see the whole manuscript), and recently, Party organizers in St. Louis. In order to maintain *Anvil's* balance, Jack chose Balch, Clark Mills (McBurney), and Winkler, all members of the St. Louis Union of Writers and Artists, as associate editors to screen the manuscripts that were pouring into the editorial offices at twenty-five and more each week.[124] Joe Jones was the art editor. Be ruthless in editing and sweet in rejecting, Jack advised.

St. Louis contributors and staff people like Wallie Wharton sought to keep *Anvil* going and were willing to contribute, in some cases their own money and voluntary labor. Nelson Algren, Meridel Le Sueur, Sanora Babb, and Erskine Caldwell continued to send their work to *Anvil*, despite the editorial changes. Balch sent the screened manuscripts to Conroy for final approval. The business offices were moved from Moberly to Wharton's apartment in St. Louis, on Nottingham Avenue. It was a workable arrangement, but Balch tangled with Mills, former editor of *Eliot*, a Washington University literary magazine, and Balch refused to let Wharton read manuscripts, despite Jack's urgings that the St. Louis staff "work in harmony." There were other complicating factors: Pete Chaunt, the CP's St. Louis district organizer, was "bearing down roughly" on the St. Louis *Anvil* staff.[125] Trachtenberg wrote Chaunt, telling him to ease up. Yet, Chaunt's criticism probably reinforced the idea among the Party's cultural commissars that *Anvil* was undependable—and dispensable. Snow acted as a liaison between *Anvil* and the Party, a role that soon placed him in editorial control of the magazine.[126] In New York, Snow said, *Anvil* could be put back on firmer footing, with the Party's help, then returned to the St. Louis group and Conroy.[127] The confusion and conflicts that bedeviled the St. Louis editors escalated into a ludicrous episode that cheered Jack's low spirits and provided Wharton with ready-made matter for satire.

Eager to increase the number of workers in the membership, Joe Jones invited an uneducated black janitor named Vanderbilt Belton to join the St. Louis John Reed Club (the Union of St. Louis Artists and Writers existed separately) based upon a letter Belton had signed to the *Daily Worker*. It is unclear what her motives were, but the letter was actually composed by Minerva Primm Wharton, Wallie Wharton's wife, who knew Belton and wished to help him. Wallie saw potential for humor in the Belton invitation, at the expense of John Reeders like Jones who, in Wharton's eyes, took his Party work all too seriously. Jones supported vigorously Belton's application, but Jack Balch objected angrily. As a result, Balch and Wharton were brought before a "court" of John Reeders and Party functionaries—a kind of farcical Soviet "Workers Court."[128] Both Wharton and Conroy, who was not present, took immense delight in telling the story of the St. Louis "trial" of Balch and Wharton.

The charge against Balch "was that he sat in a corner writing a poem during the nutpickers' strike."[129] To make matters worse, Balch's father-in-law was an outspoken Trotskyist. Wharton's pranks and mischief had made him unwelcome in JRC meetings. As a consequence, both Balch and Wharton were expelled from the club. Joining them was Jean Winkler, who resigned in sympathy with the accused. Wharton faked being angry at his expulsion; Winkler wrote an unpublished comic opera about the affair.[130] Conroy ever afterward in retelling the story referred to the incident as "Wharton, the man of sorrow, on trial for his life before the sanhedrin of the John Reed Club."[131] The kangaroo court, the denunciation, the dogmatism—these were reprehensible to Jack. Yet he continued to support the Party's aims, despite evidence of its ambivalent commitment to proletarian literature.

Jack's own literary plans pointed in new directions, as indicated in a Guggenheim application he wrote in late 1934. In early 1935, he was awarded funding to write a documentary study of workers migrating from the South to northern industrial cities like Chicago and Detroit. Jack's shift to what was then called "revolutionary reportage" was the literary equivalent of political activism.[132] In *A World to Win* (the retitled "Little Stranger"), Robert Hurley abandons his literary aspirations finally to join in the workers' struggle for rights. Similarly, many proletarian writers had turned to activism—Robert Cruden, Joseph Kalar, Ed Falkowski, and Warren Huddlestone.[133] Several writers had grown weary of trying to find publishers for their novels; most wanted to participate more actively in labor's struggle to organize. Despite mounting evidence that the proletarian episode was in decline, Jack remained confident that the worker-writer had an important role in American letters and would soon be giving his reasons to his fellow writers in New York.

* * *

By March of 1935, Snow, a lanky, mustachioed, congenial man given to anemia and stomach problems, had taken over almost entirely the editor's role in the *Anvil*. The actual control of the magazine, however, was slipping out of Snow's hands. An *Anvil* based in the East, directed mainly to New York readers, under the auspices of the Party, promoting "big-time" authors while running up frightening debts—this was the stuff of Jack's worst nightmares. And yet it was all to happen within the year. But the most terrifying specter of all—again assuming that Jack had dreamed all this during some particularly anguished night—would be the absorption of the *Anvil* by *Partisan Review*. Jack's archrivals in the little-magazine field, Rahv and Phillips, at the helm of his magazine, building up their circulation from his list, squeezing out the *Anvil*'s special flavor so that nothing of the original was left, and the editors finally turning Trotskyist? These things also were to come to pass.

Snow had reached an "understanding" with Trachtenberg that *Anvil* was now "the official fiction magazine of the Communist literary movement."[134] Snow, he wrote Wharton, as its "responsible editor . . . is taking guidance directly from the Central Committee [Trachtenberg]."[135] To counterbalance Snow's eastern bias and maintain the center of gravity in the Midwest, Jack maintained his St. Louis editorial staff (Winkler, Balch, Wharton—Mills had dropped out), who, after screening the submissions, sent the best to Snow for his decision. Snow, however, largely ignored their recommendations and appointed his own contributing editors.[136] A backlog of some thirty manuscripts still remained from those that Jack had chosen to publish in future issues. Most of these Snow simply scratched.

Snow's plans for *Anvil* were to "boom" its circulation, make it into a "big-time" literary magazine, self-sustaining and prestigious. This meant contracting with a press in New York, improving the paper and print, placing ads (usually at his own expense) in *New Masses* and elsewhere, soliciting contributions from better-known authors, featuring their names on the cover, and exaggerating circulation figures if necessary to give the impression of success. These were the features of literary prominence that Snow wished *Anvil* to display, and to achieve his goal, he sought the support of the Party's literature agencies. Trachtenberg assured him that *Anvil* would "be boomed in preference over all other radical fiction magazines," Snow reported to Conroy.[137] Furthermore, Snow said, Trachtenberg "ordered" Rahv to cooperate in promoting the *Anvil*.[138] As demonstration of this new "friendship," Rahv would review *Anvil* in the next *Partisan Review*, which he did—favorably. In return for allying *Anvil* with Party interests, Snow would receive the "fullest support of the Party literature agencies—the bookshops and the CDA."[139]

Jack had done much to help young writers, Snow acknowledged, "but that period in the career of *Anvil* is past."[140] To appear in *Anvil* now would be a mark of distinction. Those associated with it would receive their rewards as well. "We may load you with work," Snow wrote Wharton, "but don't forget that you're being watched by a whole bunch of important people and when *Anvil* gets to be the mag Trachtenberg, Bill Browder and I hope that it will, you'll be up in the front."[141] Snow's tactics in "booming" *Anvil* included announcing a forthcoming story by Kalar, then soliciting Kalar to write the story. Snow was in an expansive frame of mind, proud that he had negotiated successfully with the Party to place *Anvil* in the forefront of all cultural magazines in the movement. He had even succeeded in neutralizing Rahv, who nonetheless would still bear watching.[142] From Snow's apartment on Barrow Street, *Anvil*'s future looked bright. Snow was getting help from Clinton Simpson, a book editor and reviewer who appeared as eager as Snow to make the magazine go. Liberal Press extended credit, which made it possible to increase the print run for *Anvil* to 3,500. Willner's distribution of *Anvil*, Snow reasoned, would pay the printer's bill, which had doubled Sanford's ninety-dollar press runs. In anticipation of the Writers' Congress in late April, to which Snow had been invited, *Anvil* 12 would appear, preempting its competitor, *Partisan Review*. Trachtenberg expressed his pleasure with *Anvil* 11. *Anvil* was no longer looking "like a plaything of amateurs," he told Snow.[143]

Jack could do nothing but watch the spectacle silently from a back row and hope that his surrogate editors would perform their parts adequately. Covici-Friede rushed him to complete the manuscript of *A World to Win* for its spring list. Parts of the manuscript were in galley proof before the entire manuscript was completed. The Guggenheim had given him a reprieve financially, but he now had to show something in return for it. Gladys was laid off from her job at the Brown Shoe Company factory. The $166 Jack received from his grant each month would scarcely cover the expense of maintaining two households (the project required a great deal of travel). Yet, as he approached the trip east to the Writers' Congress, held in New York City's Mecca Temple, he sensed that finally the hour had come when in a large and influential public forum he could make his case for the worker-writer. To speak at the congress meant recognition, not for himself alone, but for the *Anvil*, for worker-writing, for a concept of literature that would be worthy of a democratic culture that values the expressions of "those who do not write."

16

The Unmaking of the Worker-Writer

Ah, what greenhorns and rubes we were then, innocent of the city's plots and counterplots in the literary domain.
—Conroy, Foolkiller talk, 2 June 1978

JACK FELT LIKE A CELEBRITY in New York, and he was somewhat awed too, as Meridel Le Sueur remarked, by the "effect of seeing faces rush toward you on the street."[1] The *New York Post* reported how "New York writers, those veterans of literary teas, and publishing trade gossip, goggled at the delegations from the South and Far West. They clustered around such famed novelists as Jack Conroy who boomed: 'He was a no good guy, bull simple, that's all.' The New York critics from the magazines and newspapers had to ask about that one. A 'bull simple guy' is somebody who is afraid of a policeman because he has been beaten up before."[2] Jack had arrived by bus on Thursday, 25 April, taken the subway to Sheridan Square in Greenwich Village, and walked to the Snows' at 54 Barrow Street. Walt and his wife shared their small apartment during the Writers' Congress with Meridel Le Sueur, Jack, Howard Rushmore, and Wallie Wharton. Snow, the tireless publicist, had arranged for Jack to be interviewed. It was an opportunity for journalists covering the congress who were looking for a proletarian bard, and they made much of it, featuring Jack in New York newspapers. Jack, affable and generous, fulfilled their expectations, as he had in 1933 when journalists sought him out in the shack on Collins Street. The *New York Herald-Tribune* reporter visited with Jack in the Snows' apartment, where he met a "brawny fellow [Jack], with tousled yellow hair and big, calloused hands" who talked as he put away "a huge mouthful of potatoes." Jack, it was reported, would go back to work in an automobile factory if a job were available.[3] The *New York World-Telegram* dwelt on his working-class credentials—born in a coal camp, railroad worker, factory hand, and so forth. A caricature of Conroy (looking like an Irish longshoreman) appeared in *International Literature* and *New Masses*, along with the faces of other Congress speakers. People were amused when during interviews he pulled written notes from his pocket. Affable and performative in small groups of friends and the curious, Jack felt strangely awkward when asked to speak before an assembly. Nelson Algren was similarly reluctant to talk before an audience. Meridel Le Sueur remembers having to prop him up to speak. Apart from Le Sueur, whose oratorical ability seemed never to flag, the midwesterners appeared ill-equipped to participate in the displays of rhetoric and response in evidence during the Congress sessions.

The congress opened on Friday, 26 April, at 8:00 P.M., at Mecca Temple (Fifty-fifth Street, between Sixth and Seventh Avenues) to an audience of some four thousand. Waldo Frank delivered the initial address, reminding the participants and the audience that the purpose of the congress was to organize a League of American Writers affiliated with the IURW, and calling upon writers to break out of their isolation, to think in terms of "we" rather than "I." The audience of writers from many nations roared its appreciation as in turn Malcolm Cowley, Earl Browder, Granville Hicks, Frederich Wolf, Mike Gold, and others spoke. Writers who felt exiled in their native land joined ex-expatriates like Cowley and Matthew Josephson in what appeared to be a demonstration of unity. A great deal of disunifying maneuvering, however, was occurring behind the curtain, so to speak, and indeed there appeared to be wide divergence concerning proletarian literature and the role of the worker in literature.[4]

Jack's turn to speak came the next morning, in the auditorium of the New School for Social Research, following speeches by Joseph Freeman, Edwin Seaver, Kenneth Burke, and Martin Russak. Heywood Broun said afterward that Jack appeared at the meeting looking "like an unmade bed."[5]

In his speech, titled "The Worker as Writer," Jack limned the obstacles confronting the worker-writer: the lack of literary training, the fatigue of labor, the choice of technique appropriate to proletarian writing. On this last point, he called for simplicity and clarity. "To me," he argued, "a strike bulletin or an impassioned leaflet is of more moment than three hundred prettily and faultlessly written pages about the private woes of a gigolo or the biological ferment of a society dame as useful to society as the buck brush that infests Missouri cow pastures and takes all the sustenance out of the soil." The homely similes, the hyperbole, the anti-intellectualism of the assertion might have entertained Missourians, as did Thomas Hart Benton's salty commentaries on the "New York aesthetes" in his abrasive rebuffs of the New York art world about the same time.[6] To many eastern critics and commentators, however, it was pure cornpone, evidence of the backwardness and sloppiness of what Murray Kempton, in his revisionist memoir, *Part of Our Time*, published in the Cold War years, called "plebeian naturalism."[7] Howe and Coser, who note that Conroy was "one of the few proletarian novelists who had ever been a proletarian," describe the "impenetrable sincerity" of his talk.[8] Jack made himself an easy target, and in a sense his comment on strike bulletins merited criticism—although Kempton's remark about Jack's "scorn of careful writing" (136) is completely off the mark—for failing to provide a suitable context.[9]

Farrell, it was rumored, invented sobriquets at the congress for Jack ("Jack Cornrow") and Gold ("Maxim" Gold).[10] In *Yet Other Waters*, in which Farrell novelized his growing alienation from the Party and the ensuing Stalinist attacks on his writing, Conroy is portrayed as a "poor yokel, Pat Devlin," a rube with brash pretensions, a worker thrust into the limelight by Party patronage, still smarting over Bernard Carr's (Farrell's) hostile review, and urging his followers at the 1935 congress to gang up on Carr.[11] Bernard won't take the bait, however. "Devlin's an oaf. I'm sorry for him. I'm sorry he can't write. Why doesn't he quit writing and become a worker?"[12] The scarcely veiled satire continues with Devlin reading the famous passage on the strike bulletin "with a Midwestern twang":

> I see red when I read of one of our writers praising a pseudoproletarian novel written by a bourgeois decadent in a velvet jacket who learned about the heroic struggle of the toiling masses in the bordellos and cafes of the left bank of Paris. But I thrill with joy when I read a simple strike leaflet. There is more of the vigor of proletarian literature in a strike leaflet, however crudely written, than there is in all the style and pseudoerudition of a college graduate's painful course from the saints to the Revolution by way of the classroom and the brothel. . . .[13]

Carr sees the "strike leaflet" passage as an attack on himself but won't respond directly, waiting his turn the next morning to argue his own case for a revolutionary literature grounded in literary tradition and freed of sectarian narrowness (i.e., leftism). In Farrell's satirical portrait, based loosely on Farrell's own experiences, the protagonist Carr is aloof from the sectarianism and Party politics of functionaries like Mark Singer (Mike Gold), which have "made" Devlin's reputation. The literary rube Pat Devlin (Conroy), on the other hand, enjoys his status, boasting to everyone of his "Loewenthal Fellowship" (Guggenheim), and grinning "foolishly" when approached by reporters seeking an interview.[14] Farrell's novel was published in 1952, too long after the actual event to affect Conroy's reception or to play a role in the Farrell-Conroy feud. Moreover, it has little value in reconstructing the actual events of the congress (supposing that was Farrell's purpose, which of course it was not). It does, however, underscore one of the underlying conflicts taking shape on the cultural left, namely that between those attempting to distance themselves from the "rough proletarians" loosely represented by Gold and those attempting to reclaim quality and value for their work according to more traditional literary standards.[15]

The strike-bulletin passage became part of the lore of the congress, later marshaled into the postwar revisionist critiques, for example, Howe and Coser's reference to Conroy's speech: that "there were, to be sure, somewhat more considered and cultivated voices heard at the congress."[16] However, these were drowned out, the two historians of the CPA argue, by those who sought to join intellectuals with the working class and preserve "the Marxian class outlook" (i.e., the Stalinists). This notion became enshrined in Kempton's remark that the "impassioned leaflet which Jack Conroy found of such transcendent moment was a Party handbill."[17] Conroy's misinterpreted strike-bulletin comment stiffened the hostility of the literary standard bearers who felt called upon to defend against rude interlopers.[18]

For not providing a context for his remarks, Jack was in some part to blame for the hostility they aroused. Underlying them was Conroy's conviction that an artist was an accomplished craftsperson, not some special figure of "exalted ability" set apart from his or her fellows. Culture embraces a whole way of life, as Raymond Williams points out, not merely those in possession of a special sensibility, which is a form of idolatry.[19] Although the remark about the strike bulletin was intended to underscore the writer's role in the labor struggle (which after 1934 was quickly gaining momentum), it merely antagonized the "considered and cultivated voices" in Conroy's audience. Yet it had important implications for writers like Jean Winkler, Le Sueur, Conroy, Cruden, Kalar, Russak, and others who, as writers, were actually involved in union struggles. The "strike bulletin" was an important instrument of communication in a strike.[20] Jack had in mind the so-called Minneapolis techniques used so effectively by Miles Dunne in the 1934 strike. In St. Louis, as mentioned earlier, Jack had a small part in the locally written and published bulletins employed in the nutpickers' and Laclede Gas Workers' strikes, providing vital communication lines of which the workers, who contributed to them, were justifiably proud.[21] There would have been less misinterpretation if Jack had spoken to fellow workers instead of fellow writers, since most members of the congress had little or no actual experience in labor organization or union activities. Lacking this experience, one might misconstrue Conroy's remarks. The incident deserves this much attention since, I believe, it throws into relief the shifting terrain, misunderstanding, and factionalism that characterized the left's cultural front in 1935.[22]

Conroy's strike-bulletin comment refers to the importance of instruments of communications linking workers in general, and to reportage. "It seemed to me," Jack commented years later, "that such a document [the strike bulletin] intrinsically would have more moment and contemporary relevance than a dozen prettily written pages about the private woes of a Parisian cocotte. I have been unjustly branded as a 'foe' of 'careful' and workman-like writing because of these misquotations and misinterpretations."[23] The response to Jack's strike-bulletin remark reveals the deep-seated ambivalence felt by many at the congress toward literary "relevance" and the role of literary tradition and aesthetics, framed within debates since ancient times on the useful and the beautiful. Most speakers at the congress appeared to hold out hope for a radical novel, a proletarian fiction; but there was no consensus on how to realize this hope, and in fact, some delegates were charting their course back into the traditions of great literature, or perhaps had never abandoned them. These tensions would soon rupture the precarious display of unity paraded at the congress, unleashing a fury of mutual recrimination and antagonism. Around the simmering kettle of conflicting aims and desires at the congress danced the figure of Farrell, provocatively honest at times, mischievous and iconoclastic, poking fun at the "walking cornfield" Conroy, misprizing the strike-bulletin speech, and eventually taking everyone by surprise in proposing to end the congress by singing the Internationale.[24] These anecdotes, of course, should be weighed against Farrell's own memories.[25]

What of Conroy's "impenetrable sincerity"? Perhaps it was so. He failed, too, to calculate the impression his speech would make on some. Lacking all pretense, naively almost, Jack praised *Those Who Built Stalingrad*, a collection of stories told by Soviet workers, recently translated into English and introduced by Gorki as "good simple truth—the truth of strong hardy men and women—Bolshevik truth."[26] The collection joined two avenues of thought in Jack's mind: his love of vigorous, readable, vivid writing, close to actual speech, characteristic of first-person narratives; and his support of the workers' republic where the voices of workers were given special cultural sanction.[27] The Soviet work is hopelessly propagandistic, a fact that Conroy foregrounded in his remarks, quoting the editors: "can we not say that their various life-stories blend together into one whole curve of growth, in an upward curve of the development and unfolding of human personality in a society where there is no such shame as the exploitation of man by man?"[28] The task that lay before anonymous toilers and obscure organizers in the United States, Jack hoped to persuade his listeners, was to create a literature that reflected their own concerns and aspirations. "Our first duty is to attempt an interpretation of those aspects of American life important to the masses, and the next duty is to communicate this material as simply and clearly as we are able to the largest body of readers we can command." Intended to make a case for worker-writing, the speech argued the instrumentality of the writer's role. To achieve this role, however, required the support of the left's cultural movement, support that was quickly evaporating as the Party sold off its proletarian stock. Moreover, Conroy's own chances for mainstream recognition of his work were slim since few radical novels had gained a large readership to the extent, say, of Sinclair's *The Jungle*. The division between popular literature and belles lettres seemed more firmly entrenched than ever in the general reader's mind.

Conroy and others hoped to improve the disappointingly low sales of proletarian novels via a proletarian book club called the Writers' Union, modeled after the phenomenally successful Book-of-the-Month Club.[29] But this plan also met with Party disapproval, despite Trachtenberg's initial support. Party cultural doyens were interested in consolidating cultural activity; efforts lying outside their dominion met censure. Marginalized by his subject matter—working-class experience from a radical perspective—and increasingly isolated from his base within the Party's revolutionary movement, Conroy enjoyed only briefly the attention that he richly deserved as discoverer of new talent (the *Anvil*) and literary pioneer in exploring working-class experience, creatively transforming this experience into literature, using appropriate genres and techniques such as worker narrative, orality, and popular literature. These were considerable achievements for a factory worker and day laborer, living on the edge of impoverishment in rural Missouri. On this point the journalists got things right.

Conroy's literary fortunes seemed very favorable at the congress, but in fact the conditions were already created that would occasion the unmaking of his long struggle to achieve recognition for worker-writing. The principal circumstances included Jack's decision to turn most of *Anvil's* editorial duties over to Snow, his identification with the proletarian movement (a categorization that proved fatal to others as well), his decision to exchange his literary strengths for conventional novelistic methods in composing *A World to Win*, and the shifting winds of literary politics, evident in the orchestrations that occurred at the Second Writers' Congress two years later. These rendered him vulnerable, unable to stave off the losses that ensued.

The coming wind-shift was anticipated in the selection process at the first congress. No worker-writers were named to the executive committee of the League of American Writers. Ironically, Jack was given the task of reading the names of nominees on the evening of the congress's close.[30] The chief aim of the congress had been achieved, Waldo Frank, the league's new head, proclaimed: "to integrate elements and forces of American cultural life which, heretofore, have been anarchic, into the beginning of a literary movement, both broad and deep, which springs from an alliance of writers and artists with the working classes."[31] Sectarianism, he concluded, was finally dead. The congress "marks an important movement," Meridel Le Sueur said in a newspaper interview, "from the growth of regional literature and regional groups which has divided American literary production and consumption to a wider function for the writer and an orientation with a class instead of a region."[32] Such were the ostensible aims of the congress, which the League of American Writers was charged to carry out. Behind the expressions of unity, however, a shift of power was taking place that sought control of the cultural discourse through systems of exclusion. The Party's decision, in Chicago, to terminate the John Reed clubs was early evidence of this centripetal shift. The *Anvil* was already feeling the effect of its pull.

While in New York, Jack and other writers marched in the May Day parade, which he recalled in vivid detail:

> It was the time of the United Front with the Irish Workers Clubs brandishing shillelahs and shouting "Free Tom Mooney and the Scottsboro Boys!" as they marched just before the resplendent white limousine of Father Divine, in which he sat regally. Flanking the limousine on foot was a bevy of angels clad in heavenly robes and banging tambourines. It reminded me of Vachel Lindsay's poem "General William Booth Enters Heaven": "The banjos rattles and the tambourines jing, jing jingled in the hands of queens." To the shouts of the Irish Workers "Free Tom Mooney and the Scottsboro Boys" the angels chanted without missing a beat on their tambourines: "Tell 'em to pray and get right with God."[33]

Next to Jack in the parade marched Thomas Bell, a worker-writer from Pennsylvania,³⁴ in a group of writers that included Dahlberg, Farrell, Algren, Gold, Benjamin Appel, Millen Brand, and Isidor Schneider, who with upraised fists cried out "we write for the working class." As the Irish Workers' Club members marched by, Jack Balch hollered, "Hooray for the micks!" Gold, standing next to him, elbowed Balch in the chest, reproving him: "Don't EVER call an Irishman a MICK, Jack! That's as bad as calling a Jew a kike or an Italian a wop!"³⁵ Conroy was surprised at Gold's reaction—in Monkey Nest the Irish miners were always called "micks" without offense taken.

Jack recalled seeing Tillie Lerner (Olsen) in a Young Communist League uniform that she had fashioned for herself, and Sanora Babb, an *Anvil* contributor, darting from the grasp of Howard Rushmore, who was smitten with her.³⁶ Babb had come to New York with the English novelist Harry Carlisle and Tillie Lerner "in a one-seat, soft top Ford roadster (and nearly froze)."³⁷ The three were delegates from the Los Angeles John Reed Club. In 1929, Sanora had moved to Los Angeles from the plains—her novel *An Owl on Every Post* describes her impoverished childhood in a Colorado sod house—to work as an Associated Press reporter, but the Great Crash left her stranded, homeless and without work. For a brief time Babb taught in a country school in western Kansas.³⁸ Supporting herself from temporary jobs, Babb pursued her ambition to write. Her early literary work had already begun to appear in little magazines, including Hagglund's *Northern Light*. A friend took her to a John Reed Club meeting where she found an outlet for her youthful idealism. She subsequently joined the Party.

Sitting on a curb in front of Mecca Temple, Richard Wright was the first to greet Sanora at the opening of the Writers' Congress. The sessions made little lasting impression on her; more memorable was the trip to New York and her return alone. The three delegates stayed in fifty-cent hotels, visited factories to talk to the workers, and looked up Nelson Algren and other writers associated with the John Reed Club in Chicago. "That trip that began so happily did not end so. We were all poor, broke, though I had $70, and paid the bills. But worse, I was a 'mere radical, an individualist' and was rather too often scorned for not being a Marxist." Babb hitchhiked alone back to California.³⁹ When she heard that *Anvil* was faltering for lack of funds, she sent money. (Tillie Lerner and Meridel Le Sueur offered their help, serving as West Coast advisory editors.)⁴⁰

Not long after the 1935 Writers' Congress, the Party sent Babb to work as an organizer in the farm fields of central California, where she became close friends with Tom Collins, the model for the government camp manager in *Grapes of Wrath,* who encouraged her to make field notes. Babb shared the notes with John Steinbeck, later turning them into a book manuscript entitled "Whose Names Are Unknown." Steinbeck, who was doing fieldwork independently on the same farms, reworked his notes into a novel and sent it to Covici-Friede. Babb sent her manuscript to Random House, which accepted it for publication. When the *The Grapes of Wrath* appeared, Random House returned Babb's manuscript; there was no market, the editors said, for two books on California migrant workers. It was a hard, bitter blow to a young female writer, particularly one of Babb's ability. Impatient with CP censors who insisted on scrutinizing her work before publication, she broke with the Party. In the 1950s, Babb endured another form of censorship; for two years she was subjected to FBI investigations. Married to James Wong Howe, a celebrated cinematographer, Babb authored two semiautobiographical novels of great warmth and vividness, and continues, well into her eighties now, to publish her poetry in leading literary journals.[41]

To help raise funds for *Anvil,* Conroy, Le Sueur, Gold, and Trachtenberg spoke at the Labor Temple on Thursday, 2 May. On the following day, Jack joined with other writers in a strike of office workers against the *American Mercury* at 730 Fifth Avenue.[42] Several of the writers participating in the strike, including Le Sueur and Balch, were arrested and given suspended sentences. Also on that day, a wire arrived at the Snows advising Jack of the death of Gladys's mother. "A militant Kelly from Ulster," she had provided a house for the Conroys and taken care of Jack, Junior, during the time Jack was writing *A World to Win.*[43] Jack left immediately for Moberly.

* * *

Conroy's presence on the speaker's platform of the 1935 Writers' Congress seemed to legitimate worker-writing in the agenda of the cultural left. Like the May Day parade, however, the Writers' Congress made a display of unity that, as the real working forces emerged, turned out to be held together with string and baling wire.

Accompanying the centripetal movement in the cultural politics of the left, signaled by the dissolution of the John Reed clubs and carried out in the "deproletarization" of the Party's cultural programs, was a growing attack on what was viewed by its detractors as "vulgarism." In a joint editorial appearing in the third issue of *Partisan Review,* Rahv and Phelps/Phillips lumped literary crudeness under leftism and associated it with the work of H. H. Lewis, Joseph Vogel, Maxwell Bodenheim, George Marlen, and other "leftists" in the movement—without mentioning Gold and others closer to the Party's center (including critics in the Soviet Union) who had, early on, championed Lewis.[44] Proletarian literature, the *Partisan Review* editors contended, demands the integration of human experience and history through a radical critical perspective and aesthetic standards.[45] The attack on Lewis was a minor sally in comparison to larger contests taking shape, such as between *Partisan Review* and *New Masses*, yet it revealed the extent to which "crude vigor" and worker-writing were coming under fire from radical intellectuals who, like Rahv and Phillips, were eager to gain advantage on the cultural front.[46]

Although *Partisan Review*, in its early issues, published literary radicals like Herman Spector, Meridel Le Sueur, Nelson Algren, Tillie Lerner, Jack Balch, Richard Wright, Grace Lumpkin, and others, some of whom Phillips would later disparage as nativist, "free-wheeling," grass-roots radicals, reflecting the "grass-roots" tradition of the John Reed Clubs, the *PR* editors' own biases were limited mainly to theoretical essays and editorial commentaries.[47] *Partisan Review* continued to publish midwestern literary radicals alongside Malraux, Horace Gregory, Gide, and Aragon. After the ninth issue, however, coinciding with the merger of *Anvil* and *Partisan Review*, the literary radicals had disappeared altogether from the magazine's pages, with the exception of Farrell, Josephine Herbst, Kerker Quinn, and Agnes Smedley, none of whom can be said to have had any close identification with the former *Anvil*. And certainly no worker-writer—the "primitive leftists" like Lewis, Conroy, Kalar, and others—was represented.[48] The implication is of course that Phillips's own role in the radical movement was "relevant" and "central." I have no interest in derogating William Phillips's (or Philip Rahv's) distinguished achievements as editors of the reborn *Partisan Review*, a subject that falls outside the scope of this study. Nonetheless, since both Rahv and Phillips have had opportunities to comment (usually negatively) on the midwestern literary radicals grouped loosely around Conroy's *Anvil*, I wish to point out that Phillips's reassessment of the radical movement reflects a tendency to force complex issues into opposing categories (two-valued reasoning), such as in his crucial distinction between "the 'folk' tradition and the 'intellectual' one," as does Rahv in his 1939 epitaph on the proletarian movement. The logic of dichotomous oppositions, deconstructionist criticism has shown us, is the logic of domination. Both lock their subjects into a partitive framework that distorts the broad range of literary expression that existed even within the relatively narrow range of the proletarian movement. Such two-valued thinking was also characteristic of Party orthodoxy in the 1930s. All of this becomes clear in retrospect when one reexamines what the two *Partisan Review* editors were saying during those early days of the magazine.

In 1934, Rahv argued for a radical literature grounded in critical principles derived from European Marxism, "for Marxism alone makes possible a dialectical, objective view of the entire process of our time."[49] By discrediting "crude" elements of "leftism" in the cultural movement, as Rahv and Phelps did in *Partisan Review* 3, and by defining a theoretical high ground whereon they took their positions as standard-bearers of literary judgment, the *PR* editors employed the tactic that had confused and angered Le Sueur at the Chicago John Reed Club convention: introduce divisions within a group or movement preliminary to taking a leadership role. These were tactics that the Communists had used in their own power struggles.[50] In a sense, the *PR* editors outmaneuvered the Party, using its own tactics. That the attack on "vulgarians" in the movement—the "populists," as they were sometimes called—was motivated in the desire to shift the basis of radical literary production to the control of an intelligentsia, through critical selection and ideological "purity," became evident several years later, when *Partisan Review* emerged afresh, after a hiatus of a year, promoting European modernism and espousing Trotskyist views.[51]

Worker-writers like H. H. Lewis figured in a small but significant way in the shift of power taking place within the Party's cultural sanctuary. It appeared that he reveled in the shock effect of his "vulgarism." "I am the boor that rises in the midst of a concert and stumbles toward the aisle," one of his early poems, quoted earlier, reads.[52] Another Lewis poem, "Symbol of Stupidity," enjoins the reader to

> Behold yon unenlightened ass
> nibbling the acres over:
> How plump the creature is, alas,
> Unstarved amid the clover. . . .[53]

By most literary standards Lewis's "Poof, No Chance to Be President" is vulgar. Walt Carmon vetoed it; yet the poem, quoted in Chapter 11, is a faithful image of Lewis's perception of his plowman-poet condition. The brazenness, the pungency of Lewis's poetry were rhetorical elements familiar to early socialist and Wobbly poets who, of an earlier era, exhibited more propriety, to be sure. The chief difference lies in Lewis's penchant for self-irony. The effect is often comic-serious, a self-parody of the plowman-poet, yet quite direct in its commentary. There are almost no political *ideas* in his verse; only political sentiments. Capitalism is rotten; the success myth a hoax; the poor ground down and ignored. Whatever one's response to his poetry—and here one's politics bear upon the question—it is evident that Lewis's work has the same effect as popular balladry of oral tradition (in contrast to popular literature of commercial sources). It is bold, memorable, and diverse in its echoes of written and oral sources. These were characteristics that won Conroy's admiration and brought Lewis to William Carlos Williams's attention. Similarly, Williams was attracted to folk artists like Wallace Gould, in keeping with his belief that art inheres in the localized event or thing.[54]

Few doubted the fervor of Lewis's convictions, particularly as expressed in poems declaring his admiration for the Soviet Experiment. But his odd behavior, his contentiousness, for instance, was proving an embarrassment to the Party. At the least suggestion of offense, he fired off an angry letter to an editor. Several years earlier *New Masses* had welcomed Lewis to its pages. As the Party began to cultivate establishment writers, however, it proved reluctant to experiment or encourage firebrands like Lewis. The Missouri boot-heel farmer-poet had become persona non grata. Lewis, like devoted believers who take issue with the church, fought against those ministers who, he felt, had corrupted the true word. The Party's desire to shed itself of an eccentric—an unguided missile—only deepened Lewis's alienation. With the advent of the Popular Front, Lewis felt freer to divest his poetry of doctrinaire sentiments; his verse widened in scope while still maintaining the vigor of his early work.[55] Ignored by the Party's cultural doyens, despite Williams's laudatory essay in *New Masses* and the prestigious Harriet Monroe poetry prize he won in 1938, Lewis grew evermore paranoid fencing with fascism's shadow-master.

The following stanza, for instance, concluding one of his unpublished wartime poems, takes measure of Lewis's skepticism vis-à-vis the great powers' motives for the terrible debacle at Stalingrad:

> It's just for propaganda, har,
> It's just for propaganda,
> This redscared globaloney war,
> It's just for propaganda.
> Stalin and Hitler peas-in-pod
> By subtle ruse of dander—
> IT'S JUST FOR PROPAGANDA![56]

A creative innovator in working-class verse, employing bold diction based upon actual speech rhythms and idioms, with humorous effect, Lewis carried forward the tradition of Wobbly poets who had broken with earlier working-class imitations of genteel poetry. He was—to use an old populist term—a "wild jackass," out of the agrarian radical mold, employing the vernacular in versified expressions of protest. Max Lieber cautioned him to tone down if he wished to continue publishing.[57] And Walt Carmon confessed to Kalar that he had to edit out Lewis's occasional "crapperinoes."[58] His temperamental response had cost him a publication in the *American Mercury*. Yet his native, militant, richly satirical humor found adherents. He was a contributing editor to *New Masses* when Gold was still in charge, and as late as 1934, a reviewer in *New Masses* praised his newest collection: "His particular gift is for epigram, terse, and earthy. . . . he needs discipline, but not the kind of discipline the nice critics prescribe."[59]

It was in fact Lewis's efforts to reinvest verse with belief, however obsolete the forms he used, that won William Carlos Williams's admiration and support.[60] Fred Miller introduced Lewis's poetry to Williams in *Blast*. Williams read Lewis's verse "breathlessly. . . . he knows writing is to be read and to be found interesting because it is well done, of good material. At bottom he's got the stuff—just like a baseball pitcher that has the stuff."[61] Williams was impressed with Lewis's ability to reinvest traditional forms, however outmoded and tired, with emotions born of strongly held belief. Moreover, Hagglund's pamphlet editions of Lewis's poetry were proof that poetry could be made accessible at low cost and sold in Woolworth stores. Williams's enthusiasm for Lewis's poetry flew in the face of his own convictions regarding poetic practice. When Lewis visited him later, Williams admitted that "praising my [Lewis's] work . . . contradicted a lifetime of poetry practice and poetic criticism. . . . he waved his hand to indicate that he was expressing a revolution in his own attitude toward his past."[62] Williams's sponsorship of Lewis served to heighten tensions between the *Partisan Review* editors and *New Masses*.[63]

There were bumps and switchbacks in the path toward publication of Williams's essay on Lewis. Williams's laudatory assessment was first submitted to Malcolm Cowley of the *New Republic*.[64] From there it went to *Partisan Review*. Despite the fact that Lewis and the *Partisan Review* editors had exchanged insults, the latter accepted the Williams essay on Lewis until they learned that part of the essay would appear in *Poetry* magazine (January 1936).[65] The editors, now including Ben Field and Edwin Rolfe, in addition to Phillips and Rahv, defended their rejection of the essay to Lewis, pointing out its publication in *Poetry* and answering Lewis's charge that they did not "print work of writers outside of New York." Moreover, they asked, what gave Lewis the idea that Williams was an expert on revolutionary literature? Williams was a "bourgeois decadent" who had dismissed, in a symposium statement that appeared in *Partisan Review* (April 1936), the likelihood of Marxism's ever taking root in America, given that it was fundamentally incompatible with "our deep seated ideals."[66] Williams's essay finally appeared in *New Masses* (23 November 1937), praising Lewis's "sincerity of belief" and the power of his poems, without arguing that they belong to "high art."[67] By allowing the essay in *New Masses,* however, Williams could no longer appear in *Partisan Review;* the terms were made by the NM editors and Williams complied with them, causing further hard feeling between the *Partisan Review* editors and Williams.[68]

For those "considerate and cultivated voices" anxious to distance themselves in the movement from the vulgarians, Lewis was a ready-made target. Wald remarks—correctly, I believe—that "there were elements of elitism inscribed in *Partisan Review*'s project from its inception. It overreacted to vulgarized Marxism by assigning high culture its virtually exclusive center of interest and was rather selective in the modernist writers it promoted."[69] Lewis flaunted his dung-stained overalls and flouted poetic convention. Balladeers in earlier revolutionary times had done likewise. Idiosyncratic, he made bold use of neologisms and burlesqued traditional verse forms. He professed a militant social consciousness, but beneath the paeans to the Soviet workers' republic was an intensely personal attachment to freeholder's rights. He saw no contradiction between his faith in Stalin and his deep, nativist loyalty to America. Like many in the 1930s who placed their hope in the Party, he had grown up poor, slept with homeless people in flea-ridden flophouses, experienced police brutality, and known lynchings in his hometown. Lewis never went to the Soviet Union, probably never met anyone who had been there until Falkowski looked him up in 1938.

Such then was Lewis's loyalty to a distant idol, an unfamiliar, closed, mysterious *Heiland* that demanded loyalty, sacrifice, and engagement. It was a framework of belief that Lewis constructed without comrades, Party cells, discussion groups, congresses, summer camps, or lectures. It is unlikely that Lewis would have tolerated the closeness of such engagement in Party activity. He was at heart individualist, nonideological, egalitarian, solitary. He bridled at what he perceived to be attempts on the part of "Eastern intellectuals" to pass judgment on his poetry. To make his way into a literary career, to gain the recognition he desperately sought, meant ascending a hierarchical scale within an unfamiliar system of production and publication. He detested the appearance of arborescent structures replacing the network of little magazines that had published his work. The frustrations he met in seeking recognition fueled his suspicion and resentment toward the eastern radical establishment. In the poem "The Noselings," Lewis vented his anger on the radical intelligentsia centered in *Partisan Review* and its parochial dismissal of midwestern writers:

> East of the Hudson, *off* in dual fashion,
> Way over yonder with culty passion,
> Some "proletarian" critics draw the shades
> And count who's who—behind the Palisades.
> What's all America to a clique of noses
> Huddled to get the blessing from their Moses?
>
> . . .
>
> Can any good come out of *Anvil*-yard?
> Can any rube be Rapply citified
> In the weird West upon the other side?[70]

From such isolation and solitude poets sometimes shape their material;
but Lewis ironized his loneliness, and redirected his energies into bit-
ing satirical verse. Unpolitical and isolated, Lewis took the bait that
was offered, the two-valued judgments such as "cultivated" versus "vulgar," "folk" versus "intellectual," and so forth.[71] They fueled his invective. The anti-Semitic innuendo in "The Noselings" was a nasty note
in the feuding, reminiscent of ugly strains in earlier battles between
nativists and immigrant sectors of American society.[72] The Missouri artist Thomas Hart Benton, attacking the hegemony of New York critics,
had also complained about the dominion of European-oriented Jewish
radicals in the arts, which of course did not make it true.[73] Benton's
attack on "Parisian aestheticism" and sectarianism in New York art circles, and the angry response his remarks generated, reveal deep cultural differences and misunderstandings that still resonate.

Lewis, along with other midwestern radicals, felt increasingly isolated from the left's cultural movement and viewed the growing centripe-
talism with alarm and consternation, as their populist grandfathers had
opposed the controlling mechanisms of eastern bankers and railroad
moguls. Jack, however, was still feeling heady from the attention he had
received in New York, in the wake of his Guggenheim grant and the
publication of *A World to Win*. Subsequent events, however, proved his
expectations premature. He too had been naive in misestimating the
reshuffling of power taking place on the cultural front. Its centripetal
force field proved irresistible.

* * *

Conroy's *A World to Win*, published 23 April 1935, appeared the same
year as Thornton Wilder's *Heaven's My Destination* (his response to
Gold's famous attack), Faulkner's *Pylon*, Wolfe's *Of Time and the River*,
Henry Roth's *Call It Sleep*, Farrell's *Judgment Day*, Algren's *Somebody in
Boots*, and Sherwood Anderson's *Puzzled America*. Jack wanted to title

the book "Little Stranger," or "A World I Never Made" (from an A. E. Housman poem), but Covici insisted on its final title and Jack acquiesced despite Lieber's warning that it "would give a lot of humorists an excellent opportunity to make quips."[74] Jack complained that the phrase sounded like Horatio Alger, but of course it was drawn from the concluding words of the Communist Manifesto.

In his two novels, Conroy makes creative use of the tensions introduced by personal dilemmas. *The Disinherited* was conceived in the proletarian nights of Jack's factory work. Hampered by fatigue and lack of time, but energized by the intimate contact with his subject, he synthesized a novel from the broken pieces of his proletarian existence. In *The World to Win*, plot dictates the order of events, the schematically developed tales of two half-brothers, Leo and Robert, who, divided by class loyalties, finally join at the conclusion in common cause. The story reveals Jack's own dilemma following the publication of *The Disinherited* when he felt pulled between the desire to attain literary recognition and the perception that some form of activism would ultimately be of more value in labor's struggle than literature. Pieces of his second novel deserve to stand on their own, such as the description of a mining accident, published separately in *Anvil* as "Down in Happy Hollow." And several individual characters and scenes are memorably drawn, such as Dogface Epperson, Monty Cass, and the taxi-dance hall, abortion, and strikebreaking episodes.[75] As in his Monkey Nest and workers' tales there are pastiches of hobo lore and lingo, folk superstition, grotesque bawdry, parodies of genteel romance fiction and fundamentalist religion, together with social commentary on mass culture. The omniscient narration is not as effective as the literary dialogization of speech genres that Conroy employs in *The Disinherited*. Straightforward exposition often dissolves into grotesque, comic description and storytelling, as if he were uncomfortable with omniscient narration and unwilling to commit himself to his subject. The montage quality of *The Disinherited* creates an openness in the narrative that contrasts with the closed, schematized quality of *A World to Win*. The latter resembles in some aspects the ideologically driven novel of Socialist Realism with its affirmative attitude toward the possibility of human development, its depiction of individual self-realization through the collective, and its "historical specificity in the depiction of reality."[76] The twin protagonists, Robert and Leo, link individual and collective destinies together in a programmatic manner familiar to the Soviet revolutionary novel after 1934.[77] This impression is reinforced by the dedication of the novel to Robert Minor, who abandoned a talented career as artist and political cartoonist to become a Party activist.[78] If *A World to Win* is in a sense Jack's "United Front" novel, the literary equivalent of Earl Browder's speech at the eighth Party convention, then he failed entirely in that purpose and betrayed his own literary strengths that were so richly (and unevenly) present in *The Disinherited*. Accepting this explanation, we are led to wonder why he altered so radically his course after *The Disinherited*, relinquishing in effect any chances for further literary recognition.[79]

Meridel Le Sueur attempted (gently) to explain what happened. The problem, she argued, was that under the commercial pressures of publication, Conroy had made use of "bourgeois" literary techniques—nineteenth-century narrative styles with their addiction to the past tense.[80] Despite the forced structure of *A World to Win*, however, Jack's "vigorous folk language . . . thrust out peculiarly from the muffled prose and past-tense telling."[81] In a letter to me years later, Le Sueur suggested that Jack had been "seduced" by his success in obtaining the Guggenheim, and that, lured by bourgeois recognition, he had made clumsy use of nineteenth-century narrative form.[82] Conroy's own success seemed tied in with the success of worker-writing; his failure meant that worker-writers were at best capable of one story, their own lives. But Le Sueur was not so pessimistic; his failure in the second novel had been to look to "bourgeois" literature for models inappropriate to working-class experience and worldviews. It was an error that could easily be rectified. *A World to Win*, then, neglected to continue the evolution of narrative styles and forms—a task in which Le Sueur herself was engaged—to advance a separate and legitimate stream of American literature whose subject is working people, their lives, concerns, and aspirations. Meridel appeared to feel the disappointment as keenly as did Jack. It was a costly but instructive lesson: narrative techniques in working-writing could not be advanced by merely looking backward. It would require what Walter Benjamin, in referring to Brecht, calls *Umfunktionierung* of techniques and forms appropriate to working-class experience, which, as I argue, Conroy partially achieved in refashioning worker narrative, sketch, and folk material in *The Disinherited*.[83]

Jerre Mangione's review appears to confirm this conclusion. Conroy, he argued, had tried to write a "novel"; he should have stayed with storytelling.[84] Mangione had in mind an essay by Robert Forsythe (a.k.a. Kyle Crichton) entitled "Down with the Novel," appearing in *New Masses* the previous spring, exactly one week before the publication of *A World to Win*.[85] Forsythe deals with the problem of the second novel: "it is not possible for every writer, proletarian or otherwise, to confine himself entirely to his reminiscences; a man may want to write more than one book in his lifetime. What remains is the novel, the horrifying specter which haunts the dreams of young authors and turns prospective artists into verbal mechanics. The thing has become a fetish."[86] The novel, he said, was a dying form and he urged young writers to invent a new literary form as a means to break free from the straitjacket of the traditional novel. "It is not that proletarian writers cannot write simply and effectively . . . it may only be that they are clinging to a form which does not fit them."[87] Better at storytelling than as novelists—it was the remark that Frank O'Connor had made about Irish writers.[88] Best at short sprints, Jack had attempted to run the long-distance course of a novel's plot.[89]

The first third of *A World to Win* is devoted to Robert Hurley's disillusioning experiences at college and later in bohemian milieus. The portrayal of Leo's younger half-brother, the "little stranger," is unconvincing, as if Conroy had deliberately set about caricaturing the pale aspirations of a middle-class aesthete.[90] With the intent of becoming a writer, Robert Hurley enrolls at the state university, is disappointed, and goes to the city, where he seeks out a bohemian cafe called the "Green Dragon" (loosely based upon the Blue Lantern in St. Louis). Disheartened by the negative judgment passed on his work by a more experienced writer, and "weary of clever people," he learns more about contemporary life on urban streets than in bohemian cafes. After several brushes with America First Vigilantes, a protofascist organization, and disagreeable experiences as a worker, he joins Leo quite by accident in a labor demonstration, which portends their reconciliation as brothers and the rising groundswell of protest favoring social justice.[91] Leo is Robert's opposite, a happy-go-lucky worker with no use for school, who marries, has more children than he can support, and loses his wife in childbirth suffered under execrable conditions.[92] In an absurdist, half-comic, half-bathetic gesture, Leo decides to commit suicide, but in an ironic turn of events he is hailed by strikers as a leader. The story explores the theme of dual consciousness, separating the two hyphenated terms of the worker-writer (Robert as writer manqué and Leo as unawakened worker), then rejoining them at the end, as if each had need of its complement for fulfillment. Divided by class loyalties and antagonistic ambitions—Robert's bourgeois literary aspirations, Leo's lowbrow, petit bourgeois attitudes—the two half-brothers are finally reconciled through growth and experience. *A World to Win* dramatizes the dual function of the working-class intellectual—as self-motivated intelligentsia and activist.[93]

Nelson Algren pointed out Conroy's sense of unease in "following the character of Robert Browning Hurley through bourgeois literary circles."[94] Jack himself had experienced briefly a "dandy" period, written poetry in the genteel manner, and felt ill-at-ease during his one semes-

ter at the University of Missouri, returning to the Wabash shops where
he picked up his tools again as a journeyman. Through the character
of Martha Darrell, Jack parodied the genteel tradition as a sterile influence in literature.[95] The episodes involving Robert's stay at the university reflect the self-consciousness and resentment of the working-class
student who, like Hardy's Jude the Obscure, harbors a reverential attitude toward learning and books. The "pallid adventures on the Bohemian fringes of the world of letters," as Granville Hicks described the
Green Dragon section, thinking Jack meant Greenwich Village, seem
inconsequential in contrast to the labor struggle going on some blocks
away.

Jack seldom departed from personal experience or knowledge in his
writing. The long episode in which Leo and his family travel west in
an old flivver, like the Oklahoma migrants of Steinbeck's *Grapes of
Wrath,* therefore strikes an incongruous note—not the trip by automobile so much as the Mormon setting in Utah. Exhausted, pressed for
time, and anxious to furnish an episode that would adequately portray
the ability of Leo and his family to survive the destitution facing migrant workers, Jack turned for help to the western historian Ray B. West,
who at the time was a young writer living in Utah. West supplied the
events of chapters 7 and 9, including the sojourn within a Mormon
community, an auto accident, beet-field labor, and portrayals of quartz
miners and Mexican workers. To assist him, Jack sent West a clipping
of a baby attacked by ants, which West used for an incident involving
Mexican migrant workers. Jack then revised the two chapters in his own
style.[96]

The reception of *A World to Win* was unenthusiastic without being
actually hostile, save for one review. Horace Gregory, a poet and the
author of *Chelsea Rooming House* (1930), savaged the "careless writing,"
the "inept" imitations of "bourgeois" verse, the inhuman characterizations, and the explicitness of the sex scenes. The review granted Conroy one redeeming virtue: his "physical exuberance" and "willingness
to write many more novels as he grows older."[97] In Jack's mind Gregory
was one of the "super-esthetes" from whom he expected little understanding.[98] Yet, the review seemed manifestly unjust. When in trouble
Jack marshaled the support of his friends. He wrote Kalar, Lewis, and
others, asking them to contact Irita Van Doren, the book editor of the
Herald-Tribune, to express their objections, and he sent his own protest letter. His letter to Dan James complained that Gregory's review
"betrays a complete lack of knowledge of working class life, such as ironically enclosing 'worker,' as applied to Leo and Terry, in quotation marks.
Also it is written from the point of view of an eastern, urban mind."[99]

At the Writers' Congress Jack had seen Farrell, Dahlberg, and Josephine Herbst together constantly, a tight group of close friends that included Horace Gregory. When Herbst's gushy review of Farrell's *Judgment Day* appeared shortly after, he suspected intellectual logrolling. His suspicions carried him further: perhaps Gregory too had joined Farrell and Dahlberg in discounting his work. "We westerners get a raw deal from such exquisites as Gregory. I saw a lot of log-rolling and back-scratching in New York."[100]

Van Doren passed Jack's letter of protest on to Gregory, who replied directly to Jack, suggesting that he not waste time answering critics but listen to workers' voices: "keep your eyes open to what is happening in the middlewest."[101] The exchange of letters was one more piece of evidence in Jack's mind of the cultural divide isolating "the Eastern, urban mind" from the vast province lying to the west of the Hudson.[102] Yet it was good advice, and Jack knew it. "The Cement King," published the following year, is a return to worker-writing: social content, literary dialogization of speech genres, first-person narration—the strengths, in sum, of *The Disinherited*. At the same time, however, Jack was moving forward into new territory, to political activism and social history.

* * *

Jack traveled to Akron and Detroit in the early summer of 1935, where he listened to factory workers and observed their situations as migrants from rural areas, homesick, yet holding on desperately to their factory jobs. Equipped with a letter from the UAW local's president, he went into the Ford factory to talk to the workers. "You can tell him your experiences in the plant," the letter said, "without any fear. . . . Please be quite open and keep nothing back that might prevent Jack Conroy from getting a true picture of your whole life and surroundings."[103] The Guggenheim grant was paying his expenses; Jack suspended temporarily his own job search. The results of his Guggenheim research appeared some ten years later when, in collaboration with Arna Bontemps, Jack wrote a study of black migration to northern industrial cities entitled *They Seek a City* (1945), based on Jack's studies and the black history project of the Illinois Writers' Project, where both writers were supervisors until the project folded in 1942.

In July, Jack headed toward Commonwealth College in Arkansas to teach a workshop in its special summer sessions for activists. Founded as a labor school in Newllano, Louisiana, in 1923, Commonwealth was subsequently moved to an eighty-acre location eleven miles west of Mena, Arkansas, in the Ouachita mountains. Expanded to 320 acres in order to become self-sustaining as a farm, the college was active in organizing impoverished sharecroppers, black and white. As a sixteen-year-old, Ray Koch moved to Commonwealth from Oregon with his parents and siblings in 1925. A few years later Charlotte Moskowitz left her studies at Syracuse University, hitchhiked to Commonwealth, joined the staff, and married Ray Koch. As executive secretary, Charlotte ("Chucky") invited Jack to participate during the summer of 1935.[104]

At Commonwealth, students and teachers shared the tasks. Jack was assigned the tending of mules used for plowing, since he was from Missouri and what Missourian would not know how to drive a mule? Following an unsuccessful trial of mule driving, Jack was assigned to cut weeds, along with garment workers from New York City who marched off to the fields singing "Solidarity Forever." When the day was finished, it was discovered that they had cut down a field of food-bearing plants. Instructed in plant lore, they grew faint in the Arkansas summer heat and lay sprawled under a tree. Jack's contribution to the shared work was to call hogs, for which his great voice, delivered from his broad chest, perfectly equipped him. Jack taught a course on "Literature and the Working Class" under the shade of a catalpa tree.[105] Marvin Sanford, Jack's printer in Newllano, was there teaching labor journalism and helping with the *Windsor Quarterly*, which had moved to Commonwealth from Four Corners, Vermont. "The summer sessions," write Ray and Charlotte Koch in their memoir of Commonwealth, "were like Chautauquas—entertainment combined with learning, plenty of stimulation available without having to do too much digging."[106] The school was devoted to providing workshops in grass-roots labor organization during the summer, attracting people like Mother Bloor, Carl Haessler of the Federated Press, various union leaders, and writers. The school had a yearly operating budget of less than nine thousand dollars, without counting labor, which was voluntary.[107]

The "physical plant" of the college itself was part of the college's unusual character. Joe Jones painted a large mural on the commons wall, depicting "the three major industries of Arkansas: mining, sharecropping, and lynchings."[108] A "Museum of Social Change," announced as "the first museum of capitalistic decay in America," contained exhibits contributed by Albert Einstein, H. L. Mencken, Erskine Caldwell, and members of the New York Athletic Club, among others, who "sent samples of their threadbare silk lingerie as proof of capitalistic collapse."[109] Like its counterparts, Brookwood Labor College in New York and Highlander School in Tennessee, Commonwealth accomplished a great deal on a limited income; in its commons and under its shade trees lectured many notable labor and literary figures, including the remarkable H. L.

Mitchell of the Southern Tenant Farmers' Union, until mounting political and religious controversy brought the college under the scrutiny of Arkansas legislators. In 1940, the offices were raided, charges of sedition were filed, and the school's property was seized.

In late July, Jack, along with Bruce Crawford, Emmett Gowen, Shirley Hopkins, and Alfred Hirsch, traveled to Alabama to test the Downs' law, which forbade the sale or distribution of "seditious" literature in Birmingham. The Downs' law had been used to harass anyone suspected as "reds" and labor organizers in Alabama at the time. The so-called "Street bill," defining sedition in such a manner that free speech itself was restricted, had passed the Alabama legislature. The announcement of the trip to Alabama (and to Georgia to ask Governor Talmadge to rescind an 1871 anti-insurrection law under which Angelo Herndon had been indicted) was publicized widely.[110]

Hirsch was a lawyer with the National Committee for the Defense of Political Prisoners, chaired by Lincoln Steffens, which sponsored the demonstration by the five activists. Crawford, who had been shot in the leg during the Harlan County mine strike in 1931, was the editor of *Crawford's Weekly* in Norton, Virginia.[111] Gowen, author of *Mountain Born* and *Dark Moon of March*, replaced Nelson Algren, who backed out at the last minute.[112] Shirley Hopkins was a wealthy liberal patron of leftist causes in whose car the five traveled.[113] It was a dangerous venture the five demonstrators undertook in 1935. There was little protection by press coverage; northern criticism of lynchings had generated bitter feelings toward "Yankee" civil rights advocates who came south. John Howard Lawson, who had been indicted on a libel charge the previous year for sending dispatches to the *Daily Worker* on a mine strike, warned Jack not to go.[114] Erskine Caldwell's reports in *New Masses* from Georgia on lynchings and mob violence brought death threats against him. "American literary men," Daniel Aaron writes, "seldom took such physical risks for political reasons before or after the 1930's. . . ."[115]

To test the constitutionality of the Downs' ordinance, the group picketed the Birmingham city hall, displaying prominently copies of *New Masses*, the *New Republic*, and so forth. The demonstrators soon began to sense that they had more to fear from vigilante action than from the police, who were aware of the negative publicity should they arrest the five. Threats were made against the activists and cars cruised menacingly around their hotel during the night. Moreover, they began to suspect that the lawyer who had made arrangements for them was acting as a double agent. Seeking protection, the group was escorted to the county line and left to continue by car to an interview in Montgomery

with Governor Bibb Graves, who had the Street bill on his desk for
signature. En route, Jack recalled, an automobile sped past, "the occu-
pants pointing suggestively at us. Ten miles south of Clanton [Alabama]
another car passed us at high speed, and leaning from the window was
a thug pumping lead at us out of a wicked automatic. He shot at least
five times and two of the bullets lodged in the fender." Returning to
Clanton, Conroy and the others took refuge in a café at noontime,
phoning the governor for protection. After much delay, the governor
sent a solicitor who questioned the five about the attack, concluding
that it had been a publicity frame-up. The highway patrol promised to
lead them out of town, one patrolmen announcing pompously that "I'll
take the bullets. I'll be right in front of you."[116] Convinced that they
were not going to receive the legal protection they were entitled to,
the group slipped out the back door as night fell, made their way to a
bus station from whence they traveled by bus, taxi, and train to Nashville, where they held a news conference.[117]

A quixotic venture, as Jack later admitted, his first involvement as
a civil rights activist was more than he had bargained on; yet the incident did create considerable publicity. The leftist press, of course, made
great capital of it.[118] New York papers reported the beating and harassment of the five, confirming that Alabama was ruled by terrorism.[119] An
editorial in the *Nation* cited the success of the demonstration, reporting that Governor Graves had subsequently vetoed the Street bill.[120]
Southern newspapers, however, gave an account that might have been
written by Governor Graves's press secretary. The *Gastonia Gazette* asserted in North Carolina that the writers had "framed up" their story
as a publicity stunt. The front page of the *Birmingham News* carried a
photo of the protesters with the caption "Self-Styled 'Liberals' Claim
Car Fired On."[121] The following day, the *Birmingham Age-Herald* reported
that Birmingham's Sheriff J. R. Hardy had "abandoned" the probe of
the shooting. "Having received their publicity," an editorial read, "let
the self-styled writers retire from the state. . . . The 'frame-up' is a weapon used only by cowards and weaklings. It deserves the severest con-
demnation. Let the writers remember that as they slink away."[122]

Emmett Gowen felt in retrospect that the Alabama venture had disgraced group members with critics and the public, casting an unfavorable shadow upon their motivations. Conroy and Bruce Crawford, however, thought otherwise. Shaken by the experience, they felt nonetheless
that a small but significant step had been taken in support of those in
the South who ultimately prevailed in securing basic constitutional
rights for blacks and whites.[123] Leanne Zugsmith novelized the affair in
The Summer Soldier (1938), in which Russell Donohue (Conroy), "a

good fellow... no airs about him," and other members of the "League for Civil Rights" endure a similar course of intimidation and terror at the hands of vigilantes with no legal redress and a great deal of bad press.[124] The Moberly paper was content to report that Jack had "recently returned from a tour of southern states."[125] Awaiting Jack when he arrived home was a letter from Snow describing *Anvil's* heavy printing debts and suggesting that a merger might soon occur. Snow's "merger," however, turned out to be a takeover, orchestrated by the Party in conjunction with the *Partisan Review* editors.

* * *

By issue 13 of the *Anvil*, Snow had attained his wish, which was to boost the magazine's circulation to near five thousand, a remarkable figure given that literary magazines in the past have exercised enormous influence with a circulation of a thousand. Snow's expansion program had run into difficulty. The key to *Anvil's* success had been flexibility; Conroy could pull back when costs became unmanageable. When income was not sufficient, Sanford printed *Anvil* on cheaper stock. This did not make a consistently high-quality production magazine, but it kept the enterprise afloat. *Anvil's* circulation increased its debts and hence its vulnerability. *Partisan Review*, struggling under its own debts and sagging sales, eyed *Anvil's* circulation hungrily. The Party's distribution agency wielded a decisive power if it chose to cease handling a magazine. Jack had in effect yielded the driver's seat to Snow. Acting, he thought, in the magazine's best interests, Snow steered *Anvil* away from the blue highways of America, onto the Lincoln Highway to New York City, and parked it in front of Party headquarters in New York, where it was stripped.[126]

Jack was preoccupied with his Guggenheim researches (or was he avoiding *Anvil's* problems?). When, in late summer and early fall, Snow was dickering with the Party about merging *Anvil* and *Partisan Review*, Jack was back in Detroit gathering material on the diaspora of black and white workers to northern factory cities. At the Writers' Congress, Trachtenberg appeared to support *Anvil*, showing up at the benefit for it that Snow had arranged. Now, however, he was the intermediary in the merger. What changed his mind? Because of the Whitcomb affair and other instances of *Anvil's* editorial independence, Trachtenberg said that *Anvil* needed Party supervision. It was agreed that Mike Gold would be appointed to the editorial staff; in this manner Snow hoped to keep the Party at arm's length since he knew Gold would not interfere.[127] Things were turning around very fast in late 1935, particularly after the Party's move to a reformist line at the Seventh Congress of the Comintern that year. The cultural nationalism that characterized the Popular Front represented a move to the right in which proletarian literature became a questionable enterprise outside the literary system and the term itself virtually disappeared except as an expression connoting inferior, propagandistic writing. Writers with established reputations were cultivated and a common front was announced in the struggle against fascism. New literary hierarchies appeared, shunting aside the tentative and frequently clumsy attempts to construct systems of literary production "created from below, where people live," to borrow Lawrence Goodwyn's apt expression.[128]

Some months before, Fred Miller, editor of the now defunct *Blast*, had warned of the move toward consolidation and hierarchy on the cultural front. Taking issue with Hicks's *New Masses* essay in which Hicks decried the "bohemian individualism and irresponsibility" that led to the creation of yet more little magazines on the left, Miller perceived an impending move on the part of the Party to squeeze out *Blast*, *Dynamo*, and *Anvil*, leaving the field to two, *New Masses* and *Partisan Review*. Where would new writers be welcomed? Miller asked.[129] *Partisan Review* courted established writers, Miller claimed. Its aim seemed to be "a bourgeois respectability superior to that of the *Atlantic Monthly*. Neophyte writers should try the conservative *American Mercury* where Conroy had got his own start, not *New Masses*, the putative magazine of the revolutionary movement."[130]

Things did not work out quite as Miller expected, yet his intuition regarding impending consolidation proved all too true. *Blast* went under, followed soon by *Dynamo*, leaving *Anvil* in direct competition with *Partisan Review*. *Partisan Review* lowered its per-issue price to fifteen cents, apparently in response to *Anvil*'s price.[131] In August, Snow intimated that a merger was in the making, but Jack apparently did not listen.[132] Snow's ulcers were acting up owing to the tremendous stress he had submitted himself to in "booming" *Anvil*, holding his newspaper job, and worrying over growing debts. He began to think about taking a rest from editorial work. He was getting little help, he said, from the St. Louis editors, including the business manager, Wallie Wharton, who was preoccupied with a baby daughter, Cornelia.[133] Yet he pointed with pride to *Anvil*'s heavy colored cover, white paper, and circulation, which he claimed exceeded in quality that of any little magazine in existence. The Liberal Press continued to give credit under an arrangement in which the Party's Central Distribution Agency returned the income from sales directly to it. Willner of the CDA had begun to handle the subscriptions, assess the bills, and collect.[134] While these events made continued publication possible, they increased the magazine's exposure to takeover. Snow made these concessions in hope of keeping the circulation figures high—circulation had become an obsession. In the July–August issue, he revealed his plan to boost sales to ten thousand, increasing *Anvil's* length to forty-eight pages. Snow was taking a terrible beating at the newsstands where *Anvil* was sold. Since issues were now being sold on commission, he had to pay for returned copies. Snow was persuaded that he could reach a break-even point, freeing *Anvil* from its debt, regaining its autonomy, and eventually returning it to Conroy's editorship. But the combination of financial burden and physical exhaustion proved overpowering, so that Snow, unwilling to cease publication, had little other choice than to discuss a merger under terms, he hoped, would prove amenable to Jack.

"This terrible summer," Snow wrote to Wharton, "has been fatal to many magazines." All the John Reed Club magazines, except *Partisan Review*, were gone. *Windsor Quarterly* was about to fold. *New Masses* was pressed financially; Orrick Johns and several others were let go. By early September, Snow was awaiting Trachtenberg's return from the Seventh Comintern Congress in Moscow in order to discuss plans for the merger with *Partisan Review*. He assured Wharton that Jack would go along with the merger "reluctantly" provided "*Anvil's* name wasn't submerged. . . ."[135] In the meantime, Liberal Press was pressuring Snow by delaying publication of *Anvil* 13. It was a form of blackmail, Snow complained. With ten dollars from Simpson and the balance promised within the week, Liberal Press printed the edition. Indentured to his creditors, Snow did what any sensible person might do under similar circumstances in order to have peace: he stopped answering the doorbell. Since there was a sufficient backlog of manuscripts, Snow decided to stop the flood of submissions by announcing he was taking a leave of absence. He would, however, continue to act behind the scenes "until the fate of *Anvil* is settled."[136] Jack, still in Detroit, was temporarily out of contact; not all of the letters reached him there but lay in Moberly waiting his return. In late September, Wharton wrote Jack in urgency. This time the message got through—or Jack decided to hear it.

Anvil's content was not up to par in recent issues, Wharton said; it was time Jack stepped in and did the editing himself. Wharton was particularly upset about a Farrell story Snow had decided to publish. None of the manuscripts recommended by the St. Louis editors, Winkler and Balch, had been selected by Snow; it was not surprising, then, that the two had turned to other things and were neglecting their *Anvil* work.[137] The "Western Office" (St. Louis) of *Anvil* felt left in the lurch by the "Eastern Office" (Snow in New York). "I can't understand," Wharton wrote, "why Walt is so insistent on having *Anvil* play second fiddle to

PR; they have a punk rating for returning scripts, acknowledging subs, etc. . . and their circulation is much smaller than ours."[138] Wharton suggested that Jack write Trachtenberg and ask for help. "I understand that he likes you, and I think that if he understood the situation thoroly [sic], PR's big bill at the printers, careless way of running office, etc., as contrasted with us, I think he should be smart enough business man to want to stake us for a little."[139]

The suggestion came too late; in his next letter, Wharton announced to Jack that the merger had already been decided. The new magazine would be called *Anvil-Partisan Review*—the word-order was crucial—with Snow, Alan Calmer, Phelps (Phillips), Rahv, and Simpson as editors. "*Partisan Review* is closer to headquarters," Wharton explained, "and it is only natural that they would get the big end on a merger; and the merger of course would draw some funds from the Party. This is probably what Trachtenberg will tell you." In fact, however, Wharton added, "it looks like a raiding party of a group of backslappers who want to feed on the juicy carcass of *Anvil*." And who was to blame but Snow for turning *Anvil* "a bit to the clique and claque side."[140]

Shocked and disillusioned, now that the reality of the merger was made plain, Jack wrote bitterly to Snow: "I view *The Anvil's* death with keen regrets. . . . I have no illusions about the character of the merged magazine. It will be *Partisan Review,* not *Anvil.*" Recalling that Trachtenberg had said at the Writers' Congress that *Anvil* "should be supported and that it should not lose its flavor," Jack wondered why "the movement" had allowed its merger with "a magazine which has been in a weaker position from the start." Jack would begin raising funds right away with Wharton to continue *Anvil* alone. "One more issue," he reasoned wistfully, "might conceivably put us over the hump." Feeling guilt, perhaps, Jack tried to explain his struggles at home: Gladys had been laid off again, and when the Guggenheim expired in several months he would have to "apply for relief to the authorities, who have been gleefully awaiting such an event since I organized an unemployed union here two years ago." Melancholy had seized Jack by the forelock: "In the past I have been able to do damned little, even for myself, let alone others."[141] It appeared his only hope now lay in applying to the recently organized Federal Writers' Project, for which he would be eligible as soon as he went on relief.

In a fit of mutual guilt and recrimination, Conroy and Snow exchanged several letters, Jack complaining that he had not been properly informed, and Snow replying with excerpts from earlier letters proving that this was not so. *Partisan Review* had won out, Snow intimated, in a competition whose conditions had been set by the Party. "Who would buy a 32-page self-cover *Anvil* for 15 cents when they could get a 64-page *Partisan Review*, with a separate, heavy cover, for the same price?"[142] Moreover, advertisements in the *Daily Worker* seemed to pay off more for *Partisan Review* than for *Anvil*. "Trachtenberg and others could well argue that the name *Partisan Review* had its sales-appeal value and could not be junked."[143] Apart from the name-recognition question, however, "*Anvil* had sold better than *PR*." As for Farrell's "Reverend Father Gilhooley" in *Anvil* 13, Snow explained that it was printed as "a peace-making gesture; Simpson wrote Farrell for a story and then we felt we could not reject Gilhooley because he would yell that the Conroy feud was still on."[144]

The decision to merge was formalized on Monday evening, 21 October, at Trachtenberg's home, in the presence of Snow, Simpson, and Howard Rushmore, representing *Anvil*, and Calmer, Rahv, and Phelps/Phillips representing *Partisan Review*.[145] Snow suggested "The Anvil Review" as the title, hoping it would ease Jack's loss. Trachtenberg, however, replied that "Anvil" was not an adjective. It was agreed to call the new magazine *The Anvil and Partisan Review*, and so it was publicized in magazines, until the first issue appeared, the title reversed, as *Partisan Review and Anvil*.[146] Conroy (in absentia), Snow, Simpson, Calmer, Rahv, and Phillips (who had abandoned his pen name) were proposed as the new editors, three from each magazine. When Snow pointed out the impossibility of Conroy, in Moberly, attending the meetings in New York, he was asked to propose someone else who would represent *Anvil*. Rahv suggested Walter Stacy, a Rahv loyalist. Trachtenberg supported Snow's veto. Snow's proposal of Edwin Rolfe, who had contributed to both *Rebel Poet* and *Anvil*, was met with acceptance. To avoid stalemates between the two combined editorial boards, a seventh member was appointed, Ben Field (a.k.a. Moe Bragin), considered a neutral candidate, friendly to both Rahv and Snow. Field was to have had a story in the nonexistent *Anvil* 14; it appeared in the first issue of *Partisan Review and Anvil*. Associate editors were named, including Balch, Winkler, Gold, Wharton, and Rushmore. Subsequently H. H. Lewis, Meridel Le Sueur, Joe Kalar, Nelson Algren, and Richard Wright were appointed, suggesting that the new magazine might well represent the old *Anvil*-ites in evenhanded balance. Such was Snow's demand, and it appeared on the night of the fateful meeting that it would prevail.[147] The magazine was to be located in the old John Reed Club office with a paid business manager named Bess Serman. Earl Browder, the CPA's chief, would announce the merger at a forthcoming banquet, hailing the new magazine's appearance. When Snow left the meeting at Trachtenberg's late that October evening, he felt satisfied that at his insistence the magazine would bear *Anvil's* name first and would be printed on quality paper, with a heavy cover, and the price held to twenty cents. There was no need to sell it any cheaper since all competition had been eliminated.[148]

At the time, the merger seemed to reconcile everyone's interests (except Jack's, but he had long since renounced the opportunity to intervene). The *Anvil's* "Whitcomb affair" had terrified Trachtenberg, who had to answer to his own bosses. From the Party's perspective, *Anvil* had proved unreliable and Jack too independent-minded. Snow was overtaxed and in debt; the "Magnificent Marchetti" had gambled on *Anvil* and lost. Rahv and Phillips were tempted by *Anvil's* circulation list (and its goodwill among subscribers). The new cultural politics under the Popular Front favored consolidation, literary prominence, "cultivated voices." Jack hoped to the very last that money could be raised to save *Anvil*, and viewed with half-disbelief plans to raise funds for the new magazine. In the end, however, he resigned himself to the inevitable. "I have some misgivings about the merger," he wrote Jack Rogers, one of the earliest contributors to Jack's magazines, "but nothing else can be done."[149] The fatalism that had served him in the past defended him once again. "I'm a little wounded," he recited to his friends in an oratorical voice, his small blue eyes twinkling, "but I am not slain";

> I will lay me down for to bleed a while
> Then I'll rise and fight with you again.[150]

In some ways it was a great relief. *Anvil* had become "a burden a real martyr would have to bear," Kalar wrote Huddlestone. "And a martyr with more cash than Comrade Jack."[151] Jack had little leisure to spend on epitaphs for the dead *Anvil*. He was thinking about his own future. On his mind too was the news of Nelson Algren's severe anguish over the poor reception of *Somebody in Boots*. There was a suggestion of possible suicide. Jack wrote many of his friends, asking them to write encouraging letters to Algren, which they did.

Snow was forced to imbibe the bitter dregs of the merger's aftermath. An editorial meeting of the new magazine was called. Rolfe arrived too late to the meeting to vote. Gold was not present, nor was Ben Field, who, Snow suspected, stayed away in order to avoid voting against Snow and Simpson—his story was due to appear in the first issue of the new magazine. Perhaps "Rahv & Co. might yank out his scheduled story."[152] The editors voted three to two to reverse the order of the title (Rahv, Phillips, and Calmer against Snow and Simpson). Outraged at the breach of the original agreement (and probably embarrassed by the defeat), Snow went straight to Trachtenberg, who had no time to see him, then to Mike Gold, who shared Snow's anger. Perceiving that things were irresolvably stacked against the *Anvil* faction, Snow resigned from the editorial board. Gold expressed his indignation in *New Masses*. "Papa Anvil and Mother Partisan," Gold wrote approvingly, had produced a "child . . . a vigorous male, retaining the best features of both parents; papa's earthy directness and mama's erudition and sensibility." Those in the Rahv-Phillips faction, however, were guilty of a "terrible mandarism." "They carry their Marxian scholarship as though it were a heavy cross. They perform academic autopsies on living books. They wax pious and often sectarian. Often they use a scholastic jargon as barbarous as the terminology that for so long infected most Marxian journalism in this country. . . ."[153] Farrell, Gold implied, was just as bad as the *Partisan Review* editors in this respect. Gold was incensed at Farrell's "sour attack" on Clifford Odets's new play, *Paradise Lost*, published in the first number of *Partisan Review and Anvil*. Gold's criticism of Rahv, Phillips, and Farrell was an early tremor, announcing growing fissures dividing the left.[154]

The split occurred roughly along a line dividing the *New Masses* camp and the Rahv-Phillips axis of *Partisan Review*. With the publication of Farrell's *A Note on Literary Criticism* (1936) it became unbreachable. Farrell's charge was vulgarism, sentimentalism, faulty critical standards on the part of inadequately prepared Marxist critics (principally Gold and Hicks). Isidor Schneider, in a reply published in *New Masses*, cited Farrell's broadside attack on bad revolutionary art as evidence of Farrell's misreading of Marx, and an indication of "a new crisis in revolutionary literature," a move to the right under the guise of the Popular Front.[155] The debate drew defenders to each side, including Edmund Wilson (for Farrell) and Calverton (critical of Farrell but outside the fray), neither party conceding. Exacerbating the rift were the infamous Moscow trials, which proved a watershed dividing the Party loyalists and the dissidents, like Farrell, Rahv, and Phillips, who, after the suspension of *Partisan Review and Anvil* in October 1936, were free to expand their criticism against "leftism" into preparations for a new offensive in which they would bear the standard of literary excellence against the philistines and barbarians. The campaign was launched in December 1937 when the revived *Partisan Review* appeared, all traces of its Stalinist past effaced, now become a cynosure for a new intelligentsia that redirected American readers' attention to literary modernism, attempted to reform vulgarized Marxism, and introduced a brilliant selection of new and neglected authors, both European and American, that assured the magazine's preeminence in American letters for decades to come.[156]

When the second American Writers' Congress convened in 1937, neither Jack nor Snow was invited to participate (although Jack attended anyway).[157] Numerous others were likewise excluded, including Farrell, who had criticized the Moscow purges. Workers were noticeably absent in what Malcolm Cowley called "the great broadening of subject matter" of the Popular Front.[158] Indeed, at the congress no mention was made of literature by or about workers, except for Albert Rhys Williams's passing encomium to the workers' correspondence movement in the Soviet Union.[159] The worker-writer was the first casualty in the Party's war against fascism, in which professional writers were mobilized.

Jack had no further part in *Partisan Review and Anvil* aside from writing one review (of Sholokhov's *Seeds of Tomorrow*). The new magazine was broader in scope but its circulation spiraled downward. By the next fall, the editors had decided to drop *Anvil* from the title.[160] Instead, they suspended the magazine. The last issue appeared in October 1936.

The Party had hoped to capitalize on Rahv's and Phillips's considerable rhetorical and intellectual skills for the purpose of promoting the consolidation of the left's cultural activities under the Popular Front. It is unlikely that the Party cultural commissars anticipated that Rahv and Phillips would act to consolidate their own power in the cultural movement and, not long afterward, side with the detested enemy, the Trotskyist opposition. In clasping the two editors to its breast, the Party had made a colossal blunder. Or perhaps, the Party was simply outmaneuvered. In losing *Anvil*, Jack lost his main chance to further causes the Party had several years earlier vigorously promoted. In abandoning *Anvil*, the Party betrayed its own interests, which, in Jack's mind, lay with working-class people. The Party had supported the workers' cultural movement, such as it was, during the early years of the Depression decade and had provided inspiration through its activities in organizing the unemployed, defending the rights of black workers, and sponsoring the John Reed clubs where young writers like Richard Wright, Sanora Babb, Erskine Caldwell, Robert Cruden, and many others had received encouragement and made contacts. Now it seemed that opportunists and careerists were insinuating themselves into the left's broad cultural alliance. In the beginning, the possibilities seemed very fresh that a new strain of literature might evolve, deriving from orality, certain types of speech acts, folk tradition, and ordinary experience, reflecting the heterogeneity of American common life. But new hierarchies were in the making; these were new arborescent structures devoted to setting norms and maintaining standards of excellence accordingly, new systems of exclusion to control discourse, such as "New Criticism," that educated several generations of students to ignore the ideological specificity of literature, mystifying a literary "work" through notions of transcendence, unity, and autonomy.

Rather than blaming the Party, Jack placed the blame on certain ambitious individuals, as if the Party were like the miners' union. You don't criticize the union; you single out for censure those who unscrupulously manipulate it to their own advantage. Jack and other midwestern radicals had participated in the effort to build a foundation for working-class literature, rooted in working-class identity with ties to the trade union movement, a literature that spoke to people's lives rather than diverted them through escapism and sensation. Writers like Joe Kalar, Meridel Le Sueur, and Conroy viewed literature as a transforming *praxis;* the old bourgeois apparatus of production and publication, with its assimilative practice, must be countered by a new "production aesthetic" of critical consciousness aimed at working people, writers, and artists, and a decentered system of literary production. Breaking with publishing practices that "created" best-selling writers and erected hierarchical scales of literary value, Conroy had started a literary magazine that welcomed new writers, spreading its roots in a multiplicity of subterranean connections throughout American social experience. The *Anvil* project was to prepare the soil for the emergence of a new literature that, Jack hoped, would be in closer contact with the experiences of ordinary people than was the dominant culture, with its devotion to prominence and literary personality, or popular culture, which bore the traces of commercialism. The experiment lasted only a short time; already, new, arborescent structures were appearing on the left.

There is a poignancy in the story, insofar as the midwestern literary radicals were trying to keep alive a literary movement, indeed a wider cultural movement, in a context that hardly nurtured it. The poignancy sharpens when one considers that the opposition finally came not so much from the dominant culture, the "bourgeoisie," but from within the Party's own ranks. It was a tragic loss if one believes that there is room in American letters for cultural diversity reflecting class, race, gender, and ethnic differences. Yet it is still possible to study this neglected and often maligned episode and to find useful models for future experimentation. The rich diversity of heteroglossia, the multiplicity of folk expression and social experience that Conroy and the midwestern radicals mapped, the nonhierarchical production aesthetic that represented a liberating deterritorialization of dominant codes and centrifugal structures—do we not find a similar process in the committees of correspondence and grass-roots democratic initiatives today? Such is the irony of history that the tragic contradictions of yesterday are often recast into the hopes of tomorrow.

17

The Writers' Project Years: Contexts of Loss

We will have to work out the salvation of America
without much help from New England.
—Reinhold Niebuhr to Kenneth Porter,
25 March 1935

WORKER-WRITING IN THE UNITED STATES has never achieved the status that, say, minority literatures enjoy today. Mike Gold's promotion, Walt Carmon's tireless legwork, and the devotion of little-magazine editors like Conroy failed to win a long-term commitment on the part of the left to worker-writing; nor did it achieve broader recognition beyond that accorded it by iconoclastic editors like H. L. Mencken. During the period between 1928 and 1932, the left's cultural apparatus showed some interest in sponsoring worker-writing; long before the Popular Front was announced in 1935, however, that interest had begun to wane. In retrospect, it appears that the Party's interest in worker-writing merely imitated Soviet initiatives, peaking roughly around the time of the Kharkov conference in 1930 and fading quickly after the demise of RAPP in 1932 and the appearance of a single union of Soviet revolutionary writers devoted to Socialist Realism. What was essentially a humanistic project—giving voice to workers' individual experiences and providing them access to the means of literary production—yielded to Party agendas and official ideology.

The roots of midwestern indigenous worker-writers like Conroy, Kalar, and H. H. Lewis lay in unionism, Debsian socialism, "wild jackass" populism, and folk expression. These were basically autonomous, independent traditions, as the midwesterners knew them; the worker-writers balked at Party "lines," top-down authority, centralization, and secrecy. UMW and Brotherhood Railway Carmen union locals conducted meetings in open forums, and leaders rose from the rank and file. Soviet models, such as the worker-correspondence movement, sponsored by workers' councils and administered by professional writers, were ill-adapted to American circumstances. The idea of organizing "shock brigades" of writers held little attraction to American workers. Poets are venerated in Russia by common people, and literacy is highly esteemed; Mark Twain is perhaps better known among Russian workers than American. Russian workers loved their Gorki and their Demian Bedni; no American counterpart ever enjoyed their popularity in the United States.[1] Popular Front cultural politicians sought the endorsement of acclaimed writers like Ernest Hemingway, who reported on the death of war veterans in a Florida hurricane for *New Masses*. A worker-writer's endorsement simply did not carry the same weight. In H. H. Lewis's case, for instance, a worker-writer had become an outright liability in the Party's eyes.

Ironically, the United States government filled a vacuum created when the left largely abandoned its sponsorship of worker-writing. The Federal Writers' Project, signed into being shortly after the First American Writers' Congress, employed writers like Conroy to undertake fieldwork, the harvest of which was an abundant variety of occupational narratives, social histories, and folklore. Despite the fact that the Party no longer considered the worker-writer useful to its aims, it viewed the Federal One arts projects as "counterrevolutionary."[2]

By the late 1930s, documentary expression was gaining widespread attention, particularly among Federal Writers' Project administrators like Ben Botkin and Henry Alsberg. Oral narrative and photographic documentation transcended rigid ideological divisions; the plight of the dispossessed found eloquent expression in the work of middle-class photographers and writers like James Agee, Ruth McKinney, and Dorothea Lange while proletarian writing languished in obscurity, the object of critical epitaphs such as Rahv's essay "Proletarian Literature: A Political Autopsy," published in 1939, in which he correctly observed that the "official Left is today primarily interested not in literature but in *authors*."[3] By 1936, Conroy had joined the growing number of documentarians exploring back roads, migrant camps, and factories to hear "the people talk."[4] His researches, he hoped, would provide material for a novel.

From his Guggenheim-sponsored interviews with migrant workers Jack planned to create "a sort of composite character representing the Negro immigrant. . . . the character will be a Negro boy of some ambition whose father has been in the upper strata of Negro labor because he is a locomotive fireman." He wrote Richard Wright to ask his help: "I wonder if you could tell me just where a Negro fireman would be found in the south, and how he would be regarded by his white fellow workmen."[5] Jack reported on his research: his interests had shifted to the "Negro question," as it was termed on the left. Conroy's naive attempt to write about southern blacks belied a sincerity of purpose, stemming perhaps from his recollections of black miners in Monkey Nest, the East St. Louis race riots of 1917, fellow workers in the Toledo auto factory, and chance encounters on the road as an itinerant worker. "You are probably too young to remember these events," Jack noted; nonetheless, he hoped that Wright might be able to provide anecdotes about his own migration northward. Covici-Friede had expressed great interest in Jack's new book-in-progress; Harold Strauss, a Covici-Friede editor, and Max Lieber both urged him to finish the manuscript quickly, sensing a rising interest among a broad readership in 1930s social topics, perhaps because of John Steinbeck's success (Covici-Friede had recently published Steinbeck's *In Dubious Battle*). Jack had even decided on a title: the novel would be called "Anyplace But Here."

In the previous fall, Conroy had applied to Henry Alsberg, director of the newly formed Federal Writers' Project in Washington, D.C., for a position. At that time writers had to prove they were on relief to be eligible. Since Conroy was still receiving Guggenheim money he was turned down. The Missouri Writers' Project in St. Louis had become a headache for Alsberg, who was sensitive to criticism that the FWP might be viewed as a high-priced boondoggle. Early in the spring of 1936, he sent Lawrence Morris, a field supervisor for the FWP, to St. Louis; Morris reported back that problems in the MOWP lay with the director, Geraldine Parker. Parker, it appeared, jealously guarded authority for herself despite the competence of her staff.[6] Morris recommended that Alsberg hire Conroy under the new nonrelief category. An "experienced writer and editor," Morris wired Alsberg, "would be very useful addition to Missouri state editorial staff which has enormous job ahead of it." The pay was $125 per month.

Jack first heard of the opening at the MOWP in Des Moines in May, when Jay Du Von, Ray Kresensky, and other members of the Midwest Literary League invited him to give a talk. Jack and Joe Jones traveled to Des Moines in Jones's car, staying in the Chamberlain Hotel. Du Von and Kresensky were members of the Iowa Writers' Project, where Jack was first introduced to Geraldine Parker, who was in Des Moines to visit her project colleagues. Parker told Jack that a position on the Missouri project would be waiting for him when he returned with Jones to St. Louis. Dale Kramer, Carroll Norling, and several members of the Iowa

Writers' Project had started a new little magazine called *Hinterland*, under the auspices of the Midwest Literary League. Influenced by the example of the *Anvil*, the editors invited new writers and welcomed controversial subjects. *Hinterland* was evidence, Jack observed to Richard Wright, of a renaissance of midwestern literature.[7] A number of *Hinterland*'s contributors and editors were former *Anvil*-ites, like H. H. Lewis, Ray Kresensky, and John Rogers.

Several years before, Jack had sent Dale Kramer to help Marvin Sanford publish the *Anvil* in the Newllano Colony printery, a job that offered little remuneration and a repetitious diet. In mock indignation, Kramer blamed Conroy for the bum steer. Kramer, on behalf of the Midwest Literary League, arranged for Jack to speak at the Unitarian church in Des Moines to members of the Farmers' Holiday Association, a populist organization of independent farmers opposed to foreclosures and to corporations' controlling land and the price of grain. A week before Jack's talk, Milo Reno, the FHA's dynamic leader, died in a sanitarium in Excelsior Springs, Missouri.[8] Introducing Jack at the meeting was an opportunity for Kramer to "settle scores" with Conroy. When Jack pulled out a written talk, Kramer said, "Give me that old manuscript. I've heard it a dozen times. I'm going to tear it up!" Jack never felt altogether comfortable speaking on a subject to an audience. Painfully he weaned himself of written texts and notes but never quite dispensed with them altogether. If formal speeches were a bane, he felt great pleasure in telling stories; much of his speechmaking was in effect a serial form of anecdotes.[9] On their return from Des Moines, Conroy and Jones took a side trip to visit the eccentric editor of *Boomer*, Axel Peterson. Peterson lived in Avery, Iowa, a tiny coal community where once Jack had thought of moving the *Anvil*.[10]

In early June, Conroy was a featured speaker in Chicago at an organizational meeting of the Midwest Federation of Arts and Professions, whose purpose, in line with efforts to promote a "Midwest renaissance," was announced in the conference title: "The Promise of Midwest Literature." Active in the federation was the Chicago Writers Group, epigone of the dismantled John Reed Club. Gathered in Foresters Hall, 1016 North Dearborn Street, on the thirteenth and fourteenth of June, the federation declared its twofold intent: to oppose fascism (in the spirit of the Popular Front) and to sponsor a new magazine called *Midwest*, which, according to a report that Conroy and Meridel Le Sueur wired to the *New York World-Telegram*, would "nourish again in the Middle West its writers and artists so they won't have to go East to be published. They will find again their own audience and be connected with their own deep roots and struggle."[11]

In his afternoon talk of the thirteenth, titled "The Writer in the Industrial Scene," Jack reviewed the successes and failures of those who had attempted in literature to portray workers' problems. Intuition and sympathy, he concluded, were more important than actual experience among workers. The implication was that the worker-writer was not to be granted exclusive rights to working-class material, a sentiment that fit the broad coalition needed to fight fascism. At the Chicago meeting, Mike Gold brought greetings from the League of American Writers and from "New York writers." Gold warned the midwesterners to avoid narrowness; the presence of Carl Sandburg, Sherwood Anderson, and Upton Sinclair was needed at the meeting. Federation members must learn to write "in a style as broad and simple as that of a Twain."[12] Such was the spirit of the Popular Front that Mike Gold, former champion of the proletarian movement, now advised radical writers to know their *Huckleberry Finn*.[13]

Meridel Le Sueur read Malcolm Cowley's long message of greeting to the federation, in which Cowley pointed out evidence of incipient fascism in the Black Legion, the Silver Shirts, and Hearst's chain of newspapers. Such evidence was frequently cited during the Popular Front in the final years of the 1930s. Spain cruelly illustrated fascist and progressive elements in conflict. Would Americans suffer a similar tragic fate?

No longer a "worker-writer" (that term had virtually disappeared on the left) or magazine editor, Conroy was now simply "a writer." Earlier distinctions of status tended to be effaced in the common literary enterprise of the Popular Front. The years 1936–38 were fallow ones creatively when Jack, beset by frustrations in his new position with the Missouri Writers' Project and financial worries at home, sought diversion among a group of mill workers and madcap writers in St. Louis.

In late June, assuming his new job at the Writers' Project, Jack stayed temporarily in a louse-infested hotel in St. Louis, then moved in with Joe Jones in the run-down mansion on the corner of Franklin and Grand streets that had been divided into apartments, providing a home and meeting-place for artists and radical activists. The summer of 1936 was scorching hot; people sought nighttime relief, sleeping in their backyards, in city parks, and on rooftops. Office workers wrapped wet towels around their necks and the wealthy rented rooms at the Chase Park Plaza Hotel, which boasted a new "refrigerated air" system. The Missouri Writers' Project members fled their offices, located on the ninth floor of the Civil Court building in downtown St. Louis, to nearby bars during long lunch-hours to seek relief. Everything seemed to be bogged down in the muggy, hot St. Louis summer, including the Missouri Writers' Project.

The project had experienced problems from its beginning the previ-

ous year. Chief among them was its director, Geraldine Parker, a political appointee. These were the years when the powerful Pendergast
machine in Kansas City controlled state politics in Missouri. With little experience, either as a writer or administrator, Parker was not able
to carry out the project's mission, which was to produce a state guidebook. Masses of documentation lay about chaotically in the office; morale was low. When Conroy signed on the project, scarcely a line of
the guidebook had been written. Talented writers and editors—the
project had several in addition to Conroy—were hamstrung. The setting scarcely boosted Jack's morale following the loss of the *Anvil* and
the critical failure of his second novel.

The working-class culture that Conroy had hoped to participate in
building as an autonomous little-magazine editor was now subsumed
within the larger agenda of the left, represented by the League of American Writers, of which he was a board member, and other Popular Front
organizations. Moreover, as noted earlier, New Deal programs, such as
the Federal Writers' Project, had removed a great deal of the animus
for a separate worker-writer movement. Age and family responsibilities
intervened, absorbing the enthusiasm and energy that Jack had invested in his editorial duties earlier in the decade. Men and women whose
writerly aspirations had been so great ten years earlier were no longer
youthful free-spirits without financial obligations. The Federal Writers'
Project offered them means of support and, in some instances, notably
the Illinois Writers' Project, work that they found interesting and useful. Conroy's participation on the Missouri project, however, slowed almost to a complete halt his progress on the black migration novel. Optimistically, he wrote Howard Wolf that "going to work for Roosevelt
and Hopkins slowed me down temporarily, but I'm at it again."[14] The
fact was that he had not produced a single manuscript page of text.

When Harold Strauss of Covici-Friede reminded him of his promise
to submit a manuscript by late spring of 1936, Jack realized the jam he
was in.[15] Financial worries stifled his desire to work on the migration
book. By the fall he had made no further progress and had sold only
one article, a sketch called "Happy Birthday to You," to *Esquire* magazine. Whenever his own work was not progressing he had a tendency
to displace some of his own ambition to succeed as a writer upon others. It was a saving grace, born of instinctive generosity, sparing him
the self-recrimination that Nelson Algren, for example, on occasion
experienced. Conroy was pleased that some of the old *Anvil* writers were
"breaking through" to major publications; and he urged Richard Wright
to finish his autobiography, two chapters of which Wright had sent him,
and send it off to Maxim Lieber.[16]

The prospects for a midwestern literature sensitive to the problems and experiences of working people seemed ever dimmer in 1936. Efforts were made on the left: the Midwest Literary League, the Chicago Writers Group, and various symposia in Chicago, Des Moines, and Minneapolis where Jack, Meridel Le Sueur, and others spoke on "the promise of midwestern literature." One group, promoting "Americanism" and allied with Popular Front ideals, talked about integrating a "usable past" with indigenous folk culture and radical expression; another, an opposing group, anti-Stalinist and eastern, associated with the *Partisan Review* after 1937, gravitated toward European modernism and critical theory.[17]

Mike Gold asked Jack to send material to *New Masses* on the Midwest. Howard Rushmore, Conroy's self-appointed protégé from Mexico, Missouri, arranged for Jack to publish a series of sketches in the *Sunday Worker Magazine* and *Progressive Weekly* based upon a humorous, eccentric folk figure named Uncle Ollie. The "Uncle Ollie" tales, modeled after one of Gladys's relatives, underscore the enduring qualities of rural folk culture in northeast Missouri, grafting folk art onto radical politics. Not only literary radicals like Conroy but mainstream composers like Aaron Copland, dramatists like Thornton Wilder, artists like Thomas Hart Benton, and writers like John Steinbeck celebrated such qualities in the common people in the Popular Front period of the late 1930s quite apart from any political agenda of the left.

Conroy's folk narratives with progressive themes, benefiting from Popular Front sponsorship, were the literary counterparts of a new "folk consciousness" manifesting itself in music, for example, in the work of Earl Robinson, Woody Guthrie, and later, the Almanac Singers.[18] Such a consciousness was anticipated well before the Popular Front, however, in Botkin's *Folk-Say*, Constance Rourke's critical studies—indeed, in Conroy's "proletarian" stories, which, by introducing humor, folk locutions, and orality spurned the conventions of proletarian literature. But dominant cultural trends and countervailing political forces marginalized expressions of "folk consciousness" in American literature. Critics and academics failed to evolve new generic definitions and critical standards beyond the acceptable range of the literary canon. And greatly diminished were the number of little-magazine editors and small presses that would accept the risks that mainstream publishers consistently refused.

The resistance that Conroy and others experienced from mainstream publishers and critics was frustrating, yet expected. Jack observed with growing bitterness, however, the spectacle of the reborn *Partisan Review*, having absorbed the *Anvil*, creating a place for itself in the dominant culture, indeed defining new trends that would dominate American literature and art for several decades.

Clinton Simpson, an editor for McGraw-Hill whom Snow had enlisted as editorial associate of the *Anvil*, was the sole remaining representative of *Anvil's* interests on the editorial board of the merged *Partisan Review and Anvil*. The magazine's editors ignored Conroy in distant Moberly; Snow resigned in disgust before the first issue appeared although his name was listed as contributing editor. With fewer stories and more emphasis on criticism, the new magazine saw its circulation drop from *Anvil's* 4,500 to 2,000, then to 700 or 800 copies when it ceased publication altogether.[19] Simpson stayed in touch with Conroy, advising him of moves to diminish the role of *Anvil* in the merged magazine. "I don't like the way the magazine is getting to be more and more the mouthpiece of Rahv, Phillips and [Alan] Calmer," Simpson confided.[20] Several months later Simpson wrote that the editors were planning to drop *Anvil* altogether from the title, along with Conroy's and Simpson's names from the list of editors. Little was left of the old *Anvil* in the magazine, and Simpson had been squeezed out of any active role; it seemed like a meaningless formal gesture when in fact the last issue, number 6, appeared in October 1936 as *Partisan Review*, listing Rahv, Phillips, and Calmer as editors. "Of course," Simpson wearily confided to Conroy, "all this is a violation of the agreement for the combination of the two magazines; but I suppose there is no use to talk about that."[21]

Conroy felt little satisfaction in the demise of *Partisan Review*. The magazine had altered greatly from its original intent; he had written off his part in it. Jack found entertainment in Nathanael West's satire, *A Cool Million*, passing it around to project members, who, weary of Geraldine Parker's incompetence, the slow progress of the guide, and the increasing criticism of the project's work by unsympathetic legislators and newspaper editorialists, were amused by West's disillusioned humor and pointed satire.[22] The spirit of boredom and frustration that pervaded the St. Louis office of the project was exacerbated by reports of open hostility on the part of U.S. Congressman Dewey Short of Springfield, Missouri. On the floor of the House, Short performed an impromptu parody of a Federal Arts Project dancer on pointed toes, to general laughter. The implication was clear: conservative legislators held artists and writers on relief in low regard.[23]

Incompetence at the director's level and the nature of the political favors system victimized talented writers on the Missouri Writers' Project. Concerned about negative publicity in Congress, Alsberg, the FWP's national director, sent a field supervisor named Frank B. Wells (and later Reed Harris) to investigate the Missouri project in the fall of 1936. Project writer Wayne Barker had found evidence of Parker's financial freewheeling, including the funding of a fancy dinner to impress the supervisor from Washington, D.C. Parker fired Barker, who had made himself unpopular with her for helping organize the St. Louis Writers' Union, prompting a sympathy strike by seventeen project writers, including Conroy. Conroy was not optimistic about the strike's outcome; unlike industrial labor strikes, he reasoned, in this strike no one stood to suffer but the participants.

In December, Conroy made a trip to Washington, D.C., to discuss the strike with Alsberg. He met Jerre Mangione, assistant director of the FWP, who was sympathetic with the striking writers' grievances but was unable to help. Joseph Gaer, whom he met in a hallway, told Jack that given Alsberg's sensitivity to legislative funding, there was little hope of resolving their claims. The strikers were able finally to force Parker's "resignation," but Alsberg, unwilling to confront the state WPA director for fear of further bad press, made no other concessions. When the strike was ended after six weeks, shortly before Christmas, Jack was hired back. It was anything but a happy conclusion. Disgusted with the lack of progress on the state guide, he thought about quitting. But where would he find work in Moberly? It was a demoralizing experience, to say the least, for an experienced writer and editor to spend fruitless days in the project offices. Chamber of Commerce boosterism ruled the project in St. Louis; good material was cast aside for fluff promoting highways and tourist attractions.

Despite deep reservations, Jack stayed on for another year, and for a time there was talk of making him director, but his leftist connections disqualified him in the eyes of the state WPA administrator. A year later the project was shut down, but it was revitalized subsequently, in June 1938, under Charles van Ravenswaay, who in the interest of "accuracy" edited out the more creative writing, including Conroy's reflections on Cape Girardeau and an unsparing portrait of southeast Missouri's Ozark people. The guide was finally printed in 1941 under the auspices of the State Highway Commission, with the approval of the Missouri Chamber of Commerce.[24]

Conroy made little headway on his documentary study of black migration. His few publications during these years included a report on a mine disaster occurring near Moberly in August 1936, which was published in *New Masses*, and a series of short sketches that Howard Rushmore arranged for publication in Party organs such as the *Champion of Youth*, a publication for young communists, the *Sunday Worker Magazine*, and the *Progressive Weekly*. One of these, "The Cement King," based upon Jack's experiences as a laborer, poignantly describes a tentative friendship between a young white worker and a black, both outcasts for different reasons.

Perhaps because he had worked so hard for so many years and now faced the uselessness of a job he was not allowed to perform competently, Jack gravitated toward the post-Prohibition bars of St. Louis. Away from his family and despondent that for the present at least he seemed thwarted in fulfilling the promise offered by his earlier work as writer and editor, Conroy sought out bohemian locales, such as Savo Radulovich's "Little Bohemia" at 220 South Fourth Street, near the river, and in rougher taverns across the river in East St. Louis, which even then was no place for the fainthearted. In Little Bohemia he met with writers and artists like Tennessee Williams, whom everyone knew as "Tom," Joe Jones, Stanley Radulovich (Savo's artist brother), and Wallie Wharton, the ex–business manager of *The Anvil*. At a union meeting in Granite City, Illinois, Jack befriended Lawrence "Bud" Fallon, a quick-witted, handsome mill worker who, like James Cagney in his movie roles, fought hard with his fists and played fast and loose with women. Through Fallon he fell in with a small group of mill workers and petty hoodlums who, like Jack, enjoyed a good laugh, although their forms of humor were, on occasion, cruel and exploitive.

The "Fallonites," as the East St. Louis toughs came to be known, began to occupy a great deal of Jack's time during the St. Louis years, 1936 to early 1938. East St. Louis in the 1930s, with its whorehouses, gangsters, and racetracks, was to other villages in Missouri and southwestern Illinois what Memphis was to Faulkner's Jefferson, Mississippi, a place where many a young Temple Drake attained maturity in the course of an evening. Mill toughs and writers seemed to enjoy special privilege there, indeed inspired a certain awe in the minds of the barkeepers and prostitutes. In this milieu Jack apparently found the spontaneity and conditions for enjoyment that he had known earlier in working-class taverns and that he yearned for as counterpart to the frustrations he encountered on the project. "I often reeled into the palatial offices of the Writers' Project," he wrote Wallie Wharton years later, "without having been to bed at all—after a long night of debauchery with the Fallonites on both sides of the river. I was able, too, to sit reasonably upright at a desk, speak semi-coherently, and even make small noises upon a typewriter at times."[25] It was a curious friendship: Jack Conroy, on the one hand, a generous, decent man who abhorred violence, a writer of compassion and humor, a progressive thinker; on the other hand, a group of small-time gamblers, mill toughs, and minor underworld figures who, in the era of tough guys, bootleggers, and hardboiled gangsters, were a dark counterpart of Jack's own personality. What then was the mutual attraction?

With the exception of Jesse Blue, all were mill or construction workers: Bud Fallon, Steve Conroy (no relation), Otto "Doc Otty Ollie Snake" Shaefer, Russ Finch, Bill "Drip" Walker. Too, all were impressed by Jack's literary achievements; here was a real author—or "arthur," as Jack liked to say, mimicking Missouri speech—a worker, like them, whose style of storytelling and explosive laughter made him the cynosure, the king of the revels. Jesse Blue was a petty mobster who carried a pistol and frightened bar patrons by his very presence. But kicking in doors and terrorizing customers were not sources of amusement for the Fallonites; rather satire, impromptu melodramas, elaborate pranks, and sacrilegious rites were their style. These were not your usual bullies; they had poetic souls, a bit twisted in places, some might have argued, but souls nonetheless. Their roguish capers attracted writers like Conroy, and eventually Nelson Algren, as Jack Kerouac was drawn to the experiences of Neal Cassady a generation later. The *Anvil* had unearthed writers among workers, convicts, and minority members; toughs like Fallon and Finch felt included in Conroy's literary world, harboring the desire that they too might become "arthurs."

Their "bard" was Wallie Wharton, the sandy-haired Scots-Irishman, who had got a job as a secretary-typist for a piston-ring company in St. Louis. Betrenia Watt Bowker, who worked on the Missouri Writers' Project during the summer of 1936, remembered Wharton as a prankster whose outrageous behavior in the bars scandalized even the jaded habitués of East St. Louis's notorious "Valley."[26] Wharton composed "odes" spontaneously at the behest of the Fallonites, satirizing the bawdry of the Valley prostitutes, middle-class mores (he had made of himself, he said, an example of bourgeois decadence), and the Communist Party. Indeed, the CP's involvement in labor organizing in St. Louis at the time is another curious facet of Conroy's relationship to the Fallonites.

Following the earlier strike activity—the marches of the unemployed, the Funsten nutpickers' strike, the International Ladies' Garment Workers' Union picketing, and so forth—St. Louis experienced the dramatic Laclede Gas Workers' Union strike in 1935 during which 152 strikers were arrested.[27] Bill Sentner, whom Jack had known as a CP district organizer in the Funsten nutpickers' strike, was now a regional vice-president of the Electrical Workers' Union, leading electrical workers in the Emerson Electric strike of 1937.[28] Bud Fallon organized in his off-hours for the fledgling CIO, arranging for Jack to talk to steel workers in the Labor Temple in Granite City.[29] Together with Josephine Johnson, Pulitzer Prize–winning novelist, Jack lectured at a labor college in St. Louis. He joined other speakers, such as Heywood Broun, in addressing a convention of the Newspaper Guild. Radical and bohemian milieus were closely linked in the St. Louis of the 1930s. There was a social dimension to artistic activity then; everyone Jack knew, including a number of wealthy liberals, was interested in improving the lot of the worker. The CP had widespread support among intellectuals and artists in the 1930s in its efforts to aid workers struggling for their rights. In sympathy with its progressive goals, Wharton, Conroy, and the Fallonites nonetheless lampooned the Party's penchant for authoritarianism and adherence to "the line." Targets of their satire were the policy of "Democratic Centralism" and the humorlessness of the Party faithful.

Fallon, for instance, had followed the shifts in Party orthodoxy and factional quarrels over the years, and seeing the potential for humor, invented his own Party faction, the "Parallel Centrists," a reference to the Party's Democratic Centralist line. Anyone opposed to Fallon's new line was a "Trotskyite-Bukharinite Wrecker." Still smarting from the Vanderbilt Belton affair and his expulsion from the John Reed Club in 1934, Wharton created a new Party hierarchy, naming it "Posterianism," in honor, as he said, of his own large bottom. In bars he recited impromptu satires, such as the following, on Party orthodoxy:

> O please stop the presses!
> It's the worst of all messes!
> I want to withdraw my review.
> I was told I should grovel
> in praise of some novel.
> I did—but now here's something new—
>
> The Party's decided
> it must be derided—
> the author, one Glotz, is passé:
> a Trotskyite rotter
> persona non grata
> and I should have known it. They say
>
> that I'd broken my glasses
> or cancelled New Masses
> or else I'd have heard of the purge.
> I remember one issue
> I made use of as tissue
> when caught with a purgative urge
>
> but I missed the denouncement,
> the sudden announcement
> that Glotz and his plots do not please.
> It's so hard to follow
> up hill and down hollow
> these whimsical Party decrees. . . .
> ("Left wing reviewer laments unfortunate review")[30]

Wharton's satires on the CP infuriated Nelson Algren, who offered Wharton a quarter for the manuscript of the poem.[31] The Belton "affair," to Wharton's mind, was an example of Party interference in literary matters, just as the Party had interceded in favor of *Partisan Review* at the cost of the *Anvil*. The Belton affair was a ridiculous tempest-in-a-teapot to Wharton—and to Jack too; however, Jack revealed his criticism of the Party privately, not in public impromptu performances such as Wharton staged in taverns. While Jack was content to poke good-natured fun at CP organizers like a German immigrant named Wagenknecht, whom he dubbed "Wagon Wheels," Wharton's humor reached further to caricature. Wallie gave nicknames to Party loyalists like Pete Chaunt's consort, Carolyn Drew, whom he called "Dialectics" Drew for her adeptness in Marxist rhetoric. Conroy was in a mood for satire following the *Anvil* takeover and what to midwestern radicals seemed overbearance on the part of New York comrades like Alexander Trachtenberg and William Browder.

Jack was drinking heavily, and much of his creative energy was devoted to comic parodies and satires, frequently in collaboration with Wharton, rather than to his documentary study of black migration. These were performed in St. Louis taverns (later in Chicago), before audiences of workers, Lumpenproletariat, and the jobless, and in the homes of wealthy liberals sympathetic to the cause of labor, such as Alice Koken, the Koken barber-chair heiress. Conroy performed a hilarious parody of Jack Balch's memoir, which had appeared several years before in an obscure magazine, *Vagaries*, turning to humor Balch's earnest recounting of his childhood in a tenement house.[32] Balch's *New Masses* story, "Take a Number, Take a Seat," about a relief applicant waiting for an interview, occasioned Conroy's samizdat parody, "Pay a Nickel, Take a Seat," about a man who enters a public restroom to find the stalls locked, and in his rage and frustration, utters a tirade in defense of communism. As "Behemoth Frittertitter," Wharton satirized Popular Front politics. A meeting of the "Midwest Cultural Alliance," he wrote in one of his countless unpublished tracts, passed around among the Fallonites and project writers, would include Communists, Republicans, Anglicans, Wobblies, Socialists, anarchists, indeed every conflicting point of view except the "Lutherans, Methodists, Baptists, Anabaptists, Christian Scientists and Latter Day Saints . . . Farmer-Laborites and Prohibition Party members," excluded for their "Northern European, Essenian and cruciferous attitude on life."[33] Party orthodoxy, temperance tracts, literary figures (like James T. Farrell) who had offended, scatological topics—all were favorite subjects of satire in the East St. Louis tavern life among the Fallonites. There, Jack was the cynosure and Wharton the bard/jester. Conroy and Fallon would chant a line in imitation of a fellow-traveler at a meeting who shouted, "Comrade Vag, five dollars from the Freiheitsgesangverein!"[34] Jack would recite in mock solemnity a verse penned by one of the group, which began:

> Barker and Balch hate the red Soviet star,
> Gladly they build a new throne for the Czar.
> Up from the steppes to the wild Balchic sea,
> Conroy's red army brings victory.

In these post-Prohibition years when people imbibed as if they were making up for lost years, Jack adapted a number of temperance tracts into a melodrama entitled, "The Drunkard's Warning," performed by the "Band of Hope Blue Blouse Theatrical Enterprises, Inc." which saw its first "full dress" performance at the Oasis bar outside of Moberly with Fallon, Wharton, and Finch in leading roles.[35] One of the "jeeps" (a Fallonite name for their girlfriends) played the part of "Little Lilly." A collective enterprise, "The Drunkard's Warning" had a number of versions to which Wharton, and later Algren, contributed lines, befitting the audience and the occasion.[36] Parodying the declining fortunes and increasing brutishness of the sottish Behemoth Frittertitter, an early version of the play ends with the helpless victim, Frittertitter's child, giving a temperance tract to the audience. A satire based upon melodrama conventions such as appear in T. S. Arthur's "Ten Nights in a Barroom," "The Drunkard's Warning" reflected Conroy's interest in nineteenth-century working-class culture and Victorian values, for example, the popular literature that emphasized values of thrift, sobriety, and industriousness.[37]

Later, in Chicago, the play evolved into a satire of James T. Farrell, who received the sobriquet James T. Barrelhouse. Jack was still smarting from Farrell's review of *The Disinherited*. The Fallonites took up Jack's cause, one of them offering to travel to Chicago to give Farrell a good thrashing, years after the review appeared. "The Drunkard's Warning" was performed many times in Chicago to raise money for the *New Anvil*, with Conroy, Red Kruck, Nelson Algren, Amalie Woldenburg, and others in the various roles. Wharton's dramatic "productions" included "Waiting for Luchinsky" (Odets's play was titled "Waiting for Lefty"), a satire of Lenin's preservation in the Red Square mausoleum, in which Stalin forces Dr. Luchinsky to eat Lenin's embalmed corpse, after which the unfortunate doctor becomes the consecrated figure of the Red Square tomb.

Wharton was cordially despised by the Fallonite jeeps, one of whom said, "If I ever see that man on the sidewalk in front of my house, I'll call the police."[38] Jack tolerated a great deal of the Fallonite pranks and foolishness such as Wharton's infamous "black mass" performed in an East St. Louis bordello; pranks were familiar to Conroy from his days in the Wabash shops and traveling with the Wobblies. He felt comfortable around working-class people, particularly storytellers or subjects of storytelling like Bud Fallon. Jack liked to recite Fallonite escapades, but these never directly entered his writing. Rather it was Nelson Algren who made use of Fallonite connections with the underworld, particularly Jesse Blue's, for story material. Jack's own literary debt to the Fallonites is less direct. He was not, he confessed, interested in writing about the kind of life they lived; that task was for Algren, who, fascinated by cardsharps, petty gangsters, and gamblers, was a careful observer of their lives.[39]

An important part of Jack remained detached from the Fallonites and their occasional cruel and violent mischief. A cry would go up in the rough working-class bars when Fallon entered: "CIO, CIO, CIO." Later in the evening, there would be a fight and Jack would be the first to take to his heels, like Falstaff, persuaded that discretion was the better part of valor. Wharton's role among the Fallonites was to entertain with his impromptu bawdy verses; the real center that held the group together, however, was Jack. He was the conciliator, "never willing," as Wharton said, "to sacrifice friendship to theory."[40] Some might argue that he was *too* accommodating.[41] The Fallonites were somewhat in awe of Jack and his literary abilities; Fallon ventured into poetry but abandoned his literary ambitions quickly. He turned what talent he had for writing to baiting Algren. Mimicking Algren's habit of note taking, Fallon wrote:

> Ain't got no Pulitzare, but I'm not the type to care,
> 'Cause I got a pocketful of notes.
>
> Never had no Guggenheim, I just don't have time,
> But I got a pocketful of notes.
> I wouldn't trade a poem of Balch's
> For a shelf of Algren's books
> And I calculate I'm worth my weight
> in Fanny Cooks.
> O lucky, lucky me! I'll wait posterity
> For I got a pocketful of notes. . . .[42]

Well into an evening Conroy, with the Fallonites' encouragement, would recite from memory Maxwell Bodenheim, Shakespeare, bawdy miners' ballads, and sentimental verse. With resonant voice, his left forearm upraised, palm slightly open and thumb touching forefinger—

the gesture of a nineteenth-century formal orator—Jack would conclude his recitation in a burst of rollicking laughter, his eyes sparkling. Gleefully recalling a Fallonite escapade and rubbing his hands together, he'd paraphrase the Irish poet Thomas Moore, "The harp that once through Fallon's hall, the soul of discord shed." Finally, too exhausted to continue his "performance" beyond a certain hour, he would stretch out on the host's couch, fast asleep.

At Jack's instigation, the Fallonite pranks began to involve bogus, frequently slanderous letters addressed to Algren and Balch, with Wharton's falsified signature, or Balch's, or that of Emerson Price, Jack's former Rebel Poet colleague who had made the mistake of visiting Jack when the Fallonites were present. Conroy hoped that Balch would respond. The letter writing soon got out of hand. Fallon, a clever imitator, wrote obscene letters to Algren, signing Wharton's name. Curiously naive and credulous at times, Algren took the bait at first; he kept a file of letters, and when the sixth letter arrived, containing crude anti-Semitic innuendoes and obscenities, he struck back bitterly.[43] Algren threatened to report Wharton to the postal authorities, and in signing the letter, underlined his actual family name, Nelson *Abraham*, persuaded that Wharton was an anti-Semite. Soon thereafter, however, Algren discovered that Fallon was the author; the tip-off was that Fallon had signed the letters "Wally" instead of "Wallie."[44] Algren wrote "Pussyface" (Fallon) a less hostile letter, pretending he did not know of the "Wally" letter, afraid perhaps of confronting Fallon directly. Algren chose rather to tell Fallon (falsely) that Jack was squealing on Fallon to those who had been the butt of his pranks, such as Emerson Price. Getting tough, Algren said he would settle when next in St. Louis (no mention of settling with Fallon).[45] Wharton, for his part, warned Fallon that he would contact postal authorities if Fallon continued.

Algren was sensitive to jests aimed his way. Nelson arranged for Jack and Bud Fallon to ride to the Second American Writers' Congress in a friend's chauffeur-driven car. Neither Conroy nor Algren had a place in the program of the congress, an indication of their standing (and that of "proletarian literature") with the cultural arm of the left by 1937.[46] Quite simply, it appeared they had been "dropped," and perhaps it was this reason that Algren felt depressed. At a downtown bar in New York, Fallon and Jack embarrassed Nelson, who was making awkward attempts to attract a young woman. Angrily Algren told the two to get home to the Midwest as best they could; he would lend them no money. Nelson later relented, lending enough to cover the bus fare, nothing more.[47]

A sour note, too, from the perspective of the organizers of the second congress, was the intervention on the part of a small group, in-

cluding Rahv, Phillips, Dwight Macdonald, Mary McCarthy, Fred Du-
pee, and Eleanor Clark, who, in announcing their break with Party regulars, attacked the Stalinist orientation of the congress, signaling their
admiration for Trotsky. The keynote of the congress was cultural nationalism and unity among bourgeois and leftist writers against fascism.
The Moscow trials precipitated a split, however, that was by no means
entirely ideological, but rather one involving questions of literary standards and the nature of personal ambition. The 1937 congress was, then,
both the pretext and the occasion for a group of radical intellectuals,
gathered around a new *Partisan Review* under Rahv and Phillips's editorship, to break with Party orthodoxy and control, and not long after
to constitute the nucleus of the New York intellectuals.[48]

The fall of Algren's and Conroy's literary fortunes in the spring of
1937 marked coincidentally the ascendancy of an emerging avant-garde
associated with literary modernism and Eurocentric criticism. It was
ironic that the cultural left in effect spawned the creation of a significant and powerful coterie of writers and artists who in determining subsequently the reputations and reception of certain major European and
American writers and artists in the postwar era gave little attention to
minority interests and working-class subjects. In giving shape to a literary canon whose systems of exclusion constitute, in Foucault's terms,
the attempt to control "the production of discourse," the *Partisan Review* editors who had once rebelled against the strictures of Party orthodoxy aided in narrowing the range of American literary expression
to a few "unapproachable giants" institutionalized in a complex web of
discursive and pedagogical practices.[49]

Perhaps the incident in the New York bar had galled Fallon, or perhaps it was just another prank; whatever the cause, Fallon continued
to harass the easily baited Algren. When Jack moved to Chicago in
1938, Fallon sent anti-Semitic letters to Meyer Levin, editor of *Esquire*,
with Algren's signature. At this point, Jack intervened, cautioning Fallon that he should desist. "I have always conducted myself as a loyal
friend and supporter of yours, and now, with glazing eyes, with the shiv
wielded by treacherous hand deep between my shoulder blade, I look
at you reproachfully and croak: 'Thou, too, Fallon! Then fall, Conroy.'"[50]

By the summer of 1937, the Missouri project had begun to discharge
its nonrelief employees to make room for the unemployed; a reduction
in Jack's pay made it clear to him that he was the next to go. Jack sought
to be transferred to the Washington, D.C., national office but was turned
down.[51] It was no great disappointment to leave the mismanaged project,
whose new director, Esther Greer, was scarcely an improvement on Parker.[52] Unedited manuscripts lay about; it appeared the guide would nev-

er be completed. Project members were sent on senseless field trips to gather material. Jack was told to map foot tours in Kansas City although the project had its own staff members there; he looked up Thomas Hart Benton and the two drank bourbon.[53] Convinced that writing ability was wasted on the Missouri project, Conroy decided to quit. The Fallonites held a farewell party in a "clubhouse" on the Meramec River. Conroy vowed he would depart St. Louis "perched on the radiator cap of Fallon's car, cherubically nude, with a copy of the Communist Manifesto in one hand, and a lot of blank paper, symbolizing the Missouri guide, in the other."[54]

The Conroys' financial situation was desperate in the fall of 1937. Jack owed the butcher, the grocer, and several doctors. To make matters worse, the Brown shoe factory let Gladys go when a large government shoe order went to Czechoslovakia.[55] Over the Christmas holidays, Jack fell quite ill; he decided to appeal to his St. Louis friends for a "Conroy Liberty Loan." The Fallonites formed a "League for the Rehabilitation of Conroy," to which several of Jack's friends, including Wayne Barker, Fallon, and Wharton, contributed. Jack kept a record and within several months was able to repay. In the meantime *Esquire* had paid fifty dollars for a story. His nephew Fred Harrison, still employed at the shoe factory, took him out for a New Year's Day drink.

Early in the new year, 1938, Jack and the Fallonites undertook their last collective prank. In a perverse way, the highwater mark of all Fallonite pranks, it brought the East St. Louis mill toughs brief national attention. Ironically, it signaled the end of a low period in Jack's life, a time of frustration and despondency, temporary relief from which he had found in East St. Louis bars in the company of the Fallonites.

Otis Ferguson had written a less than flattering review of a new collection of James T. Farrell's short stories in the *New Republic* entitled "Lillian Lugubriously Sighed," an actual phrase from a Farrell story.[56] Conroy wrote Ferguson to say that he had enjoyed the review whereupon Ferguson telegraphed Conroy, urging his support in the face of Farrell supporters offended by Ferguson's assessment. Jack and Fallon drafted a letter to the editor of *TNR*, gathering signatures from a group of East St. Louis barroom habitués, some of whom were illiterate. The round-robin letter, published in *TNR* on 12 January 1938, praised Ferguson's review. The letter might have gone unnoticed except that *Partisan Review*, unaware of the fraudulent signatures, condemned the letter and its authors, giving them the label "the East St. Louis camarilla." It was unfair, the editors said, to gang up in such a manner against "one writer."[57] The "one writer" was of course Farrell, who had gained the approbation of the *PR* editors, Rahv and Phillips, for his anti-Stalinist critiques of the dramatist Clifford Odets and others. Letters in response to the "camarilla" were printed in both magazines, including one by the critic Dwight Macdonald, who called the letter "literary lynching."[58] Succeeding well beyond Jack's expectations, the prank gave a fillip to his flagging spirits. By the time the exchange of letters tapered off, Jack had left for Chicago where his fortunes quickly turned around.

Algren persuaded Jack to move to Chicago where they could join forces to revive the *Anvil*. With money advanced from a review he had written for the *Midwest Daily Record*, the midwestern edition of the Party's *Daily World*, Jack bought a bus ticket to Chicago, arriving on a blustery March day in 1938 at Nelson and Amanda Algren's apartment, number 18, 3569 Cottage Grove Avenue, in an area known as "Rat Alley" among artists who lived there. Originally an arcade for the Columbian Exposition, Rat Alley offered cheap quarters for impecunious writers and artists like Algren, Mitchell Siporin, and others. As Jack settled in, Amanda Algren, who had a WPA job inventorying people living in tent cities in Lincoln Park, made a beef stew on Saturday nights to feed the three of them during the week. It was a chaotic ménage à trois, to say the least. Jack seemed temporarily at loose ends. Jobless and away from his family, he began to drink more. Friends, Amanda Algren said, placed pennies on his eyes as he lay stretched out on the floor. Nelson's moods cycled, from charming affability to bitter reproofs that Amanda had no business inviting friends over—the apartment belonged to him.[59]

Chicago still attracted young midwestern writers long after the Chicago Renaissance. Dreiser, Sandburg, and others had made their names there; in Chicago in the late 1930s, new literary fortunes were being made, many of them tied to the work of the Illinois Writers' Project at 433 East Erie Street in Chicago's Loop, a stone's throw from the rooming house where Sherwood Anderson wrote *Winesburg, Ohio*, the mansion where Ernest Poole had grown up, and the office where Harriet Monroe edited *Poetry* magazine. Jack deeply admired Dreiser: both had come from impoverished circumstances, struggling for recognition and acceptance, which came slowly.[60]

Algren, who was already on the Illinois Writers' Project, introduced Conroy to its director, John T. Frederick. Familiar with his work as author and editor, Frederick invited Jack to join the project, remembering Jack's generous offer to help out Frederick's failing *Midland* in 1933. Mild-mannered, serious, and conservative, Frederick admired Conroy's literary abilities but looked disapprovingly on what he considered to be Conroy's and Algren's radical tendencies. Nonetheless, Jack was hired in the special administrator category, avoiding the humiliating means test, which included an assessment of one's personal belongings. Frederick put Jack to work gathering tales from industrial workplaces. The idea came from the WPA's national folklore editor, Benjamin A. Botkin, who had edited the *Folk-Say* volumes earlier in the decade. Botkin prepared an outline for a collection to be called "American Folk Stuff" and sent it to regional editors.[61] Since Jack had joined the project, Frederick's enthusiasm for the possibilities of industrial folklore had mounted. In an early memo, responding to a piece Jack had submitted, Frederick wrote: "This is good stuff on the bridge plant—just the sort of thing we want for that phase of our subject."[62]

Botkin's inspiration, Frederick's reception, and Conroy's fieldwork were the three principal factors in shifting the project's focus from the study of folklore relics to the exploration of living lore created in the workplace. The scope of earlier project inquiry included morris dancing, cornhusking, apple cutting, and other recreations, valued more for their quaintness than for their authenticity. It is fair to say that the boost these three gave the study of industrial folklore was largely responsible for its evolution. Jack brought formidable credentials to the study of industrial folklore based upon his experience as a worker and his writing skills. Thus when Frederick assigned him to fieldwork, gathering the lore of industrial workers, Jack was able to draw from his own repertoire of tales. To supplement that material, Jack and Algren performed their "assignments" in North Clark Street bars where Wobblies, actors, circus clowns, and artisans gathered.

One of Conroy's early industrial folklore contributions to the ILWP actually appeared under Nelson Algren's name. Recasting a traditional workplace joke about an overtaxed worker who uses every moving part of his body to keep up with the pace of the job, Jack composed a short tale called "True Blue Highpockets from the Forks of the Crick," which Algren, eager to show Frederick that he was producing and not fooling around, submitted under the title "Highpockets."[63] Conroy was not one to feel possessive about his tales, and besides he owed Nelson a favor for helping him get on the project. In addition, Conroy furnished Algren with another industrial folktale entitled "Hank the Freewheeler," later published in Botkin's *A Treasury of American Folklore* under Algren's name. Algren had probably never set foot inside an auto factory; the language is entirely Conroy's.

Algren felt chagrined when Frederick complimented him on the Highpockets tale. To spare further embarrassment Algren suggested that Frederick give the industrial folklore assignments to Conroy.[64] Algren did his "fieldwork" at the racetracks and in Chicago's night court, from which he drew the material of *A Walk on the Wild Side*, *The Man with the Golden Arm*, and other novels.[65]

During 1938 and 1939, Conroy submitted ten industrial folk narratives, as well as a number of personal narratives, gathered in North Clark Street bars and elsewhere. One of these, "A Miner's Apprentice," was an oral transcription Jack made of conversations with his nephew, Fred Harrison, the "Ed" of *The Disinherited*. Frederick received the tales warmly and sought to find a commercial publisher to print them, along with other manuscripts collected on the project. Six of these tales eventually appeared in Botkin's *A Treasury of American Folklore* (1944), including the "High Diver" tale, told by a circus clown named Charlie De Melo, and "Slappy Hooper," told Jack by Harold Sullivan (also a project member), who had heard it from his father-in-law. Jack was able to reconstitute entire conversations overheard in taverns, submitting this as material to Frederick after deleting the "commonplace" from the manuscript. On Madison Avenue Jack listened to railroad tales from a retired railroader named George Walton. From itinerant workers Jack gathered work narratives of the Montana copper mines.[66] A couple of ex-typesetters named Harold Gunn and Floyd Nims gave Jack the basis of a tale he would entitle "The Type Louse." From his own experiences Conroy produced "The Demon Bricksetter," "The Boomer Fireman's Fast Sooner Hound," "The Sissy from Hardscrabble County Rock Quarries," and several others, some of which he subsequently developed into children's stories, in collaboration with Arna Bontemps.

When Fallon asked for his help in getting hired on the ILWP, Jack, ever accommodating, supplied Fallon with an unpublished manuscript written by Lawrence Lipton, which Fallon submitted to Frederick as proof of his writing ability, under the name Leo Leopold. Wharton threatened to blow Fallon's cover with Frederick, but Algren assured Fallon that he would warn Frederick of Wharton's utter unreliability.[67] Algren had little goodwill left for Wallie, particularly after the affair of the bogus letter and Wharton's satires on the Party. Moreover, Wharton had parodied Algren's poem "Program for Appeasement," appearing in the *New Anvil*. Wharton named his parody "Pogrom for a Piece of Cement."[68]

Algren and Conroy carried through their intent to revive the old *Anvil*. Determined to put the magazine on a sounder financial footing than its predecessor, and aware that it could not survive on the basis of sales alone, the two editors proposed "a collective subsidy of several hundred persons pledging from fifty cents up per month over a period of one year."[69] After that time, they hoped, it would sustain itself. To fund the start-up expenses of the *New Anvil* Algren and Conroy staged performances of "The Drunkard's Warning," sponsored fund-raising parties and lectures, including readings by Richard Wright, Langston Hughes, Sheamus O'Sheel, Peter DeVries, and Maxwell Bodenheim. Algren and Conroy had to prop up an inebriated Bodenheim in a chair for his reading, which he was not able to finish. It was no matter, since most people enjoyed seeing the once-famous poet of the 1920s drunk. At a party thrown by Stuart Engstrand, author of *The Invaders,* Bodenheim showed up tight. "He never disappointed us," Jack recalled.[70] Wharton wrote and staged "The Rise and Fall of Nick the Pander" for a *New Anvil* benefit in St. Louis but was unsuccessful in attracting the Fallonites across the river for the event. The Fallonites were laying their own plans to follow Jack to Chicago, hoping to land positions, they thought, on the Illinois Writers' Project. Writers, however, they were not.

From its inception the *New Anvil* solicited stories and poems from black and white writers. Frank Marshall Davis, poet and feature editor of the Associated Negro Press, was one of the associate editors, and the magazine was the first to publish stories by black writers Frank Yerby ("The Thunder of God") and Margaret Walker ("The Satin Dress"), both members of the ILWP, in a nationally circulated magazine. Conroy and Algren accepted early poems by Tom McGrath, and the first published story by Tom Tracy. Now long forgotten, Tracy's "Homecoming" was chosen by Harry Hansen for the O. Henry Memorial Award Prize in 1940. Edward J. O'Brien ranked the *New Anvil* fourth among literary magazines for the number of distinctive stories published. Several of the old *Anvil* contributors appeared, including Meridel Le Sueur, Algren, Jack Balch, John Rogers (woodcut prints), Benjamin Appel, and Norman Macleod; newcomers included the Kentucky folk poet Jesse Stuart, poets Karl Shapiro, John Malcolm Brinnan, Don West, and Vincent Ferrini, together with novelists Fannie Cook, Millen Brand, and others whose stories have since slipped into obscurity. Tennessee Williams and J. D. Salinger both submitted stories and were rejected. William Carlos Williams contributed two stories, one of which, "The Paid Nurse," was the lead story in the first issue, March 1939, published by Ben Hagglund, the *Anvil's* old printer, on Marvin "Dad" Sanford's press in Pelly, Texas. Prevented from joining the printers' union local, Hagglund moved to San Benito, Texas, in the Rio Grande Valley, where on a hand-set press and aided by his wife, Isabel, he published subsequent issues of the *New Anvil.*

The first number, on newsprint paper with buff ledger cover and saddle-stapling, ran 3,500 copies at a cost of $245. Hagglund showed enormous patience as payments for the printing dribbled in slowly. He had hoped to reduce costs by buying large lots of paper stock, but the record of payments barely covered rent and lights. Depending in great part upon the formula that Hagglund and Conroy had devised for the old *Anvil*—low-cost printing, self-sacrificing editors and publisher, an enthusiastic network of supporters—the magazine's prospects looked good in the spring of 1939. Direct subscriptions accounted for 750 copies of the second number; Irving Cress, of the CP's distribution agency in New York, took 500 copies.[71] Supporters like Meridel Le Sueur and Alexander Bergman distributed bundles; bookstores like Brentano's and the Gotham Book Mart in New York, together with leftist bookstores in St. Louis, San Francisco, and elsewhere, handled bundles of ten.

The Party dropped its endorsement of *Partisan Review* when the magazine reappeared in 1937. The *New Anvil*, which announced in its first issue that its purpose was to provide a creative forum for "those who do the useful work of the world" and oppose the forces of reaction, won the approval of V. J. Jerome and others in the CP's cultural hierarchy. Conroy and Algren welcomed the Party's patronage to the extent that Jack, in conflict with the editorial independence he had shown in the original *Anvil*, asked Albert Maltz whether he should send several contributors' stories to the Party's district organizer, not to censor but to test the response. Maltz said no. "You've been long enough in the movement to judge adequately whether a story is good or not, and whether it is good left or not."[72]

Coming at the end of the 1930s, on the eve of the Nazi-Soviet pact and World War II, the *New Anvil* was a late bloom of the midwestern radical culture that Jack and the *Anvil*-ites had helped create earlier in the decade. "Where in hell," wrote a contributor, "are all those guys who wrote such damn good stuff in the early 1930's—who were just beginning to make their words and their names mean something—I don't know—maybe they're still there and the words are still there, but the medium for publication just ain't."[73] By 1939, most of the radical little magazines of earlier in the decade had folded. The Nazi-Soviet pact caused the Party to close many of its bookstores for lack of clientele; literary magazines were placed at a lower priority than that given to distributing *New Masses* and the *Daily Worker*.[74] Moreover, critical realism was on the defensive. Hadn't *Grapes of Wrath* been attacked in the Oklahoma legislature and copies burned?

Benjamin Appel suggested to Jack that with the emerging prospect of war, renewed patriotism would work a hardship on writing of critical social content.[75] The task of finding fresh talent fell increasingly to new magazines like the *Kenyon Review* sponsored by universities and managed by editors in tenured positions. The *New Anvil*, on the other hand, maintained the spirit of the Old Left even as the left was badly fractured following the defeat of the Spanish Republicans and the Nazi-Soviet pact. The locus of literary patronage and readership shifted toward the universities, and the survival chances of an independent little magazine like the *New Anvil* dimmed.

Jack was unsure about the pact and its consequences despite Hag-glund's assurances that the Soviets had acted wisely in the face of France and England's desire to capture Europe within the capitalist orbit.[76] Conroy and Algren remained supporters even as many leftists aban-doned the Party. The spectacle of those who had been strong in the Communist cause now profiting from their version of "confessions of an ex-Communist" was alone cause in Jack's mind not to jump ship cry-ing mea culpa. Instinct counseled him to "stick to the union," reserv-ing judgment. He refused to sign a declaration condemning the Sovi-ets.[77] His attitude of support yet reserve toward the Party, however, often meant steering around the Party or ignoring its criticisms. For exam-ple, several in the Party's local unit criticized Conroy and Algren's light-hearted pranks and "bohemian" management of the magazine. Conroy and Algren were called before a CP official in Chicago named Frank Myers, an associate on *New Anvil's* board, to discuss editorial decisions. "He kept us waiting in an anteroom for about an hour," Jack remem-bered, "then delivered a stern lecture about the necessity of publishing material that made explicit a Marxist moral."[78]

The verve, humor, and enthusiasm with which the new magazine was organized and promoted became part of a tradition of friendship, par-ty-giving, and progressive politics among Conroy's wide circle of Chi-cago friends, continuing long after *New Anvil* withered and died in its seventh issue of August–September 1940. Alone the presence of Al-gren and Conroy as editors was sufficient to ensure an informality that welcomed unknowns possessing talent and a freewheeling atmosphere that belied the magazine's serious purpose. The publication of Richard Wright's *Native Son* gave a boost to *New Anvil's* policy of accepting con-tributions by untried writers. Conroy and Algren struggled to continue *New Anvil* in the hope of discovering others whose work might one day prove as significant as Wright's. Helpers like Christine Rowland deliv-ered copies of *New Anvil* to bookstores in the belief that it served such a purpose. A few wealthy liberals, such as Polly Spiegel, the mail-order-catalog heiress, made donations when apprised of its dedication to dis-covering and encouraging new writers.

Located in the former Burnham Building, 160 North LaSalle Street, the *New Anvil* occupied an office recently vacated by Carl Haessler, editor of Federated Press, which represented labor organizations. Earli-er, Sidney J. Harris edited the *Beacon* from the same location. Haessler had done public relations work for the Institute of Mortuary Research, leaving behind a ream of the institute's stationery, which Algren and Conroy used for *New Anvil's* correspondence, including a rejection note to J. D. Salinger, who responded to the humorous whimsy of the sta-tionery, regretting the announcement that *New Anvil* would soon cease to exist (in 1940). Wallie Wharton did not take a rejection note as graciously. Particularly galling to Wharton was the fact that *New Anvil* printed a poem, "Utility Magnate," signed by "Lawrence O'Fallon" but written by Algren as a joke.[79] Wharton wrote a scalding letter to Conroy, reminding him of Wharton's earlier labors as business manager of the old *Anvil*, and chastising him for "slavish cowardice" in seeking Party patronage. Wharton was in a bilious mood. He assailed the Communists as "conniving, bigoted, fanatical, smug, ass-kissing, baby-bombing gangsters" and anyone, including Jack, even loosely associated with the Party as their lackeys.[80] Jack dismissed the letter; he had witnessed Wharton's contumelious anger on other occasions and felt his barbs in connection with the authorship question of "The Drunkard's Warning." Notwithstanding, the two remained friends and Jack was instrumental in finding a publisher for Wharton's poetry collection ten years later.

Soon after starting his new position on the Illinois Writers' Project, Jack met Theodora Pikowsky, a fieldworker on the project. A romance developed and Jack began to spend a great deal of time at 15 E. Delaware Place, in Theo's fourth-floor loft apartment, where an "all-star cast" performed "The Drunkard's Warning" on 16 May 1938. Performances were always open to improvisation; this particular evening, however, the action spilled out beyond the dramatic frame when Red Kruck, who played Little Lily, his red hairy legs showing beneath petticoats, spied Trotskyites in the audience, leaped from the stage, and started a brawl. The ensuing pandemonium, amplified by sound effects produced by rattling tin sheets provided for the play, concluded with the landlady serving notice.[81]

Born in Russia, some ten years Conroy's junior, Theo was a bright, warmhearted Jewish woman and ardent leftist. Sanka Bristow, one of her close friends at the time, remembers Theo dressed in a peasant smock, tending generously to others' needs. Sweet-tempered, very fond of Jack and deeply interested in his literary life, she was the intellectual and sexual companion Jack apparently needed as he attempted to redirect his creative energies following a long fallow period. When Gladys learned of the affair shortly after moving to Chicago with the children some six months following Jack's arrival, she demanded a separation. Jack assured Gladys that Chicago was different from Moberly; Chicago's cosmopolitans were expected to have affairs. Gladys's response was to boot Jack out of the Conroys' shabby apartment on Thirty-ninth and Ellis. She found work in a hassock factory and prepared to raise the children without Jack's financial help, which he nonetheless continued to provide. After a year Jack returned to Gladys, who had since moved to apartment number 3 at 3866 Lake Park Avenue, where the ties were reknit. Theo, Sanka recalls, was heartbroken when the affair ended.[82]

"The Drunkard's Warning" was revived each time to fund a new issue of *New Anvil*. In its Chicago adaptation, the penitent drunk Behemoth Frittertitter, played by Conroy, became James T. Barrelhouse, a broad satire on Farrell, despite objections by Farrell's family, who complained to Conroy and Algren that performances were "causing Jimmy trouble."[83] Discarding much of Wharton's bawdry in the St. Louis version, the new collaborative version included Algren's lines such as "a bed I never made" (reference to Farrell's *A World I Never Made*) and "you Goldblatt bargain in a Marshall Field topcoat," alluding to Chicago's department store. Amalie Woldenburg had an unprofessional habit of wandering off from the performance, delaying the stage action until she could be located.

On the project and among a growing circle of friends and literary colleagues in the 1940s and 1950s, Conroy and Algren were legendary figures, revered for their literary abilities as well as their original but widely divergent personalities. At parties, the two friends acted as foils for the other, such as when they took the parts of Gypo Nolan and Frankie McPhillip, the "Devil's Twins," from Liam O'Flaherty's novel *The Informer*.[84] Jack's legendary (among his Chicago friends) capacity for drink accentuated an outgoing, bluff, friendly manner and an instinctive theatricality.[85] Jack had a big heart, and after enough drinks he would permit Algren to lead him about like a trained bear to perform his comic recitations, ignorant of the fact that Algren might be using him cruelly. Such times were painful to watch; Jack loved Algren, but Algren's interest in Jack scarcely went beyond the amusement Jack provided him—despite the fact that they had been struggling young writers together in the early *Anvil* days, shared an apartment for at time, worked as colleagues on the Writers' Project, and rambled Chicago streets together for several years. While others like the poet Frank Marshall Davis saw in Jack a profoundly decent man possessing a certain old-world gentlemanliness, Algren viewed him as an entertaining companion, oddly reserved in some ways but always "good for laughs."[86] Harold Sullivan remembered that Jack met an old friend on a street who was hungry and without a coat on a cold winter night. Jack took him in, fed him, and gave him money to go to New York, where he worked for the *Daily Worker* for a short while, renounced his leftist past, and hired on with a Hearst magazine titled *Confidential*, exposing "reds." The man was Howard Rushmore from Mexico, Missouri, who had idolized Jack as a young literary aspirant some years earlier.[87]

* * *

Jack first met Arna Bontemps in the Erie Street offices of the Illinois Writers' Project sometime in the summer of 1940. Their mutual friend was Langston Hughes, who felt the two had a great deal in common and would become friends. The folklore project had folded in 1939; in late 1940, Algren and Conroy were let go from the ILWP since, according to WPA rules, they had served longer than eighteen months. Soon after, however, they were reinstated and reassigned.

When Curtis MacDougall replaced John T. Frederick as the project director, Jack was assigned to a group exploring unorthodox religious cults such as the Nation of Islam and the Black Muslims. Headed by Katherine Dunham, an anthropology student and dancer, later celebrated for her innovative contributions to modern choreography, the group gathered material from fieldworkers assigned to attend meetings held in abandoned storefronts. Not long after Jack joined the group, Dunham resigned to continue her studies and embark upon a dancing career. Jack was then assigned to Illinois WPA Project 30068, initiated by Horace Cayton, whose purpose was to assemble what was to become the Chicago Afro-American Union Analytic Catalog.

Jack's Guggenheim research had made him eligible for the assignment, but eligibility was not always strictly observed on the project. Eligibility was in most cases the ability to write and offer proof of relief status, ascertained through the so-called "pauper's oath," a humiliating qualification, according to the project director, Curtis MacDougall, who nonetheless had to accept those sent to him by the Relief Administration through the Works Progress Administration office.[88] Working with supervisors like Jack and Arna Bontemps, who had been hired in the nonrelief category, MacDougall, a journalism professor at Northwestern University, worked hard to turn what was basically a relief program into a professional organization.

Project 30068 was located in a mansion once owned by Julius Rosenwald, who had made his fortune as a founder of Sears mail-order. Occupying adjacent offices, Bontemps and Conroy, whom MacDougall had named supervisors, were assigned to help produce a study called "The Negro in Illinois." Down the hall connecting the offices, once bedrooms in the mansion, passed fieldworkers reporting back from their researches in libraries and visits to the Moorish-American Science Temple, where whites were known as "Caucasian devils."

Gathering materials and studying black religious cults were Arthur Weinberg, later Clarence Darrow's biographer, the novelist Frank Yerby, the poet Fenton Johnson, and a host of other researchers, mainly black. Whites were not permitted access to the storefront churches. Much of the material consisted of trivial gleanings from newspapers, but some of it was of genuine scholarly value, which Bontemps and Conroy made use of for their study of black migration. Ironically, the fieldwork attracted the interest of the FBI. The bureau interviewed Conroy, suspecting that the black religious cults, whose secret rituals called for an end to the "spook" civilization of white "cavemen," were connected with the subversive Japanese Black Dragon Society. Conroy and Bontemps both denied any such links.[89]

Conroy's meeting with Bontemps proved fortuitous, for both were novelists interested in folklore and social history. Arna Bontemps was a quiet, dignified, scholarly novelist who thought out race relations carefully and without anger, caring deeply and helping where he could. Langston Hughes, more gregarious and lively than Bontemps, had known Arna as early as 1925 when both participated in the Harlem Renaissance. Some people thought of Bontemps and Hughes almost as brothers, Conroy recalled, and indeed they were lifelong friends and collaborators.[90]

Jack and Arna worked together harmoniously, discovering that their writing styles were similar and that each was willing to accept stylistic changes suggested by the other, a rare collegiality indeed among writers, who are generally sensitive about revisions from their colleagues. Within a few months following their introduction, they were already planning to remake the folktale "The Boomer Fireman's Fast Sooner Hound," which Jack had written for the project two years earlier, into a children's story, a "juvenile," to use the trade name. Moreover, they had jointly authored a zany satirical play called "The Great Speckled Bird," about two morticians, based upon an undertaker's joke that Jack had heard in 1935 from Melvin Bean, an undertaker, while waiting to take the bus in Mena, Arkansas, after leaving Commonwealth College.[91]

The Illinois Writers' Project began to disband in late 1941, a victim of underfunding and wartime exigencies. Bontemps completed his studies in library science at the University of Chicago, accepting a position at Fisk University in Nashville. Jack received unemployment benefits—one of the social legacies of the 1930s—for several months, then accepted a Julius Rosenwald Fund Fellowship in late winter of 1942.

Acting on a tip from Josephine Herbst, who was living with Dorothy Farrell in the home of Dorothy's wealthy family, the Butlers, Conroy joined Algren in one of the spinoff programs of the project, the Venereal Disease Control unit, or "Syph Patrol," as they dubbed it. Located in the Chicago Health Department building at 56 West Hubbard on the North Side, the VD control program sent Algren, Jack, and other "investigators" like Joe Velarde to taverns and suspected bordellos to deliver summonses.[92] Algren seemed to enjoy the job since it paid him to spend time in locales that furnished settings and incidents for his writing. In a typical assignment Algren and Conroy would visit a tavern on State Street to deliver a summons to a prostitute suspected of carrying a venereal disease and ordered to undertake tests. The next day she would resume plying her trade. Algren was a witty companion, but Jack did not enjoy accompanying the "poor, trembling, young black whores" to the health office. Neither were the tavern owners happy with Algren and Conroy. At least once Jack was threatened by a pimp wielding a knife and had to ask a policeman to accompany him.

Conroy found little of literary value in "Syph Patrol" work, burdened, he said, with problems of his own without having to create those for others.[93] Algren, on the other hand, seemed drawn to whorehouses, bars, and slum streets of the "neon wilderness," the subproletariat of police lineups and night court, those "cheated and betrayed by the mores of a money society," as Maxwell Geismar wrote, barroom derelicts, "creatures who once were men" (Gorki). Where Jack cocked his ear for a worker's tale, Algren made notes for *A Walk on the Wild Side* and *The Man with the Golden Arm*. "The gates of Algren's soul," Conroy once said to me, "were open on hell's side."[94]

Jack had grown up among miners, men living on familiar terms with death, whose worst offense was drink and rowdiness on a Saturday night. He had come out of a workers' world. The losers, the shipwrecked, the pimps and prostitutes, the lame and incompetent, the abandoned and homeless—these he viewed in the context of a social reality in which useful and dignified work was central. As a youth Algren had been intimidated by the "big guys," the toughs. All his life he had been fascinated by them—the gangsters, the gamblers, the losers. In East St. Louis, Jesse Blue and Bud Fallon, the "Fallonites," found Algren a job in a boiler factory. The workers badgered Algren mercilessly, driving him away after a week. Conroy had an explanation for Algren's sojourns with mill workers and semihoodlums. Frightened yet fascinated by cruelty and power, Jack said, Algren felt drawn toward the very people who would torture a sensitive youth. Algren's attraction to "hell's side" was both his personal agony and the source of his literary genius.[95]

Nelson was drafted into the army. Too old for military service, Jack worked briefly for a Civilian Defense newsletter, "Friendly Fighters," then found a position as an encyclopedia editor. The friendship between Algren and Conroy had formed through a mutuality of interests, chiefly their devotion to literature and the experience of those who, for just or unjust reasons, lived on society's margins. The catalytic effect that seemed to energize their strong personalities in one another's company created an unstable bond that would eventually break. After the war, circumstances were altered greatly for both writers. The prospect of a literature of critical realism that they had worked to foster as coeditors of the *New Anvil* was displaced by a new mood in which the sensational circumstance itself, absent a broader social context, was eagerly sought by publishers and readers. By 1949, Algren had written a best-seller and won a major book prize. The social context was still present in Algren's writing, but the sensational details of drug addiction portrayed in *The Man with the Golden Arm* gained him his fame.

18

Only a Bridesmaid:
The Chicago Years

If I ever said anything I'm sorry for, I'm glad of it.
—Moberly folk saying

CONROY'S TAVERN PROWLS, the parties, his literary and demimonde friends like Nelson Algren, Willard Motley, Frank Sandiford, and James Blake remind one of Craig Rice's detective novels, set in Chicago during the war years of the 1940s, portraying a madcap, insouciant world in which people get killed but no one is hurt. Murder was not Jack's beat but booze and conviviality attracted him to milieus that artists, barroom habitués, bohemians, workers, and writers frequented. In disreputable North Clark Street taverns, waste beer from the bar ran down the bar's gutter, derelicts slumped over their nickel beer mugs, and scarcely anyone noticed, for instance, when an old woman peed on the seat, swaying back and forth, humming to herself. Such were the locales that Conroy and Algren staked out, finding not only diversion but in certain cases subject matter for their writing.

A hard-boiled waiter in the King's Palace on North Clark, noticing a dowdy brunette feeling up her companion's leg, shouted angrily, "What the hell kind of place do you think this is?" Ignored by the tavern regulars, the comment was the kind that delighted Algren and Conroy.[1] Sometimes Algren and Conroy put on impromptu performances for the barroom patrons. On one occasion Conroy, dressed in bum's apparel, said in a loud voice to Algren, who was properly attired (by North Clark Street standards): "I went to work at fifteen!" Algren replied: "Yes and quit at sixteen!" One afternoon Ben Reitman, a social reformer and "whorehouse physician," brought students from his classes at the University of Chicago to the Pink Poodle, calling the visit a "sociological field trip."[2] Pointing out Algren and Conroy to his students, Reitman said: "*There's* a couple of regular denizens." Conroy recalled the awe and wonder with which the students scrutinized them.[3]

There was a great deal of drinking, to be sure, and illicit activity penetrated the upper reaches of Chicago political life. At Dorothy Farrell's parties wealthy patrons of art as well as writers, Fallonites, and gate-crashers mixed and alcohol flowed. Ex-members of the Illinois Writers' Project would show up, like Horace Cayton, who was Jack's peer in drinking. When Cayton had drunk enough, he would go upstairs, sleep, then reappear several hours later, rejoining the party and the drinking. A woman came to Farrell's door to complain, was invited in, drank, sang, and stayed.[4]

Jack befriended a group of theater people and writers who lived in a house at 3538 Ellis Avenue, near Cottage Grove Avenue, designed by the famous Chicago architect Louis Sullivan. Named "Karl Marx Hof" by Bud Fallon, the large, stately home housed members of the Chicago Repertory Group, including Lou "Gigi" Gilbert, and Neal and Christine Rowland, who held full-time jobs and labored in progressive causes after work. The Karl Marx Hof commune was the setting for parties in which cheap "Manhattan" beer was bought in quantities and sold for ten cents a glass to raise money for various causes such as the CP's workers' school on State Street, later the Abraham Lincoln School where Jack taught. Amanda and Nelson Algren lived just around the corner in the "Rat Alley" apartment. "Most of these people," Neal Rowland remembered, "were disenchanted ex-Communists or fellow travelers who believed in the same goals: child labor laws, the right of workingmen to organize and form unions, the right of unions to bargain collectively with management, civil rights (for blacks), forty hour week, etc."[5]

One of Jack's new friends was Willard Motley, an ex-member of the Writers' Project. Jack saw a real "comer" in Motley and encouraged him to get on with his first novel. He accepted one of Motley's earliest short stories, entitled "The Beer Drinkers," but the *New Anvil* ceased publication before it could appear. At Bontemps's home, Jack met the black poet Melvin B. Tolson, whose first volume of poems, *Rendezvous with America,* was published in 1944. Tolson, soon to be named poet laureate of Liberia, and Conroy were astonished to discover that they both had been born in Moberly.

The Ellis Avenue commune people participated with Jack in performing a rewritten version of the nineteenth-century melodrama *Ten Nights in a Barroom,* by T. S. Arthur, which extolled the work ethic and excoriated drunkenness. Sponsored by Paul Douglas, an alderman at the time and later an Illinois Senator, and the Chicago Park Commission, the performances employed both amateur and semiprofessional actors, including Bender Kinland, who was married to Dorothy Farrell's sister at the time, and Amalie Woldenburg, who named her dog "Fellow Worker." Conroy took the role of Simon Slade the innkeeper, Russell Finch (a Fallonite) played a young boy ruined by a professional gambler (Kinland), and Dorothy Farrell acted the part of the drunkard's much-abused daughter, the performance of which involved a long and demanding dying scene. Played in the Cube Theatre, a storefront building near Jackson Park, *Ten Nights in a Barroom* saw frequent substitutions, such as Bud Fallon in Dorothy Farrell's role.[6]

Chicago was still the hog butcher of the world, as Carl Sandburg had written—the pungent smell of eviscerated animal carcasses drifted over to the Conroys' home, particularly on warm summer nights. Chicago offered Jack the ready camaraderie he valued so highly. Union Station seemed to be the hub of the world; old friends and former colleagues passed through, changing trains, leaving time to visit the Conroys. There were still money problems; well into his forties now, Jack realized that book royalties would never provide him a satisfactory income. The prospect of steady employment as an encyclopedia editor brightened; he was reconciled. Gladys's job at Hillman's food store was hardly adequate to feed the family of five. And when the food workers went out on strike, there was even less income. Gladys shunned heroic roles; during one strike, however, she lay down in front of a truck to prevent its delivery.[7]

In the summer of 1943, Jack went to work at Consolidated Book Publishers, one of the several "encyclopedia mills," as Meridel Le Sueur called them, in Chicago. The director, Franklin J. Meine, had heard of Conroy's work on humor from an editorial assistant named Ruth Schaff, who had known Jack on the Writers' Project. Acting on this information, Meine promptly hired him. The author of *Tall Tales of the Southwest* (1930), Meine had assembled an extraordinary collection of southern humor; on several occasions, Meine took Jack with him to folklore meetings, paying his expenses. Located at 153 North Michigan Avenue, Consolidated produced the *American People's Encyclopedia*, which sold through the Sears catalog. For the first time in his life, Jack felt some financial security. Fifty dollars a week, with weekends free to pursue his writing, looked good to Jack, who hoped to provide sounder financial support for his family than the occasional book review and dwindling royalties offered.

Heartened by a growing demand for books on black social history,

Bontemps and Conroy began work on a book tracing the story of black migration from southern rural areas to northern factory cities. The product of their collaborative effort, to be titled *They Seek a City*, drew upon their work at the Illinois Writers' Project and the resources that the Rosenwald Foundation had deposited with the George Cleveland Hall Branch Library. By early 1944, Bontemps had put together an outline of the book. Jack and Arna wrote separate chapters, submitting them to one another's scrutiny and revising them in turn. Bucklin Moon, an editor at Doubleday, was eager to see the manuscript, but progress went slowly. During the summer vacation of 1944, both finally wrested time away from their work to concentrate on the manuscript, Arna in Nashville, Jack in Chicago. Despite the wilting heat of August, they were able to exchange chapters by the end of the month. Bontemps took the completed manuscript to Doubleday in the early fall and came home with a contract for publication in March 1945. The two collaborators had hoped desperately to win Doubleday's Carver award, which Moon implied would be theirs. Before the publisher had seen the completed manuscript, however, the award went to Fannie Cook. Nonetheless, when *They Seek a City* appeared finally in May 1945, it was received enthusiastically.

Meanwhile Hardwick Moseley, an editor at Houghton-Mifflin who had published *The Fast Sooner Hound*, signaled his desire to see another juvenile from Bontemps and Conroy. Moseley had seen Conroy's industrial folktales in Ben Botkin's *Treasury of American Folklore*, first published in 1944, and was especially impressed by Carl Sandburg's tribute to Conroy in the preface. Based upon the tale of an itinerant sign painter that Harold Sullivan had passed on to Jack, Bontemps and Conroy went to work adapting "Slappy Hooper," adding a small boy, on Arna's suggestion, to add personal conflict and vivify the incidents.

Jack was wearing six hats at the time. Curtis MacDougall, who had left the ILWP to work for the Chicago *Sun*, had gotten Jack started as a book reviewer for the paper. Reviewing under three names, he sometimes appeared thrice in a Sunday issue. Jack continued at the "encyclopedia mill," a job that proved to be steady but stupefyingly dull. On the basis of *They Seek a City*, Dr. Metz T. P. Lochard, editor in chief of the *Chicago Defender*, invited Jack to write a book review column for his newspaper, at that time the leading black paper in the Midwest. In addition to his collaborations with Bontemps, Jack was asked to put together an anthology of midwestern humor. Finally, he was hired to teach a creative writing at the Abraham Lincoln School, "the little red schoolhouse in the Loop," as the *Chicago Tribune*'s publisher, Colonel McCormick, derisively called it.

Jack began his evening teaching job at the Abraham Lincoln School in late summer of 1943, filling a position vacated by Josephine Herbst. A product of Popular Front politics and culture, the Abraham Lincoln School, at 30 West Washington Street, offered low-tuition night courses, extension courses in factories, and lectures. "We are planning a curriculum," A. D. Winspear, the school's director, wrote in an early catalog, "which will be broadly patriotic and democratic, authentically American in its content but broad as humanity in its outlook."[8] Organized by the black activist and writer William L. Patterson, the school appointed Winspear, a Rhodes Scholar who, George Bernard Shaw once said, had made the greatest contribution to scholarship on Plato in the past one hundred years, as its head.[9]

Monday evenings in the fall session of 1943, Jack offered a course entitled "Problems of the Individual Writer." Classes were held in a second-floor room in the same building where Gladys worked. Through Jack's many connections with Chicago writers, the school frequently hosted guest talks by Willard Motley, Algren, Bontemps, Richard Wright, and others. Considered one of the "bohemians," in contrast to the "approved Marxists," Conroy nonetheless won the respect of Winspear and Patterson for his achievements and commitment to progressive goals.

The erudite Winspear, who looked like a real-life Mr. Chips, tolerated Jack's "anarchic" teaching methods, which included "field trips" to the Pink Poodle in Chicago's burlesque district.[10] Jim Light, one of Conroy's writing students, later a dean at Southern Illinois University, remembered those excursions. Denizens of the Pink Poodle included Princess Rita, a midget stripper, and a piano player named James Blake whom Algren and Conroy befriended. When Blake was later sent to the Florida State Penitentiary for burglary, Conroy and Algren raised money to arrange an escape fund. The prison guard was ready to look the other way except that Blake insisted on taking his lover along with him. This proved too much for the guard, who sounded the alert. Blake made no struggle, returning quietly to prison, where he said he enjoyed the regularity of the life and arranging musical concerts for the prison chaplain. The example of Conroy and Algren turned Blake to literature; with their help and encouragement a volume of his letters from prison, entitled *The Joint*, was published by Doubleday in 1971.[11] Like his predecessor, Josephine Herbst, Jack hoped that truck drivers, waitresses, night watchmen, and workers in Chicago's war plants, with encouragement and guidance, would discover a desire to write. Again the example of Richard Wright and other unknowns whom the *Anvil* had helped lift from obscurity came to mind.[12]

The Cold War inquisitional spirit appeared prematurely in a *Chicago Tribune* attack on the Abraham Lincoln School. The paper disclosed that the school's administration, supporters, and faculty were "heavily loaded with Communists and internationalists," including a New Dealer named Marshall Field, of department store notoriety, and a novelist named Jack Conroy who had published in *New Masses*.[13] Internationalists, Communists, and New Dealers were a dreadful threesome in the eyes of Colonel McCormick. In 1943 it was easy to ridicule clumsy attempts to restrict free expression, but within several years, people would lose their jobs and go to prison on the basis of their past associations with the Left. Worse, however, was the silencing of dissenting voices, and complicit in this silencing were publishers, editors, and critics—among them people who loved literature and defended democratic values.

H. H. Lewis absorbed the tensions and contradictions of the 1940s, turning his anger and bitterness against the Party's cultural commissars, V. J. Jerome and others. The favorable, albeit erratic reception of Lewis's poetry slackened following the awarding of the Harriet Monroe prize in 1938, despite his appearances in *Poetry* and the *New Republic*. Lewis's crude vigor no longer fit the temper of the Popular Front, which was anxious to reconcile a diversity of supporters in defense against fascism.

The times and reader interests were of course quite altered in 1942 when Lewis made his final and farewell assault on the eastern (leftist) literary establishment. The tall Missouri plowman arrived in New York City with, as Alfred Kreymbourg described, "an enormous sheath of poems—songs, ballads, jingles, free verse narratives, prose rhythms—on every conceivable phase of the life of the underprivileged."[14] Kreymbourg recognized the unpolished genius in the self-tutored farmhand, recommending him to publishers. There were few little magazines of the *Anvil* type anymore. The newer magazines were cool toward "hinterland" literature, as Rahv called it. Even Walt Carmon, recently returned to the United States as a correspondent for the Union of Soviet Writers, wondered whether "Humpy" Lewis had overreached his customary unpredictability. Carmon wrote Jack that Lewis "is hard to handle. He just doesn't realize that there are other things in this world."[15] Writers in the Midwest were isolated, particularly as their reputations became tarnished by the academic critics and former leftists who set up new cultural hierarchies in New York, anxious to divorce themselves from the taint of "vulgar populism," which they assigned to radical writers from Illinois small towns, Iowa farms, and Minnesota sawmills.

Lewis took as a personal affront the sealing off of literary channels of communication with regard to the midwestern "vulgarians," not only by a new intellectual elite but by the Party's cultural commissars. His last published poem, "Insult for Insult," appearing in *Poetry* (August 1942), responded sarcastically to the indifferent reception Lewis received among functionaries like V. J. Jerome. His self-perceived abandonment by his early sponsors fostered in Lewis a persecution complex apparent in his correspondence with Jack, the one literary person he still trusted.

Letters exchanged among Conroy, Lewis, the FBI, various Senate committees, and Lewis's congressman, Orville Zimmerman of Missouri's tenth district, reveal a bizarre attempt on Lewis's part to warn the U.S. government of conspiracies by foreign agents. At the same time, mounting paranoia fueled his apprehensions that he was being hounded by government agents. It is a strange story, a tragic story really, when one reflects upon the waste of Lewis's considerable, if erratic, poetic talent. In a broader sense, Lewis's story reflects events of greater consequence unfolding in a society when artists, writers, film directors, and actors were intimidated, mentally tortured by agents and agencies of the government, on evidence that no just court would admit.

Lewis was convinced that he had uncovered a betrayal plot that led to the Pearl Harbor attack and was anxious to convey his information, involving a leftist writer of Japanese descent named Sachio Oka, to the FBI. The FBI discredited the information after some investigation; nonetheless, Lewis persisted, threatening to implicate V. J. Jerome. Conroy urged Lewis to dismiss the matter entirely. "I doubt," Jack wrote in 1945, "if the CPA will relish or credit your charges. Not only that, but many of the FBI agents are still more zealous in hunting down 'red' than Axis agents. . . . There is almost sure to be a duplication of the Palmer Raids after the war is over. If you're on the list, you'll be one of the victims."[16] Further on in the letter Conroy recalled his sense of abandonment a decade earlier by the Party's cultural apparatus: "Don't attach too much importance to that praise so long ago in the *Moscow News* when you were hailed as the only one of your kind. Many things have happened since, and even Soviet critics and the public forget. I, too, was given a lot of recognition there, called 'the American Gorki,' a translation of *The Disinherited* sold 250,000, etc., but I don't flatter myself that I am much of a figure any more."

Jack advised Lewis to get on with his creative work. Lewis's antagonism was a measure of his alienation, both from the Party that had once given him encouragement and from friends—even Conroy—who had stuck by him despite his unpredictable behavior. Years later, Lewis, living in a converted corncrib outside of Cape Girardeau, Missouri, confided to me that "agents" had welded an automobile to stilts outside his window so that its headlights shone directly in upon his bed at night. The FBI had in fact assigned a special agent to observe Lewis. Undoubtedly it was the surveillance, in addition to his pitiable isolation and paranoia, that nurtured the fantasy.[17]

Jack searched for reasons why his own creative work inspired little beyond favorable reviews. He was deeply disappointed, for instance, when Doubleday, Doran, dropped *They Seek a City* from its list several months following its publication. "The plain fact," he wrote to Bontemps, "is that Doubleday, Doran threw us to the wolves—first they didn't give us the award they had practically promised us, then they showed little or no interest in promoting the book at all."[18] When Houghton-Mifflin let *The Fast Sooner Hound* run out of stock shortly before Christmas—traditionally prime time to sell juveniles—he again accepted his destiny fatalistically. Jack unjealously observed the mounting attention paid to the work of his close friends Willard Motley, Algren, and Max Shulman. Former contributors to the *New Anvil*, like Frank Yerby, had struck it rich, while Jack was resigned to be "only a bridesmaid." Shulman, recently returned to civilian life from writing military manuals, turned out best-selling humorous books whose phenomenal sales figures and lavish royalties he reported to Jack, who labored in the encyclopedia mill and wrote book reviews to support his family.[19] It seemed that there was always a party for an author-friend celebrating the publication of a new book, attended by Conroy, who rejoiced in the event but felt evermore deeply oppressed by his own situation.[20]

It was not that Conroy lacked the opportunities (advances, editorial assistance, encouragement) that Motley and Algren had made use of to begin another novel. When Ken McCormick became editor in chief of Doubleday he offered Jack a contract to write both his literary reminiscences, to be titled "Only a Bridesmaid," and a novel based upon his experiences in Monkey Nest coal camp. Jack was doubtful whether he could meet McCormick's deadline to prepare an outline and sample chapter of each book. He had already accepted a contract from A. A. Wyn of Current Books to put together an anthology of midwestern humor. His eyes "bulged out like walnuts," however, when he heard that McCormick signed on Algren with a $6,000 advance and $60 a week for two years to write a novel. Nonetheless, Jack seemed unwilling to give up his "day job" at the Consolidated Publishers, and continued to review for the *Chicago Sun* and Lochard's *Chicago Defender*. What, we ask, held him back? Why the hesitation at the threshold of possible success?

In the summer of 1946, Bontemps and Conroy sent in the galleys for their second juvenile, based upon a Conroy folktale, called *Slappy Hooper*. Jack was momentarily free to embark on a new writing project. A. A. Wyn approached him with the idea of editing an anthology of midwestern humor, to be titled "Midland Humor," a plan suggested by

Wyn's sales representative, Larry Hill. Jack chose to accept an editorial project of this nature rather than embark on a creative project such as McCormick suggested. McCormick continued to press Jack for a book contract; not long after, Bennett Cerf, editor at Random House, likewise invited an outline and chapter from Jack. Cerf reminded Jack of their meeting some thirteen years earlier, at the first performance of Albert Maltz's *Black Pit*. Proletarian novels are "old hat" now, Cerf told Jack; he must fit the theme of a new novel to the times.[21]

Scarcely was Jack's signature dry on the contract with Wyn, effectively scotching the opportunity to write a novel, when Sengstacke, publisher of the *Defender*, announced Jack's dismissal, claiming that paper shortages forced him to reduce his staff, a pretext, Jack discovered, for hiring Sengstacke's wife in his place. Threatening to sue, Jack was offered damages, which he never collected. It was his destiny again; yet Jack seemed resigned to face the weekday toil at the "mill" and churn out reviews on weekends. Domestic problems beset him. His landlady (at 6360 Ingleside), living in filth and muttering to her dead husband and cats, kept the heat low in the Conroys' apartment in mid-January. The lack of heat sore-pressed the Conroys but failed to drive them away. When the landlady set fire to the apartment building, however, intending to smoke out her unwanted renters, in desperation Jack put a down payment on a dilapidated house at 6012 South Green Street. He was close to a psychological crisis because of "accumulated worries and work."[22]

The nation emerged from the war with greatly altered expectations. Literary tastes were changing. Existential and absurdist themes attracted intellectuals on campuses, while best-sellers, like Algren's *The Man with the Golden Arm*, published in 1949, and Mickey Spillane's novels shocked with their brutal portrayal of human depravity. After its great victories of the 1930s, the labor movement moved to the right, apparently content to assimilate and consolidate its achievements. With the passage of the Taft-Hartley legislation and the Smith act, labor leaders were anxious to distance themselves from "red subversives" within their ranks.

Jack shared few of the values of postwar America—its fetish of affluence and image-making, its vulnerability to fear and suspicion in an atmosphere charged with the specter of the bomb, McCarthyism, and HUAC.[23] The ground of Conroy's existence was loyalty to friends, cooperation with other writers (whom he considered to be colleagues rather than competitors), the "warm life" of working-class milieus and people, the creative uses of memory and orality, and dedication to progressive ideals. He was a man firmly anchored by devotion—not to

God or Marx or literary fame—but to human community. This devotion brought both solace and suffering to his life. In this devotion lay a refusal to pursue success. Recognition, however, he fervently desired, a point I return to soon.

When William Rogers—replacing A. C. Spectorsky as book editor of the Chicago *Sun*—asked contributors to swear they were neither Communists nor sympathizers, Jack stopped writing reviews for its book magazine.[24] The prevailing climate of reception was unfavorable, he perceived, to working-class themes; security, personal well-being, and self-fulfillment took precedence over questions of individual responsibility toward society. A novel about an obscure Missouri coal camp and its immigrant miners with their proud, independent resiliency and communal solidarity stood little chance of becoming a commercial success in postwar America. It is probable—at least during the Cold War years—that he showed himself more prescient in this regard than the Random House and Doubleday editors who encouraged him to return to his Monkey Nest material. Jack stood on firmer ground writing children's stories. Similarly, Meridel Le Sueur turned to children's fiction, writing books about Johnny Appleseed and Nancy Hanks, in the face of hostile postwar critics and publishers intimidated by blacklists.[25]

Jack suggested to Arna Bontemps the story of Sam Patch, a nineteenth-century folk hero celebrated for his great leaps, as the title of their next juvenile. Juveniles were money-makers. *Midland Humor*, on the other hand, had not sold well when it appeared in 1947, despite generally favorable press. Jack asked Howard Wolf, who had visited a Doubleday bookstore in Detroit: "Did they have the copy of *Midland Humor* hid under the counter and try by everything short of violence to prevent your buying it? That's the way it usually is with Conroy books. . . ."[26] Weak sales of *Midland Humor* reinforced Jack's feeling that he was destined to be "only a bridesmaid." During the early Cold War years, a new work in the *Disinherited* vein was doomed to fail in the literary marketplace. Readers sought diversion in detective fiction and hard-boiled novels depicting the underside of urban life. Algren and Motley, for example, were finding a ready market for their new novels. Jack, on the other hand, seemed unable or unwilling to produce fiction of this kind. By the end of the 1950s, Algren's and Motley's reputations had faded; readers seemed now to prefer novels offering brutal realism without the social commentary that writers like Algren, Motley, and Conroy, nurtured in the hard times of the 1930s, provided.

When he asked F. J. Meine at Consolidated Publishers for a raise, Jack was told: "You're on the regular staff." Jack replied: "Then put me on the irregular staff." Meine refused and Jack quit, moving over to work for the New Standard Education Society at 130 North Wells. In 1947, New Standard was virtually a one-man business run by Calvin Fisk, a southern Democrat and a stickler on language. One should not write, "the man was executed," he told Jack. A *sentence* is executed, but not a man.[27] Jack sensed that it was best to maintain a discreet silence about his views around Fisk and show up on time for work. Encyclopedias were not selling well and staff were being laid off. Jack felt a growing awareness that he was trapped: not enough time to write; not enough income to free himself to write. Such were the circumstances of quiet desperation, yet the fear that he could not provide for his family brought him back to his hateful cubicle every Monday. "Rush for the subway," he wrote Jim Light, "grub away at a maddeningly inept encyclopedia, rush for the subway, fall over in exhaustion and dream fitfully of better days."[28]

Algren, returned from overseas duty in the army, called Jack at the encyclopedia, proposing: "Let's go back on the syph patrol." Jack told him that the unit had shut down. Algren inquired, "Do you have to keep regular hours at the encyclopedia?" "Yes," Jack said, "I have to arrive and leave at regular times." Algren expressed relief that he could return to his typewriter, a "free" man. While Jack bitterly complained about his "dreary treadmill stint," his twenty-three years as an encyclopedia editor suggest that the constraining conditions of work played an essential role in his psyche; writing took place between times, in the interstices. Algren and Motley—neither with families—had cut loose from the workday routines of employment to write best-selling novels. They were *authors*. In the deep-lying residual consciousness of Jack's mind and emotional life, writing was still joined with work-life and with working people. While he longed to achieve Motley's and Algren's freedom to write when and where they wished, still the binding nature of the worker-writer held him in thrall.

Jack had worked at disagreeable jobs since age thirteen, except for periods of unemployment that had exacted a terrible toll. In a letter to Dale Kramer he confessed that he was "writing this . . . with one eye on the office manager."[29] It was a terrible way to live, Jack wrote Wallie Wharton. Worse, however, was the threat of being let go from the encyclopedia. He wrote between times, as he had done during the proletarian nights of factory work, but lacking now were youthful energy and the camaraderie of revolutionary movements. The 1930s radicals were older and the world was much changed. Jack was nearly fifty years of age. Family problems interceded; opportunities dwindled; and the threat of being "fingered" as a Communist loomed menacingly over him.

Jack loved Chicago. The dreariness of the encyclopedia mill was lightened by friends and the stimulus of the city. Algren and Conroy spoke for progressive causes during the Henry Wallace campaign in 1948. Booksellers like Stuart Brent, Paul Romaine, Max Siegel, and Larry Gold fostered Chicago writers and provided a forum for their new books. A visit by a writer was occasion for a memorable party at the Conroys' Green Street house. Legends grew about Jack's attraction to drink. Like Brendan Behan, he had an enormous capacity for alcohol and conviviality. "Worries and preoccupations," he wrote Wharton in April 1951, "drive me into compulsive drinking, whereas it used to be social."[30] Shouldering the responsibility for his son Tom's swings in mood, the family's impecunious circumstances, and the well-being of his daughter, Margaret Jean, whose husband, Jim Swartz, suffered health problems, Jack felt as if a "huge and festering albatross" were around his neck.

The 1950s were a period of "silences" for Jack, the expression Tillie Lerner Olsen employs to describe the cessation of creative activity owing to the demands of family responsibilities and remunerative work. "The years when I should have been writing, my hands and being were at other (inescapable) tasks."[31] It was a suffocating burden at times. Mark Harris, whose first novel Jack had reviewed favorably, recalled how he kept his promise to Gladys to return Jack from a tavern excursion by midnight—and how Jack had then slipped out the back door. "His night had now begun."[32] Late drinking bouts, however, were rare; Jack abstained from drinking for weeks at a time. A party or an old friend's visit would send him on a bender. Yet, at a gathering for Wallie Wharton—perhaps the most memorable of the parties at "Conroy's Folly" on Green Street—on 21 January 1950, Jack scarcely imbibed.

Five hundred people answered Jack's appeal to celebrate the publication of Wharton's volume of irreverent poetry, *Graphiti from Elsinore* (Decker Press, 1949), with prints by Stanley Radulovich, brother of Savo who ran "Little Bohemia" in St. Louis. "Say that I aged," Wharton wrote,

> in shabby rooms midst whores and bores
> and sentimentally reviewed my feeble runes
> as messengers in office corridors
> might whistle last year's dance hall tunes.
>
> I could have pinned my scraps upon a prayer wheel
> but in these temples neither gods nor men will hark—
> in these markets who'd hear the piping spiel
> of old men chanting in the dark?

Wharton sold more than 150 copies of his book at the party, but the Conroys' new rug was ruined and the plumbing broken. Jack vowed "never again," but the vow was quickly forgotten.

In May he gave a party for a young violinist, Anita Lipp, daughter of former *Anvil*-ite Leo Lipp, following her concert. Gertrude Abercrombie, a surrealist painter; Studs and Ida Terkel ("Studs' Place" was a hit television show in Chicago at the time); the novelist and ex–gentleman thief, Frank Sandiford; the actor Louis "Gigi" Gilbert and his wife, Martha; Harold and Aldine Gunn (brother of John Gunn, who had worked for Haldeman-Julius); Ferne Gayden (director of the South Side Art Center); the poet Gwendolyn Brooks; Margaret and Charlie Burroughs (who started the DuSable Museum of African-American History); Willard Motley; Joyce Gourfain (who wrote *Dust Under the Rug*) and her husband; the folksinger Win Stracke and his wife—all were frequent guests at Jack and Gladys's parties on Green Street. Win Stracke would sing the Wobbly song "Brady, Why Didn't You Run" and "Hallelujah, I'm a Bum," and recite the old circuit preacher's sermon, "The Harp of a Thousand Strings," which Jack had included in his *Midland Humor* anthology. Inspired by Stracke, Jack would perform "Letter Edged in Black" and "My Mother Was a Lady" in a suitably lachrymose manner. On Monday, Jack was back at his desk composing entries for the New Standard Encyclopedia. Algren, who had won the National Book Award for *The Man with the Golden Arm*, was in Hollywood negotiating movie rights. The film version of Willard Motley's novel *Knock on Any Door*, starring Humphrey Bogart, had appeared. To all appearances, Jack had abandoned writing.

Nearly everything Conroy produced after 1941, until the 1970s, was the reworking of material he had gathered from his association with the Illinois Writers' Project. The alliance with Bontemps through 1946, that is, through *They Seek a City* and *Slappy Hooper*, had been mutually productive for Bontemps and Conroy. Afterward, however, their collaborations met with increasing frustration. In 1949, the *Sam Patch* project was bogged down; the children's editor at Houghton-Mifflin, Jean Colby, insisted on putting her own imprint on the story. Weary with the project, the authors yielded to her editorial direction almost entirely. The book finally appeared in 1951, the least successful of their juveniles.

Collaboration with Bontemps comforted Jack, removing a great deal of the burden he felt in a competitive authorial system of literary production in which the bottom line seemed always to be profit. Their work together recreated the *Anvil* spirit of joining forces, of advancing shared literary interests, and reproduced the spirit of community and comradeship he had known in the 1930s. It was linked with his apparent disinclination or inability to achieve the status of professional fiction writer. Implied in his literary activities over the years was a denial of that occupation, as mentioned earlier, a refusal of "arriving," as Motley and

Algren had arrived in their professional careers. But then again, collaboration had become a deception for Jack; *Sam Patch* wasted what little time he had for other projects and concluded with little imprint of his own creativity on the book. His literary career was mired in a personal and political dilemma. As a writer he was not able to meet the expectations currently demanded of fiction. The McCarthy era, on the other hand, effectively destroyed his credibility as radical editor and activist (and the credibility of others like him) to help change those expectations, or offer an alternative to them.

* * *

In August of 1949, Bontemps's and Ken McCormick's recommendations sent Jack to Yaddo, near Saratoga Springs, New York, where he quartered with writers J. T. Powers and David Wagoner, scholars Austin Warren and Wallace Fowlie, and others.[33] Powers remembered that Jack felt awkward among the academic writers-in-residence there and squirmed under Elizabeth Ames's orderly regimen. On a weekend Jack fled the gloominess of Yaddo to Saratoga Springs to meet with Jim Light, who taught at Syracuse University. Late one night Jack recited Shakespeare from the grand staircase at Yaddo; in the morning he received a reprimand from the executive secretary.[34] Jack returned to Chicago with a rough outline of an anthology of sentimental verse, not the draft of a novel that McCormick hoped to see.

At Yaddo Jack enjoyed the company of writers like Powers and Wagoner with whom he felt immediate rapport; for the first time in years he had time to write. Yet no tangible result came of it. Nor was there any further progress the following summer when he returned to Yaddo. The constraining circumstances of everyday existence were necessary to his art, which bears witness not only to actual experience but to Conroy's linguistic ability in transforming speech into art. In his best writing, Conroy's reconstituted "voice sources" convey truths about working-class people. His stay at Yaddo underscored the alienated situation of the worker-writer: without status in postwar America, classed among lowbrow interlopers by conservative and liberal critics alike, denied access to publication, the worker-writer had little choice but to abandon literature or attempt a career as a professional writer for a middle-class readership. Choosing the latter course produces other contradictions, not the least of which is the loss of intimacy with experience that worker-writing seems to require.

A fundamental contradiction involves the nature of success itself within the authorial system of the dominant culture. Jack's failure to produce another novel, his refusal to pursue the role of author, which amounted to a refusal to pursue success, was not "failure" so much as the inability to insert himself temperamentally or otherwise into a literary system that for most of his life he had tried to furnish an alternative to or circumvent altogether. This seeming paradox is alluded to in Mark Harris's comment that "Conroy's triumph or contribution, the fruit of his witnessing, is akin to his more or less deliberate arrest of his own growth."[35] It has as much to do with the tensions and countercurrents that were the wellsprings of Conroy's creative work as it does with essential questions of reception, the status of the worker-writer, and access to circuits of literary communication. The value of worker-writing, for instance, lies in its testimonial quality, the particular nature of its relationship to historical and political consciousness. Such attributes, which are also those of critical realism, attracted few postwar readers buoyed by prospects of affluence ("There's a Ford in Your Future," an ad read, depicting a couple and their child gazing admiringly at a new Ford enclosed in a bubble) and eager to put behind them memories of hard times and wartime sacrifices. "The difficulty is that if you want to tell the real story," Ben Appel wrote Jack, "the chances are no jackpot."[36] The midwestern radicals found active detractors among revisionist historians and the radical intelligentsia associated with magazines like *Partisan Review* and *Commentary* who dominated cultural politics after the war.[37] In the new critical coinage, "truthfulness" to experience was discounted in favor of "timeless truths of the human condition." *The Disinherited*, for example, tells essential truths about how it *felt* to be homeless during the Great Depression, without pretending to the truthfulness of objective historical narrative.

A great deal has changed, of course, since literary radicals went involuntarily into internal exile. By the early seventies, a growing number of critics had begun to turn their attention to the generic forms proper to marginalized groups. New critical perspectives have revolutionized the study of marginal literatures—feminist, black, and Native American. Similarly, new critical approaches are evolving to deal with questions of class difference, transcending the dualistic ideological categories familiar to the Old Left. The study of worker-writing helps us deal with questions having to do with the ways in which historical knowledge of an era becomes personal knowledge. "The contemporary fact [Conroy] vivified," Mark Harris noted, "was the slaughter of his brothers, the degradation of his family. With what topical, salable, printable story could a literary man top that?"[38]

* * *

By 1950, it appeared that Conroy's literary career was finished. Tainted by his radical past, his work ignored or judged a failure by contemporary aesthetic standards, his output reduced to an uninspired children's book, he joined the "disappeared" literary radicals from the 1930s.[39] Other literary radicals, former *Anvil*-ites, were scarcely any better off. Joe Vogel worked in a state prison; Kalar had long ceased to write and despite his long feud with a lumber company, he set up and ran its labor relations department until his death in 1972; Lewis was a recluse; Falkowski picked up odd jobs as he could, supported in part by his wife, Helen; Corey built a house of his own design in Jack London's Valley of the Moon where he wrote on technical subjects and animal rights; Meridel Le Sueur could find a market only for her children's books; Cruden and Porter made their living as college teachers; Max Lieber moved to Mexico, then Poland to avoid appearing before an investigating committee. A member of the CP fraction of the newspaper guild, Walter Snow drifted away from the Party around 1941, entering military service during World War II. After the war Snow turned virulently anticommunist, preparing a confessional in the manner of Budenz and Rushmore, which he never published. Late in his life, however, Snow felt shame for anticommunist sentiments that shaped the crude plot of his 1952 mystery novel, *The Golden Nightmare*. Participating with Jack, Max Lieber, Granville Hicks, and Arna Bontemps in a "Semester of the Thirties" at the University of Connecticut–Storrs in 1969, Snow was able to reconfirm his attachment to the political beliefs of his youth and defend the literary work of writers on the Left in the 1930s.[40] Quite different was John Rogers's tale. Deemed a "security risk," Rogers lost his job with the government on the basis of anonymous letters written by an informer who had known Rogers in his "WPA days." As a "security risk," Rogers wrote Jack, "you are branded, like a Star of David in Hitler's Germany."[41] Suing for his job, Rogers was finally reinstated after years of enforced idleness.[42] Other former *Anvil*-ites, such as Benjamin Appel, suffered blacklisting. In refusing to sign a loyalty oath, Appel lost the sale of his book, which the Texas state school system had conditionally accepted.[43]

The work of Algren, Millen Brand, and Erskine Caldwell had fallen into critical disesteem and neglect by the end of the 1950s, despite the success of these individuals as professional writers. Revisionist literary historians joined academic critics in discounting, or simply ignoring, the literary achievements of the 1930s.[44] In the postwar years, the New Critics—Cleanth Brooks, Robert Penn Warren, John Crowe Ransom—exercised an enormous influence on literary standards of evaluation. "Close reading" became institutionalized as a critical practice in the university and in scholarly publishing. Literary magazines associated with universities took over from the independent little magazines the task of locating and fostering new writers. Viewing themselves as "literary legislators of their times," the academic magazines attracted "like-minded contributors," as Marian Janssen writes, and "published and discussed the same writers time and again."[45] Government-sponsored grants and business contributions provided funding for the arts; universities grew dependent upon grant "monies." The assignment of the grants was in certain cases politically motivated as a result of crucial appointments— for example, when William Phillips became head of the Coordinating Council of Literary Magazines, and neoconservative Irving Kristol intervened to secure William Bennett the position as head of the National Endowment for the Humanities. Reputations of writers were "made," in certain cases, by the consensus of the New York intelligentsia who made common cause with the establishment, defending high culture against the rude interlopers of popular culture, retreating, as Christopher Lasch writes, from politics.[46] Nonelitist values that Conroy as editor cherished in the Anvil—cooperation, accessibility, openness, the freedom of roughhewn thoughts and forms of expression, the democratic optimism of the Whitman tradition—retreated in the face of the "blockbuster" mentality of publishers, the confessional genre, the antisocial, antihero, and a hostile critical reception orchestrated by the cultural establishment indifferent to indigenous radical traditions.[47]

Critical attacks on "vulgarism," using terms like "populist," "provincial," "crudity," were a move to control discourse through systems of exclusionism.[48] A few critics, such as Maxwell Geismar, defended realism and indigenous radicalism against their detractors, and C. Wright Mills made a similar case for reasserting democratic traditions in the face of cultural repressiveness.[49] By the 1950s, however, worker-writers like Conroy were dismissed as "forelock-tugging rubes," as Conroy said, even by knowledgeable students of the left such as Irving Howe and Lewis Coser, who reinforced the "cultivated" versus "mindless crudity" dualistic assessment of the 1930s in their influential study of American communism, published in 1957.[50] The Cold War period, marked by anticommunist liberals' acquiescence on loyalty issues raised by Senator McCarthy, silenced numerous creative voices, privileging instead Mickey Spillane's novels in which the tough guy shoots deceitful women in the navel and leaves politics to HUAC.

The 1930s had become in the popular media synonymous with Pretty Boy Floyd, the Lindbergh kidnapping, Gone with the Wind, and dust storms, not with social justice and labor reform. Mea culpa–type confessionals like "I Was a Communist for the F.B.I." shaped Americans' image of the "evil empire."[51] The anti-red hysteria rose on occasion to absurd levels. In the early fifties, the crew of a French passenger ship was refused shore leave under a new security check law that required that each seaman answer questions about his political affiliations. Similar measures were instituted, intended to "keep Communists out of the country."[52] Rather than condemning such absurdities, establishment intellectuals were content to pursue their mission of rescuing literature from the masses, aligning themselves with CIA-sponsored organizations like the Congress for Cultural Freedom and its many affiliates, in certain notable cases making common cause with the right in support of anticommunist crusades.[53] In the name of cultural freedom, imperialist aims were served. The "elitism of intellectuals" (Lasch's expression) that "expressed itself as a celebration of American life" ignored the experience of most Americans.[54]

If Jack was "disappeared" in the minds of revisionist critics, he was on the minds of those charged with ferreting out Communist members and sympathizers. Two FBI agents showed up in the New Standard Encyclopedia office one day and said to Calvin Fisk, "Do you know you have a Communist working for you?" When shown a copy of the *Anvil*, Fisk said, "I don't care about that. He's a good editor, and I don't care about his political ideas. So if you don't have anything further, I'd like to get back to my work."[55] Louis Budenz, Jack's former editor in Chicago when he wrote reviews for the Party's *Midwest Daily Record*, fingered Jack in testimony before HUAC, but nothing came of it.[56] Howard Rushmore, on the other hand, whose anticommunist exposés appeared in *Confidential* magazine, spared Jack.

Jack confessed his anxiety to Julian Lee Rayford, who reassured him that he had nothing to worry about. "You have about as much to do with Moscow as I have to do with establishing a gas station on the Moon," Rayford wrote.[57] This was a time when literary radicals destroyed their letters in order to conceal potentially incriminating evidence. Conroy kept his, as did Kenneth Porter and others, for they realized their historical value. "Once more," he might have said with Wordsworth, "did I retire into myself," knowing the inquisitional time would pass.[58]

To earn extra cash, Jack gave a number of talks to suburban ladies' literary teas, as Algren did. At a cocktail party he attracted the attention of a newspaper columnist who wrote that he was shocked to see Conroy eating anchovies. "Back in my salad days, in mid-depression, Conroy was a hairy-chested free spirit who wouldn't have been caught dead with anchovies. . . . We newly married guys on the paper used to crowd around his table in the saloon across the street and drool wistfully at his theories on the wild, free life, unbound, uninhibited, tied to no woman's apron strings. Well, I just want the old gang to know, wherever they are, that Jack Conroy, the hairy-chested novelist, is now working for an encyclopedia and had to hurry home early last night so the wife wouldn't get sore!"[59] Conroy interiorized the humiliation of being cast into the role of a has-been. Whereas Algren lashed out at his friends, projecting his own vulnerability toward the rise and fall of his reputation, Jack sank deeper into fits of melancholy when faced with the eclipse of recognition and the foreclosure of further literary endeavors.

Jack's wounds were personal and immediate, involving family and friends. The Conroys' son Tom slept all day, unable to complete a task or stay enrolled in Roosevelt College or manage his money. In a drunken stupor he crashed through a glass door and was charged with malicious mischief. Jack paid the court costs. Married, the father of a boy, Tom grew increasingly despondent when his wife, Carolyn, left him. His erratic lifestyle had grown intolerable. Agitated over the conditions set by Carolyn and her lawyer concerning visitation rights, Tom withdrew to a basement room in his house down the street from the Conroys and overdosed on barbiturates and sleeping pills. In midsummer 1954, Jack and Gladys took Tom's body back to Moberly to bury him in the miners' cemetery at Sugar Creek. Jack wrote Arna that "the whole thing is more horrible than I ever imagined it would be."[60]

Hard on the heels of Tom's tragic death came Murray Kempton's gratuitous comment appearing in his memoir of the 1930s, *Part of Our Time: Some Ruins and Monuments of the Thirties* (1955). Extolling Farrell as an incorruptible artist, Kempton alludes to Conroy disparagingly as "a hopeless soak in Chicago," suggesting that he had "abandoned the craft of creation entirely."[61] Jack got halfway through a reply to Kempton, pointing out his omissions and errors, then decided not to send it, confiding his feelings rather to Jim Light and other close friends.[62] "It used to be that I'd trouble deaf heaven with my bootless cries about such things, but there is always my job to think of and the less I say the better. Kempton, like the editors of the scandalous *Confidential* magazine, relies upon the reluctance of his victims to bring such matters to attention in the supercharged atmosphere of the day."[63] The true story of the 1930s, Jack said, had yet to be told.

Margaret Jean's husband died, leaving three young children. Grief stricken, she was unable to leave home to return to work. In 1959, Jack and Gladys sold their Green Street house and moved to Midlothian to look after the grandchildren.[64] Sometime earlier, Gladys had quit her job at Hillman's, the grocery chain, where in 1953 she had come out on strike. Jack commuted to his encyclopedia job in the Loop by train. Margaret Jean, an attractive, gregarious redhead, remarried, but the second marriage was soon in shambles. An alcoholic, her second husband became abusive, particularly toward the children, to the point that Jack, on at least one occasion, intervened.[65] In 1962, Jack and Gladys moved back to Chicago, to an apartment on Jeffrey Boulevard.

Jack remained close to Nelson Algren, at least through 1955 when *A Walk on the Wild Side* was published. Algren had written the main part of the book—a reworked version of *Somebody in Boots*—in an upstairs room of the Conroys' Green Street home, where he lived for six weeks in 1954. Jack visited Algren and Simone de Beauvoir at Nelson's cottage on Lake Michigan's south shore, and participated in the cock-eyed scheme to spring James Blake from prison. Algren was an obsessive gambler; the Blake scheme was no better than his poker strategy. Often Jack and Nelson would meet for dinner with out-of-town visitors like Malcolm Cowley. But Algren was behaving strangely, not only toward Jack but toward other friends. Sometimes Algren showed up at the Conroys at 4:00 A.M. after a late-night carouse. In New York to talk with his agent, Elizabeth Ingersoll, Algren wrote Jack that he would mention Jack's "Rosewood Casket" manuscript to Ingersoll. *A Walk* was finally finished and an off-Broadway theater version was soon to appear.

The bright side of Algren's present mood was offset by the lingering bitterness he felt toward his reception in Hollywood, where he had gone, after New York, to discuss a film version of *The Man with the Golden Arm*. In what he hoped would be the deal of the century, Algren attempted to negotiate (without a lawyer) a handsome payment and an active role in Otto Preminger's production of the film. Preminger took Algren to the cleaners. Having purchased the rights to the novel from another producer for a nominal sum, the Viennese-born movie mogul prevented Algren, who had become a thorn in his side, from having any hand in the production of the film version. Algren, the street-smart veteran of racetracks, police lineups, and late-night poker games, thought he was putting over something on Preminger in Hollywood when he moved from the expensive hotel where Preminger lodged him to a cheaper hotel in order to pocket some of the expense money. Writing Jack from the $12.50-per-night room, Algren complained of Preminger's high-handed treatment. Among the grievances was Preminger's announced intent to release the movie before the premiere of Jack Kirkland's off-Broadway theater production of Algren's novel. In a word— the letter reveals Algren's self-ironizing humor at its best—Algren recognized he had been snookered. Algren concluded his note to Jack as the horn of Preminger's private limousine blew outside the run-down hotel. Algren was a lamb led to slaughter.[66]

Following the Hollywood fiasco Algren wrote a blistering, sardonic letter to Preminger. Jack showed Stuart Brent of Seven Stairs bookstore a copy of the letter that Algren gave him, asking Brent to guard against its publication. Instead, the entire text of the letter appeared in Brent's memoir, *The Seven Stairs*, much to Algren's chagrin. It is impossible to say exactly when the rift between Jack and Nelson began, or what caused it. One body of evidence points toward certain instances; the other argues that Algren had changed in his own attitude, having nothing to do with Jack or any other friend.[67] However, most of his close friends, with the possible exception of Studs Terkel, bore the abuse and hurt of Algren's rude distemper. The use of Frank Sinatra in the role of Frankie Machine in Preminger's film version was deeply irksome to Algren. The film lost all its value in favor of box-office appeal.[68]

Algren's growing churlishness, his unpredictable behavior, expressed itself cruelly at times, such as when he savaged (in a letter to the publisher) Frank Sandiford's novel manuscript, which appeared subsequently as *Next Time Is for Life*.[69] Subsequently, Algren performed a wrecking-ball job on Motley's new novel in 1958. Nelson seemed unable to shake the Preminger episode. He brought a lawsuit against Preminger. When it failed, his attorney filed a lawsuit against him for uncollected fees. Algren was depressed and angry, in no mood to shrug off hostile criticism of *A Walk on the Wild Side* by New York reviewers Alfred Kazin and Orville Prescott. Leslie Fiedler and Norman Podhoretz, wondering why anyone would write about bums, assigned Algren's work to the ash heap of proletarian literature.[70] The success of the theater version of his book notwithstanding, Algren seemed to lose his bearings. Temperamentally he appeared suicidal.[71] Jack wrote Jim Light of Algren's withdrawal.[72] The emotional turmoil of a deeply troubled man boiled and spilled over on Jack and others who loved Algren.

It is tempting to speculate—Jack did it to the end of his life—on what motivated Algren's remark about Jack in an interview with David Ray, published 11 June 1959 in the *Reporter:*

Q. Do you think academic studies help the young writer?

A. Hardly a serious writer with a formal education. I cite you Whitman, London, Poe, Dreiser, Sherwood Anderson, Mark Twain, Ambrose Bierce, J. C. Kornpoen.

Q. J. C. Kornpoen?

A. Not surprised you haven't heard the name. Came from the small mining community of Groveling, Missouri. Perhaps the greatest creative imagination of our day. I say "perhaps"—no one ever really knew. No way of telling for sure. You see, J. C. never wrote anything down. That was what was so great about it, Dad. He kept it all in his head! Kornpoen occupied the Chair of Make-Believe Literature at Alcoholics Anonymous. Never sold out. "No offers," he used to explain.[73]

The characterization of Jack as Kornpoen, an unachieved, besotted rural genius, hurt him deeply, not because of its content per se but because it came from Algren. Nelson knew, perhaps better than anyone else, why, after coming to Chicago in 1938, Jack had not invested his considerable creative talent in literary projects that might assure him a reputation as a best-selling writer. The reasons had to do with his unwillingness, or inability, to create fictions that lay outside his working-class experience; his financial responsibilities as family provider; and the unfavorable climate of literary reception toward the worker-writer in the postwar era. But in his present humor Algren shot wide of reasons or reasonableness.

About a year before the *Reporter* interview, James Blake, writing to Lorraine Fallon from cell number J-57 in the Florida State Prison, confirmed her feeling that Algren had gone sour. "I recall now," Blake wrote, "that in his last letters to me (some time ago), he seemed somewhat hung up, evincing a vague kind of resentment and bitterness at things in general that was totally unlike his usual cavalier attitude. One thing in particular that struck me, that the reason Conroy never made it big as a writer was because when the time came for him to decide whether to be a good guy, and not write, or a prince (spelled ———) [prick], and write, he chose to be a good guy." Jack's friends always seemed quick to defend him—such was undoubtedly the spirit of Blake's concluding and rather silly remark. More to the point is his comment on Algren's odd behavior. Others too had noticed it, and each had a separate explanation for it. Algren's change of mood, Blake suggested, had to do with the Preminger affair and the "mixed critical reception" of *A Walk*. We live in a time of "dynamic conformity," Blake concluded, when irreverence is "sadly out of style."[74] Algren seemed pulled in two directions at once: anxious about his literary status, the reputation that *The Man with the Golden Arm* had earned him, he nonetheless maintained a radical sensibility that made him suspicious of intellectuals and artists, as Maxwell Geismar argues, and excluded him from "official academic culture."[75]

Ben Hagglund wrote to console Jack soon after Ray's interview with Algren. Algren, he said, had "followed Richard Wright down the existentialist road," meaning that he had grown estranged from human feeling, nihilistic even. Algren's remark was not meant to be personal; "J. C. Kornpoen" symbolizes the fallen estate of proletarian literature, just as Algren's nihilism represents the present time. "And if you had your choice of what symbol to be, which would you choose?" Hagglund asked.[76]

The question should have been posed to Algren, for he had forced the choice, slaking off the skin of the past, and Jack with it. Jack's very being—the values inculcated in a Missouri coal camp, shaped by experience in working-class milieus, and manifested in the *Anvil*—had defined an important part of that past. In 1959, for Algren and Conroy, the 1930s had finally ended.[77]

19

Home to Moberly:
Contexts of Recovery

They certainly are raising up a generation of molly-
coddles now. The only safe thing to do is curse
Moscow, and if you do that many of your past sins
are shriven.

—Conroy, letter to Dale Kramer, 13 May 1955

BENJAMIN APPEL, a former *Anvil*-ite and the author of a documentary
study of the Great Depression, *The People Talk* (1940; 1982), looked
back upon the writers of his generation—the 1930s—and saw a clear
pattern in their lives by the early 1950s: "hack work and easy money,
unachieved promise and silence, sensational success that is a little hollow." They had been an "uncompromising group, determined to put
down on paper the story of the many Americas they knew," noted Appel. But their promise and idealism had been wasted subsequently in
the pursuit of cheap success in Hollywood, security in comfortable jobs,
and silence imposed by neglect and death. Only a few had kept steadily at the task of "writing truly."[1] One of the editors of the magazine in
which Appel's essay appeared asked Conroy for his response. Jack offered no specific written reply. In an important sense, however, the remainder of his life was devoted to "witnessing" and evaluating the work
of his generation, in a variety of forums and publications.

In the 1990s, the response to the work of Appel's generation of writers remains clouded by misapprehension and neglect. Engraved in the
work of Olsen, Le Sueur, Conroy, and Langston Hughes are the politi-
cal-historical contexts of the 1930s. Others, who gained much greater
recognition, such as Steinbeck, Wolfe, and Faulkner, were evaluated

according to transcendent values, such as universality and timeless truth, within the canonical framework of the postwar era. Viewed as autonomous works of art, their writings were conferred a certain exemption from contextual readings, as if the status of literary prominence freed them from such consideration. The ignored and reviled writers of the 1930s, however, whom Alfred Kazin claims (in his influential *On Native Grounds* [1942]) had "surrender[ed] to naturalism," were made to wear a crown of thorns—or a dunce cap. In the Cold War climate of reception, the literary expression of commitments and ideals emerging from a people's social drama during the previous decade was disparaged, tainted with the charge of treason, or simply forgotten.[2]

How this unfavorable reception was orchestrated in some part by those who had earlier labored in leftist causes has been the subject of numerous studies. By the 1950s, individualist values allied with conformist attitudes silenced cultural diversity and critical independence. In response, the Beat Generation and the "rebels without a cause" withdrew into inner exile, posing little threat to the dominant culture, creating personalized styles without political content. Unidimensional figures in popular culture, literature, and politics (Pat Boone, the Man in the Grey Flannel Suit, Senator Joe McCarthy) symbolized monolithic standards of acceptance and recognition.[3] Powerful cultural institutions, principally the "Tory Formalists" (the New Critics—Eliot, Tate, Ransom, and others) and the "Bourgeois Avant-Garde" (the New York intellectuals—Rahv, Trilling, Fiedler, and the like), as Grant Webster terms them, influenced the way literature was reviewed and taught.[4] Reputations were created like cultural artifacts in a literary system driven as much by political concerns as by literary judgment.[5] The radical intelligentsia that had regrouped around publications such as *Partisan Review* after the war enlisted George Orwell, for instance, in their Cold War crusade, identifying his novel *Nineteen Eighty-Four* in the public mind with pat notions concerning the division between the "free" Western world and "totalitarian" Soviet Russia.[6] In some cases, reputations were diminished or destroyed. The New York intelligentsia's long-standing feud with iconoclastic artist Thomas Hart Benton effectively delayed thoughtful appraisal of his work for decades.[7]

To Alfred Kazin, the young novelists of the 1930s were literary naturalists whose work evoked violence and crudity; to Maxwell Geismar, they belonged to the main tradition of native realism in American literature, a tradition that had fallen on hard times in the 1950s. Geismar's attack on the critical paternosters of the New York literary establishment was a small but significant dissenting vote against the devaluation of American literature of critical realism. "Where can a writer turn who still wants to root his work in the reality of his own time?" Geismar asked. "The disenchantment of the literary left, which in many cases has become the extreme right, hangs heavy over him."[8]

The rediscovery and reassessment of indigenous radical traditions in postwar America began quietly in the academy, not among the New York radical intellectuals, whose attention was turned toward problems occasioned by "the human condition," existential "angst," and the threat of Soviet totalitarianism. Radical subjects, such as the exclusion of blacks from political and academic life, the boycotting of talented artists and academics on the basis of hearsay, the loss of workers' rights, and "crippling cultural repressiveness,"[9] were unwelcome among publishers seized by a blockbuster commercial spirit and anxious to avoid the taint of unconformity. Walter Rideout's pioneering historical overview of American radical writers, begun as a dissertation, appeared in what Meridel Le Sueur called "the dark time" when writers threatened by HUAC investigations turned to writing juvenile, detective, and mystery stories in order to make a living. "I tried to avoid," Rideout wrote Conroy, "the angel-theory of the Thirties and the devil-theory of the Fifties." A compendium of critical readings, Rideout's *The Radical Novel in the United States* depends almost entirely on written documentation, ignoring the oral histories of individuals who played principle roles in the subjects of the study. Rideout regretted having failed to interview Jack in Chicago, less than an hour away.[10]

Daniel Aaron's seminal study *Writers on the Left* (1961) expands the scope of Rideout's literary history through extensive use of interviews and published records of writers' attitudes and opinions. But Aaron's interviews focused mainly on East Coast radicals like Joseph Freeman, ignoring many important sources—then still living—associated with little magazines like *Direction, Dynamo,* the *New Quarterly, Anvil,* the *Left,* and members of the John Reed clubs in Chicago, St. Louis, Detroit, and so forth. As a consequence, midwestern radicals received short shrift.

Rideout's and Aaron's studies heralded a reawakened interest in the 1930s at the same time they offered a solid basis for the scholarly reevaluation of long-silenced creative voices. They were followed by Gilbert's *Writers and Partisans,* Pells's *Radical Visions and American Dreams,* Swados's *The American Writer and the Great Depression,* Salzman and Zanderer's *Social Writings of the 1930s,* Klein's *Foreigners,* Wald's *The Revolutionary Imagination,* and more recent studies by Cary Nelson, Janet Zandy, Charlotte Nekola, Paula Rabinowitz, Barbara Foley, and James F. Murphy. Mainstream critics, on the other hand, have been slow to acknowledge the existence and continuity of radical literary traditions in America. Leslie Fiedler's essay, published in 1967, compartmentalized what he termed "the other thirties" in two groups: "the urban, Marxist, predominantly Jewish half" and "a provincial, Agrarian, primarily WASP tradition," that is, the Southern Agrarians. Fiedler makes no mention of literary radicals west of the Hudson River; everything north of the Mason-Dixon line and west of the Hudson apparently is beneath notice. It was a pattern familiar to Conroy, who wrote in the margin of the article, "Ever heard of Algren, you dumb cluck?"[11] Such were the powers of critical exclusion, continuing into our own time, that served to occlude the existence of hundreds of writers, many of whom have only recently emerged from obscurity—among them Meridel Le Sueur, Tillie Olsen, Joseph Vogel, Fielding Burke, Tom Kromer, Edwin Rolfe, Conroy, and Thomas Bell—thanks to the labors of a younger generation of scholars, small independent publishers, and university presses.

* * *

The 1950s brought little but disillusionment and grief to Jack. There were happy moments—for example, his visit with the Ozark folklorists Vance Randolph and his wife, Mary Celestia Parler, in Fayetteville, Arkansas. The trip to Fayetteville reunited Jack with the tramping companion of his youth, his nephew Fred Harrison, who drove Jack and Gladys to see the Randolphs. For two weeks Conroy and Randolph swapped ballads and tales.[12]

Jack had long wished for a fair reading of the 1930s, as he wrote to Dale Kramer in 1955: "The story of the literary Thirties is yet to be told."[13] Jack might try it; or he would share the materials—letters, magazines, and so forth—with a qualified person like Kramer.[14] He would resume the role of "witness to his time." Over the next several decades, Jack told fragments of the "story" to countless students, scholars, and "pilgrims," Conroy's expression for visitors come to meet the "granddaddy of all rebel poets." After 1960, he devoted himself almost entirely to making sure that one way or another the story would be told, not simply *his* story but that of a whole generation of radical writers.

Revisionist attitudes toward the 1930s had entered the work of at least two recent novelists, Jack noted in a 1960 review of William Golding's *Free Fall* and Alan Kapelner's *All the Naked Heroes.* "In each of these two novels of [about] the 1930s," Conroy wrote, "the antihero man, the antisocial man, is dominant. This, of course, is in the current mode, the antithesis of the attitude of social concern taken by many of the writers who lived and wrote during the '30s. It is as though history were being rewritten, and men and morals being surveyed from a new perspective."[15]

Jack hoped that if the neglected literature of the thirties could be made available again, a new generation of readers might gain an appreciation of his generation's work. Kennedy's election, the civil rights movement, and the growth of a new leftist constituency seemed favorable harbingers. Jack was delighted therefore when his agent, Max Siegel, persuaded Hill and Wang to republish *The Disinherited* with an introduction by Daniel Aaron, appearing in 1963. Introductions are important instruments in the recovery of lost novels, in the redemption of reputations, particularly in college courses. "Now to get enough English teachers to use it in their classes," he wrote a young writer whose manuscript he had recommended to Siegel.[16]

In August 1961, Gladys and Jack visited Willard Motley in Cuernavaca, Mexico, a trip financed with the money Jack received as settlement in a suit against an author who had plagiarized "The Fast Sooner Hound" version that had appeared in Botkin's folklore anthology. Jack bolstered Motley's shaken confidence. Gloomy in light of the negative critical reception of *Let No Man Write My Epitaph* (1958), Motley sent Jack a manuscript copy of "Let Noon Be Fair," which Jack read, offering suggestions for revisions as he had done with *Knock on Any Door* (1947). Algren's review, in which Algren remarked pettishly that Motley had moved backward since *Knock on Any Door*, "from the derivative to the imitative," stung the sensitive black writer who had been a colleague of Algren's on the Illinois Writers' Project.[17]

Shortly after the Conroys' return, Fred Harrison, whose painful World War II battle wounds left him with deep psychological scars as well, shot himself following a drunk-driving charge that, he feared, might jeopardize his job. Fred had been Jack's closest companion from Monkey Nest days; together they had "nagged the red ball," and stood in employment lines in Toledo. "This has had a profound effect on me," Jack wrote Motley.[18]

Twice in the early 1960s, once with Gladys, Jack traveled to Ireland, England, and France, where he looked up the writers J. T. Powers, Vera Brittain, and Sean O'Faolain. In Paris he met with Michel Fabre, who was helping Richard Wright's widow organize his literary papers, and with Suzanne and André Chennevière, who had translated *The Disinherited*, which ran serially in *L'Humanité* in 1947. In Ireland Jack traveled to Galway to view the statue of Gaelic poet Pairic O'Conaire, from whom, he was told, the Conroy name derives. Visiting Oxford he thought of Hardy's Jude the Obscure, who stood in reverence before the university from which, because of lack of sufficient schooling, he was denied access.

There was talk of Jack writing his autobiography. Larry Hill of Hill and Wang pushed the idea and Arna Bontemps wrote that "it might be the kind of book that would almost write itself."[19] Cooking on a front burner, however, was a new collaboration by Bontemps and Conroy to update—essentially rewrite—*They Seek a City*. The new book would bear the same title, *Anyplace But Here*, that Jack had used in his 1930s Guggenheim-sponsored researches. Bontemps and Conroy had a great deal of work to do in rewriting the new book to reflect recent black history—the Supreme Court decision of 1954, early civil rights demonstrations, the emergence of Martin Luther King, Jr., and Malcolm X, rioting in Watts. *Anyplace But Here*, appearing in 1966, received high praise from historians such as John Hope Franklin and critics such as William Katz in the *Saturday Review of Literature*. *Anyplace But Here* "illuminates" black history "with uncompromising honesty" wrote Robert Hirsch of the *Los Angeles Times*, who recommended it for "every American."[20] The book is long out of print and the events superseded by subsequent history, but the collaboration between the two authors is especially relevant today in light of racial divisions that cause many people to wonder whether blacks and whites can work together as peers.[21]

In the 1960s, a new generation of students with expectations shaped by the civil rights era and the Vietnam War provided forums for writers and editors like Jack, Granville Hicks, Meridel Le Sueur, Tillie Olsen, and others. The reappearance of *The Disinherited* in 1963 started Jack off on an odyssey of lectures and symposia in response to growing interest in the 1930s. A symposium on the 1930s under Erling Larsen's direction at Carleton College brought Jack, Malcolm Cowley, Algren, Ben Hagglund, Farrell, Ben Appel, Russell Ames, Botkin, and others together in an issue of *Carleton Miscellany*.[22] Jack lectured at the University of Washington, sponsored by the poet David Wagoner whom Jack had met at Yaddo. Former Rebel Poet Kenneth Porter invited Jack to speak at the University of Oregon. In Corvallis, Oregon, members of the ultrarightist John Birch Society passed out leaflets during Conroy's lecture at the state university, warning the audience of Conroy's communist associations. "I think the 30's revival," he wrote Dale Kramer in 1966, "is picking up a bit of speed."[23]

Jerre Mangione, who was writing *The Dream and the Deal*, a history and memoir of the Federal Writers' Project, arranged for Jack to speak at the University of Pennsylvania. At the University of Connecticut in 1969, Jack joined Max Lieber, Walt Snow, and Arna Bontemps in a symposium on the 1930s.[24] At Birmingham-Southern College he was gratified to find *The Disinherited* taught in American literature courses. Someone dubbed him "the Sage of Moberly." Jack was beginning to achieve some recognition, not alone on the basis of his earlier literary production but for his personal "testimonies" appearing as memoirs in scholarly publications, such as *Tri-Quarterly*, *New Letters*, *Negro American Forum*, *American Book Collector*, and David Madden's *Proletarian Writers of the Thirties*, and as creative sketches in *New Letters*, *December*, *Journal of Popular Culture*, and elsewhere. Jack's recompense for living long, it appeared, might be finally to have the opportunity to tell about it. The satisfaction he felt is expressed in a review he wrote of Richard H. Pells's *Radical Visions and American Dreams*, published in 1973. Pells concluded that "the fundamental tragedy of the 1930s was not that men raised the wrong issues or failed to supply satisfactory answers but that the political and psychic wounds of the decade's final years virtually paralyzed an entire generation of intellectuals. Though their capacity for artistic experimentation remained undiminished, they were as a result of these experiences unable (and perhaps unwilling) to break with political and doctrinal rigidity which permeated America following World War II."[25] Conroy's explanation of the fate of radicals who recanted their ideals eschewed Pells's paralysis thesis. It was not a question of psychology but of character. "Radicals," Conroy wrote, "sold out so cheap."[26] Edwin Seaver, Jay Du Von, Albert Halper, and others had compromised themselves. Howard Rushmore had turned informer. "Just for a handful of silver he left us," Conroy said (quoting Browning), "Just for a riband to stick in his coat." It was not enough simply to have survived the dreadful time of betrayal when men who once held ideals high were crying "mea culpa." As a survivor Jack must now, like Ishmael, tell his tale.

* * *

Perhaps the fact that they viewed themselves as survivors drew long-time rivals Conroy and Farrell together. After one last flare-up, their feud fizzled out. For years, Jack had declined to review Farrell's novels—until the appearance of Farrell's eighteenth novel, *What Time Collects*, in 1964. Jack could find no good words for it. Farrell was so incensed that he wrote a virtually illegible letter to columnist Hoke Norris at the *Chicago Sun-Times* complaining that "Jack Conroy has written more renunciations of me than he has books. On and off for 30 years, he has been having his kicks by condemning my writing." Conroy's reply: "If I've been getting my kicks in this way, I must have spent a joyless 18 years. It has been that long since I reviewed 'Bernard Clare' in the *Sun*. I thought then that the book was an ineffective one, and said so."[27] When Farrell's next novel, *Lonely for the Future*, appeared, Jack criticized it for its repetitive use of material from Farrell's earlier writings, but praised qualities in Farrell's work that (to Conroy's mind) younger novelists lacked. "I hope the cantankerous Jim Farrell appreciates it," Vasiliki Sarant, a Hill and Wang editor, wrote Jack.[28] Apparently Farrell did, for he wrote Jack: "I have never heard anyone speak badly of you. I have seen so many give up, so many sell out."[29] In another letter, Farrell said he had misjudged *The Disinherited*. The feud finally died for lack of sustenance.[30]

Similarly, Dahlberg and Conroy patched up their differences. Jack wrote Dahlberg in the late 1960s praising Dahlberg's "richly ornate style" and "knowledge of the classics and mythology."[31] Dahlberg, for his part, quoted approvingly a passage from *The Disinherited* to illustrate Depression-era indigence and saluted Jack for spurning the "grease of cupidity."[32]

For years the Farrell-Conroy feud had symbolized deeper dissensions between Party regulars (and fellow-travelers) like Mike Gold, Malcolm Cowley, and Samuel Sillen, and apostates such as Rahv, Phillips, John Chamberlain, Horace Gregory, and others. The highpoint (or lowpoint, corresponding to one's perspective at the time) was the Albert Maltz affair in 1946. Maltz expressed doubts in an essay entitled "What Shall We Ask of the Writer?" whether Farrell had been treated fairly by the Party. The view that art might serve as a weapon had now become useless, Maltz wrote. Farrell might dwell beyond the Party pale, but, Maltz argued, his novels still were of value to the left. The wrath of the Party descended upon Maltz for daring such a conciliatory stance. After a period of stern reprimand and "re-education" Maltz recanted in an apology printed in *New Masses*. Farrell had made enemies on the left, in part because of his record of debunking Party icons, in part because of his alignment with the Phillips-Rahv axis and embracing of Trotskyist views. They were not letting him off the hook.[33]

The Maltz affair was a dismal chapter in the history of the literary left. Jack had no part in it and probably would have refused if he had been asked to join Maltz's rebukers, who included Alvah Bessie, Howard Fast, and Herbert Biberman. In the face of new social realities unfolding in the 1960s and the direction American letters had taken, Jack called rather for a positive reappraisal of Farrell's work. "Maybe it's because we've grown accustomed to his ill grace," Jack wrote in his review of *Lonely for the Future*, "—maybe he looks somewhat better because of the company he keeps—but Farrell, still a man of the naturalistic '30s in spirit, should benefit from the definite (if still limited) reassessment of that period that is now under way." American letters had fallen into a sorry state. Farrell was "a more worthy candidate for the bays of posterity than William Burroughs."[34] Perhaps the solidarity Jack felt with writers of the Old Left in a period when their work was receiving renewed attention overrode the bad feeling and divisiveness that characterized earlier times. In any case, Conroy seemed to feel a restored sense of confidence and hope that he soon communicated in the first of his memoirs, entitled "Home to Moberly," published in 1968.

Jack was considering retiring from his encyclopedia job. The last years were less onerous after western historian Don Russell joined New Standard. Russell was a quiet-spoken scholar, a specialist on Buffalo Bill. During lunch breaks the two searched used-book bins on Clark Street for obscure titles on American history and folklore, swapping tales about the eccentricities of western historian E. Douglas Branch, who had worked with Jack at Consolidated Book Publishers some ten years before. The decision to retire was made for Jack when New Standard requested his resignation in October 1966 on the basis of age (he was sixty-seven). Without a pension he was forced to apply for unemployment compensation. When the benefits expired, the Conroys moved back to Moberly to settle despite Gladys's objection: "I feel I'm just going back there to die." "Madam," Jack told his wife, "you'd better die among relatives and friends than among strangers. You'll die wherever you go!"[35] Jack looked forward to the chance at long last to produce the much-anticipated autobiography.

One of Jack's first undertakings after his return was to visit Monkey Nest, in the company of the Moberly city clerk, R. W. Daly, and the thirteen-year-old son of the mine's property owner, Alfred Floyd Turner, who served as guide. Scrub trees overgrew the hillocks where the chalky mine tailings had been dumped; exposed ventilation shafts posed dangers to the unwary; a pond that fed the steam pump now furnished water to deer and raccoons. The house in which Jack was born had been moved a half-mile away.

The Conroys purchased an old stone house at 701 Fisk Avenue. In a large upstairs bedroom facing the southeast corner Jack built floor-to-ceiling bookcases to house his large library. He was soon a familiar figure on Fisk Avenue, carrying home large sacks of groceries under each arm. Few people recalled his radical associations in the early 1930s, although Jack liked to portray himself as a one-time persona non grata in his hometown. He might have been a Nobel Prize winner for all they knew—people remembered him for his unconventionality, not his literary achievements. Someone remarked, passing Jack on the street, "There's that drunk, Jack Conroy; those sacks are probably full of whiskey." Almost everyone knew he had written a book about Monkey Nest and some townspeople had actually read it. But the one bookstore in town seldom carried it in stock. When visitors came to see him, he took them to Hickman's Tavern, which belonged to Gladys's sister and brother-in-law, Agnes and Stanley Hickman. One afternoon, a client who had been refused service returned with a chainsaw and proceeded to cut the bar into two pieces. The "great chainsaw debacle" attracted the notice of a *Kansas City Star* reporter.

Jack was in touch again, as he wrote, with his native earth, like the mythic Antaeus, regaining strength. "It seems to me that not a few of our writers who began promisingly are now suspended in the sterile air of New York or Hollywood. . . . It has been too long since they touched the good earth. What I'm doing now is trying to make some sort of consensus of all I've seen and, if possible, to extract some sort of meaning from it all. These investigations and ruminations might conceivably take the form of an autobiography."[36]

An East German edition of *The Disinherited* was selling very well. Someone wrote Jack that he had found a Pakistani man reading the edition in a remote Himalayan hamlet. In 1967, Conroy and Bontemps won the Society of Midland Authors' James L. Dow Award for *Anyplace But Here*. In presenting the award, novelist Harry Mark Petrarkis recalled the help and encouragement Jack had given him much earlier. "I don't know how many other aspiring writers Jack Conroy helped," Petrarkis said, "but I will always remember the great heart of this man, the way he evidenced to a despairing young man the humanism and compassion which permeates his work and his life."[37] The Pulitzer Prize–winning poet Gwendolyn Brooks paid Jack a similar tribute in presenting him the first Literary Times Prize the same year, citing "his aid and encouragement to young writers and his overall contribution to American literature, particularly his novel, *The Disinherited*." Other honors followed: a literary award from the Missouri Library Association; an honorary doctorate from the University of Missouri at Kansas City; the Mark Twain Award from the Society for the Study of Midwestern Literature; a National Endowment for the Humanities artist's grant. The latter astonished him since, as he wrote John Rogers, a few years before he had been labeled a Communist and subjected to FBI scrutiny.[38] Moreover, he had joined other writers in signing a letter to Lyndon B. Johnson, opposing the Vietnam War.[39]

In the late 1960s, a group of progressive-minded young people from Kansas City, including Don St. Clair and Verle Muhrer, started the "Folk University," a counterculture collective enterprise that brought together folk musicians, political theorists, actors, and "cultural workers." Camp-outs were held in Kansas and Arkansas in the spirit of 1930s rural labor colleges like Commonwealth in Mena, Arkansas. St. Clair and Muhrer visited Conroy in Moberly, inviting him to speak at their cultural gatherings. Jack suggested renaming the organization "Foolkiller," after James Larkin Pearson's irreverent newspaper, published several decades earlier in Boomer, North Carolina. Pearson had written that "the best way to get a truth into a yokel is to make him open his mouth wide with laughter, and then cram the knowledge down his throat."[40]

Moving from its temporary residence on East Thirty-first Street in Kansas City, the Foolkiller organization relocated in a large factory building at Thirty-ninth and Main in the mid-1970s. There, conferences were held bringing together Old Left writers like Meridel Le Sueur, Vincent Ferrini, Tom McGrath, Conroy, Emanuel Fried, and John Rogers, and a new generation of radical writer/scholars like Norma Wilson, John Crawford, Fred Whitehead, and Harold Dellinger. Conroy wrote columns, "Musings of the Sage of Moberly," for the organization's publication. Small, independent groups like the Foolkiller in Kansas City and the Association for the Study of People's Culture in Minneapolis were important agents in reconnecting older midwestern literary radicals with younger progressive artists and scholars in the 1970s and early 1980s and making their work available through small presses and little magazines. David Ray's *New Letters* (subsequently edited by James McKinley and Robert Stewart), Curt Johnson's *December*, Fred Whitehead's *Quindaro*, Jack Miller's *North Country Anvil*, and other publications helped to restore broken communication circuits for midwest-radical writing.

The poet David Ray played an important role as editor of *New Letters* (Kansas City) in bringing attention to Conroy's work and establishing his significance. In the early 1970s, *New Letters* published an important essay on Conroy's work as editor by a Sorbonne professor, Michel Fabre. Some eight years earlier, in the course of his research on Richard Wright, Fabre had visited Jack in Chicago where during a week's stay he helped put Jack's correspondence in order and prepared his own dissertation topic on American little magazines of the 1930s. Conroy's personal memoir of little-magazine editing, "The Literary Underworld of the 1930s," Lewis Fried's interview, and Jack memories of Richard Wright appeared in *New Letters*. The role of survivor, of old rebel, in which Jack cast himself, emerged in these essays and memoirs. The role suited Jack's temperament well. Zestfully the "Sage of Moberly" inveighed against "Tricky Dick" Nixon, "Echo Chamber Ford" (Gerald Ford), "the New York Literary Mafia," and bêtes noires such as *Commentary* editor Norman Podhoretz, regaling his visitors with colorful anecdotes of "Algrenfellar" (Nelson Algren), Farrell, the Fallonites, and a host of little-known literary figures.[41] Closely guarded, however, were his feelings. Jack resisted disclosing closet skeletons; the biographical "facts" that interest scholars seldom crept into the conversations I had with him. Was he saving these for his own writing?

Boosted by the award of a Rabinowitz grant, Jack set himself the task of writing his autobiography in piecemeal sketches, published separately as they were written. The realism, humor, and vigorous language of his earliest *American Mercury* sketches were recaptured in five tales about his Monkey Nest days, composed near the end of his life. The stories begin with "The Fields of Golden Glow," which appeared in *New Letters*, and conclude prematurely with "The Kimberly Toughs," when Jack was already eighty-three. He had trouble "getting out of Monkey Nest," he confessed. The long-awaited life history would never be completed.

Jack lived long enough to experience the recovery and reappraisal of 1930s writers whose work was made available again through independent publishers like Florence Howe's Feminist Press, John Crawford's West End Press, and Lawrence Hill. Jack collaborated with Curt Johnson (of December Press) in 1973 to edit *Writers in Revolt,* an anthology of *Anvil* and *New Anvil* writing. David Ray and Jack Salzman gathered critical writings, poetry, and sketches together in *The Jack Conroy Reader* in 1979. A new edition of *The Disinherited* appeared from Lawrence Hill in 1983, and again from the University of Missouri Press in 1991. A Japanese edition appeared, in Kiyo Murayama's translation. The introduction to a collection of Conroy's sketches and folktales, *The Weed King and Other Stories* (1985), suggests new methods for reading Conroy, unlocking his work from the ideological constraints of "proletarian literature." While Jack was yet alive to witness their emergence, the rhizomes of midwestern radical culture sent up new shoots through the soil of experience. Debs, Ameringer, Le Sueur, Conroy, Benton, Smedley, Kalar, Corey, Lewis—here is a remarkable tradition of human dignity, protest, and hope that, Conroy believed, would find its counterpart in a time when ten million are out of work, despairing people riot in urban ghettos, and the homeless crowd city parks. "Is it possible," Jack wrote in 1982, "that some of those who now lose their pride and stoop low may rise up angry?"[42]

Jack received the recognition that means most to a writer: from his hometown people. In May 1985, some five hundred admirers turned out on a day that the City of Moberly proclaimed as "Jack Conroy Day" to hear Stephen Wade perform Conroy's "Fast Sooner Hound" and other Conroy folktales from his long-running show, "Banjo Dancin'," at the Arena Stage Theater in Washington.

In his last years Jack was sanguine, reflective, content. His son, Jack, and Jack's wife, Thelma, and his three grandsons, Jim, Jerry, and Jack Swartz, whom he had sent to college, were close to him; old friends, including Studs and Ida Terkel, Win Stracke, Mike Hecht, David and Judy Ray, Wallie Wharton, Betrenia Watt Bowker, Peggy Werkley, Ray and Charlotte Koch, and new friends like Carolee Hazlet, Stephen Wade, and Tom Kruck visited him in his stone house on Fisk Avenue. Aware that he would not live to finish the task of telling his own story, he dropped the storyteller's role with me, sharing his long-guarded "secrets" and giving me access to his personal archives.

There were terrible losses during these last years: his daughter, Margaret Jean, died of cancer in 1975; Jack nursed Gladys, a semi-invalid, at home until her death in 1982. "There is some kind of dreadful finality about death," he said to me after Gladys's passing. Finally, a stroke robbed Jack of his speech and the use of his writing arm. Poised, attentive, silent he lay in nursing homes for two years. His eyes, twinkling in amusement at the world and humankind, welcomed visitors in their gentle embrace. To the very end, which came in the early hours of Ash Wednesday, 28 February 1990, he was the unreconstructed rebel. On a crisp, clear spring day, John Wesley Conroy was buried in the old miners' cemetery at Sugar Creek.

Afterword

> I have never lost a sense of something that lives
> and endures underneath the eternal flux. What we
> see is the blossom, which passes. The rhizome re-
> mains.
>
> —Carl Jung

FROM AN ABANDONED GAS STATION in Texas, Nelson Algren sent Conroy early chapters of his first novel for publication in the *Anvil*. Erskine Caldwell submitted stories focusing on racial injustice. Langston Hughes anticipated Ellison's *Invisible Man* in a short story satirizing Jim Crow education. Richard Wright, then a Chicago post office worker, saw his first work published in the *Anvil*. Meridel Le Sueur and Sanora Babb contributed their perspectives on working-class women's lives. As editor, Conroy crossed gender, ethnic, race, and class lines in pursuit of his aim, which was to provide a publishing alternative in an increasingly commodity-oriented culture. Whitmanesque in its purpose, engaging diverse voices in "the powerful language of resistance . . . the dialect of common sense," the *Anvil* removed barriers between uncompromising writers and their subjects, an angry and confused people in the midst of the worst economic crisis the country had ever known.

A victim of literary politics, and in a larger sense, of commodity culture, Jack Conroy and his contributors made only tentative gains in educating readers to prefer "crude vigor to polished urbanity." The *Anvil* was one of many "little magazines" of the early 1930s, polycentric sites of literary production that spread their meshpoints horizontally, forging networks of young writers and diverse perspectives. A revolution in communication means was underway, anticipating the information society of today with its modems, networking, data bases, and electronic mail. When this "revolution" is linked to democratic forms and aims—an example is the emergence of committees of correspondence in reply to authoritarian practices—it constitutes a liberating, empowering force.

As both a shaper of midwestern literary radicalism and its product, Conroy helped initiate counterhegemonic cultural trends whose legacy is evident in the continuity of traditions that, largely unnoticed, spread their roots beneath the surface, "sprouting alike," as Walt Whitman said, "in broad zones and narrow zones, / Growing among black folks as among white."[1] Wherever neighbors in violence-torn ghettos organize to improve their lives, independent editors open their little magazines to controversial topics and unknown writers, ordinary people ignore class, race, and sex differences, forming grass-roots coalitions to resist the encroachments of powerful interest groups, writers knowledgeable of working-class people and settings share their understanding with the general reader, and publishers take economic risks in publishing them, there is evidence that the rhizome has sprouted, however tentatively.

Nadine Gordimer, the Nobel Prize–winning South African novelist, mused during a trip through upstate New York in the mid-1980s: "I drive past mobile homes and wonder: 'Who are these people? I don't meet them in American fiction.'"[2] Why are workers generally not subjects of fiction in America? The best-seller lists suggest that readers prefer the lives of the rich, the middle class, and the "Lumpenproletariat." Something in the failure of the worker to rise "to better things" seems to disturb the popular self-image.

To the extent that the worker has been largely excluded from American literature, the story of Jack Conroy is all the more remarkable. By any standard Conroy was an exceptional person. We have his story, but can we explain fully his ambition to do what few others of his talent and imagination in American literature have attempted, to forge from within the world of working-class experience, as worker-writer, the material of literary narrative and folktale?

One of the central achievements of the 1930s "proletarian" fiction and documentary art was to shift from the sociological, outsider's sympathetic scrutiny of the under class (for example, the notion of the "poor" in the 1890s) to a literary reframing of the voices of the disinherited. "Overheard" voices were reconstituted in a manner that conventional methods of literary criticism fail to decode. Conroy violated the rules of proletarian and realist literature, introducing humor, oral expression, folk perspective, and indigenous patterns of protest. When he failed, it was because he attempted to imitate conventional literary codes.

The present study is not a biography in the traditional sense. Industrial work situations are collective and collaborative. Conroy's entire life was one of sharing and participating. His narratives reveal the persona of a self-fashioned narrator-author. Emanating from within the experience he portrays, Conroy's writing also stands outside the experience, defining vantage points that offer perspectives on clichéd assumptions about working-class life. Conroy recreates rather than transcribes workers' voices, placing them democratically on the same level with the voice of his narrator. Workers recognize themselves in his stories. Worker-writing is not familiar, however, to most readers in our culture. It does not succeed in challenging generic conventions of the dominant culture simply because it is not given that kind of regard. To evaluate properly the hybrid genres of midwestern literary radicalism we need to employ methods and standards different from those linked to canon formation.

When I began this project I determined to inquire into the details of Jack Conroy's lifelong devotion to literature despite the great personal hardships and financial handicaps he endured. What led him, the son of an immigrant Irish coal miner, mainly self-taught, to turn to writing during the brief nights bounded relentlessly by days of manual labor? What prompted him to remain a worker in a society that puts a premium on social advancement and status? Who were the contributors, editors, agents, publishers, and literary colleagues of his generation, most of whose work lay buried in obscurity when I first began? What were the literary, social, political, and personal contexts in which his work evolved and was received?

The present volume answers these questions in part; however, we need to continue the task of recovering "disappeared" writers and clarifying neglected traditions. It may happen again that a generation of bright, young, and energetic men and women, uprooted, without a future, helmless and homeless, hear the voices of "those who do not write."

Notes

Introduction

1. In the 1950s, Irving Howe and Lewis Coser, for example, scornfully dismissed the "mindless crudity" of the *New Masses* under Mike Gold—in other words, the period (1928–32) when Gold encouraged and published worker-writers like Kalar, Conroy, Falkowski, Lewis, and others involved in the effort to create a literature by and for the working person. See *American Communist Party*, 257. The blacklisting of Meridel Le Sueur's work is recalled in her recent collections, *Ripening* and *Harvest*.

2. Michel Fabre, Richard Wright's biographer, suggested that I read the book and visit Conroy when my wife and I returned to the United States following a three-year teaching stint in France. Coincidentally, Conroy lived in my wife's hometown, which made things very convenient. Richard Wright said of Conroy: "All of his work has been directed singularly towards one goal: the enlightenment of the American people of the realities of the lives and potentialities of American labor, and the encouragement of the young worker-writer. From that faith and labor, he has not swerved one iota." Quoted by Fabre, *Richard Wright*, 31.

3. Meridel Le Sueur, letter to author, 29 August 1990.

4. This is also characteristic of minority literatures, as Gilles Deleuze and Felix Guattari point out in *Kafka—Pour une Littérature Mineure*, 31.

5. Weimann, *Structure and Society in Literary History*.

6. Jack Morgan, in the fall 1992 issue of *Eire-Ireland*, draws attention to Conroy's contributions as an Irish-American writer; past studies of Irish-American literature, including Charles Fanning's recently published *The Irish Voice in America: Irish-American Fiction from the 1760s to the 1980s*, have generally ignored this point. As Morgan points out, *The Disinherited* represents, perhaps better than any contemporary novel, the continuity of traditions of Anglo-Irish labor radicalism in America during the early twentieth century.

7. Whitman, "Democratic Vistas," in *Walt Whitman: Complete Poetry and Collected Prose*, ed. Kaplan.

8. I hope that readers will accept that my use of "Jack" throughout this study to refer to Conroy implies no special privilege or lack of respect. Given Jack Conroy's nature, his disavowal of formalities, it would be awkward, pretentious, and simply wrong to refer to him otherwise.

Chapter 1
Monkey Nest Mine

1. *Moberly Monitor*, 2 February 1894.

2. William Hendren, interview, 5 December 1981. At age ninety-three, when I interviewed him, Hendren still had vivid memories of Monkey Nest mine. Unless otherwise noted, this and subsequent interviews were conducted and taped by the author. Tapes and notes are in the author's possession.

3. See *The First Hundred Years* for a description of mining in the hand-loading era in northern Missouri.

4. Schweider, *Black Diamonds*.

5. Coleman, *Men and Coal*, 63.

6. Ibid.

7. See, for example, Brophy, *John Brophy*.

8. Edward MacLysaght locates Conroys in the midland counties. Mac-Lysaght, *Irish Families*, 27–28, 61. Jack felt fairly sure that his father was born in County Roscommon. The name Conroy derives from O'Mulconry, hereditary poets and chroniclers to the Connacht kings, a genealogical fact that pleased Jack.

9. The experience of the Irish immigrant in Montreal in the 1880s is described by S. Johnson, *History of Emigration*, 158–93.

10. My thanks to Père Joseph Cossette of the Archives de la Compagnie for checking the "liste des Anciens Élèves du Collège Ste.-Marie" in Montreal, the sole Jesuit college at the time. Cossette to author, 4 August 1986.

11. Jack Conroy, interview, 12 April 1982.

12. Conroy, interview in *Kansas City Star*, 11 May 1975, 2E.

13. Margaret Conroy Wisdom, interview, 7 September 1986.

14. The Wabash Railroad Company published a special map showing the connection between Montreal and Kansas City, presumably to appeal to emigrants like Tom heading for the coal fields of Illinois and Missouri.

15. Terry Coleman lists Illinois as the third most favored choice of Irish immigrants in 1855, in part because of opportunities in mining. See *Going to America*.

16. Gottlieb, "British Coal Miners," 180.

17. Gottlieb, lecture, Illinois Labor History Conference.

18. Kerby A. Miller argues that Irish-Americans were "incredibly dominant" in craft unions during this period. See *Emigrants and Exiles*, 500. On the influence of English-speaking immigrants in the early union movement, see McDonald and Lynch, *Coal and Unionism*.

19. Margaret Conroy Wisdom, interview, 7 September 1986.

20. See Winter, "Division in Missouri Methodism," on the emotionalism and democratic spirit in early Methodism.

21. Zweig, *Men in the Pits*, 168; also, see E. Thompson, *The Making*, 41–43; and Mathews, *Methodism*, 15.

22. William G. McLoughlin, Jr., writes, "there was little in Moody's sermons to appeal to the workingman." *Modern Revivalism*, 270. Also, see Fones-Wolf, *Trade Union Gospel*, 41: "Moody's faith in individual redemption led him to scorn the social reforms being advocated by immigrant and working-class leaders."

23. Fones-Wolf, *Trade Union Gospel*, xvi.

24. William G. McLoughlin, Jr., makes this point about religious revivals in *Revivals, Awakenings*.

25. Rorabaugh, *Craft Apprentice*, 39.

26. Fones-Wolf, *Trade-Union Gospel*, 196.

27. Margaret Conroy Wisdom, interview, 7 September 1986.

28. Fones-Wolf, *Trade Union Gospel*, 197.

29. Conroy, interview, 4 June 1986.

30. See Laslett, *Labor and the Left*, chap. 6.

31. See Gottlieb, "British Coal Miners"; Roy, *History of the Coal Miners*, 59–60, 323f. Martin Kane, an Irishman, edited the *United Mine Workers' Journal* (hereafter abbreviated *UMWJ*); John L. Lewis's parents were Welsh.

32. Monkey Nest mine was small and dangerous, less attractive than mines in neighboring Macon County where, in David Thelen's words, "The only people who could mine coal in the days when it was still a skilled craft were British immigrants who had acquired their skills earlier in England and Wales. The culture of Macon County coal miners was the culture of these immigrants. In 1870, 77 percent of Macon County coal miners had been born in England or Wales. . . ." *Paths of Resistance*, 6.

33. McWilliams, *Idea of Fraternity*, 543.

34. As Richard Hoggart points out, most of us encounter exceptional individuals of working-class origins and experience in locations of achievement such as the university; and afterward the differences are of less significance. "They would be exceptional people in any class," Hoggart says; "they reveal less about their class than about themselves." *Uses of Literacy*, 16.

35. The ratio of foremen to underground workers was only 1 to 114 in the hand-loading era. Dix, *Work Relations in the Coal Industry*, 14.

36. Evans, "Sketch of the Life," 7–16. This is an informative account of immigrant miners in midwestern mines in the last decades of the nineteenth century.

37. Husband's *Year in a Coal Mine*, for instance, erases the role of collective action.

38. Evans, "Sketch of the Life," 38.

39. Hoggart, *Uses of Literacy*, 262.

40. "He was the best talker there ever was in this country," says Larry Donovan's mother in Conroy's *The Disinherited*, 268. "He could persuade the miners to do anything he wanted them to." This and subsequent citations refer to the 1991 edition.

41. *Huntsville Herald*, 24 August 1906.
42. *Annual Report, 1899*, 29.
43. *Annual Report, 1900*, 151.
44. *Annual Report 1902*, 174.
45. My thanks to Charles Evans's grandson, Emerson Rice (Moberly, Missouri), who shared his memories with me.
46. *Moberly Monitor*, 5 September 1906.
47. *Annual Report 1908*, 102.
48. Ibid.
49. *Annual Report 1909*.
50. *The Disinherited*, 55.
51. *Annual Report 1909*, 170. When Evans no longer made inspections, the narrative information of the *Annual Reports* was presented simply as statistical data.
52. "Mine Accident Hurts Two," *Moberly Monitor*, 7 July 1909.

Chapter 2
Monkey Nest Coal Camp

1. Conroy, interview, 4 June 1986.
2. Conroy, "Charley Was Our Darlin'," *The Weed King*, 97. Hereafter cited as *WK*.
3. In contrast, for instance, to Lawrence's portrayal of his mother in the coal-mining village of Bestwood. See Ruderman, *D. H. Lawrence and the Devouring Mother*. Interesting parallels occur in Killingsworth's discussion of the maternal influence in Whitman's life. Killingsworth, "Whitman and Motherhood," 28–43.
4. Schneiderman's book on Jacques Lacan describes qualities that, in unlike circumstances, characterized Conroy's own life: placing ethical conduct before personal happiness; refusing to intellectualize experience; engaging a destiny which in Conroy's case won him many admirers but little success. See Schneiderman, *Jacques Lacan*, 164–82.
5. Conroy, "Fields of Golden Glow," *WK*, 81.
6. Conroy, "The Morphadite," *WK*, 116.
7. Conroy, "Kimberly Toughs," *WK*, 144.
8. Lantz, *People of Coal Town*, 150–56.
9. V. McLaughlin, *Family and Community*.
10. Sennett, *Families Against the City*.
11. Glenn Porter, foreword to Bodnar, *Workers' World*, xiii.
12. Bodnar, *Workers' World*, 1–4.
13. Vincent, *Bread, Knowledge and Freedom*, 62; Zaretsky, *Capitalism, The Family, and Personal Life*, 65.
14. Conroy, interview, 21 April 1984.
15. Humphries, "Class Struggle," 486.
16. Aronowitz, *False Promises*, 201.

17. P. Roberts, *Anthracite Coal Communities*, 11.

18. Ibid., 40.

19. Korson, *Coal Dust on the Fiddle*, 29–34.

20. Burnett, ed., *Annals of Labour*, 47–48.

21. Gaventa, *Power and Powerlessness*, chap. 3; Caudill, *Night Comes to the Cumberlands*. Also, see Carawan, *Voices from the Mountains*, 9.

22. Seltzer, *Fire in the Hole*, 18.

23. Ibid., 20.

24. Conroy, *The Disinherited*, 39.

25. Conroy, interview, November 1984.

26. For an interesting description of a midwestern coal camp (Braidwood, Illinois) see Gutman, "The Workers' Search for Power," 38–39.

27. Conroy, "Holiday at a Coal Camp," 1.

28. Ibid.

29. Ibid. In the *Chicago Sun*, "blacks" was substituted for the actual term "Niggers." Conroy, interview, 28 February 1986.

30. Hertzler, *Sociology of Language*, 36. On the notion of working-class subcultures, see R. Baker, "Labor History, Social Science," 101.

31. Conroy, "Charley Was My Darlin'," *WK*, 88.

32. Conroy, interview, 28 February 1986.

33. Conroy, "The Siren," *WK*, 127. In an interview, the Missouri painter Thomas Hart Benton, during the time when he was working on his mural in the State Capitol at Jefferson City, explained his attraction for weeds. "They grow in such immense, fascinating varieties," he told the interviewer. "Are weeds more interesting to you than people?" he was asked. "No, not more so, but equally interesting. Weeds and people are alike in many respects. They both grow in such unpredictable ways." *Kansas City Times*, 15 November 1939.

34. Conroy, "The Weed King," *WK*, 114.

35. Conroy, "The Fields of Golden Glow," *WK*, 82.

36. The expression "life-world" is from Schutz and Luckmann, *Structures of the Life-World*.

37. Lasch, *The Minimal Self*.

38. Hoggart, *Uses of Literacy*, 88. Hoggart writes of English working-class life, but I feel that his conclusion here applies also to the close-knit immigrant mining community of Monkey Nest.

39. Aaron, introduction to *The Disinherited*, xii.

40. Fishwick makes a similar point about black culture in "Where Are Uncle Remus and John Henry?" 36.

41. Conroy, "That Skinner Bottoms Winter," *WK*, 153.

42. Conroy, "Charley Was Our Darlin'," *WK*, 92.

43. Empson discusses the implications of the pastoral in real and romantic settings. See *Some Versions of Pastoral*.

44. ". . . qui se développe en évitant toute orientation sur un point culminant ou vers une fin extérieure." Deleuze and Guattari, *Mille Plateaux*, 32. Translation mine.

45. Ibid., 16.

46. See Stivale, "Literary Element," 21.

47. An apt expression I borrow from Davies, "Dark Inner Landscapes," 36–44.

48. Deleuze and Guattari, *Mille Plateaux*, 29: "avec ses Indiens sans ascendance, sa limite toujours fuyante, ses frontières mouvantes et déplacées."

49. Nye, *Unembarrassed Muse*, 205.

50. Denning, in *Mechanics Accents*, argues that such popular fiction carried encoded messages to working-class youth, empowering them in the face of a dominant culture. See also Smith, ed., *Popular Culture and Industrialism*, 420.

51. Conroy, "The Kimberly Toughs," *WK*, 143.

52. Conroy, "Down in Happy Hollow," *WK*, 158.

53. Garland, *Son of the Middle Border*, 114.

54. Conroy, interview, November 1984.

55. Garland, *Son of the Middle Border*, 112–13.

56. Conroy, "The Morphadite," *WK*, 118.

57. Ibid., 120. The emphasis on memory, "the repository of the cultural tradition in oral society," Jack Goody points out, engrains knowledge deeper than mere writing. Goody and Watt, "Consequences of Literacy," 50.

58. Kreuter, *American Dissenter*, 5.

59. Donaldson, "Rhetoric of a Small Midwestern Town."

60. Ibid., 449.

61. *UMWJ*, 25 December 1902, 1.

62. Ibid. Kelliher eventually left mining, worked briefly for the Moberly newspaper, and wrote detective novels in Kansas City. Conroy, interview, 28 February 1986.

63. *UMWJ*, 26 February 1903, 8.

64. The French novelist and poet Raymond Queneau termed such a literary reconstitution of orality "le parlé-écrit," as distinct from mere transcription.

65. *UMWJ*, 12 September 1901, 8.

66. Ibid., 6 September 1900, 3.

67. Ibid., 21 March 1901, 7.

68. Quoted by Goody and Watt, "Consequences of Literacy," 29.

69. Zumthor, "L'écriture et la voix," 239: "dans le vacuité de leur Nouveau Monde, ils maintenaient—ils maintinrent, aussi longtemps qu'il fut socialement et techniquement possible—le souffle de cette voix, cette parole vive, présence et chaleur. . . . C'est dont témoigne, à sa manière et dans son secteur, la littérature de cordel. La voix qui l'engendra, et à qui elle fait, aujourd'hui encore, à toute occasion retour, constituait le lieu fondateur de la conscience du groupe."

70. Guthrie, "Ear Players," 32–43. Spiller et al., in *Literary History*, note the rich "ministrelsy" of mining camps (713).

71. Aronowitz, *False Promises*, 60f.

72. Ibid., 70.

73. Conroy, "The Morphadite," *WK*, 115.

74. *McGuffey New Fourth Reader*, in Lindberg, *Annotated McGuffey*, 160.

75. Conroy, interviews, 28 May 1983, 27 December 1987.

76. Such popular fiction turns up in Joyce and Flaubert. In *Ulysses*, Molly

Bloom reads herself to sleep with *Ruby: The Pride of the Ring.* Joyce made use of genteel popular fiction, in matters of form and intertextuality. Hugh Kenner, "Aspects of Modernism," lecture, Humanities Research Center, University of Texas–Austin, 26 February 1991. Paul DeKock's novels diverted Emma Bovary.

77. On genteel fiction in nineteenth-century American literature, see Radway, *Reading the Romance;* Cowie, *The Rise of the American Novel,* chap. 10; Papashvily, *All the Happy Endings;* Baym, *Women's Fiction.*

78. Conroy, "The Fields of Golden Glow," *WK,* 78.

79. Conroy, "Charley Was Our Darlin'," *WK,* 89.

80. Conroy, "The Fields of Golden Glow," *WK,* 85.

81. Conroy, interview, 20 November 1987.

82. Conroy, interview, 4 June 1986; Harvey Harrison, interview, 27 November 1986.

83. Conroy, interview, 23 May 1984.

84. Conroy, "The Morphadite," *WK,* 125.

85. Conroy, *The Disinherited,* 84.

86. Ibid., 84–85.

87. Hoggart, *Uses of Literacy,* 38. Dahlberg's portrayal of his mother avoids this tendency because Lizzie's life is so utterly unconventional by most standards of working-class families. Michael Gold's attitude is reverential but realistic. At times generous, at other times prejudicial, his mother "hobbled about all day," Gold writes in *Jews without Money,* "in bare feet, cursing in Elizabethan Yiddish, using the forbidden words 'ladies' do not use, smacking us, beating us, fighting with her neighbors, helping her neighbors, busy from morn to midnight in the tenement struggle for life" (158).

88. Conroy, interview, 5 September 1986.

89. Vincent underscores the importance of literacy as a key to personal and class emancipation. *Bread, Knowledge and Freedom,* 167.

90. Conroy, interview, 31 March 1986. Jack was also in attendance when several years later Bryan spoke in Moberly's Tannehill Park on the "Making of a Man." *Moberly Monitor-Index,* 25 August 1912.

91. Conroy, interview, 21 April 1984. Laslett notes the attraction of organized miners to Debsian socialism. "The *United Mine Workers' Journal* expressed a strong interest in Debs' transition from Populism to socialism, and his declaration for socialism in the *Railway Times* of January 1, 1897, aroused so much interest that the editor felt obliged to reproduce it in full." *Labor and the Left,* 202.

92. Conroy, interview, 29 November 1980.

93. See Shore, *Talkin' Socialism,* 5. Also, see J. Graham, ed., *"Yours for the Revolution."*

94. Baratz, *Union and the Coal Industry,* 138.

95. Conroy, interview, 21 July 1985.

96. Conroy, "On *Anvil,*" 114; Margaret Conroy Wisdom, interview, 7 September 1986.

97. Margaret Conroy Wisdom, interview, 7 September 1986.

98. Conroy, interviews, 16 August, 5 September 1986; 20 November, 27 December 1987.
99. Conroy, interview, 31 October 1979.
100. Conroy, *The Disinherited*, 69; interview, 4 June 1986.
101. Conroy, *The Disinherited*, 77.
102. Gorki, *My Childhood*, 15.

Chapter 3
The Wabash Shops

1. My secondary sources here include Stokes, *Company Shops*; Reinhardt, *Workin' On the Railroad*; Licht, *Working for the Railroad*; Stover, *American Railroads*; Kirkman, *Science of Railways*.
2. Waller, *History of Randolph County, Missouri*, 169–72.
3. There was a rumor that Moberly had beat out its competitor, Montgomery City, for the Wabash machine shops by spiking its source of water when it was learned that a fresh source was an important consideration in the choice of site. "All in the Spirit of Fun, No Doubt," 312–13.
4. Conroy, interview, 4 June 1986.
5. Vincent, *Bread, Knowledge and Freedom*, 67.
6. Sherwood Anderson's Clyde, Ohio, was a railroad division point.
7. See Rorabaugh, *Craft Apprentice*.
8. Licht, *Working for the Railroad*, 18.
9. Conroy, interviews, 31 March, 4 June 1986; letter to author, 10 April 1986.
10. Conroy, "Greedy-Gut Gus, the Car Toad," *WK*, 71–72.
11. Conroy, interview, 31 March 1986.
12. Benjamin, "The Storyteller," 85.
13. For a description of ranking and work in the Wabash shops see Conroy's "Freight Car Repair Yard Pranks," *WK*, 67–69.
14. Conroy, interview, 9 September 1984.
15. Licht, *Working for the Railroad*, 106.
16. Conroy, "Kimberly Toughs," *WK*, 150.
17. Margaret Wisdom Conroy interview, 7 September 1986.
18. Conroy, letter to author, 16 August 1986.
19. For instance, Whit Burnett, editor of *Story* magazine.
20. Both Gorki and Conroy submitted their first publications while employed as railroad shopmen.
21. Foner, *Jack London*, 24.
22. Also, see Gutman, "Reality of the Rags-to-Riches 'Myth,'" 211–33.
23. Conroy interviews, 24 May 1982; 29 January 1985.
24. *Railway Carmen's Journal* 18 (December 1913): 736.
25. Caroline Elsea Werkley, interview, 22 November 1979. Also, see Werkley, *Mister Carnegie's Library*.
26. Nexö made a deep impression upon other working-class writers such as Michael Gold, who wrote: "I had always wanted to meet the great Andersen

Nexö, whose book had such a deep influence on my youth." Folsom, ed., *Mike Gold: A Literary Anthology*, 236.

27. London, *People of the Abyss*, 15.

28. London said: ". . . the hard hand of the world was laid upon me. It has never relaxed. It has left me sentimental, but destroyed sentimentalism." Foner, *Jack London*, 39.

29. In *People of the Abyss*, London measured life by a simple standard: "That which made for more life, for physical and spiritual health, was good; that which made for less life, which hurt, and dwarfed, and distorted life, was bad." Preface, 9.

30. Gorki, *My Universities*, 17.

31. Conroy, interviews, 24 May 1982; 4 June 1986.

32. Conroy recalled these memories for the *American School News* 1 (Summer 1949): 2; this was a publication of the same correspondence school that had sent him his lessons thirty years earlier.

33. Conroy, interview, 4 June 1986.

34. See Howe on this point. *Thomas Hardy*, 134–35.

35. *Railway Carmen's Journal* 19 (July 1914): 416–18.

36. Ibid. 18 (September 1913): 554–55.

37. *Semi-Weekly Monitor*, 29 September 1916, 1.

38. Conroy, interview, 9 September 1984.

39. See Aronowitz, *Working Class Hero*, on the fraternal character of early craft unions (32). Also, Brody, *Workers in Industrial America*.

40. Andrew Dawson writes: "The collectivist response on the part of the skilled workers, regardless of its particular weaknesses, posed a striking alternative to the social outlook of individualism: improvement for the skilled worker was to come not via solitary progress but through united action, through social rather than atomistic self-help." "Parameters of Craft Consciousness," 135–55.

41. See Ducker, *Men of the Steel Rails*, 126ff.

42. Alt, "Beyond Class," 58.

43. Cottrell, *Technological Change and Labor*, 41.

44. See, for instance, Ameringer, "Why Workers Go to War," 420–21. Ameringer, Eugene Debs, Scott Nearing, and other socialists contributed articles to the *Railway Carmen's Journal*.

45. Painter, *Through Fifty Years*, 155. Also, Ferris, *Moberly Libraries*. Ferris shows that a direct line can be traced from the early efforts on the part of Wabash employees for "self-improvement" to the founding of Moberly's Free Public Library where Jack spent so many hours.

46. See Dawson, "Parameters of Craft Consciousness," 135–55, for a discussion of bourgeois individualism and craft consciousness.

47. The labor leader Samuel Gompers apparently never resolved the conflict between artisan and bourgeois culture. Gompers's roots "lay in the artisan work culture, someone who remembered and engaged in the camaraderie of the workplace and the sociability of the inn. Yet, at the same time, Gompers identified with Victorian bourgeois culture; he wanted to be disciplined, sober, and respectable. . . ." Cotkin, "Caught in Cultures," 41.

48. Cottrell, *Technological Change*, 125.

49. Soon after Jack apprenticed in the Wabash shops, the BRCA succeeded in negotiating with the railroads a minimum age of sixteen. *Railway Carmen's Journal* 18 (June 1913): 374.

50. Conroy, interview, 5 June 1986.

51. Painter, *Through Fifty Years*, 150.

52. Stover, *American Railroads*, 184.

53. Conroy, interview, 5 June 1986.

54. Ibid.

55. Lottie Bly, interview, 1 April 1986.

56. Conroy, interview, 31 March 1986.

57. Such experiences apparently figured importantly among certain Missouri artists and writers of Jack's generation. Thomas Hart Benton once told Conroy that, as a boy, he purposefully would pass by saloons in Neosho. The half-doors permitted him to peer between or under to glimpse nudes painted on the wall behind the bar. Such forbidden games, Benton said, gave him inspiration to learn to paint. Conroy, interview, 26 December 1983.

58. Ferris, *Moberly Libraries*, 13.

59. Lowe, "Theatre as Moberly Has Known It," 240–43.

60. Jack was made a deacon, he said, because he "contributed $25 to a new organ for the church." Conroy, interview, 26 November 1982.

61. Conroy, *The Disinherited*, 77.

62. Merlin Bowen, letter to author, 20 July 1981.

63. E. Thompson, *The Making of the English Working Class*, 58.

64. Ibid., 59.

65. Degh, *Folktales and Society*, 73.

66. Conroy, interview, 19 July 1986.

67. Stover, *American Railroads*, 179.

68. Ibid., 182.

69. Montgomery, "'New Unionism,'" 514.

70. Ibid., 516.

71. Stover, *American Railroads*, 182–93.

72. Gary M. Fink writes: "The failure of wages to keep pace with the constant pressure of inflation produced one of the greatest periods of class consciousness and militancy in the twentieth-century history of the Missouri labor movement. The number of strikes in Missouri increased sharply in 1916, and militant strike activity continued for several years." *Labor's Search*, 62.

73. Braverman, *Labor and Monopoly Capital*, 27.

74. London, *War of the Classes*, 9.

75. Conroy, interview, 17 October 1984.

76. Conroy and Harvey Harrison, interview, 27 November 1986.

77. Conroy, *The Disinherited*, 155–56.

78. Lea, *Political Culture*, 6.

79. Conroy, interview, 19 July 1986.

80. Margaret Conroy Wisdom, interview, 7 September 1986.

81. Conroy, interview, 4 June 1986.

82. *Railway Carmen's Journal* 22 (April 1917): 195–98.

83. Fink, *Labor's Search*, 61.

84. Kennedy, *Over Here*, 70.

85. Editorial, *Railway Carmen's Journal* 19 (September 1914): 544.

86. *Railway Carmen's Journal* 23 (October 1918).

87. Ibid. 22 (April 1917): 196.

88. Ibid., 197.

89. O'Neil, *Echoes of Revolt*, 53–54; Coser, *Men of Ideas*, 127.

90. See Freeman, *American Testament*, 108f. Similar instances of intolerance led Roger Baldwin to found the American Civil Liberties Union.

91. In Mount Olive, Missouri, a mob led by prominent businessmen forced a merchant named Hein to kneel on an ice-covered street and kiss the flag forty-eight times because of alleged disloyal remarks. P. Murphy, *World War I*, 129. Also, see the *Moberly Weekly Monitor*, 8 May 1918, 1.

92. Kennedy, "Vietnam and World War I," 3.

93. On Moberly's patriotic fervor, see *Moberly Semi-Weekly Monitor*, 15 April 1917, 1.

94. Guest, "A Patriot," 141.

95. Conroy, interview, 4 June 1986. Jack's memories of intolerance and violence are corroborated by Fite and Peterson in *Opponents of War*.

96. Thomas Hickey, letter to Conroy, 27 November 1931.

97. Conroy, *The Disinherited*, 113.

98. Fink, *Labor's Search*, 71–81.

99. Montgomery, "'New Unionism,'" 516.

100. Stover, *American Railroads*, 193–97.

101. *Moberly Monitor-Index*, 5 August 1920, 9.

102. Ed Falkowski, letter to Conroy, 25 November 1977. John W. Gunn, one of Haldeman-Julius's editors, wrote "The Pocket Series with Its 500 Titles Is the Beginning of an American Culture," in *Life and Letters* (January 1924): 8.

103. Thompson, "A Vag in College," 22.

104. Conroy, interviews, 24 November 1984; 4 June 1986; 26 July 1987. Eugene Debs wrote that a youngster from a poor family who goes to college feels like a beggar. *Railway Carmen's Journal* 20 (November 1915): 722.

105. Conroy, interviews, 30 October 1982; 31 March 1986.

106. Conroy, interviews, 24 November 1984; 31 March, 4 June 1986; Agnes Kelly Hickman, interview, 31 August 1986.

107. Conroy, interview, 19 July 1986.

108. Conroy, interview, 31 March 1986.

109. Perlman and Taft, *History of Labor*, vol. 3, 515.

110. Ibid., 517–18.

111. Conroy, interview, 4 June 1986.

Chapter 4
The Great Railroad Strike of 1922

1. Thomas Hickey, letter to Conroy, 27 November 1931.

2. Dubofsky, *Industrialism and the American Worker*, 104.

3. Ibid., 132.

4. Ibid., 134.

5. Potter, *People of Plenty*.

6. Haessler, "Peace Reigns at Herrin," 13.

7. Minor, "We Want a Labor Party," 7.

8. Roy, *History of the Coal Miners*, 321.

9. Conroy, *The Disinherited*, 121.

10. Dubofsky, *Industrialism and the American Worker*, 131f.

11. J. Green, *World of the Worker*, 99.

12. *Railway Carmen's Journal* 26 (March 1921): 144; ibid. 26 (June 1921): 358–59.

13. Painter, *Through Fifty Years*, 164.

14. Conroy, "Mammon's Marionettes," *Railway Carmen's Journal* 27 (June 1922): 376.

15. Conroy, interview, 1 September 1985.

16. *Moberly Weekly Monitor*, 6 July 1922, 1.

17. Montgomery, "The 'New Unionism,'" 509–29.

18. My thanks to Orville Sittler, Moberly, Missouri, for these details. A reporter for the *Moberly Monitor-Index*, Sittler was a perceptive observer of Moberly life.

19. Conroy, interviews, 12 April, 23 December, 24 December 1982; 21 May, 24 November 1983; 9 September 1984; 1 September 1985; 28 February, 31 March, 4 June, 6 June 1986.

20. *Moberly Weekly Monitor*, 13 July 1922, 4.

21. Conroy and other shopmen tried to get farmers to join the strikers, but the farmers would not cooperate. They were experiencing hard times and some went to work in the shops. "The whole strike was a fiasco," Conroy said years later. Interview, 9 September 1984.

22. Judge J. Carr, interview, 6 June 1986.

23. Interview, Judge Richard J. Chamier, 25 December 1980.

24. Governor Hyde supported open shops the following year. His actions during the 1922 strike revealed his disposition to side with business against labor. Fink, *Labor's Search*, 103–4.

25. *Moberly Weekly Monitor*, 27 July 1922, 2.

26. Conroy, interview, 28 February 1986.

27. *Moberly Weekly Monitor*, 27 July 1922, 4.

28. Ibid.

29. Conroy, interview, 6 June 1986.

30. Conroy, letter to author, 10 April 1986; interviews, 23 December 1982; 21 May 1983; 31 March 1986.

31. Conroy, interview, 9 September 1984. The Uncle Ollie stories are included in Conroy's *The Weed King and Other Stories*.

32. Conroy, interview, 4 June 1986.

33. *Moberly Weekly Monitor*, 12 January 1922, 1.

34. Painter, *Through Fifty Years*, 169.

35. Perlman and Taft, *History of Labor*, 4:522.

36. *Moberly Weekly Monitor*, 23 November 1922, 1.

37. Ibid.

38. Ibid., 30 November 1922, 1.

39. Ibid., 7.

40. On this point see J. Green, *The World*, 33.

41. *Moberly Monitor-Index*, 5 December 1922, 2.

42. See Morray, *Project Kuzbas*. Also, "Eastward Ho!" 13.

43. *The Disinherited*, 127.

44. Conroy, "That Skinner Bottoms Winter," *WK*, 151.

45. Orville Sittler, interview, 6 June 1986. Margaret Wisdom Conroy recalled people's anger, even with the Methodist church. Interview, 7 September 1986. Also, see Conroy, interview, 1 September 1985.

46. *Moberly Weekly Monitor*, 7 December 1922, 2.

47. See Slichter, "Labor Politics," 398–404; 431–35; also, J. Green, *The World*, 101: "The defeat of the militant railroad shopmen's strike in 1922 wiped out the last vestiges of the 'new unionism.'" Also, see Davis, "Bitter Conflict."

48. Thelen, *Paths of Resistance*, 173.

49. Dubofsky, *Industrialism and the American Worker*, 134.

50. Aronowitz notes the importance of status among skilled artisans (such as the car repairmen in the Wabash shops). "In the artisanal mode, leadership in the labor process accrues to those who possess status according to their skills. . . . The craftsmen who organized unions in the early stages of capitalism were well aware of their status at the workplace." *Working Class Hero*, 12.

51. *Moberly Weekly Monitor*, 27 July 1922, 5.

52. Conroy, "Paving Gang," *WK*, 266.

53. Conroy, interview, 31 March 1986.

54. F. Vernon Lamson, interview, 7 June 1981.

55. Conroy, interview, 23 May 1984.

56. Conroy, interview, 5 October 1982.

57. Published in Banks, ed., *First-Person America*.

58. Brophy describes these new proletarians in *John Brophy*: "Nobody knows how many ex-coal miners have gone to steel, auto, rubber and other industries all through the Northeast and Midwest, but they must number hundreds of thousands. I know I was constantly meeting ex-coal miners who had taken the lead in organizing the new industries during the CIO drives of the thirties. But in the early twenties, there was nothing as hopeful as the CIO in the non-union towns, only desperation in the face of grinding poverty, and burning rage against the iron rule of the operators" (178).

Chapter 5
My Universities

1. See, for example, Casey, "The Road Kid." Also, Brevda, *Harry Kemp*, and Fox, *Tales of an American Hobo*, based upon the author's experiences in the 1920s and 1930s. For Fox, hoboing was simply a way of life without political or social motivation.

2. See Kemp, *More Miles*. A number of Jim Tully's hobo tales appeared in the *American Mercury* during the 1920s.

3. Lynn, *Adventures of a Woman Hobo*.

4. See also Hamsum's *Vagabonds*; Forster, "Despised and Rejected of Men," 671–72.

5. See N. Anderson, *The Hobo*. First published in 1923, Anderson's work is an early resource on the homeless worker. See also Foster's graphic portrayals of tramping in *Pages from a Worker's Life*, 117–24.

6. Jack was very proud of his Wobbly credentials. He admired the work of Wobbly poets, Arturo Giovannitti—especially his *Arrows in the Gale*—Covington Hall, and Ralph Chaplin, later turning to them as models for the Rebel Poet organization.

7. See Callahan, *Carl Sandburg*, 35–36.

8. Conroy published in the *Anvil* a number of Wobblies who had tramped in the 1920s.

9. Polanyi, *Great Transformation*, 163.

10. Ibid., 157.

11. Gutman, *Work, Culture and Society*, 15.

12. Lloyd E. Anderson, letter to author, 7 October 1986. Dick Jackson of the Pittsburgh–Des Moines Corporation graciously put me in contact with Anderson, who had worked as a supervisor in the P-DM steel mill in the 1920s.

13. Conroy, "Bridge Plant Initiation Ceremonial," MS (industrial folklore project), Illinois Writers' Project, 1939.

14. Conroy, *The Disinherited*, 133.

15. These experiences are told in Conroy's "Bun Grady," WK, 182–96.

16. Gladys Conroy, letter to Florence Hardy, 12 November 1924.

17. Leuchtenburg, *Perils of Prosperity*.

18. Ibid.; also, see Nye, *Midwestern Progressive Politics*, 310–11.

19. Hesseltine, *Third-Party Movements*, 174–80.

20. Weil, *Need for Roots*, 45.

21. R. Nash, *Nervous Generation*, 65–67. Also see Bernstein, *Lean Years*.

22. R. Nash, *Nervous Generation*, 66; Hesseltine, *Third-Party Movements*, 177–80.

23. Curti, *Growth of American Thought*, 678.

24. Conroy, *The Disinherited*, 209.

25. Galbraith, *Great Crash of 1929*, 155.

26. Curti, *Growth of American Thought*, 692.

27. Ibid., 674.

28. See, for example, F. Lewis, *Only Yesterday*. Nash criticizes the myths of the 1920s but ignores working-class experience altogether, for instance, in discussing Henry Ford. *Nervous Generation*, chap. 5

29. Quoted in Nye, *Midwestern Progressive Politics*, 296.

30. Conroy, *The Disinherited*, 180.

31. Conroy, "Bridge Plant Initiation."

32. Conroy, interview, 5 September 1986.

33. Berger et al., *Homeless Mind*, 12.

34. Ibid., 29.
35. Ibid., 32.
36. Ibid., 34.
37. Conroy, interview, 5 June 1986.
38. Bontemps and Conroy, *Anyplace But Here*, 345; Conroy, interview, 6 June 1986.
39. Bontemps and Conroy, *They Seek a City*, 252.
40. Conroy, interview, 23 July 1982.
41. Conroy, letter to author, 21 August 1986; also, interview, 5 September 1986.
42. Conroy, "Journey's End," in *The Jack Conroy Reader*, 4. Hereafter cited as *JCR*.
43. Gold, "Notes of the Month," 5.
44. See, for example, Ashleigh, *Rambling Kid*. Ashleigh, an Englishman, followed the grain harvests in the American west as a Wobbly.
45. Joseph Kalar, letter to Covington Hall, 18 December 1928.
46. See Carter, *Twenties in America*, 11ff., for a discussion of the "other twenties," which, while useful, ignores the traditions of literary radicalism in the 1920s.
47. Nash, *Nervous Generation*, 27.
48. Singleton, *H. L. Mencken*, 73–74. William Edge's *The Main Stem* is dedicated to "H.L.M.," "without whom these experiences had never been set down."
49. See Singleton, *H. L. Mencken*, 144, 152.
50. Caldwell, "School of Prostitution," 174.
51. Gramsci, "American and Fordism," 302.
52. Wilson, "Detroit Motors," 214–48. Gramsci makes the same observation in "Americanism and Fordism."
53. Conroy, "Bull Market," *WK*, 221.
54. The French novelist Céline, who worked as a physician in a Detroit auto factory, left a memorable description of assembly-line work in *Voyage au Bout de la Nuit*.
55. James Steele (a.k.a. Robert Cruden), *Conveyor*, 51.
56. Conroy, interview, 16 October 1986. Also, Robert Cruden, interview, 7 November 1987.
57. See Conroy's description of the subproletariat in *The Disinherited*, 187–89.
58. Dawley and Faler, "Working-class Culture," 61–75.
59. Potter, *People of Plenty*. Also, Leuchtenberg, *Perils of Prosperity*, chap. 10.
60. Paraphrase of Lynds by Brody, *Workers in Industrial America*, 64.
61. Ibid., 65.
62. Also, see Rodgers on the new consumption ethic, in *Work Ethic in Industrial America*, 121–24.
63. Zaretsky, *Family and Personal Life*, 107. Also, see Rodgers, *Work Ethic in Industrial America*.
64. Chinoy, in *Automobile Workers and the American Dream*, suggests that the aspirations of blue-collar workers were low because they lacked knowledge of occupational alternatives.

65. Jack described the incident much later in "Happy Birthday to You," *Esquire* (January 1937).

66. Conroy, interviews, 16 October 1986; 13 March 1987. About the ride back to Moberly, Jack said to me, echoing Tennessee Williams's Blanche Dubois, "I've always depended upon the generosity of strangers."

67. Gene DeGruson, curator of the Haldeman-Julius archives, Pittsburg State University, Pittsburg, Kansas, graciously permitted me access to Haldeman-Julius materials.

68. See J. Graham, ed., *"Yours for the Revolution."*

69. Herder, "Little Blue Books," 38.

70. Johnson and Tanselle, "Haldeman-Julius 'Little Blue Books,'" 41.

71. Herder, "Little Blue Books," 40.

72. *Baltimore Sun,* 22 February 1923.

73. J. Gunn, *E. Haldeman-Julius.*

74. Editorial, *Minnesota Daily Star,* 9 April 1923.

75. Quoted by Herder, "Little Blue Books," 35.

76. Adamic, "Voltaire from Kansas," 283–85, 314–16.

77. Conroy, letter to editors, *Outlook and Independent* 155 (27 August 1930): 679.

78. Wendell Johnson's book inscribed to Haldeman-Julius is in the Haldeman-Julius archive at Pittsburg State University.

79. Conroy, "For Men Must Work," *JCR,* 84.

80. Conroy, interview, 6 September 1986.

81. Conroy, "For Men Must Work," *JCR,* 81.

82. Harvey Harrison, interview, 27 November 1986.

83. Wabash shop foremen were not called out in the 1922 strike. See Painter, *Through Fifty Years,* 164.

84. Conroy, interview, 5 June 1986.

85. Conroy, interview, 27 November 1986.

86. Werkley, *Mister Carnegie's Lib'ary,* 71.

Chapter 6
Early Literary Contacts

1. See Hoffman et al., *The Little Magazine,* chap. 9.

2. See Peck, "Salvaging the Art and Literature," 128–41; also, Peck, "'Tradition of American Revolutionary Literature,'" 390–91; and Hoffman et al., 151–52.

3. Robert was the inspiration for "Hearne" of *The Disinherited.*

4. Conroy, letter to Tydings, 20 August 1926.

5. Conroy's closeness to Margaret Jean endured until her untimely death from cancer in 1975. Conroy, interview, 5 September 1986.

6. Conroy, letter to Labadie, 19 March 1924. Courtesy of the Labadie Collection, University of Michigan Library.

7. Conroy's first novel is the story of a worker-intellectual's search for an

authentic voice, pulled between bookish, self-conscious word-intoxication and the vernacular speech of a workers' world.

8. Calverton, "American Literary Radicals," 254.

9. Ibid., 254–55. Italics in the original.

10. Ibid., 256.

11. For examples of popular working-class poetry in the nineteenth century that bear close resemblance to Conroy's early verse, see James, *Fiction for the Working Man*, Appendix 1. Years later Jack referred to his early poetic efforts as "fancy dithyrambs now mercifully forgotten." "Literary Underworld," *JCR*, 154.

12. Kalar, letter to Conroy, 21 December 1928.

13. Conroy, "Broken Moon," 24. Courtesy of Cleveland Public Library, which possesses an incomplete run.

14. Conroy, "Literary Underworld," *JCR*, 152–54. The revolt against genteel standards in literature and morality has received a great deal of attention among critics, most notably Malcolm Cowley and Maxwell Geismar, pointing out H. L. Mencken's role in overturning standards. Sinclair Lewis attacked the genteel tradition in his 1930 Nobel Prize acceptance speech, citing the rebellion of Dreiser, Mencken, Anderson, and others, and naming more recent rebels, among them Mike Gold. Similarly, worker-writers divested their writing of genteel influences in order to evolve a language fitting their experience. As I argue later, Mencken's *American Mercury* and John T. Frederick's *Midland* played an important role in this regard.

15. See, for example, "Little Libbie," in Conroy's *Midland Humor*.

16. Conroy, "Tragedy," 111. The "she" must surely refer to the poetic muse, since there is no hope for *this* poem.

17. Weiss, "Give Us Poems for Workers," 22. See also Weiss, "Poetry and Revolution," 9.

18. H. H. Lewis, "Indigenous—Yet Thinking of Russia," in *Thinking of Russia*, 12. Self-taught and widely read, Lewis turned literary burlesque to radical purposes.

19. See, for instance, *Pegasus* 22 (May 1929): 41.

20. Conroy, letter to Labadie, 31 December 1926. Courtesy of the Labadie Collection, University of Michigan Library.

21. Conroy, letter to Labadie, 18 January 1927. Courtesy of the Labadie Collection, University of Michigan Library. Also, see Conroy, "H. H. Lewis: Plowboy Poet," 204.

22. Conroy, "Literary Underworld," *JCR*, 155.

23. Hagglund's description of Whitaker in *Northern Light* 1 (October 1927): 126.

24. Hagglund, "Rhythm—the Basis of All Poetry," 63.

25. *Pegasus* 16 (November 1927): 64.

26. Conroy, "The Great Spectra Hoax," 10–11.

27. Kalar, letter to Cheyney, 6 January 1928.

28. Conroy, "Rubber Heel Plant Initiation Ceremonial." Courtesy of the State Historical Library, Springfield, Illinois.

29. McGuire, "Legacy of Clarence Earl Gideon." Jack and Clarence Gideon worked in the rubber-heel plant at the same time but apparently did not know one another.

30. McGuire, "Legacy of Clarence Earl Gideon," 7.

31. Conroy, *The Disinherited*, 171.

32. Conroy, interview, 26 July 1987.

33. *Hannibal Courier-Post*, 9 September 1926, 1. Also, see Pete Daniel, *Deep'n as It Come*. A flood on the river the following year was the inspiration for Faulkner's "The Old Man."

34. Conroy, "To Eugene Victor Debs."

35. Conroy, interview, 6 May 1985.

36. *Hannibal Courier-Post*, 14 March 1927, 1.

37. Curiously, Jack London also applied for a post-office appointment—and turned it down after successfully passing an examination. Foner, *Jack London*, 37.

38. Kalar, letter to Warren Huddlestone, 17 January 1925.

39. See Kalar, letters to Conroy, 7 December, 21 December 1928. Also Gold, "Poverty Is a Trap," 18–19; Gold, Editorial, *New Masses* (hereafter abbreviated *NM*) 4 (July 1928): 2; Dos Passos, "The *New Masses* I'd Like," 20; Daniel Aaron, *Writers on the Left*, 210–11; David Peck, "The Development," chap. 3.

40. Conroy, "Rubber Heels," *WK*, 209.

41. Conroy, letter to Labadie, 6 October 1927.

42. The New Magazine Section, *Daily Worker* (27 August 1927): 1.

43. See Joughin and Morgan, *Legacy of Sacco and Vanzetti*.

44. Conroy, "The Quick and the Dead," 1.

45. George Milburn found Haldeman-Julius's publications a poor substitute for earlier socialist publications like the *Appeal to Reason*. Old-timers—those who had been part of the Appeal army—"snorted" at Haldeman-Julius's promise to provide "a literary feast for real culture-seekers who want to know the truths of science, philosophy and history and want to establish weekly contact with the vast beauties of literature and art." Milburn, "The *Appeal to Reason*," 371.

46. See F. Howe, "Where Are the Pre-War Radicals," 33–34. Howe argues that the prewar radicals are digging turnips and intellectualizing. Evangelists, on the other hand, who seek to change people, not institutions, are thriving.

47. In Haldeman-Julius publications, there appeared, among others, realistic sketches by Erskine Caldwell ("The Georgia Cracker)"; James T. Farrell ("The Filling Station Racket in Chicago)"; W. D. Trowbridge ("The Lower End of Main Street, a Realistic Picture of Life in an Average Small Town)"; Harold Preece ("Ardmore, Godly and Gauche)"; Albert Halper ("Chicago Mail Clerks)"; Gerald V. Morris ("On the Skidroad, What One Sees on Los Angeles' Street of Forsaken Men)"; O. W. Cooley ("The Damned Outfit, a Pair of Apple Pickers Fall Into a Haywire Dump").

48. David Webb, letter to Kalar, 3 December 1927.

49. *Spider* 1 (March 1928): 1.

50. Ibid. 1 (June 1928): 2.

51. Conroy, letter to Labadie, 20 April 1928.

52. Conroy, "Jo Labadie, Craftsman and Poet," 159–60.

Chapter 7
The Crucible of Experience

1. Conroy, interview, 5 September 1986.

2. Conroy, interview, 21 June 1987.

3. Aaron's comment, that Conroy's "principal reason for going to Detroit and Toledo was to gather material on automobile workers," confuses two separate periods in Jack's life. In 1928, Jack moved to Toledo to find work. Aaron probably had in mind the period of the Guggenheim grant, 1935 and 1936, when Jack made trips to Detroit and elsewhere to study migrant workers in auto factories. See Aaron, Introduction, *The Disinherited*, x.

4. Conroy, "The Atheist," 45.

5. Conroy, "Jackson Street: Toledo," 17.

6. "Tol. VF-Industries—Willys Overland Motors, Inc.," unpubl. MS. Courtesy of Toledo Historical Society archives.

7. London, *War of the Classes*, 67–68.

8. Braverman, "Work and Unemployment," 21.

9. The role of kinship and communal network in black migration from southern states is treated by Trotter, *The Great Migration*.

10. Miners from the British Isles appear to be an exception. See chap. 1.

11. Conroy, interview, 16 October 1986.

12. For an overview of the disproportionate conditions during the "age of affluence" separating workers and the affluent, see Stricker, "Affluence for Whom?" Milton writes: "The myth of the prosperous twenties, still perpetuated a half-century later by President Reagan, was not shared by the workers at the bottom of the economic ladder." *Politics of U.S. Labor*, 21–22.

13. This point is made in Gordon, Evans, and Reich, eds., *Segmented Work*, 144.

14. Conroy, interview, 26 November 1986.

15. Don Shinew, interview, 27 October 1979.

16. Bettye Zacharias Hawley, interview, 4 May 1991. One of thirteen children, Bettye Hawley was forced to leave home in the early Depression; she cleaned houses to earn enough to pay $50 for a ride to California, where she worked as a waitress, eventually owning a restaurant that served Groucho Marx and other film notables. She knew Jack only as a child, yet years later she recalled Conroy's kindness and love of play.

17. Conroy, interview, 23 November 1979.

18. Shinew, interview, 27 October 1979. Some two weeks before Don Shinew and I planned to visit the house on Byrne Road where the Conroys had lived, it had been removed, leaving a gaping hole, symbolic somehow of the effacement of individual workers' lives from history.

19. Jack recalled Don Shinew, who was then a boy, always drawing. Shinew later became an artist for the *Toledo Blade*.

20. Shinew, interview, 27 October 1979.

21. Conroy, interview, 5 September 1986.

22. Conroy, "Prosperity—Where Is It?" 4.

23. Conroy, interview, 21 June 1987.

24. Conroy, interview, 16 October 1986.

25. Conroy, "Hard Winter," *WK*, 231.

26. Conroy, interview, 16 October 1986.

27. Conroy, "Dusky Answer," 67.

28. Quoted by Cassirer, *Essay on Man*, 180–81.

29. Peck, "'The Tradition,'" 388.

30. See, for example, Kalar, letter to Huddlestone, 6 January 1925, in which Kalar cites his literary models.

31. Gold, "American Famine," 10.

32. Ibid., 11.

33. One might note a contrast with David Copperfield, who works in a bottling factory, yet harbors genteel expectations and feels unsympathetic with his work companions.

34. Kalar, letter to Conroy, 7 December 1928.

35. Kalar, letter to Covington Hall, 18 December 1928.

36. Using the term *coupure ethnologique*, Rancière writes: "Pour que la protestation des ateliers ait une voix . . . il faut que ses gens-là se soient déjà faits autres, dans la double et irrémédiable exclusion de vivre comme les ouvriers et de parler comme les bourgeois." *La Nuit des Prolétaires*, 9.

37. Rancière, *La Nuit*; see also his "Myth of the Artisan."

38. Musser, "Another Milestone," n.p.

39. Van Doren, review of *America Arraigned!* 409.

40. Gold, "May Days and Revolutionary Art," review of *May Days*, 161.

41. Kalar, letter to Conroy, 7 December 1928.

42. Conroy, "Cornwall: A Memory," 16.

43. Kalar, letter to Conroy, 7 December 1928.

44. In addition, other anthologies, lacking any explicit purpose of protest, influenced the new generation of rebel poets, for instance, Brooks et al., eds., *American Caravan*, which included Mike Gold, Stanley Burnshaw, Isidor Schneider, and Nathan Asch alongside Gertrude Stein and Ernest Hemingway.

45. See Gilbert, *Writers and Partisans*, 25.

46. Fishbein, *Rebels in Bohemia*, 18, 63–64.

47. Conroy, interview, 13 March 1987.

48. Cheyney, "The IWW," 150–51.

49. Trent, "Factory Town," *Children of Fire*, 77.

50. Conroy, letter to Verne Bright, 5 October 1928.

51. Kenneth Porter, letter to author, 30 January 1981.

52. In addition to being a poet, Porter was a precocious scholar in his field, business history. Harvard University Press published his two-volume biography of John Jacob Astor, in 1931, five years before he received his Ph.D.

53. Conroy and Cheyney, eds., *Unrest* (1929), 5.

54. Kalar, "Rebel Poets," review of *Unrest* (1929), 18.

55. Channing-Renton, letter to Conroy, 6 May 1929.

56. Bill Fudge, letter to Conroy, 25 October 1929.

57. Cheyney, letter to Porter, 23 November 1929.

58. Kalar, "Revolt," review of *Unrest* (1929), 68.

59. Kalar, letter to H. H. Lewis, 21 December 1928.

60. Kalar, letter to Conroy, 9 January 1929.

61. Kalar, "Insolent Query," unpubl. MS, ca. January 1929. Courtesy of Kalar family.

62. Folsom, "Education of Michael Gold," 231–32. While essentially correct, Folsom's remark deserves elaboration, as I attempt to provide in later chapters.

63. Kalar, NM (December 1929): 18.

64. Gold, "Write For Us!" 2.

65. Kalar, letter to editors, NM 4 (July 1928): 2.

66. Kalar, letter to editors, NM 5 (November 1929): 22.

67. Stanley Burnshaw, letter to Ruth Lechlitner, 12 February 1936. Lechlitner was the wife of Paul Corey, a midwestern literary radical whom Jack published in the *Anvil*. Letter courtesy of Paul Corey, with Stanley Burnshaw's permission.

68. Peck, "'The Tradition,'" 39.

69. Mencken served roughly the same function for Conroy as he had for Gold, publishing his early sketches, which formed the core of his first, semi-autobiographical novel.

70. Norman Macleod, interview, 16 July 1981. Macleod was closely associated with *New Masses* at different periods, ghost-editing one issue.

71. Conroy's locution. David Peck's otherwise useful essay on *New Masses* ignores Walt Carmon's contributions. See Peck, "'The Tradition,'" 385–409.

72. In *Democracy and Education* (1916), according to Leslie Fishbein, Dewey argues "that mass production fragmented the nature of work so that each worker came to view his own input solely in terms of the pay derived rather than in being able to understand the collective and social aspects of labor." Fishbein, *Rebels in Bohemia*, 67.

73. Kalar, letters to Huddlestone, 4 September 1932; January 1933. These letters are reproduced in *Joseph A. Kalar, Poet of Protest*, 147, 166.

74. Kalar, letter to Huddlestone, 19 April 1933. Kalar and Huddlestone had become acquainted through the Lone Scouts, an organization without troops or leaders, which encouraged youngsters isolated in rural areas and small towns to submit short narratives to the organization's magazine and to correspond with one another.

75. Representative texts are the following: Kramer, *Wild Jackasses*; Le Sueur, *North Star Country*; Le Sueur, *Crusaders*; Dell, "Young Poet in Davenport"; O'Hare, *Kate Richards O'Hare*; Pollack, *Populist Response*; Ameringer, *If You Don't Weaken*.

76. Billington, "Writers in Revolt," 8.

77. Shinew, interview, 27 October 1979.

78. Conroy, "Hard Winter," *WK*, 233.

79. Bernstein, *Lean Years*, 81.

80. Kalar, letter to Huddlestone, 9 October 1933.

81. Gold, "Go Left, Young Writers!" 3–4.

82. Kalar, letter to editors, (September 1929): 22.

83. Cheyney, letter to Kenneth Porter, 18 March 1929.

84. Cheyney, letters to Porter, 18 March, 11 May 1929.

85. Cheyney's poetic affinities were with the English Lake Poets, yet he was able to turn out on occasion a radical proletarian poem, such as "Bawl, Kid!" in *New Masses*.

86. Cheyney, letter to Porter, 23 June 1929.

87. Channing-Renton, letters to Conroy, 6 May 1929; 21 August 1929.

88. Conroy, letter to Emerson Price, 20 October 1929.

89. Channing-Renton, letter to Emerson Price, 18 September 1929.

90. The first curator of this collection, Agnes Inglis, an active member of the IWW, was an unusual person in her own right who corresponded with Conroy over the years. See Miles, "Agnes Inglis," 7–15.

91. Conroy, letter to Emerson Price, ca. fall 1929.

92. Sinclair Lewis in his 1930 Nobel Prize speech included Gold among the few American writers meriting the world's attention.

93. Gold, "New Program for Writers," 21.

94. Conroy, letter to editors, *NM* 5 (April 1930): 20.

95. Kalar, letter to editors, *NM* 5 (April 1930): 21.

96. "East of the Hudson" was the expression midwestern radicals often used in referring to the New York literary radicals, critics, and publishers. I discuss perceived regional differences in a later chapter.

97. Norman Macleod, letter to Conroy, 2 March 1969. Courtesy of Beinecke Library, Yale University.

98. H. Harris, "Working in the Detroit Auto Plants," 479. Also, see Edmund Wilson's reportage on the Ford plant in 1931, in *American Jitters*, 46–85.

99. "True-Blue Highpockets from the Forks of the Crick," Illinois Writers' Project (1939). I discuss the tale's authorship, misattributed to Nelson Algren, in chapter 17.

100. Technological practice, according to Garth Gillan, "is no longer the execution of work, but the planning and administration of labour in terms of the possibilities of technological production. The time and space of human labour are the time and space of the machine and its possibilities." *From Sign*, 120.

101. Conroy, "Bull Market," in *WK*, 228.

102. Conroy, interview, 4 June 1986.

103. Steele's (a.k.a. Cruden) *Conveyor* (1935) portrays these conditions. I discuss Cruden in chapters 12 and 13.

104. Steele, *Conveyor*, 164.

105. See the note on Cruden, *NM* 6 (April 1931): 23. Also, D. Anderson, "Michigan Proletarian Writers," 88–93.

106. Conroy, letter to Walt Carmon, ca. 1930. Conroy subsequently published one of Cruden's auto-factory sketches in *Anvil*. See Steele, "Own Your Own Home," which became part of *Conveyor*, published the following year.

107. Galbraith, *Great Crash of 1929*, 58.

108. Conroy, "Jackson Street: Toledo," *JCR*, 8.

109. Galbraith, *Great Crash of 1929*, 74.

Chapter 8
Exiles in Their Native Land

1. Conroy, letter to Emerson Price, ca. fall 1929.

2. Zola, *Germinal*, 499.

3. Conroy, *The Disinherited*, 215.

4. Conroy, letter to Rebel Poets, 25 August 1929.

5. Conroy, letter to Emerson Price, ca. fall 1929.

6. Rebel Poets, hectographed letter, 25 October 1929.

7. Conroy, letter to Emerson Price, ca. fall 1929.

8. Lewis maintained that he lost his traveler's checks, but Catherine Lewis Bock, Harold's sister, suspects that he was "swindled by some sharpies." "Biographical Sketch of Harold H. Lewis," unpubl. MS in author's possession. My thanks to Catherine Lewis Bock for graciously supplying biographical information. My interviews with H. H. Lewis took place during the last three years of his life, 1982–85.

9. Lewis, "Sidewalks of Los Angeles," 13. Also, Lewis, "Memoirs of a Dishwasher," 7. Haldeman-Julius published first-person narratives of life on the stem that might have served as models for Lewis. See Morris, "On the Skidroad," 76–78. Also, see James Rorty, "Anything Can Happen in Los Angeles," 6–7, 27.

10. Bock, "Biographical Sketch of Harold L. Lewis," 2.

11. Lewis's own account of his radicalization gives the flavor of his humorous self-deprecation as "plowboy poet," a title that Jack bestowed on him: "Less than ten feet from where I say this, on a run-down eighty acres four miles west of the Mississippi, in Southeast Missouri, I was born December 13, 1901, my folks being from the poor white trash of Tennessee. Dumb in books, I 'finished' the rural eighth grade with secret help from the teacher, and started riding a mule to high school. But because the town fellers guyed me, said why don't *you* stand in the stable all day and let the mule attend classes, I got plumb mad, balked, and wouldn't go to school any more. Something happened in Russia in 1917 to make me whatever I am to-day. I have published two booklets of revolutionary verse, *Red Renaissance* in 1930, *Thinking of Russia*, in 1932." Contributor's notes, *Folk-Say IV*, ed. B. A. Botkin.

12. Kalar, letter to Conroy, 7 December 1928.

13. Norman Macleod, letter to Kalar, ca. 1929.

14. Kljuev was a peasant poet who gave readings in Leningrad until his long eulogy on Lenin got him into trouble, after which he was forbidden to read publicly.

15. The question of "credentials" was always a sticky subject in the proletarian movement. True, James "Slim" Martin had been a migratory harvest hand and a structural steel worker. But these credentials alone do not necessarily define a worker-writer. When Martin was writing for *New Masses*, he was a member of the Provincetown Players and was "one of O'Neill's drinking companions." His contributions to *New Masses* "touched upon all appropriate attitudes," as Klein says. See M. Klein, *Foreigners*, 77. Also, see Klein on Martin, Gold, and the question of proletarian credentials. I give particular attention to the question in chapter 9.

16. On populism in the boot-heel, see Ogilvie, "Populism and Socialism," 159–83.

17. Calverton, *Liberation of American Literature*, 467. Calverton's book was first published in 1932.

18. *New Republic* 70 (13 April 1932): 252.

19. Benet, "Round About Parnassus," *Saturday Review of Literature* 8 (4 June 1932): 775. Conroy's reply appears in *Rebel Poet* (henceforth abbreviated *RP*) 15 (August 1932): 2.

20. Nietzsche, *Gay Science*, 298.

21. Walter Snow, letter to Kalar, 19 September 1932.

22. For an example of the thirst Rebel Poets had for communication with one another, see Kalar's letters to Huddlestone, collected in *Joseph A. Kalar, Poet of Protest*.

23. In January 1933, Graham started an anarchist monthly called *Man!* which after seven and one-half years of financial difficulty and government harassment was finally suspended. See M. Graham, ed., *Man!*, including Graham's autobiographical note, viii–xxi.

24. Conroy, letter to Walter Snow, 16 August 1930.

25. Conroy, letter to Kenneth Porter, 26 November 1929.

26. Conroy, letter to Robin Lampson, 21 December 1929. A glance at Crosby's life proves Conroy's estimation of Crosby to be naive. For instance, see Wolf's *Black Sun*.

27. Macleod, "Comment," 33.

28. Musser, *Ernest Hartsock*, 15.

29. Musser, *Poetry World* (September 1929).

30. Benjamin Musser, letter to Kenneth Porter, 31 January 1930.

31. Conroy, letter to Emerson Price, February 1930.

32. Ibid.

33. Conroy, letter to Emerson Price, ca. February 1930. Ginsberg's review is in *Contemporary Vision* 1 (Winter 1930).

34. Conroy, letter to Ralph Cheyney, winter 1930.

35. Conroy, letter to Kenneth Porter, 11 January 1930.

36. Emerson Price, letter to Robin Lampson, 1 December 1929.

37. *Toledo Blade*, 9 October 1929, 1.

38. Ibid., 3 November 1929, 1.

39. Conroy, letter to Emerson Price, ca. fall 1929.

40. Conroy, letter to Emerson Price, ca. December 1929.

41. Ibid.

42. Amidon, "Toledo," 672. The company went into federal bankruptcy three years later. Under the terms of the receivership the great bulky metal stamping presses were sold to Japan as scrap; instead, the Japanese manufacturers used them to produce tools in World War II.

43. *Toledo Blade*, 17 January 1930, 21.

44. Conroy, "Hard Winter," *WK*, 233–34.

45. Conroy, "Whistling Past a Graveyard: Toledo," 12–13.

46. Susman, "Dialectic of Two Cultures," 172.

47. Alt, "Beyond Class," 62–63.

48. J. Green, *World of the Worker*, 115. "The collapse of organized labor in the 1920's should be considered, then, in the larger context of Fordism, consumerism, and the emergence of a powerful 'new capitalism'" (119).

49. Jose Ortega y Gasset's famous attack on mass culture, *The Revolt of the Masses*, appeared in an American edition in 1932.

50. Aronowitz, *False Promises*, 119.

51. Weil, *Need for Roots*, 65.

52. Warren, introduction, in E. Roberts, *Time of Man*, xvii.

53. Ibid., xvii. Warren appears to address the "vulgar dichotomy" in which human fate is separated from specific social issues.

54. Conroy, "The Worker as Writer," *JCR*, 218–21.

55. "A Democracy," Dewey writes, "is more than a form of government; it is primarily a mode of associate living, of conjoint communicated experience." *Democracy and Education*, 87. Also, see G. Gunn, *Culture of Criticism*, 74. The distinction I wish to make is best expressed in Marx's "Six Theses on Feuerbach": "The essence of man is not an abstraction inherent in each separate individual. In reality, it is the aggregate of social relationships." Quoted by Clark and Holquist, *Mikhail Bakhtin*, 164.

56. ". . . it is the human being itself that is irreducibly heterogeneous; it is human 'being' that exists only in dialogue: within being one finds the other." Bakhtin paraphrased by Todorov, *Mikhail Bakhtin*, x–xi.

57. Conroy, letter to Kenneth Porter, 21 January 1930.

58. Conroy, letter to Emerson Price, ca. March 1930.

59. Ben Hagglund, letter to Kenneth Porter, 28 April 1930.

60. Conroy, "In Memoriam: John C. Rogers," 56.

61. Conroy, letter to Kenneth Porter, 6 April 1930.

62. Conroy, letter to Emerson Price, ca. March 1930.

63. Quoted in *Western Poetry* 1 (January 1930): 2.

64. Conroy, "Hard Winter," *WK*, 232. The concluding line has a finality equivalent to Keats's "And no birds sing."

65. Conroy, "Hard Winter," *WK*, 240.

66. Mattick, *Arbeitslosigkeit*, 17.

67. Mattick estimates that up to one-eighth of the urban population lived in these conditions.

68. Warren Huddlestone, interview with author, 29 August 1981. Huddlestone's book-length manuscript has never been published. Because of its mood

of resignation and quietism, Jack rejected Huddlestone's story "Hunger Is for Quiet Men," which was based on his experiences, but published Huddlestone's poem in *Anvil* 5.

69. Turner, *Frontier in American History*. Also, see Ray Allen Billington, ed., *Frontier Thesis*, for a discussion of the "safety-valve" function expressed in Turner's hypothesis. Kenneth Porter uses the term "social frontiers" in his dedication to his poetry volume, *The High Plains*: "To my father and mother, Scotch-Irish pioneers in the western Kansas of the '80s and on the social frontiers of the '30s." Ruth Lechlitner's poem "The Last Frontiers" describes a succession of frontiers in American history, including the social frontier of the 1930s when young men are "Idle on the home steps . . ."(20–21). Archibald Macleish's "Land of the Free," published in 1938, is perhaps the best-crafted poetic evocation of the 1930s social frontier, the counter-frontier in which people are left "wondering," the American dream shattered.

70. London's "The Class Struggle" and Hamlin Garland's portrayals of deprivation and failure on midwestern farms at the end of the nineteenth century are earlier descriptions of social anti-frontiers.

71. The distinction is Billington's. In *Land of Savagery* Billington argues that America is both a land of savagery and of promise as a consequence of shaping factors like the frontier experience. Nonetheless, he says, equality and opportunity have evolved despite "savagery."

72. The contributors read like a who's who of the midwestern little magazine circuit. Among them, H. H. Lewis, Raymond Kresensky, John Rogers, Dee Brown, Paul Corey, Kenneth Porter, Jerre Mangione, Erling Larsen, Carroll Norling, Sanora Babb, Alan Swallow, Paul Corey, Jim Hearst, Warren Huddlestone, Peter De Vries, and Alfred Morang.

73. E.g., Garland, Norris, Donnelly, Dreiser, Suckow, Quick, Sandburg. Billington, "Writers in Revolt," 8.

74. Corey, "Lurching," 45.

75. Paul Corey, interview with author, 23 September 1984.

76. These are *Three Miles Square* (1939), *The Road Returns* (1940), and *County Seat* (1941). See McCown, "Paul Corey's Mantz Trilogy," 15–26. Corey's *Acres of Antaeus* (1946) is a novel about dispossession and the attempts to create a farmers' union in the 1930s. The farm organizer, "Smiley," of *Acres of Antaeus*, is based upon John Herrman, an ardent Party member and the husband of novelist Josephine Herbst, who helped organize a streetcar strike in Omaha. (Paul Corey, interview with author, 23 September 1984.) Corey's short story "The Hunt" is reprinted in *Growing Up in Iowa*, 88–99. Also, see Meyers, *Middle-Western Farm Novel*, on Corey. Corey hated being aligned with the "farm novelists." Meyers ignores the radical implications and background of Corey's work.

77. See Lechlitner's memoir ". . . anti-war and anti-fascism . . . ," 77–82. Six of Lechlitner's poems appear in *The New American Caravan* (1936) .

78. Paul Corey, letter to Conroy, 5 April 1933.

79. Corey, "Lurching," 63.

80. Corey turned this skill into a part-time trade, publishing "how-to" articles for *Popular Mechanics* and writing a book on house construction, using native materials.

81. The "crowd" reference is to writers and critics associated with Rahv and Phillips's *Partisan Review* after 1937. Corey, interview, 23 September 1984.

82. Corey, "Lurching," 60.

83. See Mangione, *Dream and the Deal*, 149–50. Mangione includes a photo of Corey at Cold Spring.

84. A representative of the La Follette organization asked George Gallup, Corey's schoolmate at the University of Iowa, who the radicals were on campus. Gallup named Corey. Lechlitner was from a small, conservative Indiana town where her father was a staunch Republican. She fell in with a small but vocal group of campus radicals at the University of Michigan, and later at Iowa. Corey, interview, 23 September 1984.

85. Paul Corey, interview, 23 September 1984.

86. All comments by Herrman in this paragraph are from his "New Multitudes," 252–55.

87. Not all expatriate magazines published in Paris, of course, were experimentalist in matters of language and form. Harold Salemson's *Tambour* "objected strenuously to the esoteric exclusiveness of some of its contemporaries," according to Hoffman, Allen, and Ulrich, *The Little Magazine*, 80. In a manifesto published in 1930, Salemson wrote: "We demand that the artist look at his day with the point-of-view of his day, as he understands it, and without making us feel his presence in it." Quoted by Hoffman, Allen, and Ulrich, *The Little Magazine*, 84. Norman Macleod and James T. Farrell published in *Tambour*.

88. Hamovitch notes that "by 1933, modernist fiction was finding a market in the higher-paying magazines like *Scribner's*." Introduction to *The Hound and Horn Letters*, 7.

89. There was some resentment, I feel, on the part of the midwestern radicals toward the expatriates, for example, as appears in a fragment of Conroy's unpublished manuscript: "in the twenties . . . Hemingway and not a few other American writers seceded from American life and found sanctuary in the salons of Paris, where literary aesthetes were chafing under the fetters of form and asserting their right to freedom of language. . . . But the financial earthquake of 1929 brought the secessionists to grips with realism as effectively as the guns of World War I had jarred the delicate sensibilities of the pre-war poets." Unpubl. fragment, review of Hoffman, Allen, Ulrich, *The Little Magazine*, with the Conroy papers, Newberry Library.

90. In the visual arts, on the other hand, a synthesis of experimental form and social content occurred most notably, to a lesser or greater degree, in the work of Ben Shahn (e.g., the Sacco-Vanzetti paintings), Thomas Hart Benton, William Gropper, Stuart Davis, and others.

91. Marcus Klein argues that proletarian literature "was among other things a new episode in the literary modernism which had come into being at least as long before as 1912." He continues, "The sense of fact, a sense of the moral

role of literature, the sense of an adversary position within the general culture—all these constitute a great amount of what modernism meant." "Roots of Radicals," 134, 137. Klein's argument is attractive, but he fails to consider the question of readership and communication (e.g., the radicals' critique of "obscurity"), for example, the modernists' distrust of mimetic assumptions that take for granted language's ability to convey meaning. I find Dickran Tashjian's comments on the obscurantism debate in the 1930s to the point. See Tashjian, *William Carlos Williams*, 132. My own approach is to trace the radicals' reception of modernist ideas and their response to the expatriates as they appear in their correspondence and in the little magazines.

92. Lechlitner, "Verse-Drama for Radio," n.p.

93. Conroy, "What If You Don't Want to Write for Money," 11.

94. Spector, "Liberalism and the Literary Esoterics," 18–19.

95. Walter Snow, letter to Conroy, 21 July 1932.

96. *transition* 16/17 (1929). Quoted in McMillan, *Transition*, 49.

97. Paul Corey, interview, 23 September 1984.

98. Alfred Kazin addresses this point in *Starting Out in the Thirties*, generalizing it for all radical writers: "What young writers of the Thirties wanted was to prove the literary value of our experience, to recognize the possibilities of art in our own lives, to feel we had moved the streets, the stockyards, the hiring halls into literature—to show our radical strength could carry on the experimental impulse of modern literature" (15).

99. Weiss, "Give Us Poems for Workers," 22.

100. Jolas was in fact an editor of great sensitivity toward a broad range of poetic expression. See his *Anthologie de la Nouvelle Poème Américaine*, which includes Gold, Cheyney, H. L. Davis, and Sandburg along with Eliot, H. D., Frost, and Stevens.

101. Joseph Vogel, letter to author, 9 July 1982.

102. Vogel, "Defence of the American Literary Scene," 247–57. Vogel, a radical writer, was published five times in *This Quarter* during the period 1928–29—in an avant-garde magazine published in Paris whose first issue was dedicated to Ezra Pound. Little-magazine editors did not always draw lines between literary radicals and modernists.

103. Vogel, interview, 7 October 1982. Also, Vogel, letter to author, 27 September 1983.

104. Vogel's letter, captioned "Literary Graveyards," appeared in the October 1929 issue of *New Masses*. Vogel's break with *Blues* and his criticism of Pound's influence are told by Johns and Clancy in their introduction to Spector's *Bastard in the Ragged Suit*, 6–7. Also, Vogel, interview, 7 October 1982. Spector was a contributing editor of *Blues*. Great friends, Spector and Vogel later started *Dynamo*, a magazine "of revolutionary poetry."

105. First published by Knopf in 1938 to critical acclaim, then forgotten in the ensuing climate of literary reception, *Man's Courage* was republished by Syracuse University Press in 1989.

106. Pound's letter to Macleod was written from Rapallo, Italy. *Morada* 3 (Spring

1930): 90–91. The first three issues of Macleod's little magazine were published in Albuquerque; the final issue was numbered five—number four never appeared.

107. Kalar, *Morada* 3 (Spring 1930): 91–92. The matter is addressed in the Kalar-Macleod correspondence, ca. late 1929 or early 1930.

108. Pound made a crack about McKenzie's ailment when the two met in Italy. Norman Macleod, interview, 16 July 1981.

109. After the fifth number, Macleod, who in Conroy's words "carried water on both shoulders," was unable to continue publication. Conroy, interview, 23 December 1982. Macleod was among the literary radicals deeply interested in Pound and Eliot, without sharing their politics. Macleod, letter to author, 26 November 1984.

110. Similarly, Kalar praised Kreymborg's anthology, *Our Singing Strength* (1929), for bringing together in a single volume the traditions of literary experimentalism (*transition*, *Blues*, *Exile*) and those of revolt.

111. Gold, "Notes of the Month."

112. Gold, "Six Letters," 4.

113. Pound's involvement with the Italian fascists during World War II and his subsequent internment in prison and in the mental ward of St. Elizabeth's hospital were a tragic conclusion to the funny, eccentric Pound, who obviously took great delight in debating Gold. Pound's ignorance of the current American literary scene was profound, according to Archibald MacLeish in a letter to Harriet Monroe, dated November 29, 1930, quoted by Homberger, *American Writers*, 238.

114. Without putting it in the same terms (worker vs. artist), William Carlos Williams lambasted Pound and Eliot for ignoring American subjects. For a general overview of this topic, see M. Klein, *Foreigners*, and Tashjian, *William Carlos Williams*. See also, Karl, *Modern and Modernism*.

115. Homberger discusses one facet of the modernist-radical connections, occurring "east of the Hudson," in his chapter "Communists and Objectivists," *American Writers*, 163–86. Deeply affected by the economic and social crisis of the early Depression, the Objectivist poets—Oppen, Zukofsky, Reznikoff—moved into the Communist orbit, Homberger notes. "Yet as poets the Objectivists were pursuing goals which assumed the absence of integral ties between the poet and his audience. (There was no audience for the poems they wanted to write.)" Homberger, 182. The radicals discovered that their audience was limited—but for entirely different reasons.

116. See Kempf, "Encountering the Avant-Garde," 19.

117. Wilson, "Literary Class War," quoted in Homberger, *American Writers*, 149.

118. Cowley, "Homeless Generation."

119. See Hazlett, "Conversion, Revisionism," 179–88. See also Homberger's chapter "Edmund Wilson Turns Left," in *American Writers*, 141–62. Despite their backgrounds (upper-middle-class families, graduates of Ivy League schools), Cowley and Wilson felt a commitment to workers' causes in the early 1930s.

Chapter 9
Worker-Writers and Editors

1. Towey, "Hooverville," 4–11.
2. Harvey Harrison, interview, 22 September 1991.
3. *Moberly Monitor-Index*, 22 May 1931, 1.
4. Conroy, letter to Walter Snow, 16 August 1930.
5. Snow, "The Revolutionary Poet"; "Goliath."
6. Snow, "Bibliography—Walter Snow." Courtesy of the University of Connecticut–Storrs Library.
7. Symes and Clement, in *Rebel America,* argue that rebellions, not five-year plans, agree with the American radical temperament.
8. Neets, "From Our Critic in Moscow," 23.
9. Freeman, "Past and Present," in Freeman, Lozowick, and Kunitz, *Voices of October,* 20.
10. See Gold's footnote to Neets; letter to editors, *NM* 6 (November 1930): 14.
11. Neets, letter to editors, *NM* 6 (November 1930): 14. David Peck reveals Neets's identity as Joshua Kunitz. Peck, "The Development."
12. See for example, Falkowski, "In a Soviet Mining Town," 14–15.
13. See Peck, "The Development," 108, 127–29.
14. Walt Carmon's criticism of Conroy's "High Bridge" in *New Masses* is an example of "Party-mindedness," although Carmon was perhaps the least orthodox of *New Masses* editors. Carmon wrote: "There's just a tone of a romantic kind of adventurousness about it. . . ." Carmon, letter to Conroy, 16 January 1931.
15. Gold et al., "Charkov Conference," 6.
16. See Gold's "Notes from Kharkov," 5, in which he reiterates the worker-correspondence notion. Similarly, the populist forebears of the midwestern radicals had underscored regionality in connection with political differences.
17. Quoted in Aaron, *Writers on the Left,* 242.
18. Bernstein, *Lean Years,* 427.
19. Reprinted in Hughes, *The Big Sea,* 321.
20. The term "invented traditions" is from Hobsbawn and Ranger, *Invention of Tradition.*
21. Kent's *Interpretation and Genre* is useful here, particularly his comment on "culture's extra-textual concerns" (102). The role of worker narrative as a subliterary genre deserves further study.
22. See Lejeune, *Je Est Un Autre,* 206f.
23. Mencken apprenticed in the cigar-making trade, like his father and grandfather before him, and took correspondence courses (on writing); he later apprenticed in the newsroom of the *Baltimore Morning Herald.*
24. Knopf and Mencken were close friends; Mencken mentioned Conroy's writing to Knopf.
25. Quoted in Singleton, *H. L. Mencken,* 8. Hemingway wrote in *The Sun Also Rises:* "So many young men get their likes and dislikes from Mencken." As Singleton points out, however, expatriate writers generally ignored the *Mer-*

cury, and by 1930 the younger "mainstream" writers as well were no longer taking cues from Mencken. Singleton, 206–7.

26. Haldeman-Julius, "Taming of Mencken," 7.

27. Singleton, *H. L. Mencken*, 150.

28. Ford Maddox Ford criticized Mencken for his stereotypes of the Midwest. See Singleton, *H. L. Mencken*, 207.

29. Hubbell reports Mencken's saying: "Henry James would have been vastly
improved as a novelist by a few whiffs from the Chicago stockyards." Quoted
by Hubbell, *Who Are the Major American Writers?* 170.

30. Halpert, ed., *Return to Pagany*, 335.

31. Mencken, "Editorial Notes," xxxiv.

32. H. L. Mencken, letter to Conroy, 24 October 1930.

33. Conroy, interview, 21 April 1984.

34. Levy, "Some Poets to the Left," 20.

35. Ben Hagglund, letter to Conroy, 19 December 1930.

36. Ibid.

37. Conroy, introduction, *Red Renaissance*, 2–4.

38. *Moberly Monitor-Index*, 21 October 1930, 1.

39. Ibid., 6 January 1931, 1.

40. Ibid., 26 January 1931, 4.

41. Mencken's reply: "My only defense is that I didn't make Arkansas the
butt of ridicule—God did it." Ibid., 6 February 1931, 1.

42. Warren I. Susman discusses reasons for the support the Party enjoyed
from intellectuals: "The genius of the Communist movement of the 1930's was
its ability to use the obvious social and psychological needs of the period. . . . For
the first time in the twentieth century the Party had attempted to organize
writers and intellectuals and to bring them together to exchange views, political and aesthetic, to feel themselves an important part of the American scene."
"The Thirties," 247. While Susman probably has in mind the proximity of intellectuals in cities like New York and San Francisco, the same might be said
about the Party's attraction to isolated worker-intellectuals like Conroy and
Kalar in the Midwest, who felt themselves to be part of the movement without participating directly in Party activities.

43. See Kelley, *Hammer and Hoe*.

44. Conroy, editorial notes, *American Mercury* 22 (February 1931): xviii.

45. Cowley, "Old House in Chelsea . . . ," 42.

46. Warren Huddlestone, interview, 29 August 1981.

47. For example, see Huddlestone's "A Little Business Deal."

48. Raymond Kresensky, letter to Kenneth Porter, 14 June 1932.

49. Dewey, *Individualism Old and New*, quoted in R. Nash, *Nervous Generation*, 63.

50. Conroy, letter to Emerson Price, ca. 1930–31.

51. The cover of the 1930 *Unrest* is reproduced in C. Nelson, *Repression
and Recovery*.

52. Ed Falkowski, "A Sign-Post of Tomorrow," *Moscow Daily News*, ca. early
1931. The review is with the Conroy papers, Newberry Library.

53. Porter, "Anthology of Rebel Poets," 558.

54. Conroy and Cheyney, *Unrest* (1930), 11.

55. Levy, "Some Poets to the Left," 19–20.

56. Mencken, editor's notes, *American Mercury* (February 1931): xiii.

57. Conroy, interview, 13 March 1987.

58. H. H. Lewis, letter to Joseph Kalar, 1931.

59. Michael Gold, letter to H. H. Lewis, ca. 1929.

60. H. H. Lewis, "In All Hell," *RP* 1 (January 1931).

61. Conroy, interview, 30 October 1982.

62. Conroy, letter to Kenneth Porter, 6 February 1931.

63. Maxim Lieber, letter to Conroy, 9 May 1931.

64. Maxim Lieber, interview with author, 18 October 1982.

65. Conroy, interview, 21 April 1984.

66. Kalar, letter to Huddlestone, ca. April 1933.

67. Falkowski recorded his memories of the coal town, Shenandoah, Pennsylvania, in "Coal Mountain," 51–57.

68. Falkowski, letter to author, 15 March 1982.

69. Falkowski, interview, 2 April 1982. My information on Shenandoah is drawn from my visits, interviews, and Leighton, *Five Cities*.

70. For more on Brookwood, see Altenbaugh, *Education for Struggle*.

71. Falkowski, "Miners' Progress," 6. Falkowski's earliest published article appeared in *The Bookman*, about a famous Greenwich Village character named Guido Bruno.

72. See Falkowski, "In a Brown Coal Country," 75–79.

73. See Wiebe, "Deutsche Arbeiterliteratur (1847–1918)." Courtesy of Deutsche Welle, Cologne, Germany. See also Schmitt, *Beruf und Arbeit*. Helga Gallas, *Marxistische Literaturtheorie*, treats Lukacs's commentaries on Bredel, criticizing worker-writers like Bredel for "Unzulänglichkeiten" (inadequacies). Nor was Lukacs prepared to accept Brecht's radical techniques in reorienting the proletarian novel.

74. Falkowski, letter to author, 2 March 1983.

75. Christopher Isherwood's *Goodbye to Berlin* and "Cabaret" have stimulated this perception.

76. Angress, "Pegasus and Insurrection," 35.

77. Falkowski, "Das Land der guten Hoffnung," 12–16.

78. See Werner Angress, "Pegasus," 50–55. See also Gotsche, "Vorwort," in *Die Linkskurve*, 5–20; J. Murphy, *Proletarian Moment*.

79. See Magil, "European Newsreel," 10, on *Linkskurve*, which, like *New Masses*, welcomed visiting revolutionary writers from abroad.

80. Falkowski, "Amerika wendet sich nach Links," 18–20.

81. See Falkowski, "Five Year Plan Tempo," 8–9.

82. Falkowski, "Rebel Poets in Germany," 6.

83. Falkowski, "In a German Mining Town," and "Workers' Art in Germany."

84. Falkowski, "Berlin in Crimson," 10.

85. Falkowski, "In a Soviet Mining Town," 14–15; "The Soviet Political Theatre," 22.

86. For a discussion of American workers in the Soviet Union in the early 1920s, see Morray, *Project Kuzbas*. Also, Haywood, *Autobiography*; Kennell and Bennett, "American Immigrants in Russia."

87. Falkowski, untitled MS, in Falkowski personal papers. Courtesy of Falkowski family.

88. Falkowski, letter to Conroy, 22 December 1931.

89. "Promparty" was the name given to the Industrial Party, several of whose members, older engineers, were accused of sabotage and exchanging information with the "enemy," chiefly the British. The trials, lasting about two weeks, were held in the Hall of Columns of the House of Trade Unions. Falkowski, letter to author, 26 May 1982.

90. For example, Falkowski, "Red Gangway!" and "Dreams in Red," both appearing in Conroy's *Anvil*.

91. Alan Calmer, *Daily Worker*, ca. October 1933. With Conroy papers, Newberry Library.

92. Falkowski, interview, 2 April 1982.

93. Falkowski, letter to author, 22 March 1982.

94. Falkowski organized and ran the first Polish Press Agency following World War II. In this capacity he represented the Polish government at the first United Nations conference in San Francisco in 1945. Falkowski, letter to author, 2 May 1982.

95. On Spector and Russak, see the Johns and Clancy introduction to Spector, *Bastard in the Ragged Suit*. Short biographies of Spector and Russak appear in *NM* 6 (February 1931): 23, and *NM* 5 (December 1930): 22, respectively. Spector and Russak, both worker-writers, spent their lives in or near New York. Their contacts with the midwestern radicals were tangential, yet many parallels exist and deserve to be studied.

96. Falkowski's writings also appeared in *Common Ground*, *Christian Herald*, and *New Republic*.

97. Kalar, letter to H. H. Lewis, ca. December 1931.

Chapter 10
Proletarian Night

1. *Moberly Monitor-Index*, 9 February 1931, 1; ibid., 14 February 1931, 1; ibid., 20 March 1931, 1.

2. Ibid., 6 March 1931, 2.

3. Leo and Lottie Bly, interview, 5 July 1982.

4. Stella Jacoby, letter to author, 15 April 1991.

5. The expression "proletarian night" is Kalar's, in a poem of the same title. Coincidentally, it approximates the title of an important text: Jacques Rancière's *La Nuit des Prolétaires*, a study of nineteenth-century French artisans and their publications.

6. Rancière, "Myth of the Artisan," 13.

7. For Frank Kermode's interesting commentary on this point, see his re-

view of *Prodigal Sons*, by Alexander Bloom, in the *New York Times Book Review* (27 April 1986): 12.

8. See for example, Lawrence, "Autobiographical Sketch," 592–96. "As a man from the working class, I feel that the middle class cut off some of my vital vibration when I am with them. I admit them charming and educated and good people often enough. *But they just stop some part of me from working.* Some part has to be left out. Then why don't I live with my working people? Because their vibration is limited in another direction" (595). Jack London novelizes similar ambivalences in *Martin Eden*.

9. George Orwell's remark, that "there can't be lower-class intellectuals because as soon as they become intellectuals they are forced to live in a world very different from their own," is pertinent here. See Kermode, *History and Value*, 66.

10. Rancière, *La Nuit*, 89.

11. "Par quels détours," asks Rancière, "ces transfuges, desireux de s'arracher à la contrainte de l'existence prolétaire, ont-ils paradoxalement forgé l'image et le discours de l'identité ouvrière?" (By what circuitous means, did these renegades, anxious to free themselves of the constraints of proletarian existence, forge, paradoxically, an image and discourse of workers' identity?) *La Nuit*, 10.

12. Hicks, "Writers of the Thirties." MS, courtesy of the University of Connecticut–Storrs.

13. See Bakke, *Unemployed Man*; idem, *Citizens without Work*; Komarovsky, *Unemployed Man and His Family*. See also Conroy, *The Disinherited*, 180–89, 192–93; and Algren, *Somebody in Boots*.

14. Berger et al., *Homeless Mind*, chap. 2; Lea, *Political Consciousness*, 187ff.

15. Brody, *Workers in Industrial America*, 82ff. Conroy remarks about the docility of workers in the early 1930s, in an interview with Hoke Norris, "Critic at Large."

16. In subsequent chapters I discuss Kalar's, Cruden's, and Conroy's involvement in the labor movement.

17. Rancière, *La Nuit*, 10.

18. Rancière, in *La Nuit*, 9, discusses "dual consciousness" in connection with nineteenth-century French artisan-writers.

19. Kalar, "Proletarian Night," in *Joseph A. Kalar*, 48.

20. *La Nuit*, 87. A writer of gargantuan energies, such as Jack London, might compose an entire story at night while working in a factory by day, as he did in writing "Typhoon Off the Coast of China." Most aspiring worker-writers in the early 1930s, however, abandoned the effort. "The great wonder to me is that workers write at all," exclaimed Fred Miller, editor of the proletarian magazine *Blast*, after two months of delivering phone books on foot. Letter to editors, *NM* 5 (September 1930): 20.

21. H. L. Mencken, letter to Conroy, 12 February 1931.

22. In the way that, for example, the work narratives of Studs Terkel's *Working* possess social and cultural significance.

23. Stanley, "Personal Narrative," 108.

24. Ursula Münchow calls this "der Einzelne im Ganzen und das Ganze im

Einzelnen" (the particular in the whole and the whole in the particular)." *Frühe Deutsche Arbeiterautobiographie,* 61.

25. "Seuls la pratique de l'action, l'engagement politique et syndical, permettent de donner à une vie ouvrière une identité, c'est-à-dire une structure et une valeur. . . ." Lejeune, *Je Est Un Autre,* 256.

26. For example, autobiographies by working-class leaders like John Brophy, John Mitchell, and William Z. Foster. I purposely ignore accounts of working-class life authored by researchers and writers whose temporary *séjour* in working-class occupations and milieus provide material for their studies, e.g., Richard M. Pfeffer, *Working for Capitalism;* Paul Goehre, *Three Months in a Workshop;* Robert Schrank, *Ten Thousand Working Days.*

27. Brecher, Lombardi, and Stackhouse, *Brass Valley;* Schroedel, *Alone in a Crowd;* Kareven and Langenbach, *Amoskeag;* Banks, ed., *First-Person America;* Nelkin and Brown, *Workers at Risk.* The Pennsylvania folklorist George Korson was an early pioneer in the oral transcription of worker narratives. The 1930s awakened an interest in oral testimonies of work. An important sponsor was the Federal Writers' Project. See Terrill and Hirsch, eds., *Such As Us.* Also, Couch, ed., *These Are Our Lives.* Studs Terkel has made the genre well known through his transcriptions of oral interviews, such as *Working* and *Hard Times.* For a discussion of the role of documentary expression and its relation to literature and the arts, see Stott, *Documentary Expression;* Foley, *Telling the Truth.*

28. See Lovell, Jr., "Champions of the Workers"; Prestridge, *Worker in American Fiction.*

29. See the 1982 edition of the *Independent* "lifelets" by Katzman and Tuttle, eds., *Plain Folk.* While Holt hoped to provide a representative sample of workers' experiences and attitudes, the results showed that all but a black worker and a farmer's wife had aspirations of getting rich, of moving up the social scale through wealth. Nonetheless, Holt's subjects sometimes offer resistance in the workplace, hoping to improve conditions by forming unions and attempting to maintain a sense of self-worth. Introduction, xii.

30. See, for example, the famous "Cub-Pilot" chapter in *Life on the Mississippi.* It was not unusual for apprentices to keep diaries, detailing their initiation to work and conditions of employment. Printers' apprentices were frequently drawn to professional writing careers, as Rorabaugh points out in *The Craft Apprentice.* After World War I the nature of apprenticeship in most trades had so altered that men had to fake knowledge to keep a job or to get one. Most factory jobs required no such formal apprenticeship such as Twain received from Mr. Bixby.

31. See Foner, ed., *American Labor Songs;* Lomax, Guthrie, and Seegar, eds., *Hard Hitting Songs;* Fowke and Glazer, eds., *Songs of Work and Protest.*

32. See Korson, *Coal Dust on the Fiddle* and *Minstrels of the Mine Patch.* Archie Green substantiates the fact that music was an integral part of the United Mine Workers' activities from the beginning. *Only a Miner.*

33. Parrelle and Lucas, "Pick Coal Rhythm," first stanza, reprinted in Frederick, *Out of the Midwest,* 308–9.

34. On preliterary expression and black literature, see Hemenway, "Are You a Flying Lark," 122–52. See also H. Baker, *Blues, Ideology.*

35. Conroy, review of *Black Men in Chains*, in *New Letters*, 77. Ben Botkin, Jack's longtime friend, also valued the slave narratives for qualities that, he said, characterized the best writing of the 1930s. They "have the forthrightness, tang and tone of people talking, the immediacy and concreteness of the participant and the eyewitness, and the salty irony and mother wit which, like the gift of memory, are kept alive by the bookless world." *Lay My Burden Down*, xiii.

36. Conroy contributed a number of "unprintable" ballads and songs, many remembered from Monkey Nest, to Vance Randolph's "Unprintable Songs from the Ozarks," MS in the Library of Congress. The collection was published in 1992 by the University of Arkansas Press. Unfortunately the editor, J. Legman, leaves the attributions unclear, using "Mr. J.C." in place of "Jack Conroy."

37. An example is Dwyer's *Tales from the Gangway* (1923), a book that Conroy had in his library.

38. Singleton, *H. L. Mencken*, 86n.

39. Singleton notes that Mencken remembered the "birds of passage" better than the "clever pieces."

40. Singleton, *H. L. Mencken*, 212.

41. In his essay "The National Letters," Mencken criticizes writers removed from American life. Of Ring Lardner, for example, Mencken wrote in praise: "Without wasting any wind upon statements of highfalutin aesthetic or ethical purpose, he is trying to get the low-down Americano between covers." Singleton, *H. L. Mencken*, 83. See also Nolte, *H. L. Mencken*, chap. 2. Hobson writes that Mencken "preferred the broad view; his instrument was a wide-angle lens, not a microscope." Hobson, *Serpent in Eden*, 7.

42. Gold, review of *Shanty Irish*, 26.

43. Ibid. In his eagerness to locate "authentic" worker-writers Gold had published the flamboyant Slim Martin, a worker-turned-actor with the Provincetown Players. See M. Klein, *Foreigners*, 76–79.

44. Conroy liked to quote Mencken's review: "Mr. Gold stays off revolution to the very end, and then what he has to say he says very politely." Interview, 5 June 1986.

45. Conroy, review of *Jews without Money*, 14. Art Shields recalls that *Jews without Money* was circulated by workers in an artificial-silk plant in Cumberland, Maryland, where Shields worked. *On the Battle Lines*, 195.

46. *Jews without Money* sold widely despite instances of unfavorable reception on political grounds by critics on both the left and right. See Rideout, *Radical Novel*, 152.

47. Gold attacked Mencken in "An Open Letter to H. L. Mencken, Editor of the *American Mercury*," NM 7 (September 1931): 3. Some five years earlier he had held the *Mercury* up to literary radicals as a model. Gold, "America Needs a Critic," NM 1 (October 1926): 8.

48. See Milburn's *The Hobo's Hornbook* (1930), a collection of tramping lore, as well as his *Oklahoma Town* (1931). Milburn said about himself: "I am bitterly class-conscious, but I have no political affiliations." *International Literature* 5 (May 1935): 106.

49. Pells, *Radical Visions*, 101.

50. Ibid.

51. Benedict's studies viewed an individual's ties to culture in terms of accommodation, not resistance. Ibid., 113.

52. See J. Rubin, *Constance Rourke*, 45–50, for a discussion of the notion of "usable past."

53. See M. Klein, *Foreigners*, 176, and Bluestein, *Voice of the Folk*, 66; both authors underscore the importance of Rourke's work in 1931.

54. By 1930, most writers interested in folklore, including one of his former students, Zora Neale Hurston, were ignoring Franz Boas's injunction to keep ethnography and fiction apart, turning their hands to "ethnographic fictions." See Krupat, "Fiction and Fieldwork," 22–23.

55. Corey's novel, *Three Miles Square*, reveals these new currents—social protest, regional settings, humor, and sex.

56. For example, fifteen of Raymond Weeks's Missouri "folk humor" stories appeared in *Midland*. Jack admired Weeks's stories, reprinting "The Fat Women of Boone" in *Midland Humor* (1947).

57. Reigelman, *The Midland*, 42. Frederick wrote: "I believe that New York's despotism is bad: bad for criticism, because New York writers and critics know each other too well and see each other too often; bad for creative writing. . . ." Quoted by Reigelman, 43.

58. See Reigelman, *The Midland*. Also, Hoffman, Allen, and Ulrich, *The Little Magazine*, 128–33.

59. Quoted by Reigelman, *The Midland*, 35.

60. Corey, interview, 23 September 1984.

61. On Botkin's folklore work, see Hirsch, "Folklore in the Making," 4–38. A more recent folklore study that shows how folklore continues to function in a fragmented time, binding people together in spontaneous communities, is Stahl's *Literary Folkloristics*.

62. Conroy noted Botkin's powerful influence on young radical writers: "*Folk-Say*, during its short but distinguished career, published some of the most significant work of Erskine Caldwell, George Milburn, H. H. Lewis, John C. Rogers, Norman Macleod, William Cunningham, and numerous other young writers who have since attracted notice because of their ability to mirror graphically the people and terrain of some particular region." Review of *The Green Corn Rebellion*, 76.

63. Botkin, "Folk and the Individual," 129.

64. Vance Randolph's fieldwork in the Ozarks rejected all traces of antiquarians' nostalgic quest for a lost past. See Cochran, *Vance Randolph*, 1985.

65. See Tashjian, *William Carlos Williams*, 105–6, for a discussion of modernism and folk art.

66. David Whisnant calls this "manipulative cultural interventions." *All That Is Native and Fine*, 11.

67. Tashjian, *Skyscraper Primitives*, 72.

68. See Tashjian, *William Carlos Williams*, 110–12.

69. See Tashjian, *Skyscraper Primitives*. Contributors to Eugene Jolas's *tran-*

sition frequently displayed a distrust of industrial society and mass society. See McMillan, *Transition*, 30ff.

70. Nemser, "Charles Sheeler," 50.

71. Frank, *Our America*, 121–26, 179–80.

72. R. Nash, *Nervous Generation*, 73–75.

73. Botkin, "Folk and the Individual," 125.

74. Hirsch, "Folklore in the Making," 3.

75. Botkin, "Regionalism and Culture," 140–57. Botkin delivered this speech at the Second American Writers' Congress in 1937.

76. Rourke, "Significance of Sections," 148–51.

77. See "Regionalism: Pro and Con," *Saturday Review of Literature* 15 (28 November 1936): 3–4, 14, 16. For a discussion of folklore that includes industrial workers see A. Green, "American Labor Lore," 51–68.

78. I discuss this point in "Thomas Hart Benton's New York Years."

79. H. Smith, "Localism in Literature," 298–301.

80. On the contemporary regionalist debate, see Odum and Moore, *American Regionalism*, chap. 7. Two early studies that anticipated the new regionalist interest were Mumford's "Theory and Practice of Regionalism" (1928), and Carey McWilliams's *New Regionalism* (1930).

81. I borrow the term from Frye, *Critical Path*. Frye distinguishes between myths of concern and of freedom. The myth of concern has to do with certain conserving beliefs in society that are socially established. The myth of freedom, on the other hand, has to do with "non-mythical elements that are studied rather than created" (139).

82. Eric Mottram writes of "the responsibility at least some artists [in the 1930s] felt for their function in society, conceiving 'the very act of creation as one of affirmation of the value of human life' and relentlessly pursuing American experience and the truth about themselves." "Living Mythically," 285. See also, Nye, "The Thirties," 37–58; Maloff, "Mythic Thirties," 109–18.

83. Rourke argues that the "center of growth of any distinctive culture is to be found within the social organism and is created by peculiar and irreducible social forces." *Roots*, 284.

84. See Rideout, *Radical Novel*, 165–224.

85. Gramsci, *Antonio Gramsci*, 189. Also, Vladimir Propp: ". . . we study all phenomena in the *process* of their development. Folklore had existed before the emergence of the peasantry. From a historical perspective, the entire creative output of peoples is folklore. For peoples who have reached the state of class society, folklore is the output of all strata of the population except the ruling one; the latter's verbal art belongs to literature. Folklore is, first and foremost, the art of the oppressed classes, both peasants and workers, but also of the intermediate strata that gravitate toward the lower social classes." *Theory and History of Folklore*, 4–5.

86. Gramsci, *Antonio Gramsci*, 189.

87. Marcia Landy's paraphrase of Gramsci, in Landy, "Culture and Politics," 58.

88. See Flusche, "Joel Chandler Harris," 347–63.

89. These are gathered in Conroy's *The Weed King and Other Stories*. Similar patterns are evident in Conroy's "Uncle Ollie Tales."

90. Botkin, *Treasury of Southern Folklore*, viii.

91. Alan Wilde writes of the modernist writers who, he says, were incapable of accepting chaos or denying it: "in distance and detachment, in the search for order and its creation through absolute irony, . . . [we can see] the dynamics of consciousness in crisis." *Horizons of Ascent*, 49.

92. Kazin, *American Procession*, 21.

93. I distinguish "folk consciousness" here from the "folk consciousness" of which R. Serge Denisoff speaks in *Great Day Coming*. Denisoff describes how the left nurtured "folk consciousness" in the early 1930s, locating it within the organizational context of the Party.

94. See Conroy, "The Affirmative Trend," 8–9. On the other hand, "optimistic" writing, such as Paul Engle's "American Song," seemed to Jack shallow and unconvincing in the midst of the Depression. Conroy's *A World to Win* (1935) reflects the formulaic patterns of revolutionary conversion. Yet Conroy takes pains to show how the "conversion" proceeds from a change in consciousness so that the conclusion is not merely gratuitous.

95. Similarly, Meridel Le Sueur's pronouncements do not square always with her artistic vision. Her work makes fertile use of "bourgeois" literary devices and in fact was attacked by Party critics for defeatist attitudes—for instance, her "Women on the Breadlines." Similarly, her bitter rejection of New Critical values is not confirmed in the suggestiveness and open-endedness of her own writing. Referring to the New Critics, Le Sueur said at a conference in 1985: "In my time at the University of Minnesota, we had two of the most deathly corpses in bourgeois culture—Allen Tate and Robert Penn Warren. We had them both at once. Either one of them could kill you. They taught in writing, as a structure in writing, they taught ambiguity. Can you imagine? They corrupted and polluted our good middle western farm people by talking about ambiguity. You learned to write a whole story or a whole book and say nothing, mean nothing. . . . That was their ambiguity. That was a tremendous weapon. . . ." "Colonialism and American Culture."

96. Aaron, introduction, *The Disinherited*, xii.

97. In chapter 17 I discuss Conroy's literary collaboration with the novelist Arna Bontemps.

98. Quoted in Kornbluh, ed., *Rebel Voices*, 150.

99. Conroy, "Greedy-Gut Gus, the Car Toad," *WK*, 71.

100. My purpose here is to show Conroy's connections with oral tradition to support a contextual reading of uses of folklore in literature. Two interesting studies in this connection are Barnes, "Toward the Establishment of Principles," 5–16, and Cohen, "American Literature and American Folklore." Cohen suggests that literature is associated with literacy, while folklore is allied with illiteracy, the fluid text, orality. Conroy uses folklore to convey the "illiterate" world of workers, of "those who do not write." See Cohen, "American Literature," 238–47. On Wobbly speech and lore see Kornbluh, *Rebel Voices*, and A. Green, "John Newhouse, Wobbly Poet," 189–217.

101. Benjamin, "Storyteller," 87.

102. Ibid., 91, 101. Benjamin's commentary suggests the demise of story-telling in the age of information. David Craig, on the other hand, calls attention to the rich tradition of literary storytellers (Gorki, Sholokhov, O'Casey, Brecht, and others) in the twentieth century. "It appears to be a law of literary development," Craig writes, "that the more a writer identifies himself with the forces of radical change, the readier he is to go to the wellsprings of the oral tradition." *Real Foundations*, 223. To Craig's list we might add B. Traven, Alan Sillitoe, Toni Morrison, and Alice Walker.

103. The reference is to the Pre-Socratics. See Havelock, *Preface to Plato*, x.

Chapter 11
The Gathering Storm

1. *Moberly Monitor-Index*, 10 February 1931, 1.

2. Shover, *Cornbelt Rebellion*.

3. See Pollack, *Populist Response*.

4. Raymond Kresensky, letter to Porter, 2 September 1932. Courtesy of Annette Porter.

5. Charles Kelly, letter to Conroy, ca. December 1985; interview, 6 May 1985.

6. *RP* 10–12 (October–December 1931): 12.

7. Conroy, "Books Abroad," 19.

8. Conroy, "The Twilight of Capitalism," 3–4.

9. *RP* 10–12 (October–December 1931): 8.

10. Henry George Weiss, letter to Isidor Golub, 11 February 1931.

11. Conroy may have toyed with the idea of traveling to the Soviet Union at this time, in the company of H. H. Lewis. See Falkowski, letter to H. H. Lewis, December 1931.

12. See Lasch, *New Radicalism*, 274–85, where this paradox in Steffens's thinking is examined.

13. See Kennell, *Theodore Dreiser*.

14. Weil, *Need for Roots*, 153.

15. H. H. Lewis, *Thinking of Russia*, 1.

16. Rebel Poets, Conroy explained to Robin Lampson, "is catholic enough to attract all the four and seventy sects of radicalism and liberalism. Communists and liberal Christians are represented in the membership. . . ." Conroy, letter to Lampson, 21 December 1929. But several weeks later he wrote to Emerson Price: "I think our logical step is to move farther to the left. The milder radicals are not much to lose, and the better ones will stay with us." Conroy, letter to Price, ca. late December 1929.

17. Walt Carmon, letter to Conroy, [spring?] 1931.

18. Carmon, letter to Conroy, 10 June 1931.

19. Walter Snow, letter to Conroy, 18 February 1931.

20. Ibid.

21. Conroy, letter to *NM*, ca. January 1931.

22. Joseph Kalar, letter to Conroy, 10 November 1931.

23. Conroy, letters to Kenneth Porter, 4 December 1931; 30 December 1931.

24. Ed Falkowski, letter to Conroy, 26 June 1931.

25. Conroy, letter to Kenneth Porter, 6 February 1931.

26. Noah Whitaker, letter to Conroy, 22 February 1931.

27. Conroy, "*The Anvil* and Its Aims," 3–4.

28. Ralph Cheyney, "*The Anvil* and Its Aims," 3.

29. Walt Carmon, letter to Conroy, 28 April 1931.

30. Weiss wrote to Hugh Hanley (a.k.a. Emerson Price): "The only thing about pulpwood is that it pays good if you can write their tripe and click with the right magazine." Henry George Weiss, letter to Hugh Hanley, 17 February 1930. Weiss wrote for *Weird Tales, Amazing Stories, Science-Wonder Stories*, as Snow and other radicals did, for money.

31. Lewis, "Liberal," 8.

32. *New Republic* 70 (13 April 1932): 252.

33. Covington Hall, letter to Conroy, 12 November 1931.

34. Tom O'Flaherty, letter to David Webb, 9 June 1931.

35. Conroy, interview, 13 March 1987.

36. See Conroy, letter to Alice Inglis, 13 June 1931. Courtesy of the Labadie Collection, University of Michigan Library.

37. Conroy, letter to Porter, 30 December 1931.

38. Ed Falkowski, letter to Conroy, 22 December 1931.

39. Ed Falkowski, letter to Conroy, 9 February 1932.

40. Conroy, "Art Above the Battle?" 1.

41. *Moberly Monitor-Index*, 26 October 1931, 1.

42. Ibid., 27 October 1931, 1, 4.

43. Ibid., 6 November 1931, 1.

44. Tom Hackward, interview, 27 December 1978.

45. In *A Return to Pagany*, Halpert and Johns erroneously have Conroy in New York City in the summer of 1931, passing out sandwiches to workers (304).

46. Conroy, interview, 5 September 1986.

47. Conroy, "They Won't Let Us Birds Roost Nowheres," *NM* 8 (18–19 June 1933). The *bezprizorni*, a term associated with Soviet literature, was a commonplace topic of the left.

48. Max Lieber, letter to Conroy, 10 June 1931.

49. H. L. Mencken, letter to Conroy, 29 May 1931.

50. Frances Strauss, letter to Conroy, 26 August 1931. Strauss, the *New Masses* business manager, visited Conroy in Moberly in the early 1930s.

51. *NM* (April 1931): 23.

52. Lieber, "Literature and Social Commentary," 22. Courtesy of the University of Connecticut–Storrs Library. At the Storrs symposium in 1969 Lieber remembered that Hicks, at a party in V. F. Calverton's home and in the company of Lieber, Malcolm Cowley, Matthew Josephson, Edwin Seaver, and others, suddenly exclaimed, "What can I do for Communism?" Hicks had been dismissed from his teaching position at Rensselaer Polytechnic Institute.

53. Spiller et al. on the "malaise": "For this entire literary movement of the American twenties, fresh and promising, varied in talent and bold in achievement, seems to end almost everywhere on a note of negation and of exhaustion." Spiller et al., *Literary History*, 1141.

54. Yet, as Delmore Schwartz notes, another revolution was concurrently underway: "I mean the poetic revolution, the revolution of poetic taste which was inspired by the criticism of T. S. Eliot." Schwartz, "Present State of Poetry," 25. Modernist experimentation took a backseat for a time, only to eclipse the literature of social concern by the end of the decade, promoted by New Criticism in the universities and in the new academic journals of the 1940s and 1950s, a point I return to in chapter 19.

55. Commager, *American Mind*, 434.

56. Ibid., 435.

57. Hicks, *Great Tradition*.

58. On the "search for America" topic, see Preston, "Search for Roots in America." On the "road book" as subgenre, see M. Klein, *Foreigners*; Cook, *From Tobacco Road*.

59. Quoted by Reinemer, "Miscarriage of Promise," 17.

60. See Peters, "Flivver Tramps," 14–15.

61. Probably from a speech Jack gave to a John Reed Club in 1934. Unpubl. MS, untitled, in Conroy papers, Newberry Library.

62. Gorki, "Soviet Literature," in *On Literature*, 229, 243, 252. The text is Gorki's address to the First All-Union Soviet Writers' Congress of 1934.

63. See also Reuss, "American Folklore," and Denisoff, *Great Day Coming*.

64. Anthony Giddens makes a similar point about workers in his essay "Class Structuration and Class Consciousness," in which he argues that the existence of "conflict consciousness" has been more important in the labor movement than "proletarian consciousness," citing the various forms of worker resistance such as slow-down, absenteeism, sabotage, and so forth (174). The essay appears in *Classes, Power and Conflict*, 157–74.

65. See B. Nelson, *Workers on the Waterfront*.

66. Paraphrased by Brewster and Burrell, *Modern Fiction*, 298.

67. For instance, see "Blueprint for Negro Writing" (1937) in which Wright urges black writers to draw upon their own culture, e.g., sources in the black church, folklore, and so forth.

68. The "serious man," Sartre shows, is a materialist assertion (in Marx's terms) of the priority of object over subject and hence a central doctrine of revolutionary activity. But in play, Sartre argues, man "creates" himself, and is able to realize the absolute freedom that is the very being of the person. *Being and Nothingness*, 580–85. Also, see Meeker, *Comedy of Survival*, in which Meeker underscores the comic spirit, its affirmation of life and its rejections of all abstractions that exact a cost in freedom.

69. Frankfurt Social School theorists criticized realist aesthetics, according to Clas Zilliacus: "realism conceives of empirical existence as the only possible existence and, in doing so, links art to the dominant ideology; by denying that art and the observable are things apart, it deprives art of its utopian potential." "Radical Naturalism," 109.

70. Granville Hicks wrote of "Jack Conroy's intimate acquaintanceship with the proletariat" in "Revolution and the Novel," 35.

71. Joseph Kalar, letter to Conroy, 7 March 1932.

72. For instance, see Kenneth Patchen's "Joe Hill Listens," 8–9.

73. Joseph Kalar, letter to Warren Huddlestone, 6 November 1932.

74. Kalar, letter to Huddlestone, 6 November 1932.

75. Conroy, review of "Flat Tire," 10–13; also, *The Literary Workshop* 1,3 (1934): 51.

76. Conroy, "The Affirmative Trend," 8–9.

77. Scott, *Gender and the Politics*.

78. Perhaps this is the meaning of Jack's oft-quoted remark, noted earlier: "Just to see Marx's *Das Kapital* on the shelf gave me a headache."

79. Conroy, "A Note on the Proletarian Novel," 5.

80. Conroy, "The Twilight of Capitalism," 3–4. Images of decay were favorites among radical writers such as Meridel Le Sueur. Gorki wrote in his "A Letter to Workers," "The Capitalist world is decaying and the stench of its corpse contaminates all those who voluntarily or involuntarily serve its inhuman interests. . . ." In *Culture and the People*, 134.

81. Conroy, "Art above the Battle," 3.

82. Ibid.

83. An antecedent was Art Young's cartoons in the old *Masses*. "Art Young's top-hatted, pot-bellied plutocrats had their counterparts in real life and everyone knew who they were." O'Neill, *Echoes of Revolt*, 125.

84. Conroy, "New Notes," *RP* 15 (August 1932): 2.

85. See E. Thompson, *Making of the English Working-Class*, 88ff.; see also, Davidson, *Revolution and the Word*, 160.

86. Ray B. West, Jr., interview, 23 January 1990.

87. Conservative critics like Allen Tate thought otherwise. "The revolutionary art of our time," he wrote in the *New Republic* (2 August 1933), "as of all times, is an escape from reality."

88. Falkowski, letter to Conroy, 9 February 1932.

89. Paul Corey, interview, 23 September 1984.

90. An interesting historical perspective on radicalism among workers in the 1930s is provided by Verba and Scholzman, "Unemployment, Class Consciousness, and Radical Politics," 292–323.

91. In *Social Change and Cultural Crisis*, Richard Lowenthal makes the point about collapse occurring as a "consequence of the generalization and intensification of the anomic cultural crisis of the West."

92. Lewis liked to tell people that he was "an American Mercury writer." Conroy, interview, 1 September 1985.

93. Conroy, interview, 21 April 1984.

94. See chapter 8.

95. H. H. Lewis, *Road to Utterly*, 21.

96. Carmon, letter to Conroy, 5 April 1934.

97. Calverton, *Liberation of American Literature*.

98. *New Republic* 70 (13 April 1932): 252.

99. Conroy, interview, 26 December 1984.

100. Catherine Lewis Bock, "Biographical Sketch"; letter to author, 5 November 1990.

101. Weiss, letter to Lewis, ca. 1932. Bedni was a Soviet peasant poet whom Jack published, in Fania Kruger's translation, in *Rebel Poet*.

102. H. Lewis, *Road to Utterly*, 25.

103. Lewis seems to have had little or no direct connection to the populist and socialist protest movements that swept across southeastern Missouri earlier in the century. On these earlier movements, which seem to provide antecedents for Lewis's solitary vernacular protest, see Ogilvie, "Populism and Socialism," 159–83.

104. Dellinger, "Pegasus and the Plow," 6–7. Dellinger located Lewis in the early 1970s living alone in a converted corncrib, a follower of the Christian fundamentalist Herbert Armstrong.

105. H. H. Lewis, interview, 26 August 1982.

106. John Brown is a more famous example of the kind.

107. *International Literature* 1 (April 1934): 150–51.

108. Quoted in *Left Front* 1 (May–June 1934): 20. The second assertion is incontestable.

109. Falkowski, letter to Conroy, 22 December 1931.

110. Grace Stone Coates, letter to Conroy, 22 December 1931.

111. See Gilbert, *Writers and Partisans*, 113.

112. Falkowski, letter to Conroy, 22 December 1931.

113. On Wheelwright and Conroy, see Wald, *Revolutionary Imagination*, 92. The Cambridge poetry group also included Kenneth Porter.

114. A similar shift in focus occurred in *New Masses* under Gold's editorship, as noted earlier. The June 1928 issue of *New Masses* is subtitled "A Magazine for Rebels." The July issue, with Gold now as editor, has the caption "Poems and Tales by Miners, Sailors, Clerks, Carpenters, Etc."

Chapter 12
Comrade Jack

1. *Moberly Monitor-Index*, 18 May 1932, 1.

2. Ibid., 21 January 1932, 7.

3. Ibid., 11 July 1932, 1; 28 July 1932, 1.

4. Ibid., 20 November 1931, 1.

5. deFord, "Unemployed," 12.

6. See Frank Thibault, letter to Conroy, 26 December 1931.

7. Conroy used the St. Louis riot as the basis of a key episode in *A World to Win*, including an incident when one of the demonstrators hurled a tear-gas bomb at the police. The Moberly paper described the incident: "As the crowd broke and ran, several of the bolder spirits threw stones toward the police, some of whom had been temporarily blinded by a gas bomb caught by one of the men in the crowd and hurled back." *Moberly Monitor-Index*, 11 July 1932, 1.

8. Eric Homberger notes that "when examined in detail, the political commitments of American writers often seem equivocal. Their commitments are a

manuscript which they are endlessly revising. It is precisely in the space where ideological certainties and emotional desires come into conflict that the most interesting stories and essays, novels and poems, emerge." *American Writers and Radical Politics*, xi.

9. Conroy, letter to a "friend," 14 March 1932.

10. Conroy, "The Twilight of Capitalism," 4.

11. Norman Macleod, interview, 16 July 1981. Edward Dahlberg's description of a John Reed Club meeting is more fanciful than factual. Yet it corroborates Macleod's memory of struggles among its members over correct interpretation. See *The Confessions of Edward Dahlberg*, 286–89.

12. Macleod, interview, 16 July 1981.

13. Conroy, letter to John Rogers, 7 September 1971.

14. Members of the Chicago John Reed Club helped organize the St. Louis JRC. Bill Jordan, Marvin Klein, and others—altogether about twenty-five members—went to St. Louis in early 1932 to give talks and help in organizing the JRC there. Jordan, letter to Conroy, 28 February 1932.

15. Howe and Coser, *American Communist Party*, 284–97.

16. Homberger is certainly correct in asserting that "the experience of the left in American literature is scarcely comprehensible without a firm grasp of the ways in which Soviet literary policy was emulated." Homberger, *American Writers*, 140. Earlier I revealed the particular manner in which the midwestern radicals grafted Soviet examples (e.g., the role of proletarian literature, the figure of the worker-writer) to indigenous traditions, such as union activity, Socialist/Populist currents. Here I study how the CPA helped shape the worker-writer movement through its active role in organizing the unemployed and defending social causes. In later chapters I discuss the CPA's function in providing distribution outlets for little magazines and books. Finally, I examine the effect of the Party's abandonment of the worker-writer movement in the Popular Front period. While the Soviet example and the CPA are important components, at least for the period under discussion, I believe that it is necessary to consider the more important role of indigenous radical traditions in shaping midwestern radicalism and the worker-writers I study.

17. A good description of a devoted Communist Party member is Nelson, Barrett, and Ruck, *Steve Nelson*.

18. Russel B. Nye identifies certain characteristics of Midwestern indigenous radicalism, among which he lists an anarchic strain that resists ideologies and centralized control: ". . . it was virtually impossible for a single man or a small group of men to create a Midwestern movement. Traditionally, Midwestern protest came from the people first and a leader followed, or if no leader appeared, the movement proceeded without one, as did the Grange and the Farmers' Alliance. Midwest movements seemingly could not be organized from the top downward. . . ." *Midwestern Progressive Politics*, 14.

19. "Out in the Midwest of penny auctions and burning corn . . . we were far from the ideological tempests raging in New York City coffee pots. How many Marxian angels could dance on the point of a hammer and sickle?" Conroy, "Semester of the Thirties."

20. See Wixson, "Thomas Hart Benton," 191–218.

21. See Rourke, "Significance of Sections."

22. See Wilson, "Literary Class War." Wilson recalls that orthodox Communist critics attacked Gold's *Jews without Money* for its individualist point of view. In a subsequent article Wilson, quoting Trotsky, reminded such critics that the task was not to construct "an abstract culture without any real foundation," but to encourage "an actual, concrete culture." "Art, the Proletariat and Marx," 43.

23. Trotsky, letter to V. F. Calverton, *Modern Monthly* 7 (March 1933): 85.

24. Some radicals on the left were better informed but no less "backward" with respect to the evolution occurring in Soviet literary theory and practice. Homberger notes that Mike Gold held onto superannuated notions of Proletcult in his editorship of *New Masses* between 1928 and 1930. Homberger, *American Writers*, 128.

25. Weil, *Need for Roots*, 153.

26. Conroy, *RP* 14 (July 1932).

27. More attention needs to be devoted to this point. Schwartz's discussion of RAPP influence in the United States needs further clarification. See L. Schwartz, *Marxism and Culture*, chap. 3. Sergei Tretyakov's essay in *International Literature* 3 (July 1933): 54–56, for instance, praises worker-correspondence, the use of mimeo machines, and so forth, well past the official dismantling of RAPP.

28. Struve, *Russian Literature*; E. Brown, *Proletarian Episode*.

29. The Party, according to Herman Ermolaev, was now "interested in creating a literary elite from both proletarians and fellow travelers by uniting them in a single association under the watchful eye of Communist officials and writers." *Soviet Literary Theories*, 122.

30. Falkowski, letter to Conroy, 9 February 1932.

31. Carmon, letter to Conroy, 15 January 1932.

32. *NM* (February 1932): 30. Material on John Rogers generously provided by Robin Rogers.

33. Botkin published Lewis, Rogers, and solicited material from Conroy and Kalar. Botkin, letters to Conroy, 5 December, 22 April, 31 December 1932.

34. Dee and Sally Brown, interview, 24 April 1983.

35. *Quindaro* 6 (1980).

36. *Rebel Poet* exchanged ads with Jolas's *transition*. In *Rebel Poet* 17 appeared a notice of a new installment of James Joyce's "Work in Progress."

37. Seguin, "Rebel Poet and Humanity."

38. Conroy, "Art above the Battle," 3.

39. Falkowski, "Notes of a Soviet Literary School," 6.

40. Bedni's poems were, according to Struve, the "quintessence of proletarian 'agit-poetry.'" Struve, *Russian Literature*, 30.

41. *RP* 13 (March 1932): 10.

42. S. Anderson, "Machine Song," 17, 19.

43. Benet, "Round About Parnassus," 772.

44. *Nation* (16 December 1931).

45. Conroy, "The Sweet Uses of Criticism," unpubl. MS, Conroy papers, Newberry.

Notes to Pages 268–74

46. Musser, "To Young Rebel Poets," 77.
47. Carmon, letter to Conroy, 1931.
48. Conroy, letter to Porter, 12 January 1932.
49. Conroy, letter to Abernethy, 6 March 1932.
50. Mencken, letter to Conroy, 6 February 1932.
51. Conroy, letter to Abernethy, 22 March 1932.
52. Mencken, letter to Conroy, 17 March 1932.
53. Conroy, letter to Ralph F. Lozier, 7 March 1932.
54. Quoted by Kennedy, *American People*, 86–93.
55. Kresensky, letter to Porter, 14 June 1932.
56. Kresensky, letter to Porter, 2 September 1932.
57. Conroy, letter to Porter, 21 March 1932. Porter, Link, and Wheelwright started the Cambridge Poetry Forum, affiliated with the Rebel Poets.
58. Rogers, letter to Conroy, 15 March 1932.
59. Conroy, letter to Porter, 21 March 1932.
60. Mattick, *Arbeitslosigkeit*, 51.
61. Pells, *Radical Visions*, 98.
62. "Unemployment," *Fortune Magazine*, September 1932, 19.
63. Conroy, letter to editors, *Earth* (April 1932): 18.
64. Max Lieber, letter to Conroy, 20 April 1932.
65. Agnes Inglis, letter to Conroy, 21 April 1932.
66. Whittaker Chambers, letter to Conroy, 16 May 1932.
67. Conroy, letter to Richard Johns, 4 May 1932.
68. Conroy, letter to Porter, 9 May 1932.
69. Oakley Johnson, letter to Conroy, 16 June 1932.
70. Conroy, editorial note, *RP* 16 (September 1932): 2.
71. Aaron, *Writers on the Left*, 229.
72. Bill Jordan, letter to Conroy, 1 June 1930.
73. "Call to American Intellectuals to Rally Against Imperialist War!" National Conference of John Reed Clubs, 30 May 1932. Conroy papers, Newberry Library.
74. Bill Jordan, letter to Conroy, 1 June 1932.
75. Norman Abrams, letter to Conroy, 8 July 1932.
76. Carmon, letter to Conroy, 12 November 1932.
77. Ibid.
78. Philip Rahv, letter to Conroy, 27 May 1932.
79. Born Ivan Greenberg in Ukraine, Rahv came to the United States in 1922, changing his name when he joined the Party. Rahv was a rising young star in the New York radical intellectual scene in 1932.
80. Rahv, review of "Scottsboro Limited," 7.
81. Rahv, "An Open Letter to Young Writers," 3.
82. Walter Snow, letter to Grace Wellington, 5 January 1933.
83. Rahv, letter to Conroy, 22 June 1932.
84. "Minutes of the Rebel Poet's Meeting of June 22, 1932." Conroy papers, Newberry Library.
85. Rahv, letter to Conroy, 22 June 1932.

86. Ibid.

87. Leonard Spier, letter to Conroy, late July 1932.

88. Conroy, editorial notes, *RP* 15 (August 1932): 2.

89. Walter Snow, letter to Conroy, 21 July 1932.

90. Conroy, letter to Walter Snow, 26 July 1932.

91. Kenneth Porter, letter to Professor Rosenfeld, 29 November 1973.

92. Conroy, letter to John Wheelwright, 15 July 1932.

93. John Wheelwright, letter to Conroy, 26 July 1932.

94. Wheelwright, unpubl. MS with Conroy papers, Newberry Library.

95. Charlotte Moskowitz, letter to Conroy, 11 July 1932.

96. A. Heymoolen, letter to Conroy, 29 May 1932.

97. Minutes of Rebel Poets meeting, 13 July 1932. Conroy papers, Newberry Library.

98. Rahv, letter to Conroy, 4 August 1932.

99. Mencken, letter to Conroy, 18 July 1932.

100. Emerson Price, letter to Conroy, September 1932.

101. James Rorty, letter to Conroy, 2 September 1932.

102. Carmon, letter to Conroy, 12 November 1932.

103. Walter Snow, letter to John Ackerson, 13 August 1932.

104. Rahv, Kainen, Stacy, Miller, and Weber, joint letter to "Comrade Conroy," 19 August 1932.

105. Howe and Coser call Jerome "a Party hack." *American Communist Party*, 289.

106. Minutes of the Rebel Poets meeting, 29 August 1929. Conroy papers, Newberry Library.

107. Snow, letter to Conroy, 9 September 1932.

108. Rebel Poets was not alone in attracting armchair activists. Edward Laning notes that officers of the New York John Reed Club "harangued the meeting in an effort to persuade someone to go out to a plumber's union meeting in Canarsie to give a chalk talk." "The New Deal Mural Projects," in O'Connor, *New Deal Art Projects*, 81.

109. Magil displayed a supple attitude toward the issue in question. At the Kharkov conference in 1930 he had led a faction of Americans opposing the IURW's effort to enlist progressive writers among the middle class. Since that time, however, he had aligned his view with the IURW's position. See Homberger, *American Writers*, 136.

110. In the Soviet Union, RAPP had repeatedly come under Party fire for narrowing the scope of proletarian literature. RAPP leaders made the "worker-udarnik" (worker-writer) central to the proletarian literary movement at a time when the Party decided that it no longer sought proletarian hegemony in literature; that any writer could serve Party ends if he or she wrote from a socialist viewpoint. See E. Brown, *Proletarian Episode*, 164, 210–13. Lawrence Schwartz notes that the RAPP phase continued in the United States after 1932 when it was dissolved in the Soviet Union. Schwartz, *Marxism and Culture*, 8–9, 39–46.

111. Kalar, letter to Huddestone, 19 December 1932.

112. Snow, letter to Conroy, 20 September 1932.

113. Snow, letter to Conroy, 17 November 1932.

114. Spier, letter to Conroy, 1 October 1932.

115. Snow, letter to Conroy, 11 October 1932.

116. Ibid.

117. Snow, letter to Conroy, 9 September 1932. Unintentionally comic, Snow's letter to Conroy describes a farcical meeting in Spier's apartment, in which Rahv and Spier positioned for power and Jerome quietly manipulated both. Jerome pretended not to listen to the ongoing debates between Spier and Rahv, then intervened, and ever so politely demolished both with an ideological observation. Snow writes: "Rahv's eyes popped out. Opening thick lips, he sucked in his breath. Nodding his head slowly, he listened. His dark eyes showed a gleam of admiration. Here at last was a man he could learn something from. A trained Marxist."

118. Snow, letter to Conroy, 9 September 1932.

119. Olga Spier, letter to Conroy, 3 November 1932.

120. Kalar, letter to Huddlestone, 19 December 1932.

121. Howe and Coser, *American Communist Party*, 282.

122. Conroy, letter to Paul Romaine, 26 September 1932.

123. Conroy, letter to Porter, 10 October 1932.

124. Bendiner, *Just Around the Corner*, 77. Randolph County showed slightly better for the Communists than did H. H. Lewis's Cape County in southeastern Missouri, where only two cast their votes for Foster/Ford: Lewis and "my cousin-hand who works for us." Lewis, letter to Conroy, ca. November 1932.

125. Snow, letter to Grace Wellington, 3 January 1933.

126. Quoted by Harry Hansen, *New York World-Telegram*, 2 December 1933.

127. Granville Hicks, letter to Conroy, December 1932.

128. V. F. Calverton, letter to Conroy, 26 October 1932.

129. The American Library Association estimated a four million jump in library patronage by 1933. Grannis, *Publishers' Weekly*, 19–22.

130. Snow, letter to Wellington, 11 October 1932.

131. Kalar, letter to Snow, 29 September 1932.

132. James Rorty, letter to Conroy, 2 September 1932.

133. Grace Wellington, letter to Snow, 27 September 1932.

134. Jack seldom disclosed his motivations or offered reasons, other than an offhand remark such as: "I like working-class people; they're not trying to be somebody else." When asked to follow up on remarks like this (which he made very seldom), he would quote a humorous verse or change the subject.

135. Conroy, letter to Snow, ca. late fall 1932.

136. Lejeune addresses this point: "le fait de prendre en main son propre récit de vie . . . sera plus ou moins voluntairement un acte d'ascension sociale et d'assimilation à la culture dominante, même s'il se situe dans le cadre d'une lutte militante. . . ." (The fact that an artisan [worker] takes in hand his life story . . . is, more or less willingly, an act of social ascension and assimilation to the dominant culture, even if he places it within the context of militant struggle. . . .) *Je Est Un Autre*, 254.

137. Abe Aaron, interview, 7 January 1990.

138. Aaron, letter to Conroy, 23 February 1934.

139. Ibid.

140. Lovelace, letter to Leonard Spier, 6 August 1932.

141. Max Lieber, letter to Conroy, 9 January 1933.

142. Carmon, letter to Conroy, 12 November 1932. Carmon continued to serve as an intermediary for Jack, communicating shifts in Soviet literary policy and promoting American worker-writers in Moscow.

143. Conroy, letter to Porter, November 1932.

144. Snow, letter to Conroy, 22 December 1932.

145. Daniel Aaron makes a similar point in connection with radical writers. *Writers on the Left*, 88–89.

146. To devote a whole issue (no. 15) to black writers and problems was in 1932 unusual, even courageous. No black writers, however, actually contributed to the issue. (Black writers like Eugene Gordon were Rebel Poets.) Spier called upon black and white writers to join in common cause in opposing lynchings. Several of the contributors wrote poems based upon newspaper accounts of the Scottsboro Boys; Rahv used his review of Langston Hughes's "Scottsboro Limited" to polemicize; V. J. Jerome's poem "Communis' Blues" is an unintentional parody of Hughes's blues poems.

147. Whitman, Preface to *Leaves of Grass* (1855), in *Complete Poetry and Collected Prose*, 15. For a discussion of Whitman's mixed reception among the Rebel Poets, see Michel Fabre, "Walt Whitman and the Rebel Poets," 88–93.

148. W. S. Stacy's "Picket Lines on a Coal Mine," 9, is a good example of this kind.

Chapter 13
Proletarian Bull Market

1. Conroy, interview, 21 June 1987.

2. Kennedy, *American People*, 83; also, see *Fortune* 10 (October 1934): 55–56.

3. *Moberly Monitor-Index*, 31 December 1932, 4.

4. Conroy, "Bull Market," *WK*, 215.

5. Conroy, "Literary Underworld of the Thirties," lecture, Semester of the Thirties, 17 April 1969, University of Connecticut–Storrs, MS, pp. 4–6. See also Komarovsky, *Unemployed Man*. Edwin Rolfe's poem "The Sixth Winter" is a powerful evocation of contrasts between haves and have-nots; in Salzman and Zanderer, eds., *Social Poetry of the 1930s*, 236–41.

6. Conroy, *The Disinherited*, 223.

7. Pells, *Radical Visions*, 114–15.

8. "Gone West," in Salzman and Zanderer, eds., *Social Poetry of the 1930s*, 139. Similarly, Maxwell Geismar argues that Steinbeck moved from the "individualistic power-drive of the buccaneer, this more glamorous portrayal of the values of '29" [in *Cup of Gold*] to "writing of man's communal good" [in *Grapes of Wrath*]. Geismar, *Writers in Crisis*, 266.

9. Fried, "Conversation with Jack Conroy," 41–56.

10. It could be, alternatively, a three-valued system, for instance, as implied in the title *Bolshevism, Fascism and Capitalism*, by Counts, Villari, Rorty, and Baker, published by the Institute of Politics at Yale University. Fascism, the authors suggest, preys upon uncertainty; it is necessary to take a position.

11. Scheel, "Book Revue of 1933," in "The Sunday Review," *New York World-Telegram*, 31 December 1933.

12. See Marling, *Wall-to-Wall America*.

13. Brecht, "Questions from a Worker Who Reads."

14. See Fichtenbaum, *Funsten Nut Strike*. Fichtenbaum pays little attention to Sentner's role in the strike.

15. The Chicago John Reed Club's publication, *Left Front*, carried a long piece on the strike. Bronson, "The Nut-Pickers Picket," 16. For a more objective account, see Fichtenbaum, *Funsten Nut Strike*; see also Brunn, "Black Workers and Social Movements."

16. See Towey, "Hooverville." Towey glosses over the desperation of the people.

17. See A. Martin, *Tempest Maker*, on Harry Turner and the earlier bohemia. Some of my information is based upon interviews with Robert Logsdon, a labor activist in the 1930s, who remembered vividly the labor and bohemian milieus of St. Louis in the thirties. Logsdon, interview, 10 April 1984. See also Wharton, letter to Conroy, 28 August 1957.

18. Conroy, interview, 26 December 1978; Conroy, letter to author, 9 March 1977.

19. Guy Golterman, Jr., quoted by Seevers, "Blue Lantern Bohemians," 5.

20. See Johns, *Time of Our Lives*, 339. Johns was the son of George Sibley Johns, editor of the *St. Louis Post-Dispatch*. Orrick Johns lived in Greenwich Village before World War I and in Europe during the 1920s. Later head of the New York Writers' Project, he was murdered by a sailor who poured whiskey over him and set him afire after Johns rejected the sailor's effort to gain a position on the project (his submission was, in Johns's opinion, doggerel). Conroy, interview, 22 October 1978. See also Harrington, *Fragments of a Century*, on St. Louis's bohemian milieu in the 1940s.

21. Conroy, *A World to Win*, 164.

22. See, for example, Conroy's "What If You Don't Want to Write for Money," 9–13, in which Conroy suggests that the best proletarian novels will be written by workers themselves.

23. Conroy, "White Collar Writers," 31–34.

24. Plato, *Republic*, VII, 752.

25. Johns, *Time of Our Lives*, 339.

26. Conroy, NM 8 (May 1933): 30.

27. Gold, NM 4 (July 1928): 1.

28. Ibid., 2.

29. Spector, letter to Walter Snow, 17 January 1933.

30. For example, Carmon gave suggestions to Jack concerning his poem "Kokomo Joe." Emerson Price, letter to Olive Stainsby, 22 December 1929.

31. Kalar, letter to Huddlestone, 6 November 1932.

32. Wright, *White Man, Listen!* 145.

33. Dennen, "Soviet Literature."

34. See Gorki, *On Literature.*

35. O'Toole, *Structure, Style,* 9.

36. See Lemon and Reis, eds., *Russian Formalist Criticism,* 67. The editors note: "Technically, a *skaz* is a story in which the manner of telling (the normal speech patterns of the narrator—dialect, pronunciation, grammatical peculiarities, pitch patterns, etc.) is as important to the effect as the story itself."

37. Bakhtin, "Discourse Typology in Prose," 183.

38. Clark, "Little Heroes and Big Deeds," 199.

39. Artyom Vesyoly (a.k.a. Nikolay Kochkurov), according to Gleb Struve, was one of the few true proletarians in Soviet literature. A factory worker, Vesyoly used the first-person narrative and the *skaz* form. Struve, *Russian Literature,* 139–40.

40. Conroy, "The Worker as Writer," *JCR,* 221.

41. Kalar, letter to Warren Huddlestone, 7 December 1932.

42. Orvell, *Real Thing,* chap. 7.

43. Kalar, letter to Huddlestone, 4 September 1932. Mencken suggested that Kalar use George Milburn's Oklahoma sketches as a model. Kalar, letter to Conroy, 26 November 1931.

44. A good example is H. H. Lewis's "Memoirs of a Dishwasher."

45. Conroy, "What If You Don't Write for Money," 12.

46. Elistratova, "*New Masses.*"

47. See Abe Aaron, letter to Conroy, 4 April 1935. "Nelson's been ragging me alot [sic] because of my enthusiasms in this matter. He says he doesn't know what a sketch genre is. The phrase is Elistratova's." Aaron's letter, in the Conroy papers, Newberry Library, is an interesting contemporary commentary on the uses of the sketch form in proletarian fiction of the early 1930s.

48. Kalar, letter to Huddlestone, 7 December 1932.

49. Kalar, letter to Huddlestone, 4 September 1932.

50. Kalar, letter to Huddlestone, 29 September 1932.

51. Max Lieber, letter to Conroy, 9 January 1932.

52. Conroy, letter to Kenneth Porter, 17 March 1933.

53. Fred Miller, letter to H. H. Lewis, 26 February 1933. Jack wrote to Snow that Miller was trying to "stir up Lewis" but his efforts would be in vain "for we three [Lewis, Kalar, Conroy] grew up together in the literary movement and are known as the Three Musketeers, the Western Triumvirate." Conroy, letter to Snow, early 1933.

54. Snow, letter to Walt Carmon, 27 March 1933.

55. Williams, *Autobiography,* 299.

56. See F. Miller, "*The New Masses* and Who Else?" 4–5.

57. The problem was, of course, that *Anvil* and *Blast,* two similar magazines, were aimed at the same limited readership.

58. Snow, letter to Conroy, 11 October 1932; Conroy, letter to Snow, ca. October–November 1932.

59. Benjamin Musser, letter to Conroy, 17 November 1932.

60. Cheyney, "Statement."

61. Conroy, "Statement," *Anvil* 1 (May 1933): 3. The fact that Conroy reprinted both statements entirely in an essay he wrote in 1978 for *TriQuarterly* suggests that even if he no longer stood completely behind what he had written forty-five years earlier, he was certainly not ashamed of it. During the darkest days of the Depression in 1933, Conroy wrote his strongest expression of support to the Communists. He was angered by the spectacle of hunger and despair among workers in St. Louis and by the reluctance of several labor groups to join the Communist-led Unemployed Council, which was successfully organizing the jobless. Hope for the worker, he concluded, lay only in embracing the "Marxist-Leninist way." In a lengthy letter to *International Literature* Conroy suggested to his readers that the New Deal—then only several months old—was simply the old capitalist wolf offering "blandishments." "American Proletarian Writers and the New Deal," 123–26.

62. Snow, letter to Conroy, 26 November 1932.

63. "Turns With a Bookworm," Books Section, *New York Herald Tribune*, 19 February 1933.

64. *Richmond Times-Dispatch*, 5 March 1933.

65. Conroy, letter to Snow, 19 January 1933.

66. Conroy's "High Bridge" appeared with Cruden's "Men Wanted" in the same issue of *NM* (April 1931).

67. See bibliography for Cruden's worker narratives and reportage in *New Masses, Nation, National Review*. A photo and brief biographical description of Cruden appears in *NM* (April 1931): 23.

68. Conroy, "A Note on the Proletarian Novel," 5.

69. Robert and Janet Cruden, interview, 7 November 1987. In a letter to me Robert Cruden writes that "when the CIO came along I was swept up in its great campaigns, becoming a publicity man for the rubber union. That is one of the gut experiences of my life. Then came the war, and I ended up with a tank battalion on Okinawa. That is another gut experience. The war over, I found the union movement had changed. And I was shortly out of a job. What to do, with a wife and two children?" (Cruden, letter to author, 16 November 1987). Cruden later earned a Ph.D. and taught history, specializing in the Civil War and Reconstruction eras, at Lewis and Clark College until his retirement in 1978. Also, see D. Anderson, "Michigan Proletarian Writers."

70. Upton Sinclair, letter to Conroy, 4 January 1933.

71. Max Lieber, letter to Conroy, 3 March 1933.

72. Conroy, letter to Snow, 20 March 1933.

73. Mencken, letter to Conroy, 1 April 1933.

74. Conroy, interview, 30 October 1982. D. I. Polyanov, editor and founder of Bulgarian proletarian literature, writes in this issue that the Bulgarian *Anvil* would draw upon worker and peasant correspondents. They "must be the reserve from which to choose proletarian writers." *Literature of the World Revolution* 1 (1931): 122.

75. Sandburg, "The People, Yes," 617.

76. Jean Winkler, letter to Betrenia Watt, ca. 1937. Courtesy of Betrenia Watt Bowker.

77. Similarly, George Redfield, one of the *Left* editors in Davenport, Iowa, complained to Kalar of the difficulty in finding well-written revolutionary prose. Redfield, letter to Kalar, 17 April 1931.

78. Frank Nipp, interview, 30 December 1985.

79. J. W. Norrick, letter to Conroy, 12 February 1933.

80. Conroy, "The Literary Underworld of the Thirties," 159–60.

81. Walter Snow, "The Anvil and the Proletarian Short Story." Courtesy of the University of Connecticut–Storrs. The manuscript is Snow's speech to the International Labor Defense League in New York City, early 1935.

82. Snow, letter to Conroy, 17 November 1932.

83. Balch, "To the Manlovers of Our Local Four Hundred."

84. John Rogers, letter to Snow, 4 March 1933.

85. Jack wrote Snow: "Dinamov is already favorably disposed toward us, so let the galled jades [Rahv, Miller and Stacy] wince, our withers are unwrung." Conroy, letter to Snow, 20 March 1933. Clearly, it was important to Jack to gain Moscow's approval. If nothing else, Snow wrote Jack, it was necessary to forestall attacks by the Rahvites.

86. Granville Hicks, letter to Conroy, 23 May 1933. Jack scribbled in the margin of Hicks's letter: "This is true, but Alan Calmer doesn't think so." Calmer was a Marxist critic for the *Daily Worker*.

87. Carmon, letter to Kalar, 13 April 1933.

88. Conroy, letter to Snow, 23 February 1933.

89. Ben Hagglund, letter to Snow, 28 January 1933.

90. Spier, letter to Snow, ca. March 1933; Snow, letter to Clements, 15 May 1933.

91. Gold, letter to Conroy, ca. early 1933.

92. Paul Corey, letter to Conroy, 5 April 1933.

93. Hagglund, letter to Conroy, 2 May 1933.

94. Broun, "It Seems to Me," *New York World-Telegram*, 15 May 1933.

95. Snow, letter to Broun, 15 May 1933.

96. See Sherwood Anderson, James Oppenheim, and Randolph Bourne in Leslie Fishbein's *Rebels in Bohemia* for a description of that earlier conflict (52–53). Best known, of course, is Whitman's defense of the "the roughs." "I will not have in my writing any elegance or effect . . ." (Preface to *Leaves of Grass*).

97. Snow, letter to Leonard Spier, 15 May 1933.

98. Covici-Friede, letter to Lieber, 25 March 1933.

99. See, for instance, Seaver, "Literature at the Crossroads." "The revolutionary writer has his clearly defined line of action," Seaver writes, "from which he cannot depart without risking criticism for left or right deviation. . . . It carries the materialistic dialectic to all problems. It seeks, in a word, to carry out the minimum obligations agreed upon by the International Union of Revolutionary Writers at the Kharkov conference of 1930" (12).

100. Seaver, "Memorandum on *The Disinherited*." Conroy papers, Newberry Library. Seaver had thrown himself into the revolutionary struggle since the

publication in 1929 of *The Company*. By 1933, he was working on a novel ("Between the Hammer and the Anvil") that treated, from a class perspective, children made homeless by the Depression. See Seaver, letter to the editor, *International Literature* 2 (1933): 129–30.

101. Hicks, letters to Conroy, December 1932, 3 January 1933. Hicks gave each section of the book a letter grade.

102. Conroy, letter to Abernethy, 13 March 1933.

103. Lieber, letter to Conroy, 16 February 1932.

104. Conroy claimed the manuscript was rejected thirteen times. His correspondence with publishers only accounts for nine: Knopf; Random House; Scribner's; Macmillan; Simon and Schuster; Covici, Friede; Harcourt, Brace; Viking; Farrar and Rinehart.

105. See Fensch, *Steinbeck and Covici*.

106. Covici-Friede appears to be an exception, publishing Horace Gregory's *Chelsea Rooming House* in 1930, John Strachey's *The Coming Struggle for Power*, Alvah Bessie's *Dwell in the Wilderness*, and Harriet Arnow's first novel, *Mountain Paths* (1936), all books that incurred financial risk on the publishers' part.

107. Conroy, "What If You Don't Want to Write for Money," 9.

108. Norman Macleod, letter to the editor, *International Literature* 3 (July 1933): 129. At the same time that most publishers were tightening belts, Simon and Schuster commercialized the legitimate book trade. Macleod, letter to author, 26 November 1984.

109. Conroy, interview, 6 May 1985.

110. See *Fortune* 28 (November 1943), 142ff., for an early study of the mass marketing of books. Also, see Radway, *Reading the Romance*.

111. Seaver, letter to Conroy, 9 May 1933.

112. Seaver, letter to Conroy, ca. June 1933.

113. Ibid.

114. Conroy, letter to Snow, 5 July 1933.

115. Editor's note, *Windsor Quarterly* 1 (winter 1933–34): 416.

116. Haldeman-Julius, a transplant from New York City by way of Los Angeles, got his start with socialist publishers, which eventually brought him to Girard, Kansas, through his association with J. A. Wayland.

117. J. Gunn, "Pocket Series," 9–10.

118. On Davenport's socialist past, see Weinstein, *Decline of Socialism in America*, 44, 96, 238.

119. W. K. Jordan, letter to author, 15 April 1983.

120. Herbert Kline, letter to author, 10 April 1984. Mosenfelder seems to have been a black sheep in the family. John Mosenfelder, a relative, said, "Talk to the FBI, they'd know more about him!" Interview, 6 October 1985.

121. George Redfield, letter to Kalar, 10 May 1931.

122. The great Soviet filmmaker Sergei Eisenstein also contributed to this issue of the *Left*.

123. Adamic, "What the Proletariat Reads," 321–22.

124. See Shore, *Talkin' Socialism*.

125. See Shepherd, *History of Street Literature*; E. Thompson, *Making of the Working Class*.

126. Bookstores in the 1930s were willing to carry ephemeral publications, including radical magazines, in contrast to today's mass-market chain bookstores.

127. Influential literary magazines often had a much smaller circulation, such as the *Dial*, which, with never more than three hundred subscribers, published Emerson, Thoreau, and others.

128. Snow, letter to Conroy, 2 December 1971.

129. Eager to show ideological correctness, the *Left's* editors nonetheless revealed little knowledge of labor issues when they insisted that Jack make certain changes in his story "Picket Line" for *Left 2*. The time span between the strike's end and the retribution of the ex-striker, which Jack had put at one year, was implausibly long, they said. Jack complied, but replaced the detail when he incorporated the story in *The Disinherited*. See Marvin Klein, letter to Conroy, 21 October 1931.

130. Hefland, "Left, No. 1," 139.

131. Calverton, "Need for Revolutionary Criticism," 9.

132. "Left No. 2," *International Literature* 2–3 (1932): 152.

133. Max Eastman in *Artists in Uniform* (1934) underscores the humiliation of the *Left* editors in their apology to IURW. "Before these young men ever become revolutionists they will have to learn to be rebels" (27). See pages 25–26, for a brief summary of the incident. Eastman, once the great radical editor of the *Masses*, was a lapsed revolutionary from the point of view of the left in the 1930s.

134. Jay Du Von subsequently edited the *New Quarterly* in Rock Island, Illinois, and later was appointed director of the Iowa Writers' Project. According to Norman Macleod, Du Von became an FBI informer (Macleod, letter to Conroy, 31 October 1969). Marvin Klein and Bill Jordan went to Chicago to be part of the John Reed Club and publish its magazine, *Left Front*. Jordan later was a civil servant in Washington, D.C. (W. K. Jordan, letter to author, 15 April 1983). Herbert Kline (a.k.a. Klein), Marvin's brother, subsequently became a well-known theater and film producer (Klein, letter to author, April 1984). Mosenfelder continued in the furniture business. His satiric attack on left-wing intellectuals, "The Movement to the Left!," appeared in the February 1933 issue of the *American Mercury*. I have no information on the remaining Davenport radicals.

135. See Horkheimer, *Critical Theory*, 273–90.

136. Conroy, "What If You Don't Want to Write for Money," *Writer's Review* (April 1933): 9–13.

137. Benjamin makes a similar point in "Der Autor als Produzent."

138. The *bezprizorni* story in the Left press was a politicized counterpart of the boxcar or tramping sketch.

139. Conroy, letter to Howard Wolf, 19 July 1933.

140. Gold, "Notes of the Month," 5.

141. Drew, *Nelson Algren*, 62.

142. Snow, letter to Granville Hicks, 18 July 1933.

143. Drew, *Nelson Algren*, 64–65. Drew quotes Algren's talk at Sul Ross Col-

lege in which Algren placed Conroy above "Sinclair Lewis and other popular contemporaries" (65).

144. See Murrah, "Llano Cooperative Colony."

145. The Wisconsin writer August Derleth, an *Anvil* contributor, worked in the printing shop at Llano in 1934. "Llano was the 'depot' of a constant stream of dreamers, crackpots, intellectuals, and plain hoboes who came, stayed briefly, and went, and I among them. The New Deal finally made Llano superfluous, so it went under. . . ." Derleth, ". . . never cursed with the illusion . . . ," 68.

146. *Blast* ran five issues, *Dynamo*, four, *Scope*, one.

Chapter 14
"Something Great Has Begun"

1. For instance, the entire New York press reviewed it. A Covici-Friede editor wrote Jack that he had never seen so much attention given to a first novel. George Joel, letter to Conroy, 22 November 1933.

2. Canfield, *Book-of-the-Month Club News*, 59.

3. Similarly, Jesse Stuart attracted media attention with the publication of his *Man with a Bull Tongue Plow*. People were curious that a farmer could write. Hagglund wrote Jack: "you oughtn't to fool dese pipples like diss." Ben Hagglund, letter to Conroy, 2 July 1934.

4. Charles Waterfield, Jack's uncle, snapped one of the "plowboy" photos used by newspapers, including the *New York Times*, with a Brownie camera. Conroy, interview, 31 March 1986.

5. The cliché still hangs on; for instance, Eric Homberger calls Jack a "farm labourer," in *American Writers and Radical Politics*, 128. Algren once referred to Jack, after their split as friends, as "J. C. Kornpoen." It was a curious epithet, given that a deep rift existed between the rural farmers and the miners of Jack's childhood experience. Jack of course belonged with the miners. Perhaps Algren was thinking of Farrell's reference to Jack as "Jack Cornrow" at the first American Writers' Congress in 1935. I discuss the Conroy-Farrell feud below. In chapter 19 I review the Algren-Conroy split.

6. Note Lawrence H. Schwartz's remark that a writer's public stature is a cultural artifact created within a specific historical-political milieu. *Creating Faulkner's Reputation*.

7. Rebecca Farnham, a bookstore owner in Boston, wrote Jack that *The Disinherited* was the "most popular book in our lending library." Farnham, letter to Conroy, 23 June 1934. The Los Angeles Public Library purchased twenty-five copies.

8. Erskine Caldwell, letter to Conroy, 7 November 1933.

9. There were attempts at market surveys. Covici-Friede gave copies to twenty-five manual laborers, asking them to send their opinions to the publishers. Arthur Mizener tried Jack's first novel out with a group of textile workers, reporting great success. Mizener, letter to Conroy, 9 January 1935.

10. O'Sheel, "They Went Forth to Battle."

11. Conroy, interview, 2 April 1983. Elaine Hedges discusses the Party's male orientation in regard to Le Sueur in her introduction to Le Sueur's *Ripening*, 14.

12. Gold, "A Letter to the Author of a First Book," 25.

13. Wallace, review of *The Disinherited*.

14. Fadiman, review of *The Disinherited*.

15. Mencken, review of *The Disinherited*.

16. Rodriguez, review of *The Disinherited*.

17. Hicks, review of *The Disinherited*.

18. Gold, "Change the World!"

19. Farrell, review of *The Disinherited*.

20. Farrell's first story was "The Filling Station Racket in Chicago," *Debunker* 9 (January 1929): 91–93. See Farrell, letter to Haldeman, 14 June 1964.

21. Abe Aaron, letter to Conroy, 13 January 1934.

22. Jack's review of Gold's *Jews without Money*, *Earth* 1 (May 1930): 14, and Farrell's "Halfway from the Cradle," *Earth* 1 (June 1930): 1, 3, 14). As early as 1930, Farrell revealed a tendency to strike an archly independent pose and a desire to be taken seriously as a critic. See also Farrell, "Note on Contemporary American Letters."

23. Dee Brown, letter to Conroy, 21 February 1934.

24. J. Martin, *Nathanael West*, 257.

25. Herbert Klein, letters to Conroy, 27 October 1934; late fall 1934.

26. George Milburn, letter to Conroy, 10 October 1933.

27. Caldwell, letter to Conroy, 2 January 1934.

28. Grace Wellington, letter to Conroy, 27 December 1933.

29. Walt Carmon, letter to Conroy, 19 February 1934.

30. Dahlberg, review of *The Young Manhood of Studs Lonigan*, 24.

31. See Dahlberg, review of *The Death and Birth of David Markand*.

32. Conroy claimed that Farrell's uncle (by marriage) had funded the Farrells' European sojourn during the early years of the Depression. Both Conroy and Farrell were writing about the underclass, but while Farrell was able to produce his text in the amiable circumstances of Paris, Jack was sweating on a factory assembly line and digging ditches in western Missouri. Years later Jack met Farrell's patron (Roney) at Dorothy Farrell's home in Chicago. Roney told Jack that Farrell still owed the money lent him, and that Farrell had told people he earned his upkeep in Paris writing for the *New York Herald Tribune*. Conroy, interview, Conroy, 28 February 1986.

33. Granville Hicks, letter to Conroy, 23 February 1934.

34. Stanley Burnshaw, letter to Orrick Johns, 9 March 1934.

35. Henry George Weiss, letter to editors, *NM* 24 (April 1934): 21.

36. Conroy, review of *The Land of Plenty*, 52.

37. Dahlberg to "Jack," 7 June 1934. I am unable to identify "Jack."

38. Wald, *James T. Farrell*, 34–37.

39. Aaron writes: "His [Farrell's] cantankerous and didactic comments on proletarian fiction had already begun to irk some of the Left Wing critics; soon he was to engage in a free-swinging contest with *The New Masses* and ultimately break with the Stalinists." *Writers on the Left*, 287.

40. Orrick Johns, letter to Conroy, 7 March 1934.

41. Granville Hicks, letter to Conroy, 7 May 1934.

42. Stanley Burnshaw, letter to Conroy, 28 May 1934.

43. Farrell's critical attitudes at this time, according to Wald, were directed toward the Party's cultural commissars, not the Party per se. Wald, *James T. Farrell*, 31–32.

44. Stanley Burnshaw, letter to Conroy, early May 1934.

45. Conroy, letter to Burnshaw, early May 1934.

46. Burnshaw, letter to author, 18 May 1992. Burnshaw recalls that his "role was . . . to keep the Left from wasting itself in backbiting, interpersonal slander, etc., and to work in a positive way." See also Burnshaw, "Middle-Ground Writers."

47. Wald, *James T. Farrell*, 37.

48. Farrell, letter to Edgar Branch, 29 January 1974. James T. Farrell Collection. Special Collections, Van Pelt Library, University of Pennsylvania. By special permission of Cleo Paturis.

49. Brent, *Seven Stairs*, 38.

50. Drew, *Nelson Algren*, 82.

51. The feud also underscores the pitfalls in attempting to explain literary disagreements and "debates" in the 1930s in terms of ideological differences alone.

52. "U.S.S.R. Writers—to the Factories, Workers—into Literature," 105.

53. Walter Snow, letter to Kalar, 19 September 1932.

54. Conroy, "What If You Don't Want to Write for Money," 10.

55. Ibid.

56. Caplan, review of *Gender and the Politics of History*, 62.

57. Farrell, letter to Edgar Branch, 29 January 1974. James T. Farrell Collection. Courtesy of the Van Pelt Library, University of Pennsylvania.

58. Joseph Kalar, letter to Warren Huddlestone, 10 January 1936; the review appeared in *Nation* magazine.

59. Mencken, "Illuminators of the Abyss," 156.

60. Charles H. Compton's *Who Reads What* (1934), a study of readership at the St. Louis Public Library in the early 1930s, seemed to back up Cantwell. Some critics have suggested that workers are not anxious to read portrayals of working-class subjects; for instance, they feel caricatured, especially in the use of working-class dialect.

61. Conroy, "A Note on the Proletarian Novel," 5.

62. Ibid.

63. Thus most readers of Jacob Riis's *How the Other Half Lives* (1890) and Upton Sinclair's *The Jungle* (1903) had no experience of the slums or meat packing houses.

64. Lejeune writes: "Le discours sur leur vie reste contenu dans la mémoire de leur groupe. . . ." *Je Est un Autre*, 253.

65. Conroy, "A Note on the Proletarian Novel," 5.

66. Rodman, review of *The Disinherited*.

67. Forsythe, "Down with the Novel," 29–30.

68. Conroy, review of *Land of Plenty*, 52.

69. Conroy, untitled lecture, unpubl. MS, ca. 1934. Conroy papers, Newberry Library.

70. Conroy, interview with Robert Lefley, 6.

71. Conroy, "Home to Moberly," *JCR*, 139.

72. There are parallels here in what George Bisztray calls the "Gorki" model, in contrast to the "Lukacs" model. See *Models of Realism*, 59f. Lukacs, in his critique of the German worker-writer Willi Bredel, called for the use of techniques common to the great nineteenth-century realists. Conroy's writing, by contrast, utilizes discursive styles, with sources in folklore and oral storytelling, more characteristic of Gorki.

73. Soviet aestheticians explored montage as a technique for portraying the growth of political consciousness. See Denyer, "Montage and Political Consciousness," 89–111.

74. Aaron in his useful introduction to the 1963 edition of *The Disinherited* calls Conroy's first novel "picaresque." I disagree for the reasons cited.

75. Tzvetan Todorov argues that "from a structural point of view, each type of discourse usually referred to as literary has nonliterary relatives which resemble it more than do other types of literary discourse. . . . Thus the opposition between literature and nonliterature is replaced by a typology of the various types of discourse." "The Notion of Literature," 14–15.

76. Gorki, in his address to the First Soviet Writers' Congress in 1934, underscored the importance of preliterary traditions in the making of certain notable literary works: "The real history of the toiling people cannot be understood without a knowledge of their unwritten compositions, which have again and again had a definite influence on the making of such great works as, for instance, *Faust, The Adventures of Baron Münchhausen, Pantagruel and Gargantua.* . . ." A. Zhdanov et al., *Problems of Soviet Literature*, 43. This book was in Jack's library.

77. Benjamin, "The Storyteller," 87.

78. Ibid., 101.

79. See R. Martin, *Ishmael Reed*; H. Baker, *The Journey Back*; idem, *Blues, Ideology*.

80. Vivid recollections of the first day of work appear throughout the worker narratives gathered by John Bodnar in *Workers' World*.

81. Vincent, *Bread, Knowledge and Freedom*.

82. Little has been written on the subject of American worker autobiography, although a number of collections of worker narratives have appeared in the past ten years. Vincent's study and Burnett's *Annals of Labour* are limited to the English worker. I have drawn widely upon studies of English, German, French, and Belgian traditions of worker autobiography, for instance, Münchow, *Frühe Deutsche Arbeiterautobiographie*; A. Klein, *Im Auftrag Ihrer Klasse*; Lejeune, *Je Est un Autre*; Ragon, *Histoire de la Littérature Prolétarienne en France*.

83. Elizabeth Bruss's term in *Autobiographical Acts*.

84. Lejeune, *Je Est un Autre*, 249–50: "modèles exclus de l'écriture et récupérés par ceux qui la possèdent."

85. Stahl, *Literary Folkloristics*, 18.

86. Ibid., 19.
87. Lejeune, *Je Est un Autre*, 265–67: "méfiance à l'égard de l'écriture."
88. Burnett, ed., *Annals of Labour*, 10.
89. "Novel or not, just so it tells the truth," Conroy said to an interviewer. See interview with Robert Lefley, 9.
90. For the success type, see Stelzle, *Son of the Bowery*. For early worker narratives as forms of textual communication, see Foner, ed., *Factory Girls*. Other types include journalists who enter trades to learn about workers (Husband, *Year in a Coal Mine*); immigrant narratives (Ravage, *American in the Making*); and tales in which the interest is independent of the fact that the narrator is a worker (Rice, *Heaven in the Eye*).
91. See Couch, ed., *These Are Our Lives*; Lambert and Franks, eds., *Voices from the Oil Fields*. I discuss Conroy's worker narratives, collected while on the Illinois Writers' Project, in chapter 17.
92. An early collection is Ginzberg and Berman, *American Worker in the Twentieth Century*.
93. See, for example, Rubin, *The Log of Rubin the Sailor*; Denby, *Indignant Heart*; Mortimer, *Organize!*; Mers, *Working the Waterfront*.
94. See Egan, *Patterns of Experience*, on this latter point.
95. Janice Thaddeus makes an interesting distinction between closed and open autobiography. In the former, "the writer presents his life as a finished product." "The Metamorphosis of Richard Wright's *Black Boy*," 199–214. Openness characterizes the progress of Conroy's protagonist. There is little to suggest that Larry Donovan is moving toward any assigned purpose. He stumbles into a commitment only at the very end; that commitment is left open, ready for further shaping.
96. Münchow, *Frühe Deutsche Arbeiterautobiographie*, 61.
97. This tradition is much more evolved in Europe than in the United States. In the United States most worker-writing exists unedited in labor archives or on tape (or in people's perishable memories).
98. Jauss, "Alterity and Modernity of Medieval Literature," 213. The term "simple forms" is Andre Jolle's, in *Formes Simples*. Jauss discusses the origin of romance in the medieval exemplary and urges the reconstruction of "the horizon of experience of the simple forms of aesthetic experience" in order to understand a literature that may have been repressed by the canon of the dominant culture (214). On the other hand, he argues that in our age of "mass media and subcultures" certain simple forms have reappeared, such as the proverb in advertising and so forth (216).
99. Rancière, "Myth of the Artisan," 13.
100. Kalar, letter to Conroy, 7 December 1928.
101. Kalar, letters to Huddlestone, 1 June 1925; 29 September 1925.
102. Kalar, letter to Huddlestone, 20 November 1932.
103. Elvena Kalar, unpubl. MS, with Kalar papers. Courtesy of Richard Kalar.
104. Kalar, letter to Walter Snow, 29 September 1932. Courtesy of the Library, University of Connecticut–Storrs.
105. Rancière: "In a conflictual universe where the barrier of leisure, the

barrier separating the necessity of work and the luxury of thought, constitutes an essential stake, this undifferentiated sense of culture [the assumption of cultural homogeneity] is likely to miss the originality of the representations in/at play in worker discourse and politics." "Myth of the Artisan," 14.

106. Bakhtin, "Discourse Typology in Prose," 177. The various discursive styles of the characters in Conroy's writing are elements of the manner of telling, as they are in Gorki's trilogy.

107. Ibid., 176.

108. Bakhtin, *Speech Genres*, 105.

109. Lejeune says: "On est toujours plusieurs quand on écrit, même tout seul, même sa propre vie." *Je Est un Autre*, 235.

110. Ibid., 249.

111. Quoted by R. Lewis, *Picaresque Saint*, 143.

112. Bakhtin, *Dialogic Imagination*, 281.

113. Ibid., 368.

114. Roland Barthes complained of the "bad" use of the dominant culture's speech by orthodox proletarian writers who appropriate bourgeois writing and language. Barthes, "Writing and Revolution," 77ff. Likewise, George Orwell complained: "It is doubtful whether anything describable as proletarian literature now exists—even the Daily Worker is written in standard South English. . . ." *Road to Wigan Pier*, 175.

115. *New Republic* (11 October 1933).

116. Nathan Adler and Leo Hurwitz, in interviews with Alan Wald, claimed that *Dynamo* was Sol Funaroff's idea. (Wald to author, 11 October 1992.) To clarify this point I wrote to Joe Vogel, who responded that *Dynamo* "was strictly and purely an idea cooked up by Spector and me—a little magazine for the publication of prose and poetry." (Spector's *Bastard in the Ragged Suit* corroborates this point.) Later, when Vogel and Spector determined that suitable stories were not forthcoming, Funaroff suggested that the magazine exist "solely as a poetry magazine." Adler and Hurwitz "weren't around in the first stage of *Dynamo*—they weren't told about it," Vogel recalls. Letter to author, 14 September 1991. See also Herman Spector, letter to Walter Snow, 17 January 1933; Snow, letter to Conroy, 24 January 1933.

117. Johns and Clancy, in introduction, *Bastard in the Ragged Suit*, by Herman Spector, 5.

118. Joseph Vogel, interview, 7 October 1982.

119. See Vogel to Richard Johns, editor of *Pagany*, in Halpert and Johns, eds., *Return to Pagany*, 98–99, 224–25.

120. The story of Adam Wolak, an immigrant laborer who loses everything in the Depression, Vogel's novel *Man's Courage* was featured on the front page of the *New York Times Book Review* and hailed by the Party as a proletarian milestone. Vogel felt that the Party had "expropriated" his novel for its own uses. Joseph Vogel, interview, 7 October 1982.

121. Granville Hicks, letter to Conroy, 8 October 1933.

122. Rahv, "Open Letter to Young Writers," 3–4.

123. Wallace Phelps, review of *Ulysses*, 26.

124. Quoted by Salzman and Wallenstein, ed., *Years of Protest*, 19. Elsewhere Rahv wrote: "What with Jack Conroy's *The Disinherited* . . . revolutionary literature in America has reached a higher stage of development this year, setting new standards for the army of proletarian art." Rahv's review of Cantwell's *Land of Plenty*, in the *Daily Worker*, quoted in *International Review* 4 (September 1934): 157.

125. Gilbert, *Writers and Partisans*, 209.

126. Advertisement, *Left Front* 1 (January–February 1934): 20.

127. Orwell, *Road to Wigan Pier*, 175.

128. Jerre Mangione, member of the New York John Reed Club, said that Rahv and Phillips "sounded more like lawyers than writers." Lecture, Newberry Library, 23 September 1989.

129. Calmer, "Labor Press," 5.

130. Walter Snow, unpubl. MS, "The Anvil and the Proletarian Short Story," Conroy papers, Newberry Library.

131. Conroy, "What If You Don't Want to Write for Money," 12.

132. Aronowitz, *False Promises*, 124.

133. Kalar, letter to Warren Huddlestone, 19 June 1934.

134. W. Williams, "A Symposium: The Status of Radical Writing," 134.

135. "Daughter" is reprinted in Conroy and Johnson, *Writers in Revolt*.

136. Dahlberg, *Confessions*, 286.

137. Conroy, letter to Willard Maas, 6 February 1934. See also Conroy, "The Affirmative Trend."

138. Joseph North, one of the editors of *Proletarian Literature in the United States* (1935) in which Conroy was represented, liked the affirmation in Jack's writing in preference to gloomy proletarian stories. North, letter to Conroy, 3 November 1934. Jack was dismayed by the gloomy dustcover of *The Disinherited*, drawn by Murray Levin, which depicted the silhouettes of regimented, unindividuated workers walking mechanically to work in a factory.

139. Benjamin, "The Storyteller."

140. An example of this is the terrible boredom and drabness of factory work, as Sherwood Anderson points out. "There was in the factories where I worked and where the efficient Ford type of man was just beginning his dull reign this strange and futile outpouring of men's lives in vileness through their lips. Ennui was at work. The talk of the men about me was not Rabelaisian." *A Story Teller's Story*, 198.

141. See Howe and Coser, for instance, who attribute the "mindless crudity" of *New Masses* and "the left-wing regional magazines" between 1928 and 1932 to "the international Stalinist line on cultural matters." *American Communist Party*, 278.

142. Ben Hagglund, ". . . akin to revelation . . . ," 68.

143. Sanora Babb, letter to author, 18 September 1983.

144. Caldwell, letter to Conroy, 18 November 1934.

145. Masaki Fujio, letter to Conroy, ca. 1933.

146. Agnes Smedley, letter to Conroy, 17 September 1934.

147. Abe Aaron, letter to Conroy, 24 November 1933.

Chapter 15
The Road to Mecca Temple

1. Sukenick, "Eight Digressions," 472–73.
2. R. Williams, *Culture and Society*, 31–32.
3. Cowley, *Exile's Return*, 223.
4. Ibid., 300.
5. Ibid., 302.
6. Gold, *Hollow Men*, 31.
7. Melville, *Confidence Man*, 99.
8. Larsen, review of *Let Us Now Praise Famous Men*, 88.
9. One effect of the Depression, Grant Wood wrote, was to throw artists "back upon certain true and fundamental things which are distinctively ours to use and exploit. . . . Because of this new emphasis upon native materials, the artist no longer finds it necessary to migrate even to New York. . . . The great central areas of America are coming to be evaluated more and more justly as the years pass. They are not a hinterland for New York; they are not barbaric." "Revolt Against the City," in Flanagan, *America Is West*, 652–53.
10. Van Wyck Brooks searched the past for traditions that would, as Robert Weimann writes, "promote literature as the democratic conscience of the nation and form a bulwark against paleness and narrow-mindedness of New England, against the vulgar utilitarianism and puritanism of the petit bourgeois, but also against the interference and chaos of those enemies of art—capitalism and big government." *Structure and Society*, 103. Such attitudes vis-à-vis the East may appear parochial today, but they were taken quite seriously where not long before, the Populist Party had inveighed against Eastern "money power" and writers like Mark Twain and Hamlin Garland created figures who spoke with a midwestern accent. Sherwood Anderson, in *A Story Teller's Story*, described his fears and aspirations as a midwestern writer in the East (380–85). Also, see May, "Rebellion of the Intellectuals," 163–64.
11. Some forty years later, a renewed feminist movement discovered Le Sueur, whose work was reissued by editor John Crawford of West End Press.
12. Le Sueur, "Proletarian Literature and the Middle West," 135–38.
13. "A Call to All Midwest Writers," *New Writers*, 29.
14. I. Howe, "Toward an Open Culture," 26.
15. Abe Aaron, letter to Conroy, 24 November 1933.
16. Van Wyck Brooks, *America's Coming-of-Age*, 84.
17. Spero and Harris, *Black Worker*.
18. Kempton, *Part of Our Time*, 126–27.
19. See Wright, "I Tried to be a Communist," 61–62, 63. Also, Fabre's *Unfinished Quest*.
20. Elshtain, "Forgetting Who Are 'The People,'" 543.
21. Fabre, *Unfinished Quest*, 68.
22. Abe Aaron remembers Wright as a very serious young man who read pulp adventure magazines in order to develop notions of plot. "Abe," he said, "they're closer to the soil than you think." Abe Aaron, interview, 7 January 1990.

23. Kinnamon, "Richard Wright," 251. Abe Aaron, interview, 7 January 1990.

24. See Wright, "I Tried to be a Communist."

25. In a memoir of Wright, Conroy wrote: "His talents seemed to proliferate in those early days in the John Reed Club; he wrote with more confidence. Much of his disillusionment with the left-wing movement stemmed from his dismay at the arbitrary ukase of the C.P. dissolving the John Reed Clubs." Interview with Conroy, *New Letters* 38 (Winter 1971): 34.

26. Kinnamon, "Richard Wright," 250. "I am a Red Slogan," was published in *International Literature* in April of the following year, followed in June by Wright's famous poem, "I Have Seen Black Hands," in *New Masses.*

27. An antecedent exists in the IWW's desire that the working class be in possession of its own "machinery of production and distribution." On William Haywood's speech at the IWW's first meeting, in Chicago, 27 June 1905, see M. Coleman, *Men and Coal,* 78.

28. *Windsor Quarterly* (Winter 1933–34): 416.

29. Conroy, "The Literary Underworld of the Thirties," *JCR,* 151–64.

30. West, *American Authors.*

31. McLuhan, *Gutenberg Galaxy,* 163.

32. Benjamin, "Der Autor als Produzent," 101.

33. Swingewood, "Marxist Approaches to the Study of Literature," 144.

34. Benjamin, "Der Autor als Produzent," 105.

35. Schulte-Sasse, Foreword, *The Theory of the Avant-Garde,* by Peter Buerger, xvi.

36. Ibid.

37. Cowley, *And I Worked at the Writers' Trade,* 100.

38. K. Burke, *Permanence and Change,* 269–70.

39. Conroy, letters to Nelson Algren, 16 March 1934, ca. April 1934.

40. Bourne, *History of a Literary Radical,* 40.

41. Conroy, letter to Wallie Wharton, 8 November 1937.

42. Conroy, letter to author, 23 May 1978.

43. See Le Sueur's *Ripening,* Babb's *An Owl on Every Post,* Josephine Johnson's *Now in November.*

44. Meridel Le Sueur, interview, 13 June 1980.

45. McCauley later started the Seabury Press.

46. Boris Israel, "We Are Nurtured," *Anvil* 8 (September–October 1934).

47. Conroy, interview, Conroy, 21 June 1987.

48. See Conroy, letter to Tom ("Tennessee") Williams, 22 February 1934.

49. Conroy, "In Memoriam: John C. Rogers 1907–1979," 56.

50. John Rogers, "Biographical Notes," unpubl. MS, courtesy of the University of Virginia Library, by permission of Robin Rogers.

51. Self-effacing, independent-minded, and stubborn, Rogers was fired from his position as an illustrator for the Internal Revenue Service during the McCarthy era. See chapter 18.

52. Rogers, "Unreconstructed Radical," 73.

53. See Nelson and Hendricks, *Edwin Rolfe.*

54. Navasky, *Naming Names*, 40, 62; Conroy, interview, 30 October 1982.

55. See Rosemary Reurer, video tape, "Making History," Washington University, 11 November 1988. Also, John McGuire, "Where Does Labor Go from Here?"

56. Raymond Koch, letter to author, 4 September 1988.

57. "American Unemployed and Art: The Story of Joe Jones," 95–97; Johns, "St. Louis Artists Win," 28–29; Marling, "Joe Jones"; "Chronicle," 109.

58. Conroy, "Home to Moberly," *JCR*, 139.

59. Walt Carmon, letter to Conroy, 19 February 1934.

60. "Jack Conroy; American Worker-Writer," 114. On the Soviet reception of *The Disinherited*, see D. Brown, *Soviet Attitudes toward American Writing*, 72ff.

61. Orrick Johns, letter to Conroy, 5 March 1934.

62. Arthur, review of *The Disinherited*, 31. *Anvil* contributor W. D. Trowbridge wrote Jack of violence against leftist demonstrators on the part of rightwing extremists. Trowbridge, letter to Conroy, 7 February 1932.

63. Cantwell, "Literary Life in California," 49.

64. Conroy, "Young American Novelists," speech to the Workers' Modern Library, 24 March 1934.

65. Howe and Coser's term in *American Communist Party*, 226. Howe and Coser argue that the "surrender of the will" was "the most troublesome aspect of the history of American Communism."

66. Rall, "1933 and *The Disinherited*," 3.

67. John Gunn had a long affair with Marcet Haldeman-Julius, wife of the Girard publisher and niece of Jane Addams. Conroy helped Harold and his wife, Aldine, scatter John's ashes on a hillside near Freeport, Illinois, not far from Marcet (and Jane Addams). Harold brought along a case of beer and recited Keats's "Ode to a Grecian Urn" in his formal, elocutionary manner that amused Chicago friends. Conroy, interviews, 26 November 1986, 26 July 1987.

68. Pete Chaunt, note to Joe Jones, n.d., Conroy papers, Newberry Library.

69. Jack Balch, note to Conroy, 12 May 1934.

70. Joe Jones, telegram to Conroy, 4 May 1934.

71. Conroy, letter to Jones, May 1934.

72. Orrick Johns, letter to Conroy, 12 May 1934.

73. Jack Balch, letter to Conroy, 12 May 1934.

74. Wharton, letter to author, 8 December 1980.

75. See Wixson, "Jack Conroy and the East St. Louis Toughs."

76. "The Logic of Lunarcharsky Frittertitsky," unpubl. MS in Wharton archive. Courtesy of the Western Historical Manuscript Collection, University of Missouri at Columbia.

77. Ben Hagglund, letter to Conroy, 4 March 1934.

78. Robert Cantwell, letter to Conroy, 10 March 1934.

79. E. Ely-Estorick, letter to Conroy, 9 March 1934.

80. The Llano Cooperative Colony offered its printing facilities "as a laboratory for the builders of a new social order. . . . On the theory maybe that bread cast upon the waters, etc. some gladly take advantage; some repay the compliment and some thumb their nose! Others reject the opportunity as tending to

bring them into close bodily contact with something compromising, utopian, or opportunist." Marvin Sanford, letter to Walter Snow, 13 September 1934.

81. Ben Hagglund, letter to Conroy, 2 July 1934.

82. Conroy, interview, June 1981.

83. Conroy, letter to Dale Kramer, 18 October 1934.

84. Agnes Kelly Hickman, interview, 31 August 1986; Lottie and Leo Bly, interview, 1 April 1986.

85. Conroy, *Moberly Monitor-Index*, 27 October 1931.

86. Conroy, interview, 16 October 1986.

87. Johns, "Different Spring"; Rukeyser, "The Trial."

88. Editors, *The Writers' 1934 Year Book*, 12–13.

89. Goddard, "Missouri Novelist Writes in Overalls."

90. Stork, "Mr. Calverton and his Friends," 97.

91. Dinamov, letter to Conroy, Feburary 1933.

92. Calverton, letter to Conroy, 18 March 1933.

93. See Walter Snow's memory of this event in "Authors and Literature of the 1903s," Semester of the Thirties symposium, University of Connecticut–Storrs, 1969, transcript, pp. 17–22. Courtesy of University of Connecticut–Storrs.

94. Kalar wrote Conroy years later: "I thought of the good old days when you were a philosophical anarchist who thought socialist and socialism were the new conservativisms." Kalar, letter to Conroy, 24 May 1951.

95. See Whitcomb, "Writers' Fight," 143–47.

96. Walter Snow, letter to Conroy, 2 December 1934.

97. Ibid.

98. Maxim Lieber, letter to Conroy, 19 November 1934.

99. Walter Snow, letter to Conroy, 5 December 1934.

100. Sanora Babb, letter to author, 18 September 1983.

101. As pointed out earlier, Constance Rourke attempted to defend regionalist art against its critics regardless of their political orientation. See Rourke, "Significance of Sections." Similarly, in 1933, Edmund Wilson argued for a culture grounded in actual concrete practice in place of "an abstract culture without any real foundation." See Wilson, "Art, the Proletariat and Marx," 43.

102. Gorki, in Zhdanov, *Problems of Soviet Literature*.

103. Abe Aaron, letter to Conroy, 23 February 1934. See also Fabre, *Unfinished Quest*, 102–4.

104. Quoted by Klehr, *Heyday of American Communism*, 351.

105. Wright, "I Tried to Be a Communist," quoted in Fabre, *Unfinished Quest*, 105.

106. *Hinterland*, published first in Cedar Rapids, under Dale Kramer's editorship, then in Des Moines, Iowa, by the Midwest Literary League, is a particularly interesting example of midwestern radical initiative. H. H. Lewis, Raymond Kresensky, A. E. Clements, John Rogers, and other Rebel Poets/*Anvil*-ites appeared in its issues, often with Rogers's woodcuts.

107. Meridel Le Sueur, interview, 13 June 1980.

108. Conroy, interview, *New Letters* 38 (Winter 1971): 33–34. The bur-

lesque theater Conroy describes is the "Little Rialto" of Algren's *Somebody in Boots*, where Cass McKay meets Norah, the setting for their ill-starred attachment.

109. Conroy, interview, *New Letters* 38 (Winter 1971): 35.

110. Conroy, speech to the JRC conference, 1934, unpubl. MS, Conroy papers, Newberry Library.

111. Walter Snow, "The Renaissance of American Proletarian Literature," JRC conference, 1934, unpubl. MS, Snow papers. Courtesy of the Library, University of Connecticut–Storrs.

112. Conroy himself had criticized "leftists" in the revolutionary movement, to which Joseph North (of *New Masses*) replied: "Listen, Jack, you can't surprise me with anything about these leftists. This I.W.O. fellow you tell me about, how many of them are all holier-than-thou and eventually holier that the working class." Joseph North, letter to Conroy, 20 November 1934.

113. Quoted in Orrick Johns, "The John Reed Clubs Meet," *NM* 13 (30 October 1934): 25.

114. Meridel Le Sueur, interview, 13 June 1980.

115. Conroy, interview, 24 May 1982.

116. Meridel Le Sueur, interview, 13 June 1980.

117. Hicks, "Our Magazines and Their Functions," 23.

118. Walter Snow, letter to Sanford, 13 December 1934.

119. Walter Snow, letter to Conroy, 18 December 1934.

120. Walter Snow, letter to Conroy, 5 December 1934.

121. Erskine Caldwell, letter to Conroy, 26 December 1934.

122. Walter Snow, letter to Conroy, 18 December 1934.

123. Walter Snow, letter to Sanford, December 1934.

124. Conroy, letter to Clark Mills, 12 November 1934.

125. Walter Snow, letter to Sanford, 13 December 1934. Also, Snow, letter to Conroy, 18 December 1934.

126. The March 1935 issue of *Anvil* lists Snow as the New York "business office manager."

127. Walter Snow, letter to Wharton, 9 January 1935. Wharton, letters to author, August 1982, 14 September 1982, summer 1983, January 1985. Wharton, letter to Fred Whitehead, ca. November 1980.

128. See Coser and Howe, *American Communist Party*, 209ff., on the trial of August Yokinen.

129. Conroy, interview, 30 June 1984.

130. Wharton, letter to Fred Whitehead, ca. November 1980; Wharton, letters to author, 18 October 1982, 3 February 1983.

131. Conroy, letter to Wharton, 9 March 1972; Conroy, interview, 26–27 December 1987.

132. Abe Aaron, in a letter to Jack, heralded reportage and the sketch as "the coming forms." 4 April 1935.

133. Kalar joined an active CP cell in 1935, ran unsuccessfully for election as a Farmer Labor candidate in 1939, became president of the paperworkers' union local, and eventually wrote publicity for a lumber company; Falkowski

returned from the Soviet Union in the late 1930s, served in the U.S. armed forces, and was active in Polish-American relations following the war. Huddlestone went to work for the Indiana State Employment Service in 1934, "ending the Depression," served in the war, and worked for an ad agency afterward.

134. Walter Snow, letter to Conroy, 18 December 1934.

135. Walter Snow, letter to Wharton, 5 January 1935.

136. Wharton, letters to Conroy, spring 1935; late September 1935. Snow's advisory editors included Jay Greulich, Erskine Caldwell, Louis Mamet, Saul Levitt, and Alfred H. Sinks, indicating the *Anvil's* editorial center of gravity shift to the East Coast.

137. Walter Snow, letter to Conroy, 18 December 1934.

138. Ibid.

139. Ibid.

140. Ibid.

141. Snow, letter to Wharton, 1 January 1935.

142. Snow, letter to Conroy, 21 February 1935.

143. Snow, letter to Conroy, 11 April 1935.

Chapter 16
The Unmaking of the Worker-Writer

1. Conroy, lecture, Foolkiller Conference, Kansas City, 2 June 1978. Unpubl. MS, Conroy papers, Newberry Library. Enroute to the congress, Jack made stops in St. Louis (where he shared a platform with Josephine Johnson), Indianapolis, Cleveland, and Philadelphia to give lectures at John Reed Clubs and labor forums. In Akron he met with Howard Wolf of the *Beacon Journal* and gathered material on Akron's rubber industry for his Guggenheim project. See "The Book World," *Akron Beacon Journal*, 6 April 1935, 5. In Cleveland, he visited with Bob Cruden, the worker-writer turned labor activist, and his wife, Janet.

2. "U.S. Writers Quit Ivory Towers at Congress," *New York Post*, 27 April 1935.

3. *New York Herald-Tribune*, 26 April 1935, 15.

4. Granville Hicks appeared to support theoretical considerations and literary technique, noting efforts in these directions on the part of the *Partisan Review* editors. Edwin Seaver represented those who proposed that a revolutionary-proletarian viewpoint was sufficient for proletarian writing, not working-class origins or topics. Taking issue with Seaver, Malcolm Cowley distinguished between the broader category of revolutionary literature and proletarian literature, arguing that the latter is best written from within the working class on working-class subjects. Le Sueur and Jack both spoke in favor of the worker's role in writing, Meridel placing the worker-writer in the tradition of midwestern radical culture, whose immediate forbears were the Wobblies. Kenneth Burke distinguished between "workers" and "the people," foreshadowing a Popular Front theme. Trachtenberg's short speech balanced theoretical and creative concerns under the cultural wing of the Party.

5. Conroy, interview, 24 December 1986. Meridel Le Sueur's reply when I mentioned this to her: "Broun *was* an unmade bed!" Le Sueur, interview, 26 January 1985.

6. Wixson, "Thomas Hart Benton's New York Years."

7. Kempton, *Part of Our Time*, 135.

8. Howe and Coser, *American Communist Party*, 311. Conroy said later that one doesn't have to be a proletarian to write a proletarian novel, but it makes it easier. "Authors and Literature of the 1930s," lecture transcript, Semester of the Thirties symposium, University of Connecticut–Storrs, April 1969. Courtesy of the University of Connecticut–Storrs.

9. Literary craftsmanship was fundamental to Conroy's views on writing despite the fact that his own work was in places badly flawed. It was the point of his AWC talk that despite the obstacles that made attaining excellence in literary craftmanship difficult, the worker-writer had something "vital and new to communicate" and should be encouraged in his or her efforts. Conroy's goal in taking risks on young writers in the *Anvil* was to provide the experience that publication and editorial criticism offer. In short, he perceived literary craft as process, not product.

10. Farrell later denied doing so. See Farrell, letter to Alan Wald, 10 August 1974. Courtesy of Alan Wald.

11. Farrell, *Yet Other Waters*, 398.

12. Ibid., 112.

13. Ibid., 113.

14. Ibid., 110. Unquestionably Conroy's head was turned by all the attention he suddenly received and by the excitement of the congress.

15. Earl Browder, in his speech, underscored the importance of "good writing" and literary standards in revolutionary literature, a remark that in retrospect seems pointed at proletarian writers. Jack was unaware of Farrell's literary parody until many years later when a graduate student drew it to his attention.

16. Howe and Coser, *American Communist Party*, 312.

17. Kempton, *Part of Our Time*, 135.

18. Eugene Lyons imposes a similar revisionist interpretation on Jack's remark. Conroy, Lyons writes, claimed that the strike bulletin was of greater literary value than Proust's *A la Recherche du Temps Perdu*. Lyons, *Red Decade*, 135–36. The main significance of Lyons's study is that his book was one of the first to anticipate and profit from Cold War red hunting.

19. R. Williams, *Culture and Society*, xvi. Note that the Federal Writers' Project gave writers work, as it did other craftspeople. The implication is that writing is a skill, like other artistic skills—planting trees, building boats, painting landscapes.

20. It is an error to simplify the composition and activities of the labor movement in the 1930s. Within the unions, for instance, different groups were represented. The longshoremen's union gathered Wobblies, anarchists, Party members, conservatives, and others. There was no single pattern. The Party called on writers like Meridel Le Sueur to "write leaflets to become more dis-

ciplined," criticizing her for the lyrical, emotional strain of her writing, yet other writer-activists, like Winkler, ignored such demands, as explained earlier. Quotation from Pratt, "Woman Writer in the CP," 257.

21. Jean Winkler, one of Conroy's St. Louis *Anvil* editors, wrote strike bulletins for the Electrical Workers' Union. See Winkler's letters, published in *New Letters* (Spring 1991). Gilbert Mers, a longshoreman and organizer with the National Maritime Union in the 1930s, underscores the importance of such bulletins in his autobiography, *Working the Waterfront*. Mers, interview, 12 June 1991.

22. Similarly, Kenneth Burke's reference to "myths" in his address to the congress caused disagreement. Orthodox CP-ers misunderstood "myth," thinking that Burke was talking about lies, not the generic meaning. "We don't talk about myths, we talk about facts!" they retorted. But Burke was able to defend himself easily. Conroy, interview, 30 October 1982.

23. Fried, "Conversation with Jack Conroy," *JCR*, 176.

24. Conroy remembers Farrell jumping up at the conclusion of an afternoon session and shouting: "Let's everybody go out and bomb the Chase Manhattan Bank!" Paul Romaine, who chaired the closing session, saw Farrell's suggestion as a "damned Trotskyite tactic." Conroy, interview, 21 June 1987.

25. See James T. Farrell to Edgar Branch, 29 January 1974. Also, Wald, *James T. Farrell*, 32–36. Wald corrects the impression that Farrell was a "perverse left sectarian" at the congress, noting that his suggestion to sing the Internationale was approved by the delegates. Wald, "Remembering the Answers," 708.

26. Foreword, *Those Who Built Stalingrad*, 6.

27. Matthew Josephson, in his congress speech, appeared to support Conroy's use of the Soviet example, in which "cultural activities" benefit through collaboration with the working classes. "Role of the Writer in the Soviet Union," *American Writers' Congress*, 44–45.

28. Conroy, "The Worker as Writer," *JCR*, 221.

29. *New York Herald-Tribune*, 26 April 1935, 15.

30. Wald reports that Farrell objected angrily to the exclusion of working-class and ethnic writers from membership in favor of big-name writers. "Remembering the Answers," 708.

31. Quoted by Aaron, *Writers on the Left*, 285.

32. *New York World-Telegram*, 26 April 1935.

33. Conroy, "Reflections on the 1935 Writers Congress," 13.

34. Bell wrote *Out of This Furnace* and *All Brides Are Beautiful*.

35. Conroy, Foolkiller Conference, Kansas City, 2 June 1978, unpubl. MS, Conroy papers, Newberry Library.

36. Conroy, letter to Walter Snow, 17 April 1973. Babb recalls that Lerner borrowed a ragged overcoat that had belonged to Babb's father in order to look "proletarian." Babb, letter to author, 12 February 1991.

37. Sanora Babb, letter to author, 12 February 1991.

38. See Babb, letter to Conroy, 10 November 1935.

39. Sanora Babb, letters to author, 18 September 1983, 12 February 1991.

40. Babb's "Dry Summer," published in the *Anvil*, is reprinted in Conroy and Johnson, *Writers in Revolt*. See *Anvil 12* on Lerner and Le Sueur.

41. Sanora Babb, interview, 21 October 1983. Letters to author, 18 September 1983, 18 September 1990, 12 February 1991. Babb's other novel is titled *The Lost Traveller* (1958). Her work has appeared widely in *Scribner's, Southern Review, Prairie Schooner* and elsewhere. Several of her short stories were published in a collection, *The Dark Earth and Others Stories from the Great Depression* (1987). In its summer 1990 number, *Michigan Quarterly Review* published an extract from her migrant-worker manuscript, "Whose Names Are Unknown."

42. *New York World-Telegram*, 3 May 1935. Mencken had left the *Mercury* several years earlier.

43. Ibid., 9 May 1935.

44. Earlier, Rahv had praised the worker-writers. In a note to Kalar, congratulating him for a poem submitted to *Partisan Review*, Rahv mentions that Conroy won't like the editorial on account of Rahv's "crack at Lewis." Lewis, Rahv added, had gone "downhill, since that splendid piece 'Adverse Publicity' in *Left*." Rahv, letter to Kalar, 9 July 1934.

45. See Gilbert, *Writers and Partisans*, 126–43.

46. A year earlier, Rahv expressed admiration for Joe Kalar's story in the *Anvil* and solicited a story from the Minnesota worker-writer for *Partisan Review*. Rahv, letter to Kalar, 7 June 1934.

47. Phillips, "What Happened in the '30s," 204–12.

48. Phillips in his 1962 retrospective wondered how "the radical movement in this country . . . could at the same time be so marginal, so parochial, so mindless, and also so relevant and so central. I am thinking mostly of the literary and intellectual side of the radical movement—which could take Mike Gold, Jack Conroy, and Edwin Seaver as important writers. . . ." Phillips, "What Happened in the '30s," 205.

49. Rahv, "Valedictory on the Propaganda Issue," 2.

50. For instance, "leftism" was a term Lenin used to classify the opinions of those whose proposals were contrary to his own.

51. Much has been written on the *Partisan Review* and the New York intellectuals, but very little attention has been given to its absorption of *Anvil*. William Phillips passes over the subject entirely in his brief history of *Partisan Review*, "On *Partisan Review*," *TriQuarterly* 43 (Fall 1978): 130–41. For earlier discussions of the topic, see Gilbert, *Writers and Partisans*; Fabre, "Jack Conroy as Editor"; Aaron, *Writers on the Left*.

52. H. H. Lewis, "In All Hell," reprinted in *Thinking of Russia*, 16.

53. H. H. Lewis, "Symbol of Stupidity," *Road to Utterly*, 8.

54. See Tashjian, *William Carlos Williams*, 24, 106.

55. See, for instance, his sharecropper poems in the *New Republic* (27 July 1938).

56. H. H. Lewis, "Just for Propaganda." Lewis papers, Kent Library, Southeast Missouri State University. By 1943, the approximate date of this poem, Stalin had fallen from grace in Lewis's eyes.

57. Lieber, letter to Conroy, August 1931.

58. Walt Carmon, to Kalar, ca. 1934.

59. Review of *Poems* by H. H. Lewis, *NM* (16 January 1934): 28.

60. Paul Mariani reviews the Williams-Lewis relationship and its consequences with regard to *Partisan Review* and *New Masses*. See Mariani, *William Carlos Williams*, 376–79, 405–7.

61. William Carlos Williams, letter to Fred Miller, 26 September 1934.

62. H. H. Lewis, letter to Edmund Wilson, 6 August 1937. Courtesy of Yale University Library.

63. In 1935, on his only trip east, in the company of his sister Catherine and her husband, Lewis visited William Carlos Williams and his wife. "In the New York area he was the guest of the William Carlos Williamses—proudly brought Dr. Williams to the hotel to meet his kin." Catherine L. Bock, "Biographical Sketch of Harold L. Lewis," unpubl. MS, n.d., included with letter to author, 5 November 1990.

64. In rejecting the essay, Cowley wrote, "I wish we could publish this outspoken comment." Lewis wrote an insulting letter to Cowley, demanding that he explain the rejection and quoting the *Moscow News*'s praise of several years earlier. H. H. Lewis, letter to Malcolm Cowley, ca. 1935, courtesy of Yale University Library. "I have you in a well-bulwarked jam about this and I know how it hurts, Comrade Recent, expatriate from Paris, middleclass snob. Sacred Cowley of Rappism [RAPP], you are hereby rendered into hamburger."

65. The essay was announced in *Partisan Review* 1 (February 1936): 32. Harriet Monroe would not print the entire essay in *Poetry*. See H. H. Lewis, letter to Edmund Wilson, 6 August 1937. Courtesy of Yale University Library.

66. *Partisan Review* editors to Lewis, 4 February 1936. A letter to the *PR* editors, published in the subsequent issue under the caption "Sanctions Against Williams," attacking Williams, was followed by an editorial note in which the editors added their voices to the letter writer's in opposition to Williams's "direction of thought." *Partisan Review* 3 (May 1936): 30. Concerned about the editors' note, Lewis wrote Isidor Schneider, who had praised Lewis's poetry in an earlier *PR*. Schneider replied, calming Lewis's alarm. "I don't think for a moment, that there was any idea of serving a warning upon us." Schneider, letter to H. H. Lewis, 11 May 1936. Courtesy of the University of Connecticut–Storrs. Lewis sent a copy of the letter to Williams with the note: "In spite of Schneider's attitude, I believe that I enclose documentary straws in the wind which must perforce cause you suspect: that PR editors could not but have thought of your survey and NM's acceptance of it when they went so far as to suggest a boycott against you." Isidor Schneider, letter to H. H. Lewis, 11 May 1936.

67. W. Williams, "American Poet," 257–63.

68. See Mariani, *William Carlos Williams*, 406. Also, see Conroy, "H. H. Lewis, Plowboy of the Gumbo," *JCR*, 241.

69. Wald, *New York Intellectuals*, 95.

70. H. H. Lewis, "The Noselings," *Salvation*, 31. "Rapply" is a reference to the Soviet RAPP.

71. Howard Mumford Jones, in a letter to Kenneth Porter, remarks at length about "the patronizing way in which American literary historians deal with literature, however defined, stemming from beyond the Mississippi. . . . the main trouble with the West is that it is always approached from the Eastern point of view" (Howard Mumford Jones, letter to Kenneth Porter, 23 March 1979). Irving Howe includes "plebeians" from west of the Hudson River in a vital American culture. In an essay on democratic culture he writes that "it's especially difficult for us to maintain a cultivated tradition, which means first of all to stay in vital relation to the classical culture of Europe, while also welcoming plebeian newcomers from Mississippi river towns, western mining camps, and New York sweat shops. . . ." Intellectuals, writers and scholars, "must be ready to welcome into its ranks newcomers who bring along with them the unruly, the uncouth, the 'barbaric.'" I. Howe, "Toward an Open Culture," 26–27.

72. Rahv and Phillips were both Jewish. I find no other evidence of anti-Semitism in Lewis's writing. Indeed, Mike Gold and Isidor Schneider were among his most enthusiastic defenders.

73. Wixson, "Thomas Hart Benton's New York Years," 198–99.

74. Maxim Lieber, letter to Conroy, 19 December 1934.

75. The taxi dance episode was based upon Norman Dopher's visit to Moberly and his visit with Jack to Kansas City.

76. Geoffrey Hosking, quoted in Freeborn, *Russian Revolutionary Novel*, 246.

77. This thematic pattern was common to Socialist Realism. See A. Klein, *Im Auftrag*, 274–75, 562. Conroy decided against setting the action of the concluding section of the book in the Soviet Union, as for a time he apparently intended to do. See "International Chronicle," *International Literature* 2 (June 1934): 147. The "affirmative trend" was a commonplace of Socialist Realism. See Conroy, "The Affirmative Trend."

78. Coincidentally, Orrick Johns published an essay on Minor in *New Masses* (28 August 1934: 16–19), just at the time that Jack was writing his novel.

79. Harry Hansen, the *New York World-Telegram* columnist, who had written enthusiastically about *The Disinherited*, was disappointed that Jack's second novel failed to "live up to the promise of the first." It seems many other reviewers shared this disappointment. Hansen, "The First Reader."

80. Orrick Johns noted in a letter to Conroy that it was considered to be bourgeois writing if the writer used developed scenes depicting individualized characters (7 April 1934). Algren, in his review, faulted the use of past-tense narrative. "This makes for indirectness, lends a sense of unreality to many passages." *Windsor Quarterly* 3 (Fall 1935): 73.

81. Le Sueur, "Join Hand and Brain," 25.

82. Le Sueur, letter to author, 22 September 1990. "My review hurt him as it did me. We always had this between us but because we were both silent self conscious midwestern yokels we could never talk about it. . . . i thought it was goodby to his disinherited style but he never referred to it or wrote like that again."

83. Wolin, *Walter Benjamin*, 154–61.

84. Mangione, review of *A World to Win*, 109.

85. Forsythe, "Down with the Novel," 29–30.

86. Ibid., 29.

87. Ibid., 30.

88. Frank O'Connor, ed., *The Lonely Voice*, 19.

89. From notes he had scratched on the back of a letter, it is clear that he thought in terms of individual episodes, not the whole construction. See Conroy, letter to Wharton, 21 May 1934. In a letter to Kenneth Porter, he indicated that he was writing sketches and short stories with the aim of making them into a book. Conroy, letter to Porter, 28 May 1932. In fact, only three sketches were incorporated into *A World to Win* in contrast to the thirteen that comprised *The Disinherited*.

90. Harry Block, an editor at Covici-Friede, asked Jack to revise the section. Block, letter to Conroy, 12 March 1935.

91. The incident with the Vigilantes was drawn from Conroy's own experience in Foster's, a St. Louis bookstore. See Conroy, letter to "Will and Walt" (Wharton and Snow), ca. early 1935. The concluding scene, in which a black worker hurls a tear gas bomb back at the police, was reported in the *Moberly Monitor-Index*, 11 July 1932, 1.

92. The stillbirth scene is quite shocking by the standards of the time. Le Sueur defended the scene in her review, arguing that Leo and Anna are poor, improvident people who are no less human for it, and that Conroy's unsentimental detachment gives dignity and compassion to the scene.

93. Schwartz points out that the Party "never considered literary and artistic intellectuals as crucial to the success of socialism in America. The main aesthetic from the Party's point of view, then, was that the artists should ally themselves with the working class against the capitalist possessing class." *Marxism and Culture*, 9. *A World to Win* appears to support this view.

94. Algren, review of *A World to Win*, 73.

95. That is, the "genteel females turned out by small religious colleges at the close of the 19th century." Conroy, letter to Dan James, 23 May 1935.

96. The agreement was that the two writers would not reveal West's collaboration, which neither did until several months before West's death in 1990, when I asked West directly whether he had written the two chapters. He seemed astonished that I—or anyone—should know, then replied affirmatively, giving me the details of his contribution. Ray B. West, interview, 23 January 1990. My thanks to Mrs. Ray B. West for permission to make use of this interview, and to Dan Morris, who first drew my attention to the possibility that West had helped Conroy.

97. Gregory, review of *A World to Win*.

98. In his foreword to Leonard Spier's *When the Sirens Blow*, Jack had blown off steam about the "super-esthetes" who write reviews. It was better to have "something vital to say" than to follow the "traditional trappings and the vapid *trivia* affected by most young poets." Foreword, *When the Sirens Blow*, 3–4.

99. Conroy, letter to Dan James, 23 May 1935.

100. Ibid.

101. Horace Gregory, letter to Conroy, 25 May 1935.

102. Gregory's 1937 edition, *New Letters in America*, is evidence that he was looking east to Europe, not to western America, in choosing selections for the anthology.

103. William McHie, letter introducing Conroy, 20 June 1935.

104. James T. Farrell was scheduled to teach at Commonwealth the week before Jack's arrival. Ben Botkin, Mother Ella Reeve Bloor, and Charles J. Finger, publisher of *All's Well*, were also listed for that summer. See *Commonwealth College Fortnightly* (15 June 1935): 4.

105. Conroy, interview, 5 October 1982.

106. Koch, *Educational Commune*, 136.

107. Ray and Charlotte Koch, interview, June 1981.

108. Koch, *Educational Commune*, 150.

109. Ibid., 146.

110. See "Writers' Group to Study Alabama Sedition Cases," *New York Herald-Tribune*, 17 July 1935.

111. See "Class War in Kentucky," *NM* (September 1931): 23.

112. An advance news release of Hicks's *The Great Tradition* credits Algren with taking part in the Alabama demonstration. Afterward, the error became a private joke between Algren and Conroy. At parties, Nelson would talk as if he had been on the trip. Conroy, interview, 17 October 1984.

113. Hopkins was reluctant to talk about the Alabama adventure when Jack saw her again in Chicago. She wrote a proletarian novel, using the pen name Polly Bowden, entitled *The Pink Egg* (1942). Its uniqueness lies in the fact that the characters are birds.

114. John Howard Lawson, letter to Conroy, 24 June 1935.

115. Daniel Aaron, *Writers on the Left*, 304. John Howard Lawson reported on the "terror against militant workers" and "red-baiting" in Birmingham in "'In Dixieland We Take Our Stand,' A Report on the Alabama Terror," 8–9. Note also Matthew Josephson's *Infidel in the Temple* on the hazards of northern liberals and radicals going into the South (111). Blaine Owen's "Night Ride in Birmingham," 65–67, details the oppressive anti-red hysteria and vigilante action in the South. A publication called *The Southern Worker* had to be published underground; anyone caught distributing it was imprisoned.

116. Conroy, interview, 5 June 1986.

117. Conroy, "Reception in Alabama," 9, 21. Also, Conroy, interviews, 26 December 1978, 5 June 1986. The Alabama demonstration and shooting were reported sympathetically in a long article in Nashville's *Tennessean Magazine* (4 August 1935). The members of the writers' committee, it is reported, are true-blue Americans, including two native-born Southerners, and only one with a "furrin" name, hardly the sort plotting revolution. Jack went home to Moberly (Lieber had written him that the publicity of the trip might threaten his Guggenheim grant) while others in the group went to meet with Governor Talmadge of Georgia concerning the Angelo Herndon case. In the meeting with the governor was a member of the American Legion who claimed that he had incontestable evidence of Herndon's sedition; Hirsch and the others were "racketeers." Realizing the futility of the meeting, Bruce Crawford inquired about the gover-

nor's snake bite. "Some say it killed the snake," Governor Talmadge replied, snapping his suspenders. See unpublished transcript, "Interview with Governor," in Conroy papers, Newberry Library; also, Conroy, interview, 5 June 1986.

118. See "Writers Receive 'Southern Hospitality,'" *International Literature* 10 (October 1935): 106–7; Gowen, "Bigot Brigades," 5.

119. See "5 Shots Fired at 5 Liberals," *New York World-Telegram*, 30 July 1935; "Liberals Return from Dixie 'Test,'" *New York Post*, 7 August 1935; "Alabama Ruled by Terrorism, Writers Charge," *New York World-Telegram*, 7 August 1935.

120. Editorial, *Nation* (14 August 1935).

121. *Birmingham News*, 30 July 1935.

122. *Birmingham Age-Herald*, 7 August 1935, 6.

123. Conroy, interview, 3 November 1985.

124. Loosely connected to the actual events, Zugsmith's story concludes with the disillusionment of two of the fictional demonstrators: one who abandons labor causes to settle into a comfortable marriage, the other, a college professor, who concludes that the whole venture was basically futile and that artists should exercise their freedoms within the realm of art. Donohue, however, continues his involvement in Southern civil rights through lecturing and writing. Zugsmith's story, published in 1938, suggests that a certain staleness had begun to affect the radical movement, associated with the growing presence of fascism in Spain and Germany (and in the American South) and the ineffectiveness of liberal activism.

125. *Moberly Monitor-Index*, 7 December 1935.

126. One incident occurring under Snow's management deserves brief telling. Martha Dodd, daughter of the American ambassador to Germany, submitted a story titled "Red Wedding" to the *Anvil*. When the German government protested her radical activities in Berlin, Dodd withdrew the manuscript from consideration. In several newspapers it was reported, probably erroneously, that the State Department had forced the withdrawal. Conroy, letter to John Rogers, 19 November 1935.

127. In fact, Gold never showed up or took part in editorial meetings; his only impact on *Anvil* was to contribute a story for its ultimate issue.

128. Goodwyn, "The Cooperative Commonwealth," 35.

129. Hicks had suggested that the problem was between *Blast* and *Anvil;* one or the other had to go. Miller was persuaded that the aim was to eliminate all of the independent magazines.

130. F. Miller, "*New Masses* and Who Else?" 4–5.

131. Snow, letter to Wharton, 16 July 1935.

132. Malcolm Cowley remembered discussions of the League of American Writers' executive committee during the summer of 1935 at which Trachtenberg announced plans, under Party orders, to stop the publication of *Partisan Review*, along with all remaining John Reed Club publications, in order to substitute a single literary magazine under the league's auspices. Cowley claims he was able to dissuade Trachtenberg from carrying out the plan. See Cowley, "Thirty Years Later," 509.

133. Snow, letter to Wharton and Conroy, 20 August 1935. Alexandra Wharton Grannis, letter to author, 12 June 1991.

134. Snow, letter to Wharton, 16 July 1935.

135. Snow, letter to Wharton, 3 September 1935.

136. Snow, letter to Conroy, 24 September 1935.

137. Snow showed his appreciation for Balch's editorial help by publishing a Balch story in Anvil 13.

138. Wharton, letter to Conroy, late September 1935.

139. Ibid.

140. Wharton, letter to Conroy, October 1935.

141. Conroy, letter to Snow, 22 October 1935.

142. Snow, letter to Conroy, 30 October 1935.

143. Snow, letter to Conroy, 6 November 1935.

144. Snow, letter to Conroy, 30 October 1935.

145. William Phillips, in my interviews with him, seemed to have no memory of the meeting. Interview, 22 May 1990. In a letter to me, Mr. Phillips wrote: "As for the matter of the Communist Party's involvement in the merger with Anvil, as I said to you, I have no recollection of such involvement. And so far as I recall, it was done completely on our own. Moreover, the Party never interfered in matters of this kind. However, I will look up the correspondence again to see if it throws any light on this question." Phillips, letter to author, 7 July 1990. A subsequent letter from the Partisan Review's office confirmed that there is no correspondence with Conroy or Snow in the PR archives—despite the fact that Conroy had served on the editorial board of PR-Anvil. Jane Uscilka, letter to author, 10 July 1990. In a 1966 symposium, Phillips confessed that he had "suppressed" memories of the merger, resulting from his "disaffection from the Party's control." Phillips, "Thirty Years Later," 510.

146. For instance, see the ad in Art Front (January 1936).

147. Walter Snow, "That Literary 'Shotgun Marriage,'" unpubl. MS, Walter Snow papers, University of Connecticut–Storrs.

148. Snow, letter to Conroy, 30 October 1935.

149. Conroy, letter to John Rogers, 19 November 1935.

150. "Johnny Armstrong's Last Goodnight." Other times Jack would quote a long passage from Marc Antony's funeral oration, beginning, "You are not wood, you are not stones, but men. If you have tears, prepare to shed them now, . . ." parodying in mock-tragic voice his own misfortunes.

151. Kalar, letter to Huddlestone, 25 November 1935.

152. Snow, "That Literary 'Shotgun Marriage,'" 8.

153. Gold, "Papa Anvil and Mother Partisan," 22–23.

154. Cooney, Rise of the New York Intellectuals. See pp. 83ff. on Calmer's defense of Farrell.

155. Schneider, "Sectarianism on the Right," 23.

156. See Aaron, Writers on the Left, 296–303; Gilbert, Writers and Partisans, 142–87; Pells, Radical Visions, 334–62; Cantor, Divided Left, chap. 7.

157. Jack rode to New York with Algren and a new friend, Bud Fallon, an

East St. Louis mill worker, in Grace Outlaw's car. Jack recalled a disruption at the congress by a small group led by Dwight Macdonald and including Rahv, Phillips, Mary McCarthy, and others, who asked pointed questions in a morning discussion group. The *Partisan Review* "literary mafia," he said, were as thick as thieves, but in the background, obviously at odds with the congress and its program. Conroy, interview, 21 June 1987.

158. Hart, ed., *Writer in a Changing World,* 46.

159. Ibid., 137–39. Cowley later viewed the shift to established writers and the disbandment of the John Reed Clubs as "one of the origins of the great schism in the literary movement later on." "Thirty Years Later," 496.

160. Simpson, letter to Conroy, September 1936.

Chapter 17
The Writers' Project Years

1. Slonim, *Soviet Russian Literature,* 39. Russian workers my brother and I met during an extensive trip throughout the Soviet Union in 1961 pushed editions of poetry into our hands and quoted at length from them.

2. Mangione, *The Dream,* 30.

3. Rahv, *Essays on Literature and Politics,* 301.

4. The expression is also the title of ex-*Anvil* writer Benjamin Appel's collection of "American voices from the Great Depression" published in 1940.

5. Conroy, letter to Richard Wright, 10 April 1936. Courtesy of Yale University Library.

6. Memoranda, Lawrence S. Morris to Henry G. Alsberg, 25 March 1936, 28 May 1936. Courtesy of the Federal Writers' Project archive, Library of Congress, Washington, D.C.

7. Conroy, letter to Richard Wright, 10 April 1936. Courtesy of Yale University Library.

8. See Kramer, *Wild Jackasses.* See also Shover, *Cornbelt Rebellion.*

9. Interview, Conroy, 31 March 1986.

10. Interviews, Conroy, 21 July 1985; 29 January, 31 March, 19 July 1986.

11. *New York World-Telegram,* 16 June 1936. Conroy papers, Newberry Library.

12. Minutes of the meetings, Midwest Federation of Arts and Professions, 13 June 1936. Conroy papers, Newberry Library.

13. In addition to interviews with Conroy, my sources are the minutes and an unpublished manuscript by Margaret Walker, "The Midwest Federation of Arts and Professions," Illinois Writers' Project. Courtesy of the Illinois State Historical Library, Springfield.

14. Conroy, letter to Howard Wolf, 6 October 1936.

15. Harold Strauss, letter to Conroy, 18 March 1936.

16. Conroy, letter to Richard Wright, 14 November 1936. Courtesy of Yale University Library.

17. See Denning's essay on this point, "'The Special American Conditions,'" 356–80.

18. See Denisoff, *Great Day Coming*.

19. Walter Snow, letter to Conroy, 12 November 1971.

20. Clinton Simpson, letter to Conroy, ca. spring 1936.

21. Simpson, letter to Conroy, ca. August 1936.

22. Jay Martin credits Conroy as an early promoter of West's work. Martin, *Nathanael West*, 256–57.

23. Interview, Betrenia Watt Bowker, 17 March 1979. Responding to criticism of the Federal Arts and Writers' Projects, Harry Hopkins exclaimed: "Hell, those people have to eat too!"

24. See Shinkle, "Focusing on Missouri's Past," 6–10; Lipsitz, "Striking Prose," 44–46; Conroy, "Writers Disturbing the Peace," 13; "Why the WPA Writers Are On Strike," unpubl. MS, Conroy papers, Newberry Library. I summarize extensive correspondence relating to the strike and Conroy's role in the project, located in the FWP archives at the Library of Congress as well as in the Newberry's Conroy papers. A general history of the Federal Writers' Project is offered in Mangione's *The Dream* and Penkower's *Federal Writers' Project*.

25. Conroy, letter to Wharton, 14 December 1949.

26. Interview, Betrenia Watt Bowker, 17 March 1979.

27. See McGuire, "Where Does Labor Go from Here"; also, interview, Robert Logsdon, 10 April 1984.

28. See "A Yaleman and a Communist," *Fortune* 28 (November 1943). Sentner was later indicted under the Smith Act in the McCarthy era.

29. See Conroy, letter to Peggy Werkley, 14 October 1936.

30. Unpubl. MS, Wharton Collection, Western Historical Manuscript Collection, University of Missouri at Columbia. Wharton noted in the margins of the poem that he had been inspired by Conroy's humorous remarks in a bar. Conroy said, tongue-in-cheek, that it was necessary to read the *Daily Worker* every day; otherwise one risked reviewing favorably a book whose author had become a Trotskyite since the previous day's issue.

31. Wharton, letter to author, 18 October 1982.

32. Wharton, letter to author, summer 1983.

33. Wharton, "Monster Three Day Baccanalian Festival Marks Return of Eminent Middlewestern Critic," unpub. MS, Wharton Collection, Western Historical Manuscript Collection.

34. Wharton, letter to author, January 1985.

35. "Band of Hope" of course refers to the Salvation Army; and "Blue Blouse" is a reference to street theater in the Soviet Union.

36. Wharton subsequently attacked Jack for not giving credit in the byline for Wharton's contributions (Wharton, letter to Conroy, 2 May 1938). In his reply, Jack reminded Wharton of the play's collective authorship, including Algren's contributions (Conroy, letter to Wharton, 3 May 1938). Wharton's misanthropic moods were also the source of his choicest satiric humor.

37. See J. Hart, *Popular Book*, 106ff.

38. Conroy, interview, 27 July 1987.

39. Conroy's sketch "The Kimberly Toughs," written when Jack was in his early eighties, bears similarities with the Fallonite days of some forty years ear-

lier. The story tells of the "toughs'" perverse humor, misogyny, racism, and penchant for violence—the dark underside of the Fallonites—which Jack, as a novelist, had never directly treated in his writing. Artistic concerns, he felt, should not intrude upon the obligations that friendship imposed on one. For better or worse, the Fallonites had been Jack's friends during a difficult time. On Algren's attachments to the Fallonites, see Drew, *Nelson Algren*.

40. Wharton, "Sand County Sandpaper," n.d., unpubl. MS in Wharton Collection, Western Historical Manuscript Collection.

41. On this point, see Algren, letter to Wharton, ca. 1939, in which Algren claims that Balch is shrewder about judging people than is Conroy. It is significant that Conroy was willing to balance his desire for entertaining companionship that the Fallonites seemed to provide him against his personal abhorrence of their violence and criminality, in which he took no part. His relationship to Jesse Blue is especially illustrative of this precarious balance. See Conroy, letters to Wharton, 19 November 1947, 1 February 1950.

42. Quoted in Conroy, letter to author, 16 November 1985. Fanny Cook, a St. Louis liberal and the author of *Mrs. Palmer's Honey*, was a friend to Conroy and the project writers.

43. Algren, letter to Wharton, 6 December 1938; interview, Conroy, 26 December 1985.

44. Algren, letter to Wharton, December 1938.

45. Algren, letter to Fallon, December 1938.

46. Michael Gold's characterization of John Howard Lawson as a "bourgeois Hamlet" in *New Masses*, and Lawson's reply, in which he defended Conroy's *The Disinherited*, prefigure the cultural left's increasing focus on mainstream writers who supported antifascist causes in place of fellow-traveling writers, like Lawson, who were struggling (as Lawson said) to clarify their ideological development. See North, ed., *New Masses: An Anthology*, 219–29.

47. Conroy, interviews, 4 June 1986, 21 June 1987.

48. See H. Hart, ed., *Writer in a Changing World*, 225ff.; Gilbert, *Writers and Partisans*, 160–64, 178–80; Wald, "Revolutionary Intellectuals," 118–33. Phillips, "Comment," 7–9, tells (understandably) only half the story.

49. See C. Nelson, *Repression and Recovery*, 36ff.

50. Conroy, letter to Fallon, 15 December 1938.

51. Conroy, letter to Henry Alsberg, 17 July 1936.

52. Memorandum, Lawrence S. Morris to Henry Alsberg, 15 March 1938, FWP Archive, Library of Congress.

53. Jean Winkler, letter to Betrenia Watt, spring 1937. Courtesy of Betrenia Watt Bowker.

54. Winkler, letter to Betrenia Watt, June 1937. See Wixson, "Jack Conroy and the East St. Louis Toughs," 29–57.

55. Conroy, letter to Wharton, 3 November 1937.

56. Otis Ferguson, "Lillian Lugubriously Sighed," 22.

57. "Ripostes," *Partisan Review* 4 (February 1938): 64.

58. Conroy, letter to Wharton, 8 October 1964. See Conroy's account of the hoax in *New Letters* 39 (Fall 1972): 51; and Wald, *James T. Farrell*, 36–

38. Eugene Lyons, an ardent Communist who later turned virulently anti-red, referred to the hoax in his *Red Decade* (1941), citing it as an example of a "Stalinist literary tactic" that attacked Farrell in "slimy language." See Conroy, "Conversation with Jack Conroy," *JCR*, 174. "Slimy" was a favorite Stalinist expression at the time.

59. Amanda Algren, interview, 17 September 1992.

60. See Conroy's essay "Theodore Dreiser," 9–15.

61. Retitled "Nobody with Sense," the collection never appeared.

62. John T. Frederick, letter to Conroy, 14 July 1938.

63. This tale appears in Banks's *First-Person America*, 90–92, credited to Algren. If Conroy's memory is not convincing on this point, then a simple analysis of the text should prove persuasive: the style and locutions are unquestionably Conroy's. Conroy contributed a variant of "True Blue Highpockets" to Frederick, in the form of an interview Conroy conducted with Dr. Morris Finkel, a physician, who had been connected with the Ford plant in Detroit. The mss are in the Conroy papers, Newberry Library.

64. Conroy remembered that Algren "confessed" finally to Frederick that he didn't have sufficient experience in industrial settings to write industrial folklore. Interviews, Conroy, 22 October 1978, 21 June 1987.

65. Conroy recalled that Algren liked to give the impression that he didn't do anything for the Writers' Project. In truth, however, Algren wrote the Galena guidebook and submitted occupational narratives like "When You've Lived Like I Done."

66. "That Burg Called Butte," "A Job in the Couer d'Alene" [*sic*], unpubl. mss, Illinois State Historical Library, Springfield.

67. Algren, letter to "Pussyface" (Fallon), summer 1938.

68. Wharton, "Pogram for a Piece of Concrete," unpubl. ms, in Wharton Collection, Western Historical Manuscript Collection.

69. Circular, *New Anvil*, ca. April 1938. Conroy papers, Newberry Library.

70. Interview, Conroy, 26 December 1983. Destitute, Bodenheim was found murdered on 7 February 1954, along with a young mistress, in a litter-strewn New York hotel room.

71. Ben Hagglund, letter to Conroy, 7 May 1939. Also, see circulation lists in Conroy papers, Newberry Library.

72. Maltz, letter to Conroy, 1939.

73. I. J. Kissen, letter to Conroy, 17 December 1939.

74. Conroy to Wharton, 12 December 1939. Also, Hagglund to Conroy, 27 December 1939.

75. Benjamin Appel, letter to Conroy, 1939.

76. Ben Hagglund, letter to Conroy, 25 August 1939.

77. Conroy, interview, 3 November 1985. Both Conroy and Algren signed "A Statement by American Progressives," published 3 May 1938, in *New Masses*, which criticized hasty condemnations of the Moscow trials on the basis of incomplete evidence, arguing that the menace of fascism justified "drastic defense" on the part of the Soviets. Others who signed the statement, endorsing the CPA's official explanation of the trials, included Malcolm Cowley, Lillian

Hellman, Langston Hughes, Dorothy Parker, Lynn Riggs, and Henry Roth. In retrospect, they were victims of "obstinate credulity," Cowley wrote years later, not the "dupes of Stalin" portrayed by their detractors. Fervent desire to support those who opposed Hitler inclined them "not so much to excuse as to overlook the crimes of Stalin." See Cowley's memoir, "Echoes from Moscow," 1–11.

78. Conroy, "On Anvil," 128–29. Myers later recanted his Marxist principles, embracing William Buckley–style conservatism. Of the two editors, Algren showed more serious concern about the Party's support than did Conroy. Arranging a fund-raising function for New Anvil in St. Louis, Algren cautioned Fallon to impress the CP people with the magazine's responsible purpose, waiting until they were gone before performing "The Drunkard's Warning." Algren, letter to Wharton, ca. 1938.

79. See McCollum, Nelson Algren: A Checklist, 58. Algren confessed to McCollum that he wrote the poem and published it as a prank aimed at Fallon, who had aspirations to become a writer but, despite his cleverness and wit, never saw anything into print. Conroy, interview, 26 November 1986.

80. Wharton, letter to Conroy, 22 December 1939.

81. Conroy recalled that while sweeping the stairs to Theo's apartment following a performance of "The Drunkard's Warning" Algren accidentally hit one of the irate apartment dwellers with the broom handle. The tenant returned with a pistol and shot at Algren. Tenant, Algren, and Conroy were sent to jail for the remainder of the night. Conroy, interview, 29 January 1985.

82. Interviews, Sanka Bristow, 28 December 1985; Conroy, 19 July 1986. Theo's warmth and interest in Jack's creative life are evident in her two letters to Wharton, one written 20 October 1938, the other undated, Conroy papers, Newberry Library.

83. Conroy, interview, 24 November 1984.

84. See Hoke Norris's description, for instance, in "Critic at-Large," Chicago Sun-Times, 14 April 1963.

85. Merlin Bowen, letter to author, 20 July 1981. Also, see Mark Harris's review of The Jack Conroy Reader, New Republic (1 March 1980), and my reply, letter to editors, ibid. (26 April 1980).

86. Frank Marshall Davis, letter to author, 11 February 1982; Neal Rowland, letter to author, 27 September 1984.

87. Harold Sullivan, interview, 5 December 1982. Conroy said that Rushmore was his only real failure among the old Anvil-ites.

88. Curtis D. MacDougall, interview, 23 June 1981.

89. Conroy, interview, 27 December 1987. An unpubl. MS, "Allah and Race War in Chicago," by Bontemps and Conroy, together with other material gathered and written on the black history project, are with the Conroy papers at the Newberry Library.

90. Conroy, interview, 5 June 1986.

91. Conroy, interview, 1 September 1985.

92. Joe Velarde, interview, 24 June 1981.

93. Conroy, interview, 27 December 1987.

94. Geismar, *American Moderns,* 16; Conroy, interview, 26 December 1985.

95. Conroy, interview, 19 July 1986. Apart from this admission, it was un-characteristic of Conroy to speak unflatteringly of anyone who had once been a friend.

Chapter 18
Only a Bridesmaid

1. Paul Romaine, interview, 2 August 1981. Romaine and Conroy had gone together to the bar where this particular scene occurred.

2. The expression is Conroy's in his review of *The Damndest Radical.*

3. Conroy, interview, 6 June 1986.

4. Conroy, interview, 5 June 1986; Dorothy Farrell, interview, 28 May 1990.

5. Neal Rowland, letter to author, 27 September 1984. Rowland recalled the following incident: when a reporter asked Claude Lightfoot whether the CP had exploited him given that he was black, Lightfoot replied: "All the rights you take for granted today—that's what the CP meant to me in those days." Neal and Christine Rowland, interview, 16–17 September 1992.

6. Conroy, interviews, 9 September 1984, 26 December 1985, 16 October 1986.

7. Conroy, interview, 19 June 1983. Sidney Lens was the business manager for the food workers' union to which Gladys belonged.

8. Catalog, *Abraham Lincoln School, Summer Session 1943,* 3.

9. On the Abraham Lincoln School, see Patterson, *Man Who Cried Genocide.*

10. Henry Noyes, letter to author, 9 April 1981. Noyes, who taught at the Abraham Lincoln School with Jack, later founded China Books.

11. Also see Drew, *Nelson Algren,* on Blake. Blake's letters to Algren, Con-roy, and Fallon are in the Conroy papers, Newberry Library.

12. Conroy expressed this aim to Dale Harrison, published in "All About the Town," *Chicago Sun,* 4 January 1944. Although Josephine Herbst and Con-roy were on friendly terms, she portrayed him unflatteringly in *Somewhere the Tempest Fell.*

13. "7 New Dealers on Red School Faculty List," *Chicago Daily Tribune,* 14 October 1943, 2.

14. Kreymborg, "Farmhand Poet," *NM* (29 April 1942): 22.

15. Carmon, letter to Conroy, 27 March 1943.

16. Conroy, letter to H. H. Lewis, 26 January 1945.

17. The Lewis I met toward the end of his long life was a man of great per-sonal dignity, erect bearing, and old-fashioned courtesy, living, more by choice than necessity, in his one-room corncrib shack. "Tell Jack I'm a wealthy man!" he exclaimed one day, showing me a coffee-stained check for $1,500 from Yale University for letters he had received from Malcolm Cowley and Edmund Wil-son. It is altogether likely that Lewis left the check uncashed, lying in a pile of newspapers. Harold Dellinger recalled that Lewis viewed Dellinger's visit in the 1970s as the end of a "blockade" against him, since Dellinger was the first

in many years to acknowledge his literary work. See Dellinger, "Pegasus and the Plow," 6–7. Also, see C. Nelson, *Repression and Recovery*, on Lewis. It is likely, then, that the Japanese espionage plot that Lewis had fantasized was bound up with the question of literary recognition—lacking the recognition he desperately sought, he felt abandoned, turning his disappointment into a paranoic response directed at the FBI (who actually was harassing him) and at alleged plots against the United States in World War II by the Black Dragons.

18. Conroy, letter to Arna Bontemps, 13 September 1945.

19. Rather cruelly, I think, Shulman addressed a letter to Conroy, "Dear Always-A-Bridesmaid," in which he recited in dollar figures his own literary success. Shulman, letter to Conroy, 20 October 1947.

20. To Wharton he wrote: "You are right in saying that I have a lot of cause for dissatisfaction with my lot, and I am more resigned, I suppose, than contented. Every week or so I get evidence of somebody who was first published in *The Anvil*, or who has some very modest literary achievement, making the grade in a big way." Conroy, letter to Wharton, ca. early 1949.

21. Conroy, letter to Bontemps, 15 December 1948.

22. Conroy, letter to Wharton, 20 October 1946.

23. At a writers' conference in Columbia, Missouri, in the early 1950s, Algren attacked bitterly the loyalty tests and spirit of conformity of the early 1950s. Conroy and Algren had discussed these matters many times. Neither realized at the time, I think, that the public's complacency would prove a greater force than McCarthyism in eclipsing their reputations. See Algren, "Things of the Earth," 3–11.

24. Conroy, letter to Bontemps, March 1947. Rogers thought Conroy was a "tool of Moscow."

25. Holy Cow! Press has recently republished five of Le Sueur's children's books from this period in a "Wilderness Road Series."

26. Conroy, letter to Howard Wolf, 4 November 1947.

27. Conroy, interviews, 31 March, 4 June 1986; 26 December 1987.

28. Conroy, letter to Jim Light, 19 February 1948.

29. Conroy, letter to Dale Kramer, 28 April 1948.

30. Conroy, letter to Wharton, 26 April 1951.

31. Olsen, *Silences*, 38. On Walker's similar dilemma, see Olsen, 209.

32. M. Harris, review of *The Jack Conroy Reader*, 35.

33. McCormick wrote to Elizabeth Ames, director of Yaddo: "I can honestly say that I don't know of any other person who has quite so much heart for literature and so much of humanity wrapped up in one body." Letter, 2 June 1949. Copy with Conroy papers, Newberry Library.

34. Conroy, letter to Wharton, 13 August 1949.

35. M. Harris, review of *The Jack Conroy Reader*, 36.

36. Ben Appel, letter to Conroy, 3 January 1950.

37. By 1946, Conroy was already sensing a changing climate of reception, orchestrated in part, he said, by "deconverted reds." See his review of *The Partisan Reader*, edited by William Phillips and Philip Rahv.

38. M. Harris, review of *The Jack Conroy Reader*, 36.

39. Writing in 1947, Leo Gurko in *The Angry Decade* asserts that Conroy "had disappeared without a trace" (69).

40. Maurice Isserman, letter to author, 2 March 1985. Isserman, Snow's stepson, graciously granted me permission to quote from this and Snow's letters.

41. John Rogers, letters to Conroy, 6 August 1955, 1 July 1960, 2 December 1970.

42. Rogers, letter to Conroy, 30 August 1959. When Rogers's wife died in 1959, a friend said loudly at the funeral home; "She didn't die of cancer. She was killed by Joe McCarthy!" My gratitude to Robin Rogers, Rogers's daughter, for sharing her memories and granting permission to quote from Rogers's papers.

43. "Notes on Contributors," *Carleton Miscellany* 6 (Winter 1965): 127. The Appel affair received a great deal of attention, prompting an anti-oath statement by the Authors' League of America.

44. Among those discounting the achievements were Stewart H. Holbrook, *Dreamers of the American Dream* (1957), and James Wechsler, *Age of Suspicion* (1953).

45. Janssen, *The Kenyon Review, 1939–1970*, 3.

46. Lasch, *Agony of the American Left*, 57. Also, see Cooney, *Rise of the New York Intellectuals*. Wald's *New York Intellectuals* details the elitism of *Partisan Review*'s project, from 1936 on, to discount vulgarized Marxism while privileging high culture. On efforts to politicize cultural production in recent times, see Pinsker, "Revisionism with Rancor," 243–61.

47. Conroy discusses this point in "Two Authors Look Back at the '30s," his review of Alan Kapelner's *All the Naked Heroes* and William Golding's *Free Fall*.

48. For instance, Kenneth Rexroth writes condescendingly of "Midwest Populism, whose intellectual foundations never rose higher than an editorial in a Des Moines newspaper." *The Alternative Society*, 53. William Phillips's one-sentence history of *Partisan Review*'s merger with *Anvil* cites differences to explain why the combined magazine did not last: "Conroy was too populist and anti-intellectual—and *PR* decided to go it alone again." *Partisan View*, 38. One of the earliest revisionist histories of the 1930s, Eugene Lyons's *The Red Decade* (1940), listed the founders of the League of American Writers, including Conroy, Tillie Lerner Olsen, Meridel Le Sueur, Nathanael West, Richard Wright, Erskine Caldwell, Theodore Dreiser, Nelson Algren, and Langston Hughes, as "literary curiosities" for the "coming historian" (147). John Chamberlain's *Farewell to Reform* similarly devalues the work of the 1930s generation of literary radicals.

49. See, for example, Geismar's *American Moderns*. See also Geismar's essay in the *Saturday Review of Literature* (14 March 1953); C. Wright Mills, *The Power Elite*.

50. Howe and Coser, *American Communist Party*, 275–78, 311–12.

51. One of the earliest of these was Benjamin Gitlow's *I Confess: The Truth About American Communism* (1940).

52. "Anti-Red Law Will Bar 269 of Liner Crew," *Chicago Tribune*, 24 December 1952.

53. Lasch, "Cultural Cold War," 322–59. See also Lasch's chapter on "The Cultural Cold War" in *The Agony of the American Left*. James T. Farrell was one of the early supporters of the Congress for Cultural Freedom.

54. Lasch, "Cultural Cold War," 357.

55. Conroy, interviews, 9 September 1984, 27 December 1987.

56. "Budenz Says 30 Reds Had Foundation Links," *New York World-Telegram and Sun*, 23 December 1952. For commentary on the patterns of betrayal among former 1930s radicals see Malcolm Cowley, *And I Worked at the Writer's Trade*, 136–42. Edwin Seaver, in his autobiography, expresses his gratitude toward HUAC and admiration for Roy Cohen, saying how polite the members of the Special House Committee were to him. See also David McConnell, "Fund Officers, Scholars Called Reds by Budenz," *Chicago Sun-Times*, 24 December 1952.

57. Julian Lee Rayford, letter to Conroy, 8 December 1951.

58. Ernest Hemingway, for instance, felt a paranoid obsession that he was being constantly monitored by the FBI. See A. E. Hotchner, *Papa Hemingway: A Personal Memoir*. For a discussion of loyalty oaths and government surveillance of writers, see Mitgang, "Annals of Government," 47–90. For a broader discussion, see Caute, *Great Fear*; Belfrage, *American Inquisition*. Norman Macleod's letter to Conroy, 31 October 1969, scrawled in the margins of a Conroy letter, is a revealing account of the response of ex-*The Left* editors—Jay Du Von, George Redfield, William Jordan—to the Cold War inquisitions.

59. Weitzel, "Story of a Male's Decline," S2.

60. Conroy, letter to Bontemps, 22 July 1954; Leonard Karlin, interview, 23 June 1981. Karlin, Conroy's lawyer in Chicago, gave practical advice and solace to the Conroys at Tom's death.

61. Kempton, *Part of Our Time*, 132–33. The "monuments" of the 1930s, Kempton wrote, were Farrell, the *Partisan Review* editors, and others who remained independent of the Party. Kempton's characterization of Farrell is drawn in part from Farrell's *Note on Literary Criticism*.

62. A remark in a similar vein by James Wechsler in *The Age of Suspicion* (1953) implied that Jack had opportunistically associated himself with the proletarian movement. Responding several years later, Conroy wrote that after the red-hunters of the 1940s, like Eugene Lyons, "came the 'mea culpa! mea culpa!' outcries of repentant and guilt-laded retrospectivists like Murray Kempton and James Wechsler, who had been seduced by the Muscovites and wanted to save other political virgins from a life disaster." Conroy, ". . . the contemporary fact . . . ," 37. Conroy's half-completed reply to Kempton is with the Conroy papers, Newberry Library.

63. Conroy, letter to Light, 26 May 1955. Bitterly Jack discovered that writing for *Confidential* was Howard Rushmore, his friend in earlier days, who in naming names, brought grief to former colleagues on the left. See also Conroy, letters to Wharton, 5 May, 13 May 1955; Conroy, letter to Kramer, 13 May 1955.

64. Jack Swartz, Jerry Swartz, interview, 2 March 1990.

65. Jerry Swartz, Jack Swartz, interview, 3 March 1990.

66. Algren, letter to Conroy, ca. early 1955. Conroy papers, Newberry Library.

67. The rift became a kind of legend in Chicago and among Conroy's friends. It continues to be debated today. There are numerous versions, including the following: (1) Conroy made fun of Algren's attempt to move in on a blonde in a bar in New York City, embarrassing the girl. Algren left Jack and Fallon, who had come there in Algren's car, and told them to fend for themselves. (Jay Robert Nash's and Stuart Brent's versions, both wrong. The incident occurred years before at the Second American Writers' Congress in 1937, and had nothing to do with Algren's attitude toward Jack later on.) (2) Algren read in a Chicago paper in the mid-fifties that Conroy had replied to a questioner asking where Algren was these days: "lifting his pinkie somewhere with a ladies afternoon literary club." (Version from Herman Kogon, former book editor of the *Chicago Tribune*.) (3) Jack needled Algren when his advances were running out: "Any day now you'll be begging to come to work on the encyclopedia." (This version has things backwards: it was Algren's own joke on himself.) (4) Conroy made a comment about Algren going to Jazz Limited, a high-priced club in Chicago, which was quoted in the *Sun-Times*. Algren balked at any suggestion that since he had made good he now hobnobbed with the well-to-do. (5) In a Chicago bar, Conroy and others kidded Algren. Algren got sore and walked out. (Version from Agnes Hickman, Jack's sister-in-law, at Jack's funeral, indicating the extent to which the rift became a family legend as well.) (6) After an evening in the "black and tan" Club DeLiza in South Chicago, Jack, Algren, Algren's wife, Amanda, and Harold Sullivan left in Dorothy Farrell's car. Seeing Russell Finch, an ex-Fallonite, Farrell stopped her car. Amanda got out of the car and went off with Finch. Algren held everyone in Farrell's car responsible for Amanda's departure with Finch, particularly Jack since Finch had come to Chicago to visit him. (Interview, Harold Sullivan, 5 December 1982). (7) Sensitive about his reputation, and seeking approval from the establishment, Algren broke with those whom he viewed as possible detriments to his acceptance, which finally came when he was elected to the American Academy and Institute of Arts and Letters. Ironically, he died on 9 May 1981, some ten days before the induction was to take place, discovered by friends who had come to celebrate the honor.

68. Drew, *Nelson Algren*, 260–66.

69. Sandiford's editor chose to ignore Algren's letter. Interview, Frank Sandiford, 14 January 1991.

70. Drew, *Nelson Algren*, 275. It was typical of Algren to accept the judgment of "hookers and pimps" who, he said, loved *A Walk on the Wild Side*, and discount the judgment of literary critics like Kazin, Podhoretz, and Fiedler.

71. Drew recounts the events of New Year's Eve 1956, revealing Algren's suicidal despair at this time.

72. Conroy, letter to Jim Light, 5 September 1956.

73. Ray, "Talk on the Wild Side," 33.

74. James Blake, letter to Mrs. Lawrence Fallon, 24 June 1958. H. E. F.

Donohue's interview with Algren, published in a 1987 edition of *Never Come Morning*, cites Algren's perception that following *The Man with the Golden Arm* his work was no longer wanted (299–300).

75. See Geismar, "Nelson Algren," 5.

76. Hagglund, letter to Conroy, 31 August 1959.

77. Dale Kramer asked Conroy to write a piece on Algren in 1962. Jack replied: "I don't want to write anything about Algren. We were close friends for so many years that I can't yet think about him with anything but pain about his curious attitude toward me." Conroy, letter to Kramer, 25 January 1962.

Chapter 19
Home to Moberly

1. Appel, "My Generation of Writers," 5–9. Appel's refusal to sign a loyalty oath received a great deal of attention, prompting the Authors' League of America to oppose loyalty oaths.

2. In one of the earliest assessments of 1930s literary achievements, *On Native Grounds* (1942), Alfred Kazin writes that "the disorganization and demoralization of the crisis period explain why so many sincere writers [novelists of the 1930s] yielded so worshipfully to the Russian example, the marked coarsening and opportunism of literary standards, and the characteristic savagery of writers who, often mediocre enough in imagination, delighted in hitting back at life in their books as violently as life had hit them" (294). It was such generalizing assertions, together with the implication that writing is best explained by behavioral methods, that characterized the tone of numerous critical assessments in the Cold War–era of revisionism. Alan Wald discusses the strengths and limitations of Kazin's commentary on the 1930s in "In Retrospective: *On Native Grounds*," 276–88.

3. See Bellah et al., *Habits of the Heart*.

4. Webster, *Republic of Letters*.

5. Lawrence H. Schwartz argues that Faulkner's reputation was "inflated" by the collaboration of these cultural forces in postwar America. See *Creating Faulkner's Reputation*.

6. I discuss this point in some detail in "Reception Theory," 72–86.

7. See my article "Thomas Hart Benton's New York Years."

8. Geismar, *American Moderns*, 19.

9. Mills, *Power Elite*, 256.

10. Walter Rideout, letter to Conroy, 2 September 1956. "Walter had what seemed to me as a supercilious attitude toward the worker as writer," Conroy wrote Walter Snow some years after Rideout's study appeared. "I have since become acquainted with him. He now teaches at the University of Wisconsin and is a 'believer,' using *The Disinherited* in his classes." Conroy, letter to Snow, 13 October 1972.

11. Fiedler, "John Peale Bishop and the Other Thirties," 74–82.

12. Many of these appear in Randolph's *Roll Me in Your Arms*.

13. Conroy, letter to Dale Kramer, 13 May 1955. Courtesy of Newberry Library.

14. Kramer, apparently, was contemplating doing the "story." Reluctant to write about old friends, Jack offered his material to Kramer. Kramer died soon after completing *The Wild Jackasses*, a study of early midwestern radicalism. Conroy, letter to Kramer, 25 January 1962. Courtesy of Newberry Library.

15. Conroy, "Two Authors Look Back at the '30s."

16. Conroy, letter to Paul D. Bartlett, 4 November 1962. Bartlett wrote *When the Owl Cries* (1960).

17. Nelson Algren, review of *Let No Man Write My Epitaph*. Refusing to reply in kind, Motley wrote a generous, conciliatory letter to the *Chicago Tribune Magazine of Books* (1 February 1959) concerning the savage review. Algren later targeted Motley in a review of Motley's diaries, which were published posthumously. Motley was a likable, moral man, Algren wrote, but as a "literary figure, we now perceive, he does not even exist." Conroy guessed that it was a turf problem with Algren: Motley's subject matter was uncomfortably close to Algren's own. Algren sought to distance himself from Motley, particularly when literary naturalism began to fall into critical disfavor. Conroy, interview, 16 October 1986.

18. Conroy, letter to Motley, 5 February 1962.

19. Bontemps, letter to Conroy, 26 October 1962. Courtesy Bontemps estate.

20. Kirsch, review of *Anyplace But Here*.

21. Studs Terkel, in *Race*, calls race an "American obsession," one that seems to continue to dominate national politics and private conversation.

22. Characteristic of Algren's mood at the time was his submission, a letter, in which he claimed that "that time is so remote I lost interest in it long ago." "A Letter," 104.

23. Conroy, letter to Kramer, 4 May 1966. Courtesy of Newberry Library.

24. Walter Snow's articles on the symposium appear in the *Willimantic Daily Chronicle*, 15 and 16 April 1969.

25. Pells, *Radical Visions*, 368. Pells ignores the importance of regionality in literary radicalism, making no mention of the midwestern radicals, of the *Anvil* (in his discussion of *Partisan Review*), or of east-west differences.

26. Conroy, review of *Radical Visions*, 3D.

27. Hoke Norris, "Critic-at-Large," *Chicago Sun-Times*, 20 September 1964. Farrell summarizes his version of the Conroy-Farrell feud in a letter to biographer Edgar Branch in 1974. The letter is in the James T. Farrell Collection, Van Pelt Library, University of Pennsylvania.

28. Vasiliki Sarant, letter to Conroy, 27 January 1966.

29. Farrell, letter to Conroy, 2 January 1966.

30. On the Conroy-Farrell feud, see also Fried, "Conversation with Jack Conroy," 49; Aaron, *Writers on the Left*, 300; Salzman, *Years of Protest*, 277ff; Wald, *James T. Farrell*, 35ff.

31. Conroy, letter to Edward Dahlberg, 22 July 1969. Also, 19 September

1969. Courtesy of the Harry Ransom Humanities Center, University of Texas at Austin.

32. Dahlberg, *Confessions of Edward Dahlberg*, 270–71, 274.

33. See Salzman, *Albert Maltz*, 85–95.

34. Conroy, review of *Lonely for the Future*.

35. Conroy, interview, 16 October 1986.

36. Conroy, "Home to Moberly," 50.

37. "Conroy and Bontemps to Get Award for Literary Work," *Moberly Monitor-Index*, 19 April 1967, 1.

38. Conroy, letter to John Rogers, 3 November 1977.

39. "27 Writers and Scholars Here Protest War in Letter to LBJ," *Chicago Sun-Times*, 15 May 1966.

40. RP 6–7 (June–July 1931).

41. See Conroy's essay on Podhoretz and the New York intellectuals, "Making It and Faking," 272–75.

42. Introduction, *The Disinherited* (1982), xii.

Afterword

1. "Song of Myself."

2. "Where's the New Faulkner," 65. See also McElvaine, "Workers in Fiction: Locked Out," 1, 19.

Selected List of Names

NELSON ALGREN, born in Detroit, lived mainly in Chicago, giving expression to unrealized human aspirations in literary portrayals drawn from the dark underside of urban existence. Conroy published several of Algren's early sketches that became his first novel, *Somebody in Boots* (1935). Algren later helped Conroy obtain a position on the Illinois Writers' Project in Chicago, where the two writers coedited *The New Anvil* (1939–40). Algren's *The Man with the Golden Arm* (1949), which won the National Book Award, was made into an Otto Preminger film starring Frank Sinatra. Algren died on 9 May 1981, shortly after his election to the American Academy and Institute of Arts and Letters.

SANORA BABB spent a desperately poor childhood with her sister, Dorothy, in Kansas, Oklahoma, and Colorado, the setting for her novel-memoir *An Owl on Every Post* (1970). Babb used personal experience and observations, including those gathered among migrant workers in California in the 1930s, to write short stories published widely in mainstream and radical magazines like the *Anvil*. Babb's novel *The Lost Traveller* (1958) depicts her gambler father, his passion for life, and the misfortunes he brings to his family. Married to the cinematographer James Wong Howe, Babb endured FBI harassment in the 1950s. She continues to write poems and short stories for *Prairie Schooner* and other literary magazines today.

ARNA BONTEMPS, a member of the Harlem Renaissance of black writers and artists in the 1920s, was already a well-known novelist when in 1939 he met Conroy on the Illinois Writers' Project. Born in Alexandria, Louisiana, in 1902, Bontemps graduated from Pacific Union College in 1923, later earning his M.A. degree at the University of Chicago. Bontemps teamed up with Conroy to coauthor three best-selling juvenile stories and two highly regarded studies of black migration to northern industrial cities.

WALTER CARMON, a professional baseball player in his youth, was a devoted editor who promoted the writings of worker-writers like Conroy, Kalar, and

Lewis while performing the day-to-day editorial duties of *New Masses* under Michael Gold. In the mid-thirties, Carmon, with his wife, Rose, went to the Soviet Union to help edit the *Moscow News*. Carmon represented Soviet publishers in the United States after his return in the late 1930s.

RALPH CHEYNEY was the son of the noted historian Edward Potts Cheyney. Together with his wife, LUCIA TRENT, the younger Cheyney published little magazines in the 1920s devoted to introducing new poets and offered poetry correspondence courses to novices. Inspired by Marcus Graham's anthology of revolutionary poetry and the Sacco-Vanzetti executions, Cheyney and Trent founded the Rebel Poets organization, enlisting Conroy as president and editor of its publication. Cheyney and Trent later ended editorial collaboration with Conroy, citing political differences.

PAUL COREY, born in 1904 in Shelby County, Iowa, drew from his experiences growing up on an Iowa farm to write *Acres of Antaeus* (1946), describing the trials of a young farming family in the face of early manifestations of "agribusiness." Graduating from the University of Iowa in 1925, Corey spent his literary apprenticeship in Greenwich Village with his wife, the poet RUTH LECHLITNER. The Coreys built a stone house on an abandoned farm in Putnam County, New York, where he made contacts with Conroy and other little-magazine editors. Active with the League of American Writers, Corey joined the New York Writers' Project in 1939. His work, which included the comic realist novel *Three Miles Square*, was largely neglected during the period when social realism fell into disfavor following World War II. An inventor and craftsman, Corey survived by writing articles for the trade press on homesteading and cats.

ROBERT CRUDEN, born near Aberdeenshire, Scotland, on 21 April 1910, immigrated with his parents to Detroit at age twelve. At City College of Detroit, where he met his wife, Janet, Cruden wrote for the Federated Press. After three years, he left City College, which had provided him a lively forum of radical discussion, to work in an auto factory to help support his childhood family following the layoff of his father. His earliest writings, based upon his experiences on an assembly line and those of his wife as a punch press operator, were published in the *Nation* and *New Masses*. Early drafts of his only novel, *Conveyor* (1935), appeared in Conroy's *Anvil*. Cruden left the factory in 1931 to work in public relations for a rubber union in Akron. Following service in World War II, Cruden earned a Ph.D. in history and taught for many years at Lewis and Clark College.

EDWARD FALKOWSKI left school at age fifteen to enter apprenticeship in an anthracite mine near Shenandoah, Pennsylvania, joining his father and his grandfather, a Polish immigrant. A scholarship student at Brookwood Labor College from 1926 to 1928, where he wrote for the Federated Press and authored a play of mining life for the Hedgerow Theatre in Philadelphia, Falkowski shipped out to Germany, earning his passage as a busboy, to find work in the soft-coal mines of Leipzig and Rheinhausen. These experiences became subject matter for his reportages published in *New Masses* and the *Anvil*. Later he worked in Russian mines and wrote for the Soviet English-language press in Moscow. Intending to remain in the Soviet Union, Falkowski subsequently married a Russian woman, but returned to the United States in 1937 when the purge trials began. Like many others with past Communist associations, Falkowski was unable to publish his work during the Cold War or find employment. Supported in part by his second wife, Helen, a schoolteacher, Falkowski derived satisfaction in helping arrange Poland's admission to the United Nations.

BEN HAGGLUND was born in 1908 near Holt, Minnesota, where, after graduating from high school, he purchased the town's weekly newspaper and taught himself the printer's craft. Abandoning newspaper work in a fit of restlessness, he took a variety of laboring jobs throughout the Northwest. He finally returned to Holt, where he bought an old press with hand-set type and began to publish the *Northern Light*. Through his editorial contacts Hagglund became acquainted with Conroy, whose *Rebel Poet* and *Anvil* he printed, first in Holt and later in Newllano, Louisiana. With his wife, a poet and printer, Ben moved his press to the Rio Grande Valley in Texas, where they published volumes of poetry and a series of short-lived little magazines. Hagglund died shortly after visiting Conroy in the early 1970s.

WARREN HUDDLESTONE, raised in Kokomo, Indiana, got his start as a writer submitting pieces to the *Lone Scout* magazine, through which he made epistolary contact with Joe Kalar. Teaching himself to write by emulating examples from his wide reading, Huddlestone assisted his father, a housepainter, until work was no longer available in the early Depression. Unwilling to burden his parents, Huddlestone tramped around the United States, hungry and homeless, an experience that supplied material for sketches and stories submitted to editors like Conroy and Malcolm Cowley. After unsuccessful attempts to publish two novels and following his attendance at the 1935 American Writers' Congress, Huddlestone abandoned writing to work for the Indiana State Employment Service and later as a technical journalist.

JOSEPH KALAR, born in a Slovenian community in northern Minnesota, submitted juvenilia to the *Lone Scout*, the *Bohemian*, and other ephemeral magazines, hoping like Warren Huddlestone to follow in the path of Theodore Dreiser and Sherwood Anderson. Certified at age eighteen, Kalar abandoned teaching after a year in isolated Koochiching County. Unable to find employment as a journalist, he worked in paper mills and sawmills during which time he wrote prolifically for *New Masses*, *Rebel Poet*, the *Anvil*, an anthology titled *We Gather Strength* (1933), and numerous other publications. Active in union organization, Kalar became increasingly discouraged in his literary goals after 1935. Following his defeat as a farm-labor candidate for state office, Kalar worked until retirement in industrial and personnel relations for a Minnesota paper company.

RAYMOND KRESENSKY, one of ten children, a poet and Presbyterian minister from Algona, Iowa, graduated from Coe College in 1927. Restless as the pastor of small parishes in Iowa, Indiana, and Nebraska, Kresensky frequently made trips to cities like Chicago where he witnessed the desolation and poverty of the early Depression. His first volume of poems, *Emmaus* (1931), attracted some notice. His poems and short narratives appeared in the *New Republic*, the *Anvil*, *Christian Century*, and *Hinterland*, which he helped edit. Like Kenneth Porter, Kresensky held convictions that were a blend of Christian belief and radical sentiment. The state director of the Iowa Writers' Project for a time, Kresensky returned to church work and poetry for the remainder of his life.

RUTH LECHLITNER, from a conservative community in Indiana originally, was exposed to radical ideas at the University of Michigan in the early 1920s. Fired for teaching Flaubert in a New Mexico high school, Lechlitner was hired by John T. Frederick as an editorial assistant for *Midland* magazine in Iowa City, where she pursued her studies at the university. In 1928, Ruth and Paul Corey married and moved to New York, where Ruth worked for *Nation* magazine. In the 1930s Lechlitner was an editor in New York City, wrote poetry criticism for the *New York Herald-Tribune*, and published her poetry in the *New American Caravan*, *New Directions*, the *Anvil*, and elsewhere.

MERIDEL LE SUEUR, born in February 1900 in Murray, Iowa, was the daughter of Socialists who opened the short-lived People's College in Fort Scott, Kansas, where Eugene Debs and Emma Goldman spoke. Le Sueur's early stories appeared in the *American Mercury*, *Scribner's*, the *Dial*, and various radical publications. Conroy published early versions of her novel *The Girl* in the *Anvil*. A writer of lyrical beauty and bold radical convictions, a passionate speaker, trained as an actress, and a feminist, Le Sueur is enjoying overdue critical attention after a long "dark time" of suppression during the Cold War years. Her most recent book, *The Dread Road* (West End Press, 1991), is characteristic of Le Sueur's best work: individual suffering is viewed under the light of broader social and political problems.

H. H. LEWIS, born 13 January 1901, near Cape Girardeau, Missouri, worked as a mail clerk in Chicago and St. Louis. Tramping west in the early 1920s, Lewis lived penniless on Los Angeles's skid row, an experience that radicalized him politically and furnished the material for his first publications. Working as a laborer for most of his life on his family's farm, he submitted poems, sketches, and personal narratives to left-wing publications, including *New Masses* and the *Anvil*. Conroy drew H. L. Mencken's attention to Lewis, resulting in the publication of "School Days in the Gumbo" in the *American Mercury* (January 1931). Lewis achieved notoriety for his eccentric temperament and irreverent, pungent satire. Reviled by critics like William Rose Benet and championed by William Carlos Williams, Lewis won *Poetry* magazine's Harriet Monroe Prize in 1938. Lewis's caustic, earthy humor and temperamental feuding eventually cost him the support of the left movement. Conroy remained a friend long after Lewis, no longer able to attract a publisher, retired to a converted corncrib, haunted by fears of FBI intimidation and silenced as a poet.

MAXIM LIEBER, a publisher in the 1920s, was later a literary agent for Conroy, Erskine Caldwell, Langston Hughes, William Saroyan, Josephine Herbst, and others. Faced with HUAC harassment, Lieber moved to Mexico (where he edited a collection of short stories called *The American Century*), then to Poland, returning to live near Hartford, Connecticut.

NORMAN MACLEOD, born in Salem, Oregon, in 1906, grew up in Missoula, Montana, the subject of his novel *The Bitter Roots* (1941). His poetic settings and themes frequently reflect his western upbringing. His career as a little-magazine editor (*Palo Verde, Morada, Front, Maryland Quarterly, Briarcliff Quarterly, Pembroke Magazine*), a poet who appeared in both avant-garde and radical publications, and a founder of the New York Poetry Center indicates the breadth of his talent. Macleod's poetry reveals energy, experimentalism, and craftsmanship that he continued to employ even as he lay, an old, very sick man, in a Greensboro, North Carolina, nursing home.

KENNETH PORTER, born on a farm near Sterling, Kansas, in 1905, studied for the Presbyterian ministry in Kansas. He was a member of the Cambridge Poetry Forum with John Wheelwright and Seymour Link while a graduate student at Harvard University. Porter, a Rebel Poet, published his first collection of poetry, *The High Plains*, in 1938, followed by *No Rain from These Clouds* (1946). Named poet laureate of Kansas, Porter also had a distinguished career as a professor of history, concluding at the University of Oregon.

EMERSON PRICE, who also wrote under the name Hugh Hanley, was born in Dublin, Ohio, in 1902. Price was one of Conroy's first literary contacts in Ohio and served as assistant editor of the *Spider* and as the "workhorse of Rebel Poets," printing the monthly bulletin. Conroy encouraged Price to submit his story "Ohio Town" to Mencken's *American Mercury*, where it appeared in September 1931. Conroy helped place his first novel, *Inn of That Journey*, with Caxton Printers in 1939. Price served as review editor of the *Cleveland Press* for twenty-two years.

PHILIP RAHV, born Ivan Greenberg in Ukraine, immigrated to Palestine with his parents, then to Providence, Rhode Island. An ardent revolutionist in the early Depression years, Rahv was an outspoken Marxist proselytizer in the New York Rebel Poet chapter. Rahv and Wallace Phelps (a.k.a. William Phillips) became editors of the New York John Reed Club's publication, *Partisan Review*, which subsequently absorbed the *Anvil*. Renouncing ties with the Communist Party, Rahv (and Phillips) steered the *Partisan Review* into modernist waters, championing the work of Kafka, Delmore Schwartz, Eliot, and others. Breaking with *PR* in the 1960s, Rahv grew closer once again to his earlier radical views, founding *Modern Occasions* in 1970. With only a high school diploma Rahv rose to become an influential if controversial critic, a bellwether of the New York intellectuals, and a professor of literature at Brandeis University.

JOHN ROGERS was born on 11 February 1907 in Alexandria, Virginia, where he spent most of his life. An artist and writer, Rogers worked as a tree surgeon, a railway clerk, and at other jobs to support his literary artistic endeavors. He served in a series of government positions, first with the Civilian Conservation Corps as artist, then in the army during World War II, and later as an artist for the Internal Revenue Service. He was suspended from the IRS job on the basis of his past radical associations, then reinstated after a long and costly court battle. Conroy considered Rogers to be the all-around rebel: prose writer, artist, and poet. Rogers's graphic prints appeared in the *Anvil* and numerous other little magazines in the 1930s, often together with his written sketches.

WALTER SNOW's first poems were self-published in a pamphlet while he was a young mill worker in Willimantic, Connecticut. A stagehand for a brief time with the Provincetown Players, Snow apprenticed in the newsroom of the *Brooklyn Eagle*. Coeditor of the *Anvil* during its last issues, Snow wrote mystery stories to help support his family. Active in the Newspaper Guild, Snow continued to work as a journalist following military service in World War II. His collection of poems, *The Glory and the Shame* (Pequot Press), appeared in 1973, the year of his death.

JOSEPH VOGEL, born in New York City, grew up in Utica and in 1926 graduated from Hamilton College, where he won a prize for writing. His first published piece, based upon summer job experiences on a railroad gang, appeared in *American Speech*. Vogel shipped out on a cattle boat to Italy, publishing his impressions in *New Masses*. Appearing in three volumes of *The American Caravan*, Vogel gave editorial assistance to little magazines such as *Blues*, the *Morada*, and *Dynamo*. Engaged as an editorial assistant for commercial publications like *Women's Wear Daily*, he wrote three novels: *At Madame Bonnard's* (1935), *Man's Courage* (1938), and *The Straw Hat* (1940). *Man's Courage* received critical acclaim, but Vogel's growing literary reputation was soon eclipsed in the changing climate of reception. He worked for the Ohio state prison system and later taught writing at Ohio State University.

W. W. WHARTON, born in St. Louis, attended Washington University, where he helped edit a student literary magazine, the *Eliot*. His first poetry volume, *May Harvest*, was published at age nineteen. Business manager of the *Anvil*, Wharton worked as an office clerk, later as the publicist for a liquor distribution firm. Conroy assisted Wharton in finding a publisher (Decker Press) for his *Graphiti from Elsinore* (1949), a collection of satiric verse that parodies T. S. Eliot, among others. A poet of playful and often caustic humor, Wharton wrote in the bawdy, irreverent tradition of the English court wits—Sackville, Rochester, Etherege—remaining outside the institutions of poetry.

Bibliography

Interviews

Abe Aaron
Chester Aaron
Amanda Algren
Miriam Kresensky Allen
Sanora Babb
Wayne Barker
Thomas Barrett
Alvah Bessie
Leo Bly
Betrenia Watt Bowker
Stuart Brent
Kenneth Bristow
Sanka Bristow
Gwendolyn Brooks
Dee Brown
Sally Brown
Margaret Burroughs
Erskine Caldwell
Richard J. Chamier
Mike Chomyk
Gladys Conroy
Jack Conroy
Jack Conroy, Jr.
Thelma Conroy
Paul Corey
Ruth Lechlitner Corey
Len Crain

Miriam Creeden
Janet Cruden
Robert Cruden
Howard Derrickson
Douglas Downy
Edward Falkowski
Helen Falkowski
Dorothy Farrell
James T. Farrell
Vincent Ferrini
Russell Finch
Mary Forsmark
Lillian Friedman
Archie Green
Flora Mercil Hagglund
Harvey Harrison
Bettye Hawley
Agnes Kelly Hickman
Ruth Huddlestone
Warren Huddlestone
Stella Jacoby
Richard Kalar
Leonard Karlin
Charles Kelly
Herbert Kline
Marian Knoblauch-
    Franc

Charlotte Koch
Raymond Koch
Herman Kogan
Meridel Le Sueur
Harold H. Lewis
Maxim Lieber
James Light
Robert Logsdon
Leah Williams Lowe
Curtis MacDougall
Norman Macleod
Jerre Mangione
J. B. Mead
Gilbert Mers
Charles Miller
Carroll Norling
Henry Noyes
Harry Mark Petrarkis
William Phillips
Kenneth Porter
Harold Preece
Vance Randolph
David Ray
Robin Rogers
Paul Romaine
Christine Rowland
Neal Rowland

Don Russell
Frank Sandiford
Don Shinew
Win Stracke
Harold Sullivan
Jack Swartz
Jerry Swartz
Jim Swartz

Studs and Ida Terkel
W. H. Trowbridge
Edith Vanko
Joe Velarde
Joseph Vogel
Stephen Wade
Margaret Walker

Peggy Werkley
Ray B. West, Jr.
W. W. Wharton
Fred Whitehead
Margaret Conroy
Wisdom
Karin Wisiol

Manuscript Collections

Nelson Algren (Ohio State University)
Sanora Babb (Boston University)
Arna Bontemps (Syracuse University)
Benjamin A. Botkin (University of Nebraska)
Jack Conroy (Newberry Library)
Paul Corey (University of Iowa)
Edward Dahlberg (HRHC, University of Texas)
Edward Falkowski (Helen Falkowski, New York City)
James T. Farrell (University of Pennsylvania)
E. Haldeman-Julius (Pittsburg State University)
Joe Kalar (Richard G. Kalar, Coon Rapids, Minn.)
Raymond and Charlotte Koch (Wayne State University)
Dale Kramer (Newberry Library)
Meridel Le Sueur (Augsburg College)
Harold H. Lewis (Southeast Missouri State University)
Norman Macleod (Beinecke Library, Yale University)
Jerre Mangione (University of Rochester)
Willard Motley (University of Wisconsin; Northern Illinois University)
Kenneth Porter (University of Oregon)
John Rogers (University of Virginia)
Walter Snow (University of Connecticut–Storrs)
Joseph Vogel (Ohio State University)
W. W. Wharton (Western Historical Manuscript Collection, University of
    Missouri–Columbia)

Little Magazines

The following is a chronological list of little magazines of the 1920s and 1930s
that published work of the midwestern literary radicals treated in this study.
The name of each magazine is followed by its place of publication. Most of
the titles can be found in the collections of the Minnesota Historical Society
Library (St. Paul), the Wisconsin State Historical Society Library (Madison),
the Yale University Library, the University of Michigan Library, and the New
York Public Library. See also Kraus Reprints.

Haldeman-Julius publications (e.g., *Haldeman-Julius Monthly, H-J Quarterly, The Debunker,* 1922–ca. 1940). Girard, Kansas.
The American Mercury (Mencken's editorship, 1923–33). Baltimore, Maryland.
The Spider (1927–28). Columbus, Ohio.
Pegasus (1926–28). Cleveland, Ohio.
Northern Light (1927–31). Holt, Minnesota.
The Morada (1929–31). Albuquerque, New Mexico.
Western Poetry (1929–31). Holt, Minnesota.
The Midland (1915–33). Iowa City, Iowa.
Contemporary Verse (1916–29). Philadelphia.
New Masses (1926–). New York.
Blues (1929–30). Columbus, Mississippi.
Contemporary Vision (1929–31). Chicago.
Earth (1930–32). Wheaton, Illinois.
The Earth-Pamantul (1930–31). East Chicago, Indiana.
Front (1930–32). The Hague, Netherlands.
Nativity (1930–31). Columbus, Ohio.
Pagany (1930–33). Boston, Massachusetts.
Contempo (1931–34). Chapel Hill, North Carolina.
The Left (1931–32). Davenport, Iowa.
Fantasy (1931–43). Pittsburgh, Pennsylvania.
Literature of the World Revolution (1931–32). Moscow, USSR.
The Rebel Poet (1931–32). Moberly, Missouri.
The Anvil (1933–35). Moberly, Missouri.
International Literature (1932–37). Moscow, USSR.
Blast (1933–34). New York.
Kosmos (1933–35). Philadelphia.
Left Front (1933–34). Chicago.
The Magazine (1933–35). Beverly Hills, California.
The Little Magazine (1934). New York.
1933 (1933–34). Philadelphia.
The Outlander (1933). Portland, Oregon.
The Partisan (1933–34). Hollywood, California.
The Windsor Quarterly (1933–35). Four Corners, Vermont; Mena, Arkansas.
The Calithump (1934). Georgetown, Texas; Austin, Texas.
Direction (1934–35). Peoria, Illinois.
The Dubuque Dial (1934–35). Dubuque, Iowa.
Dynamo (1934–36). New York.
Hinterland (1934–36). Cedar Rapids, Iowa; Des Moines, Iowa.
Hub (1934). Cedar Rapids, Iowa.
Left Review (1934). Philadelphia.
Manuscript (1934–36). Athens, Ohio.
The New Quarterly (1934). Rock Island, Illinois.
Partisan Review (1934–). New York.
Scope (1934). Bayonne, New Jersey.
Space (1934–35). Norman, Oklahoma.

New Writers (1936). Detroit.
Greenhorn (1936–?). Philadelphia.
Midwest (1936–37). Minneapolis.
The New Anvil (1939–40). Chicago.

Newspapers

Baltimore Sun, 22 February 1923.
Birmingham Age-Herald, 7 July 1935.
Birmingham News, 30 July 1935.
Chicago Sun-Times, 15 May 1966.
Chicago Tribune, 14 October 1943; 24 December 1952.
Huntsville Herald (Missouri), 24 August 1906.
Minnesota Daily Star, 9 April 1923.
Moberly Monitor, 5 September 1906; 7 July 1909.
Moberly Monitor-Index, 5 December 1922; 21 October 1930; 6 January, 6 February, 9 February, 10 February, 14 February, 6 March, 20 March, 26 October, 27 October, 6 November 1931; 21 January, 18 May, 11 July, 28 July, 20 November, 31 December 1932; 19 April 1967.
Moberly Weekly Monitor, 8 May 1918; 12 January, 6 July, 13 July, 23 November, 30 November, 7 December 1922; 27 July 1923.
New York Herald-Tribune, 19 February 1933; 26 April, 17 July 1935.
New York Post, 27 April, 7 August 1935.
New York World-Telegram, 15 May 1933; 26 April, 3 May, 9 May, 30 July, 7 August 1935; 16 June 1936.
New York World-Telegram and Sun, 23 December 1952.
Railway Carmen's Journal, June, September, December 1913; July, September 1914; November 1915; April 1917; October 1918; March, June 1921; June 1922.
Semi-Weekly Monitor (Moberly, Missouri), 15 April 1917.
Toledo Blade, 9 October, 3 November 1929; 17 January 1930.
United Mine Workers' Journal, 6 September 1900; 21 March, 12 September 1901; 25 December 1902; 26 February 1903.

Works by Jack Conroy

Works by Conroy have been listed chronologically, where dates are known.

1921
Letter. *Railway Carmen's Journal* 26 (March): 144.
"Capital's Fifth Labor." *Railway Carmen's Journal* 26 (March): 155.
"Labor the Scapegoat." *Railway Carmen's Journal* 26 (June): 358–59.

1922
"Mammon's Marionettes." *Railway Carmen's Journal* 27 (July): 375–76.

"The Shopman's Side Again." *Moberly Weekly Monitor*, 7 December.

1927
"To Eugene Victor Debs." *Pegasus* 14 (May): 38.
"Broken Moon." *Pegasus* 15 (August): 24.
"Tragedy." *Northern Light* 1 (August–September): 115.
"The Great Spectra Hoax." *Pegasus* 16 (November): 9–11.
"Jo Labadie, Craftsman and Poet." *Northern Light* 1 (November–December): 159–64.

1928
Coeditor, with David Webb. *The Spider* 3–5, March–June.
"The Quick and the Dead." *Spider* 1 (March): 1.
"Prosperity—Where Is It?" *Spider* 1 (April): 4.
"Reviewettes." *Spider* 1 (April): 4
"The Atheist." *Pegasus* 18 (May): 45.
"Reviewettes." *Spider* 1 (June): 3.
"Cornwall: A Memory." *Verse and Song* (August): 16.

1929
Unrest: The Rebel Poets Anthology. Edited by Jack Conroy and Ralph Cheyney. London: Stockwell and Co. Includes "Journey's End" by Conroy.
"Cornwall: A Memory." In *Overseas Anthology*, edited by S. Fowler Wright. London: Poetry and Play.
"Jackson Street, Toledo." *Earth-Pamantul* (December): 17.
"Dusky Answer." *The Morada* 2 (Winter): 67.

1930
Unrest: The Rebel Poets Anthology for 1930. Edited by Jack Conroy and Ralph Cheyney. London: Studies Publications.
"Whistling Past a Graveyard: Toledo." *New Masses* (March): 12–13.
Letter to the Editor. *New Masses* 5 (April): 20.
Review of *Jews without Money*, by Michael Gold. In *Earth* 1 (May): 14.
"Books Abroad." *New Masses* 6 (June): 19.
Letter to the Editor. *Outlook and Independent* 155 (27 August): 679.
Introduction to *Red Renaissance*, by H. H. Lewis. Reprinted in *Western Poetry* 1 (September): 3–4.
"Undertone." *Northern Light* 8 (November): 3.

1931
Unrest 1931. Edited by Jack Conroy and Ralph Cheyney. New York: Henry Harrison. Includes "Dusky Answer" by Jack Conroy.
Editor. *Rebel Poet.* Numbers 1–17, January 1931–October 1932.
"Hard Winter." *American Mercury* 22 (February): 129–37.
Editorial Notes. *American Mercury* 22 (February): xviii.
"High Bridge." *New Masses* (April): 12.
"Boyhood in a Coal Town." *American Mercury* 23 (May): 83–92.
"Rebel Poets." Report to the Editor. *New Masses* 7 (June): 21.

Review of "The Road the Fiddler Went," by Joe Corrie. *Home and Abroad* 1 (Spring): 74–75.
"In the Sargasso Sea." *Rebel Poet* 6–7 (June–July): 4.
Review of *Labor and Lumber*, by Charlotte Todes. *New Masses* 6 (August): 17–18.
"The Twilight of Capitalism." *Rebel Poet* 8–9 (August–September): 3–4.
Tiazhelaia zima. *Prozhektor* 11. Translation of "Hard Winter."
Review of "Cross Country," by Solon R. Barber. *Rebel Poet* 10–12 (October–December): 11.
"Literature of the World Revolution." *Rebel Poet* 10–12 (October–December): 12.
Letter to the Editor. *Moberly Monitor-Index* (6 November 1931).
"Picket Line." *The Left* 2:57–63.

1932
Foreword to *The Unknown Soldier Speaks*, by George Jarrboe. Holt, Minn.: B. C. Hagglund.
"Mass Demonstrations and Protests." Letter to the Editor. *International Literature* 2–3:9.
"Paving Gang—On a Job in Missouri." *New Masses* 7 (20–21 February): 20–21.
"Art Above the Battle?" *Rebel Poet* 13 (March): 3.
"Passion and Pellagra." Review of *Tobacco Road*, by Erskine Caldwell. *New Masses* 7 (April): 24–25.
"Rubber Heels." *American Mercury* 25 (April): 431–40.
"He Is Thousands." *New Masses* 7 (May): 18.
"Bun Grady." *Pagany* 3 (July–September): 105–17.
Editorial Notes. *Rebel Poet* 15 (August): 2.
"The Life and Death of a Coal Miner." *American Mercury* 26 (August): 442–51.
"Pipe Line." *American Mercury* 27 (September): 98–107.

1933
The Disinherited. New York: Covici-Friede.
Foreword to *When the Sirens Blow*, by Leonard Spier. Holt, Minn.: B. C. Hagglund.
Editor. *The Anvil.* Numbers 1–13, May 1933–October/November 1935.
"Covered Wagon—Modern Style." *Common Sense* 1 (2 February): 20–21.
"American Proletarian Writers and the New Deal." *International Literature* 4:123–26.
Letter to the Editors. *Earth* 3 (April): 18.
"What If You Don't Want to Write for Money." *Writer's Review* (April): 9–13.
"The Siren." *American Mercury* 29 (May): 70–79.
"A Statement." *Anvil* 1 (May): 3–4.
"They Won't Let Us Birds Roost Nowheres." *New Masses* 8 (June): 18–19.
"Hoover City." *International Literature* 3:46–49.
"A Coal Miner's Widow." *Modern Monthly* 7 (August): 423–31.

"The American Proletarian Writers and the New Deal." *International Literature* 4:123–26.

"H. H. Lewis, Poet and Peasant." *Fantasy* 3 (Autumn). Reprinted in *The Jack Conroy Reader*, 243–46.

"Bull Market." *The Outlander* (Winter).

"Little Stranger." *Year Magazine* 2 (December 1932–April 1933): 212–18.

"Detstvo v rudnichnom poselke." *Inostrannaia literatura* 5. Translation of "Boyhood in a Coal Town."

1934

Obezdolenyi. Moscow: Moscow State Publishers. Russian translation of *The Disinherited*.

Review of "Homecoming, An Autobiography," by Floyd Dell. *Left Front* 1 (January–February): 18–19.

Review of "You Gotta Live," by Bob Brown. *Left Front* 1 (January–February): 18–19.

"They Won't Let Us Birds Roost Nowheres!" *Young Worker* 12 (13 February). Reprint from *New Masses*.

"Young American Novelists." Lecture to the Workers Modern Library, 24 March. Typescript in Conroy papers, Newberry Library.

"A Note on the Proletarian Novel." *Call of Youth* (April): 5.

Review of *The Land of Plenty*, by Robert Cantwell. *Partisan Review* 1 (June–July): 52–53.

"For Whom Do You Write?" *New Quarterly* 1 (Summer): 8.

Letter to the Editor. *New Quarterly* 1 (Summer): 24.

Review of "Flat Tire," by Bob Reed. Part 1, *Literary Workshop* 1, no. 2: 10–13. Part 2, *Literary Workshop* 1, no. 3: 51.

"White Collar Writers." *Writers 1934 Year Book and Market Guide* 5 (1934): 31–34.

"Artel' mostovshchikov." *Amerikanskaia Novella XX Veka*. Moscow. Translation of "High Bridge."

"Bezdomnye." *Amerikanskaia Novella XX Veka*. Moscow. Translation of "Hoover City."

1935

"A Coal Miner's Widow." In *Proletarian Literature in the U.S., Anthology*, edited by Granville Hicks et al. New York: International Publishers.

Foreword to *Lenin Lives*, by Henry George Weiss. Holt, Minn.: B. C. Hagglund.

"Les Déshérités." French edition of *The Disinherited*, translated by André and Suzanne Chennevière. In *L'Humanité* (published serially, February–April).

The Disinherited. Moscow: Publishing Co-operative of Foreign Workers in the U.S.S.R.

"The Worker as Writer." In *American Writer's Congress*, edited by Henry Hart. New York: International Publishers.

A World to Win. New York: Covici-Friede.

"The Weed King." *Manuscript* 2 (February): 48–59.

"For Men Must Work." *Midland Left* (February).

"Down in Happy Hollow." *Anvil* 10 (March): 7–10, 26.

"The Affirmative Trend." *Trend* 3 (March–April): 8–9.

Review of *Somebody in Boots*, by Nelson Algren. *New Masses* (16 April): 21–22. Reprinted in North's *New Masses* anthology.

"Dixie Bus Trip." *Young Worker* 12 (3 September): 73–75.

"Reception in Alabama." *Labor Defender* (September): 9–10.

Review of *The Green Corn Rebellion*, by William Cunningham. *Windsor Quarterly* 3 (Fall): 76–77.

1936

Die Enterbten. German-language edition of *The Disinherited.* Translated by Dora Wentscher. Moscow: Publishing Co-operative of Foreign Workers in the U.S.S.R.

Obezdolennyi. So Slovarem i Grammaticheskim Kommentariem. Ohrab. S. A. Kreines and S. S. Tolstoi. *Lit. Na Inostr.* Abridgement and translation of *The Disinherited*, with notes.

"A World Won." Review of *Seeds of Tomorrow*, by Mikhail Aleksandrovich Sholokhov. *Partisan Review and Anvil* 3 (March): 30–31.

"Jack Conroy Tells of a Dublin Day When 'Their Irish Rose' and James Connolly Died for Ireland." *Young Worker* 14 (7 April): 10.

"The Cement King." *Champion of Youth* (June): 7; (July): 14.

"Writers Disturbing the Peace." *New Masses* 21 (17 November): 13.

"Why the Writers Are on Strike." Typescript in Conroy papers, Newberry Library.

1937

"On-tysiachi." *Amerikanskie Rasskazy.* Moscow: Series Biblioteka ogonek. Russian translation of "They Are Thousands."

"A Groundhog's Death." *New Masses* 22 (January): 17–18.

"Happy Birthday to You." *Esquire* 7 (January): 74, 156.

"An Anthology of WPA Creative Writing." Review of *American Stuff*, by Federal Writers' Project. *New Masses* 22 (14 September). Reprinted in North's *New Masses* anthology, 239–42.

1938

Statement. In *Writers Take Sides: Letters About the War in Spain from 418 American Authors*, edited by Fannie Hurst. New York: League of American Writers.

"Home to Uncle Ollie's." *Sunday Worker Magazine* (1 January): 2, 9. All "Uncle Ollie" stories are reprinted in *The Weed King.*

"Uncle Ollie on Trial." *Sunday Worker Magazine* (29 January): 2, 9.

"Boss Tom's Throne." *Sunday Worker Magazine* (20 February): 5, 9.

"Uncle Ollie Finds a New Market." *Sunday Worker Magazine* (11 September): 2, 9.

"Rubber Heel Plant Initiation Ceremonial." Illinois Writers' Project. Typescript. Conroy's Illinois Writers' Project MSS are in the Illinois State Historical Library, Springfield.

"Bridge Plant Initiation Ceremonial." Illinois Writers' Project. Typescript.

"The Demon Bricksetter from Williamson County." Illinois Writers' Project. Typescript.
"The Boomer Fireman's Fast Sooner Hound." Illinois Writers' Project. Typescript.
"The Sissy From the Hardscrabble County Rock Quarries." Illinois Writers' Project. Typescript.
"Freight Car Repair Yard Initiation." Illinois Writers' Project. Typescript.
"Greedy-Gut Gus, the Car Toad." Illinois Writers' Project. Typescript.

1939

Editor, with Nelson Algren. *The New Anvil.* Numbers 1–7, March 1939–August 1940.
Introduction to *Inn of That Journey* by Emerson Price. Caldwell, Idaho: Caxton Printers.
"Uncle Ollie's Spite Fence." *Progressive Weekly* (22 January): 4.
"A Barrel of Fun." *Progressive Weekly* (4 June): 6.
"Young Writers Need Elbow Room: Do Little Magazines Solve Problems?" *Progressive Weekly* (24 June): 16.
"Uncle Ollie's Rabbit Hunt." *Progressive Weekly* (23 July): 6.
"The Home Town on Labor Day." *Progressive Weekly* (3 September): 1, 5.
"Miner's Apprenticeship." Illinois Writers' Project. Typescript.
"Slappy Hooper." Illinois Writers' Project. Typescript.
"Yard Number Nine." Illinois Writers' Project. Typescript.
"The Type Louse." Illinois Writers' Project. Typescript.
"The High Divers." Illinois Writers' Project. Typescript.
"Mass Production." Illinois Writers' Project. Typescript.
"North Clark Street Conversation." Illinois Writers' Project. Typescript.
"A Job in the Couer d'Alene" [sic]. Illinois Writers' Project. Typescript.
"Interview With Frank DeSoto, Boomer Sign Painter." Illinois Writers' Project. Typescript.
"No. 4 Smoke." Illinois Writers' Project. Typescript.
"The Whistle of a Freight Wafted from Afar . . . ." Illinois Writers' Project. Typescript.
"Drift Miner." Illinois Writers' Project. Typescript.
"A Burg Called Butte." Illinois Writers' Project. Typescript.
"Lute Goin's Sawmill." Illinois Writers' Project. Typescript.
"Island of Beygo-Beygo." Illinois Writers' Project. Typescript.
"True Blue Highpockets from the Forks of the Crick." Illinois Writers' Project. Typescript. Submitted under Nelson Algren's name.

1942

Bontemps, Arna, and Jack Conroy. *The Fast Sooner Hound.* Boston: Houghton Mifflin.
Bontemps, Arna, and Jack Conroy. *The Great Speckled Bird.* Typescript. In Conroy papers, Newberry Library.
"Friendly Fighters." Column in *Civilian Defense News* (1942–43). Published in Chicago.

1944

"The Sissy from the Hardscrabble County Rock Quarries"; "The Demon Bricksetter from Williamson County"; "The Boomer Fireman's Fast Sooner
Hound"; "Greedy-Gut Gus, the Car Toad"; "Slappy Hooper, World's Big-
gest, Fastest and Bestest Sign Painter"; "The Type Louse"; "The High
Divers." In *A Treasury of American Folklore*, edited by B. A. Botkin. New
York: Crown Publishers. Also, "Hank, the Free Wheeler," wrongly attributed to Nelson Algren.
Introduction to *The Caxton Printers in Idaho*, by Vardis Fisher. Cincinnati: Society of Bibliosophers.

1945

Bontemps, Arna, and Jack Conroy. *They Seek A City*. Garden City, N.Y.: Dou-
bleday, Doran.
"Happy Birthday to You." In *North, East, South, West: A Regional Anthology of
American Writing*, edited by Charles Lee et al. New York: Howell, Soskin.
"The Sissy from the Hardscrabble County Rock Quarries." In *One Side, Please*.
Chicago: Royce Publishers.
Bontemps, Arna, and Jack Conroy. "An American Original: Jelly Roll Mor-
ton." *Tomorrow* 4 (June): 26–32.
Bontemps, Arna and Jack Conroy. "Exodus Train." *Common Ground* (Spring).
Review of "Darkness and the Deep," by Vardis Fisher. *Western Review* 10 (Au-
tumn): 57–58.
"Holiday at a Coal Camp." In *Midwest Christmas Annual*, published by the
Chicago Sun, 2 December.

1946

Bontemps, Arna, and Jack Conroy. *Slappy Hooper, the Wonderful Sign Painter*.
Boston: Houghton Mifflin.
Review of *The Partisan Reader*, edited William Phillips and Philip Rahv. *Chi-
cago Sun Book Week* (15 September 1946.)

1947

Editor. *Midland Humor: A Harvest of Fun and Folklore*. New York: A. A. Wyn.
"The Little Mag." Review of *The Little Magazine: A History and a Bibliography*,
by Frederick J. Hoffman, Charles Allen, and Carolyn F. Ulrich. *New Masses* 62 (25 February): 24–25.

1948

Numerous unsigned entries. *The American Peoples' Encyclopedia*. Edited by F. J.
Meine et al. Chicago: Spencer Press, 1948–55.

1949

"Ikh tysiachi." *Takova Amerika*. Moscow: Voenizdat. Russian translation of
"They Are Thousands."
American School News 1 (Summer): 2.

1950

"Dyni." *Rasskazy ob Amerike*. Moscow. Russian translation of "Uncle Ollie"
stories.

1951

Bontemps, Arna, and Jack Conroy. *Sam Patch, the High, Wide and Handsome Jumper*. Boston: Houghton Mifflin.

1952

"Rudareva udovica." In *Deset Americkih Pripovijedaka*, edited by Janko Tampa and Dusan Curcija. Zagreb: Glas rada. Croatian translation of "A Coal Miner's Widow."

"Lute Goin's Sawmill." *100* 1 (June): 24–25.

1953

"Freight Car Repair Yard Pranks. " In *A Treasury of Railroad Folklore*, edited by Alvin Harlow and B. A. Botkin. New York: Crown Publishers.

"The Boomer Fireman's Fast Sooner Hound." In *The Arbuthnot Anthology of Children's Literature*, edited by May Hill Arbuthnot. Chicago: Scott, Foresman.

1954

"The Boomer Fireman's Fast Sooner Hound." In *The Story Parade*, edited by Esther M. Bjoland. Chicago: Standard Education Society.

1956

"The Boomer Fireman's Fast Sooner Hound"; "Slappy Hooper, Sign Painter"; "Hardscrabblers"; "Rival Divers." In *A Treasury of American Folk Humor*, edited by James N. Tidwell. New York: Crown Publishers.

1957

"The High Divers." In *The Family Book of Humor*, edited by Helen Hoke. Garden City, N.Y.: Hanover House.

1958

Bontemps, Arna, and Jack Conroy. "An American Original: Jelly Roll Morton." In *Jam Session: An Anthology of Jazz*, edited by Ralph J. Gleason. New York: G. P. Putnam Sons.

"A Coal Miner's Widow." In *The American Century: A Collection of American Short Stories Reflecting the Nature of Society in the United States*, edited by Maxim Lieber. Berlin: Seven Seas Publishers.

"The Laughing Frontier." *Westerners' Brand Book* 15 (April): 9–11, 15–16.

1960

"Two Authors Look Back at the '30s." Review of *All the Naked Heroes*, by Alan Kapelner, and *Free Fall*, by William Golding. *Chicago Sun-Times*, 6 March 1960.

1961

Bontemps, Arna, and Jack Conroy. "Sam Patch, the High, Wide and Handsome Jumper." In *The Grandma Moses Story Book*, edited by Nora Kramer. New York: Random House.

"Slappy Hooper." In *The Life Treasury of American Folklore*, edited by the editors of *Life*. New York: Time.

1963

The Disinherited. Introduction by Daniel Aaron. New York: Hill and Wang.

"Theodore Dreiser." *Inland: The Magazine of the Middle West* 40 (Autumn): 11–16.

1964

"Boyhood in a Coal Town." In *The Missouri Reader,* edited by Frank Luther Mott. Columbia, Mo.: University of Missouri Press.

1965

"Theodore Dreiser." *American Book Collector* 15 (February): 11–16.

". . . the contemporary fact . . ." *Carleton Miscellany* 6 (Winter): 36–39.

The Disinherited. Berlin: Seven Seas Publishers.

1966

Bontemps, Arna, and Jack Conroy. *Anyplace But Here.* New York: Hill and Wang.

"The Disinherited." In *The American Writer and the Great Depression,* edited by Harvey Swados. Indianapolis: Bobbs-Merrill. Reprint of part 1, chapter 7.

Review of *Lonely for the Future,* by James T. Farrell. In *Chicago Daily News,* n.d. (ca. 1966). In Conroy papers, Newberry Library.

1967

"The Hard Winter." In *Years of Protest,* edited by Jack Salzman and Barry Wallenstein. New York: Pegasus.

Die Enterbten. German-language edition of *The Disinherited.* Translated by Gerhard Bottcher and Klaus Schultz. Berlin: Volk and Welt.

1968

Review of "The Land of Plenty," by Robert Cantwell. In *Proletarian Writers of the Thirties,* edited by David Madden. Carbondale, Ill.: Southern Illinois University Press.

"Home to Moberly." *Missouri Library Association Quarterly* 29 (March): 41–50.

"Homage to Kenneth Patchen." *The Outsider* 4/5: 130–31.

"Anvil Days in Chicago." *ChicagoLand* (September).

1969

"H. H. Lewis: Plowboy Poet of the Gumbo." *December* 11: 203–6.

"A Groundhog's Death." Reprinted in *New Masses: An Anthology of the Rebel Thirties,* edited by Joseph North. New York: International Publishers.

"Literary Underworld of the Thirties." Typescript. Semester of the Thirties symposium. University of Connecticut–Storrs.

With Walter Snow and Max Lieber. "Authors and Literature of the 1930s." Typescript. Semester of the Thirties symposium. University of Connecticut–Storrs.

With Arna Bontemps. "The Negro in the City." Typescript. Semester of the Thirties symposium. University of Connecticut–Storrs.

1971

"Days of the *Anvil*." *American Book Collector* 21 (Summer): 14–19.

"Making It and Faking It on the Seaboard 'Family' Circuit." *December* 13: 272–75.

"Personal Impressions." *New Letters* 38 (Winter): 33–36. Conroy's memories of Richard Wright.

1972

"Conversation with Jack Conroy." Interview by Lewis Fried. *New Letters* 39 (October): 41–56.

"The Fields of Golden Glow." *New Letters* 39 (Fall): 5–15.

1973

Editor, with Curt Johnson. *Writers in Revolt: The Anvil Anthology 1933–1940*. New York: Lawrence Hill.

"Slave Narratives." Review of *Black Men in Chains: Narratives by Escaped Slaves*, edited by Charles H. Nichols. *New Letters* 39 (Spring): 77–80.

"Charley Was Our Darlin'." *Journal of Popular Culture* 7 (Winter): 529–36.

1974

"The High Divers." In *Fantasy: The Shape of Things Unknown*, edited by Edmund J. Farrell et al. Glenview, Ill.: Scott, Foresman.

"Musings of the Sage of Moberly." Column in *Foolkiller* (1974–79).

"The Literary Underworld of the Thirties." *New Letters* 40 (Spring): 51–72.

"Memories of Arna Bontemps, Friend and Collaborator." *American Libraries* 5 (December): 602–6.

1976

Review of *Only a Miner*, by Archie Green. In *New Letters* 43 (Fall): 126–27.

"The Morphadite." *December* 18:114–21.

"Memories of Arna Bontemps: Friend and Collaborator." *Negro American Literature Forum* 10 (Summer): 53–57.

1978

"On Anvil." *Triquarterly* 43:111–29.

Review of *Yonnondio: From the Thirties*, by Tillie Olsen. *New Letters* 45 (September): 115–16.

"Reflections on the 1935 American Writers' Congress." *Midwest Alliance* 1:13–15.

1979

The Jack Conroy Reader. Edited by Jack Salzman and David Ray. New York: Burt Franklin.

Review of *Social Poetry of the 1930's*, by Jack Salzman. *New Letters* 46 (Winter): 121–23.

1980

"Fred Harrison." In *First-Person America*, edited by Ann Banks. New York: Knopf, 1980.

"In Memoriam: John C. Rogers, 1907–1979." *Quindaro* 6–7:56.
"The Frontiers of Language." Panelist, with Meridel Le Sueur, Truman Nelson, Tom McGrath, and Fred Whitehead. *Quindaro* 8–9:27–34.

1981
"The Kimberly Toughs." *December* 23: 197–202.
"That Skinner Bottoms Winter." *New Letters* 48 (Fall): 31–38.
Afterword to *The Smile*, by Harry Bernstein. Cambridge, Mass.: West Press, 1981.
"Introduction to the Poetry of Will Wharton." *Quindaro* 8–9:19–20.

1982
The Disinherited. Introduction by Jack Conroy. New York: Lawrence Hill.

1983
Obezdolenyi. Foreword by M. Mendelsohn. Moscow: Raduga. Translation of *The Disinherited*.

1985
Preface to *Joseph Kalar, Poet of Protest*. Edited by Richard G. Kalar. Blaine, Minn.: RGK Publications.
The Weed King and Other Stories. Edited and with an introduction by Douglas Wixson. New York: Lawrence Hill.

1986
Japanese edition of *The Disinherited*. Translated by Kiyohiko Murayama.
"Kogda Rabotchi Stanovitsia Pisatelem." In *Veriu v Cheloveka*. Foreword by O. Zlobin. Moscow: Raduga. Translation of "The Worker as Writer."
Review of *The Damndest Radical*, by Roger A. Bruns. *Chicago Tribune Books* (30 November).

1990
The Disinherited. Introduction by Douglas Wixson. Columbia: University of Missouri Press.

1991
"Hard Head Hardy, a Folktale." Written collaboratively with Stephen Wade. *New Letters* 57 (Summer 1991): 125–27.

Book Reviews by Jack Conroy

Conroy wrote several hundred book reviews for newspapers over forty years, chiefly for the *Chicago Sun-Times*, *Chicago Daily News*, *Chicago Tribune*, *Kansas City Star*, and *St. Louis Post-Dispatch*. I have listed above only those I have directly referred to in the text. Many of Conroy's reviews are in the Conroy collections at the Newberry Library and the Moberly Area Community College Library.

Tape-Recorded Interviews and Readings

Unless otherwise noted, all of the following tape-recorded interviews with Conroy were conducted by the author in Moberly, Missouri. Asterisk indicates tapes
in the author's possession.

28 March 1962, 28 May 1963, 30 November 1973 (by Studs Terkel, in Chicago); 21 May 1978; 22 October 1978; 17 December 1978 (by Lon Pearson)*;
26 December 1978*; 28 December 1978*; 13 March 1979*; 26 March 1979;
30 March 1979*; 7 June 1979; 22 September 1979; 23 November 1979*; 4 May
1980*; 23 June 1980; 27 September 1980 (with David Anderson)*; 27–29 November 1980*; 21 December 1980*; 26 March 1981*; 16–17 May 1981*; 8 June
1981; 11 August 1981*; 26–27 November 1981*; 26–27 December 1981; 1
March 1982*; 12 April 1982*; 23–24 May 1982*; 5 July 1982*; 23–24 July
1982 (with W. W. Wharton)*; 1 August 1982*; 28 August 1982*; 23 September 1982*; 5 October 1982*; 30 October 1982*; 26 November 1982*; 23–24
December 1982*; 2 April 1983*; 30 April 1983*; 21 May 1983*; 28 May 1983*;
19 June 1983; 9 July 1983*; 30 July 1983*; 27 August 1983*; 1 October 1983*;
25 November 1983*; 26 December 1983*; 24 February 1984; 24 March 1984*;
21 April 1984*; 23 May 1984 (with Larry Goldberg and Charlie Kelly)*; 30
June 1984; 21 July 1984*; 8 September 1984 (by Studs Terkel with Win
Stracke)*; 9 September 1984*; 23 September 1984; 17 October 1984*; 24–26
December 1984*; 29 January 1985; 6 April 1985*; 3 May 1985*; 6 May 1985;
21 July 1985*; 1 September 1985*; 3 November 1985*; 26 December 1985*;
28 February 1986*; 31 March 1986*; 4–6 June 1986*; 4 July 1986*; 19 July
1986*; 5 September 1986*; 16 October 1986*; 26 November 1986*; 27 November 1986 (with Harvey Harrison)*; 26 December 1986*; 13 March 1987*;
21 June 1987*; 25–26 July 1987*; 20 November 1987*; 26–27 December 1987*.

Discussion of *The Disinherited*. 2 October 1970 and fall 1972. Led by Mary
  Edrich Redding, San Diego State College.*
Interview and readings. "New Letters on the Air." With David Ray, n.d. *New
  Letters*, University of Missouri–Kansas City.*
"Jack Conroy Reads from *The Disinherited*." Edited by Kay Bonetti. American
  Audio Prose Library, Columbia, Missouri.*
Interview. KWIX, Moberly, Missouri, 15 December 1979.*
Panel discussion, Jack Conroy Day, Moberly, Missouri. 22 May 1984. Margaret
  Burroughs, Ralph Gerhard, William Peden, Stephen Wade, Larry Goldberg,
  James Light, Douglas Wixson, Carolyn Werkley.*

General Sources

Aaron, Chester. *About Us*. New York: McGraw-Hill, 1967.
Aaron, Daniel. Introduction to *The Disinherited*, by Jack Conroy. New York:
  Hill and Wang, 1963.

———. *Writers on the Left*. New York: Oxford University Press, 1961.
Abraham Lincoln School, Summer Session 1943. (Catalog.)
Adamic, Louis. "Voltaire from Kansas, Portrait of E. Haldeman-Julius." *Outlook and Independent* 155 (25 June 1930): 283–85, 314–16.
———. "What the Proletariat Reads." *Saturday Review of Literature* (1 December 1934): 321–22.
"Alabama Ruled by Terrorism, Writers Charge." *New York World-Telegram*, 7 August 1935.
Albrecht, Friedrich, and Klaus Kändler. *Bund Proletarisch-revolutionärer Schriftsteller Deutschlands 1928–1935*. Leipzig: VEB Bibliographisches Institut, 1978.
Alexander, Stephen. "Art: Joe Jones." *New Masses* (28 May 1935): 30.
Algren, Nelson. "Interview." Interview by E. F. Donohue. In *Never Come Morning*, by Nelson Algren, 293–310. New York: Four Walls Eight Windows, 1987.
———. "A Letter." *Carleton Miscellany* 6 (Winter 1965): 104.
———. *Never Come Morning*. New York: Harper and Brothers, 1941.
———. Review of *A World to Win*, by Jack Conroy. *Windsor Quarterly* (Fall 1935): 73.
———. Review of *Let No Man Write My Epitaph*, by Willard Motley. In "Magazine of Books," *Chicago Sunday Tribune*, 17 August 1958.
———. *Somebody in Boots*. New York: Vanguard Press, 1935.
———. "Things of the Earth: A Groundhog's View." *California Quarterly* 2 (Autumn 1952): 3–11.
"All in the Spirit of Fun, No Doubt." *Missouri Historical Review* 46 (April 1952): 312–13.
Alt, John. "Beyond Class: The Decline of Industrial Labor and Leisure." *Telos* 28 (Summer 1976): 55–80.
Altenbaugh, Richard J. *Education for Struggle: The American Labor Colleges of the 1920s and 1930s*. Philadelphia: Temple University Press, 1990.
"American Unemployed and Art: The Story of Joe Jones, Revolutionary Artist, and His Co-Workers." *International Literature* 2 (June 1934): 95–97.
Ameringer, Oscar. *If You Don't Weaken: The Autobiography of Oscar Ameringer*. Norman: University of Oklahoma Press, 1983.
———. "Why Workers Go to War." *Railway Carmen's Journal* 18 (July 1913): 420–21.
Amidon, Beulah. "Toledo, a City the Auto Ran Over." *Survey Graphic* (1 March 1930): 656–60, 667–72, 681, 685.
Anderson, David D. "Jack Conroy Remembered: A Review Essay." *SSML Newsletter* 21 (Fall 1991): 10–12.
———. "Michigan Proletarian Writers and the Great Depression." *MidAmerica IX* (1982): 88–93.
Anderson, Nels. *The Hobo: The Sociology of the Homeless Man*. Chicago: University of Chicago Press, 1961.
Anderson, Sherwood. "Machine Song: Automobile." In *Unrest 1931*, edited by Jack Conroy and Ralph Cheyney, 17–19. New York: Henry Harrison, 1931.
———. *A Story Teller's Story*. New York: B. W. Huebsch, 1924.

Angress, Werner T. "Pegasus and Insurrection: *Die Linkskurve* and Its Heritage." *Central European History* 1 (March 1968): 35–55.

Annual Report of the State Mine Inspector, 1900. Jefferson City, Mo.: State Mining Board, 1900. Also, *Annual Reports* for 1899, 1902, 1908, 1909.

Appel, Benjamin. "My Generation of Writers." *Tomorrow* 10 (February 1951): 5–9.

———. *The People Talk: American Voices from the Great Depression.* New York: Simon and Schuster, 1982.

Aronowitz, Stanley. *False Promises: The Shaping of American Working Class Consciousness.* New York: McGraw-Hill, 1973.

———. *Working Class Hero: A New Strategy for Labor.* New York: Pilgrim Press, 1983.

Arthur, Chester. Review of *The Disinherited*, by Jack Conroy. *Dune Forum* 1 (15 January 1934): 31.

Ashleigh, Charles. *Rambling Kid.* London: Faber and Faber, 1930.

Babb, Sanora. *An Owl on Every Post.* London: Peter Davies, 1970.

———. *The Dark Earth.* Santa Barbara, Calif.: Capra Press, 1987.

———. *The Lost Traveller.* London: Victor Gollancz, 1958.

Baker, Houston A., Jr. *Blues, Ideology, and Afro-American Literature.* Chicago: University of Chicago Press, 1984.

———. *The Journey Back: Issues in Black Literature and Criticism.* Chicago: University of Chicago, 1982.

Baker, Robert P. "Labor History, Social Science and the Concept of the Working Class." *Labor History* 14 (Winter 1973): 98–105.

Bakhtin, Mikhail. *The Dialogic Imagination.* Edited by Michael Holquist. Austin: University of Texas Press, 1981.

———. "Discourse Typology in Prose." In *Readings in Russian Poetics,* edited by Ladislav Matejka and Krysyna Pomorska. Cambridge, Mass.: MIT Press, 1971.

———. *Speech Genres and Other Late Essays.* Edited by Caryl Emerson and Michael Holquist. Austin: University of Texas Press, 1986.

Bakke, Stephen. *Citizens without Work.* New Haven: Yale University Press, 1940.

———. *The Unemployed Man: A Social Study.* London: Nisbet, 1933.

Balch, Jack. *Lamps at High Noon.* New York: Modern Age, 1940.

———. "To the Manlovers of Our Local Four Hundred." *Anvil* 1 (May 1933): 8.

Banks, Ann, ed. *First-Person America.* New York: Knopf, 1980.

Baratz, Morton S. *The Union and the Coal Industry.* New Haven: Yale University Press, 1955.

Barnes, Daniel R. "Toward the Establishment of Principals for the Study of Folklore and Literature." *Southern Folklore Quarterly* 43 (1979): 5–16.

Barrett, James R., Steve Nelson, and Rob Ruck. *Steve Nelson: American Radical.* Pittsburgh: University of Pittsburgh, 1981.

Barthes, Roland. "Writing and Revolution." *Yale French Studies* 39 (1967): 77–84.

Baym, Nina. *Women's Fiction: A Guide to Novels by and About Women in Amer-*

ica, 1820–1870. Ithaca: Cornell University Press, 1978; 2d edition, with new introduction and supplementary bibliography, Urbana: University of Illinois Press, 1993.

Belfrage, Cedric. *The American Inquisition, 1945–1960.* Indianapolis: Bobbs-Merrill, 1973.

Bell, Thomas. *Out of This Furnace.* New York: Little, Brown, 1941; reprint, Pittsburgh: University of Pittsburgh Press, 1972.

Bellah, Robert N., et al. *Habits of the Heart: Individualism and Commitment in American Life.* Berkeley: University of California, 1985.

Bendiner, Robert. *Just Around the Corner: A Selective History of the Thirties.* New York: E. P. Dutton, 1968.

Benet, William Rose. "Round About Parnassus." Review of *Thinking of Russia,* by H. H. Lewis. *Saturday Review of Literature* 8 (4 June 1932): 775.

Benjamin, Walter. "Der Autor als Produzent." In *Versüche über Brecht,* edited by Rolf Tiedemann. Frankfurt am Main: Suhrkamp, 1966.

———. "The Storyteller." In *Illuminations,* edited by Hannah Arendt. New York: Schocken Books, 1986.

Berger, Peter L., Brigette Berger, and Hansfried Kellner. *The Homeless Mind: Modernization and Consciousness.* New York: Random House, 1973.

Berman, Hyman, and Eli Ginzberg. *American Worker in the Twentieth Century: A History Through Autobiographies.* New York: Free Press of Glencoe, 1963.

Bernstein, Irving. *The Lean Years: A History of the American Worker, 1920–1933.* Boston: Houghton Mifflin, 1960.

Billington, Ray Allen. *In Land of Savagery, Land of Promise: The European Image of the American Frontier in the Nineteenth Century.* New York: Norton, 1981.

———. "Writers in Revolt against Their Society." *Chicago Sun Book Week* 4 (4 May 1947): 8.

———, ed. *The Frontier Thesis.* New York: Holt, Rinehart, and Winston, 1966.

Bisztray, George. *Models of Realism.* New York: Columbia University Press, 1978.

Blake, James. *The Joint.* Garden City, N.Y.: Doubleday, 1971.

Bluestein, Gene. *The Voice of the Folk: Folklore and American Literary Theory.* Amherst: University of Massachusetts Press, 1972.

Bock, Catharine Lewis. "Biographical Sketch of Harold L. Lewis." Unpubl. MS (1990). In author's possession.

Bodnar, John. *Workers' World: Kinship, Community, and Protest in an Industrial Society, 1900–1940.* Baltimore: Johns Hopkins University Press, 1982.

Bogardus, Ralph F., and Fred Hobson, eds. *Literature at the Barricades: The American Writer in the 1930s.* University: University of Alabama Press, 1982.

Botkin, Benjamin A. *Folk-Say, A Regional Miscellany: 1930.* Norman: University of Oklahoma Press, 1930.

———. *Folk-Say IV: A Regional Miscellany.* Norman: University of Oklahoma Press, 1932.

———. "The Folk and the Individual: Their Creative Reciprocity." *English Journal* 27 (February 1938): 121–35.

———. *Lay My Burden Down: A Folk History of Slavery.* Chicago: University of Chicago Press, 1945.

———. "Regionalism and Culture." In *The Writer in a Changing World,* edited by Henry Hart, 140–57. New York: Equinox Cooperative Press, 1937.

———. *A Treasury of American Folklore.* New York: Crown Publishers, 1944.

———. *A Treasury of Southern Folklore.* New York: Crown Publishers, 1949.

Bourne, Randolph. *A History of a Literary Radical and Other Essays.* New York: S. A. Russell, 1956.

Boyden, Polly. *The Pink Egg.* Truro, Mass.: Pamet Press, 1942.

Braverman, Harry. *Labor and Monopoly Capital: The Degradation of Work in the Twentieth Century.* New York: Monthly Review Press, 1974.

———. "Work and Unemployment." *Monthly Review* 27 (June 1975): 18–31.

Brecher, Jeremy, Jerry Lombardi, and Jan Stackhouse. *Brass Valley.* Philadelphia: Temple University Press, 1982.

Brecht, Bertolt. "Questions from a Worker Who Reads." In *Bertolt Brecht Poems, 1913–1956,* edited by John Willet and Ralph Manheim. New York: Methuen, 1976.

Brent, Stuart. *The Seven Stairs.* New York: Simon and Schuster, 1989.

Brevda, William. *Harry Kemp: The Last Bohemian.* Lewisburg, Pa.: Bucknell University Press, 1986.

Brewster, Dorothy, and Angus Burrell. *Modern Fiction.* New York: Columbia University Press, 1934.

Brody, David. *Workers in Industrial America.* New York: Oxford University Press, 1980.

Bronson, John. "The Nut-Pickers Picket." *Left Front* 2 (September–October 1933): 809.

Brooks, Van Wyck. *America's Coming-of-Age.* Garden City, N.Y.: Doubleday, 1958.

Brooks, Van Wyck, et al., eds. *The American Caravan: A Yearbook of American Literature.* New York: Macaulay, 1927.

Brophy, John. *John Brophy: A Miner's Life.* Edited by John O. H. P. Hall. Madison: University of Wisconsin Press, 1964.

Broun, Heywood. "It Seems to Me." *New York World-Telegram,* 15 May 1933.

Brown, Bob. *Can We Cooperate?* Staten Island, N.Y.: Roving Eye Press, 1940.

———. *Toward a Bloodless Revolution.* Newllano, La.: Llano Publications, 1933.

Brown, Deming B. *Soviet Attitudes toward American Writing.* Princeton: Princeton University Press, 1962.

Brown, Edward J. *The Proletarian Episode in Russian Literature, 1928–1932.* New York: Columbia University Press, 1953.

———. *Russian Literature since the Revolution.* Cambridge, Mass.: Harvard University Press, 1982.

Brown, Michael S., and Dorothy Nelkin. *Workers at Risk: Voices from the Work Place.* Chicago: University of Chicago Press, 1984.

Brunn, Paul Dennis. "Black Workers and Social Movements of the 1930s in St. Louis." Ph.D. diss., Washington University, 1975.

Bruss, Elizabeth. *Autobiographical Acts: The Changing Situation of a Literary Genre.* Baltimore: Johns Hopkins University Press, 1977.

Burke, John Gordon, comp. "A Preliminary Checklist of the Writings of Jack

Conroy." *American Book Collector* 21 (Summer 1971): 20–24. (Burke's checklist contains numerous errors.)

Burke, Kenneth. *Permanence and Change*. Indianapolis: Bobbs-Merrill, 1965.

Burnett, John, ed. *Annals of Labour: Autobiographies of Working People from the
1820s to the 1920s*. Bloomington: Indiana University Press, 1974.

Burnshaw, Stanley. "Middle-Ground Writers." *New Masses* 15 (30 April 1935):
19–21.

Caldwell, Erskine. "The Georgia Cracker." *Haldeman-Julius Monthly* 4 (November 1926): 39–42.

———. "The School of Prostitution." *Some American People*. New York: Robert M. McBride, 1935.

Callahan, North. *Carl Sandburg: Lincoln of Our Literature*. New York: New York
University Press, 1970.

"A Call to All Midwest Writers." *New Writers* 1 (June 1936): 29.

Calmer, Alan. "Labor Press." Review of *Anvil* and *Blast*. *Daily Worker* (11 October 1933): 5.

———. "The Proletarian Short Story." *New Masses* 16 (2 July 1935): 17–19.

Calverton, V. F. "The American Literary Radicals." *The Modern Quarterly* 3
(September–December 1926): 251–62.

———. *The Liberation of American Literature*. New York: Octagon, 1972.

———. "The Need for Revolutionary Criticism." *The Left* 1 (Spring 1931): 5–
10.

Canfield, Dorothy. Review of *The Disinherited*, by Jack Conroy. *Book-of-the-
Month-Club News* (1934): 59.

Cantor, Milton. *The Divided Left: American Radicalism, 1900–1975*. New York:
Hill and Wang, 1978.

Cantwell, Robert. *The Land of Plenty*. New York: Farrar and Rinehart, 1934.

———. "The Literary Life in California." *New Republic* 80 (22 August 1934):
49.

Caplan, Jane. Review of *Gender and the Politics of History*, by Joan Wallach
Scott. *Nation* (9–16 January 1989): 62.

Carawan, Candie, and Guy Carawan. *Voices from the Mountains*. Urbana: University of Illinois Press, 1982.

Carr, E. H. *Twilight of the Comintern, 1930–1935*. New York: Pantheon Books,
1982.

Carter, Paul. *The Twenties in America*. Arlington Heights, Ill.: Harlan Davidson, 1975.

Casey, Patrick and Terence. "The Road Kid." *The Liberator* (July 1921): 10–
13.

Cassirer, Ernst. *An Essay on Man*. Garden City, N.Y.: Doubleday, 1953.

Caudill, Harry. *Night Comes to the Cumberlands: A Biography of a Depressed Area*.
Boston: Little, Brown, 1963.

Caute, David. *The Great Fear: The Anti-Communist Purge under Truman and
Eisenhower*. New York: Simon and Schuster, 1978.

Chamberlain, John. *Farewell to Reform*. Chicago: Quadrangle Books, 1965.

Cheyney, Ralph. "The Anvil and Its Aims, a Statement." *Anvil* 1 (May 1933): 3.

———. "Bawl, Kid!" *New Masses* 4 (July 1929): 13.

———. "The IWW." *Survey* 39 (10 November 1917): 150–51.

Cheyney, Ralph, and Lucia Trent, eds. *America Arraigned*. New York: Dean and Company, 1928.

Chinoy, Ely. *Automobile Workers and the American Dream*. Garden City, N.Y.: Doubleday, 1955.

"Chronicle." *International Literature* 1 (1935): 109. (On Joe Jones.)

Clark, J., C. Critcher, and R. Johnson. *Working-Class Culture*. New York: St. Martin's Press, 1980.

Clark, Katerina. "Little Heroes and Big Deeds: Literature Responds to the First Five Year Plan." In *Cultural Revolution in Russia, 1928–1931*, edited by Sheila Fitzpatrick, 189–206. Bloomington: Indiana University Press, 1978.

Clark, Katerina, and Michael Holquist. *Mikhail Bakhtin*. Cambridge, Mass.: Harvard University Press, 1984.

"Class War in Kentucky." *New Masses* (September 1931): 23.

Cochran, Robert. *Vance Randolph: An Ozark Life*. Urbana: University of Illinois Press, 1985.

Cohen, Hennig. "American Literature and American Folklore." In *Our Living Traditions*, edited by Tristram P. Coffin, 238–47. New York: Basic Books, 1968.

Coleman, McAlister. *Men and Coal*. New York: Farrar and Rinehart, 1943.

Coleman, Terry. *Going to America*. New York: Pantheon, 1972.

Commager, Henry Steele. *The American Mind: An Interpretation of American Thought and Character since the 1880s*. New Haven: Yale University Press, 1950.

Commons, John R., et al. *History of Labour in the United States*. 2 vols. New York: Macmillan, 1918.

Compton, Charles H. *Who Reads What?* New York: Wilson, 1934.

Cook, Sylvia Jenkins. *From Tobacco Road to Route Sixty-Six*. Chapel Hill: University of North Carolina Press, 1976.

Cooley, O. W. "The Damned Outfit, a Pair of Apple Pickers Fall into a Haywire Dump." *Haldeman-Julius Quarterly* 2 (April–June 1928): 157–61.

Cooney, Terry. *The Rise of the New York Intellectuals: Partisan Review and Its Circle, 1934–1945*. Madison: University of Wisconsin Press, 1987.

Corey, Paul. *Acres of Antaeus*. New York. Henry Holt, 1946.

———. "The Hunt." In *Growing Up in Iowa*, edited by Clarence A. Andrews, 88–99. Ames: Iowa State University Press, 1978.

———. "Lurching toward Liberalism: Political and Literary Reminiscences." *Books at Iowa* 49 (November 1988): 35–71.

Corrie, Joe. *The Road the Fiddler Went and Other Poems*. Glasgow, Scotland: Foreward Publishing, 1931.

Coser, Lewis A. *Men of Ideas: A Sociologist's View*. New York: Free Press, 1965.

Cotkin, George. "Caught in Cultures: Samuel Gompers and the Problem of the Working Class Individual in Culture." *Mid-America* 66 (January 1984): 41–48.

Cottrell, Fred. *Technological Change and Labor in the Railroad Industry*. Lexington, Mass.: D. C. Heath, 1970.

Couch, W. T., ed. *These Are Our Lives*. Chapel Hill: University of North Carolina Press, 1939.

Counts, George S., Luigi Villari, Malcolm S. Rorty, and Newton D. Baker. *Bolshevism, Fascism and Capitalism*. New Haven: Yale University Press, 1932.

Cowie, Alexander. *The Rise of the American Novel*. New York: American Book Company, 1951.

Cowley, Malcolm. *And I Worked at the Writer's Trade: Chapters of Literary History, 1918–1978*. New York: Viking Press, 1978.

———. "Echoes from Moscow: 1937–1938." *Southern Review* 20 (January 1984): 1–11.

———. *Exile's Return*. New York: W. W. Norton, 1934.

———. "The Homeless Generation." *New Republic* (26 October 1932).

———. "The Old House in Chelsea . . ." *Carleton Miscellany* 6 (Winter 1965): 40–49.

———. "Thirty Years Later: Memories of the First American Writers' Congress." *American Scholar* 35 (Summer 1966): 495–516.

Craig, David. *The Real Foundations*. New York: Oxford University Press, 1974.

Cruden, Robert."The Great Ford Myth." *New Republic* 70 (16 March 1932).

———. "1930 Model: Detroit." *New Masses* (March 1930): 4–5.

———. "No Loitering: Get Out of Production." *Nation* 128 (12 June 1929): 696–98. See also under pen name, James Steele.

Curti, Merle. *The Growth of American Thought*. 3d ed. New York: Harper and Row, 1964.

Dahlberg, Edward. *The Confessions of Edward Dahlberg*. New York: George Braziller, 1971.

———. "Portrait of the Gangster." Review of *The Young Manhood of Studs Lonigan*, by James T. Farrell. *New Masses* (24 February 1934): 24.

———. "Waldo Frank and the Left." Review of *The Death and Birth of David Markand*, by Waldo Frank. *New Masses* (23 April 1935): 22–23.

Daniel, Pete. *Deep'n As It Come*. New York: Oxford University Press, 1977.

Davidson, Cathy. *Revolution and the Word: The Rise of the Novel in America*. New York: Oxford University Press, 1986.

Davies, Christopher S. "Dark Inner Landscapes: The South Wales Coalfield." *Landscape Journal* 3 (1984): 36–44.

Davis, Colin J. "Bitter Conflict: The 1922 Railroad Shopmen's Strike." *Labor History* 33 (Fall 1992): 433–55.

Dawley, Alan, and Paul Faler. "Working-class Culture and Politics in the Industrial Revolution: Sources of Loyalism and Rebellion." In *American Working-class Culture*, edited by Milton Kantor, 61–75. Westport, Conn.: Greenwood Press, 1979.

Dawson, Andrew. "The Parameters of Craft Consciousness: The Social Outlook of the Skilled Worker, 1890–1920." In *American Labor and Immigration History*, edited by Dirk Hoerder, 135–55. Urbana: University of Illinois Press, 1983.

Debs, Eugene. *Railway Carmen's Journal* 20 (November 1915): 722.

Defanti, Charles. *The Wages of Expectation: A Biography of Edward Dahlberg*. New York: New York University Press, 1978.

DeFord, Miriam Allen. "Unemployed." *Rebel Poet* 1 (October–December 1931): 12.

Degh, Linda. *Folktales and Society.* Bloomington: Indiana University Press, 1969.

Deleuze, Gilles, and Felix Guattari. *Kafka—Pour une Littérature Mineure.* Paris: Les Editions de Minuit, 1975.

———. *L'Anti-Oedipe: Capitalisme et Schizophrenie.* Paris: Les Editions de Minuit, 1972.

———. *Mille Plateaux.* Paris: Les Editions de Minuit, 1980.

Dell, Floyd. "Young Poet in Davenport." In *America Is West,* edited by John T. Flanagan, 411–18. Westport, Conn.: Greenwood Press, 1970.

Dellinger, Harold. "Pegasus and the Plow." *Foolkiller* 3 (Fall 1976): 6–7.

Denby, Charles. *Indignant Heart: A Black Workers' Journal.* Detroit: Wayne State University Press, 1989.

Denisoff, R. Serge. *Great Day Coming: Folk Music and the American Left.* Baltimore: Penguin, 1973.

Dennen, Leon. "Soviet Literature." *New Masses* 6 (November 1931): 23–24.

Denning, Michael. *Mechanics Accents: Dime Novels and Working-Class Culture.* New York: Verso, 1987.

———. "'The Special American Conditions': Marxism and American Studies." *American Quarterly* 38 (1986): 356–80.

Denyer, Thomas. "Montage and Political Consciousness." *Soviet Union/Union Soviétique* 7 (1980): 89–111.

Derleth, August. ". . . never cursed with the illusion . . ." *Carleton Miscellany* 6 (Winter 1965): 53–57.

Dewey, John. *Democracy and Education.* New York: Free Press, 1966.

———. *Individualism, Old and New.* New York: Minton, Balch, 1930.

Dix, Keith. *Work Relations in the Coal Industry: The Hand-Loading Era, 1880–1930.* Morgantown, W. Va.: Institute for Labor Studies, West Virginia University, 1977.

Donaldson, Alice. "Rhetoric of a Small Midwestern Town." *Missouri Historical Review* 75 (July 1981): 448–562.

Dos Passos, John. "The *New Masses* I'd Like." *New Masses* 1 (June 1926): 20.

Dreiser, Theodore. *A Hoosier Holiday.* New York: John Lane, 1916.

Drew, Bettina. *Nelson Algren: A Life on the Wild Side.* New York: G. P. Putnam's, 1989.

Dubofsky, Melvin. *Industrialism and the American Worker, 1865–1920.* Arlington Heights, Ill.: AHM Publishing, 1975.

Ducker, James M. *Men of the Steel Rails.* Lincoln: University of Nebraska Press, 1983.

Eastman, Max. *Artists in Uniform.* New York: Octagon Press, 1972.

———. "The Cult of Intelligibility." *Harper's* 158 (April 1929): 632–39.

Edge, William. *The Main Stem.* New York: Vanguard Press, 1927.

Egan, Susanna. *Patterns of Experience in Autobiography.* Chapel Hill: University of North Carolina Press, 1984.

Elistratova, Anna. "New Masses." *International Literature* 1 (1932): 107–14.

Elshtain, Jean Bethke. "Forgetting Who Are 'The People.'" *Nation* (2 May 1981): 543.

Empson, William. *Some Versions of Pastoral.* New York: New Directions, 1960.

Ermolaev, Herman. *Soviet Literary Theories: 1917–1934, The Genesis of Socialist Realism.* Berkeley: University of California Press, 1963.

Evans, Charles. "Sketch of the Life of a Coal Mine Inspector, Charles Evans, as Prepared by Himself." Introduction to *Annual Report of the State Mine Inspector.* Jefferson City: Missouri State Mining Board, 1904.

Fabre, Michel. "Jack Conroy as Editor." *New Letters* 39 (Winter 1972): 115–37.

———. *Richard Wright: Books and Writers.* Jackson: University Press of Mississippi, 1990.

———. *The Unfinished Quest of Richard Wright.* New York: William Morrow, 1973.

———. "Walt Whitman and the Rebel Poets." *Walt Whitman Review* 12 (December 1966): 88–93.

Fadiman, Clifton. Review of *The Disinherited,* by Jack Conroy. *New Yorker* (2 December 1933): 88.

Falkowski, Edward. "Amerika Wendet Sich nach Links." *Die Linkskurve* 2 (July 1930): 18–20.

———. "Berlin in Crimson." *New Masses* 5 (March 1930): 10.

———. "Coal Miners' Children." *New Masses* 4 (October 1928): 6.

———. "Coal Mountain." *International Literature* 2–3 (1932): 51–57.

———. "Das Land der guten Hoffnung." *Die Linkskurve* 2 (March 1930): 12–16.

———. "Dreams in Red." *Anvil* 8 (October 1934): 3–5.

———. "Five Year Plan Tempo." *New Masses* 6 (July 1931): 8–9.

———. "In a Brown Coal Country." *Literature of the World Revolution* 4 (1931): 75–79.

———. "In a German Mining Town." *New Masses* 5 (November 1929): 5.

———. "In a Soviet Mining Town." *New Masses* 6 (October 1931): 14–15.

———. "Mine Funeral—Germany." *New Masses* 5 (January 1930): 10.

———. "A Miner's Good Morning." *New Masses* 4 (July 1928): 17.

———. "Miners' Progress." *New Masses* 4 (December 1928): 6.

———. "Moscow Theatre." *New Masses* 6 (May 1931): 22.

———. "Notes of a Soviet Literary School." *Rebel Poet* 13 (March 1932): 6.

———. "Rebel Poets in Germany." *Rebel Poet* 8–9 (August–September 1931): 6.

———. "Red Gangway!" *Anvil* 2 (October 1934): 3–6.

———. "A Request from Germany." *New Masses* 6 (April 1930): 20.

———. "The Soviet Political Theatre." *New Masses* 6 (January 1931): 22.

———. "Steel." *New Masses* 5 (February 1930): 12.

———. "Workers' Art in Germany." *New Masses* 5 (December 1929): 21.

Farrell, James T. "The Filling Station Racket in Chicago." *Debunker* 9 (January 1929): 91–93.

———. "Halfway from the Cradle." *Earth* 1 (June 1930): 1, 3, 14.

———. "A Note on Contemporary American Letters." *Earth* 1 (February 1931): 2–5.

————. *A Note on Literary Criticism*. New York: Vanguard, 1936.

————. Review of *The Disinherited*, by Jack Conroy. *Nation* (20 December 1933).

————. *Yet Other Waters*. New York: Vanguard, 1952.

Fensch, Thomas. *Steinbeck and Covici*. Middlebury, Vt.: Paul S. Eriksson, 1979.

Ferguson, Otis. "Lillian Lugubriously Sighed." *New Republic* 93 (10 November 1937): 22.

Ferrini, Vincent. *Selected Poems*. Edited by George F. Butterick. Storrs, Conn.: University of Connecticut Library, 1976.

Ferris, Forrest G. *Moberly Libraries and Literary Societies, 1872–1903*. Moberly, Mo.: Moberly Free Library, 1904.

Fichtenbaum, Myrna. *The Funsten Nut Strike*. New York: International Publishers, 1991.

Fiedler, Leslie. "John Peale Bishop and the Other Thirties." *Commentary* (April 1967): 74–82.

Fink, Gary M. *Labor's Search for Political Order*. Columbia: University of Missouri Press, 1973.

The First Hundred Years, 1879–1979, Novinger, Missouri. Kirksville, Mo.: Cooper Printing, 1979.

Fishbein, Leslie. *Rebels in Bohemia: The Radicals of the Masses, 1911–1917*. Chapel Hill: University of North Carolina Press, 1982.

Fishwick, Marshall W. "Where Are Uncle Remus and John Henry?" *Southern Quarterly* 21 (Winter 1983): 32–38.

Fite, Gilbert C., and H. C. Peterson. *Opponents of War, 1917–1918*. Madison: University of Wisconsin, 1957.

Fitzpatrick, Sheila, ed. *Cultural Revolution in Russia, 1928–1931*. Bloomington: Indiana University Press, 1984.

"5 Shots Fired at 5 Liberals." *New York World-Telegram* (30 July 1935).

Flanagan, John T., ed. *America Is West*. Westport, Conn.: Greenwood Press, 1975.

————. "Reedy of the *Mirror*." *Missouri Historical Review* 43 (January 1949): 128–44.

Fleming, Robert E. *Willard Motley*. Boston: Twayne, 1978.

Flusche, Michael. "Joel Chandler Harris and the Folklore of Slavery." *Journal of American Studies* 9 (1975): 347–63.

Foley, Barbara. *Radical Representations: Politics and Form in U.S. Proletarian Fiction, 1929–1941*. Durham, N.C.: Duke University Press, 1993.

————. *Telling the Truth: The Theory and Practice of Documentary Fiction*. Ithaca: Cornell University Press, 1986.

Folsom, Franklin. *Impatient Armies of the Poor: The Story of Collective Action of the Unemployed, 1808–1941*. Niwot, Colo.: University Press of Colorado, 1991.

Folsom, Michael. "The Education of Michael Gold." In *Proletarian Writers of the Thirties*, edited by David Madden, 222–51. Carbondale: Southern Illinois University Press, 1968.

————, ed. *Mike Gold: A Literary Anthology*. New York: International Anthology, 1972.

Foner, Philip S., ed. *American Labor Songs of the Nineteenth Century*. Urbana: University of Illinois Press, 1975.

——. *Jack London, American Rebel*. New York: Citadel Press, 1947.

——, ed. *The Factory Girls*. Urbana: University of Illinois Press, 1977.

Fones-Wolf, Ken. *Trade Union Gospel, Christianity and Labor in Industrial Philadelphia, 1865–1915*. Philadelphia: Temple University Press, 1989.

Forster C. H. "Despised and Rejected of Man: Hoboes of the Pacific Coast." *Survey* 33 (20 March 1915): 671–72.

Forsythe, Robert. "Down with the Novel." *New Masses* (16 April 1935): 29–30.

Foster, William Z. *Pages from a Worker's Life*. New York: International Publishers, 1978.

Fowke, Edith, and Joe Glazer, eds. *Songs of Work and Protest*. New York: Dover, 1973.

Fox, Charles Elmer. *Tales of an American Hobo*. Iowa City: University of Iowa Press, 1989.

Frank, Waldo. *Our America*. New York: Boni and Liveright, 1919.

Frederick, John T. *Out of the Midwest*. New York: Whittlesey House, 1944.

Freeborn, Richard. *The Russian Revolutionary Novel*. Cambridge: Cambridge University Press, 1982.

Freeman, Joseph. *American Testament*. New York: Farrar and Rinehart, 1936.

Freeman, Joseph, Louis Lozowick, and Joshua Kunitz. *Voices in October*. New York: Vanguard, 1930.

Fried, Lewis. "Conversation with Jack Conroy." *New Letters* 39 (October 1972): 41–56.

Frye, Northrup. *The Critical Path*. Bloomington: Indiana University Press, 1971.

Galbraith, John Kenneth. *The Great Crash of 1929*. New York: Avon, 1980.

Gallas, Helga. *Marxistische Literaturtheorie*. Neuwied, Ger.: Luchterhand, 1971.

Garland, Hamlin. *A Son of the Middle Border*. Lincoln: University of Nebraska Press, 1979.

Gaventa, John. *Power and Powerlessness*. Urbana: University of Illinois Press, 1980.

Geismar, Maxwell. *American Moderns: From Rebellion to Conformity*. New York: Hill and Wang, 1958.

——. "Nelson Algren: Unsung Proletarian of Letters." *Calendar* (24 May 1981): 5.

——. *Writers in Crisis*. New York: Hill and Wang, 1961.

Giddens, Anthony. "Class Structuration and Class Consciousness." In *Classes, Power and Conflict*, edited by Anthony Giddens and David Held, 157–74. Berkeley: University of California Press, 1982.

Gilbert, James. *Writers and Partisans: A History of Literary Radicalism in America*. New York: John Wiley, 1968.

Gillan, Garth. *From Sign to Symbol*. Brighton, Sussex: The Harvester Press, 1982.

Ginzberg, Eli, and Hyman Berman. *American Worker in the Twentieth Century: A History through Autobiographies*. New York: Free Press of Glencoe, 1963.

Giovannitti, Arturo. *Arrows in the Gale*. Riverside, Conn.: Hillacre Bookhouse, 1914.

Goddard, Robert. "Missouri Novelist Writes in Overalls." *St. Louis Post-Dispatch*, ca. June 1934 (undated clipping in Conroy papers, Newberry Library).

Goehre, Paul. *Three Months in a Workshop: A Practical Study*. New York: Arno Press, 1972.

Gold, Michael. "America Needs a Critic." *New Masses* 1 (October 1926): 8.

———. "The American Famine." *The Liberator* 4 (November 1921): 10.

———. "Change the World!" *Daily Worker* (29 January 1934): 43.

———. Editorial. *New Masses* 4 (July 1928): 2.

———. "Go Left, Young Writers!" *New Masses* 4 (January 1929): 3–4.

———. *The Hollow Men*. New York: International Publishers, 1941.

———. *Jews without Money*. New York: International Publishers, 1930.

———. "A Letter to the Author of a First Book." *New Masses* (9 January 1934): 25. (To Conroy.)

———. "May Days and Revolutionary Art." Review of *May Days*, by Genevieve Taggard. *Modern Quarterly* 3 (February–April 1926): 161.

———. "A New Program for Writers." *New Masses* 5 (January 1930): 21.

———. "Notes from Kharkov." *New Masses* 6 (March 1931): 5.

———. "Notes of the Month." *New Masses* 6 (October 1930): 3–5.

———. *120 Million*. New York: International Publishers, 1929.

———. "Papa Anvil and Mother Partisan." *New Masses* (18 February 1936): 22–23.

———. "Poverty Is a Trap." *New Masses* 2 (January 1927): 18–19.

———. Review of *Shanty Irish*, by Jim Tully. *New Masses* 4 (February 1929): 26.

———. "Six Letters." *New Masses* 7 (September 1931): 4.

———. "Write for Us!" *New Masses* 4 (July 1928): 2.

Gold, Michael, et al. "The Charkov Conference of Revolutionary Writers." *New Masses* 6 (February 1931): 6.

Golterman, Guy, Jr. Quoted in "Blue Lantern Bohemians," by Helen Seavers. *St. Louis Post-Dispatch*, 3 April 1969, 3, 5.

Goodwyn, Lawrence. "The Cooperative Commonwealth and Other Abstractions: In Search of a Democratic Promise." *Marxist Perspectives* 3 (Summer 1980): 8–42.

———. *The Populist Moment*. New York: Oxford University Press, 1978.

Goody, Jack, and Ian Watt. "The Consequences of Literacy." In *Literacy in Traditional Societies*, edited by Jack Goody. Cambridge: Cambridge University Press, 1968.

Gordon, David M., Richard Evans, and Michael Reich, eds. *Segmented Work, Divided Workers*. Cambridge: Cambridge University Press, 1982.

Gorki, Maxim. *Culture and the People*. New York: International Publishers, 1939.

———. *My Apprenticeship*. Translated by Ronald Wilks. Harmondsworth, Middlesex: Penguin, 1974.

———. *My Childhood*. Translated by Ronald Wilks. Harmondsworth, Middlesex: Penguin, 1966.

———. *My Universities*. Translated by Ronald Wilks. Harmondsworth, Middlesex: Penguin, 1979.

———. *On Literature, Selected Articles*. Moscow: Foreign Languages Publishing House, n.d.

———. *Problems of Soviet Literature*. Moscow: Cooperative Publishing Society of Foreign Workers in the U.S.S.R., 1935.

Gotsche, Otto. "Vorwort." Foreword to *Die Linkskurve, Berlin 1929–1932: Bibliographie einer Zeitschrift*, edited by Dieter Kliche and Gerhard Seidel, 5–20. Berlin: Aufbau Verlag, 1972.

Gottlieb, Amy Zahl. "British Coal Miners: A Demographic Study of Braidwood and Streator, Illinois." *Journal of the Illinois State Historical Society* 72 (August 1979): 179–92.

———. "The Illinois Workmen's Compensation Act, 1911: The Role of the British Immigrant Coal Miner." In *Selected Papers in Illinois History, 1980*, 63–68. Springfield, Ill.: Illinois State Historical Society, 1982.

———. Lecture. Illinois Labor History Conference. Jackson, Ill., 12 October 1985.

Gowen, Emmett. "Bigot Brigades." *Fight* (September 1935): 5.

Graham, John, ed. *"Yours for the Revolution": The "Appeal to Reason," 1895–1922*. Lincoln: University of Nebraska Press, 1990.

Graham, Marcus, ed. *Man! An Anthology of Anarchist Ideas, Essays, Poetry, and Commentaries*. London: Cienfuegos Press, 1974.

Gramsci, Antonio. "Americanism and Fordism." In *Prison Notebooks*, by Antonio Gramsci. New York: International Publishers, 1971.

———. *Antonio Gramsci, Selections from Cultural Writings*. Edited by David Forgacs and Geoffrey Nowell Smith. Translated by William Boelhower. Cambridge, Mass.: Harvard University Press, 1985.

Grannis, Chandler B. "How the Book Trace Survived the Great Depression." *Publishers' Weekly* 232 (20 November 1987): 19–22.

Green, Archie. "American Labor Lore: Its Meanings and Uses." *Industrial Relations* 4 (February 1965): 51–68.

———. *Only a Miner*. Urbana: University of Illinois Press, 1972.

———. *Wobblies, Pile Butts, and Other Heroes: Laborlore Explorations*. Urbana: University of Illinois Press, 1993.

Green, Archie, and Joyce Kornbluh. "John Newhouse, Wobbly Poet." *Journal of American Folklore* 73 (July–September 1960): 189–217 .

Green, James R. *Grass-Roots Socialism: Radical Movements in the Southwest, 1895–1943*. Baton Rouge: Louisiana State University Press, 1978.

———. *The World of the Worker*. New York: Hill and Wang, 1980.

Gregory, Horace. *Chelsea Rooming House*. New York: Covici-Friede, 1930.

———. A Review of *A World to Win*, by Jack Conroy. In "Books," *New York Herald-Tribune*, 19 May 1935.

Guest, Edgar. "A Patriot." In *Over Here*, by Edgar Guest. Chicago: Reilly and Lee, 1918.

Gunn, Giles. *The Culture of Criticism and the Criticism of Culture*. New York: Oxford University Press, 1987.

Gunn, John W. *E. Haldeman-Julius—the Man and His Work.* Girard, Kans.: Haldeman-Julius, 1924.

———. "The Pocket Series with Its 500 Titles Is the Beginning of an American Culture." *Life and Letters* (January 1924): 8.

Gurko, Leo. *The Angry Decade.* New York: Dodd, Mead, 1947.

Guthrie, Woody. "Ear Players." *Common Ground* 2 (Spring 1942): 32–43.

Gutman, Herbert. "The Reality of the Rags-to-Riches 'Myth.'" In *Work, Culture and Society in Industrial America,* edited by Herbert Gutman, 211–33. New York: Vintage, 1976.

———. *Work, Culture, and Society: Essays in American Working Class and Social History.* New York: Knopf, 1976.

———. "The Workers' Search for Power." In *The Gilded Age,* edited by H. Wayne Morgan, 31–53. Syracuse: Syracuse University Press, 1970.

Haessler, Carl. "Peace Reigns at Herrin." *Liberator* 5 (August 1922): 13.

Hagglund, Benjamin C. ". . . akin to revelation. . . ." *Carleton Miscellany* 6 (Winter 1965): 62–68.

———. "Rhythm—the Basis of All Poetry." *Northern Light* 1 (July 1927): 63.

Haldeman-Julius, Emmanuel. "The Taming of Mencken." *Haldeman-Julius Monthly* (October 1926): 7.

Hall, Covington. *Battle Hymns of Toil.* Oklahoma City: General Welfare Reporter, n.d.

———. *Dreams and Dynamite: Selected Poems.* Chicago: Charles H. Kerr, 1985.

Halper, Albert. "Chicago Mail Clerks." *Debunker* 9 (February 1929): 3–11.

———. *The Foundry.* New York: Viking, 1934.

———. *Union Square.* New York: Literary Guild, 1933.

Halpert, Stephen, and Richard Johns. *A Return to Pagany.* Boston: Beacon Press, 1969.

Hamovitch, Mitzi Berger, ed. *The Hound and Horn Letters.* Athens: University of Georgia Press, 1982.

Hansen, Harry. "The First Reader." *New York World-Telegram,* 24 April 1935.

Harrington, Michael. *Fragments of a Century.* New York: Saturday Review Press, 1973.

Harris, Herbert. "Working in the Detroit Auto Plants." In *The Thirties, A Time to Remember,* edited by Don Congdon, 477–86. New York: Simon and Schuster, 1962.

Harris, Mark. Review of *The Jack Conroy Reader,* by Jack Salzman and David Ray. *New Republic* 1 (March 1980): 35–37.

Harrison, Dale. "All About the Town." *Chicago Sun,* 4 January 1944.

Hart, Henry, ed. *American Writers' Congress.* New York: International Publishers, 1935.

———. *The Writer in a Changing World.* New York: Equinox Cooperative Press, 1937.

Hart, James D. *The Popular Book; A History of American Literary Taste.* New York: Oxford University Press, 1950.

Havelock, Eric A. *Preface to Plato.* Cambridge, Mass.: Harvard University Press, 1963.

Haywood, William D. *The Autobiography of Big Bill Haywood*. New York: International Publishers, 1929.

Hazlett, John D. "Conversion, Revisionism, and Revision in Malcolm Cowley's *Exile's Return*." *South Atlantic Quarterly* 82 (Spring 1983): 179–88.

Hefland, M. "Left, No. 1." *Literature of the World Revolution* 3 (1931): 139–43.

Hemenway, Robert E. "Are You a Flying Lark or a Setting Dove?" In *Afro-American Literature*, edited by Dexter Fisher, 122–52. New York: MLA, 1979.

Herder, Dale M. "The Little Blue Books as Popular Culture: E. Haldeman-Julius' Methodology." In *New Dimensions of Popular Culture*, edited by Russel B. Nye, 31–42. Bowling Green, Ky.: Bowling Green University Press, 1972.

Herrick, Robert. "Writers in the Jungle." *New Republic* (17 October 1934): 259–61.

Herrman, John. "The New Multitudes." *This Quarter* 1,3 (1927): 252–55.

Hertzler, Joyce O. *A Sociology of Language*. New York: Random House, 1965.

Hesseltine, William B. *Third-Party Movements in the United States*. New York: D. van Nostrand, 1962.

Hicks, Granville. *The Great Tradition*. New York: Macmillan, 1933.

———. "Our Magazines and Their Functions." *New Masses* (18 December 1934): 23.

———. Review of *The Disinherited*, by Jack Conroy. *Partisan Review* 1 (February–March 1934): 56–58.

———. "Revolution and the Novel." *New Masses* (22 May 1934): 35.

———. "Writers of the Thirties." Unpubl. MS. Semester of the Thirties Symposium, University of Connecticut–Storrs, 1969.

Hicks, Granville, et al., eds. *Proletarian Literature in the United States: An Anthology*. New York: International Publishers, 1935.

Hirsch, Jerrold. "Folklore in the Making: B. A. Botkin." *Journal of American Folklore* 100 (January–March 1987): 4–38.

Hobsbawm, Eric. *Workers: Worlds of Labor*. New York: Pantheon Books, 1984.

Hobsbawm, Eric, and Terence Ranger. *The Invention of Tradition*. London: Cambridge University Press.

Hobson, Fred, Jr. *Serpent in Eden: H. L. Mencken and the South*. Baton Rouge: Louisana State University Press, 1974.

Hoffman, Frederick J., Charles Allen, and Carolyn F. Ulrich. *The Little Magazine: A History and a Bibliography*. Princeton: Princeton University Press, 1947.

Hoggart, Richard. *The Uses of Literacy*. Boston: Beacon Press, 1957.

Homberger, Eric. *American Writers and Radical Politics, 1900–39*. New York: St. Martin's Press, 1986.

Horkheimer, Max. *Critical Theory*. New York: Herder, 1972.

Hotchner, A. E. *Papa Hemingway: A Personal Memoir*. New York: Random House, 1966.

Howe, F. C. "Where Are the Pre-War Radicals—Reply." *Survey* 56 (1 April 1926): 33–34.

Howe, Irving. *Thomas Hardy*. New York: Macmillan, 1967.

———. "Toward an Open Culture." *New Republic* (5 March 1984): 26–27.

Howe, Irving, and Lewis Coser. *The American Communist Party, A Critical History (1919–1957)*. Boston: Beacon Hill, 1957.

Hubbell, Jay. *Who Are the Major American Writers?* Durham, N.C.: Duke University Press, 1969.

Huddlestone, Warren. "A Little Business Deal." *New Quarterly* 1 (Spring 1934): 19–20.

Hughes, Langston. *The Big Sea*. New York: Thunder's Mouth Press, 1986.

Humphries, Jane. "Class Struggle and the Persistence of the Working-Class Family." In *Classes, Power and Conflict*, edited by Anthony Giddens and David Held, 470–90. Berkeley: University of California Press, 1982.

Husband, Joseph B. *A Year in a Coal Mine*. Boston: Houghton Mifflin, 1911.

Isserman, Maurice. *Which Side Were You On? The American Communist Party during the Second World War*. Middletown, Conn.: Wesleyan University Press, 1982.

"Jack Conroy: American Worker-Writer." *International Literature* 1 (April 1934): 114.

James, Louis. *Fiction for the Working Man, 1830–1850*. London: Oxford University Press, 1963.

Janssen, Marian. *The Kenyon Review, 1939–1970: A Critical History*. Baton Rouge: Louisiana State Press, 1990.

Jauss, Hans-Georg. "The Alterity and Modernity of Medieval Literature." *New Literary History* 10 (Winter 1979): 179–227.

Jerome, V. J. *Culture in a Changing World: A Marxist Approach*. New York: New Century, 1947.

Jeter, Goetze. *The Strikers*. New York: Frederick A. Stokes, 1937.

Johns, Orrick. "Different Spring." *New Masses* (24 April 1934): 10.

———. "St. Louis Artists Win." *New Masses* (6 March 1934): 28–29.

———. *Time of Our Lives*. New York: Stackpole Sons, 1937.

Johnson, Josephine W. *Now in November*. New York: Simon and Schuster, 1934.

Johnson, Richard Colles, and G. Thomas Tanselle. "The Haldeman-Julius 'Little Blue Books' as a Bibliographical Problem." *Papers of the Bibliographical Society of America* 64 (1970): 29–78.

Johnson, Stanley C. *A History of Emigration*. London: George Routledge, 1913.

Jolas, Eugene. *Anthologie de la Nouvelle Poème Américaine*. Paris: Editions KRA, 1928.

Jolle, Andre. *Formes Simples*. Paris: Seuil, 1972.

Josephson, Matthew. *Infidel in the Temple: A Memoir of the Nineteen-Thirties*. New York: Knopf, 1967.

Joughin, Louis, and Edmund M. Morgan. *The Legacy of Sacco and Vanzetti*. New York: Harcourt, Brace, 1948.

Kalar, Joseph. "Insolent Query." Unpubl. MS, ca. January 1929, in Kalar papers. Courtesy of Richard G. Kalar, Coon Rapids, Minnesota.

———. *Joseph A. Kalar, Poet of Protest*. Edited by Richard G. Kalar. Blaine, Minn.: RGK Publications, 1985.

———. "A Miner's Kid." *New Masses* 5 (February 1930): 6.

———. "Proletarian Night." In *Joseph A. Kalar*, ed. Richard G. Kalar, 48.

———. "Rebel Poets." Review of *Unrest 1929*. *New Masses* (December 1929): 18.

———. "Revolt." Review of *Unrest 1929*. *Morada* 2 (Winter 1929): 68.

Kareven, Tamara K., and Randolph Langenbach. *Amoskeag: Life and Work in an American Factory-City*. New York: Pantheon, 1978.

Karl, Frederick R. *Modern and Modernism: The Sovereignty of the Artist, 1885–1925*. New York: Atheneum, 1985.

Katzman, David M., and William M. Tuttle, Jr., eds. *Plain Folk: The Life Stories of Undistinguished Americans*. Urbana: University of Illinois Press, 1982.

Kazin, Alfred. *An American Procession*. New York: Vintage, 1984.

———. *On Native Grounds*. Garden City, N.Y.: Doubleday, 1956.

———. *Starting Out in the Thirties*. Boston: Little, Brown, 1965.

Kelley, Robin D. G. *Hammer and Hoe: American Communists during the Great Depression*. Chapel Hill: University of North Carolina Press, 1990.

Kemp, Harry. *More Miles*. New York: Boni, 1926.

Kempf, James. "Encountering the Avant-Garde: Malcolm Cowley in France, 1921–1922." *Southern Review* 20 (Winter 1984): 12–28.

Kempton, Murray. *Part of Our Time*. New York: Dell, 1955.

Kennedy, David M. *The American People in the Depression*. West Haven, Conn.: Pendulum Press, 1973.

———. *Over Here: The First World War and American Society*. New York: Oxford University Press, 1980.

———. "Vietnam and World War I." *Stanford Observer* (March 1972): 3.

Kennell, Ruth, and Milly Bennett. "American Immigrants in Russia." *American Mercury* 25 (April 1932): 463–72.

Kennell, Ruth Epperson. *Theodore Dreiser and the Soviet Union, 1927–1945*. New York: International Publishers, 1969.

Kent, Thomas. *Interpretation and Genre*. Lewisburg, Pa.: Bucknell University Press, 1986.

Kermode, Frank. *History and Value*. Oxford: Clarendon Press, 1988.

Killingsworth, Myrth Jimmie. "Whitman and Motherhood: A Historical View." *American Literature* 54 (March 1982): 28–43.

Kinnamon, Keneth. "Richard Wright: Proletarian Poet." In *Critical Essays on Richard Wright*, edited by Yoshinobu Hakutani. Boston: G. K. Hall, 1982.

Kirkman, Marshall M. *The Science of Railways, Railway Equipment*. New York: World Railway Publishing Company, 1900.

Kirsch, Robert R. Review of *Anyplace But Here*, by Arna Bontemps and Jack Conroy. *Los Angeles Times*, 10 May 1966.

Klehr, Harvey. *The Heyday of American Communism: The Depression Decade*. New York: Basic Books, 1984.

Klein, Alfred. *Im Auftrag Ihrer Klasse; Weg und Leistung der Deutschen Arbeiterschriftsteller, 1918 bis 1933*. Berlin and Weimar: Beiträge zur Geschichte der Deutschen Sozialistischen Literatur im 20-en Jahrhundert, 1972.

Klein, Marcus. *Foreigners: The Making of American Literature, 1900–1940*. Chicago: University of Chicago Press, 1981.

———. "The Roots of Radicals: Experience in the Thirties." In *Proletarian*

Writers of the Thirties, edited by David Madden, 134–57. Carbondale: Southern Illinois University Press, 1968.

Knight, Rolf. *Traces of Magma: An Annotated Bibliography of Left Literature*. Burnaby, British Columbia: Draegerman, 1983.

Koch, Raymond, and Charlotte Koch. *Educational Commune: The Story of Commonwealth College*. New York: Schocken Books, 1972.

Komarovsky, Mira. *The Unemployed Man and His Family: The Effect of Unemployment Upon the Status of Man in Fifty-nine Families*. New York: Dryden Press, 1940.

Kornbluh, Joyce, ed. *Rebel Voices: An IWW Anthology*. Chicago: Charles H. Kerr Publishing, 1988.

Korson, George. *Coal Dust on the Fiddle*. Philadelphia: University of Pennsylvania Press, 1943.

———. *Minstrels of the Mine Patch*. Philadelphia: University of Pennsylvania, 1938.

Kramer, Dale. *The Wild Jackasses: The American Farmer in Revolt*. New York: Hastings House, 1956.

Kresensky, Raymond. *The North American Mentor of Poems*. Edited by John Westburg. Conesville, Iowa: Westburg and Associates, 1965.

———. "Thirty-six Poems by Raymond Kresensky." *North American Mentor* 7 (Fall 1969): 1–50.

Kreuter, Kent, and Gretchen Kreuter. *An American Dissenter*. Lexington: University Press of Kentucky, 1969.

Kreymborg, Alfred. "Farmhand Poet." *New Masses* 28 (April 1942): 22.

Kreymborg, Alfred, Lewis Mumford, and Paul Rosefeld, eds. *The New American Caravan*. New York: W. W. Norton, 1936.

Krupat, Arnold. "Fiction and Fieldwork." Review of *Waterlily*, by Ella Cara Deloria. *The Nation* 247 (2–9 July 1988): 22–23.

Lambert, Paul F., and Kenny A. Franks, eds. *Voices from the Oil Fields*. Norman: University of Oklahoma Press, 1984.

Landy, Marcia. "Culture and Politics in the Work of Antonio Gramsci." *Boundary 2* 14 (Spring 1986).

Langer, Elinor. *Josephine Herbst*. Boston: Little, Brown, 1983.

Lantz, Herman R. *People of Coal Town*. Carbondale: Southern Illinois University Press, 1971.

Larsen, Erling. Review of *Let Us Now Praise Famous Men*, by James Agee and Walker Evans. *Carleton Miscellany* 2 (Winter 1961): 81.

Lasch, Christopher. *The Agony of the American Left*. New York: Alfred A. Knopf, 1969.

———. "The Cultural Cold War: A Short History of the Congress for Cultural Freedom." In *Towards a New Past: Dissenting Essays in American History*, edited by Barton J. Bernstein, 322–59. New York: Pantheon Books, 1968.

———. *The Minimal Self: Psychic Survival in Troubled Times*. New York: W. W. Norton, 1984.

———. *The New Radicalism in America, 1889–1963*. New York: Vintage, 1965.

Laslett, John H. M. *Labor and the Left: A Study of Socialist and Radical Influenc-*

es in the American Labor Movement, 1881–1924. New York: Basic Books, 1970.

Lawrence, D. H. "Autobiographical Sketch." In Phoenix II, edited by Warren Roberts and Harry T. Moore, 300–302. New York: Viking, 1970.

Lawson, John Howard. "'In Dixieland We Take Our Stand,' A Report on the Alabama Terror." New Masses (29 May 1934): 8–9.

Lea, James F. Political Consciousness and American Democracy. Jackson: University Press of Mississippi, 1982.

Lechlitner, Ruth. ". . . anti-war and anti-fascism. . . ." Carleton Miscellany 6 (Winter 1965): 77–82.

———. "The Last Frontiers." New Masses (16 October 1934): 20–21.

———. "Verse-Drama for Radio: A New Direction." In New Directions in Prose and Poetry 1937, edited by James Laughlin IV, 110–15. Norfolk, Conn.: New Directions, 1937.

Lefevre, Manfred. Von der Proletarischen-Revolutionärischen Literatur zur Sozialistisch-Realistischen Literatur. Stuttgart: Akademischer Verlag, 1980.

Lefley, Robert. "Panorama." Chicago Daily News, 18 May 1963, 6, 9. (Interview with Jack Conroy.)

"Left No. 2." International Literature 2–3 (1932): 145–52.

Leighton, George R. Five Cities: The Story of Their Youth and Old Age. New York: Harper and Brothers, 1939.

Lejeune, Philippe. Je Est un Autre. Paris: Editions du Seuil, 1980.

Lemon, Lee T., and Marion J. Reis, eds. Russian Formalist Criticism. Lincoln: University of Nebraska Press, 1965.

Le Sueur, Meridel. "Colonialism and American Culture." In "Our Hidden Heritage of People's Culture," edited by Fred Whitehead. Kansas City, 1985. (Mimeographed report of conference at the Foolkiller Center, Kansas City, 25–26 January 1985.)

———. Crusaders: The Radical Legacy of Marian and Arthur Le Sueur. St. Paul: Minnesota Historical Society Press, 1984.

———. Harvest. Cambridge, Mass.: West End Press, 1977.

———. "Join Hand and Brain." Review of A World to Win, by Jack Conroy. New Masses (9 July 1935): 25.

———. North Star Country. Lincoln: University of Nebraska, 1984.

———. "Proletarian Literature and the Middle West." In American Writers' Congress, edited by Henry Hart, 135–38. New York: International Publishers, 1935.

———. Ripening: Selected Work, 1927–1980. Edited by Elaine Hedges. New York: Feminist Press, 1982.

———. Salute to Spring. New York: International Publishers, 1940, 1981.

———. "Women on the Breadlines." New Masses 7 (January 1932): 5–7.

Leuchtenburg, William E. The Perils of Prosperity. Chicago: University of Chicago Press, 1958.

Levin, Daniel. Stormy Petrel: The Life and Work of Maxim Gorky. New York: Appleton-Century, 1965.

Levy, Melvin P. "Some Poets to the Left." Review of Red Renaissance, by H. H. Lewis. In New Masses 6 (February 1931): 20.

Lewis, Frederick Allen. *Only Yesterday*. New York: Harper and Row, 1959.

Lewis, H. H. "Gone West." In *Social Poetry of the 1930s*, edited by Salzman and Zanderer, 138–39.

———. "In All Hell." *Rebel Poet* 1 (January 1931): 4. Reprinted in *Thinking of Russia*, 16.

———. "Liberal." *Rebel Poet* 10–12 (October–December 1931): 8.

———. "Memoirs of a Dishwasher." *New Masses* 4 (February 1929): 7.

———. *Red Renaissance*. Introduction by Jack Conroy. Holt, Minn.: B. C. Hagglund, 1930.

———. *Road to Utterly*. Holt, Minn.: B. C. Hagglund, 1935.

———. *Salvation*. Holt, Minn.: B. C. Hagglund, 1934.

———. "School Days in the Gumbo." *American Mercury* 23 (January 1931).

———. "Sidewalks of Los Angeles." *New Masses* 4 (June 1929): 13.

———. *Thinking of Russia*. Holt, Minn.: B. C. Hagglund, 1932.

Lewis, R. W. B. *The Picaresque Saint*. Philadelphia: J. B. Lippincott, 1959.

"Liberals Return from Dixie Test." *New York Post,* 7 August 1935.

Licht, Walter. *Working for the Railroad: The Organization of Work in the Nineteenth Century*. Princeton: Princeton University Press, 1983.

Lindberg, Stanley W., ed. *The Annotated McGuffey*. New York: Van Nostrand Reinhold, 1976.

Lipsitz, George. "Striking Prose." *St. Louis Magazine* (March 1983): 44–46.

Lomax, Alan, Woody Guthrie, and Peter Seeger, eds. *Hard Hitting Songs for Hard-Hit People*. New York: Oak Publications, 1967.

London, Jack. *The People of the Abyss*. Westport, Conn.: Lawrence Hill Press, 1977.

———. *War of the Classes*. Upper Saddle River, N.J.: Literature House, 1970.

Lovell, John, Jr. "Champions of the Workers in American Literature in the 1840s." Ph.D. diss., University of California–Berkeley, 1938.

Lowe, Leah W. "The Theater as Moberly Has Known It." *Moberly: 100th Anniversary*, 240–43. Marceline, Mo.: Walsworth Company, 1966.

Lowenthal, Richard. *Social Change and Cultural Crisis*. New York: Columbia University Press, 1984.

Ludington, Townsend. *John Dos Passos: A Twentieth Century Odyssey*. New York: E. P. Dutton, 1980.

Lukács, Georg. *Essays on Realism*. Cambridge, Mass.: MIT Press, 1981.

Lynn, Ethel. *The Adventures of a Woman Hobo*. New York: George H. Doran, 1917.

Lyons, Eugene. *The Red Decade*. Indianapolis: Bobbs-Merrill, 1941.

McCollum, Kenneth G. *Nelson Algren: A Checklist*. Detroit: Gale Research, 1973.

McCown, Robert A. "Paul Corey's Mantz Trilogy." *Books at Iowa* 17 (November 1972): 15–26.

McDonald, David J., and Edward A. Lynch. *Coal and Unionism*. New York: Lynald Books, 1939.

McElvaine, Robert S. "Workers in Fiction: Locked Out." *New York Times Book Review*, 1 September 1986, 1, 19.

McGuire, John. "The Legacy of Clarence Earl Gideon." *St. Louis Post-Dispatch Magazine*, 11 November 1984, 6–10, 27.

———. "Where Does Labor Go from Here?" *St. Louis Post-Dispatch Magazine*, 28 June 1987, 6–13.

MacKinnon, Janice R., and Stephen R. MacKinnon. *Agnes Smedley: The Life and Times of an American Radical*. London: Virago Press, 1988.

McLaughlin, Virginia Yans. *Family and Community: Italian Immigrants in Buffalo, 1880–1930*. Urbana: University of Illinois Press, 1982.

Macleod, Norman. *The Bitter Roots*. New York: Smith and Durrell, 1941.

———. "Comment." *Morada* 2 (Winter 1929): 33.

———. "Poetry Takes to the Barricades." *Moscow Daily News*, 16 May 1933.

———. *Selected Poems*. Boise, Idaho: Ahsahta Press, 1975.

———. *You Get What You Ask For*. New York: Harrison-Hilton, 1939.

McLoughlin, William G., Jr. *Modern Revivalism: Charles Grandison Finney to Billy Graham*. New York: Ronald Press, 1959.

———. *Revivals, Awakenings, and Reforms: An Essay on Religion and Social Change in America, 1607–1977*. Chicago: University of Chicago, 1978.

McLuhan, Marshall. *The Gutenberg Galaxy: The Making of Typographic Man*. Toronto: University of Toronto Press, 1965.

MacLysaght, Edward. *Irish Families*. Dublin: Irish Academic Press, 1985.

McMillan, Dougald. *Transition: The History of a Literary Era, 1927–1938*. New York: George Braziller, 1976.

McWilliams, Carey. *The Idea of Fraternity in America*. Berkeley: University of California, 1973.

———. *The New Regionalism in American Literature*. Seattle: University of Washington Bookstore, 1930.

Madden, David, ed. *Proletarian Writers of the Thirties*. Carbondale: Southern Illinois University Press, 1968.

Magil, A. B. "European Newsreel." *New Masses* 6 (May 1931): 10.

Maloff, Saul. "The Mythic Thirties." *Texas Quarterly* 11 (Winter 1968): 109–18.

Malva, Constant. *La Nuit dans Les Yeux*. Brussels: Editions Labor, 1983.

———. *Le Jambot*. Brussels: Editions Jacques Antoine, 1980.

———. *Ma Nuit au Jour le Jour*. Paris: François Maspero, 1978.

Mangione, Jerre. *The Dream and the Deal: The Federal Writers' Project, 1935–1943*. New York: Avon Books, 1972.

———. Review of *A World to Win*, by Jack Conroy. *New Republic* 84 (4 September 1935): 109.

———. Untitled lecture. Symposium on the WPA Writers' Project. Newberry Library, Chicago, 23 September 1989.

Marcus, Shumuel (a.k.a. Marcus Graham), ed. *An Anthology of Revolutionary Poetry*. Introduction by Ralph Cheyney and Lucia Trent. New York: The Active Press, 1929.

Mariani, Paul. *William Carlos Williams: A New World Naked*. New York: McGraw-Hill, 1981.

Marling, Karal Ann. "Joe Jones: Regionalist, Communist, Capitalist." *Journal of Decorative and Propaganda Art* (Spring 1987): 46–59.

————. *Wall-to-Wall America: A Cultural History of Post-Office Murals in the Great Depression*. Minneapolis: University of Minnesota Press, 1982.

Martin, Alice. *The Tempest Maker*. New York: Exposition Press, 1955.

Martin, Jay. *Nathanael West: The Art of His Life*. New York: Carroll and Graf, 1970.

Martin, Reginald. *Ishmael Reed and the New Black Aesthetic Critics*. New York: St. Martin's Press, 1988.

Mathews, Horace Frederick. *Methodism and the Education of the People, 1791–1851*. London: Epworth Press, 1949.

Mattick, Paul. *Arbeitslosigkeit und Arbeitslosenbewegung in den USA, 1929–1935*. Frankfurt am Main: Verlag Neue Kritik, 1969.

May, Henry F. "The Rebellion of the Intellectuals, 1912–1917." In *The American Culture*, edited by Hennig Cohen, 159–67. Boston: Houghton-Mifflin, 1968.

Meeker, Joseph. *The Comedy of Survival: Studies in Literary Ecology*. New York: Scribner's, 1974.

Melville, Herman. *The Confidence Man*. New York: W. W. Norton, 1971.

Mencken, H. L. "Editorial Notes." *American Mercury* 18 (September 1929): xxxiv.

————. "Illuminators of the Abyss." *Saturday Review of Literature* 11 (6 October 1934): 156.

————. Review of *The Disinherited*, by Jack Conroy. *American Mercury* 30 (April 1934): 26.

Mers, Gilbert. *Working the Waterfront*. Austin: University of Texas, 1988.

Meyers, Roy. *The Middle-Western Farm Novel in the Twentieth Century*. Lincoln: University of Nebraska Press, 1965.

Milburn, George. "The *Appeal to Reason*." *American Mercury* 23 (July 1931): 359–71.

————. *The Hobo's Hornbook*. New York: Ives Washburn, 1930.

————. *Oklahoma Town*. New York: Harcourt, Brace, 1931.

Miles, Dione. "Agnes Inglis." *Dandelion* 3 (Winter 1979): 7–15.

Miller, Fred R. "*The New Masses* and Who Else?" *Blue Pencil* (February 1935): 4–5.

Miller, Kerby A. *Emigrants and Exiles*. New York: Oxford University Press, 1985.

Mills, C. Wright. *The Power Elite*. New York: Oxford University Press, 1956.

Milton, David. *The Politics of U.S. Labor: From the Great Depression to the New Deal*. New York: Monthly Review Press, 1982.

Minor, Robert. "We Want a Labor Party." *Liberator* 5 (November–December 1922): 7.

Mitgang, Herbert. "Annals of Government: Policing America's Writers." *New Yorker*, October 1987, 47–90.

Montgomery, David. "The 'New Unionism' and the Transformation of Workers' Consciousness in America, 1909–1922." *Journal of Social History* 7 (1974): 514.

Morgan, Jack. "Jack Conroy's *The Disinherited*, 1933." *Eire-Ireland* 27 (Fall 1992): 122–28.

Morray, J. P. "Eastward Ho!" *The Liberator* 5 (May 1922): 13.

———. *Project Kuzbas: American Workers in Siberia 1921–26.* New York: International Publishers, 1983.

Morris, Gerald V. "On the Skidroad: What One Sees On Los Angeles' Street of Forsaken Men." *Haldeman-Julius Quarterly* 2 (July–September 1928): 76–78.

Mortimer, Wyndham. *Organize! My Life as Union Man.* Boston: Beacon Press, 1971.

Motley, Willard. *Let Noon Be Fair.* New York: Putnam, 1966.

Mottram, Eric. "Living Mythically: The Thirties." *Journal of American Studies* 6 (December 1972):

Mumford, Lewis. "The Theory and Practice of Regionalism." *Sociological Review* 20 (April 1928): 131–40.

Münchow, Ursula. *Frühe Deutsche Arbeiterautobiographie.* Berlin: Akademie Verlag, 1973.

Murphy, James F. *The Proletarian Moment: The Controversy over Leftism in Literature.* Urbana: University of Illinois Press, 1991.

Murphy, Paul L. *World War I and the Origins of Civil Liberties in the United States.* New York: Norton, 1979.

Murrah, Bill. "Llano Cooperative Colony, Louisiana." *Southern Exposure* 1 (Winter 1974): 88–104.

Musser, Benjamin. "Another Milestone." *Contemporary Verse* 15 (November 1929).

———. Article in *Poetry World* (September 1929).

———. *Ernest Hartsock: An Appreciation.* Landover, Maryland: Dreamland Press, 1931.

———. "To Young Rebel Poets." In *Unrest 1931,* edited by Jack Conroy and Ralph Cheyney. New York: Henry Harrison, 1931.

Nash, Jay Robert. *The Innovators.* Chicago: Regnery Gateway, 1982.

Nash, Roderick. *The Nervous Generation: American Thought, 1917–1930.* Chicago: Rand McNally, 1970.

Navasky, Victor S. *Naming Names.* New York: Viking Press, 1980.

Neets, J. Q. (a.k.a. Joshua Kunitz). "From Our Critic in Moscow." *New Masses* 6 (September 1930): 23.

Nekola, Charlotte, and Paula Rabinowitz. *Writing Red: An Anthology of American Women Writers, 1930–1940.* New York: Feminist Press, 1987.

Nelkin, Dorothy, and Michael S. Brown. *Workers at Risk: Voices from the Work Place.* Chicago: University of Chicago Press, 1984.

Nelson, Bruce. *Workers on the Waterfront: Seamen, Longshoremen, and Unionism in the 1930s.* Urbana: University of Illinois Press, 1989.

Nelson, Cary. *Repression and Recovery: Modern American Poetry and the Politics of Cultural Memory, 1910–1945.* Madison: University of Wisconsin Press, 1989.

Nelson, Cary, and Jefferson Hendricks. *Collected Poems: Edwin Rolfe.* Urbana: University of Illinois Press, 1993.

———. *Edwin Rolfe: A Biographical Essay and Guide to the Rolfe Archive at the*

University of Illinois at Urbana-Champaign. Urbana: University of Illinois Press, 1990.

Nemser, Rebecca. "Charles Sheeler: Master of the Industrial Sublime." *Technology Review* 91 (April 1988): 42–50.

Nexö, Martin Andersen. *Pelle the Conqueror*. Gloucester, Mass.: Peter Smith, 1963.

Nietzsche, Fredrich. *The Gay Science*. Translated by Walter Kaufman. New York: Random House, 1974.

Nolte, William H. *H. L. Mencken, Literary Critic*. Middletown, Conn.: Wesleyan University Press, 1966.

Norris, Hoke. "A Critic-at-Large." *Chicago Sun-Times*, 14 April 1963, 20 September 1964. (Interviews with Jack Conroy.)

North, Joseph, ed. *New Masses: An Anthology of the Rebel Thirties*. New York: International Publishers, 1972.

———. *Robert Minor, Artist and Crusader*. New York: International Publishers, 1956.

Noyes, Henry. *Hand Over Fist*. Boston: South End Press, 1980.

Nye, Russel B. *Midwestern Progressive Politics*. New York: Harper Torchbooks, 1965.

———. "The Thirties: The Framework of Belief." *Centennial Review* 19 (Spring 1975): 37–58.

———. *The Unembarrassed Muse: The Popular Arts in America*. New York: Dial, 1970.

O'Connor, Frances V., ed. *The New Deal Art Projects: An Anthology of Memoirs*. Washington, D.C.: Smithsonian Institution Press, 1972.

O'Connor, Frank. Introduction to *The Lonely Voice: A Study of the Short Story*, edited by Frank O'Connor. Cleveland: World Publishing, 1963.

Odum, Howard W., and Harry E. Moore. *American Regionalism*. New York: Henry Holt, 1938.

Ogilvie, Leon Parker. "Populism and Socialism in the Southeast Missouri Lowlands." *Missouri Historical Review* 65 (January 1971): 159–83.

O'Hare, Kate Richards. *Kate Richards O'Hare: Selected Writings and Speeches*. Edited by Philip S. Foner and Sally M. Miller. Baton Rouge: Louisiana State University Press, 1982.

Olsen, Tillie. *Silences*. New York: Delacorte Press, 1978.

O'Neill, William. *A Better World; The Great Schism: Stalinism and the American Intellectuals*. New York: Simon and Schuster, 1982.

———. *Echoes of Revolt: The Masses, 1911–1917*. Chicago: Ivan R. Dee, 1989.

O'Rourke, William. *On the Job: Fiction about Work by Contemporary Americans*. New York: Random House, 1977.

Orvell, Miles. *The Real Thing: Imitation and Authenticity in American Culture, 1880–1940*. Chapel Hill: University of North Carolina Press, 1989.

Orwell, George. "The Proletarian Writer." In *The Collected Essays, Journalism and Letters of George Orwell*, edited by Sonia Orwell and Ian Angus. Vol. 2. New York: Harcourt, Brace and World, 1968.

———. *Road to Wigan Pier*. New York: Harcourt Brace Jovanovich, 1958.

O'Sheel, Sheamus. "They Went Forth to Battle." In *The Home Book of Verse, American and English*, edited by Burton Egbert Stevenson. New York: Holt, Rinehart and Winston, n.d.

O'Toole, L. Michael. *Structure, Style and Interpretation in the Russian Short Story*. New Haven: Yale University Press, 1965.

Owen, Blaine. "Night Ride in Birmingham." *New Republic* 83 (28 August 1935): 65–67.

Painter, Leonard. *Through Fifty Years with the Brotherhood Railway Carmen*. Kansas City: Brotherhood Railway Carmen of America, 1941.

Papashvily, Helen Waite. *All the Happy Endings: A Study of the Domestic Novel in America*. New York: Harper and Row, 1956.

Patchen, Kenneth. "Joe Hill Listens to the Praying." *New Masses* (20 November 1934): 8–9.

Patterson, William L. *The Man Who Cried Genocide*. New York: International Publishers, 1971.

Peck, David. "The Development of an American Marxist Literary Criticism: The Monthly 'New Masses.'" Ph.D. diss., Temple University, 1968.

———. "Salvaging the Art and Literature of the 1930's: A Bibliographical Essay." *Centennial Review* 20 (Spring 1976): 128–41.

———. "'The Tradition of American Revolutionary Literature': The Monthly *New Masses*, 1926–1933." *Science and Society* 42 (Winter 1978–79): 390–91.

Pells, Richard. *Radical Visions and American Dreams*. Middletown, Conn.: Wesleyan University Press, 1973.

Penkower, Monty Noam. *The Federal Writers' Project: A Study in Government Patronage of the Arts*. Urbana: University of Illinois Press, 1977.

Perlman, Selig, and Philip Taft. *History of Labor in the United States, 1896–1932*. Vols. 3 and 4. New York: Macmillan, 1935.

Peters, Paul. "Flivver Tramps." *New Masses* 4 (April 1929): 14–15.

Peterson, H. C., and Gilbert C. Fite. *Opponents of War, 1917–1918*. Madison: University of Wisconsin Press, 1957.

Pfeffer, Richard M. *Working for Capitalism*. New York: Columbia University Press, 1979.

Phelps, Wallace (a.k.a. William Phillips). Review of *Ulysses*, by James Joyce. *New Masses* (20 February 1934): 26.

Phillips, William. "Comment." *Partisan Review* 49,1 (1982): 7–9.

———. "On *Partisan Review*." *TriQuarterly* 43 (Fall 1978): 130–41.

———. *A Partisan View: Five Decades of Literary Life*. New York: Stein and Day, 1983.

———. "Thirty Years Later, Memories of the First American Writers' Congress." *American Scholar* 35 (Summer 1966): 495–516.

———. "What Happened in the '30s." *Commentary* 34 (1962): 204–12.

Phillips, William, and Philip Rahv, eds. *The Partisan Reader*. New York: Dial Press, 1946.

Pinsker, Sanford. "Revisionism with Rancor: The Threat of the Neoconservative Critics." *Georgia Review* 38 (Summer 1984): 243–61.

Polanyi, Karl. *The Great Transformation*. Boston: Beacon Press, 1957.

Pollack, Norman. *The Populist Response to Industrial America*. Cambridge, Mass.: Harvard University Press, 1962.

Popper, Joe. "Jack: Conversations with Author Jack Conroy, a Man Who Kept His Word." *Kansas City Star Magazine*, 27 September 1987, 10–13.

Porter, Kenneth. "Anthology of Rebel Poets." *Christian* (11 July 1931): 558.

———. *The High Plains*. New York: John Day, 1938.

Potter, David M. *People of Plenty: Economic Abundance and the American Character*. Chicago: University of Chicago Press, 1954.

Pratt, Linda Ray. "Woman Writer in the CP: The Case of Meridel Le Sueur." *Women's Studies* 14 (February 1988): 247–64.

Preece, Harold. "Ardmore, Godly and Gauche." *Debunker and the American Parade* 14 (July 1931): 2–4.

———. "The Negro Folk Cult." *The Crisis* 43 (1936): 364, 374.

Preston, John Hyde. "Search for Roots in America." In *American Points of View*, edited by William H. and Kathryn Coe Cordell. New York: Doubleday, Doran, 1937.

Prestridge, Virginia. *The Worker in American Fiction: An Annotated Bibliography*. Champaign: Institute of Labor and Industrial Relations, University of Illinois, 1954.

Price, Emerson. *Inn of that Journey*. Introduction by Jack Conroy. Caldwell, Ida.: Caxton Printers, 1939.

Propp, Vladimir. *Theory and History of Folklore*. Edited by Anatoly Liberman. Translated by Ariadna Y. Martin and Richard P. Martin. Minneapolis: University of Minnesota Press, 1984.

Putnam, Samuel. "Red Days in Chicago." *American Mercury* 30 (September 1933): 64–71.

Radway, Jance A. *Reading the Romance: Women, Patriarchy, and Popular Literature*. Chapel Hill: University of North Carolina Press, 1984.

Ragon, Michel. *Histoire de la Littérature Prolétarienne en France*. Paris: Albin Michel, 1974.

Rahv, Philip. "An Open Letter to Young Writers." *Rebel Poet* 16 (September 1932): 3–4.

———. "Proletarian Literature: A Political Autopsy." *Essays on Literature and Politics, 1932–1972*. Edited by Arabel J. Porter and Andrew J. Drosin. Boston: Houghton-Mifflin, 1978.

———. Review of "Scottsboro Limited," by Langston Hughes. *Rebel Poet* 15 (August 1932): 7.

———. "Valedictory on the Propaganda Issue." *Little Magazine* (September 1934): 2.

Rall, Jeff. "1933 and *The Disinherited*." *Industrial Worker* (22 May 1963): 3.

Rancière, Jacques. *La Nuit des Prolétaires*. Paris: Fayard, 1981.

———. "The Myth of the Artisan: Critical Reflections on a Category of Social History." *International Labor and Working Class History* 24 (Fall 1983): 1–16.

Randolph, Vance. *Roll Me in Your Arms: "Unprintable" Folksongs and Folklore*. Vol. 1. Fayetteville: University of Arkansas Press, 1992.

Ravage, Eli. *An American in the Making: The Life Story of an Immigrant.* New York: Harper and Borthers, 1917.

Ray, David. "A Talk on the Wild Side." *Reporter* 20 (11 June, 1959): 31–33. (Interview with Nelson Algren.)

Redfield, Robert. "The Folk Society." *American Journal of Sociology* 52 (January 1947): 293–308.

————. *The Little Community.* Chicago: University of Chicago Press, 1967.

"Regionalism: Pro and Con." *Saturday Review of Literature* 15 (28 November 1936): 3–4, 14, 16.

Reigelman, Milton M. *The Midland, A Venture in Literary Regionalism.* Iowa City: University of Iowa Press, 1975.

Reinemer, Michael. "A Miscarriage of Promise for the Young Writers of Iowa: A View of the Iowa Writers' Project during the Great Depression." *North American Mentor Magazine* 17 (Spring 1979): 1–20.

Reinhardt, Richard. *Workin' on the Railroad.* Palo Alto, Calif.: American West Publishing Company, 1970.

Reurer, Rosemary. "Making History." Videotape. Labor History Conference, Washington University, 11 November 1988.

Reuss, Richard. "American Folklore and Leftwing Politics, 1927–1957." Ph.D. diss., Indiana University, 1971.

Rexroth, Kenneth. *The Alternative Society: Essays from the Other World.* New York: Herder and Herder, 1970.

Rice, Clyde. *A Heaven in the Eye.* Portland, Ore.: Breitenbush Books, 1984.

Rideout, Walter B. *The Radical Novel in the United States, 1900–1954.* Cambridge, Mass.: Harvard University Press, 1954.

Roberts, Elizabeth Madox. *The Time of Man.* Introduction by Robert Penn Warren. New York: Viking, 1963.

Roberts, Peter. *Anthracite Coal Communities.* New York: Macmillan, 1904; reprint, New York: Arno Press, 1970.

Rodgers, Daniel T. *The Work Ethic in Industrial America.* Chicago: University of Chicago Press, 1978.

Rodman, Selden. Review of *The Disinherited,* by Jack Conroy. *Common Sense* (January 1934).

Rodriguez, Jose. Review of *The Disinherited,* by Jack Conroy. *Los Angeles Post-Record,* 2 December 1933, C2.

Rogers, John. "Biographical Notes." Unpubl. MS, Rogers papers, University of Virginia Library.

————. "An Unreconstructed Radical." *North Country Anvil* 7 (August–September 1973): 73.

————. "Remembering." *December* 18 (1976): 122–26.

Rorabaugh, W. J. *The Craft Apprentice, From Franklin to the Machine Age in America.* New York: Oxford University Press, 1986.

Rorty, James. "Anything Can Happen in Los Angeles." *New Masses* 1 (June 1926): 6–7, 27.

Rourke, Constance. *American Humor: A Study of the National Character.* Garden City, N.Y.: Doubleday, 1931.

——. *The Roots of American Culture*. New York: Harcourt, Brace, 1942.

——. "The Significance of Sections." *New Republic* 76 (20 September 1933): 148–51.

Roy, Andrew. *A History of the Coal Miners of the U.S.* Columbus, Ohio: J. L. Trauger, 1907.

Rubin, Charles. *The Log of Rubin the Sailor*. New York: International Publishers, 1973.

Rubin, Joan Shelley. *Constance Rourke and American Culture*. Chapel Hill: University of North Carolina Press, 1980.

Ruderman, Judith. *D. H. Lawrence and the Devouring Mother: The Search for a Patriarchal Idea of Leadership*. Durham: Duke University Press, 1984.

Rühle, Jürgen. *Literatur und Revolution: Die Schriftsteller und der Kommunismus*. Munich, 1963.

Rukeyser, Muriel. "The Trial." *New Masses* (12 June 1934): 20.

Salvatore, Nick. *Eugene V. Debs: Citizen and Socialist*. Urbana: University of Illinois Press, 1982.

Salzman, Jack. *Albert Maltz*. Boston: Twayne, 1978.

——. "Conroy, Mencken, and *The American Mercury*." *Journal of Popular Culture* 7 (Winter 1973): 524–28.

Salzman, Jack, and Barry Wallenstein, eds. *Years of Protest: A Collection of American Writings of the 1930s*. New York, Pegasus, 1967.

Salzman, Jack, and David Ray. *The Jack Conroy Reader*. New York: Burt Franklin, 1979.

Salzman, Jack, and Leo Zanderer, eds. *Social Poetry of the 1930s*. New York: Burt Franklin, 1978.

Sandburg, Carl. "The People, Yes." In *Complete Poems*, by Carl Sandburg. New York: Harcourt, Brace and World, 1950.

Sartre, Jean-Paul. *Being and Nothingness*. New York: Philosophical Library, 1956.

Schmitt, Franz. *Beruf und Arbeit*. Stuttgart: Hiersemann Verlag, 1952.

Schmitt, Hans-Jürgen, and Godehard Schramm, eds. *Sozialistische Realismuskonzeptionen: Dokumente zum 1. Allunionskongress der Sowjetschriftsteller*. Frankfurt am Main: Suhrkamp Verlag, 1974.

Schneider, Isidor. "Sectarianism on the Right." *New Masses* (23 June 1936): 23–26.

Schneiderman, Stuart. *Jacques Lacan: The Death of an Intellectual Hero*. Cambridge, Mass.: Harvard University Press, 1983.

Schrank, Robert. *Ten Thousand Working Days*. Cambridge, Mass.: MIT University Press, 1978.

Schroedel, Jean Reith. *Alone in a Crowd: Women in the Trades Tell Their Stories*. Philadelphia: Temple University Press, 1985.

Schulte-Sässer, Joachim. Foreword to *The Theory of the Avant-Garde*, by Peter Bürger. Minneapolis: University of Minnesota Press, 1982.

Schutz, Alfred, and Thomas Luckmann. *The Structures of the Life-World*. Evanston: Northwestern University Press, 1973.

Schwartz, Delmore. "The Present State of Poetry." In *American Poetry at Mid-Century*, edited by John Crowe Ransom, Delmore Schwartz, and John Hall Wheelock, 15–31. Washington, D.C.: Library of Congress, 1958.

Schwartz, Lawrence H. *Creating Faulkner's Reputation: The Politics of Modern Literary Criticism*. Knoxville: University of Tennessee Press, 1988.

―――. *Marxism and Culture: The CPUSA and Aesthetics in the 1930s*. Port Washington, N.Y.: Kennikat Press, 1980.

Schweider, Dorothy. *Black Diamonds: Life and Work in Iowa's Coal Mining Communities*. Ames: Iowa State University Press, 1983.

Scott, Joan Wallach. *Gender and the Politics of History*. New York: Columbia University Press, 1988.

Seaver, Edwin. "Literature at the Crossroads." *New Masses* 7 (April 1932): 12–13.

―――. "Memorandum on *The Disinherited*." Unpubl. MS in Conroy papers, Newberry Library.

Seevers, Helen. "Blue Lantern Bohemians." *St. Louis Post-Dispatch*, 3 April 1969, 3, 5.

Seguin, Harry. "The Rebel Poet and Humanity." *Rebel Poet* 6/7 (June–July 1931): 4–5, 10.

Seifer, Nancy. *Nobody Speaks for Me!: Self-Portraits of American Working-Class Women*. New York: Simon and Schuster, 1976.

"Self-Styled 'Liberals' Claim Car Fired On." *Birmingham News*, 30 July 1935.

Seltzer, Curtis. *Fire in the Hole: Miners and Managers in the American Coal Company*. Lexington: University Press of Kentucky, 1985.

Sennett, Richard. *Families Against the City: Middle Class Homes of Industrial Chicago, 1872–1890*. Cambridge, Mass.: Harvard University Press, 1970.

Shepherd, Leslie. *The History of Street Literature*. Newton Abbot, Eng.: David and Charles, 1973.

Shields, Art. *On the Battle Lines, 1919–1939*. New York: International Publishers, 1986.

Shinkle, Florence. "Focusing on Missouri's Past." *St. Louis Post-Dispatch Sunday Magazine*, 8 February 1987, 6–10.

Shore, Elliott. *Talkin' Socialism: J. A. Wayland and the Role of the Press in American Radicalism, 1890–1912*. Lawrence: University Press of Kansas, 1988.

Shover, John. *The Cornbelt Rebellion: The Farmers' Holiday Association*. Urbana: University of Illinois Press, 1965.

Sinclair, Upton. *The Jungle*. New York: Doubleday, Page, 1906.

Singleton, M. K. *H. L. Mencken and the American Mercury Adventure*. Durham, N.C.: Duke University Press, 1962.

Slichter, Sumner H. "The Labor Politics of American Industries." *Quarterly Journal of Economics* 43 (May 1929): 398–404, 431–35.

Slonim, Marc. *Soviet Russian Literature: Writers and Problems, 1917–1977*. New York: Oxford University Press, 1977.

Smedley, Agnes. *Daughter of Earth*. New York: Feminist Press, 1973.

Smith, Henry Nash. "Localism in Literature." In *Folk-Say, A Regional Miscellany, 1930*, edited by B. A. Botkin, 298–301. Norman: University of Oklahoma Press, 1930.

―――, ed. *Popular Culture and Industrialism, 1865–1890*. New York: New York University Press, 1967.

Snow, Walter. "The Anvil and the Proletarian Short Story." Unpubl. MS in Snow collection, University of Connecticut–Storrs.

———. "Bibliography—Walter Snow, Novelist, Poet and Journalist." Unpubl. MS in Snow collection, University of Connecticut–Storrs.

———. *The Glory and the Shame*. Coventry, Conn.: Pequot Press, 1973.

———. *The Golden Nightmare*. New York: Austin-Phelps, 1952.

———. "Goliath." *New Masses* 5 (January 1930): 10.

———. "The Revolutionary Poet." *New Masses* 4 (October 1928): 19.

———. "That Literary 'Shotgun Marriage.'" Unpubl. MS in Snow collection, University of Connecticut–Storrs.

Spector, Herman. *Bastard in the Ragged Suit*. Edited by Bud Johns and Judith S. Clancy. San Francisco: Synergistic Press, 1977.

———. "Liberalism and the Literary Esoterics." *New Masses* 4 (January 1929): 18–19.

Spector, Herman, Joseph Kalar, Edwin Rolfe, and S. Funaroff. *We Gather Strength*. New York: Liberal Press, 1933.

Spero, Sterling D., and Abram L. Harris. *The Black Worker: The Negro and the Labor Movement*. New York: Atheneum, 1972.

Spier, Leonard. *Poker Faces and Other Poems*. Charleston, Ill.: Prairie Poet Books, 1982.

———. *When the Sirens Blow*. Introduction by Jack Conroy. Holt, Minn.: B. C. Hagglund, 1933.

Spiller, Robert E., et al. *Literary History of the United States*. New York: Macmillan, 1963.

Stacy, Walter S. "Picket Lines on a Coal Mine." *Rebel Poet* 8/9 (August–September 1931): 9.

Stahl, Sandra Dolby. *Literary Folkloristics and the Personal Narrative*. Bloomington: Indiana University Press, 1989.

Stanley, David H. "The Personal Novel: Folklore as Frame and Structure for Literature." *Southern Folklore Quarterly* 43 (1979): 107–20.

Steele, James (a.k.a. Robert Cruden). *Conveyor*. New York: International Publishers, 1935.

———. "Own Your Own Home." *Anvil* 8 (September–October 1934): 25–27.

Stelzle, Charles. *A Son of the Bowery*. New York: George H. Doran, 1926.

Stivale, Charles J. "The Literary Element in *Mille Plateux*: The New Cartography of Deleuze and Guattari." *SubStance* 44–45 (1984): 20–34.

Stokes, Durward T. *Company Shops: The Town Built by a Railroad*. Winston-Salem: John F. Blair, 1981.

Stork, A. "Mr. Calverton and His Friends: Some Notes on Literary Trotskyism in America." *International Literature* 3 (July 1934): 97.

Stott, William. *Documentary Expression and Thirties America*. New York: Oxford University Press, 1973.

Stover, John F. *American Railroads*. Chicago: University of Chicago Press, 1961.

Strachey, John. *The Coming Struggle for Power*. New York: Covici-Friede, 1933.

Stricker, Frank. "Affluence for Whom?—Another Look at Prosperity and the Working Classes in the 1920s." *Labor History* 24 (Winter 1983): 5–33.

Struve, Gleb. *Russian Literature under Lenin and Stalin, 1917–1953*. Norman: University of Oklahoma Press, 1971.

Suggs, Jon Christian, and Douglas Wixson, comps. "Jack Conroy." In *Bibliography of American Fiction, 1919–1988*, edited by Matthew J. Bruccoli. New York: Facts on File, 1992.

Sukenick, Ronald. "Eight Digressions on the Politics of Language." *New Literary History* 10 (Spring 1979): 472–73.

"Summer Courses Announced." *Commonwealth College Fortnightly* 11 (15 June 1935): 1, 4.

Susman, Warren I. "A Dialectic of Two Cultures." *Nation* (16 February 1985): 172–74.

———. "The Thirties." In *The Development of an American Culture*, edited by Stanley Coben and Lorman Ratner, 215–60. Englewood Cliffs, N.J.: Prentice-Hall, 1970.

Swingewood, Alan. "Marxist Approaches to the Study of Literature. In *The Sociology of Literature: Theoretical Approaches*, edited by Jane Routh and Janet Wolff, 131–49. Staffordshire, Eng.: University of Keele Press, 1977.

Symes, Lillian, and Travers Clement. *Rebel America: The Story of Social Revolt in the United States*. New York: Harper, 1934.

"A Symposium: The Status of Radical Writing." *A Year Magazine* (1933).

Tashjian, Dickran. *Skyscraper Primitives: Dada and the American Avant-Garde, 1910–1925*. Middletown, Conn.: Wesleyan University Press, 1975.

———. *William Carlos Williams and the American Scene, 1920–1940*. Berkeley: University of California Press, 1978.

Tate, Allen. "Poetry and Politics." *New Republic* (2 August 1933).

Terkel, Studs. *Hard Times*. New York: Pantheon, 1970.

———. *Race*. New York: The New Press, 1992.

———. *Working*. New York: Pantheon, 1972.

Terrill, Tom E., and Jerrold Hirsch, eds. *Such As Us: Southern Voices of the Thirties*. Chapel Hill: University of North Carolina Press, 1978.

Thaddeus, Janice. "The Metamorphosis of Richard Wright's *Black Boy*." *American Literature* 57 (May 1985): 199–214.

Thelen, David. *Paths of Resistance: Tradition and Dignity in Industrializing Missouri*. New York: Oxford University Press, 1986.

Thompson, E. P. *The Making of the English Working Class*. New York: Vintage, 1964.

Thompson, Lloyd S. "A Vag in College." *Liberator* (July 1923): 22.

Thompson, Robert. "An Interview with Jack Conroy." *Missouri Review* 7 (Fall 1983): 148–72.

Those Who Built Stalingrad; as Told by Themselves. Moscow: Cooperative Society of Foreign Workers in the U.S.S.R., 1934.

Todorov, Tzvetan. *Mikhail Bakhtin: The Dialogical Principle*. Minneapolis: University of Minnesota Press, 1984.

———. "The Notion of Literature." *New Literary History* 5 (Fall 1973): 14–15.

"Tol. VF-Industries—Willys Overland Motors, Inc." Unpubl. MS in Toledo Historical Society Library, Toledo, Ohio.

Tolson, Melvin B. *A Gallery of Harlem Portraits.* Edited by Robert M. Farnsworth. Columbia: University of Missouri Press, 1979.

Towey, Martin G. "Hooverville: St. Louis Had the Largest." *Gateway Heritage* 1 (Fall 1980): 4–11.

Trent, Lucia. "Factory Town." *Children of Fire and Shadow.* Chicago: Robert Packard, 1929.

Tretyakov, Sergei. "Words Become Deeds." *International Literature* 3 (July 1933): 54–56.

Trotsky, Leon. Letter to V. F. Calverton. In *Modern Monthly* 7 (March 1933): 85.

Trotter, Joe William, Jr. *The Great Migration in Historical Perspective.* Bloomington: Indiana University Press, 1991.

Trowbridge, W. D. "The Lower End of Main Street, a Realistic Picture of Life in an Average Small Town." *Haldeman-Julius Quarterly* 2 (July–September 1928): 149–54.

Turner, Frederick Jackson. *The Frontier in American History.* New York: Henry Holt, 1920.

"Unemployment." *Fortune* 5 (September 1932): 19.

"U.S.S.R. Writers—to the Factories, Workers—into Literature." *Literature of the World Revolution* 1 (June 1931): 104–7.

"U.S. Writers Quit Ivory Towers at Congress." *New York Post,* 27 April 1935.

Van Doren, Mark. Review of *America Arraigned!,* edited by Lucia Trent and Ralph Cheyney. *Modern Quarterly* 4 (May–August 1928): 409.

Verba, Sidney, and Kay Lehman Scholzman. "Unemployment, Class Consciousness, and Radical Politics: What Didn't Happen in the Thirties." *Journal of Politics* 39 (1977): 292–323.

Vincent, David. *Bread, Knowledge and Freedom: A Study of Nineteenth-Century Working Class Autobiography.* New York: Methuen, 1981.

Vogel, Joseph. *At Madame Bonnard's.* New York: Alfred A. Knopf, 1935.

———. "A Defence of the American Literary Scene." *This Quarter* 1, no. 4 (1928): 247–57.

———. *Man's Courage.* Syracuse: Syracuse University Press, 1989.

———. *The Straw Hat.* New York: Modern Age Books, 1940.

Wald, Alan M. "In Retrospective: *On Native Ground.*" *Reviews in American History* 20 (1992): 276–88.

———. *James T. Farrell: The Revolutionary Socialist Years.* New York: New York University Press, 1978.

———. *The New York Intellectuals: The Rise and Decline of the Anti-Stalinist Left from the 1930s to the 1980s.* Chapel Hill: University of North Carolina Press, 1987.

———. "Remembering the Answers." *Nation* (26 December 1981): 708.

———. *The Responsibility of Intellectuals.* Atlantic Highlands, N.J.: Humanities Press, 1992.

———. *The Revolutionary Imagination: The Poetry and Politics of John Wheelwright and Sherry Mangan.* Chapel Hill: University of North Carolina Press, 1983.

———. "Revolutionary Intellectuals: Leon Trotsky and *Partisan Review* in the 1930s. *Occident* (Spring 1974): 118–33.

Wallace, Margaret. Review of *The Disinherited*, by Jack Conroy. *New York Times Book Review*, 26 November 1933.

Waller, Alexander H. *History of Randolph County, Missouri.* Cleveland: Historical Publishing, 1920.

Warren, Paul (a.k.a. Frank Sandiford). *Next Time Is for Life.* New York: Dell, 1953.

Webster, Grant. *The Republic of Letters: A History of Postwar Literary Opinion.* Baltimore: Johns Hopkins University Press, 1979.

Weil, Simone. *Cahiers.* Paris: Plon, 1970; 1971; 1974.

———. *The Need for Roots.* New York: Harper and Row, 1971.

Weimann, Robert. *Structure and Society in Literary History.* Baltimore: Johns Hopkins University Press, 1984.

Weinstein, James. *The Decline of Socialism in America, 1912–1925.* New York: Monthly Review, 1967.

Weiss, Henry George. "Give Us Poems for Workers." Letter to the Editors. *New Masses* 4 (July 1929): 22.

———. "Poetry and Revolution." *New Masses* 4 (October 1929): 9.

Weitzel, Tony. "Story of a Male's Decline: Women and Anchovies." *Chicago Daily News*, 2 May 1952, S2.

Werkley, Caroline E. *Mister Carnegie's Lib'ary.* New York: American Heritage Press, 1970.

West, James L. W., III. *American Authors and the Literary Marketplace since 1900.* Philadelphia: University of Pennsylvania Press, 1988.

Wharton, Walter W. *Graphiti from Elsinore.* Prairie City, Ill.: Decker Press, 1949.

———. "The Logic of Lunacharsky Frittertisky." Unpubl. MS in Wharton collection, Western Historical Manuscript Collection, University of Missouri–Columbia.

———. "Monster Three Day Baccanalian Festival Marks Return of Eminent Middlewestern Critic." Unpubl. MS in Wharton collection, Western Historical Manuscript Collection, University of Missouri–Columbia.

———. "Sand County Sandpaper." Unpubl. MS in Wharton collection, Western Historical Manuscript Collection, University of Missouri–Columbia.

"Where's the New Faulkner?" *U.S. News and World Report*, 27 January 1986, 65.

Whisnant, David. *All That Is Native and Fine: The Politics of Culture in an American Region.* Chapel Hill: University of North Carolina Press, 1983.

Whitcomb, Robert. "The Writers' Fight: History of the Writers's Union." *Latin Quarterly* 1 (Fall 1934): 143–47.

Whitehead, Fred, and Verle Muhrer, eds. *Freethought on the American Frontier.* Buffalo, N.Y.: Prometheus Books, 1992.

Whitman, Walt. *Walt Whitman: Complete Poetry and Collected Prose.* Edited by Justin Kaplan. New York: Library of America, 1982.

Wiebe, Phillip. "Deutsche Arbeiterliteratur (1847–1918)." Unpubl. MS, courtesy of Deutsche Welle, Cologne.

Wilde, Alan. *Horizons of Ascent*. Baltimore: Johns Hopkins University Press, 1981.

Williams, Raymond. *Culture and Society, 1780–1950*. New York: Columbia University Press, 1983.

Williams, William Carlos. "An American Poet." In *New Masses: An Anthology of the Rebel Thirties*, edited by Joseph North, 257–63. New York: International Publishers, 1972.

———. *Autobiography*. New York: Random House, 1951.

———. "A Symposium: The Status of Radical Writing." *A Year Magazine* (1933): 134.

Wilson, Edmund. *The American Jitters*. New York: Charles Scribner's, 1932.

———. "Art, the Proletariat and Marx." *New Republic* 76 (23 August 1933).

———. "Detroit Motors." In *The American Earthquake*. Garden City, N.Y.: Doubleday, 1964.

———. "The Literary Class War." *New Republic* 75 (4 May 1932) and (11 May 1932).

Winkler, Jean. "William Marion Reedy and the Mirror." *St. Louis Review* 2 (11 February 1933).

Winter, Hauser. "The Division in Missouri Methodism in 1845." *Missouri History Review* 37 (October 1942): 1–18.

Wixson, Douglas. "From Conroy to Steinbeck: The Quest for an Idiom of the People in the 1930s." *Mid-America* 8 (1981): 135–50.

———. "From the Crucible of Experience: Jack Conroy in Toledo." *Midwest Miscellany* (Spring 1980): 44–60.

———. Introduction to *The Disinherited*, by Jack Conroy. Columbia: University of Missouri Press, 1991.

———. Introduction to *The Weed King and Other Stories*, by Jack Conroy. Westport, Conn.: Lawrence Hill, 1985.

———. "Jack Conroy." In *Encyclopedia of American Humorists*, edited by Stephen Gale, 98–104. New York: Garland, 1988.

———. "Jack Conroy and the East St. Louis Toughs, 1936–38." *New Letters* 57 (Spring 1991): 29–57.

———. "Jack Conroy and Industrial Folklore." *Missouri Folklore Society Journal* 6 (1985): 462–66.

———. "Jack Conroy, Sage of Moberly." *Book Forum* 6 (Fall 1982): 202–6.

———. "Jack Conroy, Worker-Writer; A Retrospective, 1898–1990." *Against the Current* 30 (January–February 1991): 44–47.

———. "*The Rebel Poet, The Anvil, The New Anvil*." *American Literary Magazines: The Twentieth Century*. Westport, Conn.: Greenwood Press, 1992.

———. "Reception Theory and the Survival of Orwell's *Nineteen Eighty-Four*." *North Dakota Quarterly* 55 (Spring 1987): 72–86.

———. "Red Pens from the Village: Jack Conroy's *The Anvil* and *The Left*." *Mid-America* 11 (1984): 42–55.

———. "Thomas Hart Benton's New York Years." In *Thomas Hart Benton, Artist, Writer, Intellectual*, edited by R. Douglas Hurt and Mary K. Dains, 191–218. Columbia: State Historical Society of Missouri, 1989.

Wolf, Geoffrey. *Black Sun: The Brief Transit and Violent Eclipse of Harry Cros-by*. New York: Random House, 1976.

Wolin, Richard. *Walter Benjamin: An Aesthetic of Redemption*. New York: Columbia University Press, 1982.

Wood, Grant. "Revolt Against the City." In *America Is West*, edited by John T. Flanagan, 648–60. Westport, Conn.: Greenwood, 1975.

Wright, Richard. "I Tried to Be a Communist." *Atlantic Monthly* 174 (August 1944): 61–62, 63.

———. *White Man, Listen!* Garden City, N.Y.: Doubleday, 1957.

"Writers' Group to Study Alabama Sedition Cases." *New York Herald-Tribune* (17 July 1935).

"Writers Receive 'Southern Hospitality.'" *International Literature* 10 (October 1935): 106–7.

"A Yaleman and a Communist." *Fortune* 28 (November 1943): 146–48, 212, 214–15, 221.

Zaretsky, Eli. *Capitalism, The Family, and Personal Life*. New York: Harper and Row, 1976.

Zhdanov, A., M. Gorky, N. Bukharin, K. Radek, and A. Stetsky. *Problems of Soviet Literature: Reports and Speeches at the First Soviet Writers' Congress*. Edited by H. G. Scott. Moscow: Co-operative Publishing Society of Foreign Workers in the U.S.S.R, 1935.

Zilliacus, Clas. "Radical Naturalism: First-Person Documentary Literature." *Comparative Literature* 31 (Spring 1979): 97–112.

Zola, Émile. *Germinal*. Translated by Leonard Tancock. New York: Penguin Books, 1954.

Zugsmith, Leanne. *The Summer Soldier*. New York: Random House, 1938.

Zumthor. Paul. "L'écriture et la voix." *Critique* 394 (March 1980): 228–39.

Zweig, F. *Men in the Pits*. London: Victor Gollancz, 1949.

Index

Aaron, Abe, 287, 300, 318, 331, 355, 360–61, 364, 375, 379, 540n47, 552n22

Aaron, Daniel, 33, 227, 272, 409, 475, 477, 507n3, 546n39, 548n74

Abercrombie, Gertrude, 462

Abernethy, Milton A., 267, 268

Abraham Lincoln School, 451, 453–55

Ackerson, John. *See* Jarrboe, George

Adamic, Louis, 108, 198, 317, 338

Addams, Jane, 107, 554n67

Addis, Eliza Jane. *See* Conroy, Eliza Jane

Addis, William "Pip," 44, 45, 47, 50–51, 63, 68, 87, 89, 93, 106, 110, 210, 241, 284

Adler, Nathan, 550n116

AEAR. *See* Association des Écrivains et Artistes Révolutionnaires (AEAR)

AFL. *See* American Federation of Labor (AFL)

AFRW. *See* American Federation of Railway Workers (AFRW)

Agee, James, 421

Akron *Beacon Journal*, 557n1

Alabama demonstration against Downs' law, 409–11, 564–65nn112–17

Alcohol use: of Addis, 44, 51; of Conroy, 429, 432–33, 445, 451, 461, 468, 481; and industrial workers' culture, 105; melodramas on, 433, 440, 444–45, 451–52, 568n36, 571n78; of miners, 50; during Prohibition, 133, 137, 150; of railway workers, 50, 51, 54, 59; and temperance, 58–59

Alfred Knopf. *See* Knopf, Alfred

Algren, Amanda, 438, 451, 576n67

Algren, Nelson: at Abraham Lincoln School, 454; and Alabama demonstration against Downs' law, 409, 564n112; at American Writers' Congress (1935), 395; at American Writers' Congress (1937), 5, 566n157; as *Anvil* contributor, 322, 384, 486; as *Anvil-Partisan Review* associate editor, 415; attraction to toughs and losers, 448; biography of, 581; in *Carleton Miscellany*, 478; and Communist party, 443, 571n78; on Conroy, 365, 544–45n143; on Conroy's *A World to Win*, 405, 562n80; Conroy's anecdotes of, 2, 483; and "The Drunkard's Warning," 433, 568n36, 571n81; early publications of, 72; and Fallonites, 430, 434–36, 448; and Farrell, 335–36; friendship with Conroy, 59, 438, 445, 448, 450–51, 469; and Hollywood, 469–70; home in Chicago, 451; at Illinois Writers' Project, 438, 439, 440, 446, 477, 570nn63–65; at John Reed Clubs national conference (1934), 379, 380; and League of American Writers, 574n48; literary success of, 449, 457, 458, 459, 460, 462, 471; and McCarthyism, 573n23; at May Day parade,

Trained as an engineer at MIT, DOUGLAS WIXSON continued his studies in Germany, later earning a Ph.D. in English literature at the University of North Carolina–Chapel Hill. He taught American and English literature for twenty-five years in the United States and France. Professor Wixson left university teaching in 1992 in order to devote his time to writing and to archival work. He edited and furnished the introductions to recent editions of *The Disinherited* and *The Weed King and Other Stories* by Jack Conroy, and has written on Thomas Hart Benton, Thornton Wilder, Bertolt Brecht, George Orwell, and Shakespeare's *King John*, among other topics.